A GUIDE TO

IN THE
NATIONAL ARCHIVES

Compiled by Howard H. Wehmann
Revised by Benjamin L. DeWhitt

NATIONAL ARCHIVES AND RECORDS ADMINISTRATION
WASHINGTON, DC

Published for the
National Archives and Records Administration
By the National Archives Trust Fund Board
1989

Library of Congress Cataloging-in-Publication Data

Wehmann, Howard H.
  A guide to pre-federal records in the National Archives.

  Bibliography: p.
  Includes index.
  1. United States. National Archives—Catalogs. 2. United States—
History—Colonial period, ca. 1600-1775—Sources—Bibliography—
Catalogs. 3. United States—History—Revolution, 1775-1783—
Sources—Bibliography—Catalogs. 4. United States—History—
Confederation, 1783-1789—Sources—Bibliography—Catalogs. I. DeWhitt,
Benjamin, 1941-   . II. United States. National Archives and Records
Administration. III. Title.
CD3045.W44   1989   016.973   88-600400
ISBN 0-911333-75-4

Cover: *The Destruction of Tea at Boston Harbor, 1773.* Copy of
lithograph by Sarony & Major, 1846. 148-GW-439

CONTENTS

PREFACE

The National Archives and Records Administration offers this book, *A Guide to Pre-Federal Records in the National Archives*, at a time when the United States is commemorating the bicentennial of its institutions of government. Described in it are the holdings of the National Archives that relate directly to, or were created during, the period before the Constitution went into effect on March 4, 1789.

It is the primary responsibility of the National Archives to see that records created by or gathered in the process of our government's activities are both preserved and made available for use. Guides such as this one have been prepared at the National Archives since 1940 when the first general *Guide to the Material in the National Archives* was published. Over time, new editions of this general guide have been published and supplementary guides have been prepared focusing on specific subsets of Archives holdings. In this latter category are the *Guide to Federal Records Relating to the Civil War* (1962), *Civil War Maps in the National Archives* (1964), *Guide to the Archives of the Government of the Confederate States of America* (1968), *Guide to Cartographic Records in the National Archives* (1971), *Guide to Materials on Latin America in the National Archives of the United States* (1974), *Guide to Records in the National Archives of the United States Relating to American Indians* (1981), and most recently, *Black History: A Guide to Civilian Records in the National Archives* (1984). All of these publications are intended to make the valuable records that document government functions better known and more accessible.

The reader will discover that the records discussed here document subjects ranging far beyond the government under the Articles of Confederation. They reflect a wide variety of human concerns, desires, prospects, plans, and problems. It is our hope that those who seek to understand the nation's past will recognize these pre-federal records as a unique and valuable resource.

DON W. WILSON
Archivist of the United States

INTRODUCTION

The purpose of this guide is to assist the researcher in locating within the National Archives of the United States those records that were created in, or are related directly to, the pre-federal period of U.S. history—all of the time before the Constitution went into effect on March 4, 1789. The guide is not a comprehensive listing of every such document, but an attempt to identify and describe bodies of records that consist of or contain such documents.

The National Archives of the United States consists of permanently valuable records of the federal government. They are housed in the National Archives Building in Washington, DC; in the Suitland Annex in the Washington National Records Center Building in Suitland, MD; in the Pickett Street Annex in Alexandria, VA; in 11 National Archives regional archives; and in Presidential Libraries.

The term "pre-federal" in the title of this guide suggests that the records described herein pertain to the government of what became the United States and its activities before the initiation of the federal system under the Constitution. That is indeed the case for the great majority of the records. Most do apply directly to the United States as governed first by the authority of the Continental Congresses and then under the Articles of Confederation. There are, however, a significant number of records that relate to other areas of the New World, such as Canada, British colonies in the Caribbean, the Danish Virgin Islands, and Spanish colonies in North America. It is obvious that March 4, 1789, is of little significance with regard to those records that do not apply to the British colonies that became the 13 original states. However, since the vast majority of the records under consideration here are in the narrowest sense pre-federal, the construct of the period is applied to all records pre-dating March 4, 1789. In every case—and there are many—in which bodies of records possess a continuity that passes that date, that fact is noted and the pre-federal records are described in their full context.

In some cases records dating from the 19th century are described in this guide. In all cases they relate to pre-federal events, such as military service during the Revolution or financial commitments made by the government. Examples of records related to each, respectively, are pension and bounty-land application files and records of payments on military salaries, claims against the government, or government loans solicited to pay debts incurred in pre-federal times.

Some 19th- and 20th-century records that are related to the pre-federal period have been left out of this guide. Their relationship is only that they are about the period; they are not of it. These include some records of memorial commissions, which often sponsored the production or assembled copies of maps, illustrations, and other documents pertaining to pre-federal, especially Revolutionary War, times. There are also federal records that were assembled in agencies as reference collections. Both of these types of records contain information about pre-federal affairs that is often ephemeral, of questionable value, or very easily available from sources other than the National Archives. In many cases, these sources are published or are well-known collections that are throroughly catalogued. In those few cases in which the records of memorial commissions or the agency reference collections contain records created in the pre-federal period or information that is hard to find elsewhere, they are described in this guide.

It is necessary to explain two classes of terms used in this guide. References are made to the "continental government" and the "Continental Congress" in full awareness that a strict observance of fact would dictate "continental and confederation governments" and "First Continental Congress," "Second Continental Congress," and "Confederation Congress," respectively. The shortened forms are used for convenience and to save precious space and thus a little cost. Care has been taken to see that no confusion concerning the records results from this decision. Indeed the longer forms are used when absolutely necessary for clarity. Also, the choice between "American" and "United States" (used as a modifier) has been made with care. Many records, especially those predating 1776, pertain to the Canadian or Caribbean colonies of Britain as well. Thus the term "American" herein may be taken to include Canadian and, occasionally, Caribbean records along with those relevant to British colonies south from Massachusetts on the North American continent. The term "United States" is confined to the area of the 13 original states and the western territories. These distinctions most often arise regarding records of commercial affairs.

The basic organizational unit to which all records in the National Archives are assigned is called a record group (RG), and each record group is arbitrarily assigned a number. A record group most frequently consists of the records of a single agency, such as the U.S. Customs Service (RG 36). The records of the head of an executive department and units with department-wide responsibility may be assigned to a general record group such as General Records of the Department of State (RG 59). Records of a number of different government agencies or activities are sometimes brought together on the basis of similarity of function or other relationship. An example of a collective record group is Records of Boundary and Claims Commissions and Arbitrations (RG 76).

The National Archives endeavors to keep records in the order in which they were maintained by the creating agency, in the belief that this best preserves their integrity and interrelationships. This is true of pre-federal records, although their age and a natural interest in them in many cases has led to changes in their custody, location, and arrangement over the years. In such cases they nearly always are maintained in the order in which they were arranged when received by the National Archives. Agency filing systems were designed for administrative purposes and not for the benefit of future researchers. A major reason for the preparation of guides such as this is to assist subject-oriented researchers in understanding the complexities of recordkeeping systems and in locating material of interest among large quantities of records.

Within record groups, the basic archival unit of control for records is the series, which is a body of records arranged in some serial order or logically grouped together for some other reason. For many record groups, the National Archives has prepared inventories or preliminary inventories, which describe the records series by series. Typical information in an entry includes series title, covering dates, quantity, type of records, and perhaps some indication of content.

Many pre-federal records, because of their age and their association with the origins of the United States, already have been described or indexed in considerable detail. This guide attempts to take that work into account by reference to useful and readily available finding aids that already exist, and by offering descriptions that are arranged in new ways or written from different viewpoints. Every effort has been made to avoid repeating work already done well. This is especially true in RG 360, Records of the Continental and Confederation Congresses and the Constitutional Convention, which deserves discussion as a whole, separate from the subject chapters.

Record Group 360

Records of the Continental and Confederation Congresses and the Constitutional Convention

---

Records in RG 360 are not organized in ways that reflect the identity, structure, or function of each of the continental and confederation congresses. They are arranged as bound by intervening custodians, primarily by type of record—such as journals, committee reports, correspondence, memorials, and petitions—and thereunder chronologically, alphabetically, or by subject. Most of the records of the Continental and Confederation Congresses are arranged into 196 numbered units called "Items" of a type which have been, in other record groups, called series by the National Archives. They are traditionally referred to by item numbers in this body of records. These Papers of the Continental Congress will be referred to hereafter as "PCC." There are also miscellaneous records that are not among the numbered series, hereafter referred to as "Miscellaneous PCC." The records consist of the journals of Congress; reports of its committees; memorials and petitions; papers submitted by state governments; and correspondence of its president and other officers with diplomatic representatives abroad, officers in the Continental Army, state and local officials, and private persons. Included are drafts and copies of the Declaration of Independence, the Articles of Confederation, the Northwest Ordinance, the Constitution, and other documents instrumental in molding the new government; drafts of treaties and commercial agreements; papers relating to expenditures and to domestic and foreign loans; reports on military affairs during the Revolutionary War; and papers relating to Indian treaties and tribes.

There is no consistent one-to-one relationship between or among items, bindings, and volumes. Also the date span of an individual item may often encompass all continental and confederation congresses. On the other hand, groups of closely related records, even some originally from the same body of documents, may be in widely separated items as now defined. Some items and volumes within items are made up of records of disparate subjects and types. Therefore it should not be assumed that all records of a given type are to be found in a particular series, nor that the title of a series always accurately reflects either its total or principal contents.

The documents are all accessible for research through three National Archives Microfilm Publications: *Papers of the Continental Congress, 1774-1789,* (M247, 204 rolls); *Miscellaneous Papers of the Continental Congress, 1774-1789,* (M332, 10 rolls); and *Records of the Constitutional Convention of 1787* (M866, 1 roll). There is also a 38-volume printed edition of the manuscript journals (Items 1-8), *Journals of the Continental Congress, 1774-1789,* (1904-37), hereafter referred to as JCC. *Index: Journals of the Continental Congress, 1774-1789* (1976), hereafter referred to as *Index: JCC*, covers the printed journals. The remainder of the records (Items 9-196 and Miscellaneous PCC) are covered by *Index: The Papers of the Continental Congress, 1774-1789* (1978), hereafter referred to as *Index: PCC*. That publication does not index two items (17 and 184) because they are themselves indexes prepared in the pre-federal period; nor does it index the manuscript journals.

Because of the relative ease of access to records in RG 360, and especially because of the existence of the published subject and name indexes, these records are treated differently in this guide from those in other record groups. Their descriptions are more general than for those of records in other record groups and are located immediately following the introduction to each subject chapter. That placement is an attempt to put the records outside of RG 360 into the context of the better-known, heretofore more easily accessible, records in RG 360. Economy dictates the brevity of RG 360 descriptions, as does a conviction that the aforementioned publications provide excellent access, even to the level of subject indexes, to these important records. Item numbers are given, where relevant, to assist the researcher. Appendix B provides a listing of PCC Item numbers, in order, with guide paragraph citations for each, listed in the order in which they appear in the text.

Several finding aids for pre-federal records provide the researcher with help beyond that provided in this guide. They are mentioned in appropriate chapters and listed in the bibliography at the end of the guide. One, however, contains descriptions of records that cut across the subject categories of these chapters, and thus deserves discussion here.

SPECIAL LIST NO. 26

Special List No. 26, Pre-Federal Maps in the National Archives: an Annotated List (1975) is available without charge from: Publications Sales Branch (NEPS), National Archives and Records Administration, Washington, DC 20408. It describes maps that can reasonably be identified as having originated during or before 1790, as copies or facsimiles of maps from that period, or as later maps that portray areas or events during that period. The entries in the publication are divided into three classes: atlases, maps encompassing two or more colonies or states, and maps of areas within individual colonies or states. Categories under the section for areas within individual colonies and states include the 13 original states and Florida, Louisiana, Maine, Ohio, Vermont, and the District of Columbia. Each entry contains title, date of creation, size, file or sheet number if applicable, record group designation, and a description of the nature and provenance of the map. The descriptions are more detailed than corresponding descriptions in this guide. File designations are given in the entries to facilitate identification and location of the records.

This *Guide to Pre-Federal Records* employs the record group as its basic unit of arrangement within broad subject chapters. Rather than assign numbers to the chapters, we have encoded the key words in their subjects into two-letter designators, such as MI for records of military affairs, FI for records of fiscal affairs, and CC for general records of the Continental Congress. The chapters are in alphabetical order according to these designators. This places them serendipitously in some logical order, with fiscal and commercial subject chapters, and military, naval, and pension subject chapters together, for example. More important, it will help the researcher to locate the many cross references more easily. In each chapter the descriptions are arranged in numerical order by record group numbers, with one exception. As stated above, because RG 360 is so basic to the understanding of pre-federal records, contains a majority of such records, and is already well described in other sources, decriptions of records in it precede those of all other record groups in each chapter. This and the general introduction to each chapter that immediately precedes it, are an attempt to put the pre-federal records on that general subject in some perspective. The chapter introductions focus on the authorities, functions, and practices of the continental government, but contain some other relevant information.

In this guide, series titles appear in boldface type. This and other important elements of the format are illustrated in the following key.

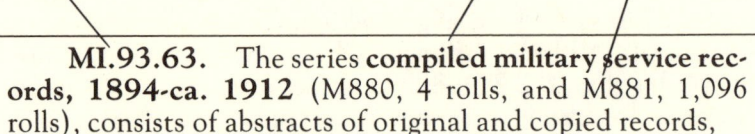

> **MI.93.63.**   The series **compiled military service records, 1894-ca. 1912** (M880, 4 rolls, and M881, 1,096 rolls), consists of abstracts of original and copied records,

1. **MI.93.63.** is an example of a unique composite number assigned to each paragraph in the guide:
   MI. is the subject chapter designation (records of military affairs).
   93. is the record group number. (In chapter introductions this number will be **0.**)
   63. is the number of the paragraph for that record group in that chapter.
   These full paragraph numbers are used in the cross references, the appendixes, and the index. This composite number should by cited by researchers when requesting records.

2. **Boldface type** is used for the title of a series of records within a record group and for the dates of those records. Information about the volume and arrangement of the records follows the boldface type. Most expressions of volume are given in linear feet. Volume is not given if records have been microfilmed.

3. "M880" and "M881" are the numbers of National Archives Microfilm Publications. Most of these microfilm publication numbers begin with M, but some begin with T. They are listed by number in Appendix A, with full titles and other information. Copies of many microfilm publications are available in the regional archives of the National Archives in cities around the country. For many of the microfilm publications there are descriptive pamphlets (see Appendix A) that are available without charge from: Publications Sales Branch (NEPS), National Archives and Records Administration, Washington, DC 20408.

Most of the records or the microfilm publications are readily available and researchers are not required to make arrangements in advance to consult them. Some records, however, may be temporarily unavailable (they may be being reproduced for another researcher, for example). It is suggested, therefore, that before traveling any extended distance to visit a repository, researchers write and describe as specifically as possible the subject of their interest and the records they may wish to consult.

CHAPTER CC

General Records of the Pre-Federal Period and the Continental Congress

CC.0.1. In response to Great Britain's Intolerable Acts of March-May 1774 several colonies called for an inter-colonial congress to adopt common measures of response. On June 17, 1774, the Massachusetts House of Representatives suggested that a congress be held at Philadelphia in September. In all colonies except Georgia a variety of public bodies elected delegates to that proposed meeting. Those 56 delegates assembled at Carpenter's Hall in Philadelphia on September 5, 1774. The "Continental Congress," as it came to be known to distinguish it from the "provincial" congresses held in various colonies, adopted numerous resolves denouncing the British acts. It also adopted the "Association" by which the delegates pledged that the colonies they represented would cut off imports from and exports to Great Britain at staged intervals throughout the coming year. Congress adjourned on October 26, 1774, but not before preparing addresses to the King and the British and American peoples and resolving to meet again on May 10, 1775, if by that date American grievances had not been redressed. When Congress reassembled on that day a de facto state of war existed.

CC.0.2. The "second" Continental Congress was not created as a governing body any more than was the first, but events conspired to make it one. On May 15, 1775, it resolved to put the colonies in a state of defense; on June 14 it resolved to raise a number of rifle companies to march to the aid of Massachusetts militiamen besieging the British in Boston; and on June 15 it elected George Washington Commander in Chief of the Continental Army. By the end of 1775 Congress had issued $2,000,000 in bills of credit to support the army, named commissioners to negotiate treaties of peace with the Indians, established a post office department, launched a military expedition into Canada, authorized the creation of a navy, and appointed a committee to correspond secretly with "our friends" abroad.

CC.0.3. During the next five years, Congress continued to exercise the powers of an independent government without the benefit of a written constitution. When Richard Henry Lee offered his famous resolution for independence on June 7, 1776, he also proposed that a "plan of confederation be prepared and transmitted to the respective colonies for their consideration and approbation." The

Declaration of Independence was adopted soon, but the Articles of Confederation presented to Congress on July 12, 1776, by a committee headed by John Dickinson, were debated off and on for more than a year. On November 15, 1777, the Articles of Confederation were adopted by Congress, but ratification by the states was not completed until March 1, 1781.

CC.0.4. The Continental Congress was a unicameral body, with members, referred to as delegates, elected by and representing state governments. The early members were chosen at irregular intervals and in differing numbers, mostly by popular conventions or by the popularly chosen branches of state legislatures. Article 5 of the Articles of Confederation provided for the annual election of delegates "in such a manner as the legislature of each state shall direct," with not less than two nor more than seven to be sent from each state. The same article called for Congress to meet on the first Monday in November of each year. Voting in Congress was by states, each having one vote regardless of the size of its delegation. Through June 1783 Congress held sessions mainly in Philadelphia. From January 1785 until its demise they were in New York City.

CC.0.5. As the only central organ of government for the rebellious colonies, Congress exercised executive and judicial as well as legislative powers. To conduct a war on land and sea, to raise money and purchase supplies at home and abroad, and to direct other necessary activities, it established subordinate bodies capable of executive action. At first these consisted mainly of special and standing committees of its own members, but these quickly proved ineffective because of rapid turnover in membership, lack of expertise, political infighting, and other problems. Boards composed of combinations of members and non-members were tried next, but were found inadequate for the same reasons. Not until 1781 were executive departments, with heads who were not also members of Congress, established for the major functions of managing the military, foreign, and fiscal affairs of the continental government. It was also in 1781 that Congress established the first judicial body made up of individuals other than members of Congress. Both the executive and the judicial agencies, however, were far from the independent branches of government they became under the federal system. The Continental Congress created and dispensed with them at will, subject only to certain limited provisions of the Articles of Confederation. The origins and operations of specific continental executive and judicial agencies are discussed in more detail in the introductions to subsequent chapters.

CC.0.6. Two officials played very important roles in the overall functioning of the pre-federal government—the President and the Secretary of Congress. The President was a member of Congress who was elected to preside over its meetings. Although possessed of no independent executive authority, such as the President of the United States would later hold, he could wield influence because of the honor of his position. The chief duties of the President, in addition to presiding over meetings of Congress, were to serve as a channel for communications sent and received by Congress and to act as an official host on its behalf for foreign and domestic dignitaries. He also signed circular and other letters sent by Congress as a body, signed documents authorizing the disbursement of public funds, and transmitted congressional ordinances and other documents to executive agencies until that duty was transferred to the Secretary of Congress in 1782. He was provided with a personal secretary, a steward, and household servants. The position of President of the Continental Congress was filled 16 times by 13 individuals throughout the pre-federal period.

CC.0.7. The position of Secretary of Congress was held by a single individual, Charles Thomson, throughout the existence of the Continental Congress. It was a position of numerous and varied duties that changed with the establishment, reorganization, and dissolution of the executive and judicial agencies of Congress. The chief responsibility of the secretary was to prepare the journals of the daily proceedings of Congress and to maintain custody of its central records. Related jobs included supervising the printing of the journals and providing attested copies of congressional resolves and other public papers to members and other persons. Congressional resolutions of January 28, 1782, and an ordinance of March 31, 1785, spelled out the duties of the Office of the Secretary in detail, directing, among other things, that the secretary should attend congressional meetings and read the public despatches, committee reports, and other papers to be considered; transmit to the heads of executive departments all papers referred to them by Congress as well as copies of all congressional resolutions, ordinances, and other enactments; keep registers of petitions, memorials, and other communications received by Congress and registers of treaties, conventions, and ordinances; authenticate acts and proceedings not requiring authentication by the President of Congress; keep the Great Seal of the United States and affix it to documents as directed by Congress; and transmit resolutions, ordinances, and other enactments to the states and correspond with them about their execution. Other tasks performed by the secretary at various times included attesting military commissions, issuing privateer commissions, and making reports to Congress on matters referred to him for an opinion. He was assisted by the Deputy Secretary of Congress and a few clerks.

CC.0.8. Matters were usually brought to the attention of Congress by some form of written communication. Congress then referred each concern to a committee or executive agency for a report on the course of action to be taken. That report might be adopted in whole or in part, amended, rejected, or returned to the originator for revision. Congress usually expressed its will in the form of resolutions (resolves), which were laws insofar as Congress had the physical power or moral authority to enforce them. Many of the reports of committees and other bodies, as well as motions of individual members, that were submitted to Congress were cast in the form of resolutions to be adopted. Congress also issued brief orders and lengthy ordinances, usually reserving the ordinances to establish and reorganize government agencies and to promulgate important and complex administrative regulations and procedures.

CC.0.9. On two occasions in the pre-federal period congressional committees acted for limited periods and with limited powers as the central government of the United States. The first such instance was during the winter of 1776-77 when Congress fled to Baltimore in anticipation of the capture of Philadelphia by the British. It then established the Executive Committee to transact business in Philadelphia while it met in Maryland. On April 26, 1784, Congress, then sitting in Annapolis, resolved to adjourn on June 3 and reassemble in Trenton, leaving the Committee of the States to act on its behalf in the interval. The composition and powers of that committee were provided for in the Articles of Confederation.

CC.0.10. Much has been written of the weaknesses of the pre-federal government of the United States, especially as it existed under the Articles of Confederation. It represented, in fact, a league of 13 sovereign states rather than a single nation. Possessing only those powers expressly or implicitly delegated to it by the states, the Continental Congress needed a large voting majority to enact measures of any importance. Thus it lacked such basic powers as those required to regulate interstate and foreign commerce, collect revenues directly from the people, and enforce its enactments through coercive measures. In spite of these limitations the Continental Congress waged and won a global war, established firm diplomatic and commercial relations with a number of foreign countries, provided for the governing and disposition of a vast western territory, and assisted in the creation of a successor government.

Record Group 360
Records of the Continental and Confederation Congresses and the Constitutional Convention

CC.360.1. Record Group 360 consists primarily of PCC (M247, 204 rolls), and Miscellaneous PCC (M332, 10 rolls).* For additional information about those bodies of records and indexes thereto, see the introduction.

RECORDS OF THE FOUNDATIONS OF PRE-FEDERAL GOVERNMENT

CC.360.2. The Articles of Association of the Continental Congress, signed on October 20, 1774, is a three-page document in Miscellaneous PCC (M332, roll 10). Its first and last pages are reproduced in *The Formation of the Union* (1970), and it is also a frontispiece in the first volume of *JCC*.

CC.360.3. Two series in PCC contain records related to the drafting and passage of the Articles of Confederation. **History of the Confederation, [n.d.]** (Item 9, M247, roll 22), is primarily a record of the congressional proceedings that pertain to adoption and ratification of the Articles. Much, but not all, of the information in the series is also in the rough journals (see **CC.360.10.**). Many of the motions, resolutions, and votes are also documented in the 127 pages of **Articles of Confederation, with plans and drafts of treaties and other miscellaneous records, 1775-84** (Item 47, M247, roll 61), but the series consists largely of drafts of the Articles, including that presented to Congress by Benjamin Franklin on July 21, 1775.

CC.360.4. Instructions to delegates to the Continental Congress from North Carolina and Virginia, sent by their respective state assemblies in April and May 1776, are in Miscellaneous PCC (M332, roll 10). Both documents instruct the representatives to favor independence and foreign alliances and were read before Congress on May 27, 1776. The Virginia instructions are reproduced in *The Formation of the Union*. Also in Miscellaneous PCC are Richard Henry Lee's resolution for independence, June 7, 1776, and the proposal to appoint a committee to prepare a declaration of independence, June 10, 1776 (M332, roll 10).

*For a complete list of National Archives Microfilm Publications cited in this guide, see Appendix A.

CC.360.5. The engrossed Declaration of Independence (M332, roll 10) is on permanent display in the Exhibition Hall of the National Archives in Washington, DC. It is a single sheet of parchment engrossed by order of a congressional resolution of July 19, 1776. Signed on August 2, 1776, and subsequent dates, it contains the signatures of 56 delegates to the Continental Congress, arranged for the most part in groups according to state. The first printed copy of the Declaration, the John Dunlap engraving of July 4-5, 1776, contains only the printed signatures of John Hancock, then President of the Continental Congress, and Charles Thomson, Secretary of the Continental Congress. It is in the rough journals (see **CC.360.10.**). Both documents are reproduced in *The Formation of the Union*. See **CC.59.2.** for descriptions of other records related to the Declaration of Independence.

CC.360.6. The engrossed Articles of Confederation (M332, roll 10) was produced under a congressional order of June 27, 1778. It was signed by representatives of eight states on July 9, 1778, and the remaining states ratified it one at a time until the last signature was affixed on March 1, 1781. The document consists of a roll of six sheets of parchment stitched together and originally fastened at each end to a wooden roller. The first and last sheets are reproduced in *The Formation of the Union*.

CREDENTIALS, OATHS, AND RELATED DOCUMENTS

CC.360.7. The series **credentials of delegates from each state to the Congress, [n.d.]** (M332, rolls 8 and 10), consists of 13 volumes and 70 portfolios, primarily attested copies of state legislative proceedings, or extracts thereof; letters; and certificates of election or appointment. They are arranged into two subseries according to physical form, thereunder by state, and thereunder chronologically. Fair copies of the credentials, arranged chronologically, are in **record of credentials, 1781-89** (Item 179, M247, roll 196), a record kept by the Secretary of Congress.

CC.360.8. **Oaths of allegiance, 1776-89** (Item 195, M247, roll 201), is a series which consists of oaths taken by military officers and civilian officials of the pre-federal government, including the staff of Continental Congress, commercial agents, interpreters, and Indian agents. About half of the oaths are those of military personnel. It is indexed by a pre-federal volume (Item 184, M247, roll 196), but that document is incomplete and not entirely accurate. A better index, prepared at the Library of Congress, presumably when this series was bound, is "Card Index #3" (M247, roll 3). Waldemaier's

Some of the Earliest Oaths of Allegiance to the United States of America (1944) is an index to this series and the series described in **MI.93.18.**, which consists entirely of oaths of military officers.

CC.360.9. Commissions issued by the continental government to U.S. citizens, authorizing them to perform such functions as negotiating boundary disputes, arranging commercial relations with other nations, and treating with Indians, are in **record books, registers, and indexes kept by the Secretary of Congress, 1775-89: form book [n.d.]** (Item 182, M247, roll 196).

JOURNALS OF THE CONTINENTAL CONGRESS

CC.360.10. The principal daily record of the Continental Congress, excepting those matters which were of a sensitive enough nature to appear only in the "secret journals," is the series **rough journals, 1774-89** (Item 1, M247, rolls 8-14). Of the 38 volumes in the series only number 15 is missing, and its entries are included in the other journals, primarily the transcript journals (see **CC.360.11.**). The rough journals contain many marginal notes, which include references to other journals, reminders concerning payments due on the basis of congressional action, indications of actions taken on congressional resolutions or other acts, and instructions to contemporary printers. The rough journals are the basis for JCC. See also **CC.360.20.**

CC.360.11. The **transcript journals, 1775-79** (Item 2, M247, rolls 15-17), consist of 10 volumes of the rough journals revised for printing, on the order of the Continental Congress. They are sometimes called the "corrected journals."

CC.360.12. There are also two other documents among Miscellaneous PCC, both called "Minutes of the Congress." They cover similar periods—May 10-July 27, 1775 (M332, roll 9), and May 10-June 22, 1775 (M332, roll 10). They are written in a different hand from all the other journals, most of which were done by Charles Thomson, and have textual variations when compared to other journals covering the same period. They are either additional contemporary copies or copies made in the process of publishing congressional journals in the early 19th century.

CC.360.13. All of the other journals of the Continental Congress are described here in tabular format. The following table indicates their titles and dates of coverage, their location in PCC and its published microfilm version, which other copies of the journals they duplicate (by item number), and whether they contain materials found nowhere else.

Title, Dates	Item No. of PCC: Roll No. of M247	Also in Item No.	Unique Material?
Secret domestic journal, 1775-87	3:18	1, 4, 6	No
Secret foreign and domestic journal, 1780-86	4:18	3, 5	No
Secret foreign journal, 1775-88	5:19	1, 4, 6	Yes
Imperfect secret journal, 1776-88	6:20	3, 5	No
Rough secret journal, 1776-79	6A:20	6	Yes
More secret journal (copy), 1781-82	7:21	7A	Yes
More secret journal (original), 1781-82	7A:21	7, 5	Yes
Secret journal, 1776-83	8:21	1, 3	Yes

Of all the journals listed, only the rough secret journal (Item 6A, M247, roll 20) contains material not used in JCC.

CC.360.14. There is also a **journal of the Committee of the States, [1784]** (Item 10, M247, roll 22), kept by the committee provided for under the Articles of Confederation, which constituted the national government while Congress was adjourned, June 4-August 19, 1784. It is included in JCC.

RECORDS SUPPLEMENTARY TO THE JOURNALS

CC.360.15. **Motions made in Congress, 1777-88** (Item 36, M247, rolls 42-43), is a four-volume series consisting of motions, many in rough form with additions and deletions noted, most of which were offered to Congress as resolutions. Many bear notes indicating the results of congressional votes on them. They are in generally chronological order and most of them appear in JCC. **Other reports of committees of Congress, 1776-88: reports of the Committee of the States, [1784]** (Item 32, M247, roll 39), contains a similar record for the period mentioned in **CC.360.14.**

CC.360.16. **Abridged resolves of Congress, 1777-86, with a detached list of abridged resolves, 1775-76** (Item 178, M247, roll 195), consists of lists of resolutions, including appointments of military officers, formation of congressional committees, and designation of agents of the Continental Congress, such as loan officers and Indian agents. The resolves of 1775-76 are listed in groups by general subject categories and thereunder chronologically; the others are in generally chronological order.

CC.360.17. Four series in PCC contain registers of reports received by the Secretary of Congress from boards, offices, and committees of Congress. They are:

1. **record books, registers, and indexes kept by the Secretary of Congress, 1775-89:** lists, 1775-85 (Item 183, M247, roll 196);
2. **record books, registers, and indexes kept by the Secretary of Congress, 1775-89: despatch books, 1779-89** (Item 185, M247, roll 197);
3. **record books, registers, and indexes kept by the Secretary of Congress, 1775-89: committee book, 1781-85** (Item 186, M247, roll 197); and
4. **record books, registers, and indexes kept by the Secretary of Congress, 1775-89:** registers of reports from boards, offices, and committees (Items 189-191, M247, roll 198).

CC.360.18. Two books kept by Charles Thomson list the documents he gave to members and officials of Congress for distribution to the states and to agents of Congress. They are:

1. **record books, registers, and indexes kept by the Secretary of Congress, 1775-89: memorandum book for 1783-85** (Item 181, M247, roll 196) and
2. **record books, registers, and indexes kept by the Secretary of Congress, 1775-89: memorandum book for 1785-88** (Item 187, M247, roll 198).

CC.360.19. Copies of congressional ordinances which are signed by the President of Congress and attested to by the Secretary of Congress are in the series **copies of ordinances of the Confederation Congress, 1781-88** (Item 175, M247, roll 194).

CC.360.20. The unsigned orders and resolutions of the Congress contained in the series **sundry motions and resolves of Congress, 1785-86 and 1788** (Item 123, M247, roll 140), are not included in the rough journals (see **CC.360.10.**) or JCC.

LETTERBOOKS OF PRESIDENTS AND THE SECRETARY OF CONGRESS AND RELATED RECORDS

CC.360.21. The letterbooks of the Presidents of Congress, containing copies of the letters they sent, are in five series of PCC. In chronological order, they are:

Names	Dates	No. of Vols.	Item No. of PCC: Roll No. of M247
John Hancock	1775-77	2	12A:23
Henry Laurens	1777-78	2	13:23
John Jay and Samuel Huntington	1778-80	1	14:24
Samuel Huntington	1780-81	1	15:24
Samuel Huntington, Thomas McKean, John Hanson, Elias Boudinot, Thomas Mifflin, Richard Henry Lee, and Arthur St. Clair	1781-87	1	16:24

There are no letterbooks for the terms indicated in which the following individuals served as President of Congress:

Name	Term of Office
Peyton Randolph	September 5, 1774-October 22, 1774
Henry Middleton	October 22, 1774-October 26, 1774
John Hancock	November 23, 1785-June 6, 1786
Nathaniel Gorham	June 6, 1786-November 1786
Cyrus Griffin	January 22, 1788-November 1788

CC.360.22. **Letterbooks of the Secretary of Congress, 1779-89** (Item 18, M247, roll 25), consists of two volumes of copies of letters sent by Charles Thomson, which also contain a few of the secretary's accounts, 1783-86. A separate series (Item 17, M247, roll 25) consists of a 147- page list of the letters, with those to states listed separately from the others. It also contains Thomson's index to the letterbooks.

CC.360.23. **Letterbook of the Executive Committee of the Second Continental Congress, 1776-77** (Item 133, M247, roll 144) was kept by the committee assigned to conduct the business of the Congress in Philadelphia while the body adjourned to Baltimore.

LETTERS AND OTHER COMMUNICATIONS
RECEIVED BY CONGRESS

CC.360.24. Two large series of memorials and petitions addressed to Congress are described in **PE.360.2.-PE.360.4.** Other communications received by Congress which relate primarily to one or a few subjects, such as letters and reports from army officers (see **MI.360.7.-MI.360.28.**), are described in the relevant subject chapters of this guide.

CC.360.25. The letters received by the Executive Committee in Philadelphia from the President of Congress during the time Congress met in Baltimore are among those in **letters of John Hancock, and miscellaneous papers, 1774-85** (Item 58, M247, roll 71).

CC.360.26. The series **miscellaneous letters addressed to Congress, 1775-89** (Item 78, M247, rolls 90-104), consists of 24 volumes of documents on a very wide variety of subjects. They are generally arranged alphabetically by the surname of the writer or the first signer in cases of multiple correspondents. Many of them are mentioned in relevant subject chapters of this guide. An alphabetically arranged card index to the names of senders and some other persons associated with the documents in this series, "Card Index #2" (M247, roll 3), was prepared while the records were at the Library of Congress.

CC.360.27. Letters and other documents sent to Congress by state governors and other officials, committees of safety, and state legislatures are in a group of series, the whole of which is nearly as large as the series of miscellaneous letters to Congress. They are called State Papers and are also cited in relevant subject chapters of this guide. The 14 series are:

States or Subjects	Dates	Item No. of PCC: Roll No. of M247
New Hampshire and Rhode Island	1775-88	64:78
Massachusetts	1775-87	65:79
Connecticut	1775-89	66:80
New York	1775-88	67:81
New Jersey	1775-88	68:82

States or Subjects	Dates	Item No. of PCC: Roll No. of M247
Pennsylvania	1775-91	69:83
Maryland and Delaware	1775-89	70:84
Virginia	1775-88	71:85
North and South Carolina	1776-88	72:86
Georgia	1777-88	73:87
"Acts of the Thirteen States"	1775-88	74-76:88
Territorial disputes between Pennsylvania and Connecticut	1780-85	77:89
Trade regulations	1786	77:89
Petitions about the Indiana region	1779-83	77:89

REPORTS OF COMMITTEES OF CONGRESS AND RELATED RECORDS

CC.360.28. There are 21 series of committee reports in PCC. Most are described in the relevant subject chapters of this guide. The following seven relate to the functioning of the Continental Congress or deal with truly national or general concerns:

Subject(s)	Dates	Item No. of PCC: Roll No. of M247
Administration of Congress and design of the Great Seal	1775-88	23:31
Functioning of the executive departments	1776-86	28:35
Inquiries into the functioning of the executive departments	1782-85	188:198
Communications with the states	1777-88	20:29
Relations with the states and days of fasting and thanksgiving	1775-86	24:31
The Committee of the States (see **CC.360.14.**)	1784	32:39
Postponed committee reports	1777-88	31:38

Charles Thomson's index to the committee reports is in Item 17 of PCC (see **CC.360.22.**).

GENERAL AND MISCELLANEOUS RECORDS OF THE SECRETARY OF CONGRESS

CC.360.29. Miscellaneous PCC contains four sets of records from the office of the Secretary of Congress which consist mostly of lists and registers by which Charles Thomson and his staff kept track of routine congressional affairs. They are:

1. Lists of letters and committee reports on various subjects, 1775-88 (M332, roll 9), which are arranged by categories, usually the names of correspondents;
2. Various papers, including copies of resolves of Congress, 1774-87 (M332, roll 9), many of which appear to be 19th-century copies and are in no discernible order;
3. Copies of letters of commendation and recommendation, 1778-88, and one original letter, 1773 (M332, roll 9), which are arranged in chronological order; and
4. Receipts for documents removed from the office of the Secretary of Congress, 1780-88 (M332, roll 9), which are mostly for copies of the journals of Congress sent to national and state government officials, military officers, and others.

CC.360.30. In PCC are four series of similar records:

1. **letters and papers of Charles Thomson, 1781-89** (Item 49, M247, roll 63), which contains drafts of many congressional resolutions and other records in no discernible order;
2. **register of incidental accounts, 1785-89** (Item 146, M247, roll 156), which pertains to expenses, including salaries, in the secretary's office;
3. **reports of the Secretary of the Confederation Congress, 1785-88** (Item 180, M247, roll 196), part of the proceedings of the Congress; and
4. **... records of the Office of Congress, 1781-89, ...** (Item 55, M247, roll 68), see **FI.360.10.** and **FO.360.42.**

CC.360.31. The series **returns of inhabitants of various states and miscellaneous papers, 1774-86** (Item 177, M247, roll 194), contains some of Thomson's accounts, miscellaneous documents, and tables showing the population of several states at various times. The states and years are:

Connecticut	1782
Maryland	1782
Massachusetts	1783
New Hampshire	1775, 1783
New Jersey	1784
New York	1786
Rhode Island	1774, 1783
South Carolina	1782

Some of the state tables also show estimates of the number and value of buildings. The New York table contains a bit of information on that colony's populations in 1756 and 1771. See also **LA.360.8.**

CC.360.32. The series **papers kept by the office of the Secretary of the Continental Congress, papers relating to fiscal affairs, and broadsides issued by the Continental Congress, 1775-88** (M332, rolls 9 and 10), contains 3 feet of broadsides, most of which are duplicates. There are two sets, only the first of which is microfilmed in M332. It is labeled "incomplete," and covers only 1775-78. The other subseries contains as many as 100 copies each of some documents. The broadsides cover a wide variety of subjects and include ordinances, treaties, and reports. The "incomplete" subseries is arranged in chronological order. A complete list of the broadsides of the Continental Congress, including depositories that hold them, is in the bibliographic notes in the last volume for each year in JCC. Originals of many of the broadsides are scattered throughout PCC.

INDEXES TO PCC

CC.360.33. Most of the indexes to specific series or related groups of series in PCC are described with the records to which they pertain. Most are also much less useful than *Index: PCC* and *Index: JCC* (see the introduction).

CC.360.34. Nine bound manuscript indexes to PCC were prepared in the Department of State while the records were in its custody. All but one are microfilmed in M247, some twice—once as indicated below and once again on the same roll as the records to which they pertain. They are:

Vol. No.	M247 Roll No.	Subject(s)
1	4	committee reports
2	4	reports and letters of executive depts.
3	4	letters of the Presidents and the Secretary of Congress
5	4	various records (The title is illegible, but many varied series are indexed.)
6	5	state papers
7	5-6	foreign and domestic correspondence
8	7	letters and papers of general officers and the Quartermaster and Commissary Generals' Depts.
9	7	memorials and petitions

Volume 4 of the indexes was transferred from the Department of State to the War Department with the records to which it pertains and is now among the registers described in **MI.93.15.**

OTHER RECORDS

CC.360.35. The series **intercepted letters, 1775-81** (Item 51, M247, roll 65), is made up of documents sent by British subjects in England and America to British officials, relatives, and friends, but intercepted in transit by representatives of the continental government. They contain information on persons, events, and conditions throughout the United States and in Britain's loyal American colonies. Many are described in the relevant subject chapters of this guide.

CC.360.36. The series **various proposals on locating the seat of government and printing the journals, 1777-89** (Item 46, M247, roll 60), covers the subjects in its title as well as proposals and cost estimates regarding publication and printing of a Bible by the Continental Congress. The records concerning location of the seat of government include letters, maps, and proposals sent to Congress by many states and towns.

CC.360.37. **Miscellaneous papers, 1770-89** (Item 59, M247, rolls 72-73), contains four volumes of records including proposals, administrative records of Congress, and keys to ciphers used by the continental government. Many of the miscellaneous records are described in relevant subject chapters of this guide.

Record Group 11

General Records of the
United States Government

CC.11.1. This record group consists of the Constitution of the United States, the Bill of Rights and other amendments, and related records; laws of the United States and related records; international treaties and agreements; Indian treaties; presidential proclamations, executive orders, and other presidential documents; rules and regulations of federal agencies; electoral records; and records pertaining to the Great Seal of the United States.

CC.11.2. Part of the series **dies of the U.S. seal, 1782-1909**, is the first die of the Great Seal of the United States, which was cut in 1782 and used until about 1841. Proposals for the design of the seal were made in the Continental Congress as early as July 1776, but the design used was not adopted until June 20, 1782. The first die was cut in brass and consists of an obverse only. For other records relating to the seal see **CC.360.28.**

Record Group 45

Naval Records Collection of the Office
of Naval Records and Library

CC.45.1. The Naval Records Collection was begun in 1882 when the Librarian of the Navy Department, then in the Office of Naval Intelligence, began to collect for publication naval documents relating to the Civil War. In the early 1900s the office began collecting records of naval bureaus and records relating to naval personnel and operations before 1861. In 1906 an act (34 Stat. 579) required that all naval records in executive departments relating to public and private craft engaged in the Revolutionary War be transferred to the Secretary of the Navy. For further information on the Naval Records Collection, see **NA.45.1.**

CC.45.2. The Archives Section of the Office of Naval Records and Library created a newspaper file consisting of four series. Many of the records are accompanied by memorandums stating that they were given to the department or to the Secretary of the Navy by naval officers or other individuals. Only one series, **English and Irish newspapers, 1733-1811,** contains originals of pre-federal newspa-

CHAPTER CN

Records of the Constitutional Convention

CN.0.1. Commissioners representing the states of Virginia and Maryland met at Mount Vernon in March 1785 to resolve mutual problems pertaining to navigation of the Potomac River and the Chesapeake Bay. They also drafted an agreement recommending to their respective legislatures uniform commercial regulations and imposts, and annual conferences on common commercial problems. On January 21, 1786, the Virginia legislature invited all the states to discuss commercial problems at a convention to be held at Annapolis. Nine states accepted the invitation, but only delegates from New York, New Jersey, Delaware, Pennsylvania, and Virginia attended the meeting. Although it only lasted a short time, September 11-14, 1786, the meeting led to the significant proposal to go beyond consideration of commercial problems and discuss a way to "devise such further provisions as shall appear . . . necessary to render the constitution of the . . . Government adequate to the exigencies of the Union," at a convention of all the states in Philadelphia in May 1787.

CN.0.2. Five states had already named delegates to the proposed convention when the Continental Congress cautiously endorsed the proposal of the Annapolis Convention on February 21, 1787. Congress resolved that "it is expedient that . . . a convention of delegates who shall have been appointed by the several States be held . . . for the sole and express purpose of revising the Articles of Confederation and reporting to Congress and the several legislatures such alterations and provisions therein as shall when agreed to in Congress and confirmed by the States render the federal Constitution adequate to the exigencies of Government and the preservation of the Union." The Philadelphia convention did not begin until May 25, nearly two weeks after it was scheduled to start, because a quorum of seven states was not present until then. George Washington was elected President of the Convention and William Jackson, who had served as Assistant Secretary of War, was named its secretary.

CN.0.3. The history of the Constitutional Convention may be divided into a number of fairly distinct periods corresponding to the introduction, consideration, and refinement of various plans of government. On May 29 Edmund Randolph of Virginia proposed 15 resolutions comprising the Virginia Plan of union, which went beyond revising the Articles of Confederation and proposed a new national government. From May 30 until June 13 the convention, as a committee of the whole, debated the Virginia Plan, and then presented 19 resolutions based upon it. The smaller states opposed that set of resolutions on the particular basis of its provision for proportional rather than equal representation of the states in a national legislature. Therefore, on June 15 William Paterson introduced the New Jersey Plan, nine resolutions, stressing retention of a revised Articles of Confederation, which conferred greater powers upon the Continental Congress. For four days beginning June 16 the convention debated the merits of simply amending the Articles of Confederation or of framing an entirely new national government. On the last day, June 19, 1787, by a vote of seven states to three, the delegates decided to become a true constitutional convention.

CN.0.4. A clause-by-clause consideration of the Virginia Plan ensued, but early in July an impasse occurred over the question of representation in the new legislature. On July 16 the deadlock was broken by the Great Compromise, by which a bicameral body would have an upper house with equal representation from each state and a lower house with membership and voting based on the population of each state. The convention then proceeded to produce 23 "fundamental resolutions" based mainly on the Virginia Plan and forming a rough draft of the Constitution as finally adopted. A Committee of Detail presented the delegates with a further draft of 23 articles on August 6. Clause-by-clause refinement, in which such details as terms of office were decided, went on until September 10. Then a Committee on Revision of Style and Arrangement was instructed to prepare the final draft. That draft was submitted to the convention on the 12th; examined and amended September 13-15; adopted and ordered to be engrossed on the 15th; and adopted and signed on September 17, 1787. The Constitutional Convention then adjourned.

CN.0.5. The engrossed, signed Constitution, with related resolutions of the convention and a covering letter from George Washington, was received by the Continental Congress at New York on September 20. Eight days later Congress resolved to transmit the proposed instrument of government to the legislatures of the several states for submission to special ratifying conventions. On December 7, 1787, Delaware was the first state to ratify. Others followed suit, and on June 21, 1788, New Hampshire became the ninth to do so. Since, by Article VII of the Constitution, it was to become operative when ratified by nine states, the President of the Continental Congress "reminded" that body of the significance of New Hampshire's action on July 2, 1788. Accordingly, on September 13, 1788, Congress adopted an ordinance setting dates for the election of the President of the United States and the convening of the first federal Congress under the Constitution. Thus the nation's pre-federal period came to a close on March 4, 1789, when the first Congress provided for by the Constitution convened.

Record Group 360

Records of the Continental and Confederation Congresses and the Constitutional Convention

CN.360.1. Record Group 360 consists primarily of PCC (M247, 204 rolls), and Miscellaneous PCC (M332, 10 rolls).* For additional information about those bodies of records and indexes thereto, see the introduction.

CN.360.2. Most of the records in RG 360 that pertain to the Constitutional Convention are in National Archives Microfilm Publication M866 (1 roll), although some are in M247 and M332.

RECORDS IN PCC AND MISCELLANEOUS PCC

CN.360.3. Records pertaining to the Annapolis Convention of 1786 (see **CN.0.1.**) are in **State Papers, 1775-91: . . . papers relating to trade regulations for the United States, 1786** . . . (Item 77, M247, roll 89). They consist mostly of a covering document, in the hand of Thomas Jefferson, for the proceedings described in **CN.360.4.**, and official copies of the resolutions of Virginia, Delaware, New Jersey, Massachusetts, New York, and Pennsylvania. The series contains about 60 pages in no discernible arrangement.

CN.360.4. The proceedings of the Annapolis Convention are included in Miscellaneous PCC (M332, roll 10). Two of its six pages are reproduced in *The Formation of the Union* (1970). It bears the holographic signatures of the delegates from all five states. The official copy of the report of the convention to Congress, with a cover letter by John Dickinson, is bound as pages 187-194 of volume 8 of the series described in **CC.360.26.**

CN.360.5. The record book labeled "Ratifications of the Constitution [of the United States of America, 1786-1791]" (M332, roll 10), was created by Benjamin Bankson, a clerk in the office of the Secretary of the Continental Congress, who made copies of documents re-

---

*For a complete list of National Archives Microfilm Publications cited in this guide, see Appendix A.

lated to the Constitutional Convention as a reference volume for Charles Thomson. The volume is often called "Bankson's Journal." It includes documents pertaining to all of the conventions leading up to the 1787 meeting in Philadelphia, as well as administrative documents concerning the convention itself and the subsequent ratification of the Constitution and the Bill of Rights. Only that portion of the volume containing copies of the credentials of members of the Constitutional Convention has been reproduced in M866. The originals of the credentials have never been found, and Bankson's Journal provides the best copies. Originals of the ratification documents are in RG 11.

THE OFFICIAL RECORDS OF THE CONSTITUTIONAL CONVENTION

CN.360.6. The records described in **CN.360.7.-CN.360.11.** are designated the "Official Records of the Constitutional Convention" because they were delivered by William Jackson to George Washington on the evening of September 17, 1787, the last day of the convention. President Washington subsequently deposited them with Secretary of State Timothy Pickering on March 19, 1796.

CN.360.7. Letters and enclosures received by the Constitutional Convention (M866, 1 roll), consist of five items. One is from a committee of citizens of Rhode Island concerning that state's failure to send delegates to the convention. Another is from James McHenry, a delegate from Maryland, explaining his need to visit a seriously ill brother in Baltimore. A third is from Jonas Phillips to the members of the convention, informing them of the difficulties encountered by Jewish inhabitants of Philadelphia. The other two concern permission granted to the convention by the Library Company of Philadelphia to borrow books.

CN.360.8. Journal of the Constitutional Convention, May 14-September 17, 1787 (M866, 1 roll), consists of four bound volumes. They are entirely in the hand of the Secretary of the Convention, William Jackson, except for some marginal annotations by George Washington in the first two volumes. They consist of:

1. a formal journal of the proceedings of the convention, May 14-September 15, 1787 (153 pages);
2. a journal of the proceedings of the Committee of the Whole House, May 30-June 19, 1787 (28 pages);
3. a record book containing the voting record of the convention, in tabular format, by states (8 pages); and
4. loose sheets of voting tabulations (later bound into 9 pages).

The voting tallies are both recorded in such a way as to make it difficult to assign votes to specific questions. See the descriptive pamphlet to M866 for a more detailed explanation.

CN.360.9. Virginia (Randolph) Plan as Amended: Two Endorsed Copies (M866, 1 roll) consists of two versions of the plan, both in the hand of William Jackson. The first contains 18 unnumbered resolutions; the second 19 numbered resolutions. The second appears to have been slightly amended by the Committee of the Whole House. Each of the plans is written on the front and back of two pages. For an earlier draft of the Virginia Plan see **CN.360.12.**

CN.360.10. The First Printed Draft of the Constitution, Reported to the Convention by the Committee of Detail (M866, 1 roll) consists of seven pages bearing marginal notes by Washington and others and an endorsement by Timothy Pickering. It was used by Washington after August 6, 1787, when the Committee of Detail delivered its report to the convention.

CN.360.11. Draft of the Letter From the Convention to Congress, to Accompany the Constitution (M866, 1 roll) consists of three pages and an endorsement agreed upon by the convention on September 12. Another copy is in Bankson's Journal (see **CN.360.5.**).

RECORDS RETAINED BY DELEGATES TO THE CONSTITUTIONAL CONVENTION

CN.360.12. David Brearley was Chief Justice of New Jersey and a delegate to the Constitutional Convention. Documents which he acquired while attending the convention (M866, 1 roll) were transmitted to the Department of State in 1818 by Gen. Joseph Bloomfield, his executor. They consist of:

1. population estimates for the states (2 pages and an endorsement), dated September 27, 1787, which were probably used earlier to apportion the members of the proposed House of Representatives;
2. the Virginia Plan, consisting of 15 resolutions as originally submitted by Randolph on May 29, 1787 (4 pages);
3. the New Jersey Plan, consisting of 11 resolutions as amended and submitted June 15, 1787 (7 pages);
4. a plan of government submitted to the convention by Alexander Hamilton on June 18, 1787, with notes by James Madison, Paterson, Brearley, and others (3 pages plus endorsement);

5. the report of the Grand Committee presented by Elbridge Gerry on July 5, 1787, which led to the Great Compromise on representation in the legislature (1 page plus endorsement);
6. the first printed draft of the Constitution, reported to the convention by the Committee on Detail, August 6, 1787, printed off center with annotations in the left margin (7 pages plus endorsement); and
7. the printed draft of the Constitution presented to the convention by the Committee on Revision of Style and Arrangement, September 13, 1787, with annotations (4 pages plus endorsement).

CN.360.13. An original motion, two pages in the hand of Elbridge Gerry (M866, 1 roll), concerns the method of electing the chief executive. It recommends the proportions of the total vote that were to be allowed each state legislature.

Record Group 11
General Records of the United States Government

CN.11.1. This record group consists of the Constitution of the United States, the Bill of Rights and other amendments, and related records; laws of the United States and related records; international treaties and agreements; Indian treaties; presidential proclamations, executive orders, and other presidential documents; rules and regulations of federal agencies; electoral records; and records pertaining to the Great Seal of the United States.

CN.11.2. The engrossed **Constitution of the United States, 1787**, is the document ordered by the Constitutional Convention to be handwritten on parchment on September 15, 1787. It consists of four sheets of parchment accompanied by a single parchment sheet containing the resolution of the convention, September 17, 1787, directing that the Constitution be transmitted to the Continental Congress and thereafter submitted to ratifying conventions of the states. Pages one and four of the Constitution are on permanent display at the National Archives in Washington, DC.

CN.11.3. **The Bill of Rights and ratifications, 1789-90**, are reproduced in National Archives Microfilm Publication M338 (1 roll). The Bill of Rights is on a single sheet of parchment, which is on permanent display at the National Archives in Washington, DC. It is the original joint resolution of the First Congress, September 25, 1789, proposing 12 amendments to the Constitution. The instruments of ratification from 11 states for the Constitution and for the 10 proposed amendments which were adopted are in a separate bound volume.

Record Group 59
General Records of the Department of State

CN.59.1. The Department of Foreign Affairs was established by an act of July 1789 and two months later was designated the Department of State by the same Congress. It was assigned such functions as preserving and publishing laws and treaties, keeping the seal of the United States, and serving as custodian of the records of the United States previously held by the Secretary of Congress. The department was also in charge of territorial affairs from 1789 to 1873.

CN.59.2. Among the records of the Bureau of Rolls and Library in the series **miscellaneous documents printed, ca. 1780-1932**, is a pamphlet titled "Some Observations on the Constitution." It is in the style of a letter addressed by James Monroe to the persons who elected him to be a delegate to the Constitutional Convention. It contains annotations which are thought to have been made by Monroe in the process of correcting printer's errors.

CN.59.3. Another series among the records of the Bureau of Rolls and Library is **manuscript copy for John Quincy Adams' edition of the Journal of the Constitutional Convention, 1818-19.** It consists mostly of fair copies of documents made in preparation of the publication of *Journal, Acts and Proceedings, of the Convention, Assembled at Philadelphia, Monday, May 14, and Dissolved Monday, September 17, 1787, which formed the Constitution of the United States* (1819), which was provided for by Congress in 1818 (3 Stat. 475). The manuscript as prepared for publication contains copies of some documents from as early as 1787 that are neither in the published journal nor among other records in the National Archives. These include a copy of a letter by Secretary of State Timothy Pickering, March 19, 1796, describing all of the official records of the convention received by him from George Washington, and a copy of a letter of June 1787 describing the forces in Rhode Island supporting and opposing the convention.

CHAPTER CO
Records of Commercial Affairs

CO.0.1. On September 19, 1775, the Continental Congress established the Secret Committee to import arms and ammunition. This committee was the beginning of a limited involvement in commercial affairs by Congress. As in other areas of government responsibility, such as foreign relations and fiscal management, Congress did not place complete authority to act in its behalf in the hands of any one subordinate body. Special committees were appointed from time to time to make special purchases and to assess the state of trade.

CO.0.2. Because purchases of foreign goods could not be made with continental currency, the Secret Committee purchased tobacco and other American products and shipped them overseas to exchange for the supplies necessary to conduct the war. To some extent this committee shared with the Marine Committee and the Board of Admiralty supervisory authority over the Continental Navy and the sale of prizes taken by continental warships and privateers. Supplies obtained by the Secret Committee were distributed to the Board of War and the Marine Committee.

CO.0.3. To assist the Secret Committee in its functions, agents were appointed both at home and abroad. Silas Deane, one of the committee's early members, was sent to France in 1776 to procure supplies. His conduct in the post, or at least opinions concerning his conduct, led to and fed one of the first and deepest factional rifts in the Continental Congress. Participants in the dispute rallied behind either Deane or Arthur Lee of Virginia, who also served Congress in France. Thomas Morris was made an additional European agent of the committee, and in 1777 Oliver Pollock was appointed its agent in New Orleans. The committee also dealt with American merchants both by purchasing imported goods and by contracting to purchase commodities to send them abroad in exchange for supplies.

CO.0.4. By July 1777, the membership of the Secret Committee was down to two, and the Congress replaced it by appointing the Committee of Commerce, which was vested with the same powers. It was reestablished on December 14, 1778, but, like the earlier Secret Committee, it declined over the next 3 years. After 1781 the commercial affairs of the confederation government usually were handled by the Superintendent of Finance, the Secretary for Foreign Affairs, or special committees.

CO.0.5. Letters received by the Continental Congresses from so-called commercial agents but directed mainly to the Committee for Foreign Affairs and the Secretary for Foreign Affairs are described in the chapter on foreign affairs, as are records pertaining to the negotiation of commercial treaties between the continental and confederation governments and foreign nations (see especially **FO.360.29., FO.360.31., FO.360.41., FO.360.48., FO.360.51.-FO.360.52.,** and **FO.360.64.-FO.360.65.**).

CO.0.6. The chapter on judicial affairs contains descriptions of bodies of records in which commercial affairs are prominent, usually as the subject of litigation. Among those records are case files concerning prize and salvage actions both during and before the Revolution, which are described in **JU.360.2., JU.21.2., JU.21.6.-JU.21.7.,** and **JU.267.2.-JU.267.5.** Also, some cases in which debts to Loyalist merchants were at issue are described in **JU.49.2.**

Record Group 360

Records of the Continental and Confederation Congresses and the Constitutional Convention

CO.360.1. Record Group 360 consists primarily of PCC (M247, 204 rolls) and Miscellaneous PCC (M332, 10 rolls).* For additional information about those bodies of records and indexes thereto, see the introduction.

CO.360.2. The series **other reports of committees of Congress, 1776-88: on the Clothing Department; reports of the Commissioners of Accounts for the Clothing, Hospital, and Marine Departments; reports of the Committee of Commerce; and miscellaneous reports, with lists of postponed reports, 1777-88** (Item 31, M247, roll 38), contains records concerning mainly the shipment of goods to and from the United States, including such subjects as payment of agents, outfitting of vessels, consignment of cargoes, purchase of supplies, reimbursement for losses, and disposition of prizes. They are dated in the early fall of 1778, near the beginning of a particularly violent period in the Deane-Lee controversy. Included are a few miscellaneous records, notably a set of resolutions summon-

---

*For a complete list of National Archives Microfilm Publications cited in this guide, see Appendix A.

ing William Carmichael before Congress for questioning about the conduct of Silas Deane. Carmichael had served both Arthur Lee and Deane in France, but he was in Congress representing Maryland by the time of the congressional inquiry. The reports are in a roughly chronological arrangement by date of report or action thereon, with some records from 1777-78 appearing after the 1781 entries.

CO.360.3. The series **copies of other reports of committees of Congress, 1777-88: reports of the Committees of Conference with the Commander in Chief at Cambridge, 1775, and Valley Forge, 1778-79, and the proceedings of the Convention of Committees at New Haven, 1778, and Hartford, 1779-80** (Item 33, M247, roll 40), largely consists of official copies of three "conventions of state committees" concerning trade, prices, currency depreciation, and support for the Continental Army. Included also are letters from the committees to the President of Congress. The records are arranged chronologically by date of convention.

CO.360.4. Documents concerning Pollock's activities as U.S. commercial agent in New Orleans are in the series **letters and papers of Oliver Pollock, 1776-85, 1792** (Item 50, M247, roll 64). Included are correspondence with the Continental Congress respecting his duties and payment due him for his services, reports by and to congressional committees, and testimonials and other documents from merchants in New Orleans. Information about the opening of New Orleans to American commerce, disposition of British prizes brought by U.S. citizens to that port, the chartering and outfitting of U.S. vessels, purchase and shipment of goods to the east coast and up the Mississippi River, and Spain's entrance into the war against Great Britain is found in the records. Arrangement is by subject of Pollock's dealings with Congress and thereunder chronologically.

CO.360.5. The series **records and accounts of Silas Deane, Beaumarchais, and Arthur Lee, 1776-84, and letters and a memorial relating to American trade in the French West Indies, 1788-89** (Item 54, M247, roll 67), contains proposals by a resident of Port-au-Prince, St. Domingue (Haiti), sent to the Secret Committee through Secretary of Congress Charles Thomson. Rey, a French citizen and merchant, argues in favor of trade between the United States and the French West Indies in spite of the protestations of merchants in metropolitan France. He contends that France alone cannot fill its colonies' needs and discusses duties, prices, and goods as well as individual U.S. merchants he has met in Philadelphia and Port-au-Prince. Arrangement is generally chronological with English translations following the French originals. The records pertaining to Deane, Lee, and Beaumarchais are described in **FI.360.67.**

Record Group 15
Records of the Veterans Administration

CO.15.1. The first federal Congress passed an act on September 29, 1789, providing for payment of military pensions to Revolutionary War veterans and their dependents—the first in a long series of pension laws. For further information see the chapter on pensions and bounty lands (**PE.0.1.**).

CO.15.2. The "Day Book of the Firm of Wadsworth and Carter, April 27, 1781-November 13, 1782" (1 vol.—240 pp.), is a part of **pension and bounty-land warrant application files based on Revolutionary War service** (M804, roll 2670). It is not known to which case it pertains. The document was kept at Hartford, CT, and contains debit and credit entries for various persons and firms concerning the trade and transportation of such supplies as foodstuffs, wood, livestock, and feed. Entries exist for other assets and liabilities. Jeremiah Wadsworth was a Hartford merchant who served in 1778-79 as Commissary General of Purchases for the Continental Army. John Carter was a Newport, RI, businessman. Each entry usually shows the date, the person or firm involved, the supplies or services exchanged, and their value. Ledger numbers are present, but refer to no document found in the National Archives. Arrangement is chronological by date of entry.

Record Group 26
Records of the U.S. Coast Guard

CO.26.1. Treasury Department officials were responsible for maintenance of lighthouses from 1789 until the creation of the Light-House Board in 1852. Aids to navigation, which includes lights and other warning devices, became the responsibility of the Coast Guard in 1915.

CO.26.2. Unbound material at the end of the 14-volume series **correspondence and other records of the Light-House Service pertaining chiefly to the location, building, and maintenance of lighthouses, 1765-1852,** dates from the pre-federal period. It was assembled for an exhibit at the Library of Congress commemorating the 100th anniversary of the Light-House Service in 1939. The records directly concern the establishment of two lighthouses, at Cape

Henlopen, DE (1765), and at Philadelphia (1785). Other documents relate to colonial laws for the building of lighthouses in Massachusetts (1715-71), Delaware (1763), and New York (1761), and to proposed lotteries to support lighthouses at New London, CT (1761), and Sandy Hook, NY (1763). The records are arranged according to the geographic location to which they pertain.

Record Group 27

Records of the U.S. Weather Bureau

CO.27.1. Meteorological observation systems and records in the federal government began in the Office of the Surgeon General in 1818 and the Smithsonian Institution in 1847. All pre-1818 weather records were kept by private citizens, but those that came into federal custody have been placed in this record group.

CO.27.2. The merchant vessel *Empress of China*, under Capt. John Green, sailed for China from New York City on February 22, 1784, with a cargo of ginseng and other articles of commerce. A log apparently kept by the ship doctor is abstracted in 11 pages of volume 524 of the series **abstracts of ship logs, 1842-93.** When and from what source the log was copied is unknown, but it contains information on navigation, weather, food supplies, sighting and catching of birds and other marine wildlife, land sightings, and celebrations of special events and holidays. The series was compiled as records of marine observations.

Record Group 36

Records of the U.S. Customs Service

CO.36.1. The Customs Service, established in July 1789, became part of the newly created Department of the Treasury in September 1789. The functions of the service relate to import and export of merchandise, collection of tonnage taxes, entrance and clearance of vessels, regulation of vessels in coastal and fishing trades, and protection of passengers. Its records include some prefederal documentation.

RECORDS FOR CONNECTICUT

CO.36.2. Pre-federal customs records for the colony and state of Connecticut consist of four series, two each located at the National Archives in Washington, DC, and at the regional archives in Boston. **Record of inward and outward foreign and coastwise manifests, New Haven, CT, 1762-1801**, shows the names of vessels and masters, dates of entrance or clearance, types and tonnage of vessels, number of guns, size of crews, dates and places of building, dates and place of registration, names of owners, ports of embarkation and destination, cargoes, and dates and places where bonds were given. There are four volumes titled "Foreigners Outwards," "Foreigners Inwards," "Coasters Inwards," and "Coasters Outwards," each arranged chronologically by the dates of entrance or clearance beginning 1762, 1762, 1790, and 1776, respectively. These records are indexed by **index to and record of outward foreign manifests, 1762-1802,** arranged alphabetically by name of vessel.

CO.36.3. Similar information is found in the series **abstracts of tonnage duties, New Haven, CT, 1788-1802,** a single volume pertaining mainly to a tax collected under the federal government on the tonnage of vessels entering U.S. ports. A small part, however, also accounts for money collected under an act of the Connecticut legislature from July 1788 to July 1789. The collections in both cases were used to maintain lighthouses.

CO.36.4. In the regional archives in Boston is a one-volume series containing a record of vessels registered at New Haven from April 30, 1763, to June 2, 1767, and May 29, 1778, to June 26, 1789. **Journal, New Haven, CT, 1763-67, 1778-1802,** shows the names, types, and tonnages of the vessels; the dates and places built; the names of the owners and masters; and the dates of registration. The information is arranged in no discernible order. Among the vessels registered in 1764 was the *Fortune*, owned by Benedict Arnold, then a New Haven merchant.

CO.36.5. Also at Boston is **impost book, New Haven, CT, 1784-93**, a volume containing an account of impost duties on goods imported into the county of New Haven from other states as well as from foreign countries. Listed are the amount of duties, the account of the collector with the state of Connecticut, and accounts of goods, with their duties, imported into Milford, Derby, Branford, and Guilford. The entries are arranged in no discernible order. Records for New York (see **CO.36.13.**) also contain a few bonds and oaths of ship owners originating in Connecticut.

RECORDS FOR MARYLAND

CO.36.6. A number of separate entries exist as pre-federal records for the colony and state of Maryland. The four-volume series **record of fees collected, 1789-1857**, contains three sections with pre-federal entries. The first and largest of these (21 pages in volume 1220b) consists of an account of goods sent to other parts of the United States from the ports of Annapolis, Oxford, and Patuxent (sometimes consolidated as the "Patuxent District"), and the "enumerated duties" paid thereon during quarter-year periods from August 3, 1745, to the quarter ending September 29, 1764. This account book records the date of clearance; the name, tonnage, and type of each vessel; its master's and shipper's names; the number of crew carried; the destination; the amounts of goods carried; and the amount of duty received. Only tobacco cargoes are recorded. The most frequently listed destinations are Boston, Rhode Island, Barbados, and New York. For many quarters, no exports are shown. Pages 36a-38 of the same volume (1220b) consist of two accounts of the collector of the Patuxent District for duties collected on imported rum, sugar, and molasses from the quarter ending July 5, 1762, to June 8, 1765. The volume as a whole is arranged in generally chronological order, with most of the entries dating after 1789 beginning at the back of the volume. The pre-federal entries are mainly in chronological order by quarter-year periods and thereunder by dates of transactions. Another volume in the same series, titled "Manifest Book, 1745-1849," is a chronological account of cargo manifests, lists of exports, and duties on imports for Oxford, Patuxent, and, later, Annapolis kept by naval officers.

CO.36.7. Another series, **records of entrances and clearances, 1780-81**, contains a list that appears to have been a leaf in an unidentified record book. The information recorded is similar to that in the tobacco cargo accounts in E1220b, but includes various kinds of goods cleared from April 18, 1780, to January 1, 1781, in the Patuxent District. Arrangement is chronological by date of transaction.

CO.36.8. The remaining Maryland records are for the port of Baltimore. At the beginning of the series **records of entrances and clearances, Baltimore, MD, 1780-1939**, are four volumes recording vessel clearances from January 1, 1780, to May 1, 1786, and three volumes recording entrances from August 1, 1782, to November 28, 1785, and May 2, 1786, to April 7, 1788. Entries generally show the name, type, and size of each vessel; the date of entrance or clearance; the master's and owner's names; the number of guns and men carried; the kind and quantity of cargo; and the place to or from which the vessel was bound. Some records contain information on securities and bonds, the date and place the vessel was built, and when and where registered. They are arranged chronologically in volumes recording either entrances or clearances. In the same series is a journal of the "Naval Office" in Baltimore ("Journal for Liber B, 1785"), containing a chronological record of transactions pertaining mainly to duties paid on imported and exported goods and on tonnage, abatement on duties, drawbacks on reshipped goods, and bonds. The single volume has no apparent relationship to other customs records extant at the National Archives.

CO.36.9. Three large series in RG 36 contain small sets of pre-federal records. Only seven pre-federal documents, which are found as loose papers at the beginning of the series, are in **returns of weighers, Baltimore, MD, 1863-70.** They contain more information on cargoes than on vessels and individuals. Three lists of individual and company names with amounts of money next to them, probably dating from 1784, are in **lists of debts owing and valuation of property.** Presumably the entries signify sums due to and by the unidentified persons or organization that compiled the list. There are also entries for the "Naval Office" and an "Adventure to Kanetuck." Some contain information about the value of realty and personalty owned. One estimate concerning property contains references to "G Washington." In the first volume of the series **records of fees collected, Baltimore, MD, 1787-89, 1809, 1877-1907**, is a ledger of accounts from November 1787 to April 1789 for business firms and individual merchants in that city. Entries pertain mainly to duties paid on imports and tonnage, to drawbacks and abatements, and to bonds. Dates, amounts of payments, and persons concerned are also given. There are accounts for entities other than persons and vessels, for example the State of Maryland, the port of Baltimore, and the "Light House." There are references to related record books, the location of which has not been determined. Arrangement is by account and thereunder chronological by the dates of transactions. Records for New York (see **CO.36.13.**) also contain a few bonds and oaths of ship owners originating in Maryland.

RECORDS FOR MASSACHUSETTS

CO.36.10. Certificates of registry were issued by the federal government to U.S. merchant vessels of 20 tons and more to entitle them to engage in foreign trade. A half-dozen similar documents issued by the State of Massachusetts at Salem, Beverly, and Ipswich, 1784-87, are found at the beginning of the series **certificates of registry, Salem and Beverly, MA, 1784-1801.** The generally chronological records reveal the name, type, tonnage, and origin of each vessel; the names of master and owner; and the place and date of registry.

CO.36.11. The series **records of clearances, 1789-1802**, contains a two-sheet "Abstracts of Imports and Exports, 1783-1791, at the Port of Salem, Massachusetts." Endorsed as showing imports and exports "previous to the 1st Jany '92," each abstract lists a large and varied number of articles and gives the quantities annually imported (1783-91) or exported (1784-91) of each article. Commodities listed include food and drink, cotton, tobacco, lumber, oil, candles, furniture, hides, cordage, iron and steel, hemp, padlocks, hand spikes, and ginseng. Each abstact is arranged to be read vertically by kind of article and horizontally by year.

RECORDS FOR NEW YORK

CO.36.12. At the beginning of the series **miscellaneous certificates of registry, New York, NY, 1784-1802**, are about a dozen unbound certificates issued from 1784 to 1788. Most were transacted at New York City, but also present are documents issued in the States of Maryland (Patuxent), Connecticut (Middletown), and Massachusetts (Dartmouth and Boothbay). Arrangement is roughly chronological by date of issuance.

CO.36.13. Among the records in **bonds and oaths of ownership of vessels, New York City, NY, 1785-1803**, are another near dozen pre-federal certificates of registry issued for the most part at New York City. Also present, however, are documents originated in Connecticut and Maryland. The records are arranged alphabetically by the names of the vessels.

RECORDS FOR NORTH CAROLINA

CO.36.14. Four paper-covered volumes constitute the series **bonds for the export of non-enumerated goods and iron and lumber, Edenton, NC, February 1773-June 1775**. A typical bond for nonenumerated goods is a printed form with information filled in for the names of the master of the vessel and his surety (often an Edenton merchant), the name and build of the vessel, the amount of the bond, and signatures of the parties and witnesses. The bonds for iron and lumber have the same information as well as the destination of the vessel added. In many cases of both types, signatures have been torn away and are missing. The purpose of the bonds was to prevent the export of goods in violation of certain provisions of the British trade acts respecting the places where exported goods could be landed. Arrangement is generally chronological within each volume.

CO.36.15. The series **inward foreign manifests** contains an unstitched, paper-covered volume of printed forms that were completed by hand. The typical completed form includes the name, build, and tonnage of a vessel; a statement that it was British-built; the nationality of the owners of the vessel and cargo; the number of crew and their nationality; the name of the master and his nationality; the place from which the vessel came; the kinds and amounts of items constituting the cargo; and the signatures, with dates, of the master and one or more witnessing officials. Nearly all entries involve ships from British North American colonies. Some other information is often present, apparently derived from certificates of registry. Arrangement is chronological by date of entry.

RECORDS FOR PENNSYLVANIA

CO.36.16. The first volume of **impost books, Philadelphia, PA, 1783, 1789-1865, 1897-1901**, contains entries dated August 12-September 15, 1783. Each gives the date of entry, the name and build of the vessel on which goods were imported, the master's name, the place from which the vessel came, the name of the consignee, the kinds and quantities of goods, the value of the goods, the duty thereon, and the total duty paid. Among the consignees listed are Robert Morris, Stephen Collins, Alexander Nesbit & Co., Tench Coxe, Stephen Gerard, William Shippen, "De Marbois," and Charles Thomson. Goods listed include wine, sugar, coffee, tea, molasses, limes, cloth, furniture, and a case of "Fiddles." Arrangement is chronological by entry.

CO.36.17. In the series **records of money received and disbursed, Philadelphia, PA, 1787-88, 1790-1854, 1861-62**, a volume bearing the title "Case B[ook]" covers the period January 1, 1787, to July 25, 1788. Under untitled columns are given a date, the name of a person or company (presumably the consignees of unspecified goods), the name and build of a vessel, the name of the presumed master, and two sums of money. Among the names of the supposed consignees are Robert Morris, William Bingham, Charles Thomson, and Benjamin H. Phillips. Although the series is arranged chronologically, the pre-federal volume is arranged alphabetically according to the first letter of the surnames of the supposed consignees and thereunder chronologically.

RECORDS FOR RHODE ISLAND

CO.36.18. The series **accounts and abstracts of duties, Newport, RI, June 1768-July 1776 and 1795-1815**, consists largely of pre-federal records. The 32 bound volumes of accounts were kept by the collector of the customs at Newport. They mainly concern duties on goods arriving from other ports. Information given includes the names of vessels, dates of entry, names of masters and merchants, names of ports from which the vessels sailed, descriptions of the kinds and quantities of the cargoes carried, and the duties paid on various kinds of goods, such as sugar, wine, molasses, and coffee. Other accounts in the volumes include those pertaining to seizures of vessels by the collector; the expenditures of the collector for such things as office supplies, rent, and salaries; and duties on exported tobacco. Arrangement is generally chronological.

Record Group 41

Records of the Bureau of Marine Inspection and Navigation

CO.41.1. Navigation laws were passed by the first federal Congress in 1789 and were enforced by customs officers under the supervision of the Treasury Department. The function remained under the Secretary of the Treasury until 1934 when it was tranferred to the Department of Commerce.

CO.41.2. Certificates of registry issued at Annapolis from 1774 to 1776 are in the first 48 pages of the first volume in the series **certificates of registry for various ports, 1789-1920.** Typically these manuscript copies of certificates include the name, residence, and occupation of the vessel owner; the name, type, tonnage, and date and place of construction of the vessel; the name of the master; the signatures of the owner, the Governor of Maryland, and the collector of customs; and the date signed. Some of the earlier certificates refer to Annapolis as part of the Patuxent District. Many of the vessel owners are identified as Baltimore merchants. The records are arranged chronologically by date of issue.

Record Group 45

Naval Records Collection of the Office of Naval Records and Library

CO.45.1. The Naval Records Collection was begun in 1882 when the Librarian of the Navy Department, then in the Office of Naval Intelligence, began to collect for publication naval documents relating to the Civil War. In the early 1900s the office began collecting older records of naval bureaus and records relating to naval personnel and operations during the American Revolution. For further information see **NA.45.1.**

CO.45.2. The papers of Nathaniel Shaw, a New London, CT, merchant who also served during the Revolutionary War as a naval agent for his state and for the Continental Congress, are found in the series **subject file of the U.S. Navy, 1775-1910**, of the Naval Records Collection. These negative microfilm copies (35mm) of his records were made by the Navy Department about 1930 from the originals in the Yale University Library. They include 16 lists, ca. 1930, of documents, each headed "Shaw Collection Catalogue." Most of these list documents in roughly chronological order from 1775 to 1784, and the filmstrips are believed to be arranged in the same order as corresponding lists. Nathaniel Shaw died on April 15, 1782, and copies of letters sent after that date are signed by his brother Thomas. The Shaw Papers mainly consist of original letters received and letterbook copies of letters sent by the Shaws from and to other merchants, continental and state officials, military and naval officers, and other persons. Subjects include the shipment and sale of goods; the procurement and distribution of military and naval supplies to the Continental Army and Navy; Continental and British Army and Navy operations in and around Connecticut and New York City; the fitting out of U.S. warships and privateers; the activities of U.S. privateers, including the *General Putnam* owned by Nathanial Shaw; and preparations for the Penobscot expedition. The papers are in the subgroup of the Naval Records Collection called Loose Papers Assembled from both Official and Private Sources and Combined to Form New Series, 1648-1927.

CO.45.3. A vessel, the *Alliance*, made a trading voyage to Canton, China, and back, presumably from Philadelphia, from June 21, 1787, to September 15, 1788. The frigate was formerly a part of the Continental Navy, having been sold by the government in Philadelphia in 1785. In the series **logs and journals of American priva-**

teers and merchant vessels, 1776-1867, is a negative photostatic copy of a journal kept aboard the *Alliance* by Richard Dale. It includes meteorological, navigational, and geographical information; reports of conditions and activities of the crew; and accounts of activity ashore in China. The vessel visited or sighted St. Helena, the Cape of Good Hope, Madagascar, Sumatra, Formosa, Macao, and Whampoa. At Canton, its captain, Thomas Read, exchanged ginseng for tea, chinaware, silk, and other goods. The same volume contains photostatic copies of two journals of two much shorter voyages made on an unidentified vessel under a Capt. Dickson—from Bombay to Macao, August 21-October 2, 1787, and from Madras to Whampoa, June 10-July 27, 1788. These journals are similar in format and subject matter to that of the *Alliance*, but their origin and relationship to the latter has not been determined. The series is in the subgroup Records of Citizens of the United States, 1775-1908, and is arranged in the order of the voyages described and thereunder chronologically.

Record Group 55
Records of the Government of the Virgin Islands

CO.55.1. The Danish West Indies consist of many small, uninhabited islands in addition to the three main islands—St. Thomas, which was settled by the Danes in 1672; St. John, occupied in 1717; and St. Croix, purchased by Denmark from France in 1733. Except for 1807-15, when England held them, they were under Danish rule until purchased by the United States in 1917. Danish records relating to the cession and the rights and property of the inhabitants of the islands were given to the United States by the treaty of cession. They have not been translated.

CO.55.2. The Danish West India and Guinea Company administered the islands until they became Danish royal colonies in 1754. The company's records, 1672-1740, are part of National Archives Microfilm Publication T952 (19 rolls). They consist of:

1. general records, 1672-1703 (roll 1);

2. general privy council records, 1703-14 and 1723-54 (rolls 2-3);

3. privy council records for St. Thomas, 1732-54 (roll 4), and for St. Croix, 1744-54 (rolls 4-5);

4. "Journals of Happenings at St. Thomas," 1686-1714 (rolls 5-8); and

5. "Report books" for St. Thomas, 1723-1741 (rolls 9-12), St. John, 1734-42 (roll 12), and St. Croix, 1735-40 (roll 13).

CO.55.3. There are also numerous customs records for the pre-federal period in National Archives Microfilm Publication T39 (22 rolls). They consist primarily of journals containing accounts of arrivals and clearances at the ports of:

1. Christiansted, St. Croix, 1746-52, 1761-69, and 1771-89 (rolls 1-13);

2. Fredericksted, St. Croix, 1760-82 (rolls 17-20); and

3. Salt River Bay, St. Croix, 1783-85 (roll 21).

CO.55.4. There are also miscellaneous records (T39, roll 22), which include:

1. annual reports of exports to Copenhagen and foreign ports, 1783-89;

2. annual reports of Danish ships visiting St. Croix, listed by name of captain, indicating cargo and weight, 1783-89;

3. abstracts indicating the name, captain, type, and ports of origin and destination of ships visiting the islands, 1778-1807;

4. accounts of sugar exported to places other than Denmark, 1778-83;

5. abstracts of imports, 1774-79, 1782, and 1786; and

6. accounts of slaves imported to the islands at Christiansted, St. Croix, 1778-80.

Record Group 59

General Records of the Department of State

CO.59.1. The Department of Foreign Affairs was established by statute in July 1789 and 2 months later it was designated the Department of State by the same Congress. It was assigned such functions as preserving and publishing laws and treaties, keeping the seal of the United States, and serving as custodian of the records of the United States previously held by the Secretary of Congress. The department was also in charge of territorial affairs from 1789 to 1873.

CO.59.2. The series **territorial papers, 1764-1873,** is divided into several subseries, one for each territory. At the beginning of a volume in the Oregon territorial papers is "Correspondence and Other Records Pertaining to the Voyage of Captains John Kendrick and Robert Gray from Boston to the Northwest Coast of North America, 1787-1823." The object of the voyage was to obtain sea otter furs on the northwestern coast of North America and trade them in China for other goods. In the course of the mission, Robert Gray became the first U.S. citizen to circumnavigate the globe. Instructions to Kendrick, who was overall commander of the ship *Columbia* and the sloop *Lady Washington*, from a representative of "the owners," although undated, appears to be an original document written in 1787. Also present are a few originals and copies of letters dating from March 28, 1792, to May 28, 1798, received by Joseph Barrell, the owners' agent, from Kendrick and his clerk concerning tracts of land purchased on the voyage. Another group of documents, dating from 1816 to 1823, consists mainly of original letters to Charles Bullfinch from various persons who had information about the Kendrick-Gray voyage. Bullfinch was seeking deeds to the land in question on behalf of the surviving owners and heirs of owners. Also present are 19th-century copies and extracts of many of the original documents. Arrangement is generally chronological.

CO.59.3.   The first volume in the series **cashbooks, 1785-95, 1820-25, 1856-1918, 1921-25**, was begun in the continental Department of Foreign Affairs under Secretary John Jay and continued in use after the establishment of the federal government. The book is divided into two parts. The first and largest contains debit and credit entries showing the receipt and expenditure of money by the office and the Department of State for 1785-95. Most expenditures during that period were made for supplies and services, such as chairs and other furniture, blank books and paper, wood and coal, candles, the printing of official forms, binding books, cleaning and repairs, moving expenses, newspapers, books of state laws, newspaper advertisements, postage, and wages of a doorkeeper and several translators. The office was located in New York City during the pre-federal period. Each entry generally gives the date, the name or position of the person paying or receiving the money, the purpose for which the money was received or expended, and the amount. Names of persons mentioned frequently in these entries include Francis Child (printer), Samuel Loudon (stationer), Elizabeth Holt (newspaper publisher), Robert Hodge (bookbinder), and Joseph Fream (supplier of furniture). Considerable office supplies of various kinds were also received from George Remsen, John Remsen, Peter Goelet, and Hugh Gaine. Entries for the federal period in the first part of the volume occasionally relate to the earlier period, as in the case of one for September 11, 1790, for cash paid to the "Rev. Dr. Gros" for services "since his appointment as German interpreter in September 1786." These later entries also show expenses incurred in moving the Department of State from New York City to Philadelphia. The entries are in generally chronological order. The remainder of the volume is described in **FO.59.19.**

Record Group 71
Records of the Bureau of Yards and Docks

CO.71.1. The Bureau of Yards and Docks in 1862 replaced the Bureau of Naval Yards and Docks, established in the Navy Department by an act of August 31, 1842. Both were responsible for design, construction, and maintenance of all naval public works and utilities.

CO.71.2. In the series **fiscal records, 1832-1946,** is found "Ledger B of the Firm of Peterson and Taylor," covering the period December 2, 1783, to December 11, 1787. The ledger contains accounts for persons, firms, stores, and ships. Entries in the accounts pertain mainly to the sale and receipt of goods and the payment and receipt of money for travel expenses, freight charges, rent, and other purposes. A typical entry usually shows the date of a transaction, the name of the person or thing involved, and the amount of money credited or debited to the account. Most of the transactions recorded took place in the area of Chesapeake Bay. The entries are arranged by account and thereunder chronologically by date of entry. An index of names of accounts, but not of names mentioned in entries, is included. Ledgers "A" and "C" referred to in this volume are not found in the National Archives. A pre-federal "Invoice Book" kept by the same firm is among Records of Naval Districts and Shore Establishments (RG 181), described in **CO.181.2.**

Record Group 76
Records of Boundary and Claims Commissions and Arbitrations

CO.76.1. This collective record group was established for segregated files relating to internal boundaries, claims, and arbitrations received from the Department of State and international commissions. Certain classes of spoliation claims of U.S. citizens against France, growing out of seizures of U.S. merchant vessels during the wars of the French Revolution, were assumed in 1800 by the U.S. government in consideration of release by France of certain treaty obligations. Not until January 20, 1885, did Congress act to authorize the U.S. Court of Claims to adjudicate such cases. See **CO.123.1.-CO.123.5.** for that court's records relating to pre-federal affairs. The State Department assisted claimants and the court in gathering documentary evidence for settlements. The records contain some documents pre-dating the French Revolution.

CO.76.2. "Correspondence and Accounts of Jonathan Nesbitt, 1781-97," is part of the series **unsorted papers, 1781-93.** Nesbitt was a member of a well-known merchant family of Philadelphia. His papers, consisting of one volume and some unbound records, are mainly unsigned copies of letters sent from Philadelphia; Dumfries, VA; Amsterdam, the Netherlands; and other places from 1785 to 1797. A few ledger style business accounts dated 1781-85 are also present, as is a copy of a letter from John Paul Jones to John Ross dated August 25, 1785; Nesbitt was the bearer of the original letter. The unbound documents consist mainly of letters received and a few copies of letters sent by Nesbitt; they are dated at Philadelphia, London, Paris, and elsewhere, 1789-97, especially 1794-96. A number of the letters received are in French. Subjects of the letters sent and received include voyages of the ships *Heer Adams* and *Hannibal* and other business matters, Nesbitt's debts and health, family matters, the French Revolution and war in Europe, Jay Treaty negotiations, and invitations to social events received by Nesbitt from a lady friend and other persons in England. There are a number of references in the letters to Robert Morris and Thomas Barclay. The records are arranged in no discernible order.

Record Group 78
Records of the Naval Observatory

CO.78.1. The Naval Observatory was established in 1830 as the Naval Depot of Charts and Instruments. The organization derives and furnishes the national time, maintains continuous astronomical observations, and develops, inspects, and services astronomical, navigational, and aerological instruments.

CO.78.2. In the series **records of the Naval Observatory, 1840-1943**, are copies of "Sailing Orders to Michael Driver, December 12, 1759." They are endorsed as having been presented to Matthew Fontaine Maury, the Superintendent of the Observatory, in 1856 or 1857, but the donor's name is illegible and no letter of transmittal has been found. The single sheet is dated at Salem, presumably in Massachusetts, and signed only by "yr Frend and Employer." Driver was apparently the captain of a ship employed by a merchant of that place. He was instructed to proceed to various islands in the Caribbean, his actual visitations depending in part on wind and market conditions.

Record Group 79

Records of the National Park Service

CO.79.1. The National Park Service was established in the Department of the Interior by an act of August 25, 1916, and was given charge of national parks and monuments. In subsequent government reorganizations, the service was given control of such establishments as national seashores, historical parks, recreation areas, and some military and battlefield parks and sites. Early records associated with many of these sites are in this record group.

CO.79.2. The Potomac Company was chartered by the states of Maryland and Virginia in 1784 and organized in 1785 with George Washington as its president. Its object was to improve the navigation of the Potomac River by deepening the channel and building canals around falls. The company never succeeded, and in 1828 its property was transferred to the newly founded Chesapeake and Ohio Canal Company, which proposed to build a canal from Washington, DC, to the navigable waters of the Ohio River or one of its tributaries. The pre-federal records of the Potomac Company make up about 26 inches of the 116 linear feet of the series **records of the Potomac Company and the Chesapeake and Ohio Canal Company, 1785-1938.**

CO.79.3. "Payrolls, Receipts, Accounts, Inventories, and Miscellaneous Financial Records of the Potomac Company, 1774, 1785-1829," were compiled by treasurers of the company beginning with William Hartshorne in 1785. The pre-federal parts consist mainly of payrolls, receipts for pay, accounts for supplies furnished the company, receipts for supplies received by the company, and inventories of tools and other company equipment and supplies. A 1774 notice to the public, soliciting subscriptions to a plan for removing obstructions to navigation, is endorsed by George Washington and lists Washington, George Mason, John Hanson, and other prominent men of Virginia and Maryland as trustees. An estimate of expenses for the project is also endorsed by Washington as "Mr. Jno. Ballendines

Estimate." Payrolls generally show the pay period covered, the place at which the work was done, names of employees, occupations of employees, number of days worked by each individual, wage rate, money due, signatures or marks of payees, and signature of the witness to the payment. Work sites included Great Falls, Shenandoah Falls, and Seneca Falls. Most of the persons listed on the rolls were laborers, carpenters, smiths, and their overseers; a few women are listed as cooks, washers, and suppliers of horses and wagons. Supplies mentioned include food and drink, clothing, shoes, leather, canvas, needles, tools, iron, coal, tar, gunpowder, and medicine. Arrangement is roughly by record types and subjects and thereunder generally chronological.

CO.79.4. Only three documents from the pre-federal period are in the 1 inch of "Legal Records of the Potomac Company, 1774, 1787-1828." One is an 11-page memorandum, undated and unsigned, endorsed "Colo. Mason's Remarks on the Bill for Poto. Navign.," probably referring to George Mason. The other two documents are a certificate of transfer of stock and an account for shoes and clothing made or repaired for the company from September 1788 to February 1789. Letters received and copies or drafts of letters sent by company treasurer William Hartshorne of Alexandria, VA, and a few accounts and receipts for supplies furnished the company are among "Letters Sent and Received, Supply Accounts and Receipts, Reports of the President and Directors, and Miscellaneous Records of the Potomac Company. May 6, 1785-August 1, 1828." There are no reports of the president and directors of the company to the stockholders for the pre-federal period among these records, and no records, of any kind, dated 1787 or 1789.

CO.79.5. Found in the volume "Minutes of Annual and Other Meetings of Stockholders of the Potomac Company, May 17, 1785-August 1, 1796" are accounts of meetings at Alexandria, VA, and Georgetown, MD. Some of the minutes include copies of the reports of the president and directors to the stockholders. The minutes of the first meeting show that company stock was subscribed to at Richmond, Alexandria, and Winchester in Virginia, and at Annapolis, Georgetown, and "Frederick town" in Maryland. Stockholders who are listed include Horatio Gates, Charles Lee, Daniel Carroll, William Hartshorne, and Alexander Henderson as well as George Washington, Thomas Johnston, Thomas Sim Lee, John Fitzgerald, and George Gilpin, who were elected directors of the company. Volume A of the three-volume "Minutes of Meetings of the President and Directors of the Potomac Company and Minutes of Meetings of Stockholders, May 30, 1785-August 25, 1828," covers the period until February 14, 1807. For the pre-federal period it contains only minutes of meetings of directors of the company and a few copies of letters, orders, reports, advertisements, and agreements written or prepared under their direction. Some of these documents were signed by George Washington. Arrangement of all the minutes is generally chronological by dates of meetings and documents. This record group also contains a positive and a negative photostatic copy of volume A and a draft of the minutes of the stockholders meeting of August 4, 1788, found in "Minutes of Meetings and Resolutions of the President and Directors and of the Stockholders of the Potomac Company, August 5, 1788-February 17, 1806."

CO.79.6. Although the account books of the company are fairly extensive, pre-federal material in them is sparse. Most is in "Waste Book of the Potomac Company. June 20, 1785-January 18,1800." A typical entry shows the date, the person or thing concerned in the transaction, the amount involved, and the account to be debited. The ledger to which entries were posted is not among the records in the National Archives. Among the pre-federal entries in the wastebook are entries pertaining to payment for stock; purchase of food, tools, iron, gunpowder, wood, tar, medicine, and stationery; purchase of "Indented" servants; hire of blacks; unspecified expenses of George Washington; capture of runaway servants; construction of boats; and travel and legal expenses. Arrangement is generally chronological. In "Stock Ledger of the Potomac Company. October 23, 1787; July 13, 1789-August 9, 1828," there is one pre-federal entry from 1787 concerning the sale of a share of stock by Thomas Bealle to James Orme. The same sale is also recorded in the company's wastebook, and a certificate of transfer for the sale is among the company's legal records.

Record Group 92

Records of the Office of the Quartermaster General

CO.92.1. During the pre-federal era, Quartermasters General were regarded as field staff officers appointed to the principal armies. Like the Quartermaster General's Department of the U.S. Army, created by Congress in 1818, they were responsible for efficient systems of supply, movement of armies, and accountability of officers and agents charged with moneys or supplies.

CO.92.2. Among suppliers of military forces in the United States during the pre-federal period were Stephen Collins & Son, Philadelphia merchants, and William Barrell, a New England and

Philadelphia merchant whose estate was administered by Collins. In 1913 three boxes of records of the firm of Collins & Son were transferred from the office of the depot quartermaster at Philadelphia to the Library of Congress. Six Collins and Barrell documents in the National Archives are believed to have been a part of those records inadvertently omitted from the transfer. They are part of the series **correspondence, reports, returns, bills, accounts current, statements, receipts, vouchers, and contracts, 1794-1842.** They relate to routine commercial events in both firms in 1766, 1769, 1775, and 1789-90.

Record Group 93
War Department Collection of Revolutionary War Records

CO.93.1. The act of August 7, 1789, that established the War Department provided that the Secretary of War should have custody of all books and papers in the Office of the Secretary at War (who had headed the Department of War created in 1781 by the Continental Congress), including papers of the earlier Board of War. For a more detailed account, including loss of records by fire and accessions from government and other sources, see **MI.93.1.**

CO.93.2 Part of the series **numbered record books, 1775-98**, is a subseries pertaining to business and other personal matters and containing accounts for various persons, firms, and goods. "The Ledger of Personal Accounts of B. H. Phillips, June 17, 1778-August 13, 1783" (M853, roll 35), has debit and credit entries showing the date of transaction, the name of the person or thing involved, and the amount of money debited or credited. Among the entries are those for expenses for trips to Liverpool, Whitchurch, and the Isle of Man; purchase and repair of clothing; board; salary; business commissions; and the cost of shipping goods. There are several references to the sloop *Success*. B. H. Phillips is probably Benjamin H. Phillips of Curacao, mentioned in several accounts of Samuel Hodgdon, Commissary General for Military Stores for several years during the Revolutionary War. Arrangement is by account and thereunder chronological by date of entry. The volume is indexed.

CO.93.3. Among the papers in the series **miscellaneous unnumbered records, ca. 1709-1913** (M926, 1 roll), is "Journal of Supply Accounts Kept at Albany, N.Y. September 23, 1758-February 17, 1760." This journal, many pages of which are missing, appears to have been kept by a merchant. It contains a record of food, clothing, writing materials, and other supplies debited to military officers, enlisted men, physicians, and persons for whom no rank or title is shown, including a few women. Among the persons having accounts are General Amherst, General Gage, and Philip Schuyler. A few credit entries are also present in the volume. The military and medical personnel were presumably part of the British Army, which used Albany as a base during the French and Indian War. Approximately the first one-fifth of the 495-page journal is missing, as are many pages in the remaining section. The ledger to which entries were posted is not in the National Archives. A name index accompanies the records. Arrangement is chronological by date of entry.

CO.93.4. In the same series is "Memorandum Book Containing Invoices of Cloth and Articles of Clothing to be Sold at Public Sale. August 30, 1757-October 17, 1758" (M926, 1 roll). The name of the person who created it and the location of the business establishment concerned is not known. Each invoice or group of related invoices generally shows to whom the goods listed were sent for sale "at Vendue," the date, and the kinds and quantities of goods involved. Thomas Lawrence and Daniel Rundle are the only persons named as recipients of the goods. The items sent include linen, calico, chintz, handkerchiefs, bandannas, and tea. Arrangement is chronological by date of invoice.

CO.93.5. For descriptions of other Revolutionary War account and memorandum books which contain both military and private commercial records see **MI.93.23.-MI.93.26.** For records concerning the purchase of military supplies from private commercial sources see **MI.93.37.-MI.93.41.** and **MI.93.46.-MI.93.47.**

Record Group 94
Records of the Adjutant General's Office

CO.94.1. The Continental Congress of June 17, 1775, appointed the Adjutant General of the Continental Army. From the disbanding of the army in 1783 until 1792, there was no such permanent position in the War Department. An act of March 5, 1792, created the position of adjutant, whose responsibilities included the duties of inspector.

CO.94.2. An "Account Book and Related Papers of Peter Anspach and Charles Bitters, September 1, 1784-December 3, 1792; January 12 and March 20, 1801," consisting of one volume and loose papers, is found in the **post-Revolutionary War papers, 1780-1815**. During the Revolution, Peter Anspach served under Quartermaster General Timothy Pickering in various capacities and helped settle his accounts after the war. The first two sections of the volume contain journal entries made at Oystershell Point and "New York," September 1, 1784-November 1785 and November 1788-September 23, 1790. Entries concern wood, butter, apples, tea, chocolate, snuff, indigo, nails, tobacco, paper, hats, and other goods. There are many references to the sloop *Betsy*. In general, each entry in the first two sections shows the date of the transaction, the name of the person or firm involved, the goods or services exchanged, and their monetary value. There are postings to and from a ledger and a wastebook not found in the National Archives. The remaining three sections of the volume consist mainly of accounts of individuals from April 26, 1785, to December 3, 1792. The entries therein pertain to linen, food and drink, wood, clothing, hauling wood, "work with a team," and other goods and services. The loose papers in the volume consist of additional accounts of individuals, 1786-92, and documents concerning the settlement of Anspach's estate in 1801. The volume is arranged by section as described, with the loose papers at the back of the volume. Entries in the first two sections are further arranged in chronological order. The accounts of individuals are generally arranged randomly by the name of the person having the account and thereunder chronologically.

Record Group 107

Records of the Office of the Secretary of War

CO.107.1. The act of August 7, 1789, that created the Department of War entrusted to the Secretary of War the responsibility of recruiting, provisioning, and regulating U.S. military and naval forces.

CO.107.2. Part of the series **letters received by the Secretary of War, unregistered series, 1789-1861**, is "Records Pertaining to Business Activities of James Wilkinson. August 7, 1788-1790s" (M222, roll 1). These presumably were enclosures to one or more communications received by the secretary, but the covering letter or letters have not been identified. The earliest document pertaining to Wilkinson is a contract of August 7, 1788, for carrying on a trade in tobacco and other articles between the District of Kentucky in Virginia and New Orleans. Also present for the pre-federal period is an account of Wilkinson with New Orleans merchants for sales made on his behalf. Additional accounts and other documents pertaining to Wilkinson's business affairs from September 1789 through the 1790s are scattered throughout the early part of the series. The records are arranged chronologically by year and thereunder alphabetically by the initial letter of the surname of the writer or subject.

Record Group 123
Records of the U.S. Court of Claims

CO.123.1. The U.S. Court of Claims was established by an act of February 24, 1855, to hear claims against the United States based on any law of the Congress, regulation of an executive department, or contract with the government, including all claims referred to the court by Congress. In 1863 the court was granted temporary jurisdiction in cases arising from depredations committed by French warships and privateers upon U.S. commerce, chiefly from 1793 to 1801. Investigation of those cases produced records from as early as 1783, which are in the series **records of French spoliation cases, 1885-1908.**

CO.123.2. In the late 18th century, the mercantile firm of Alexander Henderson, Robert Ferguson, and John Gibson operated a chain of stores on both sides of the Potomac River below present-day Washington, DC. A "Tobacco Invoice Book of the Firm of Henderson, Ferguson, and Gibson. July 1784-December 1794; March 20-May 15, 1797," was kept at their store in Port Tobacco, MD. In 1888 it was filed as evidence in French spoliation claims case No. 2161 (the Brigantine *Catherine*; Samuel Cazneau, master) by the administrators of Ferguson's estate. The volume contains an invoice for part of a tobacco shipment captured by a French privateer in 1797. Another volume submitted as evidence in the same case is "Tobacco Invoice Book and Letter Book of the Firm of Henderson, Ferguson, and Gibson. July 1787-June 1794; March-May 1797; February 24, 1801-May 10, 1803." The records contain information similar to that in the other invoice book of the same firm. The invoices in the two volumes do not appear to be duplicates. All letters included in the second volume were written after the pre- federal period. Arrangement of the volumes is chronological by date of invoice or letter.

CO.123.3. Submitted as evidence in the French spoliation claims case No. 926 (the brig *Mercury*; George Lee, master) was the "Waste Book of Henry Troup of the Firm of Worthington and Troup, January 3, 1789-January 26, 1798." Henry Troup and Henry

Worthington were merchants of Baltimore, MD. The case arose out of the capture by a French privateer in 1797 of a ship partly owned by them. The claim was pressed by the administrator of Troup's estate. The pre-federal part of the volume consists of six pages containing entries made in London for the period January through March 1789. Entries pertain principally to personal expenditures of Troup for rent, food and clothing, travel, household furnishings, bank stock, and a house in Baltimore. They were made at London; Portsmouth; Easton, MD; Philadelphia; and Baltimore. Each gives the date of the transaction; the name of the person or thing involved, showing which is to be debited and to what account; and the amount of money concerned. The account book to which the entries were posted is not among the records in the National Archives. Arrangement is generally chronological by date of entry, with some entries for 1790 at the end of the volume after the entries for 1798. A daybook or journal, 1796-99, and a letterbook, 1797-99, were also submitted as evidence in the case.

CO.123.4. Capture of the ship *Eunice* (Thomas Seal, master) by a French privateer in 1797 gave rise to French spoliation claims case No. 852 in 1888. John Quinby, a merchant of Falmouth, MA, was the owner of the vessel captured. "Ledger A of John Quinby. November 14, 1781-September 1808" was submitted by the administrator of his estate as evidence in the case. It contains accounts for persons, firms, ships, and places. The entries usually give the date of the transaction, the name of the person or thing involved, the nature of the transaction, and the amount of money concerned. Some of the accounts include memorandums. Entries within accounts concern such matters as wages, rent, unspecified work on various ships, "surveying" wood, loading ships, construction of a sawmill and gristmill, and transportation of wood to Portland. Other goods mentioned include flour, tea, rum, coffee, sugar, corn, buttons, paper, indigo, silk, calico, molasses, beef, shoes, tobacco, hay, and candlesticks. Arrangement is by name of account. The volume contains an index, arranged alphabetically by the first letter of names of accounts (surnames, if persons); it does not index names mentioned within accounts. There are references to wastebooks not among the records in the National Archives.

CO.123.5. "Waste Book A of the Office of Joseph Taylor. Mar.-Aug. 1784; Feb. 1795-Feb. 1796," originated in a marine insurance office in Boston, MA. In 1886 this volume was submitted by the administrator of Taylor's estate as evidence in French spoliation claims case No. 3722 (the ship *Governor Bowdoin*; Daniel Oliver, master). The firm had insured a ship that was captured by French privateers in 1797. The pre-federal part is 11 pages of entries made at New York pertaining mainly to the purchase and shipment of food and other goods in 1784. Taylor's role, if any, in this earlier business is not known. Each of the entries shows the date of the transaction, the name of the person or thing involved, who or what was to be debited, and the amount of money concerned. A related account book to which the entries were posted is not among the records in the National Archives. Among goods involved are tar, turpentine, flour, sugar, corn, lemons, butter, rum, cider, oats, potatoes, apples, oranges, and wine. Arrangement is chronological.

Record Group 181

Records of Naval Districts and Shore Establishments

CO.181.1. Soon after its beginning in 1798, the Navy Department created navy yards and other shore establishments.

CO.181.2. Among the records of the Washington Naval Ship Yard, District of Columbia, is "Invoice Book of the Firm of Peterson and Taylor. July 1783-July 1792; Mar. 1823." The volume was begun at Duck Creek Roads (now Smyrna), DE, and contains a memorandum indicating that the firm moved to Alexandria, VA, on December 20, 1785. The volume consists mostly of statements of merchandise bought by the firm between 1783 and 1792. A statement usually shows the date of purchase; the source, kind, and quantity of goods; and the unit and total cost. Occasionally a seller's name is followed by a place name, such as New York, Georgetown, or Chesterton. The volume also contains two inventories of goods. Included in goods purchased are foodstuffs, textiles, sewing supplies, clothing, shoes, tableware, tools, building materials, books, glass objects, snuff, rugs, blankets, saddles, combs, medicines, leather, paper, indigo, and watches. Arrangement is generally chronological by date of statement or inventory. Another book of the same firm is described in **CO.71.2.**

CHAPTER FI
Records of Fiscal Affairs

FI.0.1. The development of the continental fiscal establishment was characterized by much experimentation. It began in 1775 with the appointment by Congress of the customary committees to deal with particular matters most pressing at any moment. In June, for instance, a committee was established to arrange for the printing of continental currency. In July another committee was appointed to estimate certain expenses. On July 29th, two "joint treasurers of the United Colonies" were provided for. These officials usually were referred to thereafter as the "Continental Treasurers." On September 25, 1775, a "committee of accounts" composed of one member of Congress from each colony was established, "to whom all accounts against the Continent are to be referred, who are to examine and report upon the same, in order for payment." This standing committee usually was referred to as the "Committee of Claims" thereafter. The payments for services and supplies could be authorized only by Congress as a body after receiving the reports of the committee.

FI.0.2. Two very important events related to fiscal affairs in 1776 were the establishment, on February 17, of a "standing comittee of 5 . . . for superintending the treasury" and, on April 1, of a "treasury office of accounts." The former came to be known as the "Board of Treasury," and among the duties initially assigned it were the examination of the accounts of the continental treasurers, the employment and instruction of "proper persons for liquidating the public accounts," and the control of the issuance of continental currency. The board, headed by the Auditor General, who was charged with "stating, arranging, and keeping the public accounts," was to report to Congress on its activities. Other significant actions pertaining to fiscal administration were taken by Congress in 1776. On July 30, the Committee of Claims was abolished and all unsettled accounts and claims were referred to the Board of Treasury. The committee was directed to deliver its books and papers to the Auditor General. On August 6 the number of continental treasurers was reduced from two to one. A domestic loan was authorized on October 3, with "a loan office [to] be established in each of the United States, and a commissioner, to superintend such office [to] be appointed by the said states respectively . . . ." The loan officers, as they came to be called, were to deliver interest-bearing "loan office certificates"—the war bonds of the

Revolution—to those persons who lent their money to the government, pay the interest due, "answer all draughts of the treasurer to the amount of the cash which they shall, at any time, have in their hands," and keep the necessary records of their transactions. The loan officers were an important part of the fiscal system throughout the pre-federal period, obtaining and maintaining funds for the use of the continental government subject to the order of Congress.

FI.O.3. It was not until September 26, 1778, that a substantial alteration was made in the system of continental fiscal management. A long string of resolutions adopted on that day established the offices of Comptroller, Auditor, and Treasurer, and two "chambers of accounts" each consisting of three "commissioners." The Auditor was to receive accounts for liquidation and settlement and refer them to one of the chambers for examination and settlement. The commissioners of the Chambers of Accounts were to return accounts to the Auditor, who could hear appeals from their decisions. The Comptroller was to receive the accounts and related vouchers for filing and entry in the books of account and to draw bills on the Treasurer for balances due on audited accounts and on orders of Congress. The Treasurer was to receive and keep public funds and issue money on the above-mentioned bills. The Board of Treasury supervised these several offices and officials.

FI.O.4. Less than a year later there was an even more fundamental reorganization. By an ordinance adopted on July 30, 1779, the Board of Treasury was changed from a standing committee of Congress to a mixed body to be made up of two members of Congress and three "commissioners" who were not members of Congress. The board was to have "the general superintendence of the finances of the United States, and of all officers entrusted with the receipt and expenditure or application of all the public money, bills of exchange or loan office certificates. . . ." Also provided for in the ordinance were the Auditor General, the Treasurer, two Chambers of Accounts, and six auditors for settling claims and accounts "arising in the army." The duties of the board and the various subordinate fiscal offices were set forth in detail. The former was to inspect the treasury, prepare estimates of public expenses, and "instruct in their duty all offices concerned in the finances or accounts." The Auditor General sent to and received from the Chambers of Accounts claims and accounts against the United States for settlement; he also assumed the former Comptroller's responsibility for establishing accounting procedures. The Treasurer was to "receive and keep the monies of the United States, and issue them on bills drawn by the President of Congress or Board of Treasury." Loan officers were to make returns of money in their hands arising from loans or other sources to both the Treasurer and the Board of Treasury and make payments according to the Treasurer's instructions. The "auditors of the army" were to reside with the "main army" and "detachments of the army" and settle military accounts in the field.

FI.0.5. This new arrangement did not work well, and over a period of many months in 1781 still another system of fiscal management was conceived and implemented. On the seventh of February, Congress resolved that there be a "superintendant [sic] of Finance" in charge of fiscal affairs in place of the Board of Treasury. He was to "examine . . . the state of the public debt, public expenditures, and the public revenue, to . . . report plans for improving and regulating the finances, . . . to direct the execution of all [fiscal] plans . . . adopted by Congress . . . , to superintend and control the settlement of all public accounts, [and] to direct and control all persons employed in procuring supplies for the public service. . . ." Since a considerable amount of time elapsed before Robert Morris took the office, the Board of Treasury was authorized, July 24, 1781, to continue "in the discharge of the duties heretofore entrusted to them." On September 11, however, an ordinance was passed providing that the functions and appointment of the commissioners of the Board of Treasury and of the Chambers of Accounts, the Auditor General, auditors, and certain other fiscal officials and employees were to cease on September 20, 1781. To replace them a comptroller, treasurer, register, and several auditors were to be appointed "in aid of" the Superintendent of Finance. Once again the duties of the subordinate officers were specified. The Comptroller of the Treasury was given final authority in the settlement of accounts as audited first by the auditors; he was also empowered to prescribe the methods of accounting to be used. As usual, the Treasurer was to receive and keep public moneys and issue them on warrants drawn by the President of Congress or the Superintendent of Finance. The Register of the Treasury was a new officer who was to keep the accounts of both receipts and expenditures.

FI.0.6. The duties of the Superintendent of Finance, or the "Financier" as he was sometimes referred to, were numerous, varied, and often difficult. He was directed to make provision for the support of the civil list, to give attention to the question of paying interest on loan office certificates, to correspond with the ministers of the United States abroad upon subjects relating to finance, to dispose of funds obtained or to be obtained from Europe according to congressional resolutions, and to provide transportation for supplies secured. He also was empowered to export and import goods, money, and other articles on account of the United States. Other duties were assigned to him from time to time, such as ascertaining the value of a ration for the army and preparing circular letters to the states on the condition of the public finances and the necessity of complying with continental requisitions. He was instructed to lay before Congress every 6 months a statement of moneys borrowed and bills emitted and to prepare a report on the state of commerce together with a plan for protecting it.

FI.0.7. It was under the administration of the Superintendent of Finance that numerous commissioners were appointed to liquidate and settle the various classes of accounts of the continental and confederation governments, both domestic and foreign. Resolutions adopted by Congress on February 20, 1782, provided for the appointment of a commissioner for each state, to be nominated by the superintendent and approved by the respective state governments, "with full power finally to settle the accounts between the State for which he shall have been nominated, and the United States . . . ." These same commissioners were also "fully empowered and directed to liquidate and settle, in specie value, all certificates given for supplies by public officers to individuals, and other claims against the United States by individuals for supplies furnished the army, the transportation thereof and contingent expenses thereon, within the said State . . . ." On the 27th of the same month Congress resolved that five other commissioners be appointed "for the settlement of accounts under the direction of the superintendent of the finances, namely, one for the quartermaster's department, one for the commissary's department, one for the hospital department, one for the cloathier's [sic] department, and one for the marine department . . . ." And on November 18, 1782, it was resolved that "a commissioner be appointed . . . with full power and authority, to liquidate and finally to settle the accounts of all the servants of the United States, who have been entrusted with the expenditure of public money in Europe, and all other accounts of the United States in Europe."

FI.0.8. Unhappy with the failure of Congress to adopt certain plans of his, and under constant attack by critics, Robert Morris returned his commission as Superintendent of Finance to the government on November 1, 1784. Some months earlier, on May 28, 1784, an ordinance of Congress had provided that, upon the Financier's expected departure from office, a new Board of Treasury consisting of three commissioners was to be established and assume all current powers of the superintendent. The board commenced operating in 1785 and continued to function throughout the remainder of the prefederal period and during the first months of the federal government. Changes in the subordinate fiscal administrative structure during these last years of the Confederation included abolishing the offices of the Comptroller and the Auditor and transferring their powers and duties in September 1787 to the Board of Treasury. On March 24, 1786, Congress resolved that the commissioners of the five depart-

cause the central government was forced to flee Philadelphia several times during the Revolutionary War, the recordkeeping functions were often disrupted and difficult to maintain. Also, fires in the Treasury Department in 1801, 1814, and 1833 may have destroyed some of the records, including certain auxiliary wastebooks cited in the journals.

FI.0.12. Thus pre-federal fiscal records were subjected to scattering processes that appear to have started almost as soon as the new federal government began to function in 1789. Government organization continued to change, and the obligations incurred under the continental and confederation governments continued well into the next century. Thus it is not surprising that records which were, upon creation, closely related in the accounting process are now found in separate record groups. This applies both to postings, which now occasionally cross record group lines, and to sets of record books that, once intact, may now be found in different record groups. Every effort has been made to provide cross references in the following descriptions to account for such cases.

FI.0.13. Some records pertaining to European loans to the United States during the pre-federal period are described in this chapter; others are in the chapter on foreign affairs, according to their nature. Records concerning negotiation of commercial treaties and loans by agents of the continental and confederation governments with foreign nations are described in the chapter on foreign affairs. The chapter on naval affairs also contains some records related to these loans since ship captains were often entrusted with executing some matters concerning foreign affairs.

Record Group 360

Records of the Continental and Confederation Congresses and the Constitutional Convention

FI.360.1. Record Group 360 consists primarily of PCC (M247, 204 rolls) and Miscellaneous PCC (M332, 10 rolls).* For additional information about those bodies of records and indexes thereto, see the introduction.

---

*For a complete list of National Archives Microfilm Publications cited in this guide, see Appendix A.

ments be removed and their duties vested in a single commissioner supervised by the Board of Treasury. On May 8, 1786, however, Congress decided to vest the business in two commissioners, one for the Quartermaster and the Commissary Departments and the other for the remaining three departments.

FI.0.9. Despite the relatively large and complex administrative organization developed over the years to handle the fiscal problems of the pre-federal government of the United States, it should be emphasized that Congress as a body always retained ultimate authority over its agents and frequently concerned itself with small, even trivial, matters in various areas of government, including finance. Congress continued, to the end of the Confederation, to appoint special committees, including grand committees made up of one member of Congress from each state, to devise plans for financing government operations, and to perform other duties in connection with fiscal matters.

FI.0.10. The accounting methods used by the continental and confederation governments resulted in the creation of the following principal bookkeeping records: the wastebook, a chronologically arranged record in which all fiscal transactions were first posted; the blotter, another chronologically arranged record that was begun January 16, 1782, and replaced the wastebook as the initial posting record on January 2, 1787; and the journal, the final, chronologically arranged account book in which all fiscal transactions were entered alphabetically by title of the account or by name of accountable officer. Various miscellaneous subsidiary accounting books, some of which record receipts and expenditures of the central government or pertain to a particular function or specific person's accounts, were also created.

FI.0.11. Under authority of the funding act of August 4, 1790 (1 Stat. 138), the federal government assumed the debts of the continental and confederation governments (known collectively as the Old Government) and of the 13 original states; the old debts were to be refinanced with the "loan of 1790." It was essential, therefore, that records of the Old Government be made available to Treasury Department personnel for auditing and the settling of accounts and claims. (Because records pertaining to the 1790 funding act concern obligations incurred by pre-federal governments, they are included in this guide.) Joseph Nourse, Register of the Treasury from 1781 to 1828, had custody of the older records, maintaining them as a separate series and recording, during his federal service, transactions resulting from activities of the Old Government. This explains why the blotters and journals contain entries with dates later than 1789. Be-

REPORTS AND LETTERS OF FISCAL AGENCIES AND OFFICERS

FI.360.2. Reports of the Board of Treasury, 1776-81 (Item 136, M247, rolls 145-147), include, in addition to reports from the Board of Treasury established July 30, 1779, those of its predecessor, the Standing Committee on the Treasury, and of the Committee for Accounts (or of Claims), Commissioners for Claims, Commissioners for Adjusting Accounts, commissioners of the Chambers of Accounts, the Auditor General, and a few special committees of Congress. Most of the reports in these five volumes pertain to the disbursement of public funds for the pay of troops, for supplies, for salaries of public officials, and for settlement of claims for goods and services already provided. Frequently addressed problems include operation and organization of fiscal offices, monetary and credit policy of the new nation, and special situations regarding military expenditures. Many of the documents are endorsed with such information as the title of the official or body that produced them, the report date, the date read in Congress, and action taken by Congress.

FI.360.3. Reports with enclosures sent by Comptroller of the Treasury James Milligan to the President of Congress and the Board of Treasury in 1785-86 and letters from him to Members of Congress Elbridge Gerry and Hugh Williamson in 1785 are found in the first 61 pages of **other reports of committees of Congress, 1776-88: letters from the Comptroller of the Treasury and claims of Canadian refugees, with a few reports thereon, 1783-86** (Item 35, M247, roll 41). Also present are a letter from Milligan as Auditor General in 1780 and a report from commissioners of the Chambers of Accounts in 1779. The letters from Milligan to Congress are endorsed with such information as the writer's name, the date, the subject, the date read, and action taken; most of the other documents are endorsed similarly. All are arranged in roughly chronological order.

FI.360.4. Bound as three volumes is the series **letters and reports from Robert Morris, Superintendent of Finance and Agent of Marine, 1781-85, with an appendix, 1776-78, 1781-86** (Item 137, M247, rolls 148-150). Most of Morris' letters were sent to the President of Congress, but some are addressed to the Secretary of Congress, congressional committees, and the chairman of the Committee of the States. A few letters and reports are joint communications from Morris and the Secretary at War. Those from Morris to Congress were written by him as Superintendent of Finance and Agent of Marine and are intermixed both as to type of communication and the office from which he wrote. The whole series relates largely to such matters as adjustment of accounts between individual states and the continental and confederation governments, the foreign debt of the United States, and the purchase, sale, and outfitting of ships. However, the subjects addressed are as numerous and varied as expected in the records of an important government official during critical times. The 462-page appendix contains letters addressed chiefly to the President of Congress by George Clymer, Robert Morris, and George Walton, who were appointed as a committee to conduct the business of the Second Continental Congress in Philadelphia after it left for Baltimore in December 1776. The series also includes material produced by Morris as a member of Congress and of the Marine Committee, and in an unofficial capacity in 1785-86. Subjects include fiscal and monetary policy, military and foreign affairs as they relate to the government's finances, and the Deane-Lee controversy. Endorsements containing names, dates, and action taken are common. Arrangement is generally chronological. Item 17 of PCC contains a chronological list of letters and reports sent to the Continental Congress by the Superintendent of Finance (see **CC.360.22.**).

FI.360.5. Records of the third Board of Treasury, established in 1784 to take the place of Superintendent of Finance Morris, are in **reports of the Board of Treasury, 1784-88** (Item 138, M247, roll 151). The three commissioners of the board, elected after several persons declined the office, were Arthur Lee, Walter Livingston, and Samuel Osgood. Many of the reports in the four bindings concern settlement of accounts for salaries, supplies, and services. A good number of those were made on memorials and petitions (described in **PE.360.2.-PE.360.4.**) that concerned financial matters and were referred by Congress to the board. Most of the reports are endorsed with the date of the report, the date read in Congress, and information about action taken. They are arranged in generally alphabetical order by the first letter of the surname of the first person mentioned in the title of the report; thereunder arrangement is generally chronological by report date.

FI.360.6. More reports from the same board are in **reports of the Board of Treasury on applications from states and various other subjects, 1785-89** (Item 139, M247, roll 152). They concern fiscal relations between the United States and individual states. Many were made on motions and letters referred to the board by Congress. Most are endorsed with subject, the date read in Congress, and action taken; they are arranged in generally chronological order. The first of two volumes in **letters of the Board of Treasury, 1785-88** (Item 140, M247, roll 153), contains mainly transmittal letters for the reports of the board mentioned in the previous two series. The letters in the second volume are dated May 14, 1785-November 17, 1788. The enclosures that accompanied many of the letters are still present and include a wide variety of foreign and domestic fiscal subjects confronted by the board. These include an estimate of the interest due on the foreign and domestic debt; a statement of money due the confederation government by the states; a statement of expenses for the "Presidents Household" from 1782 to 1785; originals and copies of letters received by the board from the Treasurer of the State of New York, commissioners of accounts and various state loan office commissioners, and commissioners of loans in the Netherlands; and a report by the board on the desire of a group of Dutch merchants to purchase the U.S. debt owed to France. Most are endorsed as usual and are arranged chronologically within each volume.

FI.360.7. The series **other reports of committees of Congress, 1776-88: on the Clothing Department; reports of the Commissioners of Accounts for the Clothing, Hospital and Marine Departments; reports of the Committee of Commerce; and miscellaneous reports, with lists of postponed reports, 1777-88** (Item 31, M247, roll 38), contains reports of the departments indicated, dated January 1785-June 1788, which reflect the reorganization of the five departments that took place in 1786. The documents have routine endorsements and are arranged in loose chronological order. Part of Miscellaneous PCC is the series **papers relating to specific states** (M332, rolls 7 and 10), which contains "Original correspondence and other papers relating to settlement of Virginia's claim against the United States 'for the Northwestern territory ceded to Congress,' 1787-88." By Virginia's deed of cession of its territory northwest of the Ohio River to the United States, March 1, 1784, it was provided that three commissioners be appointed to settle Virginia's claims to reimbursement by the United States for expenses incurred by the state in acquiring and defending the ceded territory. The commissioners' report consists of documentation supporting its determination that $500,000 be awarded to Virginia. A 250-page statement of evidence in the many aspects of the case includes copies of the various documents cited. Considerations included the value of services rendered the nation by Virginia troops, the effects of depreciation on values, and the impact of Indian depredations. Correspondents in the Virginia state committee dealing with the commissioners include George Mason, John Marshall, and Benjamin Harrison.

REPORTS OF CONGRESSIONAL COMMITTEES

FI.360.8. The series **other reports of committees of Congress, 1776-88: reports on the operation of the Board of Treasury and the national finances, 1776-88** (Item 26, M247, roll 33), covers a great variety of subjects including the operational responsibilities of the three Boards of Treasury and related fiscal officers, as well as monetary and funding proposals and problems. Related reports are described in **FI.360.2.**, **FI.360.5.**, and **FI.360.6.** At least two separate committees on estimates and "ways and means" appear to have produced the reports in the series **other reports of committees of Congress, 1776-88: reports on the public debt in 1781 and estimates of expenses with related papers, 1779-81** (Item 34, M247, roll 41). The reports refer to and are followed by a variety of documents pertaining to government finances. The reports are endorsed with the date and subject; most of the other records are more fully endorsed. **Other reports of committees of Congress, 1776-88: reports on the Commissary Department, domestic loans and loan offices, loss of certain Army posts, treaties, foreign loans [in Spain, France, and the Netherlands], and courts of appeal, 1776-86** (Item 29, M247, roll 36), contain records related to fiscal affairs, which are bound as pages 154-218 of the first binding and pages 219-227 of the second binding. Most of these reports and motions are endorsed with a number and with such other information as the subject, the date delivered, the date read, the names of committee members and makers of motions, the date assigned for consideration of reports, and the nature and dates of subsequent action on reports and motions, such as debate, passage, and referral to committees. They are arranged generally chronologically.

FI.360.9. **Accounts of the Register's Office, 1781-83** (Item 142, M247, roll 155), contain foreign (Spanish, French, and Dutch) and domestic accounts copied by the Register of the Treasury for the use of the Committee on the Treasury appointed July 2, 1782, by Congress to inquire into the proceedings of the Department of Finance. Since the investigation was broad the subjects of the accounts are numerous and varied. Most of the documents are endorsed with numbers assigned to them and brief descriptions of their subjects, and they are arranged in related groups. The committee report is found in **reports of committees on applications of individuals, 1776-89** (Item 19, M247, rolls 26-28), the first volume of which contains a name and subject index to the reports.

OTHER RECORDS

FI.360.10. Congressional investigations of fiscal affairs or irregularities account for some of the records in this record group. Among **letters and papers of Thomas Paine, 1779-85, records of the Office [of the Secretary] of Congress, 1781-89, and records relating to the passing of counterfeit money, 1776** (Item 55,

M247, roll 68), are some 20 pages of documents concerning examinations and confessions of two confessed counterfeiters and other suspects, including affidavits of witnesses who appeared before the committee of observation of Morristown, NJ, in April 1776. The methods of making and passing counterfeit bills are described. The remaining records in the series are described in **FO.360.42.** and **CC.360.30.**

FI.360.11. In **papers respecting unsettled accounts, 1788, and returns of stores, 1783-84** (Item 143, M247, roll 155), are four groups of records. The first consists of letters and related records from the Board of Treasury to a congressional committee concerning the settlement of the accounts of the Secret Committee for 1775-77, money issued from the treasury during the Revolutionary War for which no appropriations appeared in the journals of Congress, and money received and disbursed on behalf of the United States in France during the war. The second group pertains to medical supplies. The third group consists of lists of accounts for money paid by the Hospital, Clothing, Marine, Quartermaster, and Commissary Departments to individuals and official bodies. The fourth group consists of lists, in French, of loan office certificates and continental money deposited in French consulates at Boston, Baltimore, and Philadelphia from 1779 to 1784. Information given includes certificate numbers and dates, amounts, states of issue, names of depositors, dates of deposit, and names of original issuees. The records are arranged by groups in the order described, except that the last two groups are somewhat intermixed.

FI.360.12. The investigation records in **letters and reports, 1781-88, from John Pierce, Paymaster General and Commissioner for Army Accounts, and records relating to investigations of Treasury offices, 1780-81** (Item 62, M247, roll 76), are found in both the first and second bindings of the two-volume set. They pertain principally to two sets of charges: those of the Treasurer of Loans against two of the commissioners of the Board of Treasury, and those of the latter pair against certain commissioners of the Chambers of Accounts. The Treasury Board commissioners were accused of insolence in office, issuance of incorrect orders, and alteration of records, among other things. Their charges against the commissioners of the Chambers of Accounts included neglect of duty, indolence, incapacity, and partiality. Also involved in the charges and countercharges were a clerk of the Chambers of Accounts and Charles Lee, Secretary of the Board of Treasury. The records consist mainly of minutes of a committee that met in October 1780 to conduct the investigation. Some of the letters of Congress are endorsed with such information as the writers' names and the date read before Congress as a whole or in committee, but many have no endorsements.

FI.360.13. Records that can be loosely defined as planning documents are also found among the holdings in Record Group 360. **Estimates and statements of receipts and expenditures, 1780-88** (Item 141, M247, roll 154), exist mainly for quarterly periods from November 1784 through 1787, with related statements for expenditures in or for particular departments or purposes. Also present for 1782-88 are documents concerning fiscal relations with the states, French and Dutch accounts and loans, and detailed estimates of military, naval, and other expenditures. **Estimates and other papers relating to the treasury, 1780-88** (Item 144, M247, roll 156), contain similar records, including papers relating to the grand committee appointed by Congress to consider the national debt. Among them is a report in Thomas Jefferson's handwriting, delivered April 5, 1784, concerning the use of western lands to be ceded by the states as a source of government revenue. Other records concerning the public debt, estimates of future monetary needs, and accounts of expenses for 1781-86 are in **book of estimates** (Item 12, M247, roll 22).

FI.360.14. Miscellaneous PCC contains **papers relating to foreign affairs**, a part of which is "bills drawn on Monsieur Ferdinand le Grand, banker in Paris, by Robert Morris, Superintendent of Finance, 1782-83" (M332, roll 5). These records consist of a paper jacket that lists numbers and face values of bills and that contains all of the bills except one. Each bill was printed to show the place of issuance and the name of the person on whom drawn, and then filled in by hand with a number, the date, the amount to be paid, the period of time after which it was payable, the name of the payee, and Morris' signature. The payees, including Benjamin Franklin, John Jay, Henry Laurens, Francis Dana, R. R. Livingston, and John Adams, were U.S. diplomatic personnel, and the bills may represent salary payments to them. **Copies of bonds required by commissioners appointed to the Board of Treasury, 1785 and 1787** (Item 131, M247, roll 143), contain fair copies of the bonds and oaths of Samuel Osgood, Walter Livingston, and Arthur Lee, and relevant congressional ordinances and resolutions. Most of the originals are in **papers kept by the Office of the Secretary, papers relating to fiscal affairs, and broadsides issued by the Continental Congress** (M332, roll 9). In the same series is "Note Book No. 3 'Containing Printed and Written Notes Commencing with Book Y and Ending with Book No. 11'" (M332, roll 9), which may have been compiled in the office of the Superintendent of Finance and is possibly related to the "account of all the Notes which have been issued by me," which is referred to in a report of Superintendent Robert Morris to the President of Congress, November 10, 1783. That report is described in **FI.360.4.**

Record Group 39
Records of the Bureau of Accounts (Treasury)

FI.39.1. The Bureau of Accounts was created in the Treasury Department in 1940 to succeed the Office of the Commissioner of Accounts and Deposits, which had been established in 1920 to coordinate the work of divisions engaged in accounting transactions and the deposits of public funds. Some records of the bureau's predecessors date to the pre-federal period. Among the bureau's functions are maintaining a unified system of central accounts, producing central financial reports, and furnishing technical guidance and assistance to Treasury Department bureaus.

FI.39.2. Pre-federal records in the subgroup General Treasury Records, 1775-1945, include the series **foreign ledgers, public agents in Europe** (M1004, rolls 1-2). The ledgers were intended to serve as a record of the "Accounts between the Public and the Persons who have done Public business in Europe." It is likely that the ledgers were kept by Thomas Barclay in his capacity as a commissioner for settling U.S. accounts in Europe. Many accounts close with a date from May 1784 to July 1787 and the word "Paris." Some contain reference to dates as late as 1798, to entries in the "books of the Old Government," and to federal government auditors' reports and statements. There are accounts in the ledgers for U.S. ministers and other diplomatic representatives, including John Adams, Silas Deane, C. W. F. Dumas, Benjamin Franklin, John Jay, Thomas Jefferson, Arthur Lee, and Henry and John Laurens. European firms and merchants, and other persons, with whom the United States had dealings include Caron de Beaumarchais, Le Ray de Chaumont, John de Neufville & Son, J. D. Schweighauser, Joseph Gardoqui & Sons of Bilbao, Willink & Staphorst, De la Lande & Fynje, Ferdinand Grand of Paris, Gourlade & Moylan, William Bingham, John Bondfield, Thomas Barclay, Jonathan Williams, Alexander Gillon, John Paul Jones, and Robert Morris. Transactions recorded pertain to such specific matters as the purchase of supplies and their shipment to America, traveling and other living expenses of U.S. diplomats in Europe, delivery of tobacco to the Farmers General of France, payments for building the ship *Indian* at Amsterdam, and postage and courier expenses. Dates and amounts of money involved in individual transactions are provided. Arrangement is by account title, with transactions under a particular account generally in chronological order.

FI.39.3. Each of the first two volumes of **miscellaneous account books, 1775-89** (M1014, roll 23), contains letters—the first from Superintendent of Finance Robert Morris (1781-84) and the second from Register of the Board of Treasury Joseph Nourse (1784-89)—presenting, summarizing, and explaining the accounts therein. Both volumes consist principally of groups of accounts for quarterly periods documenting the receipts and expenditures of the U.S. government. Those in the first volume mainly cover the period January 1, 1781-June 30, 1783, with the accounts for the last quarter incomplete. Preceding the 1781 entries is a "Sketch of an Account of Loans, Subsidies, and Grants of Money in France" from January 31, 1777, and an account for Ferdinand Grand at Paris beginning June 4, 1777. The accounts in the second volume cover mainly quarterly periods from November 1, 1784, to September 12, 1789. Following them is a report on Robert Morris' tenure as Superintendent of Finance, which summarizes the numbered accounts in the first volume and other numbered accounts not present in either volume.

FI.39.4. A typical group of accounts for a quarterly period consists of a general account of receipts and expenditures for that quarter and subordinate, more detailed, accounts of specific receipts and expenditures. Separate subordinate accounts include those for taxes received, expenditures for the civil list, various military expenditures, and "Expenditures of the Marine." Others, especially for the period when Morris was Superintendent of Finance, include accounts of the United States with Dutch and French bankers. Accounts of expenditures for the civil list include names, titles, and salaries of specific officials and employees of various continental agencies, as well as sums spent for office rent, printing the journals of Congress, purchase of newspapers and stationery, and other expenses of the Continental Congress. Transactions recorded under other account titles also usually include dates and amounts of money involved. Arrangement is by quarterly periods and thereunder by account with chronological entries.

FI.39.5. **Surety bonds of government officials responsible for collection and disbursement of public money, 1783-1925,** contain only two pre-federal entries: a May 1783 payment by Clement Hall and Joseph Day to the "Deputy Quarter-Master" and a receipt for a payment made in February 1785 by John Anderson to Andrew Dunscomb, who was probably an assistant commissioner of army accounts. The series also contains two bonds of Robert Morris dated May 24, 1796, pertaining to money due by him to the continental government and a signed proposal by Morris for making payment. The documents are arranged chronologically in three subseries (1783-1910, 1910-15, and 1916-25) and thereunder alphabetically by the surnames of persons for whom there are bonds. There is an alphabetical name index to the series.

FI.39.6. The series **reports on certificates loaned, 1798-1803**, although currently in RG 39, is a continuation of the series of the same name in RG 217. For a full description of that series see **FI.217.16**.

FI.39.7. Two volumes from the 19th or early 20th century contain information relating to pre-federal fiscal affairs and are found in **registers of outstanding liabilities, sinking fund, and securities issued on the public debt, 1777-1921.** "Copies of Certificates of Indebtedness Issued to Individuals by the U.S. Government from 1778 to 1833" consists of manuscript copies of certificates issued by the Register's Office, state loan offices, and federal banks. These copies may have been recorded for reference as to the form of the various certificates issued. They are arranged in generally chronological order except that some unbound copies of certificates duplicating those copied into the volume proper are at the front of the volume. "Appropriation Account of Redemption Temporary Loans, of Revolutionary Debt, Public Debt and Statement of Accrued Interest on the Foreign Debt, 1790-1818," mainly shows the sums of money appropriated by the U.S. government from 1791 to 1818 to pay the principal and interest of the "Revolutionary Debt." Figures for annual interest payments and purchases of U.S. government stocks are included. At the back of the volume is a "Statement of Accrued Interest on Foreign Debt to January 1st 1790," which concerns interest on foreign loans dating as far back as 1781. The volume is arranged in two sections as described and thereunder in generally chronological order.

Record Group 53
Records of the Bureau of the Public Debt

FI.53.1. From 1776 to 1817, subscriptions to government loans were handled by commissioners heading state loan offices. These institutions were established in each state under supervision of the Continental Congress and continued under the federal government. In 1817 the duties of the state loan offices passed to the Second

Bank of the United States, and upon expiration of its charter in 1836 to a succession of offices in the Treasury Department.

CENTRAL TREASURY RECORDS

FI.53.2. Twenty-four numbered and chronologically arranged accounts are in **ledger of accounts of Ferdinand Grand with the United States, 1777-85** (M1004, roll 3). They show money received and disbursed on behalf of the United States by Ferdinand Grand, "Banker in Paris." Each account covers a specific period of time from several weeks to as many as 11 months and ends with the copied signature of Thomas Barclay, who had signed them at Paris on July 1, 1784, and September 10, 1785. A letter from Barclay to John Jay, September 10, 1785, states that Grand's accounts "are at length settled . . . ." A copy of a letter from Benjamin Franklin to Barclay, July 11, 1785, concerning Grand's accounts is also present. Debit entries in the ledger show money received by Grand on various dates and derived from various sources, including loans from France and loans raised in the Netherlands. Credit entries show disbursements for many different purposes, including salaries, rental of lodgings, and travel and other expenses of U.S. diplomatic representatives and employees. Among them are Arthur Lee, Silas Deane, Francis Dana, William T. Franklin, Benjamin Franklin, Thomas Jefferson, and John Paul Jones. Other outlays include expenses connected with ship construction and the purchase of arms; the purchase of copying machines for the Continental Congress and books for the Secretary for Foreign Affairs; payments to U.S. citizens who were prisoners of war, foreign military officers, and U.S. naval officers; and payment of bills of exchange drawn on the Joint Commissioners to the Court of France.

FI.53.3. **Record of accounts current with state loan office commissions, 1775-83, 1799-1802**, is part of the subgroup General Treasury Records, 1775-1945. The first of two volumes, labeled volume 160, was presumably once part of a larger central treasury series, the other volumes of which have not been located. It consists of a number of accounts for each of the state loan offices covering varying periods from October 1778 through March 1783 and based on returns and accounts submitted by the loan office commissioners. Included are accounts for loan office certificates on hand and issued (names of issuees are not given), bills of exchange on hand and paid out for interest on loan office certificates, bills of exchange sold, and money received from lottery agents. The second volume, labeled volume 161, consists mainly of quarterly loan office accounts of a summary nature for payments on the funded debt from January 1799 through September 1802. Volume 160 is generally arranged by loan offices in geographic order from north to south, thereunder by type of account, thereunder by whether entries are debits or credits, and thereunder chronologically by date of entry. Volume 161 is arranged for the most part chronologically by quarter and thereunder by loan offices. The first volume alone is reproduced on M1014, roll 23.

FI.53.4. **Journals for the "United States Lottery"** refer to a lottery authorized by the Continental Congress in November 1776 for the purpose of raising money for military operations. The journals list individual ticket numbers and the corresponding prize amounts, from $20 to at least $5,000 for each of four classes in the lottery. The journals are arranged in numerical order by volume numbers (not the original order); the principle by which the ticket numbers are arranged within individual volumes has not been determined. Names of ticket holders are not given.

FI.53.5. Three items obviously from the pre-federal period are, however, impossible to identify further as to origin or precise function. "Index to Unidentified Account Book of the Revolutionary War Period, 1780 or later" is a volume containing references to a loan office certificate account; an emission of money made pursuant to a Continental Congress act of March 18, 1780; Robert Morris; the state of Pennsylvania; and various accounts with the United States. It appears to be an index to accounts in a ledger, possibly one kept by the Pennsylvania Loan Office, but the record indexed has not been found among those in the custody of the National Archives.

FI.53.6. "Transfer Ledger, ca. 1781," a paper-covered volume of undetermined administrative origin, contains accounts for various private persons, companies, vessels, states, Continental Congress officials and committees, and other entities. Most of the accounts contain only one entry each, showing a debit or credit balance transferred from a page in a group of ledgers identified only by letter titles. One account contains a memorandum dated May 1781 indicating that the ledger was relevant to business of the Congress and "the Treasury Board." Arrangement is by titles of accounts, which vary widely in subject. An incomplete index to account titles is at the beginning of the volume.

FI.53.7. "Account Current Book A, 1791" contains accounts of continental officials and employees, Continental Congress committees, and other persons and entities with the government based on transactions that occurred as early as 1775 and as late as January 1789. Notes in the volume presumably signify the settlement or closing of the accounts by the Register of the Treasury. Many accounts also include explanatory memorandums by the Register, some recommending certain actions to the Comptroller of the Treasury. The accounts are based on the series of ledgers described in **FI.217.7.**-**FI.217.8.**, and all appear to be for balances due to the United States.

RECORDS OF LOANS AND LOAN OFFICES

FI.53.8. Approximately 240 series, beginning with records of state loan offices established in the 13 original states by a Continental Congress resolution of October 3, 1776, pertain to subscriptions to domestic loans to finance the Revolution. The loan offices were continued in operation under the federal government until their duties and records of the sale and redemption of public securities and other matters were tranferred to the Second Bank of the United States in 1817. The charter of the bank expired in 1836, and its functions and records were transferred to the Treasury Department by statute. Interfiled among the pre-federal loan office records are records created by commissioners appointed by the Continental Congress to settle debts due from the United States to individual states ("Commissioners for Adjusting the Public Accounts") and records of other commissioners appointed to settle accounts of certain military staff departments and the Marine Department. Records of pre-federal loan offices and certain commissioners appointed to settle accounts are microfilmed for the states, with beginning dates indicated:

Connecticut	M1005	1777
Delaware	M1008	1777
Maryland	M1008	1777
Massachusetts	M925	1777
New Hampshire	M1005	1777
New Jersey	M1006	1777
New York	M1006	1777
Pennsylvania	M1007	1776
Rhode Island	M1005	1781

Extant records for Georgia, North Carolina, and South Carolina begin only in 1790, 1791, and 1791, respectively (see **FI.53.9.**). Records for Virginia begin in 1777 but have not been microfilmed. The most numerous type of pre-federal record series, present for most of the states, consists of registers of loan office certificates and public debt certificates issued by loan officers and commissioners for settling accounts. These give such information as the certificate date, the name of the issuee, and the monetary amount represented by each certificate issued. Other series beginning before 1789 and present for one or more states contain similar data and include registers of interest payments on loan office and other certificates of governmental indebtedness, registers of continental currency withdrawn from circulation, and registers of canceled loan office certificates. Letterbooks, journals, and ledgers of the loan offices are also present, and the correspondence and accounts include information about such additional activities of the offices as the disbursement of continental funds, sale of bills of exchange, and receipt of money from lottery agents. Office expenses are also recorded.

FI.53.9. Among the records created by the loan offices and the federal banks in and after 1789 are many that relate to the debts of individual states and the issuance of stock for loans to fund loan office and other kinds of certificates of indebtedness issued in the pre-federal period. Record series pertaining to these loans include subscription registers, registers of paid and unclaimed interest, journals and related ledgers, receipts for interest paid, and registers and abstracts of interest payments. Also among these loan office and federal bank records for the federal period are some that relate in whole or part to the payment of pensions to Revolutionary War veterans, including registers of pensioners and records of pension payments. The records are arranged in geographical order by state from north to south. The quantity of series for each state varies from 3 for Delaware to 43 for Virginia. The series for each state are further arranged mainly chronologically by the dates of the records, in the case of the pre-federal records, and by the dates of the loans to which the records pertain, in the case of records created later. The internal arrangement of the records within a particular series varies by type. Loan office records pertaining to the loan of 1790 have been microfilmed for the following states:

Connecticut	T654
Delaware	T784
Georgia	T694
Maryland	T697
Massachusetts	T783
New Hampshire	T652
New Jersey	T698
North Carolina	T695
Pennsylvania	T631
Rhode Island	T653
South Carolina	T719
Virginia	T696

There are also accounts for New York, none of which has been microfilmed.

FI.53.10. Central Treasury [Department] records relating to the loan of 1790 (T786, 1 roll) and **old loan records relating to selected loans of the period 1795-1807** (T787, 6 rolls) are records kept in the federal Treasury Department as distinguished from similar records originating in loan offices and the first Bank of the United States (see **FI.53.8.-FI.53.9.**). They document subscriptions to various early domestic loans of the federal government, transfers of stock issued in connection with such loans, and payment of interest on such stock. Among the stocks for which there are records are those issued under the funding act of August 4, 1790, for funding the pre-federal debt, and "exchanged" and "converted" 6-percent stocks of 1807 and exchanged 6-percent stock of 1812, issued to refinance the stocks of 1790. There are also a few volumes for the period 1792-98 pertaining to the "registered debt," involving evidences of pre-federal indebtedness that were not turned in for stocks under the act of 1790 but on which interest was paid. Kinds of records present include ledgers of accounts of stockholders, registers of transfers, and records of interest payments and unclaimed dividends. Many volumes pertain to more than one loan.

FI.53.11. Card index to "Old Loan" ledgers of the Bureau of the Public Debt, 1790-1836 (M521), provides a starting point from which to trace subscriptions to early U.S. domestic loans, including the loan of 1790, as recorded in selected loan ledgers maintained by the Treasury Department proper and certain loan offices. The only ledgers indexed are those for the New York Loan Office, the Pennsylvania Loan Office, and the Treasury Department. They are among the series described in **FI.53.8.-FI.53.10.** (Many of the ledgers in those series contain contemporary indexes in each volume.) A typical index card gives the name of a stockholder, the kind of stock held, the ledger volume and page number containing an entry for that stockholder, and the name of the state in which the loan office was located if reference is to a loan office record. The index cards are arranged in three parts, the first for individual domestic stockholders (including partnerships), the second for foreign holders, and the third for corporate holders, such as banks and insurance companies. Arrangement within each part is alphabetical by the initial letter of the company name or surname.

RECORDS OF THE SETTLEMENT OF PRE-FEDERAL ACCOUNTS

FI.53.12. Report of the Commissioners of the Public Debt, June 29, 1793, is the final report of Commissioners William Irvine, John Kean, and Woodbury Langdon, who were appointed under the act of August 5, 1789 (1 Stat. 49), to settle the accounts between the United States and individual states arising from expenditures by the latter for the "general or particular defense" during the Revolutionary War and from advances made to the states by the general government. The largest part of the report contains accounts for each state that show the total amount of expenditures credited to it, an amount representing advances to it by the continental and confederation governments, the amount of its debt assumed by the federal government, and the resulting balance. Accompanying each such account, with the exception of that of New Hampshire, is a list of moneys advanced to each by the general government in old emissions, mainly from 1775 to 1782. Included in these lists are the dates of such advances; the names or positions of the payees, including Continental Congress members, state governors, state treasurers, and military officers; and computations of the specie value of and interest due on the advances. The accounts and related lists for individual states are in geographical order by state from north to south. Following the accounts and related lists is the report proper of the commissioners, which is signed and addressed to the President of the United States and shows, among other things, the gross amounts of expenditures credited to each state, with interest; the amounts charged against each state, with interest, for advances from the continental and confederation governments and for the debt of each state assumed under the acts of August 4, 1790, and May 8, 1792 (1 Stat. 281); a statement of the population credited to each state; and the balances, with interest, either due to certain states by the United States or due the United States by the remaining states.

FI.53.13.   **Late government balances as struck on the treasury books, 1775-89** (M1014, roll 22), were probably compiled in the office of the Register of the Treasury Department under the federal government. The contents of the one volume consist of a list of selected accounts taken from ledgers "A," "B," and "C" described in **FI.217.7.-FI.217.8.** Shown for each is an account number, the page of the ledger containing the account, the title of the account, and the amount or amounts of the debit or credit balance or balances for the account in bills of exchange, specie, old emissions, and new emissions. Each account listed has a notation regarding its status in red ink with dates as late as 1797. Accounts in the ledgers for which there are corresponding entries in this volume contain notations in red ink giving the amount of the balance and the debit or credit account number as listed in this volume. Arrangement is according to the debit or credit character of the balances and thereunder, for each type of balance, numerically by the pages of the ledger where the accounts are recorded in full.

FI.53.14. Records of personal debtor accounts remaining open on the books of the Old Government, 1775-89 (M1014, roll 22), apparently were compiled also in the office of the Register of the Treasury Department under the federal government. Volume 1 of the four volumes is actually a "Book of Creditor Accounts." All four volumes are based on the ledgers described in **FI.217.7.-FI.217.8.** and show, for each account listed, the page of the ledger containing the account, the title of the account, the amount or amounts of the balances involved, the form of the balance (bills of exchange, specie, old emissions, or new emissions), and "Remarks," which include references to numbered auditor's reports and statements admitted and certified by the Comptroller of the Treasury as late as 1798. There are also references to pages in the wastebooks and blotters described in **FI.217.2.-FI.217.4.**

FI.53.15. "Register of Certificates of Indebtedness Issued and Delivered by Edward Chinn, Commissioner for Adjusting the Public Accounts of the United States in Rhode Island, 1783-86," gives for each certificate a number, date of issue, the name of the person or persons to whom due, the date due, the monetary amount represented by the certificate, and the date delivered. Many certificates are listed as having been delivered not to the persons to whom due but to a Maj. "E. Haskell" on September 9, 1788. The purposes for which payments were made are not stated. Most of the entries in the volume were crossed out at an unknown later date and were annotated and explained in the registers of "Pierce's certificates" (issued by Paymaster General and Commissioner for Army Accounts John Pierce) described in **MI.53.5.** Records of commissioners appointed to settle the accounts of the United States in other states are scattered among the loan office and related records described in **FI.53.8.-FI.53.9.** Arrangement is ordinal by certificate number.

FI.53.16. Regulations and forms, 1790-1815, constitute three volumes relating to loans made before 1837. They contain manuscript copies of forms and related instructions, rules, and regulations prescribed for use in matters involving financial transactions. They were employed by the Treasury Department and other executive departments and subordinate agencies and officials, such as the Accountant of the War Department, army paymasters, the Superintendent of Military Stores, the Secretary of State, the Navy Department, and land offices. Approximately the first 30 pages of the first volume contain copies of numerous numbered or lettered forms and related instructions sent to state loan office commissioners by the Secretary of the Treasury in September 1790 for use in connection with operations under the funding act of August 4, 1790. Included are forms and instructions for a stock subscription register and for a register of certificates of domestic debt received from nonsubscribers to the loan of 1790; for the three kinds of 3- and 6-percent stock certificates; for receipts for stock; for a certificate to be issued to nonsubscribers; and for journals, ledgers, and accounts. Forms concerning the funding of the assumed state debt, a loan for the payment of the foreign debt, other federal government loans, the payment of invalid pensioners, and the transfer and replacement of stock issued under the 1790 act are also present in the three volumes.

FI.53.17. The series **record of account of commissioners of loans and abstract of stock funded, 1790-94**, contains records related to the loan of 1790 for funding the pre-federal debt. The first section of the volume consists of a list of accounts for stock issued at the state loan offices arranged numerically by account number. Each entry shows whether stock was issued for funded or unfunded debt, the name of the loan officer, the month and year for which the account was rendered, and an auditor's report number. The accounts and auditor's reports referred to have not been located. The second section of the volume pertains specifically to stock issued by loan offices and by the Treasury Department pursuant to the funding act of August 4, 1790. This second section is also arranged by account number; it shows the dollar amounts for each of the three different kinds of 3- and 6-percent stock issued by each office and the department during the period covered.

FI.53.18. What appears to be much of the same data, arranged mainly by office, is recorded in the one-volume **account of stock funded at the Treasury [Department] and at the offices of the [state] loan commissioners, 1790-96**. It consists principally of a list for the department and for each of the state loan offices arranged geographically from north to south. Shown mainly are the dollar amounts of 3- and 6-percent stock issued, usually on a monthly basis, under the funding acts of 1790 and 1792. There are also references to related numbered loan office accounts and auditor's reports that have not been located. A summary statement following each separate list shows the total amount of stock of that kind funded in individual states and at the Treasury Department, and the grand total of stock of that kind issued. A table of contents is at the front of the volume.

FI.53.19. The single-volume series **statements relating to the assumed debt that was subscribed at the state loan offices, 1791-94**, consists principally of a statement for each of the 13 original states showing the amounts in dollars of 3- and 6-percent stock issued monthly by state loan offices from September 1791 to March 1794. The stock was issued to fund the pre-federal debt of each state as assumed by the U.S. government under the federal funding acts of

August 4, 1790, and May 8, 1792. Preceding these statements is a summary statement showing the amounts assumable for each state (totaling $21,500,000) and the total amount of stock actually issued for each state under the act of 1790 (totaling $18,328,186). Following the statements is another summary statement of the amount of stock issued for each state "at the several Loan Offices," which includes a breakdown by types of stocks issued. The volume also contains an account of the amounts owed to the United States by certain states and vice versa, and a recapitulation of the census of 1790.

FI.53.20. "Auditor's Certificates for the Funded Debt of 1790, 1790-91," forms the beginning of the series described in more detail in **FI.53.9.**, presumably having become separated from the other volumes in that series in the course of their use by the Treasury Department. It comprises those certificates of the funded debt of 1790 that were issued by the federal government in return for certificates of public debt issued by the Continental Congress, the Confederation Congress, or the state loan offices. Each certificate shows the number of certificates held by an individual before the funding operation, their face value, their specie value, and the value of the "1790 certificates" issued in lieu thereof. An alphabetical index, apparently of 19th-century origin, is included in the single volume. Persons who turned in certificates and are recorded in the volume include George Washington, Elias Boudinot, Andrew Craigie, and the trustees of Dickinson College.

FI.53.21. "Auditor's Certificates for the Treasury Credit, Aug.10-Sept.18, 1790" forms volume "D" of the series described in detail in **FI.217.15.**; it presumably became separated from the other volumes in that series during their use by the Treasury Department. The volume contains partially pre-printed reports, arranged numerically, from the Auditor to the Comptroller of the Treasury. It comprises statements of credit due to holders of certificates of public debt issued before 1790. Among the persons listed who turned in certificates are John Jay, as well as Peter Anspach for Timothy Pickering.

FI.53.22. Register of state loan office certificates, 1791-99, mainly records loan office certificates (called "Certificates of Public Debt") that had been issued before 1789 by the Georgia and South Carolina Loan Offices and that, upon presentation to the Auditor in the 1790s, were transmitted to the current commissioners of loans of the two states, presumably for examination regarding their authenticity. For each certificate listed the following information is usually given: certificate date and number; date presented to the Auditor; names of current holder and agent, if any; name of current loan commissioner to whom transmitted; name of loan officer who originally issued the certificate; name of original holder; date of commencement of interest on the certificate; face value; rate of exchange; and specie value. For many groups of certificates, total values have been computed and there are marginal notations. Arrangement is generally chronological by date of presentation of certificate to the Auditor.

FI.53.23. "Lists of Outstanding Loan Office Certificates, n.d.-1799," contains separate lists of the numbers and amounts of certificates of indebtedness issued by the several state loan offices and by the continental officers empowered to issue them, including commissioners of army accounts, state loan officers, and the five supply departments of the army. The lists are arranged by type and thereunder by state loan offices arranged from north to south. Entries for certificates paid before June 12, 1799, are canceled by a red line drawn through them.

FI.53.24. "Statement of Outstanding Loan Office and Final Settlement Certificates, 1816-34," comprises a list of loan office and other certificates outstanding on April 15, 1816, and a statement of the account on September 6, 1825.

OTHER RECORDS

FI.53.25. "Alphabet Books, Old Government, 1777-96" (M1014, roll 22), constitutes a contemporary index to the names of the accounts in the ledgers described in **FI.217.7.-FI.217.8.** Shown for each account title are the page or pages on which it appears and often the words or abbreviations "Specie," "O.E." (old emissions), "N.E." (new emissions), or "B.E." (bills of exchange) to indicate its monetary basis. Arrangement is alphabetical by the first letter of the surname of a person or other account title and thereunder by the designations of the ledger volumes indexed, A through D.

FI.53.26. Photostats of a continental bill of exchange (1779) with excerpts from journals of the Continental Congress regarding the issue constitute a series among an aggregation of miscellaneous correspondence and reports. The principal item is a report prepared in connection with an original continental bill of exchange of 1779 that was submitted to the Treasury Department by a citizen in 1931 with a request for information about its history and value. It consists mainly of typewritten copies and extracts of Continental Congress resolutions, orders, and reports, 1777- 78, and extracts of correspondence of Benjamin Franklin, John Jay, John Adams, and others, 1781 and 1783, concerning the use of the bills, which were drawn on the Joint Commissioners to the Court of France under legislation first enacted on September 9, 1777. Also present is a photostatic copy of the bill, correspondence with another holder of such a bill, a copy of an account dated 1785 that lists canceled bills drawn on a "Commissioner of the United States at Paris," a copy of a statement prepared in 1788 listing groups of bills of exchange that had been printed for the Continental Congress by Hall & Sellers from 1778 to 1781, and other related papers.

FI.53.27. "Sample Pages from Blank Books of Certificates of the Office of Finance, 1783" (M1014, roll 23), is among the records of the former Division of Public Moneys of the Treasury Department. It is a paper-covered volume of 100 pages, each of which is imprinted with three notes. On each of the first 50 pages are notes for 5, 10, and 15 dollars; on each of the remaining 50 pages are notes for 20, 50, and 100 dollars. Except for the varying evaluation, the printed part of each note is the same. Each is watermarked with the words "US NATIONAL DEBT" and a letter of the alphabet. In the margin along the spine of the book is a space for the number of each note to be entered. The notes were presumably designed to be issued in payment of financial obligations of the confederation government, with marginal stubs to be kept as a record of issuance. This volume appears to be an unused example of the books of 6-month notes referred to in the record described in the last entry in **FI.360.14.**

Record Group 55

Records of the Government of the Virgin Islands

FI.55.1. The Danish West Indies consist of many small, uninhabited islands in addition to the three main islands—St. Thomas, which was settled by the Danes in 1672; St. John, occupied in 1717; and St. Croix, purchased by Denmark from France in 1733. Except for 1807-15, when England held them, they were under Danish rule until purchased by the United States in 1917. Danish records relating to the cession and the rights and property of the inhabitants of the islands were given to the United States by the treaty of cession. They have not been translated. Pre-federal fiscal records for St. Croix are included in general ledgers, 1741-1850, and tax lists, 1743-1850.

Record Group 56
General Records of the
Department of the Treasury

FI.56.1. The Department of the Treasury was established by an act of September 2, 1789, which directed the Secretary of the Treasury to prepare plans for improving and managing revenues and supporting public credit, prepare and report expenditure and revenue estimates, superintend the collection of revenues, manage accounts, and grant warrants for money issued from the treasury. This record group includes records of the Office of the Secretary and its subdivisions and those of units performing service functions for the entire department.

FI.56.2. "Account Book of George Washington as Commander-in-Chief of the Continental Army, 1775-83," was prepared by George Washington in his own hand as a record of his official expenses as Commander in Chief of the Continental Army during the Revolution. On or about July 1, 1783, he presented it and related documents serving as vouchers to the continental government. The first and major part of the volume consists of entries dated at intervals of from several days to several weeks throughout the war showing amounts of money received and disbursed by Washington or on his behalf. Money was received mainly from the Paymaster General and his deputies. Funds were disbursed for a wide variety of purposes, including "household expenses," expenses of the general and certain aides for various travel, "secret services," the purchase of military equipment for Washington's personal use, presents to Indians, wages of servants, and money advanced by Washington to various military officers. A few entries are supported by explanatory footnotes by Washington. The second part of the volume, labeled "Recapitulation or Generl Statement," summarizes Washington's accounts for the entire period and related supporting accounts of steward Ebenezer Austin, housekeeper Mary Smith, Maj. Caleb Gibbs, and Capt. William Colfax. Gibbs and Colfax were successively in command of Washington's personal guard and disbursed much of the money entered in the first part of the volume under household expenses.

FI.56.3. Arrangement within the first part is chronological and within the second mainly by title of account and thereunder chronological. Related account books, including one retained by the general, which in part duplicates that described above, are among the George Washington Papers in the custody of the Library of Congress.

Many facsimile editions of the account book Washington submitted to the continental government have been published.

Record Group 59
General Records of the Department of State

FI.59.1. The Department of Foreign Affairs was established by an act of July 27, 1789. An act of September 15, 1789, gave the department additional functions, including custody of records of the United States previously held by the Secretary of Congress, and changed its name to the Department of State. The department was in charge of territorial affairs from 1789 to 1873.

FI.59.2. A pamphlet entitled "Propositions Respecting the Coinage of Gold, Silver, and Copper, June 2, 1785" (M116, roll 1) is part of the **territorial papers, 1764-1873**, and is bound as part of a volume in the Florida papers subseries. It was compiled from several documents (including a report by a committee of Congress, May 13, 1785; a letter written to the President of the Confederation Congress by Superintendent of Finance Robert Morris; and "Notes on the Establishment of a Money Mint" by Thomas Jefferson) and was printed by John Dunlap. An annotated copy of the pamphlet with an endorsement by Charles Thomson is on page 323 of the volume described in **FI.360.8.**

FI.59.3. "Records Pertaining to the Settlement of Accounts between the United States and France Based on Pre-Federal Loans and Other Transactions, 1790-97," is part of **letters, accounts, and contracts relating to European loans, 1782-1805.** The principal item is a portfolio containing fair copies of accounts between the United States and France "as finally adjusted" and certified correct by Register of the Treasury Department Joseph Nourse on April 14, 1797. The accounts pertain to money due from the United States to France for various loans and supplies received from 1781, and to money due the United States from France for supplies furnished by the former to the French "Marine" from 1778 to 1780 "under the agency of John Holker." In connection with the supplies furnished to the French, there is a list of kinds and amounts of provisions delivered, other disbursements made, and payments by Holker. In addition to the portfolio of accounts there are related records, mainly fair copies of correspondence between French and U.S. government officials in 1794-95 concerning the pre-federal loans, supplies, and the tobacco agreement entered into by Benjamin Franklin and Silas Deane with the Farmers General of France in 1777. A schedule of remittances on French loans from 1790 to 1792 is also present.

FI.59.4. Documents concerning loans entered into by John Adams as Minister to the Netherlands with "certain money Lenders under the negotiation of Messieurs Wilhelm and Jan Willink, Nicolaas and Jacob Van Staphorst, and de la Land and Fynje, Merchants in Amsterdam," are also a part of the series. The contracts are for two loans, each for 1 million Dutch guilders, in June 1782 and June 1787. Arrangement of the series is chronological.

Record Group 93
War Department Collection of Revolutionary War Records

FI.93.1. The act of August 7, 1789, that established the War Department provided that the Secretary of War should have custody of all books and papers in the Office of the Secretary at War, who had headed the Department of War created in 1781 by the Continental Congress, including papers of the earlier Board of War. For a more detailed account, including loss of records by fire and accessions from other government and nongovernment sources, see **MI.93.1.**

FI.93.2. In the series numbered record books, 1775-98, is the subseries "Record of Accounts of the Commissioner's Office for Settling the Accounts of the Quartermaster General's Department, May 1786- March 1789 and April 1790" (Number 101, M853, roll 24). The single volume records money paid to fulfill obligations of the Quartermaster Department remaining from the Revolutionary War. Most of the accounts are for supplies and services, but there are also some for the redemption of certificates and currency and for reimbursement to officers for money advanced from their private funds. Most of the entries for 1786-89 are dated at the commissioner's office in New York City. They are followed by 11 pages of entries for April 1790 under the heading "Auditors Office," which also pertain to accounts of the Quartermaster Department, many of them accounts with states. The volume is arranged chronologically.

FI.93.3. In the same series is "Letters Sent by Joseph Howell, War Department Accountant, Jan. 2-Dec. 30, 1794" (Number 137, M853, roll 19). It contains copies of letters sent by Howell as an official of the federal government relating to the inspection and settlement of pay, subsistence, and other accounts of military officers with the War Department. Some of the accounts concern service during the Revolution. Correspondents include the Secretary of War, the Auditor and the Comptroller of the Treasury Department, other federal officials, state governors and other state officials, military officers and former officers, and widows of officers. The volume is arranged chronologically.

Record Group 186

Records of the
Spanish Governors of Puerto Rico

FI.186.1. Spain ceded Puerto Rico to the United States by the Treaty of Paris of December 10, 1898. The cession included rights to the official archives and records on the island, which the United States agreed to preserve and make available for use. After inspection of the records at the Library of Congress in 1900-1901, many important administrative records were returned to San Juan, PR. Most of them were destroyed by a fire at the Archivo Historico in 1926. None of the records in this record group have been translated into English. Records from the 18th century are sparse and fragmentary; although the number of records in the record group increases for each decade until the 1860s.

FI.186.2. The only series that consists entirely of fiscal records from before 1789 is a single document, **contador oficial de las cajas de la ciudad [San Juan] e isla [records of the official accountant for Puerto Rico], 1782.** The records described in **CC.186.2.-CC.186.3.** also contain some information on fiscal affairs in Puerto Rico.

Record Group 217

Records of the Accounting Officers of the
Department of the Treasury

FI.217.1. This record group contains the records of officers responsible for settling federal and pre-federal accounts before 1921.

CENTRAL TREASURY RECORDS

FI.217.2. The series **wastebooks, 1776-86** (M1014, rolls

1-3), is made up of six volumes designated with letters from A through F. Headings at the tops of the pages show that these books were kept in the Treasury office from April 16, 1776, to March 4, 1780; in the Auditor General's office from March 14, 1780, to September 20, 1781; and in the Register's office until December 31, 1786. An entry usually includes the date, the titles of the accounts to be credited and debited, the name of the transaction or transactions covered by the entry (including such information as names of persons and purposes of expenditures), the amount or amounts of money involved, and a marginal number or numbers, possibly referring to a voucher or statement. There are also some cross-references to various lettered wastebooks called Auxiliary Books for Funded Debts, the location of which is not known. Some entries in volume A have marginal numbers corresponding to pages in the rough journals of the Continental Congress (see **CC.360.10.**). Many, and presumably all, of the entries in the wastebooks were posted to the journals described in **FI.217.5.**, but details were often dropped from the corresponding journal entries. For the general subject matter of the wastebook entries, see the description of the corresponding journals and ledgers in **FI.217.5.-FI.217.8.**

FI.217.3. Wastebook F contains a memorandum dated at the Register's office, New York, December 31, 1786, announcing his determination that the wastebooks and blotters kept in the office are redundant. He further says that "expense to the public will be saved by altering the mode pursued," in effect discontinuing the wastebooks (**FI.217.2.**) and making the blotters (**FI.217.4.**) the books of original entry to be posted to the journals (**FI.217.5.**). The remainder of volume F, which continued to be kept at the Register's office, New York, contains pages 1376-1471 (January 2-June 8, 1787) of journal D missing from the series of journals described in **FI.217.5.**

FI.217.4. The series **blotters, 1782-1810, 1824** (M1014, rolls 4-11), is a set of volumes numbered 1 through 17. Some appear to consist of two or more originally separate volumes; they were compiled in the Register's office mostly from January 16, 1782, to September 4, 1810. Volume 2, although similar in format to the other volumes, apparently did not belong to the set as originally compiled, as its page numbers and dates partly overlap those of the first and third volumes. Entries for 1789 and subsequent years pertain to the pre-federal period. Volume 9 contains the same memorandum that appears in wastebook F described in **FI.217.2.-FI.217.3.** This memorandum indicates that the blotters were begun in January 1782 as a set of books of original entry from which the wastebooks were to be compiled. At the end of 1786, however, the wastebooks were discontinued, the blotters having proven adequate in themselves as a source of entries to the journals described in **FI.217.5.-FI.217.6.** For the types of information present in the blotter entries and for the subjects of the individual transactions within the entries, see the descriptions of the wastebooks (**FI.217.2.-FI.217.3.**) and journals (**FI.217.5.-FI.217.6.**), respectively. Marginal references found in the blotters are similar to those in the wastebooks.

FI.217.5. The series **journals, 1776-79** (M1014, rolls 12-17), consists of seven volumes labeled A through D and "ID," "KO.G.," and "O.G." These books were kept in the Treasury office, the Auditor General's office, and the Register's office from April 1776 to January 1796 according to the form of continental, confederation, or federal government fiscal offices in force at any given time. The set of volumes is paged 1-3395, with a gap in journal D of 86 pages found in wastebook F described in **FI.217.2.-FI.217.3.** There is also a gap of about 266 pages between journals "KO.G." and "O.G."—apparently a missing volume covering a period in the 1790s. The entries for August 5, 1824, and September 2, 1854, in volume "ID" are relevant to pre-federal affairs.

FI.217.6. A journal entry usually includes the date; the titles of the ledger accounts to be debited and credited; information about the one or more transactions covered by the journal entry, such as names and civil titles or military ranks of persons to whom money was disbursed, and the purposes; the amount or amounts of money involved; and references in the left-hand margin to the page numbers of the ledgers to which the entries were posted. In some postings not all of the information in the journals was carried to the related ledgers described in **FI.217.7.-FI.217.8.** The entries in the journals were themselves carried, sometimes with details of transactions omitted, from the wastebooks and blotters described in **FI.217.2.-FI.217.4.** Some journal entries contain cross-references to wastebooks called Auxiliary Books for Funded Debts, the location of which is not known. Subjects of the entries vary greatly, including civil and military affairs, and are further discussed in the description of the ledgers in **FI.217.8.** Arrangement is generally chronological by date of transaction.

FI.217.7. A set of ledgers, dated 1777-89 (M1014, rolls 18-21), consists of four volumes, A through D, and is part of **general Treasury ledgers, 1777-1919.** Information in a typical account includes its title, usually with the civil or military office or military rank and organization specified in the cases of accounts of individuals; one or more debit and credit transactions showing the dates and amounts of money involved; and references to the page numbers in the journals (**FI.217.5.-FI.217.6.**) from which the entries were posted. Arrangement is by the titles of accounts, which appear to have been entered in the volumes in roughly chronological order. Entries under a single account are generally in chronological order. Entries dated as late as 1795 occur in the first three volumes, and entries dated as early as 1782 are in the last volume. The general scheme, however, is:

Volume A	1776-81
Volume B	1781-84
Volume C	1785-91
Volume D	1792-1810

At the front of each volume is an alphabetically arranged index to account titles, which is of 19th- or 20th-century origin. For a separate index to the titles of the accounts in all four ledgers, see **FI.53.25.**

FI.217.8. Many of the accounts are for military officers of the Continental Army line and staff serving under the commands of the Quartermaster General, the Commissary General of Purchases, the Commissary General of Prisoners, the Commissary General of Issues, the Commissary General of Military Stores, the Clothier General, the Paymaster General, and the Director General of Hospitals. Continental civil officials and employees for whom there are accounts include the Secretary at War; the Agent of Marine; superintendents, commissioners, and Indian agents; state loan office commissioners; lottery agents and managers; receivers of continental taxes; continental and commercial agents; members of navy boards; U.S. diplomatic and consular representatives, such as John Adams, Benjamin Franklin, Silas Deane, and Thomas Barclay; Deputy Secretaries Roger Alden and George Bond of the Office of the Secretary of Congress; postal officials; commissioners of the Chambers of Accounts; commissioners appointed to settle accounts; the secretary to the Superintendent of Finance; and various clerks. There are also accounts for particular states and delegates from particular states to Congress; state treasurers; emissions of continental money, loan office and lottery certificates, and bills of exchange; various U.S. ships; army contractors; various committees of Congress; regiments and battalions; British prisoners of war (collectively); expenses of Gen. Benedict Arnold's "table"; the "Funded Debt"; the civil list; the president and directors of the Bank of North America; the "Navy of the United States"; "Pensions, Annuities, and Grants"; and "Lands Granted." Accounts for individuals other than those already named include Charles Thomson, Robert Morris, George Washington, William Bingham, Capt. John Barry of the frigate *Alliance*, John De Neufville and Son, David Claypoole (printer to Congress), Caron de Beaumarchais, Christopher Ludwick ("Director General of Bakers"),

Otis & Henley ("Agents Clothiers Boston"), Wilhem and Jan Willink, and Nicholas and Jacob Van Staphorst.

FI.217.9. The warrants of the Board of Treasury on the Receiver of Continental Taxes for Virginia are part of **early warrants, 1786-1830.** The warrants of January 1786, March 1787, and May 1788 were signed by the commissioners of the Board of Treasury and called for payments to be made to the Treasurer of the United States.

FI.217.10. A four-sheet list headed "Register of Certificates issued from the Treasury" and signed by Joseph Stretch is among records of the First Auditor of the Treasury Department. It lists certificates issued July 15-September 15, 1786, in amounts varying from less than $10,000 to more than $12,000 that were issued to various persons. For each such certificate the following information is given: date of issuance, name of person in whose favor issued, date from which interest was to commence, and amount. The purposes for which the certificates were issued are not given. Arrangement is chronological by date of issue.

RECORDS OF LOANS AND LOAN OFFICES

FI.217.11. **Records of and pertaining mainly to the Virginia Loan Office, 1778-1834,** are dated mostly from the 1790s through the first decade of the 19th century and consist of certificates of funded and assumed debt issued under the loan of 1790 and apparently transmitted by the Virginia Loan Office to the Treasury Department. They involve cases of transfer of ownership; warrants concerning tranfers to Virginia of "stock" from the loan of 1790 that was on the books of other loan offices and the Treasury Department; powers of attorney for transferring public debt stock and for collecting interest thereon; and unsigned receipts for interest. Approximately 5 percent of the records date from or relate directly to the pre-federal period. These include blank and canceled certificates; instructions for recordkeeping; abstracts, reports, and summaries of Virginia Loan Office business; warrants from the Board of Treasury and Congress; and auditors' reports. Some of the pre-federal documents were submitted to the federal government by former Virginia Loan Office Commissioner John Hopkins in 1823. Others appear to be from the records of continental fiscal bodies, such as the Board of Treasury. The records are arranged for the most part in roughly chronological order by year and thereunder by type of record, but the pre-federal and related records are scattered throughout the series.

FI.217.12. **Certificates of funded debt and related records of the Rhode Island Loan Office, 1790-1805,** consist mainly of certificates of funded debt (including the assumed debt) issued by the Rhode Island Loan Office under the loan of 1790 for funding the pre-federal debt of the United States. Assignees turned in the certificates for new ones or sought transfer of the debt due them to the books of another loan office or of the Register of the Treasury Department. The faces of the debt certificates include a number; the issue date; the name, city of residence, and occupation of the issuee; the amount; the interest rate; and the interest commencement date. The backs contain the assignment statement, which usually includes the name, city of residence, and occupation of the assignee; the assignment date; and the receipt of the assignee to Rhode Island Loan Office Commissioner Jabez Bowen for a new debt certificate or for a certificate of transfer. Arrangement is alphabetical by the surnames of the issuees of the debt certificates, with the exception of some miscellaneous papers that are filed in no discernible order at the beginning of the series.

RECORDS OF THE SETTLEMENT OF PRE-FEDERAL ACCOUNTS

FI.217.13. **Miscellaneous treasury accounts of the First Auditor (formerly the Auditor) of the Treasury Department, September 6, 1790-1894** (M235, 1,170 rolls, through 1840 only), contain records that pertain to a great variety of expenditures by the federal government, including money disbursed in the settlement of accounts and claims originating in activities before 1789. For instance, there are accounts and related records concerning pay due to various officers and enlisted men of the Continental Army and Navy, money due to civilians who performed services for the continental and confederation governments, invalid pension and half-pay payments to Revolutionary War veterans and their widows, redemption of pre-federal loan office certificates, and payment of prize money to the heirs of John Paul Jones and of persons who served under his command in 1779. Among other kinds of records present are certificates of the First Auditor certifying sums due, memorials and petitions of claimants to the U.S. Congress, reports of committees of the U.S. Congress on claims, depositions of persons supporting claims, and originals and copies of pre-federal documents presumably submitted in support of claims. Examples of the latter include a printed pass issued to a private in Pulaski's Legion in 1779, a bill dated 1780 for painting and gilding military caps, three loan office certificates issued by the Maryland Loan Office around 1779, and copies of reports of Continental Congress committees and of other Continental Congress records. Arrangement is numerical according to numbers assigned to the accounts and related records in the order registered. Many of the early accounts are missing, and the records are not indexed. For certain accounts pertaining to pension payments removed from this series to form a separate series, see **PE.217.6.**

FI.217.14. **Register of audits of "Miscellaneous Treasury Accounts" (First Auditor's Office), 1790-1894** (T899, 1 roll, through March 1814 only), consists of 19 volumes. These records register accounts described in **FI.217.13.** An entry generally gives an account or report number, the name of the government employee or claimant involved, the date the account was approved, and the nature of the account. Volumes 1-3 for 1790-1838 and volumes 17-19 for 1881-94 are arranged numerically by account numbers. Entries in the other volumes are arranged alphabetically by the initial letter of the surnames of employees and claimants and thereunder numerically by account numbers.

OTHER RECORDS

FI.217.15. **Reports on canceled certificates, 1789-93,** make up six volumes among the records of the Public Debt Division of the Office of the Auditor of the Treasury Department. Designated A through G (D is in RG 53), they contain numbered reports of the Auditor to the Comptroller certifying the receipt of various kinds of "Certificates of Public Debt" for which individuals were entitled to credit, with interest, on the books of the Treasury. The certificates themselves were presumably surrendered under section 10 of the act that authorized the loan of 1790. They were transmitted to the Comptroller with the reports and destroyed by the British in 1814. Each report includes the name of the certificate holder and often that of an agent who actually turned in the instruments; the quantity and kinds of certificates; the values of the certificates in old emissions or specie; the total quantity of certificates and their total value; and the date from which interest was to be computed on the total. Kinds of certificates issued include loan office certificates; final settlement certificates issued by the Paymaster General and commissioners of army accounts; and other settlement certificates and evidences of public debt, such as lottery tickets, of the kind described in **FI.217.16.** Residences (city or state and county) and occupations of certificate holders are sometimes given. Most of the printed reports in volume G were not completed, indicating that it was the last book in the series. Volume D is described in **FI.53.21.** Within each volume the reports are generally numerically arranged. References in some volumes indicate that separate indexes to their contents once existed, but none has been found.

FI.217.16. Reports on certificates loaned, 1790-98, are contained in 24 volumes in the same source as **FI.217.15.** They are designated A through Z (there were apparently no volumes J and V) and mainly contain numbered reports of the Auditor to the Comptroller certifying:

1. the receipt of various kinds of certificates of public debt issued by the continental and confederation governments; and

2. the entitlement of the persons turning them in (under the act that authorized the loan of 1790) to 3- and 6-percent stock certificates ("certificates of funded debt").

The certificates themselves were transmitted with these reports to the Comptroller and were destroyed by the British in 1814. Each report includes the quantity, kinds, and values (in old emissions or specie) of the public debt certificates received from any one person as well as the total quantity of certificates, the total interest due, the total value including interest, and the monetary amount of each new 3- and 6-percent stock issued. The kinds of certificates received, as shown mainly by the names and positions of the issuers, include loan office certificates; final settlement certificates issued by Paymaster General and Commissioner for Army Accounts John Pierce; certificates issued by Jonathan Burrall, Benjamin Walker, and other commissioners appointed to settle accounts of certain military staff departments, such as the Quartermaster Department and the Marine Department; certificates issued by commissioners appointed by the Continental Congress to settle accounts of the United States in particular states; certificates issued by officers of the Quartermaster Department; certificates issued by Joseph Nourse, Register of the Treasury Department; indents of interest issued under the Board of Treasury; continental currency; and lottery tickets. For many holders of certificates, a city or state and county of residence are given.

FI.217.17. Volume A contains a printed form that varies somewhat from those in the other volumes. It is probably a stray volume from a different series, no other volumes of which have been found. It contains reports that pertain to the same kind of public debt certificates and holders but that do not indicate that any stock was issued under the loan of 1790. Instead, these reports state that the certificates were deposited in various state loan offices (mainly New York) and transmitted by the commissioners of those offices to the Auditor, who entitled the holders to credit on the books of said loan offices for the sums involved. The most likely true volume A of this series is in RG 53 — see **FI.53.20.** In volume Z of this series the reports are entirely handwritten and pertain to surrendered "Certificates of Public Debt" (not further described) for which the holders were entitled to payment or stock under provisions of an act of June 12, 1798 (1 Stat. 562). A continuation of the reports in volume Z is described in **FI.39.6.** Reports within each volume are arranged sequentially according to numbers assigned as received.

FI.217.18. Also among records of the Public Debt Division of the Office of the First Auditor of the Treasury Department is **Auditor's reports on registered debt, 1799-1837.** This series contains copies of reports that were sent by the Auditor to the Comptroller of the Treasury Department. Each report certifies that the Auditor has received from an individual or his agent one or more "Certificates of the Registered Debt" for which specie and funded debt certificates were payable at the Treasury Department under the act of June 12, 1798. The certificates thus turned in presumably had been issued by the federal government to holders of pre-federal certificates of public debt who had declined or failed to turn them in for funded debt certificates under the provisions of the loan of 1790. Information contained in the reports includes names and residences (city or state) of certificate holders; the names of their agents, if any; the total value of the certificate or certificates turned in, broken down by principal and interest due thereon; and an assigned number. The presence of unused forms at the back of the volume suggests that it constitutes the entire series of reports on registered debt. Arrangement is sequential according to numbers assigned as received. Inserted loosely at the front is a partial index, arranged alphabetically by the first letter of surnames, to names of certificate holders and their agents.

FI.217.19. **Indemnity bonds with related documents pertaining mainly to the replacement of federal securities, 1791-1867,** are among records of the first Comptroller of the Treasury Department. They consist mainly of bonds executed by individuals beginning in 1791 and promising to indemnify the department from future claims in return for the replacement of lost, stolen, or destroyed U.S. government securities and obligations, or for the payment of interest thereon, including stock issued under the loan of 1790. They include "Certificates of Registered Debt" issued by Register Joseph Nourse, 1783-88; final settlement certificates; and certificates issued to foreign officers who served the United States in the Revolutionary War. Related papers have sometimes become separated from the bonds to which they pertain. The records are generally arranged chronologically by the year of bond issue.

FI.217.20. Register's certificates for interest due foreign military officers on arrears of pay, and related records, 1784-1809, consist principally of certificates numbered and issued by the Register's Office from April to July 1784 under a Continental Congress resolution of February 3, 1784. The resolution directed the Superintendent of Finance to take measures to remit annually to certain foreign officers, including those of the "late corps of engineers" and Brigadier General Armand's "legionary corps," the interest on sums due them as pay. The certificates give the name of the officer to whom money was due, the principal sum due, the interest to be paid, and the manner and place of payment of interest. On the faces of the certificates are notations showing interest paid for various years. On the backs are assignments of the certificates to the Treasurer of the United States pursuant to section 5 of the act of May 8, 1792, which authorized the discharge of both the principal and interest represented by the certificates. The assignments were made from 1792 to 1798, with one in 1805, and are signed mainly by the issuees or their attorneys (Robert Morris is among the latter). The records are in roughly chronological order.

CHAPTER FO
Records of Foreign Affairs

FO.0.1. The foreign relations of the 13 unhappy British colonies were conducted from September 1774 until late 1775 by the Continental Congress. During that period the Congress drafted and sent petitions to King George III and addresses to the inhabitants of Great Britain and other British colonies concerning grievances. On November 29, 1775, Congress resolved "that a committee of five be appointed for the sole purpose of corresponding with our friends in Great Britain, Ireland, and other parts of the world, and that they lay their correspondence before Congress when directed." On the same day it appointed the first members of the "Committee of Secret Correspondence," as it came to be known.

FO.0.2. The committee promptly established communications with various persons in Europe to learn the disposition of foreign powers toward the rebellious colonies and to obtain other useful information. Among these "friends" of the United States were Arthur Lee of Virginia, then residing in England, and Charles William Frederick Dumas, a native of Switzerland residing at The Hague in the Netherlands. In March 1776 the committee sent Silas Deane to France to procure arms and ammunition and to ascertain whether that country would enter into an alliance with the new nation. It was from these beginnings that the overseas branch of the continental and confederation governments grew.

FO.0.3. On April 17, 1777, Congress resolved that the name of the Committee of Secret Correspondence be changed to the Committee for Foreign Affairs. Under its new name it continued to serve primarily as a channel of communications, a link between Congress and its representatives and agents abroad. Congress, as a whole and through numerous committees, formulated foreign policy in both its broad outlines and its details, appointed and recalled U.S. overseas representatives, and prepared their instructions. The Committee for Foreign Affairs had no significant independent power, but simply executed the orders of Congress. Even carrying out its rather limited functions, the committee proved less than adequate because of factionalism, membership turnover, and absenteeism. Much of the work fell on the shoulders of sometime-chairman James Lovell. Writing to Arthur Lee in August 1779 he confided: ". . . there is really no such

Thing as a Com'tee of foreign affairs existing—no Secretary or Clerk—further than that I persevere to be one and the other." (Thomas Paine had been elected secretary of the committee in April 1777, but was dismissed January 16, 1779.) John Jay expressed an understanding of Lovell's plight in a letter to him of October 27, 1780: "What with [committee members'] clever wives, or pretty girls, or pleasant walks, or too tired, or too busy, or you do it, very little is done . . . ."

FO.0.4. By then the Committee for Foreign Affairs had practically expired. Congress resolved to replace it on January 10, 1781, with "an office . . . for the Department of Foreign Affairs," headed by a "Secretary for foreign affairs," and spelled out in some detail the duties of the official. He was to "keep and preserve all the books and papers belonging to the Department of Foreign Affairs"; "receive and report the applications of all foreigners"; correspond with ministers of the United States at foreign courts, with ministers of foreign powers in the United States, and other persons, "for the purpose of obtaining the most extensive and useful information relative to foreign affairs, to be laid before Congress when required"; and "transmit such communications as Congress shall direct" to U.S. ministers and other persons in foreign countries. On February 22, 1782, Congress specifically authorized the first Secretary for Foreign Affairs, Robert R. Livingston, to correspond with U.S. and foreign consuls, and many other of his duties were spelled out with more precision than previously. After this act of 1782, communications from U.S. ministers abroad came regularly to the secretary, who submitted them to Congress; the replies of Congress also went through the secretary. Congress continued to appoint special committees to consider diplomatic communications, and all matters of any significance were referred to Congress by the Secretary for Foreign Affairs. After the secretary's position had been vacant for nearly a year, John Jay was elected to fill it on May 7, 1784, and served for the remainder of the pre-federal period.

FO.0.5. The staff of the continental foreign affairs establishment in the United States varied little in size and composition throughout the pre-federal period; it was neither large nor complex. In a letter to Congress dated January 25, 1782, the first Secretary for Foreign Affairs, Robert R. Livingston, mentioned that he had appointed two clerks, who were "barely sufficient to do the running business of the office . . . five copies, besides the draft, being necessary of every foreign letter or paper transmitted." On March 1, 1782, Congress authorized the secretary to appoint two "under secretaries," but resolved in April 1785 that there was to be but one such subordinate official. A few interpreters and a doorkeeper-messenger were also employed in the home office.

FO.0.6. At certain times the President and the Secretary of Congress also took part in the conduct of foreign affairs. Exasperated by not receiving timely communications from the Committee for Foreign Affairs, Benjamin Franklin wrote testily to Chairman Lovell on August 10, 1780: "My chief letters will . . . for the future, be addressed to the President till further orders." During much of the interim between the departure of the first Secretary for Foreign Affairs and the commencement of official duties by the second—June 1783 to December 1784—the Secretary of Congress kept the records of the Department of Foreign Affairs, as he had done earlier when the Committee for Foreign Affairs gradually disbanded. During that time the President of Congress and special committees were also active in foreign affairs.

FO.0.7. The overseas component of the continental foreign affairs establishment was also rather small, although at times somewhat complicated because of the appointment of particular individuals, such as John Adams and Benjamin Franklin, to fill two or more different posts. The first appointments were made in late 1775 and early 1776 when Silas Deane, Charles W. F. Dumas, and Arthur Lee were sent as "secret agents" to France, Switzerland, and London respectively. Publicly acknowledged appointments began on September 26, 1776, when Silas Deane, Benjamin Franklin, and Thomas Jefferson were elected "commissioners to the court of France." The principal object of this "Joint Commission" was to negotiate a treaty of amity, commerce, and alliance with France, but the members were also expected to borrow money, obtain armed vessels, and perform various other tasks not of a strictly diplomatic nature. Jefferson declined his appointment and was replaced by Arthur Lee in October 1776. Towards the end of 1777 Deane was recalled and replaced by John Adams. On September 14, 1778, Congresss dissolved the Joint Commission to the Court of France and replaced it with Benjamin Franklin as Minister Plenipotentiary.

FO.0.8. Congress sent other individuals as representatives of the United States to European courts during the Revolution. Among these were Ralph Izard, chosen "commissioner" to Tuscany, May 7, 1777; William Lee, sent to treat with the Emperor of Germany at Vienna and the King of Prussia at Berlin, May 9, 1777; John Jay, made Minister Plenipotentiary to Spain to negotiate treaties of alliance, amity, and commerce, September 27, 1779; and Francis Dana, commissioned minister resident to Russia, December 19, 1780.

FO.0.9. The Joint Commission to Negotiate a Treaty of Peace with Great Britain was created on June 14, 1781. John Adams, John

Jay, Benjamin Franklin, Thomas Jefferson, and Henry Laurens were elected to the commission. On May 12, 1784, Congress appointed the Joint Ministers to Negotiate Treaties of Amity and Commerce with European Countries and the Barbary States—Adams, Franklin, and Jefferson. Jefferson subsequently assumed the additional post of Minister to France, replacing Franklin; and to Adams went the additional duty of Minister to Great Britain. Adams previously had been appointed Minister to the Netherlands. When he went to Paris in October 1782 as a member of the Joint Commission to Negotiate a Treaty of Peace with Great Britain, he was succeeded in the Netherlands by Dumas, who acted as charge d'affaires although never formally commissioned as such by Congress.

FO.0.10. The continental Department of Foreign Affairs and its diplomatic and consular representatives abroad continued to function for several months after the commencement of operations by the federal government in 1789. Even after the first federal Congress established a "Department of Foreign Affairs" on July 27, 1789 (1 Stat. 28), John Jay continued to serve as secretary. In February 1790 Thomas Jefferson returned from France and assumed leadership of the renamed Department of State.

FO.0.11. Records pertaining to U.S. firms and private individuals engaged in international trade during the pre-federal period are described in the chapter on commercial affairs. U.S. representatives to European nations sought to acquire ships and supplies for the Continental Navy. These activities are reflected in some of the records in the chapter on naval affairs. The fiscal affairs chapter contains descriptions of some records involving accounts and settlements of international loans and trade. Records pertaining to the settlement of international boundaries are described in the chapter on land and exploration. The chapter on pensions and other claims contains desciptions of records related to claims involving foreign individuals and governments.

Record Group 360

Records of the Continental and Confederation Congresses and the Constitutional Convention

---

FO.360.1. Record Group 360 consists primarily of PCC (M247, 204 rolls), and Miscellaneous PCC (M332, 10 rolls).* For

*For a complete list of National Archives Microfilm Publications cited in this guide, see Appendix A.

additional information about those bodies of records and indexes thereto, see the introduction.

LETTERS AND REPORTS SENT BY THE COMMITTEE OF SECRET CORRESPONDENCE, THE COMMITTEE FOR FOREIGN AFFAIRS, AND THE SECRETARY FOR FOREIGN AFFAIRS

FO.360.2. **Other reports of committees of Congress, 1776-88: reports of the Marine Committee and the Board of Admiralty, 1776-81** (Item 37, M247, roll 44), consists of 104 pages that are copies of letters sent, mainly by the Committee of Secret Correspondence, to U.S. ship captains, U.S. diplomatic couriers and representatives, European merchants, and other persons from May 30 to December 29, 1776. There are also a few copies of letters sent by the Marine Committee and the Secret (commercial) Committee to the same classes of persons. All but three of the letters, which are arranged chronologically, were sent from Philadelphia.

FO.360.3. Both originals and contemporary copies are in the series **letters of the Committee for Foreign Affairs and of Robert R. Livingston, Secretary for Foreign Affairs, 1776-83** (Item 79, M247, roll 105). It contains letters from the Committee of Secret Correspondence as well as the two sources named in its title. The first volume consists of Livingston's letters preceded by copies of the two committees' correspondence, the originals of which are bound in the second volume, labeled "appendix to volume 1." This second volume contains a table of contents. The subjects of the letters are routine, and they are arranged chronologically within the sections described. See also **FO.360.8.**

FO.360.4. Letterbooks of correspondence sent by Secretary for Foreign Affairs Livingston are in two series, **transcripts of the foreign and domestic letters of Robert R. Livingston, 1781-83: transcripts of the foreign letters** (Item 118, M247, roll 139) and **transcripts of the foreign and domestic letters of Robert R. Livingston, 1781-83: transcripts of the domestic letters** (Item 119, M247, roll 139). The foreign letters are addressed mainly to U.S. diplomatic and consular representatives abroad, to French officials, and to a few private citizens of foreign nations, such as the Marquis de Lafayette and Jan Willink. Enclosures referred to are not included and some letters are partially in cipher. These copies of the secretary's letters, unlike those described in **FO.360.3.**, include notes indicating the number of copies sent, to whom sent, and the method of conveyance. The foreign letters are arranged in generally chronological order with an index to surnames of addressees included at the end of the volume.

FO.360.5. The domestic letters series includes some letters received by Livingston and some transmittal letters for reports described in **FO.360.6.** The originals of his letters to Congress, including some not found in this series, are in the part of Item 79 of PCC described in **FO.360.3.** Domestic letters of Livingston's successor, John Jay, are described in **FO.59.2.**

FO.360.6. **Transcripts of the reports of John Jay, 1785-89** (Item 124, M247, roll 141), contain a number of reports from Jay's predecessor, Livingston, for 1782-83. The three volumes contain fair copies of reports and related documents, the originals of most of which are bound in the volumes described in **FO.360.8.-FO.360.10.** There are some original reports and related documents bound in those records for which there are no copies here. Endorsements are not copied in these report books. For the subjects of the copied reports and related documents, see the descriptions of the original reports. The copies are arranged in generally chronological order with a chronologically arranged descriptive list at the end of each volume.

FO.360.7. Miscellaneous PCC (M332, roll 5) contains drafts of a few letters and reports by Livingston. Most are letters from him to the President of Congress, but also present are drafts for letters to Louis XVI, the French Minister to the United States, and Joseph Nourse; a draft letter of recommendation; and drafts of reports to Congress. The records are in generally chronological order.

LETTERS AND REPORTS RECEIVED BY CONGRESS FROM THE SECRETARY FOR FOREIGN AFFAIRS

FO.360.8. The letters and reports from Secretary for Foreign Affairs Livingston to Congress are in the series described in **FO.360.6.** Unlike the copies in Livingston's letterbooks (**FO.360.4.-FO.360.5.**), they contain endorsements indicating the date written, the subject, the date read in Congress, and other action taken, such as referral to committee (the names of whose members are often given). They are arranged in generally chronological order. At the beginning of each of the two volumes is a contemporary "descriptive list" of the contents.

FO.360.9. **Letters from John Jay, Secretary for Foreign Affairs, 1785-88** (Item 80, M247, roll 106), when sent, contained enclosures that Jay transmitted either upon the request of Congress or as part of his normal procedure for consideration by that body. The majority of such enclosures, however, no longer accompany the letters. A number have been found scattered among other items of PCC according to their origin or subject matter. A few are still present in this series. The letters are endorsed with such information as the writer's title; the date; the subject or the nature of enclosures; a number assigned to the letter; the date read in Congress; and the dates and nature of subsequent action taken by Congress, such as referral to a committee (members named) or referral back to the Secretary for Foreign Affairs or to the Board of Treasury or the Secretary at War. Many of the letters also are endorsed to show that on a certain date the enclosures were separated from them and returned to the Secretary for Foreign Affairs. The records are arranged in generally chronological order.

FO.360.10. **Reports of John Jay, 1785-88** (Item 81, M247, roll 107), covers a great variety of subjects related to diplomatic, commercial, and foreign affairs. The largest group on one subject concerns negotiations with Don Diego de Gardoqui of Spain over the Florida boundary and free navigation of the Mississippi River by the United States. Jay's reports are endorsed in the customary manner to indicate subject, date, and congressional and foreign office action. The first two of the three volumes are arranged in chronological order; the third is not. Contemporary fair copies of many of the reports are in the series described in **FO.360.6.**

LETTERS AND OTHER COMMUNICATIONS RECEIVED FROM U.S. DIPLOMATIC AND CONSULAR REPRESENTATIVES AND AGENTS ABROAD

FO.360.11. Documents received by the Congress and the Secretary for Foreign Affairs from U.S. representatives abroad make up a very large volume of records. They are scattered in many series throughout PCC and Miscellaneous PCC. Access to them by the name of the writer or writers of the correspondence is relatively easy using *Index, PCC*. Those index entries are arranged alphabetically by the surname of the writer(s) and principal subject (person) of the correspondence, and thereunder chronologically by date written. Each entry contains a brief indication of the nature of the document, including general subjects and location from which sent.

FO.360.12. In this guide such documents are briefly described in a tabular arrangement. They are grouped as series or subseries according to the places or functions to which the writers were assigned by the continental or confederation government. This does not mean that the correspondence in each series or subseries was sent from one particular location; it does mean that all documents relate to the writer's assignment to the indicated location or function. Thus the correspondence might have been sent from a place other than the one under which it is listed, and its date might fall outside the period in which the writer served in the capacity indicated. When a series or subseries contains correspondence of one writer who acted in more than one capacity the series or subseries is cited under all of the relevant locations and functions. This scheme is used here because it supplements the citation arrangements available in existing finding aids, such as *Index: PCC* and pamphlets accompanying National Archives Microfilm Publications M247 and M332.

FO.360.13. The following tables are arranged alphabetically by the location to which the foreign service officer was assigned, with joint commissions and ministries and commissioners assigned to multiple locations following after the last location entry. For countries to which several officers were sent, such as France, the location of the highest ranking diplomat(s) is listed first, with other sites of missions following immediately thereafter in alphabetical order by city. Under each location or function table are columns indicating the writer(s) of the correspondence, the year(s) in which written, the item (series) of PCC where filed (when relevant), and the microfilm publication and roll numbers where the document is reproduced. Correspondence that was sent jointly by more than one officer is listed last in each section under the heading "The Commissioners." Most of the citations to M332 are for sets of documents consisting primarily of contemporary copies, but all of those entries contain at least a few original or unique documents.

Writer(s)	Dates	PCC Item Number	Microfilm Pub: Roll
FO.360.14. *ALGIERS*			
John Lamb	1785-87	91	M247:119
John Lamb	1786	—	M332:3
FO.360.15. *BERLIN*			
William Lee	1775, 77-79, 82	90	M247:118
FO.360.16. *FRANCE — Paris*			
Thomas Barclay	1782-88	91	M247:119
Benjamin Franklin	1776-88	82	M247:108-9
Thomas Jefferson	1785-89	87	M247:115
John Laurens	1778-82	165	M247:182
John Laurens	1781	—	M332:3

Writer(s)	Dates	PCC Item Number	Microfilm Pub: Roll
FO.360.17. *FRANCE — Bordeaux*			
John Bondfield	1779-81, 85	92	M247:120
John Bondfield	1779-80	—	M332:3
FO.360.18. *FRANCE — Nantes*			
Jonathan Williams	1777-78, 80	90	M247:118
Jonathan Williams	1780, 81	—	M332:3
FO.360.19. *GREAT BRITAIN*			
John Adams	1785-87	84	M247:113
Francis Dana	1780-81	89	M247:117
Francis Dana	1780-81	—	M332:2
Wm. S. Smith	1785-87	92	M247:120
FO.360.20. *MARTINIQUE*			
William Bingham	1777-81	90	M247:118
Parsons, Alston & Company	1780-81	90	M247:118
Parsons, Alston & Company	1780-81	—	M332:3
FO.360.21. *MOROCCO*			
Thomas Barclay	1785-88	91	M247:119
Thomas Barclay	1782-90	—	M332:3
FO.360.22. *THE NETHERLANDS*			
John Adams	1780-88	84	M247:111-3
John Adams	1780-83,85	—	M332:1
Chas. W. F. Dumas	1776-96	93	M247:121-2
Chas. W. F. Dumas	1779-87	115	M247:137
Chas. W. F. Dumas	1777-82	—	M332:2
Henry Laurens	1778-82	89	M247:117
Henry Laurens	1781-82	—	M332:3
FO.360.23. *RUSSIA*			
Francis Dana	1780-83	89	M247:117
Francis Dana	1780-83	—	M332:2
FO.360.24. *SPAIN — Madrid*			
William Carmichael	1776-91	88	M247:116
William Carmichael	1780-86	—	M332:2
John Jay	1781	89	M247:117
John Jay	1781	—	M332:3
Arthur Lee	1777-80	83	M247:110
Arthur Lee	1777-79	—	M332:3
FO.360.25. *SPAIN — Bilbao*			
Joseph Gardoqui & Sons	1779-80	92	M247:120
Joseph Gardoqui & Sons	1780, 85	—	M332:5
FO.360.26. *SPAIN — Cadiz*			
Richard Harrison	1780-83	92	M247:120
Richard Harrison	1782	—	M332:3

Writer(s)	Dates	PCC Item Number	Microfilm Pub: Roll
FO.360.27. *TUSCANY*			
Ralph Izard	1780-83	89	M247:117
Ralph Izard	1777, 79	—	M332:3
FO.360.28. *VIENNA*			
William Lee	1775, 77-79, 82	90	M247:118
FO.360.29. *COMMISSIONER "FOR SETTLING PUBLIC ACCOUNTS IN EUROPE"*			
Thomas Barclay	1782-88	91	M247:119
FO.360.30. *JOINT COMMISSION TO NEGOTIATE A TREATY OF PEACE WITH GREAT BRITAIN*			
John Adams	1782-83	84	M247:112-3
John Adams	1782-83	—	M332:1
Benjamin Franklin	1781-83	82	M247:108-9
John Jay	1781, 83-84	89	M247:117
Henry Laurens	1781-84	89	M247:117
Henry Laurens	1781-84	—	M332:3
The Commissioners	1782-84	85	M247:114
FO.360.31. *JOINT COMMISSION TO THE COURT OF FRANCE*			
John Adams	1777-78	84	M247:111
Benjamin Franklin	1776-85	82	M247:108-9
Benjamin Franklin	1777-85	—	M332:2
Arthur Lee	1776-80	83	M247:110
Arthur Lee	1777-79	—	M332:3
The Commissioners	1777-79, 85	85	M247:114
FO.360.32. *JOINT MINISTERS TO NEGOTIATE TREATIES OF AMITY AND COMMERCE WITH EUROPEAN COUNTRIES AND THE BARBARY STATES*			
John Adams	1784-88	84	M247:113
John Adams	1785-87	91	M247:119
John Adams	1785	—	M332:1
Thomas Jefferson	1785-87	87	M247:115
Thomas Jefferson	1784-87	91	M247:119
The Commissioners	1784-86	86	M247:114

FO.360.33. Fair copies of correspondence to the Congress and the Secretary for Foreign Affairs from U.S. officials abroad exist as 13 series or subseries in 11 items of PCC. Because of missing documents and a general absence of endorsements, six of those series or subseries which consist of copies contain less information than the corresponding originals. Seven contain more information than the corresponding originals and are noted in the following table.

Writer(s)	Information That Exceeds Originals	PCC Item Number	Microfilm Pub: Roll
John Adams	none	104	M247:130-131
Wm. Carmichael	none	108	M247:134

Writer(s)	Information That Exceeds Originals	PCC Item Number	Microfilm Pub: Roll
Francis Dana and H. Laurens	a few documents	109	M247:134
Silas Deane and A. Lee	all of Deane's correspondence	102-103	M247:128-129
Chas. W. F. Dumas	none	115	M247:137
Benjamin Franklin	none	100	M247:127
Ralph Izard and Wm. Lee	a few documents	102	M247:128
Ralph Izard and Wm. Lee	none	105	M247:132
John Jay	a few documents	110	M247:135
Thomas Jefferson	a few documents	107	M247:133
Joint Comm. to Negotiate a Treaty of Peace with Great Britain	a few documents	106	M247:132
Joint Comm. to the Court of France	a few documents	102	M247:128
Joint Comm. to the Court of France	none	105	M247:132

RECORDS PERTAINING TO FOREIGN DIPLOMATS IN THE UNITED STATES

FO.360.34. The largest group of records from foreign diplomats during the pre-federal period are those that originated with French representatives. Letters received by the Congress from France's first Minister Plenipotentiary to the United States are found in four series in RG 360. Originals, which contain the customary congressional endorsements and are often accompanied by English translations, are in **letters from ministers of France in the United States, 1778-84: letters from Sieur Conrad Alexandre Gerard, 1778-79** (Item 94, M247, roll 123). Copies of these letters are in the other three series, although none bear the information contained in the endorsements on the originals. Miscellaneous PCC (M332, roll 5) contains a nearly complete set of copies of the original letters and enclosures plus a few minor documents not found among those in Item 94. **Transcripts of letters from Sieur Conrad Alexandre Gerard and the Chevalier Anne C. de la Luzerne, 1779-83** (Items 111-114, M247, roll 136), consist of copies of the original letters and enclosures plus congressional documents, such as reports, resolutions, orders, and papers related to Gerard's appointment and formal reception. The Gerard letters in Item 114 are the likely source of another set of copies in Item 111. The documents in all four series are arranged in generally chronological order.

FO.360.35. Letters to the Continental Congress from Gerard's successor are in the series **letters from ministers of France in the United States, 1778-84: letters from the Chevalier Anne C. de la Luzerne, 1779-84** (Item 95, M247, roll 123). Like Gerard's, these letters bear the usual endorsements and are occasionally accompanied by English translations. Copies, minus the endorsements, are in **transcripts of letters from Sieur Conrad Alexandre Gerard and the Chevalier Anne C. de la Luzerne, 1779-83** (Item 111- 114, M247, roll 136). Item 113 also contains a few relevant congressional reports and resolutions and minutes of oral communications from Luzerne to the Secretary for Foreign Affairs. Item 112 seems to have been copied from Item 113, but contains a few unique congressional documents. Miscellaneous PCC (M332, roll 5) contains only six documents—copies and drafts of reports and correspondence, all found in PCC.

FO.360.36. **Letters from Holker, Barbe-Marbois, Forest, and Moustier, 1778-90** (Item 96, M247, roll 123), are bound in a volume of some 500 pages. Francois de Barbe-Marbois served as secretary of legation under Luzerne and then as charge d'affaires. Approximately 75 pages of documents relevant to his service are dated July 1784-July 1785. The next Minister Plenipotentiary was Comte de Moustier, who served from 1788 through 1790. About 130 pages of correspondence, notes, and reports relate to his tenure. Some 280 pages concern the activities of French Consul and Agent de la Marine Royale Jean Holker. He was an official observer for France early in the pre-federal period and also procured supplies for the French Navy in American waters. Disputes arose concerning his purchase of flour in Delaware in 1779 and grew to involve the issues of freedom of the press, governmental regulation of prices, and currency depreciation. A wide variety of documents about this incident and Holker's other activities date from June 1778 through March 1781. The remainder of the volume, about 15 pages, consists of letters to the Secretary for Foreign Affairs from Antoine de la Forest, French Vice Consul General and Consul for Pennsylvania and Delaware. They are dated from January through October 1786 and, like the other sets of correspondence in the series, are accompanied by some English translations.

FO.360.37. Records pertaining to Spanish representatives to the United States are found in three series of RG 360. Primary is the one-volume series **letters and papers relating to Spain and to the Barbary States, 1779-95: letters from Don Diego de Gardoqui, Encargado de Negocios from Spain, 1785-89, and other letters**

pertaining to relations with Spain, 1780-87 (Item 97, M247, roll 125). Many of the letters bear congressional endorsements and are accompanied by English translations. A few relevant reports, treaties, and decrees are also present. Many of the letters and enclosures are copied in the series **transcripts of the correspondence between John Jay and Don Diego de Gardoqui, and sundry acts and proceedings of Congress pertaining to the negotiations, 1785-89** (Item 125, M247, roll 142), but that series includes a few documents found nowhere else. Miscellaneous PCC contains only one original letter (M332, roll 5) from Gardoqui to Jay, of June 30, 1876, accompanied by an English translation and note. The only other document is a copy of one found in PCC, Item 97.

FO.360.38. Communications and enclosures from the Minister of the Netherlands to the pre-federal United States, and some English translations thereof, are in the series **letters from Pieter Johan van Berckel, 1783-88, and Franco Petrus van Berckel, 1789-96** (Item 99, M247, roll 126). The records related to the Dutch minister for the early federal period are bound in the same volume. The entire series is arranged in generally chronological order.

FO.360.39. Letters and memorials received from John Temple, Consul General of Great Britain in the United States are part of the series **letters from William S. Smith and others, 1779-89** (Item 92, M247, roll 120). Most of the documents pertain to the affairs of imprisoned and other Loyalists and were sent to Secretary Jay.

FO.360.40. Copies of commissions and patents of foreign consular officials appointed to serve in the United States are found in two series, **copies of the commissions of foreign consuls, 1778-87** (Item 128, M247, roll 143), and **copies of the commissions and letters of credence of foreign consuls, 1778-1821** (Item 129, M247, roll 143). Most of the documents are copied in the languages of the originating countries. The first series contains congressional resolutions and other relevant documents. Both series have a generally chronological arrangement.

OTHER LETTERS AND COMMUNICATIONS RECEIVED

FO.360.41. Some applications for consular positions and for ship passports (called sea-letters) are in the series **proposals on locating the seat of government and printing the journals, 1777-89** (Item 46, M247, roll 60). The requests for consulships (Feb. 1783-Mar. 1787) occupy 44 pages of the volume and consist of documents from various sources supporting the applications of Reuben Harvey for a position in Ireland, Gaspard Voght in Germany, Moses Myers in

Amsterdam, and Uriah Forrest in England. Information about the applicants' mercantile and military careers is included. Applications for ship passports (Feb. 1788-Feb. 1789) make up 58 pages of the volume. They are for 12 ships, most of which were bound for China, India, and unnamed ports in the East Indies from Boston, Providence, New York City, and Philadelphia. The Secretary for Foreign Affairs was authorized to grant passports to ships that were bound on long voyages and owned and navigated by U.S. citizens, on condition that they carried U.S. cargoes and crews. Therefore these records contain information offering proof that the vessels met those conditions. Copies of the applications for ship passports are found in the records described in **FO.360.60.**

FO.360.42. The series **letters and papers of Thomas Paine, 1779-85, records of the Office of [the Secretary of] Congress, 1781-89, and records relating to the passing of counterfeit money, 1776** (Item 55, M247, roll 68), contains about 100 pages of documents, mostly from Paine, relating to an inquiry into his publication of information about secret French aid to the United States. The records from the Office of the Secretary of Congress consist of some 100 pages of correspondence from Secretary of Congress Charles Thomson to the Secretary for Foreign Affairs concerning the conduct of foreign affairs. The remaining records in the series are described in **FI.360.10.**

FO.360.43. Some records sent to Congress by Frenchmen other than diplomatic representatives are found in RG 360. Miscellaneous PCC contains 14 documents from Louis XVI (M332, roll 5), 13 of which are originals. A few are accompanied by copies or translations. Subjects include births and deaths in the royal family, credentials of diplomats, financial assistance, the services of the Marquis de Lafayette, and presentation to Congress of portraits of the king and queen. A small group of documents from Etienne d'Audibert, "consul for foreign nations not represented by consuls in Morocco," dated 1778-80, are also in Miscellaneous PCC (M332, roll 5), as are a few copies of correspondence from the Marquis de Lafayette (M332, roll 5).

FO.360.44. The series **letters and papers of bankers in Holland and contracts for loans, 1779-90** (Item 145, M247, roll 15), consists of 310 pages of documents from the Dutch mercantile firms of John de Neufville and Son, Wilhem and Jan Willink, Nicolaas and Jacob van Staphorst, and De la Lande and Fynje. Nearly all concern loans and commercial services for the United States performed, offered, or sought by the merchants in the Netherlands. Among the papers of John de Neufville and Son is a note of December 10, 1781, written in pencil to the Secretary of Congress by Henry Laurens during his imprisonment in the Tower of London. Miscellaneous PCC also contains several documents from all four Dutch firms (M332, roll 4), but all save three are copies of letters found in PCC, Item 145.

REPORTS OF CONGRESSIONAL COMMITTEES

FO.360.45. Other reports of committees of Congress, 1776-88: on foreign affairs, 1776-86 (Item 25, M247, roll 32), consist mainly of reports made by various committees to which Congress referred matters concerning foreign affairs. The reports, which fill four bindings, are arranged in generally chronological order and cover a wide variety of subjects.

FO.360.46. Occupying 47 pages of **other reports of committees of Congress, 1776-88: on the Commissary Department, domestic loans and loan offices, loss of certain army posts, treaties, foreign loans, and courts of appeal, 1776-86** (Item 29, M247, roll 36), are reports concerning foreign loans and treaties. They are dated 1778-88, with no documents for 1780-82 and 1786-87.

TREATIES, TRADE AGREEMENTS, AND RELATED RECORDS

FO.360.47. The loan contract treaties of 1782 and 1783 between the United States and France are in **letters and papers of bankers in Holland and contracts for loans, 1779- 90** (Item 145, M247, roll 156). The series also contains two tobacco contracts of 1777 between the Joint Commission to the Court of France and the Farmers General of France.

FO.360.48. Copies of much of what is in Item 145 are in the series **a record of foreign treaties and contracts, 1778-88** (Item 135, M247, roll 144). This two-volume series also contains instruments of ratification for several other pre-federal treaties and loan contracts. Indian treaties included in it are described in **IN.360.3.**

FO.360.49. Articles of Confederation, with plans and drafts of treaties and other miscellaneous records, 1775-84 (Item 47, M247, roll 61), contain an unratified consular convention with France and treaties and commissions pertaining to foreign affairs. Also included is a report presented to Congress by John Adams on July 18, 1776, setting forth a "plan of treaties" as a guide to the new nation.

FO.360.50. Miscellaneous PCC contains drafts of two trea-ties (M332, roll 5). A seven-page document is an earlier version of the draft of a proclamation "declaring a cessation of arms," presented to Congress by Secretary for Foreign Affairs Livingston on April 11, 1783. The version presented to Congress is among the records de-scribed in **FO.360.3.** and **FO.360.8.**

FO.360.51. The second draft treaty is in fact a form based on a congressional resolution of May 11, 1784. That resolution followed one of May 7, 1784, in which Congress commissioned John Adams, Benjamin Franklin, and Thomas Jefferson to negotiate treaties of am-ity and commerce with various European states and the Barbary States. This draft follows the prescribed form, with Denmark filled in as the proposed signatory.

FO.360.52. Also in Miscellaneous PCC (M332, roll 5) is a manuscript copy, in French and English, of the treaty of amity and commerce between the United States and Prussia of September 10, 1785. It includes the ratifying language of Congress of May 17, 1786.

FO.360.53. Some copies of instructions from Massachusetts to its delegates in Congress concerning the peace treaty with Great Britain are part of Miscellaneous PCC (M332, roll 7). They consist of a resolution by the state legislature that interest not be paid on certain debts due British subjects and an order of the legislature instructing the delegates to obtain information from Congress concerning provi-sions of the peace treaty with Great Britain relating to payment of such debts. Miscellaneous PCC (M332, roll 7) also contains some copies of records from the state government of Virginia pertaining to the cessation of hostilities in 1783, and the treatment of British citi-zens and their property in that state at that time.

MISCELLANEOUS RECORDS OF THE OFFICE OF THE SECRETARY FOR FOREIGN AFFAIRS

FO.360.54. The series **daily journal or despatch book of the Office of [the Secretary for] Foreign Affairs, 1781-83** (Item 126, M247, roll 142), consists of entries for letters and enclosures that were received and sent, and for letters that were referred to and from Congress, by the Department of Foreign Affairs during the time that Robert R. Livingston was secretary. There are also occasional ab-stracts of letters and copies of resolutions pertaining to foreign affairs. An entry for a letter may give such information as the name of the writer or the addressee, the date, a serial number, the number of cop-ies, the name of the person or ship carrying the letter, and a brief de-scription of the subject. The entries are in chronological order.

Letterbook copies of the letters entered in this journal are described in **FO.360.4.** Originals are among the records described in **FO.360.3.**

FO.360.55. On January 25, 1782, Secretary Livingston wrote to the President of Congress requesting that his powers be enlarged and enclosing a "resolve" to that effect. Congress referred the letter to a special committee, which reported, on February 22, a reorganization plan for the Department of Foreign Affairs. A draft of the committee report and proposed ordinance constitute a single 10-page document found in Miscellaneous PCC (M332, roll 5).

FO.360.56. **Daily journals or despatch books of the Office of [the Secretary for] foreign affairs, 1784-90** (Item 127, M247, roll 142), are two volumes similar to the one described in **FO.360.54.** They were begun when John Jay took office as Secretary for Foreign Affairs in the confederation government and continued while he served as Acting Secretary for Foreign Affairs and Acting Secretary of State in the federal government. For many of the transactions recorded in these volumes, cross-references were made to other record books of the Deparment of Foreign Affairs where the full texts of documents were copied. Those records are described in **FO.59.2.-FO.59.5.** and **FO.360.6.**

FO.360.57. Miscellaneous PCC contains lists of and receipts for letters and other records transferred from the Office of the Secretary of Congress to the Office of the Secretary for Foreign Affairs (M332, roll 5). They are dated May 13, 1785-September 10, 1788. Also present is an undated and unsigned list of letters and other records pertaining to foreign affairs received from the Committee for Foreign Affairs. It apparently refers to records of the committee transferred to the Office of the Secretary for Foreign Affairs about the time the latter began to function in October 1781.

FO.360.58. **Resolve books, 1785-89: resolve book of the Office of [the Secretary for] Foreign Affairs, 1785-89** (Item 122, M247, roll 140), consist mainly of copies of orders and resolutions of the Second Continental Congress and a few by the Senate of the first federal Congress. Included are printed copies of the Indian Ordinance of 1786, the Northwest Ordinance, the Constitution, and acts establishing the Department of Foreign Affairs and the Department of State. Entries are generally arranged in chronological order.

FO.360.59. **Copies of commissions and letters of credence of foreign ministers and consuls, 1778-87** (Item 129, M247, roll 143), are the copies of the credentials that were kept in the

Office of the Secretary for Foreign Affairs. Similar documents are described in **FO.360.40.**

FO.360.60. Similarly, the series **copies of applications for passports or sea-letters, 1788-93** (Item 130, M247, roll 143), was kept in the secretary's office and are copies, minus endorsements, of the records described in **FO.360.41.**

FO.360.61. A number of records described in the fiscal affairs chapter relate wholly or largely to expenditures in connection with the conduct of foreign relations and the settlement of related accounts. See especially **FI.39.2.** and **FI.53.2.** Other records pertaining to foreign affairs and likely maintained in the Office of the Secretary for Foreign Affairs are now found in the various journals of the Continental Congresses (Items 1-8, M247, rolls 8-21), which are described in **CC.360.10.-CC.360.14.**

RECORDS OF U.S. REPRESENTATIVES ABROAD

FO.360.62. Transcripts of letters from Arthur Lee, William Lee, Ralph Izard, and the Joint Commissioners of the United States to [the Court of] France, 1776-80 (Item 102, M247, roll 128), is a four-volume series that contains, in the third and fourth volumes, letters received by the representatives named and a few enclosures. Copies of letters sent by them are listed in **FO.360.33.**

FO.360.63. Transcripts of letters from Benjamin Franklin, John Adams, and others, 1776-88: transcripts of letters addressed to Charles Dumas from John Adams, Benjamin Franklin, and others, 1780-83 (Item 101, M247, roll 127), are contemporary copies of correspondence and a few enclosures received by the U.S. representative in the Netherlands. The great majority of them are from Adams and Franklin, but some 20 other correspondents are represented in the two volumes. Letters sent by Dumas are listed in **FO.360.22.**

FO.360.64. Copies of correspondence with representatives of foreign powers, proposed treaties, and periodic reports to Congress are found in **letterbooks of the Joint Commissioners [Ministers] for the Formulation of [to Negotiate] Treaties of Amity and Commerce [with European Countries and the Barbary States], 1783-85** (Item 116, M247, roll 138). The series also contains minutes of the proceedings of the joint ministers. Many of the letters received and drafts of treaties are in French and are not translated. Originals of much of the outgoing correspondence are in the records described in **FO.360.31.** (Item 86, M247, roll 114).

FO.360.65. John Adams and Thomas Jefferson were appointed to negotiate treaties of amity and commerce with Morocco and Algiers, either personally or through agents. Thirty-five pages of their instructions to agents are in **transcripts of instructions to Thomas Barclay and John Lamb, 1785** (Item 117, M247, roll 138). Other documents, such as credentials and letters of introduction, were copied into the volume.

FO.360.66. In Miscellaneous PCC (M332, roll 5) are invoices, accounts, and other records of Jonathan Williams and John Daniel Schweighauser, who were agents of the United States in Nantes, France (1778-81). Most of the records concern supplies shipped to the United States, and there is one account for the sale of a prize captured by a continental warship.

OTHER RECORDS

FO.360.67. **Records and accounts of Silas Deane, Beaumarchais, and Arthur Lee, 1776-84, and letters and a memorial relating to American trade in the French West Indies, 1788-89** (Item 54, M247, roll 67), contain correspondence and other documentation concerning Congress' investigation of the affairs of Deane, agent of the United States and member of the Joint Commission to the Court of France. Lee alleged that Deane had profited from the procurement of supplies through the French agent Pierre Augustin Caron de Beaumarchais. The arrangement of the records is apparently based on the investigators' judgment of which documents were closely related. The other records in the series are described in **CO.360.5.**

FO.360.68. In Miscellaneous PCC are records believed to have been submitted as evidence with requests for settlement of accounts and claims made by the firm of John de Neufville and Son, and their heirs, against the U.S. government between 1781 and 1815. The records, consisting of a bound volume and several unbound documents, include correspondence to and from a wide variety of persons in the United States and Europe, and a few related legal and financial papers. Some concern the naval activities of John Paul Jones and the equipping and outfitting of ships under his command. Many letters are in French or Dutch, not accompanied by translations. Some letters are in cipher, generally decoded into French. The bound volume contains a table of contents. The series is arranged by correspondent and thereunder chronologically.

FO.360.69. **Letters and papers relating to Spain and to the Barbary Powers [States], 1779-95: papers relative to the Barbary Powers [States], 1779-92** (Item 98, M247, roll 25), include documents pertaining to the negotiation of a treaty of amity and commerce with Morocco and the release of U.S. seamen captured when the brig *Betsey* was seized by Moroccan pirates. Many of the documents are in French, Italian, and Spanish. Some are translated. Miscellaneous PCC contains some contemporary copies, in Spanish, of letters concerning the *Betsey* (M332, roll 5).

FO.360.70. Also in Miscellaneous PCC (M332, roll 5) are a printed copy and a translation of an edict of Louis XVI providing for payments due on loans held by France in the Netherlands. The original and a signed copy are in the records described in **FO.360.44.**

Record Group 11

General Records of the United States Government

FO.11.1. This record group consists of the Constitution of the United States, the Bill of Rights and other amendments, and related records; laws of the United States and related records; international treaties and agreements; Indian treaties; Presidential proclamations, Executive orders, and other Presidential documents; rules and regulations of federal agencies; electoral records; and records pertaining to the Great Seal of the United States.

FO.11.2. The subgroup International Treaties and Related Records, 1778-1974, contains the series **perfected treaties, 1778-1945.** The term "perfected" indicates that a treaty was ratified and went into force. In this series any agreement between the United States and a foreign nation or citizen thereof is called a treaty. This includes the loan contracts with private Dutch merchants and bankers, although they are not treaties in the usual sense.

FO.11.3. The perfected treaties series is divided into two subseries. "American originals" usually consists of an original treaty signed by the negotiators; related records, such as documents defining the powers of the negotiators, correspondence between U.S. and foreign officials, attested contemporary copies and translations of the treaty, photostatic copies of the U.S. instrument of ratification made from originals in foreign archives, and copies of contemporary publications in which the treaty was published; and memorandums concerning the treaty made by Hunter Miller, Editor of Treaties for the Department of State, in 1929-30. The subseries "exchange copies" usually contains an instrument of ratification, including the text of the treaty, signed by the chief of state of the foreign signatory, to which is attached that country's seal.

FO.11.4. Both subseries are arranged by "treaty series numbers," which, in the case of pre-federal and other early treaties, are based on an alphabetical arrangement by the names of the foreign nations concerned and are thereunder arranged chronologically by date of treaty. Pre-federal treaties are interfiled with those ratified after March 4, 1789. They are all bilateral. There are five with France, three with Great Britain, two with the Netherlands, and one each with Morroco, Prussia, and Sweden.

FO.11.5. Only one pre-federal treaty exists in **unperfected treaties, 1803-1967.** It is a photostatic copy of an agreement to a consular convention with France signed on July 29, 1783, by Benjamin Franklin and Count Vergennes, but rejected by the Continental Congress on October 3, 1786. The original, signed by the negotiators, is among the records described in **FO.360.49.**

Record Group 53
Records of the Bureau of the Public Debt

FO.53.1. From 1776 to 1817, subscriptions to government loans were handled by offices of the commissioners of loans established in the states under supervision of the Continental Congress and continued under the federal government. In 1817 the duties of the loan offices passed to the Second Bank of the United States, and upon expiration of its charter to a succession of offices in the Department of the Treasury.

FO.53.2. The series **miscellaneous accounting records, 1775-1835** (M1004, roll 3), contains "Ledger Book of Monies Received and Expended for which the Secretary of [for] Foreign Affairs is Accountable, 1782-83." The first section of this single volume consists of salary accounts for agents of the United States and lists the countries in which they operated, covering March 1782-April 1783. The remaining sections contain a list of bills of exchange sent to official diplomatic representatives abroad and ledger accounts for those representatives and employees. Information in the accounts includes the titles of the positions of the persons, dates of payment, and the rate at which the bills were purchased. There are accounts for Benjamin Franklin, John Jay, John Adams, Henry Laurens, William Carmichael, Francis Dana, Charles W. F. Dumas, and William T. Franklin. For related records see **FI.53.4.**

Record Group 55
Records of the Government of the Virgin Islands

FO.55.1. The Danish West Indies consist of many small, uninhabited islands in addition to the three main islands— St. Thomas, which was settled by the Danes in 1672; St. John, occupied in 1717; and St. Croix, purchased by Denmark from France in 1733. Except for 1807-15, when England held them, they were under Danish rule until purchased by the United States in 1917. Danish records relating to the cession and the rights and property of the inhabitants of the islands were given to the United States by the treaty of cession. They have not been translated.

FO.55.2. The pre-federal records of the Danish governors include letters sent to foreign officials, 1774-84, and drafts of letters sent to Denmark, 1778-1831.

Record Group 59
General Records of the Department of State

FO.59.1. A Department of Foreign Affairs was established by an act of July 1789, and 2 months later it was designated the Department of State by the same Congress. It was assigned such functions as preserving and publishing laws and treaties, keeping the seal of the United States, and serving as custodian of the records of the United States previously held by the Secretary of Congress. The department was also in charge of territorial affairs from 1789 to 1873.

LETTERS SENT BY THE SECRETARY FOR FOREIGN AFFAIRS

FO.59.2. The pre-federal records in **domestic letters (letters sent), 1784-1906** (M40, 171 rolls), consist of four bound volumes entitled "American Letters" (M40, rolls 1-4). These manuscript volumes constitute Item 120 of PCC but, because the last binding was continued in use by the Department of State under the federal government, they became part of RG 59. They are successors to the records described in **FO.360.4.-FO.360.5.** (PCC, Item 119). During the 19-month gap between these two series, June 1783-December 1784, there was no incumbent Secretary for Foreign Affairs, and some domestic letters of the kind normally written by that official were sent instead by the President of the Continental Congress, copies of whose outgoing correspondence are described in **CC.360.21.** The letters in Item 120 by John Jay were written in both his capacities as Secretary for Foreign Affairs under the confederation government and Acting Secretary of State for the federal government, December 22, 1784-January 2, 1790.

FO.59.3. These four volumes consist mainly of copies of letters, notes, and other communications sent and received by the secretaries to and from persons located in the United States. The principal classes of correspondents for the pre-federal period are continental officials and bodies, such as the President and Secretary of Congress and the Board of Treasury; state governors and presidents; and diplomatic and consular representatives of foreign nations in the United States. Many letters addressed to the President of Congress, the Board of Treasury, and state executives are transmittal letters for documents, or copies thereof, received from U.S. and foreign diplomats and private foreign citizens. Documents in foreign languages are accompanied by English translations. Subjects of the documents are greatly varied. Bound in the front of each volume is a contemporary index keyed to the names of senders and recipients of communications, including writers and addressees of enclosures. Brief summaries of the subjects of documents are a part of these index entries. The documents in the bound volumes are arranged chronologically.

FO.59.4. Instructions, 1785-1906, consisting of 214 volumes, contain a single volume entitled "Foreign Letters" (M61, roll 1), which was begun in the pre-federal period but continued in use under the federal government (January 1785-March 1793). Like the domestic letters (**FO.59.2.-FO.59.3.**), it was originally in PCC, as Item 121, but became a part of RG 59. The volume was a successor to the records described in **FO.360.4.** (PCC, Item 118). Also like the domestic letters series, there is a gap between June 1783 and December 1784, when there was no incumbent Secretary for Foreign Affairs and instructions to U.S. representatives abroad were sent by the President of the Continental Congress. Copies of those instructions are in the Presidential letterbooks described in **CC.360.21.** John Jay's letters in "Foreign Letters" were written in both his federal capacity as Acting Secretary of State and as Secretary for Foreign Affairs under the confederation government. His last letter is dated March 3, 1790. The remainder in the volume are by Secretary of State Thomas Jefferson.

FO.59.5. The letters pertain to all phases of U.S. relations with foreign governments and also relate to the general administration of diplomatic posts. Most are addressed to diplomatic and consular representatives and other agents of the United States in Europe. Some are partially in cipher with "explications" following the coded parts. Enclosures were also copied into the volume. An alphabetically arranged index at the back of the volume lists addressees and some subjects of letters and gives brief summaries of the contents of many of them. The correspondence is in chronological order.

LETTERS AND OTHER COMMUNICATIONS RECEIVED BY THE CONTINENTAL CONGRESS AND THE PRESIDENT OF THE UNITED STATES

FO.59.6. Copies of letters to Congress from William Bingham, U.S. commercial agent at Martinique, are found in the series **territorial papers, 1764-1873** (M116, roll 1), in the Florida subseries. They are dated from October 13, 1777, to July 12, 1779, but there are no letters for 1778. Other copies of all of the letters and enclosures are in the more complete file of Bingham's correspondence described in **FO.360.20.**

FO.59.7. Among the records of the Department of State's Bureau of Rolls and Library is the series **indexes to volumes, 1778-84, on the Revolutionary War.** It consists of two paper-covered volumes, one of which is a partial name and subject index to letters received by the Continental Congress from John Adams. The other is to letters received from Benjamin Franklin. The indexes are to the copies of correspondence found in PCC, Items 104 (Adams) and 100 (Franklin), which are described in **FO.360.33.** They appear to have been compiled at the time the copies were made. Arrangement is alphabetical by the item indexed.

FO.59.8. The series **communications from heads of foreign states, 1778-1903,** contains several documents that date or relate to the pre-federal period. It consists mainly of "ceremonial letters" sent to the Continental Congress or the President of the United States announcing births, deaths, and marriages of sovereigns and other members of royal families; letters of condolence and congratulation; letters of credence and recall of diplomatic representatives; and other letters of a ceremonial nature. Examples are: a letter from the "Burgermeister and Council of Hamburg," Germany, of March 28, 1783, offering congratulations on peace and setting forth the advantages of trade with Hamburg; a contemporary translation of a letter from the Emperor of Morocco to the Basha of Tripoli, August

17, 1788, requesting him to make peace with the United States; a letter of condolence from the French National Assembly, June 2, 1790, on the death of Benjamin Franklin; and a letter from King George IV of England, January 31, 1820, announcing the death of George III. Many of the unbound letters are in the form of scrolls, are framed under glass, or have ornate and unusual covers and containers. Those that are bound are arranged by name of country and thereunder in generally chronological order. Ceremonial letters from Louis XVI before 1789 are in RG 360 (see **FO.360.43.**).

FO.59.9. Communications received concerning European loans to the United States during the pre-federal period are among records described in the chapter on fiscal affairs. See especially **FI.59.3.**

LETTERS, REPORTS, AND OTHER COMMUNICATIONS SENT AND RECEIVED BY THE DEPARTMENT OF STATE PERTAINING TO THE PRE-FEDERAL PERIOD

FO.59.10. Instructions, 1785-1906, the pre-federal part of which is described in **FO.59.4.-FO.59.5.**, contain copies of instructions from the federal Department of State to U.S. diplomatic representatives in foreign countries that relate to pre-federal affairs. As used by the Department of State, the term "instructions" embraces communications that merely convey or seek information or transmit enclosures as well as those that actually set forth directions for action to its representatives abroad. For the years through 1801 the volumes include instructions to U.S. consular officials as well as diplomatic representatives. Some letters to foreign diplomats, heads of state, and private citizens are also present. Examples of pre-federal subjects in the federal records include: ratification and amendment of the Constitution; the death of Benjamin Franklin; the dispute with Spain over navigation of the Mississippi River; negotiation of Jay's and Pinckney's treaties; the disposition of money suspected to have been paid by the French government to Beaumarchais in 1776 as part of a gift to the United States; confiscation of British property in Virginia during the Revolutionary War; and participation of Indians in the war and the subsequent negotiation of treaties with them by the United States. Enclosures include copies of correspondence dated as early as 1780. There are indexes or registers in most of the volumes predating 1870. For details of the complicated arrangement of this series and its relation to other series, see the accompanying pamphlets for the National Archives Microfilm Publications *Foreign Letters of the Continental Congress and the Department of State, 1785-1790* (M61), *Diplomatic and Consular Instructions of the Department of State, 1791-*

1801 (M28), and *Diplomatic Instructions of the Department of State, 1801-1906* (M77).

FO.59.11. Reports of the Secretary of State to the President and Congress, 1790-1906, consist of 22 volumes of reports (manuscript, typewritten, and printed) on a wide variety of subjects. The earliest volumes contain a number of reports on matters originating in or pertaining to the pre-federal period. Subjects include confirmation of land titles of French Canadian settlers at "Post Vincennes" (later Indiana) under a congressional resolution of August 29, 1788; the capture in 1785 of the U.S. schooner *Maria* and ship *Dauphin* and their crews by Algerians; general relations with the Barbary States; negotiations with Spain regarding navigation of the Mississippi River; the carrying away of slaves by the British at the end of the Revolutionary War and other violations of the peace treaty of 1783; and the cod and whale fisheries of the United States. Included in the reports are copies of correspondence of U.S. diplomatic agents concerning U.S. citizens held captive in Algiers, statements of Algerian naval strength from 1786, and statistical tables containing data on the cod and whale fisheries of the United States and other nations as far back as the year 1577. Arrangement of the series is generally chronological. Some of the early volumes contain subject indexes.

FO.59.12. Original letters, with enclosures, received by the Department of State from sources other than U.S. and foreign diplomatic and consular officials make up the series **miscellaneous letters (letters received), 1789-1906** (M179, 1,310 rolls). Letters received by the President of the United States and copies of letters sent by the Secretary of State to the President are also included. The series covers a wide range of subjects relating to both foreign and domestic affairs, some of which pertain to pre-federal matters. Among the communications received are letters from Governor George Clinton of New York, March 5, 1793, concerning "Antient [sic] Indian treaties" and papers pertaining to Indian affairs that were in the possession of Sir John Johnson at the beginning of the Revolutionary War; from several persons seeking confirmation of or compensation for services in the Revolution; from Andrew G. Fraunces to the President, August 19, 1793, with related documents, concerning provisions issued to Indians in 1787-88; from Gales & Seaton, September 20, 1819, concerning the printing of the records of the Constitutional Convention; from A. M. de Neufville, July 15, 1792, setting forth claims of her husband, John de Neufville, against the United States for advances of money and supplies during the Revolutionary War; from the Register of the Treasury, December 21, 1816, on the destruction by fire of Revolutionary War claims records in 1814; and from Thomas B. Wait, May 24, 1819, and October 5, 1820, returning "papers" relating to the

Constitutional Convention and to the printing of the secret journals of the Continental Congress.

FO.59.13. Also interfiled in this series are approximately 800 drafts or retained copies of letters sent to various persons by George Washington, mainly as President of the United States, and by his secretary, Tobias Lear, 1789-97. Five of these are dated between January 1 and March 2, 1789, and mainly concern the prospect of Washington's election as President and requests for appointments. The series is arranged in two groups, bound and unbound records, and thereunder in generally chronological order. The Department of State published *Calendar of the Miscellaneous Letters Received by the Department of State. From the Organization of the Government to 1820* (1897), which lists and abstracts the letters for the period cited in alphabetical order by writers and, occasionally, by subjects.

FO.59.14. The series **despatches, 1789-1906,** with enclosures, relates to all phases of U.S. diplomatic relations with foreign countries and to the administration of U.S. diplomatic posts. Most of the documents are originals, but a number of the earliest volumes contain contemporary copies made by the Department of State. Some despatches, especially in the 1790s, concern matters originating in or otherwise pertaining to the pre-federal period. Thus, despatches from U.S. representatives in Portugal (M43) and France (M34) concern U.S. citizens held prisoner in Algiers. Other despatches from France relate to ratification of a consular convention with the United States and a decree of the French National Assembly, June 11, 1790, declaring a period of mourning over the death of Benjamin Franklin. Despatches from Spain (M31) and Great Britain (M30) pertain to disputes of the United States with the two countries over navigation of the Mississippi River and the northeastern boundary of the United States and to negotiation of Pinckney's and Jay's treaties. The first volume of despatches from Russia (M35) contains copies and extracts of correspondence and other documents in French and English, dated 1779-1807, that deal with the activities of the "Illinois and Wabash united land companies" in the United States. The 2,202 volumes of the series are arranged alphabetically by country or groups of countries; the despatches are in generally chronological order. Two series of registers to these volumes, **register of despatches, 1789-1870,** and **register of despatches from U.S. diplomatic officers and of notes from foreign missions, 1870-1906**, are also in RG 59 and have been microfilmed with the despatches of the countries to which they relate. Each register is arranged alphabetically by country and lists and summarizes the despatches thereunder chronologically.

FO.59.15.   Miscellaneous despatches, 1792-1849, consist mainly of letterpress and other duplicate and triplicate despatches received by the Department of State from U.S. ministers abroad. A press copy of a long letter and numerous enclosures sent by Secretary of State Jefferson to George Hammond, the British Minister to the United States, May 29, 1792, concerns problems arising out of the peace treaty of 1783, such as British evacuation of military posts in U.S. territory, confiscation of Loyalist property, debts due British subjects, and the carrying away of slaves by the British at the end of the war. Other pre-federal documents include copies of 1786 correspondence on negotiations for a treaty with Morocco and a press copy of an undated memorandum entitled "An examination into the Boundaries of Louisiana," which refers to events as early as 1673 and as late as 1803. The series is arranged mainly by names of diplomatic representatives.

FO.59.16.   Original communications and enclosures received by the Department of State from foreign legations and embassies in the United States are in **notes from foreign missions, 1789-1906.** Only a few early notes and enclosures from representatives of a few nations have been found to pertain to events that occurred in or are otherwise related to the pre-federal period. In the correspondence from representatives of the Netherlands (M56) are copies and translations of credentials of Dutch diplomats who were appointed during the pre-federal period and served beyond it. The first two volumes of Spanish notes (M59) include a note concerning assistance rendered to Americans in Algiers in 1785; a copy and English translation of a treaty between Spain and the "Talapuche" Indians at Pensacola, June 1, 1784; and notes pertaining to negotiations between Spain and the United States over navigation of the Mississippi River, boundaries, and Pinckney's treaty. Bound with the notes received from representatives of France (M35) are a translation of a 1793 note concerning the attitudes of France in 1783-87 toward the question of the navigation of the Mississippi River and the adoption of the U.S. Constitution. Another note of December 3, 1794, concerns a claim of a Frenchmen, Le Breton des Chapelles, against the state of Virginia arising out of a financial transaction with Oliver Pollock as an agent of that state during the Revolution. A number of British notes (M50) in the early and mid-1790s concern the imprisonment in Massachusetts of a British subject, Thomas Pagan, for privateering activities on behalf of Great Britain during the Revolution; non- execution by both Britain and the United States of the peace treaty of 1783 with respect to such provisions as payment of debts due British subjects by U.S. citizens and evacuation of military posts held by the British in U.S. territory; ratification of Jay's treaty; and determination of the northeastern boundary of the United States along the St. Croix River. Scattered among these notes, mainly those for 1795, are a number of copies, made in Montreal in 1791-92, of several pre-federal documents concerning Indian affairs, 1760-89. The series is arranged alphabetically by country and thereunder chronologically. There are no indexes or registers for the notes dated before 1812.

FO.59.17. **Despatches, 1789-1906**, consist of despatches and enclosures sent to the Department of State by consular representatives abroad. A few volumes begin with originals or copies of correspondence of U.S. agents and private citizens dated before 1789. The first volume of despatches from Algiers (M23) includes a list of gifts given to the Dey of Algiers and subordinate officials that was enclosed in a letter in 1785 and copies of letters, 1786-87, concerning the captivity of U.S. citizens in Algiers, efforts to effect their release, Algerian naval operations, and the relations of Algiers with various European states. The first volume of despatches from Alicante, Spain (T357), contains a letter to Secretary for Foreign Affairs John Jay from Robert Montgomery, August 5, 1788, concerning political events in Algiers and the prospects for peace negotiations between that state and the United States. In the first volume of despatches from Havana (T20) is a letter from Oliver Pollock to the Secretary for Foreign Affairs, December 14, 1783, concerning the shipment of gold to Spain, a revolt in "Santa Fe," and U.S. trade with Cuba. Some other despatches and related correspondence, although dated in the early 1790s, pertain to events that occurred in or otherwise relate to the pre-federal period. For example, the volumes of despatches from Algiers (M23), Alicante (T357), Hamburg (T211), Lisbon (T180), London (T168), and Marseille (T220) for that period include documents about sending supplies to captives in Algiers, their health, and communications with them. The series is arranged alphabetically by name of the consular post and thereunder chronologically. There are no indexes or registers for the period before 1827. For Department of State instructions to U.S. consular officials, see **FO.59.4.** and **FO.59.10.**

FO.59.18. **George Washington's correspondence with his Secretaries of State** (M570, 1 roll) is part of the Papers of George Washington purchased by the U.S. government in 1834 and placed in the custody of the Department of State. When most of the Washington Papers were transferred to the Library of Congress in 1904, these three letterbooks were retained by the Department of State because of their close relation to its activities in the 1790s. Although they consist mostly of copies of correspondence between the President and the Secretaries of State after the pre-federal period, the copied enclosures include correspondence dated before 1789. Many of the letters sent are signed by Tobias Lear, the President's private secretary. Among the subjects of the correspondence are diplomatic and other matters, the origins of which predate the establishment of the federal government in 1789. Among those are ratification of a consular convention with France; recognition of Phineas Bond as British "commissary for commercial affairs" in the United States; relations with Morocco; the capture in 1785 by the Algerians of the ship *Dauphin* and the schooner *Maria*, both captained by U.S. citizens; a survey of a tract of land between Lake Erie and the northern boundary of Pennsylvania; salaries and allowances of U.S. diplomats abroad; and ratification and amendment of the Constitution. The series is in generally chronological order. There is a partial name and subject index to the first letterbook at the beginning of that volume.

OTHER RECORDS

FO.59.19. The first volume in the series **cashbooks, 1785-95, 1820-25, 1856-1918, 1921-25,** was begun in the office of Secretary for Foreign Affairs John Jay and continued in use after the establishment of the federal government. As a result, it was separated from most of the other records of the Secretary for Foreign Affairs that became numbered items in PCC. The book is divided into two parts. The first and largest contains debit and credit entries showing the receipt and expenditure of money by the office and the Department of State for 1785-95. A more detailed description of the entries is found in **CO.59.3.** The volume was discontinued as a cashbook in 1795, but was used from 1799 to 1801 as a register of passports issued to persons going to St. Domingo. That part of the volume shows the names of the passport issuees, their destination, remarks concerning their citizenship, reasons for seeking passports, names of persons who recommended them, and the dates of issuance. The cashbook entries begin at the front of the volume; the passport entries at the back. Each of the two parts is arranged in generally chronological order.

FO.59.20. A substantial part of the private and public papers bequeathed by Benjamin Franklin to his grandson, William Temple Franklin, was taken to England in 1791 and used in preparing his *Memoirs of the Life and Writings of Benjamin Franklin* (1817-18). W. T. Franklin died in 1823, and in 1851 the papers were purchased by Henry Stevens, an American bookseller in London. The U.S. government bought the papers from Stevens in 1882 and deposited them in the Bureau of Rolls and Library of the Department of State. In 1903 and 1922 they were transferred to the Library of Congress. Also part of the 1882 purchase were 19th-century copies of the papers, an "index" to the collection, and a few related printed works. All of these remained with the Department of State when the papers went to the Library of Congress.

FO.59.21. Records concerning the purchase of the Franklin Papers, 1881-83, include correspondence and despatches concerning the legal and physical transfer of the papers to the U.S. government; lists of documents in the collection; reports on the purchase; and published works concerning the papers and the purchase. **Stevens' transcripts of Franklin Papers, n.d.** (24 vols.), consist of printed and typewritten copies of Franklin's correspondence and other papers. The printed copies appear to be from Jared Sparks' 10-volume *The Works of Benjamin Franklin* (1836-40) and his 6-volume *Diplomatic Correspondence of the American Revolution* (1857). The transcripts are annotated to show such information as the location of the document among bound volumes of the Franklin Papers, type of document (such as draft or original), textual corrections, and the volume and page number of the work from which the printed transcript was taken. **Register of transcripts of Franklin Papers, n.d.,** consists of 2 feet of 4- by 8-inch slips. They are printed forms with information entered on them by hand. It includes the title of the Franklin document or the names of the sender and receiver if the document is a letter; the date of the document; the subject of some of the letters; the type of document, such as original, draft, or entry in a letterbook; the number of words in the document; the Stevens Collection series number and the volume and page number within the series; the portfolio number of the copy of the document; and the volume and page number of the document as printed in the two aforementioned works by Jared Sparks. The slips are arranged in generally chronological order except for some at the front and back of the file for documents the dates of which could not be determined.

FO.59.22. Also part of the records of the Bureau of Rolls and Library is **manuscript copy of U.S. diplomatic correspondence, 1783-89.** The series consists of copies of original records in PCC. They were made in the process of publishing the first or subsequent editions of the seven-volume *Diplomatic Correspondence of the United States from the Treaty of Peace, 1783, to the Adoption of the Constitution, 1789* (1833-34). Included among the records are letters sent and received by U.S. diplomats, as well as correspondence of the President of the Continental Congress and the Secretary for Foreign Affairs. Tables of contents for the documents and copies of documents in Item 145 of PCC are also present, as are a few original Continental Congress records. Arrangement is mainly alphabetical by the names of the principal diplomats and other persons whose correspondence is included.

FO.59.23. Another series from the Bureau of Rolls and Library, **miscellaneous manuscripts, ca. 1756-1918**, contains a facsimile copy of a letter, dated December 23, 1776, in which Benjamin Franklin, Silas Deane, and Arthur Lee introduce themselves to the Count de Vergennes as representatives of the United States with power to negotiate a treaty of amity and commerce with France. They request an audience for the purpose of presenting their credentials. Another series from the bureau, **miscellaneous documents, 1206-1932, printed, ca. 1780-1932,** contains a four-page copy of "A Bill to Enable His Majesty to Conclude a Peace, or Truce, with the Revolted Colonies in North America," 1782.

Record Group 84

Records of the Foreign Service Posts of the Department of State

FO.84.1. Diplomatic agents were sent to European courts early in the Revolutionary War, but the first permanent diplomatic representative was not appointed until 1778, and the first consul in 1780. Diplomats often served in a consular capacity until the creation of an independent consular service in 1792. The records of many posts are incomplete, especially for the early years. Many officers, upon leaving their post, took their correspondence with them, regarding it as personal property. Other records have been lost through such means as fires and adverse climatic conditions. Among post records, the instructions received from the Department of State and copies of despatches thereto are largely duplicated in the records of the department (RG 59).

FO.84.2. Only one pre-federal document is extant in RG 84. At the beginning of the series **miscellaneous correspondence** in the subgroup Records of the United States Embassy at Paris, France, 1788, 1794-1935, is a printed form, in French, dated May 1, 1788, at Port-au-Prince, Haiti, referring to duty on slaves. Records of the continental foreign service post in Paris during Benjamin Franklin's tenure there are described in **FO.59.21.-FO.59.22.**

Record Group 186
Records of the
Spanish Governors of Puerto Rico

FO.186.1. Spain ceded Puerto Rico to the United States by the Treaty of Paris of December 10, 1898. The cession included rights to the official archives and records on the island, which the United States agreed to preserve and make available for use. After inspection of the records at the Library of Congress in 1900-1901, many important administrative records were returned to San Juan, PR. Most of them were destroyed by a fire at the Archivo Historico in 1926. None of the records in this record group have been translated into English. Records from the 18th century are sparse and fragmentary; although the number of records in the record group increases for each decade until the 1860s.

FO.186.2. Records pertaining to foreign representatives in Puerto Rico are in the series **consules y gobiernos extranjeros, 1766-1894** (10 ft.), which consists of 53 files, one for each location that sent a representative to the island. The series is arranged alphabetically by the Spanish names of the locations. Documents for the pre-federal period are in the files for the following locations:

Antigua	1781-1830
Coruna	1783-92
Curazao	1762-1838
Estados Unidos	1779-1830
Guayra	1778-1809
Londres	1768-1819
Merida de Yucatan	1766-1810
Mexico	1766-1812
San Eustachio	1762-68
San Tomas	1762-1858
Santa Fe	1769-1810
Santa Lucia	1782
Tortola	1784-1823

Record Group 200
National Archives Gift Collection

FO.200.1. This record group includes gifts of personal papers, historical manuscripts, and audiovisual and other nontextual materials donated to the National Archives and Records Administration. The National Archives Act of June 18, 1934, the Federal Property Administrative Services Act of 1949, as amended, and the National Archives and Records Administration Act of 1984 authorized the acceptance from private sources of material appropriate for preservation by the U.S. government as evidence of its functions, policies, decisions, procedures, and transactions. Records in RG 200 have been donated by a wide range of business and cultural organizations and institutions and by many individuals.

FO.200.2. A facsimile copy of a British broadside announcing the signing of the preliminary treaty of peace of March 25, 1783, is in this record group. It announced that despatches addressed to the Continental Congress contained news of the signing of "preliminaries" to a general peace at Paris, on January 20, 1783, and the consequent cessation of hostilities. The original was published at New York City by James Rivington, "Printer to the King's Most Excellent Majesty." This copy contains a statement dated December 10, 1898, certifying that it was compared with "the original broadside in the collection in the first Senate House of the State of New York, situate at Kingston," and found correct.

FO.200.3. The gift collection also contains a portrait of Pieter Johan van Berckel, who was the first Minister of the Netherlands to the United States. This black and white engraving (3.5 by 5.5 inches) was likely used as an illustration in a book. The engraver was Reiner Vinkeles (1741-1826) of the Netherlands.

CHAPTER IN

Records of Indians and
Indian Affairs

IN.0.1. The administration of Indian affairs in the continental and confederation governments derived from the British system. The pre-federal government of the United States regarded Indian tribes as much like foreign governments, as had the royal government and the colonies. The superintendents of Indian affairs, for example, were in effect ambassadors who observed events, negotiated treaties, and sought to keep peace between settlers and Indians. On July 12, 1775, the Continental Congress resolved that there be three Departments of Indian Affairs, one each for the northern, middle, and southern sections of the colonies, and that a body of three or more Commissioners of Indian Affairs for each such department manage relations with the Indians therein. The principal responsibility of these commissioners was the maintenance of peaceful relations between the Indians and the continental government. Throughout the pre-federal period temporary commissioners were also appointed from time to time for the negotiation of treaties with Indians.

IN.0.2. Within Congress, Indian affairs were referred to special and standing committees on Indian affairs, but after 1779 the duties of a standing committee seem to have been performed by the Board of War. Article 9 of the Articles of Confederation included the provision that the "united states in congress assembled shall . . . have the sole and exclusive right and power of . . . regulating the trade and managing all affairs with the Indians, not members of any of the states, provided that the legislative right of any state within its own limits be not infringed or violated."

IN.0.3. An ordinance of August 7, 1786, significantly altered the management of relations with the Indians, providing for the division of the "Indian department" into a northern and southern district, each to be headed by a Superintendent of Indian Affairs. These officials were to receive instructions from and report to the Secretary at War. Their duties included the licensing of persons to trade with the Indians.

IN.0.4. There were additional persons employed by Congress in connection with Indian affairs, including agents such as John Allan, who was assigned to the Indians in Nova Scotia and the tribes to the north and east thereof. Appointed in 1777, Allan was sometimes referred to as being in charge of the "Eastern Indian Department." Other agents were George Morgan, at Fort Pitt, and Joseph Martin, agent for the Cherokee Nation. The Governor of the Northwest Territory and continental military officers stationed in the west also played important roles in Indian affairs.

IN.0.5. *Guide to Records in the National Archives of the United States Relating to American Indians* (1981) contains a separate section on pre-federal records. Since that publication treats the records primarily in their relationship to the subject of American Indians, this guide seeks to view the records primarily in the context of their relationship to pre-federal affairs. Thus, many references to Indians will be found throughout the other subject chapters of this guide, often with as much descriptive detail as will be found in this chapter. This occurs, for example, when records concerning commerce with Indians exist (see **CO.93.3.**), or when fiscal records relate to government expenditures on Indian affairs (see **FI.360.7., FI.56.2.,** and **FI.217.8.**). Such references will be noted in this chapter with cross-references under the appropriate record groups.

Record Group 360

Records of the Continental and Confederation Congresses and the Constitutional Convention

IN.360.1. Record Group 360 consists primarily of PCC (M247, 204 rolls), and Miscellaneous PCC (M332, 10 rolls).* For additional information about those bodies of records and indexes thereto, see the introduction.

RECORDS KEPT OR PRODUCED BY CONGRESS

IN.360.2. The series **other reports of committees of Congress, 1776-88: on Indian affairs and lands in the Western Territory, 1776-88** (Item 30, M247, roll 37), contains about 250 pages of reports and related documents that are the work primarily of special committees appointed from time to time to consider specific questions concerning Indian affairs. They are often in reponse to letters sent by such officials as superintendents and commissioners of Indian affairs. Related documents interspersed include correspondence, mo-

---

*For a complete list of National Archives Microfilm Publications cited in this guide, see Appendix A.

tions, and copies of resolutions and speeches. Subjects of the reports and related documents vary greatly in detail, but generally involve treaty negotiations with the Indians; the demarcation of boundaries; petitions on behalf of individual Indians; and the appointment, instructions, salaries, accounts, and terms of service of such continental officials as Indian commissioners, superintendents, and agents, and the Governor of the Northwest Territory. Most of the reports and motions are endorsed with the subject, date submitted, names of committee members, and notes on actions taken. They are arranged in roughly chronological order.

IN.360.3. Copies of treaties with Indians are found in two series of RG 360. They are interspersed throughout **a record of foreign treaties and contracts, 1778-88** (Item 135, M247, roll 144). **Copies of Indian treaties, 1784-86** (Item 174, M247, roll 194), include six treaties—those with the:

1. Six Nations, at Fort Stanwix, October 22, 1784;
2. Wyandot, Delaware, Chippewa, and Ottawa Nations, at Fort McIntosh, January 21, 1785;
3. "Shawanoe Nation," at the mouth of the Great Miami, January 31, 1786;
4. Cherokees, at Hopewell, VA, November 28, 1785;
5. Chickasaw Nation, at Hopewell, January 10, 1786; and
6. Choctaw Nation, at Hopewell, January 3, 1786.

The series is arranged in the order described.

IN.360.4. References to Indian affairs are found scattered throughout the general records of the Continental Congress, described in **CC.360.10.-CC.360.37.**, and Miscellaneous PCC. Such references are most easily accessible throught the use of *Index: PCC.* See also **FO.360.58.** and **LA.360.6.**

COMMUNICATIONS TO CONGRESS

IN.360.5. **Memorials addressed to Congress, 1775-88** (Item 41, M247, rolls 48-52), and **petitions addressed to Congress, 1775-89** (Item 42, M247, rolls 53-56), include several appeals related to Indians (see **CC.360.2.-CC.360.4.**). For a separate memorial with documents pertaining to relations with Indians in the west see **LA.360.2.**

IN.360.6. The series **records relating to Indian affairs, 1765-89** (Item 56, M247, roll 69), consists of a single volume of about 500 pages. The first 84 pages are a copy, made in 1765, of a journal reporting a conference held at Johnson Hall, NY, between Superintendent of Indian Affairs Sir William Johnson and representatives of the Six Nations and the Delawares. Most of the record consists of transcripts of speeches made by Johnson and various Indian leaders, including Killbuck and Squash Cutter of the Delawares and Gaustrax of the Senecas. Subjects include boundaries between Indian and British lands, the delivery of prisoners taken by the Indians, compensation for assistance given to the British by Indians, and complaints about the encroachment of white settlements in Indian territory. Most of the rest of the volume consists of letters, with enclosures, addressed mainly to the President of Congress. They concern such subjects as the appointment of commissioners to negotiate treaties, the progress of messengers sent to invite western Indians to a treaty conference, the friendliness or hostility of particular tribes, the difficulty of establishing peace when settlers occupied Indian lands, the inadequate congressional appropriations for treaty negotiations, the need for troops to protect settlers and to keep settlers out of Indian territory, Indian hostilities, and the role of the British in influencing Indians against the United States. There are also copies of speeches made by and to Indians, letters concerning the visit to Congress in 1786 of the Seneca chief Cornplanter, and drafts of ordinances concerning the disposal of western lands and the regulation of Indian affairs. Most of the documents bear routine endorsements such as date of receipt, committee referred to, and action taken. The series is arranged into a few groups based on general subjects, such as relations with particular tribes, a specific series of negotiations, the ordinances, and Cornplanter's visit, and thereunder in generally chronological order.

IN.360.7. A later conference held with the Six Nations is recorded in **proceedings of the commissioners appointed by the Second Continental Congress to negotiate a treaty with the Six Nations of Indians, 1775** (Item 134, M247, roll 144). The series consists mainly of the transcripts of speeches made by the commissioners and Indian leaders at a conference at Albany, NY, August 25-September 1, 1775. Although trade, land claims, roads, and missionaries were discussed, the main purpose of the talks was to explain the causes of the war with Great Britain with the hope of securing Indian neutrality. Related documents include records of meetings with other Indians in the area at about the same time and Congressional resolutions regarding the resulting treaties. The series is in generally chronological order.

IN.360.8. In the series **letters of John Hancock, and miscellaneous papers, 1774-85** (Item 58, M247, roll 71), are about 35 pages of letters and enclosures, 1783-85, from Col. John Allan, Superintendent of Indian Affairs in the Eastern Department. The letters concern Indians, like the Penobscots, who lived along what became the northeastern border of the United States, and deal with such subjects as the encroachment of British settlers on their land and the disputed boundary between the United States and Canada. They are in generally chronological order, and routinely endorsed by congressional staff.

IN.360.9. Some other letters to Congress and related documents concerning Indian affairs are found in three series of PCC. **Letters and papers relating to Canadian affairs, Sullivan's expedition, and the Northern Indians, 1775-79** (Item 166, M247, roll 183) contain correspondence concerning the 1779 effort of Gen. John Sullivan against Indians who were harassing settlers on the frontier of New York and Pennsylvania, visits by Indian leaders to Congress, exchanges of prisoners, and enrollment of Indian youths at Dartmouth College. Tribes referred to include the Senecas, Cayugas, Mohawks, Oneidas, Tuscaroras, Onondagas, and Delawares. **Letters and other records relating to charges against Gen. J. Sullivan and Dr. J. Morgan, and to British advances in the Mohawk Valley, 1776-79** (Item 63, M247, roll 77), contain a few letters concerning the military successes of the British and their Indian allies in 1777. See **LA.360.3.** for letters concerning Indian activities in the area of the Seven Ranges in Ohio during land surveys there in the late 1780s.

IN.360.10. Much correspondence concerning Indian affairs is scattered throughout other series in PCC and Miscellaneous PCC. Access to it is best gained through use of *Index: PCC*. The following list indicates the PCC items with the most such records:

1. **State papers, 1775-91** (Items 64-77, M247, rolls 78-89), which consist of letters received by Congress from governors and other officials of the states, from committees of safety, and from state legislatures. The papers from Georgia, Massachusetts, New York, North and South Carolina, Pennsylvania, and Virginia contain records about Indian affairs.

2. **Letters and reports from Maj. Gen. Henry Knox, Secretary at War, 1785-88** (Items 150-151, M247, rolls 164-165).

3. Several series of correspondence to Congress from military officers (Items 152-165, 169-173, M247, rolls 166-182, 186-193), especially that of Brig. Gen. James Clinton, Maj. Gen. Horatio Gates, Maj. Gen. Nathanael Greene, Brig. Gen. Edward Hand, Lt. Col. Josiah Harmar, Col. George Morgan, Maj. Gen. Philip Schuyler, Brig. Gen. John Stark, Maj. Gen. John Sullivan, and Gen. George Washington. For descrip-

tions of the series and locations of the letters of specific individuals see **MI.360.7.-MI.360.28.**

4. **[Miscellaneous] letters addressed to Congress, 1775-89** (Item 78, M247, rolls 90-104).

5. **Intercepted letters, 1775-81** (Item 51, M247, roll 65), which consist of British correspondence intercepted by U.S. citizens during the Revolution.

OTHER RECORDS

IN.360.11. Returns of inhabitants of various states, and miscellaneous papers, 1774-86 (Item 177, M247, roll 194), contains census returns for inhabitants of Rhode Island, 1774 and 1783; Connecticut, 1782; and New York, 1786, which indicate the number of Indians in those colonies or states.

IN.360.12. The fiscal records described in **FI.360.2., FI.360.5.-FI.360.7.**, and **FI.360.13.** contain accounts and entries dealing with continental expenditures on Indian affairs.

Record Group 11
General Records of the United States Government

IN.11.1. This record group consists of the Constitution of the United States, the Bill of Rights and other amendments, and related records; laws of the United States and related records; international treaties and agreements; Indian treaties; presidential proclamations, executive orders, and other presidential documents; rules and regulations of federal agencies; electoral records; and records pertaining to the Great Seal of the United States.

IN.11.2. The series **Indian treaties, 1722-1869** (M668, 16 rolls), consists of handwritten treaties, usually accompanied by related documents. The word "treaty" used in the context of pre-federal Indian affairs refers to both formal agreements and the proceedings of meetings held with Indians which led to no formal agreement. The pre-federal treaties and related records in this series consist of documents pertaining to seven pre-Revolutionary Indian treaties and nine produced under the continental and confederation government (M668, roll 2). All of the documents related to events before the Revolution are copies obtained from the British. A few early federal Indian treaty files contain documents pertaining to pre-federal affairs. The whole series is published as National Archives Microfilm Publication M668 (16 rolls). The treaty files are arranged chronologically and indexed by place and tribe in a separate series (M668, roll 1).

Record Group 15
Records of the Veterans Administration

IN.15.1. The First Congress of the United States passed an act on September 29, 1789, providing for payment of military pensions to Revolutionary War veterans and their dependents—the first in a long series of pension laws. For further information on pensions and bounty lands, see the relevant subject chapter. For Veterans Administration records related to militia activities against the Cherokees, 1787-88, see the case files and pension applications described in **PE.15.11.**

Record Group 29
Records of the
Bureau of the Census

IN.29.1. The Census Office was established in 1902 as a permanent bureau in the Department of the Interior. Before that year a census office had been established for each decennial census and disbanded when work on that census was finished. The first nine censuses were taken by U.S. district marshals. The 1790 census returns were submitted directly to the President.

IN.29.2. Part of the general records of the Census Bureau in the **published record set of decennial census maps, [n.d.],** is a facsimile of a 1771 map "inscribed" by Guy Johnson to William Tryon, "Captain General and Governor in Chief of the Province of New York." It shows the "Country of the Six Nations" and depicts physical features, a boundary line settled with the Indians in 1768, and the locations of white and Indian settlements. It is further described in National Archives Special List No. 26, *Pre-Federal Maps in the National Archives: An Annotated List* (1975)—see the introduction.

Record Group 49
Records of the Bureau of Land Management

IN.49.1. The Office of the Secretary of the Treasury and the Register of the Treasury handled disposition of the public domain until April 25, 1812, when the General Land Office was established in the Department of the Treasury. The General Land Office was moved to the Department of the Interior in 1849 and consolidated with other functions in 1946 to form the Bureau of Land Management. For a record of the bureau pertaining to pre-federal Indian affairs see the first map listed in **LA.49.20.**

Record Group 56
General Records of the Department of the Treasury

IN.56.1. The Department of the Treasury was established by an act of September 2, 1789, which directed the Secretary of the Treasury to prepare plans for improving and managing revenues and supporting public credit, prepare and report expenditure and revenue estimates, superintend the collection of revenues, manage accounts, and grant warrants for money issued from the treasury. This record group includes records of the Office of the Secretary and its subdivisions and those of units performing service functions for the entire department. For an account book of George Washington that contains entries for presents to Indians see **FI.56.2.**

Record Group 59
General Records of the Department of State

IN.59.1. The Department of Foreign Affairs was established by an act of July 1789 and 2 months later was designated the Department of State by the same Congress. It was assigned such functions as preserving and publishing laws and treaties, keeping the seal of the

United States, and serving as custodian of the records of the United States previously held by the Secretary of Congress. The department was also in charge of territorial affairs from 1789 to 1873.

IN.59.2. Filed at the end of the series **miscellaneous letters (letters received), 1789-1906**, are letters from Andrew Pickens, Jacob Reed, Benjamin Guerard, and Richard Beresford to the Continental Congress which pertain to pre-federal Indian affairs in the southern states, 1783-84. The four letters mainly concern regulation of trade with the Creeks and Cherokees; the reaction of those two tribes and the Choctaws and Chickasaws to encroachments by whites on their lands; a Cherokee peace treaty and land cession of 1777; and "drafts" of boundaries between South Carolina and the Cherokees, Catawbas, and North Carolina. The records are arranged chronologically. They were not microfilmed with the rest of the series of miscellaneous letters (M179).

IN.59.3. In the records of the department's Bureau of Rolls and Library, in the series **miscellaneous manuscripts, ca. 1756-1918**, are two items pertaining to pre-federal Indian affairs. One is an illuminated parchment commission in French issued at New Orleans in 1761, by which the Governor of the Province of Louisiana, Louis de Kerlerec, appointed the Cherokee chief Okana-Stote "captain and great medal chief of all the detachments which shall go to war against the enemy and in the service of the French Nation." The other is a positive photostatic copy of a handwritten petition of December 18, 1767. In it several merchants at Pittsburgh ask Sir William Johnson, Superintendent of Indian Affairs in the Northern District of North America, for action against unlicensed traders who had "forced a settlement" at Redstone Creek and allegedly murdered a Delaware chief. The entire series is arranged chronologically.

IN.59.4. For other records of the Department of State pertaining to pre-federal Indian affairs see **FO.59.10., FO.59.12., FO.59.16., LA.59.5.**, and **LA.59.9.**

Record Group 75

Records of the Bureau of Indian Affairs

IN.75.1. The Bureau of Indian Affairs was established in 1824 within the War Department, which since the establishment of the federal government had exercised jurisdiction over Indian affairs in both their civilian and military aspects.

IN.75.2. The subgroup Records of the Office of the Secretary of War Relating to Indian Affairs includes, in the series **letters received, 1800-23**, a small set of letters and related records pertaining to relations between the state of Georgia and the Creek Nation, 1784-85. The documents concern boundaries between white and Indian lands, the role of the Creeks as British allies in the Revolutionary War, and conflicts rising from the spread of white settlements. The records are arranged chronologically.

IN.75.3. The subgroup Central Map File, 1800-1939, consists of four series of manuscript, published, annotated, and photoprocessed maps containing a wide variety of information about Indians and Indian lands. A few, all dating from after 1800, pertain to pre-federal times. They show Choctaw, Chickasaw, and Creek villages in British West Florida; cessions of Indian lands in western New York; and Indian towns on the Ohio and Muskingum Rivers. These and other maps in the series are listed under the states or other geographic areas to which they pertain in National Archives Special List No. 13, *List of Cartographic Records of the Bureau of Indian Affairs* (1954).

Record Group 77

Records of the Office of the Chief of Engineers

IN.77.1. The Corps of Engineers, U.S. Army, was established by an act of March 16, 1802, to organize a military academy at West Point. In 1818 the Chief Engineer of the Corps was directed to fix his headquarters at Washington, DC, as the Office of the Chief of Engineers in the War Department. For a series containing records describing Mandan Indian communities in the 1780s see **LA.77.2.**

Record Group 93

War Department Collection of Revolutionary War Records

IN.93.1. The act of August 7, 1789, that established the War Department provided that the Secretary of War should have custody of all books and papers in the Office of the Secretary at War, who had headed the Department of War created in 1781 by the Continental

Congress, including papers of the earlier Board of War. For a more detailed account, including loss of records by fire and accessions from other government and nongovernment sources, see **MI.93.1.**

IN.93.2. The large series **numbered record books, 1775-98** (M853, 41 rolls) has references to Indian affairs scattered throughout, but four volumes in it have more than others. One book of Timothy Pickering's letters as Quartermaster General (Number 88, M853, roll 28) contains entries for expenditures on presents to Indians. Two of Gen. John Sullivan's orderly books (Numbers 27 and 31, M853, rolls 4 and 5) contain orders issued during a punitive expedition against the Iroquois in the Wyoming Valley in 1779. The correspondence of Gen. Edward Hand (Number 156, M853, roll 17) contains numerous references to Indian affairs around Fort Pitt and in other parts of the west in 1776 and 1778. Included are letters to U.S. and Spanish military officers and to Indians, as well as some letters written by Col. George Morgan, an agent for Indian affairs and Deputy Commissary General of Purchases for the Western District. For a general description of the series and indexes to the records in it see **MI.93.8.-MI.93.9.**

IN.93.3. **Miscellaneous numbered records ("manuscript file"), 1775-84** (M859, 125 rolls), also has scattered references to Indian affairs. Most notable are those records dealing with the western activities of George Rogers Clark in 1779 and with Fort Pitt in 1780. For a general description of the series and name and subject indexes thereto see **MI.93.10.-MI.93.13.**

IN.93.4. The records microfilmed in *Revolutionary War Rolls* (M246, 138 rolls) contain a few scattered records of Indians who served in the military and of troops who served in campaigns against the Indians. Some examples are listed in *Guide to Records in the National Archives of the United States Relating to American Indians* (1981). For a general description of the rolls and access to them see **MI.93.14.-MI.93.15.**

IN.93.5. Indian records are also in the series **photographic copies of state records, ca. 1775-83** (see **MI.93.58.-MI.93.59.**). Some Virginia records concern the activities of George Rogers Clark on the northwestern frontier. The North Carolina records contain many references to the Cherokees.

IN.93.6. For other RG 93 records related to pre-federal Indian affairs see **CO.93.3.**, **MI.93.27.**, and **MI.93.55.**

Record Group 94

Records of the Adjutant General's Office

IN.94.1. The Continental Congress of June 17, 1775, appointed the Adjutant General of the Continental Army. From the disbanding of the army in 1783 until 1792, there was no such permanent position in the War Department. An act of March 5, 1792, created the position of adjutant, who was also to serve as inspector. For RG 94 records related to pre-federal Indian affairs see **MI.94.4.**, **MI.94.8.**, **MI.94.11.**, and **MI.94.15.**

Record Group 98

Records of U.S. Army Commands, 1784-1821

IN.98.1. For records of U.S. Army commands related to pre-federal Indian affairs see the first series described in **MI.98.3.** and the first series described in **MI.98.4.**

Record Group 217

Records of the Accounting Officers of the Department of the Treasury

IN.217.1. This record group contains the records of officers responsible for settling federal and pre-federal accounts before 1921. For treasury records related to pre-federal Indian affairs see the general Treasury ledgers described in **FI.217.7.-FI.217.8.**

Record Group 233

Records of the U.S. House of Representatives

IN.233.1. The U.S. House of Representatives was created by article I, section 1, of the Constitution. Although it shares legislative power with the Senate, the House originates all bills for raising revenue and, by custom, general appropriation bills. The House has sole power to impeach U.S. civil officers, and judges elections, returns, and qualifications of its members. For a cartographic record related to pre-federal Indian affairs see **LA.233.2.**

Record Group 267
Records of the
Supreme Court of the United States

IN.267.1. The Supreme Court of the United States, provided for in article III, section 1, of the Constitution, was established by authority of the Judiciary Act of 1789. This record group also contains records of the pre-federal Court of Appeals in Cases of Capture and its predecessors. For cartographic records related to pre-federal Indian affairs see **LA.267.2.**

CHAPTER JU
Records of Judicial Affairs

JU.0.1. By the mid-18th century, the principal judicial institution in England's American colonies was the vice admiralty court. Such courts had been established around 1700, when the British government sought to enforce the Navigation Acts of 1696 and to see that the king was not defrauded of his revenues. As dissatisfaction with British rule grew, juries in America became reluctant to convict their fellow colonials. Therefore the crown increasingly used vice admiralty courts, which functioned without juries, to recover penalties and forfeitures imposed by the Navigation Acts. These courts were authorized directly by the crown, and all judicial appointments were subject to the approval of the First Lord of the Admiralty.

JU.0.2. Vice admiralty courts had jurisdiction over three types of cases: ordinary marine cases, mainly suits for salvage and wages of seamen; prize cases; and cases arising out of breaches of various acts of trade and navigation. The authority to appoint commissions, sometimes designated special courts of admiralty, for the trial of piracies and other maritime felonies was given to the royal governors of the American colonies in 1700 by an act of William III to more effectively suppress piracy.

JU.0.3. The continental and confederation governments exercised limited judicial powers through two systems of courts: the Court of Appeals in Cases of Capture and its predecessors, and ad hoc courts for hearing cases involving either disputes between states or private rights to land claimed under grants of two or more states.

JU.0.4. The origin of the Court of Appeals in Cases of Capture lay in the need arising soon after the beginning of the Revolution to determine the legality of seizures of enemy vessels and cargoes as prizes by continental warships and other U.S. vessels and to provide for their disposal. On November 25, 1775, Congress authorized the capture of prizes and provided that prize cases should be commenced in state admiralty courts with a right of appeal to Congress. At first this appellate jurisdiction was exercised through ad hoc committees, the first of which was named on September 9, 1776. On January 30, 1777, the Standing Committee on Appeals was established. Congress replaced that committee with a three-judge "court of appeals" on January 15, 1780, and formalized it as the Court of Appeals in Cases of Capture by a resolution of May 24, 1780. The court, which was composed of members of Congress, met irregularly, according to the amount of business to be done. Its last meeting was in May 1787 in Philadelphia. Prize case appeals were at first lodged with the Secretary of Congress; but after May 24, 1780, they were submitted to the Register of the Court of Appeals in Cases of Capture and "all papers touching appeals in cases of capture, lodged in the office of the secretary of Congress, [were] delivered to and lodged with the register of the Court of Appeals."

JU.0.5. Courts for hearing, on appeal, "all disputes now subsisting or that hereafter may arise between two or more states concerning boundary, jurisdiction or any other cause whatever," were provided for by the Articles of Confederation. Each such dispute was to be heard by a special court established for that case alone. Members of the court were to be elected by Congress through an elaborate procedure set forth in article 9 of the Articles. Article 9 also provided that "All controversies concerning the private right of soil claimed under different grants of two or more states . . . shall on the petition of either party to the congress . . . be finally determined as near as may be in the same manner as is . . . prescribed for deciding disputes respecting territorial jurisdiction between different states." A number of disputes involving state governments were brought before Congress, and various actions were taken. Only one, however, led to an actual meeting and decision of the ad hoc court. The case, heard in 1782, concerned the conflicting claims of Pennsylvania and Connecticut to land within the borders of the former.

JU.0.6. The administrative organization for the Northwest Territory included three judges, but no separate body of records produced by them is known to exist among the holdings of the National Archives. Proceedings of Continental Army and Navy courts-martial and courts of inquiry are part of records described in the military and naval affairs chapters; see especially **MI.360.6., MI.360.8., MI.45.4., MI.53.4., MI.93.20., MI.93.25., MI.93.52., NA.360.13.,** and **NA.45.32.**

Record Group 360

Records of the Continental and Confederation Congresses and the Constitutional Convention

---

JU.360.1. Record Group 360 consists primarily of PCC

(M247, 204 rolls) and Miscellaneous PCC (M332, 10 rolls).* For additional information about those bodies of records and indexes thereto, see the introduction.

RECORDS PERTAINING TO
THE COURT OF APPEALS IN CASES OF CAPTURE
AND PREDECESSOR BODIES

JU.360.2. Because appellate jurisdiction for prize cases was vested in congressional committees beginning in 1776 and then transferred in 1780 to a court appointed and overseen by Congress, similar records, with overlapping dates, exist in both RG 360 and RG 267 (see **JU.267.2.-JU.267.5.**). The series **claims for captured vessels, 1777-84** (Item 44, M247, roll 58), consists of records of prize cases heard on appeal from state courts by committees of Congress, 1777-80, and by the Court of Appeals in Cases of Capture, 1780-84. Among the records are memorials and petitions of claimants; decrees and decisions of admiralty courts of various states; state maritime acts; clearance papers, bills of lading, arrival certificates, and cargo manifests of ships; affidavits pertaining to the ownership of vessels; correspondence of shipowners; and congressional committee reports. Most of the records are endorsed with such information as the name of the claimant, the date read, the committee to which referred, and action taken. Arrangement is for the most part by case, with records for each case in roughly chronological order.

JU.360.3. In the series **other reports of committees of Congress, 1776-88: on the Commissary Department, domestic loans and loan offices, loss of certain army posts, treaties, foreign loans, and courts of appeal, 1776-86** (Item 29, M247, roll 36), are about 50 pages of reports made by the Standing Committee on Appeals. The reports are on cases heard on appeal from state court decisions and on the establishment of the Court of Appeals in Cases of Capture to replace the standing committee. Most of the reports and a few of the related documents are endorsed with such information as the subject, date delivered or read, and the nature and dates of subsequent action. Arrangement is generally chronological.

JU.360.4. **Records relative to seizure and confiscation of property, 1777-86** (Item 45, M247, roll 59), pertain to appeals made to the Continental Congress by shipowners claiming illegal seizure of their vessels and cargoes. The series includes petitions and memorials, affidavits of ownership, and copies of correspondence with

---

*For a complete list of National Archives Microfilm Publications cited in this guide, see Appendix A.

U.S. agents abroad. Some of the documents are in French or Dutch, some of which are translated into English. The records are arranged into two groups consisting of records on U.S. vessels seized by foreign governments and on property of citizens of neutral countries seized by U.S. privateers.

RECORDS PERTAINING TO TERRITORIAL DISPUTES BETWEEN OR INVOLVING STATES

JU.360.5. The series **state papers, 1775-91: papers relating to claims of territory by Pennsylvania and Connecticut, 1780-85; papers relating to trade regulations for the United States, 1786; and petitions about the Indiana region, 1779-83** (Item 77, M247, roll 89), contains three sets of records on judicial matters involving states as parties. Pages 167-245 of the single-volume series include memorials and petitions concerning claims to grants and purchases of land from the Six Nations, grants of land to the Ohio Company, and grants of land to officers who served in the regiment raised by Virginia in 1754. Other documents concern the jurisdiction of the Continental Congress respecting a dispute between the state of Virginia and the Vandalia and Indiana Companies. Claimants include "sundry Inhabitants of Great Britain, Virginia, and Maryland," such as George Washington and Arthur Lee; Samuel Wharton and Benjamin Franklin, jointly; and William Trent and others calling themselves the "Vandalia and Indiana Companies." Neither of the two sets of records is in any discernible order.

JU.360.6. Pages 1-104 and 246-493 of the same volume (Item 77 of PCC) concern the dispute between Connecticut and Pennsylvania over land lying within the boundaries of Pennsylvania. A "Court of Commissioners" was constituted in 1782 to hear the case under article 9 of the Articles of Confederation. It decided in favor of Pennsylvania. These records consist of three distinct groups. The first is the formal record of the proceedings of the court, which met at Trenton from November 12 to December 30, 1782. The second group of documents was submitted to Congress or the court from October 1781 to December 1782 by the two states involved. The last group, approximately 40 documents dated December 1782-May 1785, pertain to a situation bordering on civil war in the disputed counties (Wyoming and Northumberland) between Pennsylvania citizens and persons who had settled under Connecticut auspices. The proceedings are in generally chronological order; the other two groups of records are ordered by numbers assigned to the documents.

JU.360.7. Miscellaneous PCC contains a group of records (M332, roll 5) similar in content, but not copies of, the documents in Item 77 that relate to the Connecticut-Pennsylvania dispute. The commissions of the members of the court appointed to settle the controversy are in Miscellaneous PCC (M332, roll 7).

JU.360.8. Residents of the New Hampshire Grants, an area claimed by both New York and New Hampshire, declared themselves independent on January 16, 1777, at Westminster. Adopting the name of Vermont in June 1777, they petitioned the Continental Congress on a number of occasions for admission to the Confederation. New York disputed both Vermont's right to independence and the right of Congress to admit new states. Vermont did not become a state until 1791. The series **other reports of committees of Congress, 1776-88: committee reports and other records on claims of New York and Vermont to the New Hampshire Grants, 1776-84** (Item 40, M247, roll 47), contains copies of pre-Revolutionary War documents pertaining to the grants, such as royal proclamations and orders, petitions of inhabitants of the area to the Governor of New Hampshire seeking support, and a map showing the northern border of Massachusetts as fixed in 1740; letters to the Continental Congress concerning New York's claim to the region, lawlessness of the militia in the area, the military activities of the Green Mountain Boys, and the proceedings of the Provincial Congress of New York; letters to Congress from Governor Thomas Chittenden of Vermont and from agents sent by Vermont to the Congress; papers concerning the claim of the state of New Hampshire to the area; and reports of committees of Congress. The records are arranged for the most part in chronological order.

OTHER RECORDS

JU.360.9. Miscellaneous PCC contains four other documents related to pre-federal judicial affairs (M332, roll 7). Three are copies, signed by John McKesson, clerk of the "Supreme Court of Judicature of the State of New York," of judgments of the court in 1785 in suits brought against the imprisoned Richard Lawrence by Jonathan Morrel and Samuel and John Broome. Lawrence was a resident of Staten Island who had served the British during the Revolution as a ship carpenter. The suits were filed after the war by New York residents whose property he had taken or destroyed in the course of his service to the British. One of Lawrence's attorneys was Alexander Hamilton; Samuel and John Broomes' attorney was Aaron Burr. The copies of these judgments were obtained by Secretary for Foreign Affairs John Jay after the British government had formally inquired into the actions taken against Lawrence and suggested that they might be a violation of the treaty of peace of 1783. The other document is a record of judgments of the same court, meeting at Albany in April, May, and November 1783, in cases involving the indictment of more than 100 persons for "adhering to the enemies of the state" during the Revolutionary War. All of the judgments were against the defendants, none of whom appeared.

Record Group 21

Records of District Courts
of the United States

JU.21.1. U.S. district and circuit courts were created by the Judiciary Act of 1789 under the constitutional provision that the judicial power of the United States be vested in a supreme court and in such inferior courts as the Congress may establish. This record group includes records of federal district and circuit courts and those of their predecessors, such as courts of U.S. territories and colonies that became states. Original records in this record group generally are located in the National Archives regional archives responsible for the region in which the respective court is or was located.

JU.21.2. The series **papers extracted from the files in 1916, 1685-1838**, consists of documents selected by U.S. District Judge Charles M. Hough from the records of the Vice Admiralty Court of the Province of New York, the Admiralty Court of the State of New York, and the U.S. District and Circuit Courts for the Southern District of New York. The documents are mounted in a large volume for better preservation; some were later removed from the volume and placed in manila envelopes. The series contains specimens of libels, pleadings, interrogatories, writs of execution, and other documents intended to illustrate admiralty practices of the various courts and to show the similarity between the procedure of the Vice Admiralty Court of the Province of New York and that of the federal district court as well as shipping articles, letters of marque, manifests, certificates of clearance, muster rolls, bottomry bonds, and other shipping documents of diverse kinds. Included among the pre-federal documents are four depositions filed in proceedings held in 1685 before Governor Thomas Dongan, who by his commission had the powers of a vice admiral. There are also complaints, affidavits, warrants of arrest, minutes of testimony, and other papers filed by or before commissions appointed for the trial of piracies in 1769-70 and 1774. The documents are arranged numerically from 1 to 135. The series **list of "papers extracted from the files in 1916," n.d.**, enumerates them in order. The records are held by the regional archives in New York.

JU.21.3. Minutes of the Vice Admiralty Court of the Province of New York are in the series **minutes, 1701, 1715-17, 1723-57, 1758-74**, also located at the regional archives in New York. The three volumes show the time and place of each session, the names of the presiding judges, the final decrees and orders of the court, the entering of stipulations for libelants' and claimants' costs, the swearing in of witnesses, the assignment of counsel, and related matters. Two pages of entries in volume 1 relate to proceedings of the Commission for the Trial of Piracies and Felonies on the High Seas, composed of the lieutenant governor and members of the Council of the Province of New York, rather than proceedings of the vice admiralty court. Entries are arranged chronologically by dates of the sessions.

JU.21.4. Depositions of witnesses examined before Robert Hunter, Governor and Vice Admiral of New York, and members of the Council of the Province of New York relative to acts of piracy and robbery committed on the high seas and to the illegal harboring of the pirates Richard Caverly and Jeremiah Higgins make up the series **records pertaining to a piracy case, 1717.** The records give information about the plundering of vessels, the forceful detention of crews, and other acts of maritime lawlessness. Included among them are a warrant for the arrest of the escaped pirates and an account of the expenses allowed for their apprehension. The documents, appoximately 1 inch, are arranged chronologically and housed at the regional archives in New York.

JU.21.5. Also at the regional archives in New York is the series **miscellaneous records, 1746-72**, which originated with the Vice Admiralty Court of the Province of New York. The records consist of a manuscript copy of standing interrogatories administered by the court in 1746 to masters, pilots, and other persons found aboard vessels seized as prizes; a printed copy of an act of the British Parliament "for the Encouragement of Seamen and the more speedy and effectual Manning [of] His Majesty's Navy," 1757; a manuscript copy of a parliamentary act to "explain and amend" the aforementioned act and to promote "the better prevention of Piracies and Robberies by Crews of private ships of war," 1759; a letter received by Richard Morris, a judge of the court, from William Franklin, Governor of the Province of New Jersey, complaining of the seizure of vessels within the boundaries of New Jersey for violations of the trade laws and their removal to the New York court for condemnation and sale, 1764; and a copy of the will of Robert Quick, 1772. The records are arranged chronologically.

JU.21.6. Another series from the Vice Admiralty Court of the Province of New York and located at the regional archives in New York is **case papers, 1757-75.** This approximately 2 feet of records consists of libels, monitions, claims and answers, interrogatories, depositions, court orders, and other papers filed in prize cases, 1757-62; suits relating to seamen's wages, 1761-72; salvage cases, 1768-70; actions arising out of evasions of customs regulations, 1760-75; cases involving cruel and unusual treatment of seamen, insubordination and mutiny, and assault upon passengers in an immigrant vessel for publicly objecting to a short allowance of food, 1758-63; and "miscellaneous cases," including proceedings initiated by the "Surveyor of His Majesty's Woods in America" against individuals for cutting down white pine trees reserved for masts for Royal Navy vessels, 1758-71. The prize case records are the most numerous and consist of libels, processes, pleadings, interrogatories, orders, and decrees of the court; accounts of sales of condemned property; bills of costs; and other papers originating in the court during the course of suits. There are also papers found on board prizes at the time of their capture and delivered to the court, such as charter parties, muster rolls, instructions from owners to captains, invoices of goods laden on the vessels, certificates of clearance, and logs. Some of the seized documents are in French and Dutch; most of these are accompanied by English translations. Documents filed in the customs suits and the ordinary marine cases are generally those that reflect the progress of the case through the court.

JU.21.7. Case papers of the Court of Admiralty of the State of New York, 1784-88 (M948, 1 roll), consist of libels, monitions, stipulations, claims and answers, replications, depositions, writs of appraisement, orders and decrees of the court, and related papers filed in suits arising out of violations of customs regulations, salvage actions, and claims for seamen's wages. Other "miscellaneous" cases concern actions involving maritime contracts, such as bottomry, repairs to vessels, and marine insurance. Alexander Hamilton appeared as a proctor in a number of the cases. Arrangement is by the categories described. The records are located at the regional archives in New York. Other records from the Court of Admiralty of the State of New York are described in **JU.21.2.**

JU.21.8. The series **British vice admiralty minute books, 1716-63** (M1180, rolls 1-3), records the activities of the Vice Admiralty Court of the Province of South Carolina with respect to ordinary marine cases, such as suits for salvage and seamen's wages, prize cases, and cases involving alleged violations of navigation and trade acts. Recorded also are the activities of special commissions, appointed by the royal governor and sometimes designated as special courts of admiralty, that heard and judged cases of piracy, felony, or robbery committed on the high seas. The four volumes give the time and place for each court session, the names of the presiding judges, and information about the swearing in of witnesses, assignment of counsel, motions, and court orders and decrees. Volume 3 contains a partial table of contents; volume 4 a complete one. Arrangement throughout the four volumes is chronological by date of session. There are no records for 1731-35 and 1750-51. The records are located at the regional archives in Atlanta.

JU.21.9. Final record book of the Admiralty Court, State of South Carolina, 1787-89 (M1180, roll 3), documents 16 cases concerning seamen's wages, bottomry, debt, piracy, and salvage in which Judge William Drayton presided. Recorded in addition to the orders and decrees of the court is information on the time and place of sessions, names of parties and witnesses, appointment of court officers, and the admittance of attorneys or proctors, one of whom was Gen. Charles Cotesworth Pinckney. The pre-federal cases occupy the first 155 pages of the volume. The remaining pages contain admiralty minutes of the U.S. district court (M1182, 4 rolls). Arrangement is chronological by the date each case closed. The records are at the regional archives in Atlanta.

JU.21.10. The series **unidentified case papers, 1753-1911**, is part of the records of the U.S. Circuit Court for the Eastern District of Pennsylvania. It consists of deeds, letters, recognizances, depositions, newspaper clippings, and other documents not clearly identified with particular cases but believed to have been filed originally in connection with the prosecution of law, equity, and criminal cases in the circuit court. Included are six pre-federal documents: three leases dated 1740, 1746, and 1769; two letters from 1786 and 1787; and a 1783 deed. The series is arranged chronologically by the dates of the documents, with undated documents at the end. The records are located at the regional archives in Philadelphia.

JU.21.11. From the U.S. Circuit Court for the Southern District of Georgia is the series **"miscellaneous style" case papers, 1790-1860**, which covers all cases of appellate and original jurisdiction heard by the court before the Civil War. One case dating from events beginning in 1777 involved South Carolina merchant Robert Farquhar, who sold military supplies to the state of Georgia. He died before obtaining payment, and in 1791 his executor, Alexander Chisholm, brought suit in the circuit court to recover the amount owed. Unsatisfied with the lower court's decision that the state was immune from suit, Chisholm took the matter to the Supreme Court, where it was heard as *Chisholm v. Georgia* and led to the 11th amendment to the Constitution. For Supreme Court records on the case, see **JU.267.8.** Other cases in this series involve land disputes with origins in the pre-federal period. Some files contain pre-federal documents. These include a land grant in St. Mary's Parish, 1768; a "Delineator Plat" (map) of land in St. Andrew's Parish, 1772; and a will signed and sealed in London in 1776. The series is arranged by case letters and box numbers. There is an alphabetical index to the names of plaintiffs and defendants. The records are located at the regional archives in Atlanta.

Record Group 45

Naval Records Collection of the Office of Naval Records and Library

---

JU.45.1. The Naval Records Collection was begun in 1882 when the Librarian of the Navy Department, then in the Office of Naval Intelligence, began to collect for publication naval documents relating to the Civil War. In the early 1900s, the office began collecting older records of naval bureaus and records relating to naval personnel and operations during the American Revolution. For further information see **NA.45.1.**

JU.45.2. The series **proceedings of the "Maritime Court for the Middle District of the State of Massachusetts Bay," 1777-80**, is a positive photostatic copy of volume 159 of the "Massachusetts Revolutionary Archives." It was copied in the State House at Boston as part of the project described in **NA.45.1.** The single bound volume consists mainly of summaries of libels seeking condemnation of vessels taken as prizes by U.S. privateers, the verdicts of juries, and decrees of the judge in each case before the court. The summaries set forth the circumstances of the capture of prizes including dates, places, and names of persons and vessels involved. Other information includes the date and number of the libel, the names of the judges and jury members, the date and place of the court session, and sometimes court costs and the fact that an appeal was made. The more than 100 cases are arranged in generally chronological order by dates of court sessions. Included in the volume is a partial index to names of vessels libeled in the proceedings.

Record Group 55

Records of the Government of the Virgin Islands

JU.55.1. The Danish West Indies consist of many small, uninhabited islands in addition to the three main islands— St. Thomas, which was settled by the Danes in 1672; St. John, occupied in 1717; and St. Croix, purchased by Denmark from France in 1733. Except for 1807-15, when England held them, they were under Danish rule until the United States purchased them in 1917.

JU.55.2. Danish records relating to the cession and the rights and property of the inhabitants of the islands were given to the United States by the treaty of cession. They have not been translated. The judicial and police records of St. Croix include public notices, contracts, and petitions, 1771-1818.

Record Group 59

General Records of the Department of State

JU.59.1. The Department of Foreign Affairs was established by an act of July 27, 1789, and 2 months later was designated the Department of State by the same Congress. It was assigned such functions as preserving and publishing laws and treaties, keeping the seal of the United States, and serving as custodian of the records of the United States previously held by the Secretary of Congress. The department was also in charge of territorial affairs from 1789 to 1873.

JU.59.2. Among the records of the Department of State's Bureau of Rolls and Library is the series **miscellaneous manuscripts, 1756-1918.** It contains copies of Connecticut court records pertaining to debts owed by U.S. citizens to British subjects, such as Loyalist merchants, 1784-88. These copies, most of which were certified as true copies by the court clerk, include a petition, a writ, a summons, statements of plaintiffs and defendants, judicial decisions, and other records of proceedings in three cases heard by the Connecticut Superior Court sitting at New Haven, Danbury, and Hartford.

Record Group 186
Records of the
Spanish Governors of Puerto Rico

JU.186.1. Spain ceded Puerto Rico to the United States by the Treaty of Paris of December 10, 1898. The cession included rights to the official archives and records on the island, which the United States agreed to preserve and make available for use. After inspection of the records at the Library of Congress in 1900-1901, many important administrative records were returned to San Juan, PR. Most of them were destroyed by a fire at the Archivo Historico in 1926. None of the records in this record group have been translated into English. Records from the 18th century are sparse and fragmentary; although the number of records in the record group increases for each decade until the 1860s.

JU.186.2. Although the series **tribunal de gobiernos [governor's tribunal], ca. 1754-1824** (4 in.) is a record of the executive officers of the island, it primarily concerns their performance of judicial functions. There are also records pertaining to judicial affairs among the other series described in **CC.186.2.-CC.186.3.**

Record Group 267
Records of the
Supreme Court of the United States

JU.267.1. The Supreme Court of the United States, provided for in Article III, section 1, of the Constitution, was established by authority of the Judiciary Act of 1789. This record group also contains records of the pre-federal Court of Appeals in Cases of Capture and its predecessors.

RECORDS OF THE COURT OF APPEALS IN CASES OF CAPTURE AND PREDECESSOR BODIES

JU.267.2. Since appellate jurisdiction for prize cases was vested in congressional committees beginning in 1776 and then transferred in 1780 to a court appointed and overseen by Congress, similar records, with overlapping dates, exist in both RG 267 and RG

the court that were not heard or tried. Arrangement is generally chronological.

JU.267.5. Miscellaneous court records, 1777-89 (M162, roll 15), consist of records that were not or do not appear to have been associated with particular appeals cases. Among them are copies of minutes of the court and of minutes, resolutions, and a committee report of the Continental Congress; lists of cases pending in the court; correspondence; and other papers relating to the court's business. The records are arranged chronologically.

JU.267.6. Following the last of the miscellaneous court records, in a folder labeled "Miscellaneous Letters found among the prize cases," is a half-inch of unarranged documents, 1778-90. They pertain to a legal dispute involving the value of a continental certificate of indebtedness acquired by Postmaster General Ebenezer Hazard. Most of the correspondence and related documents were exchanged by Hazard with his attorney Elias Boudinot and with Samuel Forman, Benjamin Thompson, and Azariah and James Dunham, 1786-87. Also in the folder is an undated Continental Navy recruiting broadside. The items in the folder are not reproduced in M162.

RECORDS OF THE
SUPREME COURT OF THE UNITED STATES

JU.267.7. Depositions, maps, copies of legislative acts, letters, and other documents related to cases whose titles are not known are in the series **papers and exhibits related to unidentified cases, 1788-1930.** The pre-federal documents in the series are all dated 1788 and consist of copies of correspondence concerning the survey and location of bounty land in the Northwest Territory for Virginia continental and state troops, and cession of part of that territory to the United States by Virginia. The series is arranged chronologically by the dates of documents, with some undated documents at its beginning.

JU.267.8. In the subgroup Original Jurisdiction Records of the Supreme Court is the series **case files, 1792-1951.** These are files of cases involving states as parties in connection with such matters as financial claims and boundaries and suits for writs of habeas corpus, mandamus, and prohibition. The records include bills of complaint, answers, exhibits, affidavits, orders, judgments, and correspondence. Several have roots in pre-federal events or conditions. Among the many famous cases for which there are files is *Chisholm* v. *Georgia*, the origin of which is described in **JU.21.11.** The half-inch of papers related to the case in this series consists of a copy of an ac-

360 (see **JU.360.2.-JU.360.4.**). The National Archives Microfilm Publication *The Revolutionary War Prize Cases: Records of the Court of Appeals in Cases of Capture, 1776-1787* (M162, rolls 1-15), constitutes a valuable source of information for the naval, commercial, and legal history of the Revolutionary era. Among the records in this series of case files are petitions and memorials to the Continental Congress; copies of congressional resolutions pertaining to prize cases; attested copies of lower court proceedings; libels; notices of hearings; monitions; depositions and affidavits; interrogatories; briefs; bonds; notices of appeal; petitions for rehearings; statements of court costs and the register's fees; decrees; opinions; copies of state, colonial, and royal statutes and proclamations; and documents found on prize vessels, such as certificates of registry, crew lists, shipping articles, repair bills, bills of lading, invoices, manifests, logbooks, journals, account books, consort agreements, letters of marque and reprisal, private mail in transit, and correspondence of the crew and passengers of vessels. The quantity and kinds of documents in the files vary greatly; for a few cases no papers are present. There are originals and copies of correspondence and other documents sent to and from various well-known figures, including Alexander Hamilton, Benedict Arnold, Capt. John Barry of the *Alliance*, Benjamin Franklin, and John Laurens. The records of two cases include private letters addressed by residents of British-occupied New York to friends and relatives in Halifax, Nova Scotia. Another case involves the British occupation and evacuation of Boston. The records are arranged mainly by numbers that were assigned to the cases in the 19th century. Records relating to further proceedings in a few prize cases are in the series described in **JU.267.9.**

JU.267.3. The descriptive pamphlet for National Archives Microfilm Publication M162 contains lists that facilitate use of the records described in **JU.267.2.**, **JU.267.4.**, and **JU.267.5.** First is a list of cases in numerical order, with brief summaries of the circumstances and actions in them. This is followed by a list of cases by name of state or colony from which the appeal was made. Next is a section listing members of the Continental Congress who served on special committees to hear appeals, the Standing Committee on Appeals, and the Court of Appeals in Cases of Capture. Finally, there is a list of cases indexed alphabetically by the names of each party.

JU.267.4. The series **miscellaneous case papers, 1772-84** (M162, roll 15), consists of papers that have not been identified with any of the cases constituting the main series of case files described in **JU.267.2.** The 21 items include correspondence, privateer commissions, pleadings, and other documents pertaining to cases referred to

count, 1777, showing money due by the state of Georgia to Robert Farquhar for clothing and other goods, and of depositions and other documents, dated mainly 1793-94, that document the legal effort to obtain payment. All of the records in the series are grouped by court terms arranged chronologically; within term groups they are arranged alphabetically by case through 1909.

JU.267.9. Case files, 1792-1952 (M214, 96 rolls), covers cases in which the Supreme Court had appellate jurisdiction. These files include petitions for writs of error and certiorari, transcripts of record from lower courts, copies of records of the pre-federal Court of Appeals in Cases of Capture, exhibits, briefs, depositions, motions, orders, decrees, judgments, and correspondence. There are more than 55,000 files. Among the subjects of cases related to pre-federal times are privateering and prizes, debts of U.S. citizens to British subjects, ownership of land in the United States by British subjects, and provisions of the 1783 treaty of peace pertaining to such debts and land ownership disputes. A few pre-federal documents, such as invoices, accounts, and bills of sale, are in early case files. Also present are some printed copies of pre-federal state laws. Transcripts of record from lower courts include testimony taken in the pre-federal period. The series is arranged numerically by case numbers through the 1933 term. National Archives Microfilm Publication M214 reproduces case files for the period 1792-1831 only; another (M408, 20 rolls) provides an index to the series through 1909. That series, **card index to case files, 1792-1909**, is arranged alphabetically by names of parties to cases. In cases with more than one plaintiff or defendant, not all parties are indexed.

CHAPTER LA

Records of Land and Exploration

LA.0.1. Most of the records of the continental and confederation governments pertaining to land and related subjects concern cessions of western land claims by the states, the establishment and operation of the territorial government in the Northwest Territory, and the survey and disposal of lands in that region.

LA.0.2. John Dickinson's draft of the Articles of Confederation, read in Congress on July 12, 1776, proposed limiting the western boundaries of the states. The idea was rejected in committee. On December 15, 1778, Maryland, a state with no claim to western lands, announced her refusal to ratify the Articles until such lands were ceded to Congress by the states having claims. On February 1, 1780, the legislature of New York ceded that state's claims. Other states followed suit. Among them was Virginia, whose cession of her claims to the area north of the Ohio River on January 2, 1781, led Maryland to sign the Articles of Confederation late in February 1781. The Virginia cession of 1781 was rejected by Congress in 1783, but a revised offer made later that year was accepted on March 1, 1784. In that agreement Congress reserved certain tracts of the ceded western lands as Virginia bounty land. The ceding of western lands was not completed until June 16, 1802, when the Georgia legislature ratified the Articles of Agreement and Cession of April 24, 1802, between the state and the United States.

LA.0.3. On the day the Continental Congress accepted Virginia's revised cession of western lands, a committee headed by Thomas Jefferson proposed a plan for the temporary government of the entire west, including division of the territory into states. The slightly amended report was adopted on April 23, 1784, but was never put into effect. It served, however, along with a committee report of September 19, 1786, as the basis for an "Ordinance for the government of the territory of the United States North West of the river Ohio" adopted by Congress on July 13, 1787. The Northwest Ordinance, as it became known, provided that the territory would be governed initially by a governor, secretary, and a court of three judges to be appointed by Congress. Ultimately, from three to five states were to be formed from the region, each to be "on an equal footing with the original States, in all respects whatever. . . ." The Secretary of the

Northwest Territory was to "keep and preserve the . . . public records of the district and the proceedings of the governor . . . and transmit authentic copies . . . every six months to the Secretary of Congress."

LA.0.4. With the cession of western lands by the states to the continental and confederation governments, establishment of procedures for the survey and disposal of the new public domain became a matter of concern to the Congress. The basic administrative arrangements for marking out and disposing of this land were set forth in the Land Ordinance of May 20, 1785. This "Ordinance for ascertaining the mode of disposing of Lands in the Western Territory" provided for the rectangular survey of land in the area west of Pennsylvania and north of the Ohio River. The Geographer of the United States, Thomas Hutchins, was to supervise a team of surveyors, one from each state, in dividing the land into "ranges" of 6-mile-square townships beginning on the west bank of the Ohio River. To begin with, seven ranges of townships were to be surveyed. Plats of the surveyed land were to be transmitted to the Board of Treasury. The land was to be sold in lots of 640 acres minimum at no less than $1 an acre, except for parts reserved for bounty-land grants to Continental Army veterans, lands for Canadian and Nova Scotian "refugees," and other purposes. Surveying commenced in 1785. By 1787, four ranges had been completed, despite problems with Indians. After an interval, the survey of the Seven Ranges was resumed in 1788, but completed only after the death of Hutchins, which occurred on April 28, 1789.

LA.0.5. During the later years of the pre-federal period, several extensive tracts of land in the public domain outside of the Seven Ranges were sold. Under the direction of the Reverend Manasseh Cutler, a group of Revolutionary War veterans from New England organized the Ohio Company of Associates. The group signed a contract on October 27, 1787, for 1,500,000 acres on the Ohio and Muskingum Rivers. Another contract was made in 1788 with Judge John Cleves Symmes for a tract between the Great and Little Miami Rivers. Also in 1788 Congress granted a "donation" of 400 acres to each head of family who had settled in the Illinois country before 1783, a provision that applied to some 150 French families. The same privilege was extended to other early western settlers in 1790. The granting of bounty land to Revolutionary War veterans is discussed more fully in the introduction to the chapter on pension, bounty-land, and other claims records.

LA.0.6. The Reference Map Collection of the Cartographic and Architectural Branch of the National Archives is meant to supplement the cartographic materials among the government records held by the National Archives. It consists mainly of published atlases and originals and facsimile copies of individually published maps of both governmental and private origin. It contains some material related to the pre-federal period, which is not further mentioned in this guide because all of it is described in some detail in National Archives Special List No. 26, *Pre-Federal Maps in the National Archives: An Annotated List* (1975). See the introduction for information about Special List No. 26.

Record Group 360

Records of the Continental and Confederation Congresses and the Constitutional Convention

LA.360.1. Record Group 360 consists primarily of PCC (M247, 204 rolls), and Miscellaneous PCC (M332, 10 rolls).* For additional information about those bodies of records and indexes thereto, see the introduction.

LA.360.2. The series **memorials of the inhabitants of Illinois, Kaskaskia, and Kentucky, 1780-89** (Item 48, M247, roll 62), consists of memorials and petitions, mostly from French settlements in the Illinois region, mainly Kaskaskia, Cahokia, Post Vincennes, La Prairie du Rocher, and St. Philipp, and from other places in the areas that later became the states of Illinois, Indiana, Kentucky, and Tennessee. Some of the communications bear hundreds of signatures. Subjects include the title to land; grievances of the Kentuckians against Virginia, and their desire for statehood; Indian depredations in the Kentucky region; the establishment of local governments; a dispute between Virginia and Pennsylvania over western lands; and Roman Catholic Church property and activities in the Illinois region. Prominent among the records are several letters and memorials to Congress from Bartholomew Tardiveau, "Agent for the french & American inhabitants of Poste Vincennes & the Illinois." Documents written in French are usually accompanied by English translations. Most of the records are endorsed with the name or group designation of the writer or writers, the date written, the date read in Congress, and action taken. Arrangement is mainly by the regions in which the records originated or to which they pertain. A few of the reports of congressional committees described in **LA.360.4.** pertain to some of the petitions from the Illinois region.

---

*For a complete list of National Archives Microfilm Publications cited in this guide, see Appendix A.

LA.360.3. The series **letters from Joseph Carleton and Thomas Hutchins, 1779-88, and records relating to military affairs** (Item 60, M247, roll 74) contains about 180 pages of letters written by Hutchins, July 1781-August 1788, in his capacity as Geographer of the United States. Addressed for the most part to the President of Congress and written mainly from Philadelphia, New York City, Pittsburgh, and various camps near and along the Ohio River, the letters pertain to such subjects as the surveying of land near Trenton, NJ, for the purpose of establishing a "Federal Town"; the surveying of boundary lines between Pennsylvania and Virginia and between Massachusetts and New York; the surveying of the Seven Ranges under the ordinance of May 20, 1785; the hostility of the Indians toward that project and their depredations in the region; salaries of Hutchins and the surveyors; and the proposed survey of western Lake Ontario by boat. Numerous enclosures are included, such as copies of Hutchins' instructions to subordinates, summaries of intelligence received by him mainly concerning the attitudes and activities of Indians, and copies of communications from Indians. Tribes mentioned include the Wyandots, Delawares, Senecas, Tuscarawas, Miamis, Cherokees, Mingoes, and Shawnees. The letters are endorsed with the writer's name, the date written, the date read in Congress, and action taken. The letters are arranged generally in chronological order. Other records in the series are described in **MI.360.4.** and **MI.360.43.**

LA.360.4. Two of the three bound volumes of **other reports of committees of Congress, 1776-88: on Indian affairs and lands in the western territory** (Item 30, M247, roll 37) contain some 360 pages of committee reports and motions by members of Congress pertaining to cession of western lands, petitions from settlers in the west (see **LA.360.2.**), and the surveying of the public lands. In addition to reports and motions there are related documents, such as drafts of deeds of cession, copies of state legislative acts, annotated drafts of the Northwest Ordinance, and communications to Congress from Indian leaders concerning title to land. Subjects are extremely varied. Most of the reports are endorsed with such information as the subject, names of members, date read or delivered, and the nature and dates of subsequent action. Most of the motions are endorsed with such information as the maker's name, the date, the subject, and names of committee members referred to. Some of the records are also endorsed with numbers corresponding to the numerical list of documents and groups of documents described in **CC.360.22.** (Item 17). They are arranged generally in numerical order according to that list, with unnumbered documents interspersed.

LA.360.5. A part of Miscellaneous PCC are seven portfolios containing deeds and related records of cession of western lands to the United States by the states of Connecticut, Georgia, Massachusetts, New York, North Carolina, South Carolina, and Virginia (M332, roll 7). The records concerning Georgia, Massachusetts, and North Carolina are related to cessions made after 1789. The pre-federal deeds of cession were witnessed by Charles Thomson, Roger Alden, Benjamin Bankson, Jr., Henry Remsen, Jr., and a few other persons. Besides setting forth the limits of the territory ceded, some of the deeds contain provisions pertaining to such subjects as monetary reimbursements to be made to the ceding state; establishment of land offices in the ceded territory; confirmation of existing land titles, such as those granted by the Spanish government and the British government of West Florida and the titles of French and Canadian settlers of the "Kaskaskies" and St. Vincents; extinguishment of Creek Indian land titles; formation of new states; the preservation of slavery; and allocation of bounty land to Continental Army veterans and troops who served under George Rogers Clark. The records are arranged alphabetically by state. For records pertaining to the settlement of Virginia's claims for reimbursement based on her northwestern land cession, see **FI.360.7.** For fair copies of many of the documents in these seven portfolios, see **LA.76.5.**

LA.360.6. **Copies of ordinances and other papers relating to the western territory of the United States, 1787-88** (Item 176, M247, roll 194), constitute a manuscript volume presumably kept in the Office of the Secretary of Congress. Among the copied records are the Northwest Ordinance; the oaths of allegiance and office of Governor Arthur St. Clair and territorial judges John Cleves Symmes, Samuel Holden Parsons, and James Mitchel Varnum; and an ordinance of July 9, 1788, concerning the disposal of land in the western territory. The other records copied, most of which are congressional resolutions and orders based on committee reports, pertain to such matters as territorial officials; preparations for dealing with the Indians; treatment of Frenchmen, Canadians, and others who settled in the territory before 1783; Georgia and Virginia cessions; surveys to be made by the Geographer of the United States; the conveying of land for the use of Christian Indians at the towns of Gnadenhutten, Shoenbrun, and Salem to the Moravian "Society for propagating the Gospel among the Heathen"; and the transfer of land on the southern shore of Lake Erie from the United States to Pennsylvania. About four-fifths of the volume is blank. It is arranged generally in chronological order.

LA.360.7. For petitions, memorials, committee reports, and other records pertaining mainly to territorial disputes between or involving states that were brought to the attention of the Continental Congress for settlement, see **JU.360.5.** Similar records pertaining to requests for bounty-land and other land grants are scattered throughout the memorials and petitions described in **PE.360.2.-PE.360.4.**

LA.360.8. The series **returns of inhabitants of various states, and miscellaneous papers, 1774-86** (Item 177, M247, roll 194), contains estimates of the number of square miles of land and the number of acres of water in the United States and the western territory. See also **CC.360.31.** and **IN.360.11.**

Record Group 11
General Records of the
United States Government

LA.11.1. This record group consists of the Constitution of the United States, the Bill of Rights and other amendments, and related records; laws of the United States and related records; international treaties and agreements; Indian treaties; Presidential proclamations, Executive orders, and other documents; rules and regulations of federal agencies; electoral records; and the Great Seal of the United States.

LA.11.2. Part of the series **perfected treaties, 1778-1945**, among the "American originals" file (see **FO.11.3.**) for the Treaty of Guadalupe Hidalgo of 1848 (Treaty Series 207), is a manuscript copy of "Plan del Puerto de S. Diego en la Costa Setentl. de Californs," which is a copy of a plan of the port of San Diego, CA, originally prepared in 1782. It was made by Juan Pantoja, second sailing master of a Spanish fleet, and published in a Spanish atlas in 1802. It is mentioned in the 1848 treaty between the United States and Mexico in connection with the southern border of California. The few land features shown include the "Presidio de S. Diego" and the "Mision de S. Diego."

Record Group 42
Records of the Office of Public Buildings and
Public Parks of the National Capital

LA.42.1. The Office of Public Buildings and Public Parks for the National Capital originated in 1791 when the Commissioners of the District of Columbia were appointed to plan and construct a capital city. In 1800, after the capital was moved to Washington, DC, the office was abolished, and its functions resided in a succession of different agencies. The last such successor was abolished in 1933, and its functions were assumed by the Public Buildings Service and the National Park Service.

LA.42.2. Among the records of the Office of Public Buildings and Grounds is the series **numbered file of maps and plans of Washington, DC, 1771-1927.** It consists mainly of originals and copies of manuscript and published maps, and plans of the city and parts thereof showing streets, lots, public buildings and grounds, and proposed improvements. Included are several 19th- and 20th-century copies of plans of the projected towns of Hamburgh and Carrollsburgh within the present boundaries of the District of Columbia. The plan of Hamburgh shows the town as planned in 1771, and that of Carrollsburgh as "recorded" in 1773. Most of the copies show numbered lots and proposed streets superimposed over the 19th- or 20th-century city street layout. The file is arranged numerically according to numbers assigned in no discernible order.

LA.42.3. Also among the records of the Office of Public Buildings and Grounds is a "deed book" pertaining mainly to land purchases in the District of Columbia by the United States, including a list of deeds to lots in Carrollsburgh issued and recorded between August 1771 and April 1776. The names of owners are included, as well as descriptions of the boundaries and size of the various lots, streets, and alleys in the town as it was surveyed in October 1770 (recorded in July 1773). The documents appear to be copies made from the records of Prince Georges County, MD. The volume also contains pre-federal patents and deeds to the various parcels of land in Virginia from which stone was quarried to build the U.S. Capitol and other public buildings in Washington, DC. These include land in Stafford County, "Brent's Island" in Acquia Creek, and "Wiggingtons Island." The documents are arranged in no discernible order.

LA.42.4. The records of the Commissioners for the District of Columbia include a volume of deeds of trust of property owners in Hamburgh and Carrollsburgh. It consists mainly of conveyances from 1792 and 1793, but one is dated October 1, 1771. By it Jacob Funk, the founder of Hamburgh, sold two lots to John Shelman. A typewritten list at the front of the book contains references to the names of all of the individuals who were parties to deeds.

Record Group 49

Records of the Bureau of Land Management

LA.49.1. The Office of the Secretary of the Treasury and the Register of the Treasury handled disposition of the public domain until April 25, 1812, when the General Land Office was established in the Department of the Treasury. The General Land Office was moved to the Department of the Interior in 1849 and was consolidated with other land-related agencies in 1946 to form the Bureau of Land Management.

RECORDS OF THE CONTINENTAL AND CONFEDERATION GOVERNMENTS

LA.49.2. Among the records of the Mails and Files Division of the General Land Office is a letter of July 26, 1788, from Thomas Hutchins, Geographer of the United States, to the Board of Treasury. It was written at New York City and transmitted a "Plan of the seven Ranges . . . with the Surveys and Descriptions appertaining thereto, also a calculation of the Townships and Fractional parts of Townships in the Fifth, Sixth, and Seventh Ranges." The "calculation" is the only document mentioned that still accompanies the letter. The "Surveys and Descriptions" are likely the records described in **LA.49.3.-LA.49.4.** The location of the "Plan" is not known. Two documents accompany the records. One is an undated typewritten paper, entitled "American Rectangular Surveys," pertaining in part to Hutchin's role in the evolution of that survey system. The other is an undated typewritten document which contains information about Hutchins' subsequent career and an extract from the journal of a British officer for June 25, 1762, in which Hutchins is referred to as a British ensign. Hutchins was an officer in the British Army when the Revolutionary War began. In London at the time, he asked to be relieved of his commission, since he refused to fight against his fellow colonials. He was therefore held as a prisoner in England throughout the conflict.

LA.49.3. The records of the Division of Surveys of the General Land Office contain the series **headquarters office township plats of the public land surveys, 1785-1946.** In the series are eight volumes of township plats and field notes prepared in connection with the survey of the Seven Ranges under the Land Ordinance of May 20, 1785. They were compiled by a team of surveyors under the direction of Thomas Hutchins. The Seven Ranges of townships were located in what became the eastern part of the state of Ohio. Drawn to the scale of 1 inch to ½ mile, a typical plat shows the range and township number, the number of acres in the township, the scale, the name of the surveyor, and the exterior boundaries of the township including intersecting watercourses. Some also show the home state of the surveyor and the date surveyed, the subdivision of the township into numbered lots, and, for some of those lots, the names of purchasers, the acreages, and the dates purchased. Each of the first seven volumes contains manuscript field notes for the townships in a particular range. Information recorded in these consists mainly of a description of the boundaries of the several townships making up a range, including the timber cover, quality of the soil, boundary markers, crop possibilities, "Meanders" of the Ohio River, and the name of the surveyor. The eighth volume appears to be an incomplete collection of copies of all of these field notes. The plats in the series are arranged numerically according to the range numbers and thereunder numerically according to the township numbers. Two items accompany them. One is a 20th-century facsimile copy of a "plat" of all seven ranges published about 1795; the other is an undated sheet of "diagrams" of the Seven Ranges, each showing the area in its entirety and the location of each numbered township.

LA.49.4. Also among the records of the Division of Surveys is the series **plats of the survey of meridians, base lines, and township exteriors, 1786-1918.** The 33 pre-federal plats are all in one volume of this 116-volume series. Information given in the written description for each plat includes the range and township numbers, the scale, the number of acres in the township, the name of the surveyor and sometimes his home state and the year of his survey, branches of rivers and other watercourses present along the township boundaries, boundary markers, the quality of the soil, timber cover, and the kinds of crops that might be raised. The plats are arranged numerically by the numbers of the ranges and thereunder numerically by the numbers of the townships, with a significant number of townships missing.

RECORDS PERTAINING TO EUROPEAN COLONIAL SETTLEMENT IN NORTH AMERICA

General records

LA.49.5. The series **land entry papers of the General Land Office, 1800-1908,** consists, for the most part, of documents submitted or prepared by persons seeking land from the federal government and by officials of U.S. district land offices. The documents were forwarded to the office in Washington, DC, as evidence that all requirements for the issuance of a patent in a particular case had been fulfilled, and for final action. The records are arranged for the most part alphabetically according to the names of the public land states. Thereunder they are filed mainly alphabetically by the names of the district land offices that were established in those states; thereunder by the various kinds of classes of entries, including files of "miscellaneous papers"; and within classes in numerical order according to numbers assigned to individual documents or groups of related documents making up an entry transaction. The public land states consist of most of the states other than the original 13 and the states formed out of them. Among the records for the land office at St. Stephens, AL, are documents pertaining to land claims based on French, British, and Spanish grants, including requests for confirmation of claims, registers of claims, opinions of commissioners on confirming claims, and copies of petitions for land and other title papers. Many of the documents are in French or Spanish with English translations. The records for the land office at Kaskaskia, IL, include statements of claims that came within the provisions of acts of June 20, 1788, and March 3, 1791. These acts granted donations: the first act to heads of families who held lands received by virtue of concessions under British and French rule, and the second act to persons who had actually cultivated and improved land. The records for the land office at Washington, MS, include plats and notices of claims by virtue of letters patent and warrants of survey from British and Spanish officials. There is no overall index to this series, but indexes are available for a number of individual states.

LA.49.6. One subseries within the same series is not based on records pertaining to a single public land state. "Private land claim papers, 1789-1908," consists of claims made to the federal government on the basis of grants or settlements that occurred before the United States acquired sovereignty over the area concerned. They include claims based on grants from foreign governments, by descendants of those grantees, by U.S. citizens who settled lands with the permission of foreign governments, and by those who purchased lands acquired earlier by such grantees or settlers. The records are made up of case files arranged alphabetically by the names of states and thereunder numerically by claim numbers. Types of documents present include copies and translations of original grants, notices of claims, plots, deeds, transcripts of court proceedings, and correspondence. Among the records are a number pertaining to claims based on pre-federal land transactions. For example, there are records concerning grants made near Kaskaskia, IL, by Col. John Wilkins, as British commander at Fort Chartres, to John Edgar and John M. St. Clair,

April 12, 1769; grants of farm lands adjacent to Detroit dating back to 1700; the Orange Grove Land Tract near Mobile, AL, which was claimed by John Forbes and Company on the basis of a British government grant in 1767; claims by the heirs of Robert Farmer based on French grants in 1738; a claim by the heir of Nicholas Boudin based on a French grant in 1713; and land claims of the French fur-trading family of Auguste and Pierre Chouteau. Separate indexes are available for many of the states. They index names of claimants alphabetically by surname.

LA.49.7. The subgroup Records of Boards of Commissioners for Hearing Private Land Claims, 1803-74, consists of several dozen separate series, now part of the records of the Private Land Claims Division of the General Land Office. Boards of commissioners were established in various regions of the United States by acts of Congress beginning March 3, 1803, to hear and make findings on claims to land based on grants from foreign governments or settlement in areas administered by such governments before the acquisition of those areas by the United States. Among claims heard were those based on grants, patents, and survey orders and warrants issued by the British, French, and Spanish governments before 1789; "donations" of land by the U.S. government to settlers in the Illinois country before 1783; and settlement of lands under Georgia acts of 1783 that created Bourbon County. The records of the several boards are intermingled with other records of the Private Land Claims Division, the whole of which are arranged for the most part in roughly alphabetical order according to the names of the present states to which they pertain. Some individual series contain or are accompanied by indexes to names of claimants. Original pre-federal land records of foreign governments that came into the custody of the Private Land Claims Division, and certain other records of the division pertaining in large part to pre-federal land transactions, are described in **LA.49.8.-LA.49.19.**, arranged by geographic region.

British West Florida records

LA.49.8. The series **records relating to British West Florida land claims, 1760-1800,** comprises about nine inches of records of the Private Land Claims Division of the General Land Office. A number of petitions of the mid-1770s were written by Loyalists who had fled the rebellious British colonies to the northern part of Florida. In general, petitions include information about when and whence petitioners came to West Florida. Among the related records are field notes of surveys, inventories of estates, various commissions, and land grants. There are but a few records dated after 1780. The records are arranged alphabetically by the first letters of the surnames of the petitioners, warrantees, and other persons who signed or are otherwise associated with the documents.

LA.49.9. Records of the Private Land Claims Division also contain 2 inches of miscellaneous records in the series **British West Florida land records, 1770-79.** These are mostly about land and defense and consist mainly of original British records, 1767-79. Included are petitions for land, usually on behalf of former military personnel; passes permitting individuals to travel through British territory; and some minutes, correspondence, and records of the Council of the Province of West Florida. The records are arranged in no discernible order.

LA.49.10. The division's records also contain the two-volume series, **copies of conveyances to land, Pensacola, Florida, 1765-66.** The volumes contain land grants, deeds of sale, and other documents received by the "Register & Naval officer of West Florida." There are also a few bonds, deeds of sale for slaves, and other legal documents. Each volume is arranged chronologically with some overlap in dates between the two.

LA.49.11. Abstracts to land grants in British West Florida exist among the records of the division in two forms—**alphabetical abstracts of British grants in West Florida, 1765-70** (2 vols.) and **abstract of British grants of land in West Florida, 1766-77** (1 vol.). The first series is arranged alphabetically by surnames of grantees; the second chronologically by date of grant. Both versions contain columns, not always filled in, for the entry of information about a particular grant. This generally includes the name or names of the original grantees, the date of the petition for land, the date granted, the date a warrant was issued, lot numbers, the number of acres granted, and the date the grant was registered or recorded.

Illinois country and Michigan records

LA.49.12. A small series in the records of the Private Land Claims Division, **Illinois, Kaskaskia—miscellaneous records, 1723-1809**, contains originals and copies of records pertaining to the Illinois country, 1722-1807. Many are certified as having been copied in 1809 from files of the recorder's office at Kaskaskia, Randolph County, Illinois Territory. All of the pre-federal documents are copies. Included are Maj. Gen. Thomas Gage's "Declaration" of December 30, 1764, concerning the cession to Great Britain of the "Country of Illinois" by the peace concluded at Paris, February 10, 1763; Gage's proclamation of April 1772 ordering settlers to withdraw from settlements on or beyond the Wabash River; and documents from 1722 and 1768-86 concerning land titles. The records are in French and English; most of those in French are accompanied by English translations. They are arranged numerically by assigned numbers.

LA.49.13. Among the division's records is the series **Michigan, Detroit—miscellaneous records, 1707-1810,** containing originals and copies of records pertaining mainly to land grants and claims in and around Detroit, 1707-1825. Many relate to claims submitted to the Register of the U.S. Land Office at Detroit. Included are copies of French land grants in the area beginning in 1707; copies of British grants, 1781-82; and correspondence and other records from after 1789, but dealing with pre-federal grants and claims. The records are arranged in no discernible order.

Louisiana Territory records

LA.49.14. The Private Land Claims Division also received a volume of copies, which is the series **translated court and other records relating to British, French, and Spanish documents relating to land claims records in Alabama, 1715-1812** (M1382, roll 1). On the first page is a statement that the records were translated and copied, 1840-41, pursuant to an 1833 act of the Alabama legislature. The documents include numerous petitions to various governors of Louisiana requesting land, land grants, deeds of sale of land by private persons, and orders to surveyors from governors. The volume is arranged chronologically by the dates of the documents recorded. It contains an index arranged alphabetically by the first letter of the surnames of the officials and other persons conveying land.

LA.49.15. **"Six Livre[s] Terrien,"** 1766-97, are volumes among the division's records that include copies of land grants and records of surveys in and about the then village of St. Louis. Volumes 1, 3, and 5 contain tables of contents that list the names of persons to whom the entries in each volume pertain. There is also an untranslated single-volume copy of all six volumes. It contains an index to persons granted land or associated with the transactions, arranged alphabetically by surname. An additional volume is an abstract and English translation of the original six volumes, produced and certified as accurate in 1809. It contains six sections, one for each of the original books. Each section contains a heading describing in brief the overall contents of the book abstracted. Following each heading are columns containing the page number in the original book for a particular entry therein, the name of the person to or for whom land was granted or surveyed, the current owner's name, the dimensions of the land, the date land was granted, the location of the land, and remarks. All of the columns are not always filled in for each entry, especially the column showing the current owner. The entries are arranged in numerical order according to the numbers of the original books and thereunder numerically by the page numbers of those books.

LA.49.16. The three-volume series **record of a concession by the Spanish government to land in Louisiana Territory, 1788-1800** (M1382, roll 1), contains documents that are written in Spanish and French. Most are memorials and decrees addressed to or signed by Charles Dehault Delassus, "lieutenant goeverneur de la haute Louisiane," and Zenon Trudeau, "Comdt. Civil et Militaire du Poste et District de St. Louis" and "Teniente de Governador de la partida occidental de Illinois." Only a few documents are from the pre-federal period. There is a table of contents at the front of the first volume.

LA.49.17. A one-volume series, **record of a concession of land in the District of St. Genevieve, Louisiana (Missouri), 1788-1804** (M1382, roll 1), was, as shown on its title page "executed by Order of Amos Stoddard 1st Civil Commandant of Upper Louisiana." It consists principally of copies of petitions for land, decrees, certificates, and other documents, mainly in French and Spanish, that were received or issued by various French and Spanish officials in connection with grants of land. Most of the documents date from 1799 to 1804. The volume is arranged in numerical order, 1-50, each number assigned to a set of documents pertaining to a specific grant.

California and New Mexico records

LA.49.18. The records of the Private Land Claims Division also contain the one-volume series **index to Spanish documents, New Mexico, ca. 1800-50**, compiled around 1846. It lists grants, wills, inventories of estates, petitions for land, and other land-related documents associated mainly with Spanish-surnamed individuals and with occasional towns, settlements, or similar entities, including El Paso and Santa Fe. Each entry gives a document number, its date, its "index number," and the name of the person or entity associated with it. The location of the documents is not known. They are probably records of the Spanish and Mexican governments of New Mexico. The index is arranged alphabetically by the first letters of surnames or entities.

LA.49.19. The two-volume series **private land claims and pueblos claims in New Mexico, 1883**, includes translations of

Spanish grants and other documents from as early as 1714. The records were filed with the Surveyor General of New Mexico in support of private claims. Names of claimants in the two volumes are indexed alphabetically by surname in "Old Index of Private Land Claims in New Mexico, Arizona, and Colorado," 1858-1905.

CARTOGRAPHIC RECORDS ORIGINATING IN OR PERTAINING TO THE PRE-FEDERAL PERIOD

LA.49.20. The series **manuscript and annotated maps,** often referred to as the "Old Map File," consists mainly of maps of the United States as a whole and of individual states and parts thereof. They document the historical development of the country and the disposal of public lands. Relatively few items pertain to the pre-federal period. They are presented here in tabular form:

File number	Date	Subject(s)
M-Fla.-1	ca. 1780	West FL, around Pensacola, Mobile, and New Orleans, showing Indian (Choctaw and Chickasaw) settlements and roads.
M-Ind.-9	ca. 1821	Donations to heads of families in the Vincennes Dist. under cong'l acts of 1788 and 1791.
M-La.-14	1884	An area along Lake Pontchartrain showing grants made to Louis C. LeBreton in 1757 and 1764.
M-Ohio-1	ca. 1789	Exterior lines of a tract sold to "Messrs. Sargent & Cutler."
M-Ohio-2	ca. 1789	Purchase made by W. Sargent and M. Cutler as agents of the Ohio Co.
M-Ohio-5	n.d.	Part of OH, showing tracts reserved for VA Rev. War veterans, purchases of the Ohio Co., the 7 Ranges, and land for refugees from Can. and N. Scotia.
M-Ohio-20	n.d.	"Plan of lands appropriated" by Congress for the refugees from Can. and N. Scotia.
M-Ohio-22	n.d.	"Virginia Military Lands" in Ohio.

Fuller descriptions, including information on scale, may be found in National Archives Special List No. 19, *List of Cartographic Records of the General Land Office* (1964). Both the Old Map File and the description of it in Special List No. 19 are arranged with maps of the entire United States first, followed by each state in alphabetical order. Under the United States and each state section the maps are generally in chronological order, with numbers assigned accordingly.

LA.49.21. Another series decribed in Special List No. 19 is **field notes and related records**, usually referred to as "Old Case 'F' File." Most of the records are bound into volumes and arranged in order of assigned numbers. The records pertaining to pre-federal affairs are:

File number	Date	Subject(s)
F-93	1792-94	Field notes for "the Symmes' Purchase in Ohio."
F-96	n.d.	Field notes for land set aside in Ohio for refugees from Can. and N. Scotia.
F-97	n.d.	Township plats of land set aside in OH for refugees from Can. and N. Scotia.
F-100	1813	2 vols. of field notes taken along the meridian line through the VA military reservation in OH.

The records mainly contain information about the location of boundary lines, the physical character of the land surveyed, the quality of the soil, and the type of vegetation present. Names of grantees and settlers are seldom given.

Record Group 58

Records of the Internal Revenue Service

LA.58.1. The Office of the Commissioner of Internal Revenue was established in the Treasury Department by an act of July 1, 1862, to help finance the Civil War. During the periods 1791-1802 and 1813-17, the Treasury Department collected internal revenue taxes through an office headed by the Commissioner of the Revenue.

LA.58.2. The series **manuscript, annotated, and printed maps relating to St. Helena's Parish and to part of St. Luke's Parish, SC, 1855-95,** includes an undated manuscript item entitled "An Exact Copy of an original Map of the City of Beaufort S.C." Written on it is a statement that the original "dates prior to 1800 perhaps by 30 years." It shows mainly streets, lot numbers, and names of lot owners. There is also an undated but presumably 19th-century tracing of a "plot" made in 1785 "of a Tract of Land on Port Royal Island in St. Helena Parish and Granville County" granted to William James Ferguson in 1767. The series is arranged roughly in chronological order.

Record Group 59

General Records of the Department of State

LA.59.1. The Department of Foreign Affairs was established by an act of July 1789 and 2 months later was designated the Department of State by the same Congress. It was assigned such functions as preserving and publishing laws and treaties, keeping the seal of the United States, and serving as custodian of the records of the United States previously held by the Secretary of Congress. The department was also in charge of territorial affairs from 1789 to 1873.

TERRITORIAL PAPERS

LA.59.2. **Territorial papers, 1764-1873,** is a large series made up of several subseries, one for each territory. The two-volume subseries, microfilmed as *State Department Territorial Papers, Territory Northwest of the River Ohio, 1787-1801* (M470, 1 roll), contains original letters and enclosures from the Secretary of the Territory to officials of the confederation and federal governments. The enclosures include copies of laws, appointments, correspondence, and other official records of the territorial government. An original imprint of the Northwest Ordinance, with the holograph signature of Secretary of Congress Charles Thomson, is at the beginning of the first volume. During the pre-federal period the correspondence was sent to Thomson by the territorial secretary. Subsequent letters from the territorial secretary to the U.S. government were addressed directly to the President. A number of these contain copies of surveying instructions, lists of settlers, and other documents relating to the pre-federal period, especially in connection with the confirmation of land titles of French and other inhabitants of the region who had settled there in or before 1783. The subseries is arranged chronologically. Most of these documents have been published in volumes 2 and 3 of *The Territorial Papers of the United States* (1934). These published volumes are reproduced in the National Archives Microfilm Publication of the same name (M721, roll 2).

LA.59.3. One volume in National Archives Microfilm Publication M471 (1 roll), contains a copy of the proceedings of the government of British West Florida pertaining to land grants. The proceedings, which are undated but appear to be from 1778, consist of summaries of several petitions to the government seeking grants of land, and the decisions made concerning them. Several of the petitioners claimed to be Loyalists who had been forced for that reason to leave land and other property in Georgia and Virginia. Their claims apparently were made under a proclamation of the governor of the province of West Florida, November 11, 1775. The records are arranged by petitioner. For related records see **LA.49.8.** and **LA.49.11.**

LA.59.4. The first part of the first volume in *State Department Territorial Papers, Territory of Orleans, 1764-1813* (T260, 1 roll), contains instructions and other issuances of Don Alexander O'Reilly, Governor and Captain-General of Louisiana, 1764, 1769-70. They consist mainly of a few original pamphlets and other documents concerning civil and criminal legal procedures, the administrative organization of the provincial government, fees of public officials, land grants, and other matters. These documents were published by O'Reilly in 1769-70 to familiarize the French inhabitants of Louisiana with Spanish laws following the cession of the province from France to Spain in 1762. They are in French and include undated English annotations and translations. Preceding the first imprint is the manuscript, "Chronological Series of Facts relative to Louisiana," which contains information about wars, treaties, explorations, settlements, and other subjects from 1673 to 1803. There is also a manuscript copy of part of a letter of April 21, 1764, from Louis XV to "M. D'Abbadie, director general and commandant for his majesty in Louisiana," instructing him to deliver to the King of Spain all of the French possessions in North America not ceded to Great Britain. The documents associated with Governor O'Reilly are in no discernible order. The last part of the same volume contains copies, in Spanish, of documents from the Spanish government's archives called "Papers relative to the transfer of Louisiana." Some of the documents were printed, at O'Reilly's order, in the pamphlet described above, but others, such as a list of governors of Louisiana from 1772 to 1800 and nominations by the King of Spain of various persons to be governor during that period, are not. The copies at the end of the volume are arranged mainly by numbers assigned to the documents.

RECORDS OF THE BUREAU OF ROLLS AND LIBRARY

LA.59.5. The series **history of the French in Louisiana, 1700-24, n.d.**, consists of two copies of "Journal Historique, Concernant l'Etabliussement des Francais a la Louisianne" by Benard de La Harpe, and related correspondence. Jean Baptiste Benard de La Harpe, a French military officer, based his history on his own exploration, 1718-22, and on information "Tire' des Memoires de Messieurs D'Iberville & de Bienville, Commandants pour le Roi au dit pays." There are references in the work to events as early as 1510, and to many of the Indians in the region. At the end of one of the volumes is a certification that it was copied from the original in 1805. At the back of the same volume are copies of three letters written in 1805-6 by Spanish to U.S. civil and military officials concerning the dispute between the two countries over the Texas-Louisiana border and the history of Spanish and French activities in that region. The journal apparently was used by the governments in discussions concerning that boundary. It was published at New Orleans in 1831 in French; an English translation is in *Historical Collections of Louisiana* (1846-53).

LA.59.6. A part of the series **miscellaneous documents, printed, 1206-1932**, is a pamphlet entitled *Documents Relative to Louisiana and Florida . . .*, n.d. It contains English translations of copies of Spanish records, 1770-1806. The Spanish records were received by the State Department from the Spanish Secretary of State through the U.S. Minister to Spain, C. P. Van Ness. The first five documents are from 1770-88 and include correspondence of Spanish officials and royal orders. They pertain to such subjects as land grants, appointments of local officials, and trade. Many of the letters and other documents dated after 1789 also pertain to land grants under royal orders and intructions issued before that year. The documents are arranged chronologically. These printed translations are based largely on the records described in **LA.59.4.**

LA.59.7. About 150 pages of accounting records of the vice-regal treasury in New Spain are among the unbound records of the Bureau of Rolls and Library. Most of the documents are from 1772 and show payments made by administrators of "colegios" in Mexico City, "Tepozotlan," Zacatecas, and California missions, for grain consumed by their respective establishments. A few of the records contain references to dates as late as 1784. There is no discernible arrangement.

LA.59.8. There is a receipt from Lord Fairfax to George Washington and Fielding Lewis for quitrents paid on land by George Carter, deceased, March 18, 1769, among the records in **miscellaneous manuscripts, 1765-1918.** It shows the quit rents owed by Carter on approximately 27,500 acres from 1764 to 1768, less rent covered by prior payments or eliminated for other reasons, and the final balance due and paid in 1769. The location of the land is not given.

LA.59.9. The one-volume series **journal of Mason and Dixon, 1763-68** (M86, 1 roll), consists largely of an original manuscript journal kept in the field by Charles Mason. He and Jeremiah Dixon were English scientists hired by the proprietors of the colonies of Pennsylvania and Maryland in 1763 to survey their common boundary, a subject of dispute since the previous century. The major part of the journal consists of entries by Mason concerning details of the work done on the survey of the border in question. A number of entries concern efforts by Sir William Johnson to get the consent of the Six Nations to the western portion of the survey. Specific Indian tribes mentioned include the Mohawks, Onondagas, Senecas, Delawares, Tuscaroras, Mingoes, and Shawnees. There are also entries made by Mason during private trips through Pennsylvania, Delaware, Maryland, New York, New Jersey, and Virginia. At the beginning of the volume are copies of correspondence of Secretary of State Hamilton Fish, 1876-77, pertaining to the purchase of the journal from Judge Alexander James of Nova Scotia and a few original survey notes, 1762-67. At the end are a certificate, signed by Charles Thomson, admitting Mason to membership in the "American Society held at Philadelphia for promoting useful Knowledge," and an original letter of November 14, 1768, received by Mason and Dixon from Thomas Penn. A few other documents are interspersed among the leaves of the journal. Information about related records in depositories other than the National Archives is included in the pamphlet accompanying National Archives Microfilm Publication M86.

OTHER RECORDS

LA.59.10. The series **domestic letters (letters sent), 1784-1906**, in the subgroup Miscellaneous Correspondence, contains a report of the Secretary of State to the President of the United States, December 19, 1791 (M40, roll 4). This original document, signed by Thomas Jefferson, pertains to the sale to Pennsylvania of a tract of land owned by the United States between Lake Erie and the state's northern boundary. The sale was authorized by the Continental Congress in resolutions of June 6 and September 4, 1788. Accompanying Jefferson's report are related documents, including an original, signed letter received by President George Washington from Governor Thomas Mifflin of Pennsylvania, December 15, 1791, which Washington had referred to Jefferson; copies of letters received by the governor and the secretary of the commonwealth from the comptroller general and attorney general of Pennsylvania; copies of extracts of proceedings of the Pennsylvania General Assembly and Council, 1787-88; and copies of correspondence between the Pennsylvania delegates to the Continental Congress and the Board of Treasury, July and August 1788. The records are arranged in the order described.

Record Group 60

General Records of the Department of Justice

LA.60.1. The Department of Justice was established by an act of June 22, 1870, which continued and expanded the legal and administrative duties of the Attorney General. These had been provided for by an act of September 24, 1789, which gave the Attorney General the power to conduct suits in the Supreme Court, give opinions on questions of law at the request of the President or heads of departments, and make recommendations to the President on appointments and pardons.

LA.60.2. In the series **letters received, 1809-70**, are copies of a land grant, deed, survey, and other records, 1664-1784, relating to an island in the Delaware River near Wilmington called The Pea Patch. The documents are enclosures to a letter dated July 7, 1819, that was received by the Attorney General of the United States concerning the contested title to the island, on which military fortifications were being built. Included among the copies of pre-federal documents are a grant of certain land in America by Charles II to the Duke of York, 1664; a deed to New Castle and the adjacent region in Delaware given to William Penn in 1682 by the Duke of York; and a survey of The Pea Patch, 1784.

Record Group 76
Records of Boundary and Claims Commissions and Arbitrations

LA.76.1. This collective record group was established for segregated files relating to international boundaries, claims, and arbitrations received from the Department of State and international commissions.

RECORDS RELATING TO INTERNATIONAL ARBITRATIONS

LA.76.2. The subgroup Records Relating to International Arbitrations, 1854-1925, consists of more than 200 series of textual and cartographic records. They were created or acquired by the Department of State and various international commissions and pertain mainly to the arbitration of boundary disputes. Included are cases in which the United States was a party and in which it acted as arbitrator. Although the earliest arbitration was in 1854, more than a dozen series include records, both originals and copies, dating as far back as the 16th century. The entire subgroup is arranged in two sections—those cases in which the United States arbitrated and those cases in which the United States was a party. In each section, aggregations of series pertaining to a particular dispute are chronologically arranged according to the dates of the successive arbitrations. For any one arbitration, the records are in no discernible order. Arrangement of documents and maps within individual series varies.

LA.76.3. Arbitrations conducted by the United States for Central and South American countries produced the largest number of pre-federal records in the subgroup. There are maps of the world, the Americas, the West Indies, and individual Latin American countries dating from as early as 1523. Many are copies. Sources of the originals are often given and include archival depositories in Spain, Portugal, and France. There are also manuscript and printed copies of textual records originating before 1789. These include correspondence of Spanish colonial officials; decrees, orders, and appointments of Spanish rulers; journals of colonial surveying parties; and treaties between European powers. Sources of original documents copied are often given. Occasional documents predating 1789 are present. In some cases, English translations of documents in foreign languages are in the files.

LA.76.4. Similar types of records relating to the pre-federal period are also found in lesser quantities among arbitration records pertaining to disputes in which the United States was a party. Records of the Bering Sea Claims Commission, 1896-97, and the North American Fisheries Arbitration at The Hague, 1910, contain such records, although all are copies.

LA.76.5. Among the records of West Florida in the sub-group is the series **lands purchased and ceded to the United States, 1781-1800.** Whether it was begun in pre-federal times or later has not been established, but the contents pertaining to the pre-federal period consist principally of fair copies of documents related to the cession of western lands to the United States by New York, Virginia, Massachusetts, Connecticut, and South Carolina, 1781-87. There are also a copy of a deed, a plat, and related documents dated in July 1776 conveying "Billings Port" in New Jersey to George Clymer and Michael Hillegas for the use of the continental government. The volume is arranged generally in chronological order. For originals of western and other land cession documents for the pre-federal period, some of which are endorsed as having been recorded in this book, see **LA.360.5.**

LA.76.6. The series **laws of the western territory, 1788-92**, contains contemporary fair copies of territorial laws presumably made from the copies transmitted to the confederation and federal governments and bound in the volumes described in **LA.59.2.** Subjects of the laws include establishment and regulation of the militia, prison administration, and fees of territorial officials. The book is arranged chronologically. Somewhat more than half of the volume is blank.

LA.76.7. The three-volume series **proceedings of the territorial governors, 1788-93**, consists of two volumes containing copies of the journals of the Governor of the Northwest Territory and of transmittal letters to the Secretary of the Territory, the Secretary of Congress, and the President. All were presumably copied from the original letters and enclosures described in **LA.59.2.**

RECORDS RELATING TO THE INTERNATIONAL BOUNDARIES OF THE UNITED STATES

LA.76.8. Another subgroup, Records Relating to the International Boundaries of the United States, 1794-1952, consists of more than 500 textual and cartographic series. They were created or acquired by the Department of State and various international commissions and pertain principally to the determination of the northern and southern borders of the continental United States, including Alaska. In addition to correspondence, journals, and other records of the ongoing activities of the various commissions and other bodies concerned, there are dozens of series that consist of or include textual and cartographic evidence, both originals and copies of documents and maps, submitted by parties in boundary negotiations. Some date back to the beginning of the 17th century.

LA.76.9. The majority of pre-federal records in this subgroup are the result of cases in which the United States was in dispute with Great Britain over its northeastern boundary. For example, the records of the commission established under article V of the Jay Treaty of 1794 contain a series of five original imprints of various editions of John Mitchell's map of the British and French dominions in North America. This map was first published in 1755, and a version of it was used by the peace negotiators in 1782. Other series of the records of the same commission contain original letters sent to State Department officials in 1790 and 1796 by Benjamin Franklin, John Adams, and John Jay, which contain their recollections as treaty negotiators.

LA.76.10. Among the records of an arbitration by the King of the Netherlands under a U.S.-British convention of 1827 is a series of maps attached to the American statement. The maps include pre-federal originals and copies printed and dated as early as 1763. These depict the world as a whole, North America, the northeastern part of the United States, and the province of Quebec.

LA.76.11. An original imprint of the aforementioned 1775 edition of Mitchell's map, said to have been at one time the property of Baron von Steuben, is among the records of the commission established under article VI of the Webster-Ashburton Treaty of 1842 between the United States and Great Britain.

LA.76.12. In the records of the international boundary commission provided for in the U.S.-British convention of 1906 are series containing originals and copies of pre-federal printed and manuscript maps of the world, Asia, Africa, Europe, and the Americas dated as early as 1719.

LA.76.13. Throughout the subgroup, series of formal reports, proceedings, memorials, and arguments and replies of commissions and parties include manuscript and printed copies and extracts of pre-federal documents, such as correspondence of British and colonial officials and commissions of colonial officials; British land grants in Nova Scotia; colonial legislative proceedings; and pertinent treaties. An occasional original pre-federal document is present. The overall arrangement of the subgroup is geographical according to whether the series pertain to the southern or northern borders of the United States and thereunder according to specific sections of those borders. The series are further arranged chronologically according to the dates of the commissions and arbitrations. Within series arrangement varies. Many of the pre-federal maps in this subgroup are individually described in National Archives Special List No. 26, *Pre-Federal Maps in the National Archives: An Annotated List* (1975). See the introduction for further information about Special List No. 26.

Record Group 77
Records of the Office of the Chief of Engineers

LA.77.1. The Corps of Engineers, U.S. Army, was established by an act of March 16, 1802, to organize a military academy at West Point. In 1818 the Chief Engineer of the corps was directed to fix his headquarters at Washington, DC, as the Office of the Chief of Engineers in the War Department. The army topographical engineers were placed under the chief's supervision from 1818 to 1831 and again in 1863. Responsibilities of the Office of the Chief of Engineers have included producing and distributing army maps, building roads, planning camps, constructing and repairing fortifications and other installations, maintaining and improving inland waterways and harbors, and approving plans for the construction of bridges, wharves, piers, and other works over navigable waters.

LA.77.2. In the series **letters and papers received (irregular series), 1789-1831**, is a single document consisting of extracts from the journals of James Mackay and John Evans concerning western exploration in 1787 and 1795-97. The two were employed by the Spanish government to explore and open to commerce the upper Missouri River region. Some years later extracts of their journals were prepared by John Hay, a resident of Cahokia, IL, for the use of the Lewis and Clark Expedition. These documents appear to be a 19th-century copy of Hay's work. Most of the extracts concern Mackay's and Evans' travels in the 1790s, but there is also information about a journey made by Mackay in 1787 to Mandan Indian communities on the Missouri River. Mackay reported on the friendly reception he received and gave a few details about the tribe's trade and agriculture.

LA.77.3. The series **civil works (headquarters) map file** of the Office of the Chief of Engineers is made up of maps prepared by engineer or other army units or acquired from other government agencies or other sources. These originals and copies of manuscript and published maps pertain mainly to the continental United States. Among the items relevant to the pre-federal period are:

File Number	Date	Subject(s)
A1, B1/1, and B1/2	1776	Charts of Penobscot Bay and Boston Harbor published by J. F. W. Des Barves.
Ama 38	ca. 1767	Original Spanish manuscript map of northern Mexico and the southwestern U.S.
Ama 135	n.d.	Manuscript map of the Pacific coast from San Francisco Bay to Prince William Sound, AK, showing landfalls by Spanish explorers, 1774-79.
D70	n.d.	New York City as surveyed, 1766-67, pub. by Jeffreys and Faden.
E18	1776	Chart of Delaware Bay and River, pub. by William Faden.
H47	1822	Manuscript tracing of a 1733 map of NC
L 5	n.d.	Manuscript copy of a 1701 plan of Pensacola harbor.
L53/1	n.d.	Manuscript plan of St. Augustine, East FL, as surveyed in 1777.
M2	1778	Copy of manuscript plan of Lake Pontchartrain, LA.
P424	1749	Manuscript tracing of a map of New France made by the Jesuit mathematician Bonnecamps.
R8	1813	Manuscript map of Sandy Hook bar showing the position of the British fleet and works in July 1778.
U.S.3	1776	Map of the provinces of NY and NJ based on the observations of C. J. Sauthier and B. Ratzer.
U.S.4	1777	Pub. chart of Narragansett Bay, RI, showing American fortifications.
U.S.6	1778	Map of the western parts of VA, PA, MD, and NC, published by Thos. Hutchins.
U.S.8	1780	Map of SC and part of GA based on surveys of Wm. De Brahm, John Stuart, and others.

The file is arranged according to alpha-numeric and numerical designations assigned to the maps primarily on the basis of their relation to particular geographic regions or to a few special subjects, such as boundaries and roads. More detailed individual descriptions of these and other pre-federal and related maps in the civil works map file are available in National Archives Special List No. 26, *Pre-Federal Maps in the National Archives: An Annotated List* (1975) and National Archives Special List No. 29, *List of Selected Maps of States and Territories* (1971). For more information on Special List No. 26 see the introduction.

Record Group 92
Records of the Office of the Quartermaster General

LA.92.1. During the pre-federal era quartermasters general were regarded as field staff officers appointed to principal armies. Like the Quartermaster's Department, created by Congress in 1818, they were responsible for efficient systems of supply, movement of armies, and accountability of officers and agents charged with moneys or supplies.

LA.92.2. A copy of a plan of New Orleans "sur les Manuscrits du Depot des Cartes de la Marine Par N. B. Ingr. de la M. 1744" (map 107, sheet 12) is part of a series known as the **post and reservation file, 1820-1905.** It is an engraved copy made in 1827 from a plan originally prepared by Jacques Nicolas Bellin. Features shown include buildings, streets, parks, and the moat surrounding the city. A key identifying the principal buildings is also present.

Record Group 121
Records of the Public Buildings Service (GSA)

LA.121.1. The Public Buildings Service designs, constructs, manages, maintains, and protects most federally owned and leased buildings. It is also responsible for the acquisition, utilization, and custody of General Services Administration (GSA) real and related personal property. It was established in 1949 to supersede the Public Buildings Administration.

LA.121.2. **Title papers, 1838-1968**, is a series of records documenting the purchase or other acquisition of buildings and building sites by and for the use of the federal government. The series is arranged alphabetically by state or territory, thereunder alphabetically by city or other locality, and thereunder mainly alphabetically by building or site designation. The records include deeds, surveys, abstracts of title, and correspondence. There is about 1 foot of originals and copies of documents, 1682-1812, that pertain to the pre-federal period. These records—deeds, wills, title abstracts, plats, and others—relate to the following cities and buildings:

Annapolis, MD	Post office
Baltimore, MD	Old courthouse and old customhouse
New York City, NY	Old assay office, also known as Federal Hall
Philadelphia, PA	Old courthouse, customhouse, and mint
York, PA	Old post office
Charleston, SC	Customhouse, old post office, and old courthouse
Alexandria, VA	Post office

Also among the early records are two original parchment indentures, 1682, by which William Penn conveyed 2,875 acres of land in Pennsylvania to John Simcock. For a list of the localities and the buildings or sites therein for which there are title papers, see National Archives Special List No. 30, *Title Papers of the Public Buildings Service* (1972).

Record Group 233

Records of the
U.S. House of Representatives

LA.233.1. The U.S. House of Representatives was created by Article I, section 1, of the Constitution. Although it shares legislative power with the Senate, the House originates all bills for raising revenue and, by custom, general appropriation bills. The House has sole power to impeach U.S. civil officers, and judges elections, returns, and qualifications of its members.

LA.233.2. A copy of a map of Lake Superior and the northern parts of Lakes Michigan and Huron made in 1670-71 by Jesuit missionaries (Ex. Doc. No 69, 10th Cong.) is part of the series **published maps of the House of Representatives.** It was published at Paris in 1672. It shows the location of a few missions, rivers, and Indian nations in the vicinity.

Record Group 267
Records of the
Supreme Court of the United States

LA.267.1. The Supreme Court of the United States, provided for in Article III, section 1, of the Constitution, was established by authority of the Judiciary Act of 1789.

LA.267.2.   Maps and charts, 1851-1946, is a series of cartographic materials submitted as exhibits in cases of both original and appellate jurisdiction before the Supreme Court. Most concern disputes between two states or between a state and another party. A number of early maps of the gulf coast region, ca. 1764, were submitted to the court in 1904 by Louisiana in connection with the case *Louisiana* v. *Mississippi.* These maps, mainly photocopies, contain references to dates as early as 1700 and include such features as settlements, forts, Indian villages, roads, the Mississippi and other rivers and watercourses, offshore soundings, and a town plan of New Orleans. Exhibit No. 37 of New York in the case of *Massachusetts* v. *New York*, 1925, is a copy of a 1771 map of New York. Map L2 in the case of *Vermont* v. *New Hampshire*, 1936, is a negative photostatic copy of a map of Vermont by William Blodget, 1789. An original of this map is in the series described in **LA.77.3.** The series of cartographic materials submitted to the Supreme Court is arranged for the most part in chronological order by dates of cases and thereunder numerically by numbers or other designations assigned to individual items. All of the maps mentioned above are described in more detail in National Archives Special List No. 26, *Pre-Federal Maps in the National Archives: An Annotated List* (1975). For more information about Special List No. 26 see the introduction.

CHAPTER MI
Records of Military Affairs

MI.0.1. During the first year of the Revolutionary War the Continental Congress managed military affairs. It acted as a body, sometimes referring specific matters, such as the need to prepare recruiting instructions or to procure cannon, to numerous ad hoc committees. On June 12, 1776, Congress established a five-member standing committee called the Board of War and Ordnance. Among the numerous duties of the board were "forwarding all despatches from Congress to the colonies and armies, and all monies to be transmitted for the public service by order of Congress"; preserving "all original letters and papers, which shall come into the said office by order of Congress, or otherwise"; and superintending the raising, equipping, and "despatching" of continental troops. The Board of War and Ordnance soon began to do work previously performed by ad hoc committees, but it could act upon no matter of importance without the knowledge and consent of Congress as a whole, to whom the board reported its recommendations. Moreover, Congress continued to appoint ad hoc committees to deal with military affairs from time to time throughout the pre-federal period. During the winter of 1776-77 the Executive Committee at Philadelphia also played a role in military administration.

MI.0.2. The work of the Board of War and Ordnance proved too much for its members, who were fully occupied with other official congressional duties. Therefore, on October 17, 1777, a Board of War, consisting of three commissioners not members of Congress, was established with duties and powers very similar to those of its predecessor. It was provided that the new board "execute all such matters as they shall be directed, and give their opinion on all such subjects as shall be referred to them by Congress: and, in general, to superintend the several branches of the military department; and if, at any time, they think a measure necessary for the public service, to which their powers are incompetent, they shall communicate the same to Congress for their direction therein."

MI.0.3. For a time both the old Board of War and Ordnance and the new Board of War functioned simultaneously. That fact and the practice, even before October 1777, of referring to the first body as the Board of War has made it difficult at times to determine which of the two is being referred to in the journals and other records of the Continental Congress. It compounds matters that both boards, as well as the later Office of the Secretary at War, were also sometimes referred to as the War Office.

MI.0.4. Several changes in the composition of the Board of War were made after its creation. On November 24, 1777, two additional commissioners, also not members of Congress, were authorized. On October 29, 1778, Congress resolved that the board would consist of three commissioners who were not members of Congress and two who were. Thirteen months later Congress resolved that "the departments of the quartermaster general and of the commissaries general of purchases and issues, be for the future under the superintendency and direction of the Board of War. . . ."

MI.0.5. Congress established in February 1781 the Office of the Secretary at War—one part of the general administrative reorganization of that year. The duties and powers of the office included execution of all resolutions of Congress respecting military preparations, transmittal of all orders and resolutions relative to the "military land forces of the United States," preparation of estimates of funds needed for recruiting and paying troops and purchasing supplies, and countersigning military commissions. Until the secretary assumed the office, the Board of War was authorized to perform its functions.

MI.0.6. No Secretary at War actually began to act until after the American victory at Yorktown in October 1781. After the Continental Army was disbanded the principal responsibility of his office was to oversee the conduct of Indian relations and maintain peace on the frontier. From time to time the powers and responsibilities of the secretary were enlarged. On April 10, 1782, the distribution of military clothing and the care of prisoners of war were placed under his direction. On July 25, 1785, the Quartermaster General's Department was abolished; its work subsequently devolved on the War Office. The supplemental western land ordinance of July 9, 1788, provided that the Secretary at War issue bounty-land warrants to Continental Army veterans entitled to them. Despite the enlargement of his powers and responsibilities during this period, the secretary was still obliged to obtain the advice or approval of Congress before acting on many matters.

MI.0.7. By mid-1788 the War Office was conducted by the Secretary at War, three clerks, and a messenger. There had been an assistant secretary, but the office was discontinued in 1786. By the end of 1788 there were fewer than 700 officers and enlisted men in the continental military service.

MI.O.8. The Continental Army originated in 1775 when Congress adopted the military units of the New England colonies that were besieging Boston. Congressional resolutions of November 4, 1775, increased the army on paper to 20,372 soldiers and standardized regimental size. Each regiment was to contain 728 men in 8 companies, each consisting of 1 captain, 2 lieutenants, and 87 men. Additional regiments, which sometimes contained fewer men, were later authorized for such purposes as the Canadian campaigns and the defense of the southern states. Many of the authorized regiments were never at full strength.

MI.O.9. A major reorganization of the Continental Army came on September 16, 1776, when Congress ordered the enlistment of 88 battalions (regiments) for the duration of the war. The units were apportioned among the states, which were to recruit the soldiers and appoint the officers, although the officers would be formally commissioned by Congress. Some of the units raised as a result of this resolution bore designations as state regiments; others were numbered as continental regiments.

MI.O.10. In December 1776 Congress authorized General Washington to raise "from any or all of these United States" 16 infantry battalions "in addition to those already voted . . . ." These "additional regiments" were enlisted regionally, although some were chiefly or solely from one state. They were designated by the names of their commanding officers. Many were subsequently consolidated and adopted into the various "State Lines," taking designations as state regiments.

MI.O.11. The army was reduced to 80 battalions, each containing 585 men, by congressional authorization in 1778. In October 1780 Congress ordered that after January 1, 1781, the Continental Army would consist of 4 regiments of cavalry or light dragoons, 4 regiments of artillery, 50 regiments of infantry, and 1 regiment of artificers. Finally, on June 2, 1784, the Continental Congress directed the commanding general to discharge all troops in the service of the United States, retaining only 80 privates, with a proportionate number of officers, to guard the stores at Fort Pitt, West Point, and other magazines.

MI.O.12. An infantry regiment in the Continental Army typically consisted of 8 to 10 companies, each commanded by a captain. Field officers usually included a colonel, a lieutenant colonel, and a major. A regimental staff was made up of an adjutant, quartermaster, surgeon, surgeon's mate, paymaster, and chaplain. Infantry regiments were often called simply regiments or battalions. Cavalry and artillery regiments were organized in a similar manner. A company of cavalry was frequently called a troop. An artillery company contained specialized soldiers, such as bombardiers, gunners, and matrosses. Artificers were civilian or military mechanics and artisans employed by the army to provide services. They included blacksmiths, coopers, carpenters, harnessmakers, and wheelwrights.

MI.0.13.   Many military records related to the pre-federal period are described in *Guide to Genealogical Research in the National Archives* (revised 1985). That publication contains separate chapters on military, naval, and other categories of records, with thorough descriptions and directions on how to use them to develop genealogical information. Anyone planning to consult pre-federal records for genealogical information should use that guide.

MI.0.14.   There are some maps and other cartographic records pertaining to military affairs among the records described in **LA.0.6.** and **LA.77.3.**

Record Group 360

Records of the Continental and Confederation Congresses and the Constitutional Convention

MI.360.1.   Record Group 360 consists primarily of PCC (M247, 204 rolls) and Miscellaneous PCC (M332, 10 rolls).* For additional information about those bodies of records and indexes thereto, see the introduction.

LETTERS AND REPORTS RECEIVED BY CONGRESS FROM THE BOARD OF WAR AND THE SECRETARY AT WAR

MI.360.2.   The series **reports of the Board of War and Ordnance, 1776-81** (Item 147, M247, rolls 157-160), consists of six volumes of reports, memorials, and petitions on matters that were referred to the board by Congress or that came to the board's attention in other ways. Some reports contain comments on a number of subjects and bear marginal notes for each topic indicating whether Congress agreed, disagreed, or postponed action. Subjects of the reports include recruitment, training, and disposition of troops; commission-

---

*For a complete list of National Archives Microfilm Publications cited in this guide, see Appendix A.

ing and promotion of officers; procurement and distribution of military supplies; defense of frontier settlements against Indian attacks; treatment of prisoners of war; and problems relating to supervision of departments of the army. Many reports are endorsed to show the date considered by Congress and action taken. They are arranged generally in chronological order.

MI.360.3. A few additional reports of the board, submitted in late 1781, are in **letters from the Board of War and Ordnance, 1780-81** (Item 148, M247, roll 161). Volume 1 of the two-volume series contains letters of the board, with related documents. Volume 2 mainly contains reports with related documents. Subjects covered by both volumes are very similar to those in Item 147 (**MI.360.2.**). Both letters and reports bear endorsements that usually give the date read in Congress and frequently the names of persons or bodies to whom subjects were referred by Congress. Within each volume the records are arranged generally in chronological order.

MI.360.4. The series **letters from Joseph Carleton and Thomas Hutchins, 1779-88, and records relating to military affairs** (Item 60, M247, roll 74), contains 159 pages of letters, mostly to Congress, from Joseph Carleton, Secretary and Paymaster of the Board of War and Ordnance. Carleton also was the person primarily responsible for conducting the affairs of the War Department during the interim between the tenure of Secretaries at War Benjamin Lincoln and Henry Knox, October 1783-April 1785. His letters concern such matters as an estimate of supplies needed by Gen. George Rogers Clark for an expedition into Indian country, discharge of invalid pensioners from the Northern Army under a congressional resolution of 1782, and an estimate of funds for the subsistence of commanding officers at Albany, Fort Pitt, and West Point. Most of the letters are endorsed with such information as the date written, the date read, and action taken. They are arranged generally in chronological order. Thomas Hutchins was Geographer of the United States. His letters are described in **LA.360.3.** The other military records in this series are described in **MI.360.43.**

MI.360.5. The series **letters and reports from Maj. Gen. Benjamin Lincoln, Secretary at War, 1781-83** (Item 149, M247, rolls 162-163), concerns matters on which the secretary was asked to report or about which he sought the advice or approval of Congress. Subjects include moving troops; providing quarters for prisoners of war; procuring uniforms, provisions, and ammunition for the Southern Army; developing procedures for the promotion of officers; developing plans for the retirement of officers and enlisted men; locating and constructing magazines and arsenals; disbanding the Invalid

Corps; and hiring out prisoners of war as laborers. The three volumes also include a few reports of committees of Congress appointed to consider Lincoln's reports and a few relevant resolutions of Congress. Most of the letters and reports bear endorsements giving the date of the communication, the subject, the date read in Congress, and action taken. The entire series is generally in chronological order.

MI.360.6. Similarly arranged and endorsed are the documents in the series **letters and reports from Maj. Gen. Henry Knox, Secretary at War, 1785-88** (Items 150-151, M247, rolls 164-165). Item 150 contains letters through October 1787, in two volumes. Volume 3 makes up the second series, Item 151, and contains the remainder of Knox's letters through July 1788 and all his reports, 1785-88. The letters convey information to or request advice from Congress. They often transmit copies of Knox's correspondence with Richard Butler, Superintendent of Indian Affairs for the Northern Department; Brig. Gen. Josiah Harmar, commander of the troops on the frontiers; Arthur St. Clair, Governor of the Northwest Territory; and officers stationed in the Ohio Valley. The reports relate to military administration, negotiations with the Indians, distribution of land in the Ohio Valley to Revolutionary War veterans, court-martial procedures, and other subjects. They also contain recommendations on memorials and petitions.

LETTERS AND REPORTS RECEIVED BY CONGRESS FROM (MOSTLY GENERAL) OFFICERS AND HEADS OF STAFF DEPARTMENTS OF THE CONTINENTAL ARMY

MI.360.7. Correspondence from officers of the Continental Army to the Continental Congress and its officers and members makes up a large body of records in RG 360. *Index: PCC* entries give a brief description, including the date, location from which sent, subject, and recipient of each letter. They are listed under the names of the writers, which are merged into all other entries in the index and are arranged alphabetically by surname and thereunder chronologically. This guide lists the correspondence in a tabular format, also arranged alphabetically by the writer's surname, which gives his rank and position, the date span of the series or subseries of correspondence, the PCC item number, the microfilm publication roll number, and the quantity of the records.

MI.360.8. The writers addressed the bulk of their correspondence to the Congress as a body, generally through its president. There is also a significant number of letters sent to the Secretary of

Congress, the various War Offices, committee chairmen, and members of Congress. Very nearly all the correspondence listed is by the writer indicated. That of General McIntosh, however, contains one significant letter, signed by several brigadier generals, protesting the promotion of Thomas Conway to major general in 1778. The letters of Gen. John Paterson are all cosigned by Gen. Enoch Poor, for they all concern defense of their conduct at Fort Ticonderoga and requests for a court-martial. The single letter from Col. Samuel Patterson was sent to Brig. Gen. William Smallwood and forwarded by him to Congress. A few other series contain a small number of letters from subordinates to the officers listed, who in turn forwarded them to Congress. The subjects covered by the correspondence are many and varied, including matters related to many civil concerns and Indian affairs, as well as military matters. They are most easily determined at a general level by consulting the descriptive pamphlet accompanying National Archives Microfilm Publication M247 or *Index: PCC.*

MI.360.9. All of the correspondence was bound into volumes in the 19th century and consists mostly of originals, with a few contemporary copies, especially the entire subseries concerning Gen. Ethan Allen. All of the documents are in English except those from General Pulaski, which are in French. Nearly every series or subseries contains enclosures. Some of this is correspondence to the officers that they forwarded to Congress. There are many references to enclosures that no longer accompany the correspondence. Some of those documents are scattered among other items of PCC.

MI.360.10. Most of the correspondence is endorsed, usually by Secretary of Congress Charles Thomson, with a document number, the name and rank of the writer, the date and place from which written, the date received or read, the nature of the action taken by Congress, and the subject of the letter. Generally the larger series or subseries of correspondence are fully endorsed, but many of the smaller ones have endorsements lacking a subject indicator and document number. All are arranged chronologically except that for General Du Coudray, which is in no discernible order. For letters from the Marquis de Lafayette concerning foreign affairs, see **FO.360.43.** Many letters from line and staff military officers are in the series **[miscellaneous] letters addressed to Congress, 1775-89** (Item 78, M247, rolls 90-104); see **CC.360.26.**

MI.360.11. The table consists of four columns. The first contains the writer's name and rank. The rank listed first is that under which the author wrote the first letter in the series. A rank resulting from a subsequent promotion is listed in parentheses where relevant. Ranks and titles connected by the word "and" indicate positions held concurrently. Each officer has one entry except John Pierce, whose correspondence is filed in two separate items of PCC. A paragraph number is inserted after every fourth entry for convenience in cross-referencing and indexing. The dates in the second column indicate those of the bulk of the correspondence. A few series contain single letters with dates falling on either side the span given here. All of the records are reproduced in M247, for which the corresponding roll numbers are given in column 3. They are preceded by the PCC item number, separated by a colon. The last column indicates the quantity of the correspondence of each individual. This is usually given in number of pages, but when the amount reaches one or more bound volumes, the number of volumes is given.

Writer(s): rank	Dates	Item No. of PCC: Roll No. of M247	Volume of Records
MI.360.12.			
William Alexander, Lord Stirling: Col.(Maj. Gen.)	1775-79	162:179	242 pp.
Ethan Allen: Brig. Gen.	1781	164:181	8 pp.
Charles Armand, Marquis de la Rouerie: Col. (Brig. Gen.)	1777-84	164:181	168 pp.
John Armstrong: Brig. Gen.	1776-78	162:179	37 pp.
MI.360.13.			
Benedict Arnold: Col. (Maj. Gen.)	1775-80	162:179	208 pp.
Ephraim Blaine: Deputy Commissary Gen. and Comm'y Gen. of Purchases	1776-81	165:182	128 pp.
James Clinton: Brig. Gen.	1778-79	163:180	12 pp.
Thomas Conway: Brig. Gen. (Maj. Gen.)	1777-78	159:178	58 pp.
MI.360.14.			
Philippe Charles Tronson Du Coudray: Maj. Gen.	1776-77	156:176	93 pp.
Louis L. Duportail: Brig. Gen. (Maj. Gen.)	1778-82	164:181	32 pp.
Horatio Gates: Brig. Gen. (Maj. Gen.)	1775-82	154:174	2 vols.
Nathanael Greene: Maj. Gen. and QM Gen.	1776-85	155:175	2 vols.

Writer(s): rank	Dates	Item No. of PCC: Roll No. of M247	Volume of Records
MI.360.15.			
Edward Hand: Brig. Gen.	1777-78	159:178	45 pp.
Josiah Harmar: Lt. Col. (Brig. Gen.)	1784-85; 1788-89	163:180	111 pp.
William Heath: Maj. Gen.	1775-82	157:177	1 vol.
Robert Howe: Brig. Gen. (Maj. Gen.)	1776-85	160:178	203 pp.
M.360.16.			
Baron Johann De Kalb: Maj. Gen.	1777-79	164:181	28 pp.
John Laurens: Col.	1778-82	165:182	21 pp.
The Marquis de Lafayette: Maj. Gen.	1777-81	156:176	259 pp.
Charles Lee: Maj. Gen.	1776-80	158:177	162 pp.
MI.360.17.			
Andrew Lewis: Brig. Gen.	1776-77	159:178	46 pp.
Benjamin Lincoln: Maj. Gen.	1777-80	158:177	390 pp.
David Luckett: Lt.	1785	163:180	22 pp.
Alexander McDougall: Maj. Gen.	1776-81	161:179	60 pp.
MI.360.18.			
Lachlan McIntosh: Brig. Gen.	1778-81	162:179	53 pp.
Hugh Mercer: Brig. Gen.	1776	159:178	95 pp.
Thomas Mifflin: Maj. Gen. and QM Gen.	1776-80	161:179	78 pp.
Richard Montgomery: Brig. Gen.	1775	161:179	122 pp.
MI.360.19.			
George Morgan: Gen.	1776-84	163:180	missing
John Morgan: Director-Gen. and Chief Physician of the Medical Dept.	1776-80	63:77	208 pp.
William Moultrie: Brig. Gen.	1778-82	158:177	100 pp.
Peter Muhlenberg: Brig. Gen.	1777-79	163:180	8 pp.

Writer(s): rank	Dates	Item No. of PCC: Roll No. of M247	Volume of Records
MI.360.20.			
Lewis Nicola: Col.	1779-80	163:180	226 pp.
John Nixon: Brig. Gen.	1778	163:180	4 pp.
William Palfrey: Paymaster Gen.	1776-80	165:182	151 pp.
Samuel H. Parsons: Brig. Gen.	1777-79	161:179	24 pp.
MI.360.21.			
John Paterson: Brig. Gen. and Enoch Poor: Brig. Gen.	1777-78	163:180	8 pp.
Samuel Patterson: Col.	1778	163:180	4 pp.
Charles Pettit: Asst. QM Gen.	1778-81	192:199	136 pp.
Timothy Pickering: QM Gen.	1777-84	192:199	140 pp.
MI.360.22.			
John Pierce: Col. and Deputy Paymaster Gen. (Paymaster Gen.)	1780-83	165:182	127 pp.
John Pierce: Paymaster Gen. (Comm. of Army Accounts)	1784-88	62:76	254 pp.
Casimir Pulaski: Brig. Gen.	1778-79	164:181	115 pp.
Israel Putnam: Maj. Gen.	1776-78	159:178	138 pp.
MI.360.23.			
Arthur St. Clair: Col. (Maj. Gen.)	1776-83	161:179	52 pp.
Philip Schuyler: Maj. Gen.	1775-85	153:172-3	3 vols.
William Smallwood: Brig. Gen.	1778	161:179	48 pp.
Joseph Spencer: Maj. Gen.	1777	161:179	12 pp.
MI.360.24.			
John Stark: Brig. Gen.	1778; 1781	162:179	10 pp.
Adam Stephen: Brig. Gen.	1776-77	162:179	18 pp.
Friedrich von Steuben: Maj. Gen. and Inspector Gen.	1777-85	164:181	190 pp.
John Sullivan: Brig. Gen. (Maj. Gen.)	1776-79	160:178	343 pp.

Writer(s): rank	Dates	Item No. of PCC: Roll No. of M247	Volume of Records
MI.360.25.			
William Thompson, Brig. Gen.	1776-81	159:178	64 pp.
Artemas Ward: Maj. Gen.	1775-76	159:178	34 pp.
George Washington: Gen. and Commander in Chief	1775-84	152:166-71	11 vols.
Anthony Wayne: Col. (Brig. Gen.)	1776-81	161:179	62 pp.
MI.360.26.			
George Weedon: Brig. Gen.	1777-80	159:178	18 pp.
David Wooster: Brig. Gen.	1775-76	161:179	72 pp.

MI.360.27. Fair copies of letters sent to Congress by general officers, for which there are also series of originals, are in four series, all titled **transcripts of letters from [officer's name and dates].** The officers are Gen. George Washington (Item 169, M247, rolls 186-188) and Major Generals Schuyler (Item 170, M247, roll 189), Gates (Item 171, M247, roll 190), and Greene (Item 172, M247, roll 191). All four series are missing copies of a few of the letters found in the originals (Washington, **MI.360.25.**; Schuyler, **MI.360.23.**; and Gates and Greene, **MI.360.14.**). The three series for Gates, Greene, and Schuyler also contain copies of a few documents that are not found among the originals. Schuyler's series also contains copies of his correspondence with subordinates. The quantity of records in all of the series of copies is roughly equal to that of the corresponding series of originals.

MI.360.28. The series **letters of Nathanael Greene, with various papers relating to the Quartermaster's Department, 1778-80** (Item 173, M247, rolls 192-193), consists of documents purchased by the Department of State in 1833. They generally do not duplicate other items of PCC concerning Greene's activities as Quartermaster General. Volume 1 of the five in the series consists mainly of returns submitted to Greene by deputies in his department. Volumes 2 and 4 contain copies of letters, 1779, from Greene to his deputies and others concerning the department's activities. Reports submitted to the Quartermaster General by his deputies and other officers are in volume 3. Volume 5 consists chiefly of letters received, 1780.

REPORTS AND OTHER RECORDS OF COMMITTEES
SENT BY CONGRESS TO THE ARMY

MI.360.29. The series **other reports of committees of Congress, 1776-88: reports on the Committees of Conference with the Commander in Chief at Cambridge, 1775, and Valley Forge, 1778-79, and the proceedings of the Convention of Committees at New Haven, 1778, and Hartford, 1779-80** (Item 33, M247, roll 40), contains reports, correspondence, minutes, and other records of three congressional committees sent to confer with General Washington concerning military administration and conduct of the war. In addition to the two locations listed in the series title, one of the committees met with the Commander in Chief in Philadelphia, 1778-79. The records of each of the three committees are arranged chronologically and total nearly 300 pages. More than 250 pages of other records relating to the committee sent to Valley Forge are included in the one-volume series **letters and papers relative to the Quartermaster's Department, 1777-84** (Item 192, M247, roll 199). Included are 60 pages of original correspondence from Congress to the committee.

MI.360.30. The first 56 pages of the one volume constituting the series **letters and papers relating to Canadian affairs, Sullivan's expedition, and the northern Indians, 1775-79** (Item 166, M247, roll 183), consist of the records of two committees sent by Congress to investigate military affairs. One subseries is a 1775 report of the committee appointed by Congress to confer with General Schuyler at Fort Ticonderoga. Another consists of letters sent to Congress by a committee sent to investigate and report on affairs in Canada, May 1776.

MI.360.31. Records of a committee appointed in April 1780 to go to General Washington's headquarters and assist in effecting reforms of the military establishment are found in two series of PCC. **Record book of the Committee to Headquarters, 1780** (Item 11, M247, roll 22), consists of one volume containing the committee's final report and proceedings and copies of its correspondence. Three volumes make up the series **other reports of committees of Congress, 1776-88: letters and other records of the Committee to Headquarters (Philip Schuyler, John Mathews, and Nathaniel Peabody) appointed to confer with the Commander in Chief, 1780** (Item 39, M247, roll 46).

REPORTS OF OTHER COMMITTEES OF CONGRESS

MI.360.32. Committees of Congress, either standing or ad hoc, were assigned from time to time to investigate military matters. Often this was the result of memorials, petitions, or inquiries from outside Congress. Such activity produced 15 groups of records, consisting of both series and subseries, which are presented here in tabular form. The groupings were determined by the 19th-century custodians of the records. Most are series and contain several reports, each from a different committee, and some related records. The proportion of related records to reports is much greater in the records concerning peacetime military establishments and the Philadelphia Mutiny than in the other categories. Nearly all of the reports and a few of the related documents are endorsed with a date, a subject, a document number, an indication of the action taken by Congress, and, less frequently, the names of committee members. Only the subseries concerning the activities of Quakers is entirely lacking in endorsements. Many reports have marginal notes indicating such things as congressional agreement on or postponement of the matter annotated. All of the 15 series or subseries are arranged chronologically by the dates of the reports with related documents interspersed, except the one concerning Quakers, which has no discernible arrangement.

MI.360.33. The four columns of the table contain, for each series or subseries, a general subject indicator, dates of the reports, item number of PCC and roll number of National Archives Microfilm Publication M247 in which the records are found, and the quantity of records in pages or volumes. The series or subseries are arranged in the table alphabetically by general subject.

Subjects(s)	Dates	Item No. of PCC: Roll No. of M247	Volume of Records
Army operations, supplies, and personnel	1775-83; 1785	21:30	1 vol.
The Board of War	1776-81	27:34	1 vol.
The Clothier General's Department	1778-82	31:38	93 pp.
The Commissary General's Department	1777-80; 1784	29:36	153 pp.
The Inspector General's Department	1780; 1782	22:30	18 pp.

Subjects(s)	Dates	Item No. of PCC: Roll No. of M247	Volume of Records
The Medical Department	1777-82	22:30	90 pp.
Military posts, loss of	1776-78	29:36	72 pp.
The Paymaster General's Department	1776; 1780; 1784; 1787	22:30	14 pp.
Peacetime military establishments	1783-84	38:45	206 pp.
The Philadelphia Mutiny	1783-86	38:45	1 vol.
Prisoners of war	1776-79; 1781-83; 1786	28:35	123 pp.
Quakers, charges against and imprisonment of, mainly on suspicion of corresponding with the enemy	1776-78	53:66	38 pp.
The Quartermaster General's Department	1777-85	22:30	85 pp.
Recruitment of troops for the defense of the western territory	1785-87	30:37	28 pp.
Secretary at War, Office of the	1781-88	27:34	1 vol.

OTHER SUBJECT-RELATED RECORDS

MI.360.34. PCC and Miscellaneous PCC contain several other series or subseries, in many cases brought together by their 19th-century custodians, that are not primarily congressional committee reports or correspondence but are related by the subject to which each group of documents pertains. Since the subjects are too diverse for them to be described in tabular form, they are presented here in paragraphs arranged by larger subject headings.

MI.360.35. Records in several series pertain directly to British military activities during the Revolutionary War. **Papers and affidavits relating to the plunderings, burnings, and ravages committed by the British, 1775-84** (Item 53, M247, roll 66), consist of about 130 pages of records on the stated subjects. They are arranged roughly according to subject. Interspersed are several documents that seem to bear no relation to British activities. **Letters and papers concerning the Convention Troops, 1777-80** (Item 57, M247, roll 70), concern the 5,700 British troops taken prisoner at Saratoga after the surrender of Gen. John Burgoyne to Generals Gates and Heath in

October 1777. Under the terms of the Convention of Saratoga of October 17, 1777, they were pledged to be returned to England and not to serve again in America. The records, bound into one volume, are arranged chronologically, and many bear endorsements. Some 140 pages of records about efforts by British and U.S. representatives to arrange exchanges of prisoners, including the Convention Troops, are in the series **letters and documents relative to exchange of officers, narration of a journey to the western country, and other documents, 1777-88** (Item 167, M247, roll 184). The records are generally in chronological order.

MI.360.36. The series **records and letters relating to the trial of certain counterfeiters in New York and to the British evacuation of New York, 1783** (Item 52, M247, roll 66), totals some 175 pages, consisting mainly of copies of correspondence between British commander Sir Guy Carleton and George Clinton, Governor of New York. In addition to the case of the counterfeiters, the subjects include treatment of Loyalists; exchange of prisoners of war; British confiscation of property, including slaves and "archives"; and confiscation of Loyalist property. The records are in no particular order. "Inspection rolls of Negroes carried away by the British upon the evacuation of New York City" are two volumes in Miscellaneous PCC (M332, roll 7). Another inspection roll and copies of the correspondence between Carleton and U.S. commissioners overseeing the "embarkation of Negroes at New York City" make up 36 pages of item 53 of PCC, described in **MI.360.35.**

MI.360.37. Two series in RG 360 contain groups of records about specific military campaigns. **Letters and other records relating to charges against Gen. J. Sullivan and Dr. J. Morgan, and to British advances in the Mohawk Valley, 1776-79** (Item 63, M247, roll 77), contain 36 pages concerning Sullivan's unsuccessful raid against the British on Staten Island and 68 pages about the British advance down the Mohawk Valley and capture of Fort Ticonderoga. All three events took place in the late summer of 1777. **Letters and papers relating to Canadian affairs, Sullivan's expedition, and the northern Indians, 1775-79** (Item 166, M247, roll 183), include 64 pages of documents on a proposed, but never completed, expedition into Canada to be led by the Marquis de Lafayette in 1778 and 242 pages on preparations for a campaign against the Six Nations to be led by Maj. Gen. John Sullivan in 1779. All four subseries on real or proposed military campaigns are arranged in no particular order.

MI.360.38. The series **copies of letters and papers relative to the trial of Capt. Richard Lippincott, 1782** (Item 194, M247, roll 200), appears to be a supplement to the correspondence of Gen.

George Washington (see **MI.360.25.**). Lippincott was a member of the Associated Loyalists who was accused of killing a prisoner. The series consists of correspondence and copies of the proceedings of his trial sent to Washington by Sir Guy Carleton, British commander during the occupation of New York.

OTHER RECORDS

MI.360.39. Copies of a congressional resolution of April 14, 1777, revising the articles of war are in Miscellaneous PCC (M332, roll 9).

MI.360.40. The series **letters and reports, 1781-88, from John Pierce, Paymaster General and Commissioner for [of] Army Accounts, and records relating to investigations of the Treasury office, 1780-81** (Item 62, M247, roll 76), contains a 12-page "declaration" by Col. Benjamin Flower, dated August 19, 1778, concerning his conduct as Commissary General of Military Stores.

MI.360.41. **Papers respecting unsettled accounts, 1788, and returns of stores, 1783-84** (Item 143, M247, roll 155), contain returns of medical supplies held by the Continental Army at Albany and Philadelphia in early 1784 and of stores of military supplies held at various places in 1783-84. The inventory was requested by Congress as part of its effort to prepare a report on the operation of the Board of Treasury (see also **FI.360.11.**).

MI.360.42. In Miscellaneous PCC (M332, roll 10) is a map of the siege of Yorktown prepared by Jean Baptiste Gouvion, a Continental Army lieutenant colonel of engineers who played an important role in that campaign. It shows the positions of U.S., French, and British forces, the siege and defensive works constructed by both sides, topographical features, roads and streets, and buildings. A brief chronology of the siege, from September 28 to October 17, 1781, is written on the map.

MI.360.43. The series **letters from Joseph Carleton and Thomas Hutchins, 1779-88, and records relating to military affairs, [1777-90]** (Item 60, M247, roll 74), contains 110 pages of documents, 1777-90, consisting largely of plans for reorganizations of the Continental Army; proposals for raising specific kinds of troop units; and plans, drawings, and maps of various towns, harbors, fortifications, buildings, and troop positions. The letters are described in **MI.360.4.** and **LA.360.3.**

MI.360.44. Blank U.S. Army commissions, from 1777 to 1778, are among Miscellaneous PCC (M332, rolls 9 and 10). One is framed for display purposes.

MI.360.45. A number of records pertaining wholly or partly to military expenditures are described in the chapter on records of fiscal affairs. For example, see the reports of the various commissioners of military departments (**FI.360.7.**), the records of the commissioners appointed to settle the accounts of the military departments (**FI.93.2.** and **FI.217.16.**), and the reports sent to Congress by the Board of Treasury and other fiscal agencies and officials (**FI.360.2.-FI.360.6.**).

Record Group 15
Records of the Veterans Administration

MI.15.1. The first Congress of the United States passed an act on September 29, 1789, providing for payment of military pensions to Revolutionary War veterans and their dependents—the first in a long series of pension laws. For further information on pensions and bounty lands, see the relevant subject chapter.

MI.15.2. Registers of final payment certificates for military service issued by Paymaster General and Commissioner for Army Accounts John Pierce, 1783-87, were published beginning in 1786. RG 15 contains an incomplete set (volumes 3-4) of the eight-volume publication. For a complete set see **MI.53.5.**

Record Group 39
Records of the Bureau of Accounts (Treasury)

MI.39.1. The Bureau of Accounts was created in the Department of Treasury in 1940 to succeed the Office of the Commissioner of Accounts and Deposits, which was the last in a long line of predecessor agencies. Some records of those predecessors date to the pre-federal period. Among the bureau's functions are maintaining a unified system of central accounts, producing central financial reports, and furnishing technical guidance and assistance to Treasury bureaus.

MI.39.2. **Journal of expenditures relating to the armies of the continental and confederation governments, 1776-84** (M1015, roll 1), was probably centrally maintained in the Paymaster General's Department. Most of the accounts are for the period 1779-81 and concern continental military organizations, especially regiments, and individual line and staff officers of the Continental Army. Most of the transactions recorded pertain to money, clothing, and unspecified articles received by the organizations or individuals having accounts. These organizations or individuals used the money they received for the pay and subsistence of officers and men, for expenses of recruiting, and for supplying Continental Army staff departments. In addition to the dates given for most of the transactions, there are often notes indicating volume and page numbers to which entries were posted. However, no such books have been identified. Included in the ledger are accounts for numerous military units in all 13 states. Arrangement is by titles of accounts, thereunder by debit and credit entries, and thereunder in general chronological order.

Record Group 45

Naval Records Collection of the Office of Naval Records and Library

MI.45.1. The Naval Records Collection was begun in 1882 when the Librarian of the Navy Department, then in the Office of Naval Intelligence, began to collect for publication naval documents relating to the Civil War. In the early 1900s, the office began collecting older records of naval bureaus and records relating to naval personnel and operations during the American Revolution. All of the entries for RG 45 in this chapter describe copies of records in state and private collections that were placed in the Navy Department under the act of 1913 mentioned in **NA.45.1.**

MI.45.2. The one-volume series **"Virginia Journal of the General Assembly," 1776**, is a negative photostatic copy that, in spite of its title, was kept by the Privy Council, also known as the Council of State, in Virginia. It consists of daily entries of business, each beginning with the date and the names of the members present and ending with the copied signatures of those members. Attendees include John Page, Dudley Digges, Bartholomew Dandridge, John Blair, and Benjamin Harrison, Jr. Actions of the council include such orders as those issuing warrants for the pay of military and naval personnel; authorizing purchases of arms, provisions, and other military and naval supplies; authorizing a commission to a state naval officer; ordering that the Declaration of Independence be "solemnly proclaimed" at the capitol in Williamsburg; and directing that persons be paid for rendering services to the state, such as transportation of troops and blacksmithing. Also recorded are the receipt and registration by the council of warrants from the Virginia State Navy Board in favor of various persons, the issuance of permits to persons and vessels for the export of goods from the state, and transmittal of letters of Virginia's delegates to the Continental Congress. Copies of some instructions to military and naval officers are included. The journal is arranged chronologically, with a number of pages missing.

MI.45.3. **Massachusetts records pertaining to the Penobscot expedition, 1779**, is a single volume copied from volume 145 of the "Massachusetts Revolutionary Archives" in February 1915. It consists mainly of "Orders of Council respecting the Penobscot Expedition," July 1-August 26, 1779, which contains many orders of the Massachusetts Board of War; copies of general orders, July 21-August 13, 1779, taken from the "Adjutant's Book" and certified by the expedition's adjutant general, Jeremiah Hill; and depositions of a number of participating military and naval officers concerning the military and naval operation of the expedition, made before a court of inquiry in September and October 1779. Among the depositions are those of Massachusetts Brig. Gen. Solomon Lovell, who was in charge of the troops; Capt. Dudley Saltonstall of the Continental Navy, who commanded the naval forces; and Lt. Col. Paul Revere, who was in charge of the expedition's artillery. The volume is arranged in parts as described and thereunder generally in chronological order.

MI.45.4. The series **orderly book of Josiah Fletcher, Adjutant of Col. John Jacob's First Massachusetts State Regiment of Foot (the "Cavendish Regiment"), 1778**, is a one-volume negative photostatic copy. The first and largest part of the volume contains general, brigade, and regimental orders, May 9-December 16, 1778, issued at various places in Rhode Island and Massachusetts, including Swansey, Middletown, Freetown, Tiverton, Providence, Portsmouth, Little Compton, and "Camp before Newport," by Gens. John Sullivan, Ezekiel Cornell, and James Varnum, and by Colonel Jacobs and other officers commanding Jacobs' regiment. Subjects of the orders include troop movements and dispositions; erection of gun batteries; patrols by "Watch Boats"; engagements with the enemy; the issuance of clothing, provisions, and ammunition to troops; the granting of furloughs; company roll calls and troop returns; instructions for the use of signs and countersigns and for performing guard duty; appointment of officers of the day; appointment and announcement of the results of courts-martial for the trial of deserters and other persons; a court of inquiry into the conduct of certain officers of Jacobs' regiment for "Insulting the Inhabitants and Taking away their Beds"; and the celebration of the "Feast of St. John" by Freemasons. The second part of the volume consists principally of weekly regimental returns for Jacobs' regiment, May 6-December 24, 1778. Information contained in each return, in addition to the date and the location of the regiment, includes the name of the officer commanding; the names of the company commanders; and the numbers of officers and men in each company who were present, "Wanting," sick, on command, on furlough, dead, deserted, and discharged. Many officers are named. The book is arranged in two parts as described and thereunder in generally chronological in order.

MI.45.5. **Minutes of the Massachusetts Board of War, 1776-81**, consist of five volumes of photostatic copies of volumes numbered 148, 149 (parts 1 and 2), and 150 (parts 1 and 2). The minutes document the daily proceedings of the Massachusetts Board of War, consisting mainly of orders issued in connection with its dual function of managing both the military and naval forces of the state. Recorded are orders that military supplies of various kinds, including cannon, ordnance stores, provisions, and medicines, be delivered or transported to various places, individuals, or vessels, and that payments be made on the accounts of persons who furnished supplies or performed various services for the state, such as unloading a prize vessel or building and loading vessels. One order specifies the rates of pay of house carpenters, blacksmiths, armorers, and wheelwrights to be employed as artificers at "the Labratory" [sic]. The series is arranged chronologically if viewed in the following order: volume 148; volume 149, part 1; volume 150, part 1; volume 149 part 2; volume 150, part 2. Volumes 148 and 149 have indexes to persons mentioned in the minutes recorded in those volumes.

MI.45.6. **Letters received by the Committee of Safety of the Massachusetts Provincial Congress, 1775**, are negative photostatic copies of pages from volume 193 of the "Massachusetts Revolutionary Archives." The letters are variously addressed and include some to the Committee of Safety and some to Dr. Joseph Warren as president of the "Massachusetts Congress." Among the writers are the selectmen and committees of several Massachusetts towns, the Rhode Island legislature, a group of persons at Montreal, and individuals such as John Hancock and Timothy Pickering. Subjects include the evacuation of Boston; a request from Hancock, made while traveling to the Continental Congress in Philadelphia, for information about the conduct of British troops; requests by towns for troops and military supplies; recommendations for military appointments; offers of assistance by Rhode Island and Connecticut; an outbreak of smallpox at Charlestown; and the enlistment of troops, purchase of boats, and procurement of military supplies. The letters are generally in chronological order.

Record Group 49
Records of the Bureau of Land Management

MI.49.1. The Offices of the Secretary of the Treasury and the Register of the Treasury handled disposition of the public domain until April 25, 1812, when the General Land Office was established in the Department of the Treasury. The General Land Office was moved to the Department of the Interior in 1849 and consolidated with other functions in 1946 to form the Bureau of Land Management.

MI.49.2. Virginia records pertaining to Revolutionary War military and naval service, 1776-87, were copied in about 1832 from a volume among the records described in **PE.15.8.-PE.15.10.** titled "Virginia Claims: Communications from Officers of the State of Virginia and General Government." Included are extracts from the proceedings of a board of officers that met in Richmond, VA, in 1783 from the journal of the Virginia State Navy Board; abstracts from lists of warrants issued to Virginia veterans based on half- pay schedules; a list of officers who served in the Illinois Regiment under George Rogers Clark; a record of expenditures for "Colonel Crokett's" regiment; a payroll for the Virginia schooner *Patriot*; and abstracts of a muster roll of Capt. Robert George's Company of Artillery serving in the Illinois Department. The records are arranged chronologically by the dates on which they were copied.

Record Group 53
Records of the Bureau of the Public Debt

MI.53.1. From 1776 to 1817, subscriptions to government loans were handled by offices of the commissioners of loans established in the states under supervision of the Continental Congress and continued under the federal government. In 1817 the duties of the loan offices passed to the Second Bank of the United States, and upon expiration of its charter to a succession of offices in the Department of the Treasury. All of the records from RG 53 described in this chapter are from the subgroup General Records from the Central Treasury Records.

MI.53.2. The first three series (**MI.53.2.-MI.53.4.**) are records submitted to Paymaster General and Commissioner for Army Accounts John Pierce as evidence of Revolutionary War service. The two-volume series **"Sundry Army Accounts, Albany,"** **1776-80** (M1015, roll 2), mainly contains entries for military expenditures in New York state and Canada, including pay of troops; purchase of arms, provisions, and clothing; recruiting expenses; prize money for prizes taken in the St. Lawrence River; and expenditures made in connection with prisoners of war. The volume contains accounts for individuals including Deputy Adjutant General John Trumbull; Deputy Paymaster General Jonathan Trumbull, Jr.; Deputy Paymaster General Morgan Lewis; Gens. Richard Montgomery, David Wooster, Benedict Arnold, Philip Schuyler, John Sullivan, Horatio Gates, and Benjamin Lincoln; Dr. Jonathan Pots; Commodore Jacobus Wynkoop; and many other military line and staff officers and private persons. There are also accounts with headings such as "Victualling Account," "Pay of the Army," and "General Hospital." A separate section of the volume concerns private business accounts in the early 19th century. Both sections are arranged by account and thereunder chronologically.

MI.53.3. **Company record of the 1st Pennsylvania Line Regiment, 1779-80,** is a single volume containing a payroll, a muster roll, a list of absentees for the regiment, and accounts of money paid or due to the officers and men of the regiment, March 1779-March 1780. Information given in the accounts includes the name and rank of individuals paid or due money, dates and amounts of payments, and whether persons due payment were dead, deserters, discharged, resigned, or sick. Arrangement is chronological by 2- and 3-month periods and thereunder by company.

MI.53.4. **Company book of Capt. Aaron Ogden, 1782-83,** consists mainly of muster rolls of Ogden's Company of the 1st New Jersey Regiment, January-October 1782, and accounts for enlisted men, January 1782-March 1783. Also included are registers of furloughs, courts-martial, and deserters; statistical returns for company supplies and personnel; and a size roll of the company for 1782, which includes the age, height, birthplace, residence, trade, enlistment date, and race of all company members. The records are arranged in no discernible order. A partial table of contents is at the front of the single volume.

MI.53.5. **Records relating to the certificates of indebtedness issued by the Paymaster General, 1783-87** (M1015, rolls 5 and 6), consist of eight volumes. Four are a complete set of *Register of the Certificates, Issued by John Pierce, Esquire, Paymaster General, and Commissioner of the [for] Army Accounts, for the United States* (1786). The other four volumes include an incomplete set, volumes 3 and 4, of the same; a manuscript register, from the 1780s, for about 300 of the certificates; and a copy of the register as published in condensed form in *Seventeenth Report of the National Society of the Daughters of the American Revolution* (S. Doc. 988, 63d Cong., 3d sess., 1915). Under resolutions of the Continental Congress of June 20 and July 4, 1783, John Pierce was authorized to settle all accounts between the United States and officers and men of the Continental Army and to give them interest-bearing certificates showing the sums due them. Certificates were issued for pay, commutation, currency depreciation, and other sums due. The complete set of registers published by Child lists certificates numbered 1 to 93846 issued from July 11, 1783, to March 2, 1786. Annotations next to most of the entries indicate that specific certificates were ultimately registered, canceled, or funded by their holders at state loan offices or "at the Treasury." The incomplete set (volumes 3 and 4) of Pierce's registers contains only a few annotations pertaining to the identity of certificate holders. The volumes published in 1786 are arranged sequentially by certificate number from volume 1 through volume 4. The condensed version published in 1915 by the DAR is arranged alphabetically by the surnames of certificate holders and thus serves as an index to the 1786 (complete) edition. It also contains background information about the issuance of Pierce's certificates and a list of blocks of certificate numbers showing states or military units of the soldiers to whom they were issued.

Record Group 59

General Records of the Department of State

MI.59.1. The Department of Foreign Affairs was established by an act of July 1789 and 2 months later was designated the Department of State by the same Congress. It was assigned such functions as preserving and publishing laws and treaties, keeping the seal of the United States, and serving as custodian of the records of the United States previously held by the Secretary of Congress. The department was also in charge of territorial affairs from 1789 to 1873.

RECORDS OF THE BUREAU OF ROLLS AND LIBRARY

MI.59.2. Two volumes, each a separate series, were presented to the Department of State by Daniel R. Goodloe in 1883. Both, he said, were "rescued from the flames by a boy . . . sixteen years old on the night of the 24th August, 1814, when the Capitol and other public buildings were destroyed by the British forces." Approximately one-half of every page of the first volume is missing, according to Goodloe, because of "exposure to the weather, in an out-house." That book, **statements of accounts of paymasters of Virginia, Maryland, and Delaware, 1782-84,** shows accounts for many paymasters and other officers of the states named, as well as Pennsylvania, Massachusetts, and Connecticut. Typical entries in the accounts pertain to pay of officers, recruiting expenses, payments of bounty money to enlisted men, and expenses connected with the capture of deserters. Others relate to such matters as the care of sick troops, the purchase of equipment, travel expenses, and "Secret Service" activities. At the front of the volume is an index of accounts that includes names of accounts missing because of the physical deterioration of the record.

MI.59.3. The second volume donated by Goodloe, **Revolutionary War account book ("North Carolina Line"), 1784,** contains brief accounts for individual officers giving their rank and entries mainly for pay, subsistence, clothing, and equipment. A typical entry shows the source of the money or supplies, the value of the transaction, and the dates of entries and periods for which money was due. Many of the accounts contain entries that are inexplicable. The entries were obviously posted to or from another account book that has not been identified. An index at the front of the volume is arranged alphabetically by the surnames of the officers having accounts. The physical characteristics of the book, as well as the handwriting and the format of entries, is almost identical to the volume of accounts for Georgia officers described in **MI.93.36.**

MI.59.4. The series **Revolutionary War journal, 1779-82,** is an original manuscript journal of the travels of Alexander Church, Richard Ramsey, and Zephaniah Halsey, members of the New York Quartermaster Department. The three men were officers assigned to the Continental Horse Yard, and the entries document their travels as they delivered horses to various components of the Continental Army and performed related services. There are gaps from a few days to several months when "Nothing Remarkable" occurred, but the journal contains commentary on such events as the hanging and beheading of a deserter, the treason of Benedict Arnold and the hanging of Major Andre, and the siege and surrender of the British at Yorktown. The trio traveled mostly in New York, Pennsylvania, and

New Jersey, but also through Baltimore, Annapolis, and Richmond on the way to and from Yorktown. Private accounts and records relating to Halsey's activities as a farmer and local official in New York state, 1793-1831, follow the journal. The volume appears to have been submitted as part of a pension application file among the records described in **PE.15.4.-PE.15.6.**; how the Department of State acquired custody of it is unknown.

MI.59.5. In the series **miscellaneous documents printed, ca. 1780-1932**, is a facsimile, of late 19th- or early 20th-century origin, of a letter from George Washington to the Governor of Maryland. Written from "Camp near York," in October 1781, the letter informs the governor of the surrender of the British Army under General Cornwallis at Yorktown, thanks him for his aid, and gives estimates of personnel and supplies captured and plans for the disposition of the prisoners in Virginia and Maryland.

MI.59.6. In the series **miscellaneous manuscripts, ca. 1756-1918**, is a blank warrant issued by Lieutenant Governor Robert Dinwiddie of Virginia in 1756. It bears Dinwiddie's signature and spaces for the name of the person to whom it was to be issued and the date. The warrant was authorized by an act of the colonial legislature of October 27, 1755, for the trial of mutineers, deserters, and other offenders against military law.

MI.59.7. Memorandum on the command of Washington's "Life Guard," ca. 1876, is a brief series consisting of a report written in the Bureau of Rolls and Library in reponse to a written inquiry concerning whether Maj. Bartholomew von Heer, in addition to Caleb Gibbs and William Colfax, was ever commander of the Life Guard. It concludes that von Heer was rather the commander of the Independent Light Dragoons, whose duties included maintaining order in camp and apprehending deserters. The unit itself was composed largely of Germans who had deserted from the British Army. With the report is a letter from "E. B." to his wife, April 24, 1789, describing the welcome given President Washington by the inhabitants of New York City on the preceding day.

OTHER RECORDS

MI.59.8. The series **territorial papers, 1764-1873**, is divided into several subseries, one for each territory. The Florida territorial papers contain an eight-page pamphlet, *Plan for Conducting the Hospital Department of the United States* (M116, roll 1), that was printed at Philadelphia by David C. Claypoole. It sets forth a plan adopted by the Continental Congress on September 30, 1780.

Records of the Office of the Chief of Engineers

MI.77.1. The Corps of Engineers, U.S. Army, was established by an act of March 16, 1802, to organize a military academy at West Point. In 1818 the Chief Engineer of the corps was directed to fix his headquarters at Washington, DC, as the Office of the Chief of Engineers in the War Department. The army's topographical engineers were placed under the chief's supervision from 1818 to 1831 and again in 1863. Responsibilities of the Office of the Chief of Engineers have included producing and distributing army maps, building roads, planning camps, constructing and repairing fortifications and other installations, maintaining and improving inland waterways and harbors, and approving plans for the construction of bridges, wharves, piers, and other works over navigable waters.

CARTOGRAPHIC RECORDS

MI.77.2. All of the pre-federal records of military affairs in RG 77 are maps or plans of military installations. All are listed in National Archives Special List No. 26, *Pre-Federal Maps in the National Archives: An Annotated List* (1975). For a full description of that publication and its arrangement, see the introduction.

MI.77.3. *Faden Atlas of the American Revolution* (1793) consists mainly of maps produced during and shortly after the Revolution by William Faden of England to illustrate battles and other operations in that conflict. Included are maps and plans depicting fortifications, battles, campaigns, sieges, and skirmishes throughout the 13 original states. The copy in the National Archives consists of plates published in 1793 that were used in preparing a second publication of the atlas in 1845. There is a table of contents at the front of the volume and all of the plates are listed in National Archives Special List No. 26 (see the introduction).

MI.77.4. In the series **War Department map collection** are four maps pertaining to pre-federal military affairs. Two of them consist of undated, but apparently early 19th-century, variant engravings of a "Map of the Country which was the scene of operations of the Northern Army; including the Wilderness through which General Arnold marched to attack Quebec" (WDMC Maine No. 59 and WDMC Maine No. 60). The third item is a photocopy of a map of the siege of Yorktown published in 1787 (WDMC Va. No. 181). The other is a photoprocessed topographical map of the Yorktown siege produced at the U.S. Artillery School at Fort Monroe in 1880 (WDMC Va. No. 28).

MI.77.5. The series **fortifications map file** contains manuscript, published, annotated, and photoprocessed maps and plans, mainly of permanent coastal and other forts in the United States and its territories and possessions. Most of the documents date from after 1790, but there are over 20 originals and copies of pre-federal maps, most of which pertain to military matters. For more detailed descriptions see National Archives Special List No. 26 (described in the introduction).

MI.77.6. Two sets of plans related to pre-federal military affairs are in the series **letters received, 1826-66**, both under the file designation F-206, 1836. They are for Fort George, FL, and Fort Independence, NY.

Record Group 92
Records of the Office of the Quartermaster General

MI.92.1. During the pre-federal era, Quartermasters General were regarded as field staff officers appointed to the principal armies. Like the Quartermaster's Department of the U.S. Army, created by Congress in 1818, they were responsible for efficient systems of supply, movement of the army, and accountability of officers and agents charged with moneys or supplies.

MI.92.2. Part of the subgroup Bound Volumes of the Philadelphia Supply Agencies, 1795-1858, is the one-volume series **receipt books of Samuel Hodgdon, Assistant Commissary General and Commissary General of [for] Military Stores, June 9-November 15, 1781** (on M927, 1 roll). The receipts are mainly those of officers and other employees of the Commissary General of Military Stores' Department and of other persons who provided services or supplies to the department. Among the receipts are those of male and female workers in the "Laboratory in Fifth Street" who were paid for making musket cartridges and balls. There are many receipts from persons who received money for cleaning and repairing muskets or for providing raw materials and finished goods, such as muskets, cartridge paper, sheepskins, wood, files, linseed oil, cartridge boxes, gunners' belts, cannon, haversacks, shot and shells, cavalry swords, bayonets, spirit levels, and bullet molds. One individual received money on July 5, 1781, for "reducing one pound steel to dust for making Fireworks to commemorate the anniversary of Independence." There are several receipts from a blacksmith, a "Tinman," and a "turner" for work performed. Most receipts include the place and date executed; a description of the services or goods supplied; the amount of the payment and its form, such as specie, Spanish milled dollars, or new emission money; and the signature or mark of the person paid. The book is arranged in two sections beginning at its front and back, respectively, and proceeding toward the middle. Within each the arrangement is generally chronological. For other receipt books of Samuel Hodgdon, see **MI.93.46.**

MI.92.3. A part of the series **miscellaneous records, 1818-57**, is "Table Shewing the Annual Expence to the U States of an Officer of Each Rank, in the Army." This document appears to be a copy of a record originally created in the Quartermaster General's Deparment of the Continental Army. It lists several dozen ranks and individual staff offices, such as major general, colonel, surgeon, chaplain, adjutant, aide-de-camp, major of brigade, clerk, Quartermaster General, apothecary, paymaster, and Commissary General of Military Stores. For most of the ranks or offices the annual pay and quantity and value of rations, forage, wood, servants, public horses, and wagons allowed are shown, with the resultant total annual expense of maintaining an individual holding that position. There is no discernible arrangement.

MI.92.4. The single-volume series **manuscript history of the Quartermaster Department, 1774-1868**, was submitted to the Quartermaster General of the U.S. Army by Bvt. Col. H. A. Royce in 1868 and was issued in printed form "for information of officers of the Department" as General Order No. 8 of the Quartermaster General on February 5, 1869. It consists mainly of extracts of and statements based on published laws and official correspondence, and secondary sources, documenting the organizational history of the Quartermaster Department. Biographical sketches of the Quartermasters General are also included in the footnotes, and at the end is a list of the heads of the department from 1774 to 1868, showing their names, ranks, titles, dates of appointment, and states from which appointed. An updated version of this sketch was published as *A Sketch of the Organization of the Quartermasters' Department from 1774 to 1868* (1876).

War Department Collection of
Revolutionary War Records

MI.93.1. The act of August 7, 1789, that established the War Department under the federal government provided that the Secretary of War should have custody of all books and papers in the Office of the Secretary at War, who had headed the Department of War created in 1781 by the Continental Congress. The inherited documents also included papers of the pre-1781 Board of War. A fire of November 8, 1800, in the building occupied by the Secretary of War, destroyed many of the records. Further losses came in 1814 when British troops occupied Washington, DC, and burned government buildings. What remained of the War Department's records pertaining to the pre-federal period were in a fireproof room, but most were destroyed or carried away by persons who entered the room after the fire.

MI.93.2. Thus there were few records of the Revolutionary War in the custody of the War Department until 1873 when Secretary of War William Belknap purchased a private collection from Professor Charles A. Joy of Columbia University. It primarily consisted of records associated with Timothy Pickering, Quartermaster General of the Continental Army from 1780 to 1785, and Samuel Hodgdon, an assistant quartermaster in Pennsylvania who also served as Commissary General of Military Stores during the latter part of the war. Secretary Belknap also obtained smaller quantities of Revolutionary War records from other persons, but the collection remained in War Department custody only until 1888. In that year the records were sent to the Department of State in connection with a proposal to publish the archives of the pre-federal government.

MI.93.3. In 1889 the War Department established the Record and Pension Division (renamed the Record and Pension Office in 1892) to take custody of the records of the volunteer armies of the United States and transact the business of the department connected with them. When Col. Fred C. Ainsworth became chief of the new Record and Pension Office, he recommended to Congress that other executive departments of the federal government be directed to transfer to the War Department whatever military records of the Revolutionary War period were in their possession. As a result, the records sent to the Department of State in 1888 were returned to the War Department. They were accompanied by personnel returns, oaths of allegiance, and other military records taken from the State

Department's George Washington Papers. The War Department also received military records of the Revolution from the Pension Bureau of the Interior Department and the Treasury Department's Office of the Auditor for the Interior Department in a number of transfers that occurred between 1894 and 1913 (see **PE.15.3.**).

MI.93.4. Two additional accessions of importance early in the 20th century substantially completed the War Department Collection of Revolutionary War Records. In 1909 some records pertaining mainly to the activities of the Quartermaster General's Department were received from Henry G. Pickering, the great-grandson of Timothy Pickering. In 1914-15 the War Department supplemented its original records by making photographic copies of Revolutionary War records in the possession of individuals and institutions in several states (see **NA.45.1.**).

MI.93.5. Because of the history of loss, scattering, and government reacquisition, the records in Record Group 93 are not organized in any way resembling their original order. They were organized as they were received by the War Department and placed into five large bodies of records. Many were put into two large files of unbound material. One consists of muster rolls, returns, pay lists, guard reports, and other records showing the military service of persons in particular organizations (see **MI.93.14.-MI.93.16.**). These are reproduced on microfilm as *Revolutionary War Rolls, 1775-1783* (M246, 138 rolls). The other unbound set is reproduced as *Miscellaneous Numbered Records (The Manuscript File) in the War Department Collection of Revolutionary War Records, 1775-1790's* (M859, 125 rolls), and consists of letters, receipts for pay, supply returns, and other records of a miscellaneous character (see **MI.93.10.-MI.93.13.**). Some bound records were taken apart and their contents added to this set. The photographic copies of records made in 1914-15 were kept together and constitute a third major aggregation of records in RG 93 (see **MI.93.58.**). A fourth major part of the collection consists of about 230 orderly books, letterbooks, receipt books, journals, ledgers, bound lists of soldiers, and other bound records. Most of these were rebound into uniform bindings by the War Department and numbered to form the series microfilmed as *Numbered Record Books Concerning Military Operations and Service, Pay and Settlement of Accounts, and Supplies in the War Department Collection of Revolutionary War Records* (M853, 41 rolls); they are described in **MI.93.8.-MI.93.9.** Information taken from all of these records was written on cards and used to produce the fifth major set of records in RG 93, compiled military service records (see **MI.93.63.-MI.93.65.**). These are reproduced as two National Archives Microfilm Publications, *Compiled Service Records of American Naval Personnel and*

Members of the Departments of the Quartermaster General and the Commissary General of Military Stores Who Served During the Revolutionary War (M880, 4 rolls) and *Compiled Service Records of Soldiers Who Served in the American Army During the Revolutionary War* (M881, 1,096 rolls).

MI.93.6. In the context of the entire pre-federal holdings of the National Archives it is necessary to describe the War Department Collection of Revolutionary War Records both as these five sets of records and their indexes, and as bodies of records which, even though they sometimes are bound in separate volumes or unbound in separate series, are related by origin, general subject, or record type. Thus this section on RG 93 will in some cases contain more than one reference to a single series, or even subseries, as each is viewed from a different perspective. Many pre-federal records merit this descriptive treatment for similar reasons, but RG 93 is the most extensive and complex case of all. (See also the RG 93 section of Chapter FI, Records of Fiscal Affairs, and the RG 45 section of Chapter NA, Records of Naval Affairs.)

MI.93.7. The descriptions of the War Department Collection in this guide will be more general than those for records in all other record groups except RG 360 because the descriptive pamphlets for the 16 National Archives Microfilm Publications of RG 93 records are relatively detailed and readily available. War Department volume numbers and microfilm publication and roll numbers are given to help locate the records because they are the access keys that will remain constant for as long as the records exist. Indexes that are a part of RG 93 generally were created in the 19th or early 20th centuries and fall into three types. First are those that cover all the records in a series. Others index records that are related but in different series. The third type are indexes to subseries. All will be described, or at least mentioned, at the point at which the relevant records are described.

RECORDS OF THE CONTINENTAL ARMY: GENERAL

The numbered record books and the manuscript file

MI.93.8. The series **numbered record books, 1775-98** (M853, 41 rolls), is one of the five major divisions of the War Department Collection of Revolutionary War Records and mainly consists of records received from the State, Treasury, and Interior Departments between 1893 and 1913. Most of the records are stamped to show when and from whom they were received by the War Department. Included are orderly books, which make up about one-third of the series; oaths of allegiance and office; military commissions; lists of military officers and enlisted men of various states and organizations; and letterbooks, receipt books, and account books of various Continental Army staff departments. Most of the record books were created during the Revolution but some were continued in use or begun in the early postwar years, and a few are copies of pre-federal documents that were made after 1800. The principal subjects, broadly defined, include the service, pay, and settlement of accounts of individual officers and men; procurement and distribution of supplies; and military operations. In spite of the varied origins, subject matter, and physical types of the 199 volumes, the War Department numbered them in the order in which they were received. Thus, closely related records are not always consecutively numbered. For example, the letterbooks of Quartermaster General Timothy Pickering are in volumes 82-88, 90, and 123-127. Individual volumes, groups of related volumes, and even parts of volumes are described in numerous other entries in this chapter according to the administrative origins, subject matter, or physical types of the records. To assist in locating records, the volume numbers will hereafter be cited with the microfilm publication and roll number (as in Number 133, M853, roll 64).

MI.93.9. The numbered record books are indexed in several ways. A single alphabetical personal name index serves most of the 199 volumes as well as two other series—the "manuscript file" (see **MI.93.13.**) and photographic copies of state records (see **MI.93.58.**). It was created on cards by the Record and Pension Office of the War Department. Numbered record books not covered by this index were omitted for any one of four reasons: because the information in them was included in the compiled service records (see **MI.93.64.**), applied only to British troops (see **MI.93.60.- MI.93.62.**), made no reference to individuals, or was duplicated in other volumes that were indexed. The index is available as National Archives Microfilm Publication M847 (39 rolls). A much smaller subject-based card index to the same three series also exists, but has not been microfilmed. It contains entries mainly for ships, places, and organizations. The series **index to series 5 ("catalog and subject index of record books of Revolutionary War")** (M853, roll 1) is divided into two parts. One, entitled "Catalogue of Books," lists the 199 numbered record books in numerical order and outlines the contents of most of them. A second part, entitled "Subject-Index of Record Books," is an alphabetically arranged index to subjects and some persons mentioned in the numbered books. Each entry refers to a volume and page number. Among the numbered record books are 62 slim volumes that index individual volumes in the series. They are located throughout the series, each accompanying the volume it indexes (M853, 41 rolls).

MI.93.10. The series **miscellaneous numbered records ("manuscript file"), 1775-84** (M859, 125 rolls), was created by the War Department mostly from unbound records that did not fit any of three other series—numbered record books (**MI.93.8.-MI.93.9.**), photographic copies of state records (**MI.93.58.**), and muster rolls and related personnel records (**MI.93.14.-MI.93.16.**). The manuscript file also contains some bound records that were unbound and placed in it and a few paper-covered volumes that were deposited in it intact. The War Department began the manuscript file in 1898 and added to it as late as 1937. Many of the records bear annotations indicating when and from whom they were received by the department. The main sources were other executive departments, state governments, and private citizens. About two-thirds of the documents are originals, most of which date from the Revolutionary War years. The remaining one-third are manuscript and printed copies of Revolutionary records produced mostly in the 1890s.

MI.93.11. The principal subjects of the records are the service, pay, and settlement of accounts of individual military officers and enlisted men; procurement and distribution of military supplies; and military operations. Records on those subjects, usually numbering in the hundreds of documents for each type, include pay accounts and related records; orders for, accounts of, and receipts for supplies; oaths of allegiance and of office, military commissions, resignations, and enlistment papers; and correspondence, orders, and reports of staff and field officers and heads of Continental Army staff departments. The descriptive pamphlet for National Archives Microfilm Publication M859 contains a detailed list of the principal kinds of records in the manuscript file, a chronological list of the sources of the records, and an outline of the arrangement of the series.

MI.93.12. The manuscript file is arranged into three numbered subseries. Each subseries is arranged in four classes based on the states or organizations to which the records pertain:

1. records of troops of particular states, including both continental and militia forces;

2. records of continental troops not affiliated with particular states;

3. records of Continental Army staff departments; and

4. miscellaneous records pertaining to none or more than one of the other three classes.

Although the numbers assigned to documents in the series run from 1 to 50208, only about 35,500 discrete items are present. Documents 31756-31862 were transferred to the Navy Department in 1906. Some have been found among the records described in **NA.45.2.-NA.45.16.** Numbers 35501-49983 of the manuscript file were reserved for what became instead the series of photographic copies of state records described in **MI.93.58.** Numbers 50000-50201 were assigned to the numbered pension and half-pay application files that are now among the records described in **PE.93.4.** Lesser gaps are also present in the numbering of the documents in the manuscript file, and there are a few unnumbered records at the end of the series.

MI.93.13. The manuscript file is one of three series covered by the first index (M847, 39 rolls) described in **MI.93.9.**, which is to personal names in the records. The subject index mentioned immediately after the name index in **MI.93.9.** also applies to the manuscript file but is much smaller and less useful than the cards reproduced in M847. An even smaller index, consisting of 1 foot of cards, contains manuscript file document numbers for individuals for whom there are oaths, commissions, and resignations. It is arranged alphabetically by surname.

Returns, rolls, and related records

MI.93.14. The single-series microfilm publication *Revolutionary War Rolls, 1775-1783* (M246, 138 rolls), contains originals and copies acquired by the War Department mainly in the late 19th and early 20th centuries from a variety of sources. Many bear stamps showing the date received or copied and the source. The records are for units of the Continental Army, state troops, and miscellaneous bodies. Included are muster rolls and payrolls; returns of troops; general, monthly, weekly, and field returns of the main army under Washington; lists of officers; pay abstracts; clothing accounts; and guard reports. Information contained in the records includes the names of individual officers and enlisted soldiers, the organizations in which they served, and their periods of service; the places where organizations were stationed; and the number of troops present and troops not present for various reasons, such as those discharged, deserted, "on command," on furlough, and dead.

MI.93.15. The records are arranged in three sections: state organizations, including continental troops affiliated with particular states; continental organizations not affiliated with particular states; and miscellaneous units, such as the army under Washington. Within the first section the records are arranged alphabetically by name of state. For a more detailed description of the records see the descriptive pamphlet for M246, which includes a table of contents listing each unit for which records exist. The first roll of the microfilm publication contains a register compiled in 1906 that is arranged similarly, but also includes, for each unit, its date of formation, names of commanding officers, the location of its records, and, occasionally, the types of records present. One foot of cards makes up another register, also similarly arranged, that was prepared by the Office of the Adjutant General around 1930. It is not a part of M246 and generally contains less information than the microfilmed register. There are also two series, **register of muster rolls** and **register of muster rolls and payrolls,** that were compiled while the Revolutionary War rolls were being rolled and wrapped in numbered bundles in the Pension Office. Since the records are no longer arranged as they were when indexed, these registers are of only passing interest.

MI.93.16. The series **copies of rolls of officers of the Continental Army, 1775-79,** probably was made sometime after 1905. The rolls show the name and rank of officers and usually the dates of appointment or promotion to the rank shown. Often the date of dismissal, resignation, or death is also given. The rolls are arranged generally by branch of service, thereunder by regiment or other unit, and thereunder by order of rank. A brief statement of information concerning a unit usually precedes its roll. Another series, **returns of the 6th Massachusetts Battalion, July 1779-July 1780** (M913, roll 1), consists of a single volume kept by Lt. Samuel Frost. It contains weekly and monthly returns, field returns, and descriptive returns that give each soldier's name, age, height, complexion, color of hair and eyes, occupation, place of birth, and residence. Details of the precise status of personnel are given in weekly, monthly, and inspection returns, and on some those absent are named with the reason for absence and the location of the absentee given. Arrangement is generally chronological. Returns and similar personnel records are also found as enclosures to letters from Continental Army officers to the Continental Congress (**MI.360.7.-MI.360.28.**), in the manuscript file (**MI.93.10.**), and as part of other larger bodies of records in RG 93.

Commissions, oaths of allegiance and office, and related records

MI.93.17. The subseries "commissions and resignations, 1775-80" (Number 169, M853, roll 13), contains commissions of individuals from New York, Pennsylvania, Rhode Island, and Virginia into organizations of the Continental Army and into state service, including militia. Some resignations of commissions and requests for permission to resign, addressed to George Washington, are also present, as well as certificates and letters of paymasters and commanding officers, mainly respecting the accounts of officers desiring to resign. The records are arranged by state. There are additional commissions and oaths among the records in Item 195 of PCC (M247, roll 201); see **CC.360.8.**

MI.93.18. Four volumes of the numbered record books (**MI.93.8.**) consist of original printed and manuscript oaths of allegiance and fidelity and oaths of office taken mainly by line and staff officers of the Continental Army in accordance with a resolution of the Continental Congress of February 3, 1778. Many of the oaths were taken at Valley Forge in May 1778, including the oath of allegiance taken by George Washington. Others were subscribed to at White Plains, New Brunswick, Bethlehem, and other places in 1778. This subseries, "oaths of allegiance and fidelity and oaths of office, 1778" (Numbers 165-168, M853, roll 12), also contains certificates of witnessing officers attesting to the taking of oaths by others. Information contained in the oaths varies but generally includes the name of the subscriber, his rank or office, his organization, the date, the name and rank of the witness, and the place where the oath was taken. Witnesses who signed oaths include Generals Washington, von Steuben, Pulaski, Wayne, and Muhlenberg. The approximately 1,200 oaths in these volumes are numbered and arranged numerically. Most are grouped to some extent by states and regiments. A published index to these four volumes is described with another series, consisting mostly of oaths of civilian officials, in **CC.360.8.**

MI.93.19. A name index to both the commissions and resignations (**MI.93.17.**) and the oaths of allegiance and fidelity and of office (**MI.93.18.**) was produced around 1930 by the Office of the Adjutant General. It is a subseries (M853, roll 1) consisting of 1 foot of 3- by 8-inch cards, and it also indexes related records in the manuscript file (**MI.93.10.**). A typical entry gives an individual's name, rank, organization, and the volume and page numbers or manuscript file document numbers of pertinent oaths, commissions, and resignations. Arrangement is alphabetical by surname.

Orderly books

MI.93.20. The subseries "orderly books, June 23, 1775- September 17, 1783" (Numbers 12-76 and 193-197, M853, rolls 2-11), comprises the largest aggregation of records of a particular kind in the numbered record books (**MI.93.8.**). A few of the 70 volumes are actually fragments of 2 or more orderly books bound together. The books contain orders that reflect many levels of command, including the orders of George Washington, Commander in Chief of the Continental Army, and those of commanders of various wings, divisions, brigades, garrisons, detachments, battalions, and regiments. Most of the orders are by officers of the Continental Army, but some were issued by officers commanding state troops or militia. Many are repeated in two or more volumes because different organizations recorded the same orders emanating from higher commands in addition to the orders of their own commanders. Among the subjects of orders are announcements of appointments, promotions, and reprimands; findings of courts-martial and courts of inquiry; designations of officers of the day and other persons or organizations assigned to special duty; instructions relating to troop movements, camp regulations, discipline, distribution of supplies, and maintenance of equipment; and notices of acts of the Continental Congress and state legislatures pertaining to military affairs. A number of the books contain lists of officers and men and personnel memorandums of various sorts in addition to orders.

MI.93.21. The subseries of orderly books is arranged numerically. Within each volume, orders usually appear in chronological order. Normally, for any particular date, general orders are recorded first, followed by wing, division, brigade, and regimental orders in descending order of command level. The second part of "catalogue and subject index . . ." (M853, roll 1), described in **MI.93.9.**, is the principal subject index for the orderly books as a group. A page-by-page breakdown of the orders in each volume is available for most of the volumes in the first part of the same index. It generally gives the names of officers issuing orders, the places at which orders were issued, and their dates. For volumes 13, 15-16, 21, 23-24, 26, 28, 30-36, 40-50, 52-63, 65, 67-70, and 73-75 of the orderly books there are also separate unbound indexes to personal names and some subjects; and volumes 12 and 17 have indexes bound in them (M853, various rolls). These appear to have been prepared while the records were in Department of State custody, 1888-94. Another index (M853, roll 1) was prepared in two sets around 1930 by the Adjutant General's Office. The first is arranged alphabetically by the names of officers issuing orders. The second is arranged mainly alphabetically by levels of command—battalion, brigade, division, garrison, regiment, wing, and miscellaneous. The entries in each set give the dates and the places of issuance of orders as well as the location of the records.

MI.93.22. The series **printer's proof and related notes for "Orderly Books of the Continental Forces, and Official Records of the Quartermaster's Department of the Revolutionary Army, 1775-83," 1884-88**, consists of two sets of page proofs, 1877-78, with printer's notes and notes of contemporary War Department personnel concerning the collection of material and publication of a planned series of volumes of orderly books. No quartermaster records were printed, and the volume appears never to have been published. In 1888 the entire collection was transferred to the Department of State, which may account for the failure to complete the project. The orders in the two sets of page proofs are generally in chronological order, covering June 23, 1775-June 14, 1779. For other orderly books that occupy parts of volumes used primarily for other purposes, see **MI.93.17.** and **MI.93.26.** A few orderly books are among the pension and bounty-land application files described in **PE.93.2.** More than 100 originals and copies of Revolutionary War orderly books are among the holdings of the Library of Congress.

Account books and other company record books

MI.93.23. The one-volume series **personal accounts and military records of Capt. Eleazer Curtis, 1776-1833**, was received by the War Department from the Pension Office in 1913. From May to December 1775, Curtis was a captain in the 4th Connecticut Regiment. Most of this volume contains accounts of a private business nature, but it also contains soldier's receipts for bounty and billeting money, receipts for arms and accouterments, and acknowledgments of enlistment, 1776-77. There is a name index to the private accounts.

MI.93.24. "Record of clothing, arms, ammunition, and accoutrements, Maj. James Hamilton's Company, 2nd Pennsylvania Regiment, 1780" (Number 150, M853, roll 40), mainly shows the kinds and amounts of clothing and equipment issued to enlisted men. The entries are arranged by rank and thereunder roughly in alphabetical order by surnames. The last page contains personal accounts dated 1786.

MI.93.25. Another volume, "records of Captain Thomas Mighill, March 1775-May 1777" (Number 174, M853, roll 17), contains a variety of records and accounts kept by Mighill for his company, which served in Col. Samuel Gerrish's Massachusetts Regiment in 1775 and in the 26th Continental Regiment in 1776. Included are payrolls, lists of officers and enlisted men in the company, reports of courts-martial, clothing accounts, records of payments for supplies, and receipts for payments. There is no discernible arrangement.

MI.93.26. "Memorandum, account, and orderly book, Capt. Thaddeus Weed's Company, 2nd Connecticut Regiment, August-November 1781 and 1785-1813" (Number 158, M853, roll 17), mostly consists of private accounts dated 1785-1813. It also contains lists of supplies received by the officers and enlisted men of the company in 1781; a list of those who received 1 month's pay in "Colonel Hamilton's Battalion," September 7, 1781; orders of George Washington and battalion orders, October 2-16, 1781, issued at Yorktown and places not named; a return of Weed's company for August-November 1781; an undated account of clothing purchased for the officers of Colonel Hamilton's battalion; and battalion orders, November 22, 1781. The Hamilton referred to is apparently Lt. Col. Alexander Hamilton, commander of a light infantry battalion composed of companies drawn from various regiments at Yorktown in 1781. This volume appears to be an account and orderly book kept by Lt. Cornelius Russell of Weed's company in 1781 and continued in use by him after the war as a private account book. The Revolutionary War entries generally begin in the front of the volume and proceed toward the middle. The private account entries mainly begin at the rear of the volume and proceed toward the front.

Letterbooks, account books, and miscellaneous correspondence of military officers

MI.93.27. The subseries "letters sent and orderly book, Brig. Gen. Edward Hand, October 1776 and April-August 1778" (Number 156, M853, roll 17), was apparently begun as an orderly book since it contains copies of a few orders issued in 1776 in the vicinity of New York City by Hand (then a colonel), George Washington, and unidentified officers. In 1778, beginning at the opposite end, the volume was used as a letterbook, and the greater part of it contains about 90 pages of copies of letters sent and of a few letters received by Hand. Subjects include relations with the Indians, the protection of settlements along the frontier, the supply of provisions and stores, deserters, and prisoners. A few letters were sent by George Morgan, who was an agent for Indian affairs and Deputy Commissioner-General of Purchases for the Western District. Nearly all of the letters were sent from Fort Pitt. Both the letterbook and the orderly book parts of the volume are arranged chronologically. An index to names in the letterbook, presumably prepared by the Record and Pension Office of the War Department, is in the volume. Both the letters and orders are covered by the first two indexes described in **MI.93.9.** For letters written by Hand in 1777-78 and 1781-83, see **MI.360.14.** and **MI.93.52.**, respectively. For other orderly books, see **MI.93.20.-MI.93.22.**

MI.93.28. The series **ledger of accounts, 4th New York Regiment, 1775-77**, consists of one volume kept by Capt. Henry Beekman Livingston. It shows amounts of money debited and credited to accounts of enlisted men, officers, and other persons. Entries were made in connection with pay, distribution of supplies, recruiting expenses, and other matters. They are arranged mainly by names of persons with accounts, but there are also accounts for "Government" and "State of New York." The volume contains an index to the names of accounts.

MI.93.29. The subseries "account book of Capt. William Scull, 11th Pennsylvania Regiment, January-May 1777 and January-June 1778" (Number 157, M853, roll 21), contains in its first part a few accounts of money paid by Scull. Given are dates of payment, amounts paid, and sometimes the purposes and recipients of the payments, which were made for board, horse hire, expenses incurred in pursuing deserters, and purchases of clothing, forage, provisions, and other supplies. The accounts are arranged by names of persons for whom there are accounts. The remainder of the volume contains receipts for pay signed by Scull's surveying assistants. These are arranged generally in chronological order.

RECORDS OF THE CONTINENTAL ARMY: OF AND PERTAINING TO ARMY STAFF DEPARTMENTS

MI.93.30. For original letters received, copies of letters sent, and many other records of the Paymaster General, Quartermaster General, Commissary General of Military Stores, and other Continental Army staff departments, see the manuscript file described in **MI.93.10.** For letters and reports received by the Continental Congress from heads of the departments, see **MI.360.7.-MI.360.28.** For records pertaining to the settlement of accounts of Continental Army staff departments, see **MI.360.40.-MI.360.41.** and **FI.360.11.-FI.360.12.**

Paymaster General's Department, including the Commissioner of Army Accounts and subordinates

MI.93.31. Correspondence of major officials in the Paymaster General's Department is found in two places in RG 93 and one place in PCC. A subseries in the numbered record books, "letters sent by John Pierce, Paymaster General and Commissioner of Army Accounts, April 1786-May 1788" (Number 134, M853, roll 18), is arranged generally in chronological order. Additional letters and reports from Pierce to Congress are in Item 62 of PCC, described in **MI.360.40.** and **FI.360.12.** The three volumes, "letters sent and received by Joseph Howell, Assistant Commissioner of Army Accounts and Commissioner of Army Accounts, October 1784-January 1789" (Numbers 135, 136, and 138, M853, roll 19), contain copies of letters and reports of Howell as Assistant Commissioner and as Commissioner of Army Accounts. An index in each volume indexes the names of correspondents, but not the names of persons mentioned in letters and reports. All three sets of correspondence, both Pierce's and Howell's, contain copies of letters and reports sent to subordinates and superiors in the department, members of the Continental Congress, the President and the Secretary of Congress, governors and other state officials, the Secretary at War, the Board of Treasury, and former military officers. Subjects include claims for pay, issuance of final settlement certificates, frauds, and related matters concerning the settlement of accounts of officers and enlisted men.

MI.93.32. Journals, ledgers, and other general records of pay and accounts for the Continental Army are in three volumes, all of which contain entries that generally show to whom payment was made and the date, purpose, and amount:

1. "Paymaster General's ledger of accounts with officers of the army, 1775-78" (Number 143, M853, roll 24), shows the dates and amounts of money debited and credited to accounts while James Warren and William Palfrey were the Paymasters General. A few accounts are in the names of states. The book is arranged by titles of accounts.

2. "Account book of the pay office, Paymaster General's Department, 1783-84" (Number 141, M853, roll 24), apparently was kept by Joseph Howell in the Paymaster General's Department at Philadelphia. It records payments made to officers and enlisted men of various regiments in settlement of their accounts for pay, rations, subsistence, and other claims arising from Revolutionary War service. The 321 entries are arranged numerically.

3. "Record of disbursements, Paymaster General's office, New York, 1788" (Number 142, M853, roll 23), is apparently a record of settlements effected in 1788 of accounts relating to the Revolutionary War period. The 302 entries are arranged numerically.

MI.93.33. Receipt books, registers, and other records in RG 93 document the issuance of final settlement certificates that were issued under a resolution of July 4, 1783, by the Continental Congress. That act authorized Paymaster General John Pierce to adjust and settle all accounts between the United States and the officers and men of the Continental Army that remained unpaid at the end of the Revolutionary War. Over 95,000 certificates were issued. Because the total amount of indebtedness to an individual was not consolidated, a soldier often received more than one certificate. For contemporary printed and manuscript registers of certificates issued, see **MI.15.2.** and **MI.53.5.**

MI.93.34. Four receipt books extant in the War Department Collection of Revolutionary War Records clearly were issued by Pierce, his successor, or his assistants. The first two are "receipt books of John Pierce and Joseph Howell, Paymasters General and Commissioners of Army Accounts, July 1783-August 1785 and August 1787-August 1790" (Numbers 146-147, M853, roll 20). Howell succeeded Pierce in July 1788. Other volumes are "receipt book of George Reid, Assistant Commissioner of Army Accounts, Charleston, SC, April 1785-January 1786" (Number 145, M853, roll 20), and "receipt book of John White, Assistant Commissioner of Army Accounts, Annapolis, MD, August-November 1785 and March 1786" (Number 147 1/2, M853, roll 20). The certificates in all four volumes were issued for settlement of accounts of officers and enlisted men of the Continental Army for pay and subsistence, commutation, forage, recruiting expenses, gratuities, and other money due them. The dated receipts show the purpose of the payment, the amount, and the certificate number. Some certificates were issued to agents representing regiments or other groups. Each volume is chronologically arranged according to the dates of the receipts.

MI.93.35. While the certificates issued by Reid and White (**MI.93.34.**) were executed under their authority as Pierce's assistants, such was not clearly the case for those in volumes 171-172 of the numbered record books (**MI.93.8.**). Those books contain certified copies from "payroll books A and B" recording amounts paid in 1784-92 by the United States to Pennsylvania officers and men who served in the Continental Army. The volumes were certified as correct copies by the auditor general of Pennsylvania in 1818. Otherwise they are similar to the volumes described in **MI.93.34.**

MI.93.36. Records of pay and accounts pertaining to particular organizations and states are in five volumes of the numbered record books (**MI.93.8.**). "Ledger of final settlements of officers' accounts, 1775-85" (Number 178, M853, roll 23), apparently was kept by John White, Assistant Commissioner of Army Accounts at Annapolis, MD. Many entries are undated. The volume is arranged by the names of officers, most of whom were from Maryland, and contains a name index. "Ledger of money accounts with officers of the North Carolina Line, 1777-83" (Number 136 1/2, M853, roll 23), was kept by Ebenezer Jackson, Assistant Commissioner of Army Accounts for North Carolina. Entries are arranged by names of officers for whom there are accounts. A name index is included. "Paymaster General's record of money due to officers and enlisted men of Connecticut, Massachusetts, and New Hampshire regiments, and to Capt. Robert Walker's Company of Col. John Lamb's Artillery Regiment, 1779-80" (Number 170, M853, roll 24), contains a record of money due officers and enlisted men who deserted or who were killed, wounded, captured, invalided, transferred, discharged, executed, or otherwise absent from their units. An entry gives the individual's name, his rank, the reason for his absence, the amount due him, and sometimes the amount paid and the warrant number. A few notes contain references to dates as late as 1793. The entries are arranged by regiments in no particular order, and thereunder by companies. The book also contains a name index to officers commanding the regiments and companies. "Account book of payments made to officers and men of the Virginia Line by Lt. Charles Stockley, 1782-83" (Number 139, M853, roll 22), contains a record of payments made to officers for pay and subsistence, 1782-83, and to enlisted men for pay, 1783. Marginal notes refer to dates as late as 1794. The volume is arranged in two sections, officers' accounts and those of enlisted men. "Record of accounts of Georgia officers and enlisted men and of members of the Hospital Department of the Southern Army, 1782-84" (Number 140, M853, roll 22), probably was kept in the office of the Paymaster General or the Commissioners of Army Accounts. The accounts for Georgia officers and men are in the first part and are followed by accounts for physicians, surgeons, mates, stewards, clerks, and other members of the Hospital Department for the Southern Army. Entries are for pay, rations, subsistence, clothing, and other expenses, and also usually show the date of payment, the name of the official from whom payment was received, and the amount. They are arranged within each part by the names of persons having accounts. A name index is in the volume.

Quartermaster General's Department

MI.93.37. Much of the correspondence of the Quartermaster General of the Continental Army is in the 13-volume subseries of the numbered record books (**MI.93.8.**) "letters sent by Col. Timothy Pickering, Quartermaster General, August 1780-July 1787" (Numbers 82-88, 90, and 123-127, M853, rolls 25-28). These volumes contain copies and a few drafts of letters sent by Pickering and some copies of letters sent by deputy quartermasters. Correspondents represented in the volumes include military and naval officers, civilian contractors, the President and members of the Continental Congress, the Board of War, the Treasury Board, state governors and other state officials, the Secretary at War, George Washington, Thomas

Jefferson, Robert Morris, the Marquis de Lafayette, and other prominent persons. Subjects include appointment and pay of department personnel, procurement and transportation of supplies, preparations for marches, establishment of camps, repair of roads and bridges, sale of surplus supplies and livestock, complaints against the army regarding damage to private property, shortages of money, repair of equipment, and settlement of accounts. Each volume is arranged generally in chronological order. With the exception of a few letters in volume 90, no letter appears to duplicate another. All of the volumes contain name indexes except volume 90, for which there is a separate accompanying name and subject index, one of the 62 volumes described at the end of **MI.93.9.** For letters received by Pickering as Quartermaster General, see the manuscript file described in **MI.93.10.** For letters received by the Continental Congress from Pickering, see **MI.360.21.**

MI.93.38. "Register of letters received by Col. Timothy Pickering, Quartermaster General, May-August 1781" (Number 89, M853, roll 26), gives a number for each letter received and additional information, such as the name of the writer and his office or rank, the date of the letter, the date it was received, the date it was answered, its substance, and action taken. The entries are arranged alphabetically by initial letter of correspondents' surnames and thereunder chronologically by the receipt dates of the letters. Some of the letters registered are in the manuscript file described in **MI.93.10.** Another register of letters received by Pickering, January-May 1781, is in the series described in **MI.93.70.**

MI.93.39. Ledgers and other financial records of the Quartermaster General's Department in the War Department Collection of Revolutionary War Records are in 12 volumes of the numbered record books (**MI.93.8.**). "Ledger of receipts and disbursements, Quartermaster General's Department, 1776-79" (Number 98, M853, roll 32), shows cash receipts and disbursements made in the department while it was headed by Thomas Mifflin and Stephen Moylan, and for a short time thereafter. Included are entries for wage and supply payments, travel and express expenses, salvage costs, wagon hire, and bounties, which are arranged by the names of persons for whom there are accounts and thereunder chronologically. A name index is included. Five volumes make up the subseries "records of disbursements, Quartermaster General's Department, 1780-84" (Numbers 95, 97, 187, and 190-191, M853, roll 31). They generally show for each disbursement the place and date, the payee, the purpose, and the amount. Disbursements were made for wages of department employees; travel, transportation, and recruiting expenses; wagon and team hire; postage; pasturage; enlistment bounties; and costs of manufacture or supply of clothing, shoes, forage, wood, nails, kettles, provisions, paper, rope, and other items. The places where disbursements were made include Philadelphia, Totowa, Newburgh, "Camp at Philipsburgh," "Camp near York, State Virginia," New Windsor, Williamsburgh, and Head of Elk. Each volume is arranged generally in chronological order. Many of the entries in volume 190 are also recorded in the one volume constituting the series **ledger of Quartermaster General accounts, 1780-83** (M926, 1 roll). Another volume, "record of receipts and expenditures, Quartermaster General's Department, August 1780-March 1784" (Number 192, M853, roll 31), is divided into two parts. The first contains a ledger showing money debited and credited to various accounts, such as those for wagoners, express riders, and department personnel, and two lengthy accounts of disbursements in the Quartermaster General's Department "with the Main Army" for August 1780-June 1782. The second part of the volume is a cash ledger primarily for September 1781-June 1783. Volume 190 contains, in addition to disbursement entries, several accounts that list the names of persons who purchased public property in 1782-83 and shows the dates of purchase, prices paid, and kinds of property.

MI.93.40. Two other volumes make up the subseries "monthly registers of quartermaster accounts settled, 1780-84" (Numbers 188 and 189, M853, roll 24). Given are the names and positions of persons employed by the Quartermaster General's Department, the dates of settlement of their accounts, and the dates through which settlements extended. Each book is arranged alphabetically by the first letter of surnames. "Receipt book of Peter Anspach, January-November 1782" (Number 183, M853, roll 31), contains signed receipts for payments made by Quartermaster General Timothy Pickering through paymaster Peter Anspach for wood, forage, and other supplies. Each such receipt states the purpose and amount of the payment involved. They are arranged numerically. Entries related to the numbered receipts in this volume are in the ledgers of disbursements and expenditures described in **MI.93.39.**

MI.93.41. Other quartermaster financial records in the numbered record books (**MI.93.8.**) are two books kept by Timothy Pickering. "Miscellaneous accounts and receipts of Col. Timothy Pickering, Quartermaster General, 1781-83" (Number 179, M853, roll 32), is a small, pocket-size volume containing a few receipts signed by persons who received money from Pickering for express and other services, and a few informal statements of money lent and repaid and of provisions and other supplies procured. Entries were made at Williamsburg, "Camp near York," and New Windsor. Arrangement is roughly chronological. "Records of accounts of Col. Timothy

Pickering, Quartermaster General, 1781-90" (Number 186, M853, roll 32), contains nine accounts involving routine activities of the department. Notations dated 1789 and 1790 at the end of several of the accounts in this volume are signed by Peter Anspach and indicate that he was engaged in settling Pickering's accounts.

MI.93.42. There are a few general records of the Quartermaster General's Department other than correspondence and financial records. The series **miscellaneous records of the Quartermaster General's Department, 1775-83**, consists of a great variety of documents, totaling about 100 separate items, such as rolls and returns of wagoners, carpenters, and teamsters; ordnance returns; returns of quartermaster stores on hand, manufactured, or needed; and estimates of costs for military units of various sizes. Some documents are not dated. There is no discernible arrangement. The records in this series pertaining to the Quartermaster General's Department are reproduced in National Archives Microfilm Publication M926 (1 roll); those pertaining to military stores are reproduced in M927 (1 roll); the other records have not been microfilmed. The descriptive pamphlets for M926 and M927 include detailed lists of the records filmed. "Estimates and requirements for money, men, and materials, Quartermaster General's Department, 1781-83" (Number 103, M853, roll 29), contains estimates of carriages, horses, and oxen needed by the army; estimates of camp equipment to be furnished by states; returns of officers and other employees of the department; estimates of money needed by the department; and documents on related subjects, such as construction costs and the availability of and specifications for supplies. The volume is arranged chronologically, but not all of the items are dated. It contains an incomplete subject index and is accompanied by a separate paper-bound name and subject index of 19th-century origin. The series **return of public property belonging to the Quartermaster General's Department, April 1, 1782** (M926, 1 roll), shows kinds and quantities of public property on hand, in use, in need of repair, and unfit for further service in Massachusetts, Rhode Island, Connecticut, New York, New Jersey, Pennsylvania, and with the Main Army. Kinds of property listed include horses, wagons, carts, and related equipment; naval vessels and stores; camp equipment; artificers' tools and equipment; building materials; clothing; and stationery. The volume is arranged by kinds of property.

MI.93.43. Records kept by or associated with subordinate quartermaster officers may be presented in tabular form. All entries but one are reproduced on National Archives Microfilm Publication M853.

Name: Position	Dates	M853 Roll No.	Numbered Rec. Bk. Vol. No.
Peter Anspach: clerk and paymaster, QM Gen's Dept.	1777-79	32	164
Stephen Clapp: Captain, company of artificers	1781-82	32	182
Thomas Grant: Ass't QM, PA	1780-83	32	177
Hugh Hughes: Dep. QM, NY	1780-82	24	185
Nathaniel Nason: Lt. and QM to Vose's Rgt. of Light Infantry	1781	none	none
Charles Russell: Ass't Dep. QM, VA	1781-82	30	102, 107-109, 160

Samuel Hodgdon served as assistant quartermaster in Pennsylvania as well as Commissary General of Military Stores. Records produced by him in both capacities are interspersed and described in **MI.93.45.**

MI.93.44. Accounts, returns, and other records of quartermaster and other supplies delivered to, on hand for, and needed by particular military organizations may also be presented in a table. Those for "certain Massachusetts, Connecticut, and Rhode Island organizations" are for forage only. The other three are all for quartermaster stores, ordnance, and other supplies. The descriptive pamphlets to the microfilm publications cited contain fuller descriptions of the records.

Unit(s)	Dates	Microfilm: Roll No.	Numbered Rec. Bk. Vol. No.
The Artillery Brigade	1781-83	M853:32	184
3d and 8th Massachusetts Regiments	1779-83	M853:32	149
8th and 9th Massachusetts Regiments	1779-82	M913:1	none
"Certain Massachusetts, Connecticut, and Rhode Island organizations"	1780-82	M853:32	180-181

Commissary General of Military Stores' Department

MI.93.45. The correspondence of the Commissary General of Military Stores is in the subseries "letters sent by Samuel Hodgdon,

Commissary General of Military Stores and Assistant Quartermaster, July 1778-May 1784" (Numbers 92-93 and 110-111, M853, roll 33), among the numbered record books (**MI.93.8.**). For the most part these volumes contain copies of letters sent by Hodgdon as a deputy and commissary of military stores, field commissary of military stores, Commissary General of Military Stores, and assistant quartermaster in Pennsylvania. There are also a few copies of letters sent by Benjamin Flower, the Commissary General of Military Stores from July 1776 to April 1781, and by Deputy Commissary of Military Stores Richard Frothingham. The letters are addressed to members of the department, the Board of War, the Secretary at War, state governors, the Continental Congress, military officers, and other persons. Subjects include procurement, shipment, repair, and sale of military stores; estimates of stores needed and on hand; construction of ordnance installations; and payment and discharge of employees. Hodgdon held the position of assistant quartermaster under Quartermaster General Timothy Pickering in addition to Commissary General of Military Stores. The records are generally in chronological order. Volumes 92, 93, and 110 include name indexes. There are separate name and subject indexes of 19th-century origin accompanying volumes 92, 93, and 111. For a report concerning the Commissary General of Military Stores' Department see **MI.360.40.**

MI.93.46. Ledgers, receipt books, pay orders, and other general financial records of the Commissary General for Military Stores' Department take up 11 volumes of the numbered record books (**MI.93.8.**) plus one volume in the manuscript file. The subseries "ledger of Samuel Hodgdon, 1777-98" (Number 152, M853, roll 35), contains accounts pertaining to officers of the department, the Quartermaster General, and other persons. An entry usually shows the date and the nature of the transaction. The official accounts concern wage and subsistence payments; payments for shot, shells, clothing, food, and other supplies; rent; and travel and other expenses. Entries for the period after the Revolutionary War appear to concern private business matters. Number 144 of the two-volume "ledgers of accounts with officers and other persons, 1778-92" (Numbers 100 and 144, M853, roll 36), shows amounts of money debited and credited to the accounts of officers and employees of the department, Quartermaster General Timothy Pickering, the naval commissioners of Pennsylvania, the trustees of Carpenters' Hall, iron masters, merchants, and other persons; to states; and to accounts of the department for salaries, incidental expenses, and supplies. There is an index to the names of persons and other entities for which there are accounts. Number 100 contains accounts that are also in Number 144. Many of the transactions that make up the accounts in this subseries were recorded initially in Number 96 of the numbered record books (see **MI.93.47.**). The eight volumes of "receipts, Samuel Hodgdon, Commissary General of Military Stores and Assistant Quartermaster, October 1778-September 1779 and March 1780-November 1789" (Numbers 77-81 and 104-106, M853, roll 34), contain records for money paid to employees and other persons for wages due as employees of the department; for hire of land, buildings, tools, and teams; for pasturage; for manufacturing or otherwise furnishing ammunition boxes, fuses, lanterns, hats, drums, swords, cartridges, files, musket balls, wood, coffins, trumpets, books, and other articles; for repairing muskets; for travel expenses; and for the transportation of supplies, baggage, and prisoners. A few receipts are for supplies rather than money. Arrangement is generally chronological. Number 104 contains a name and subject index, and there is a separate paper-bound name and subject index to Number 105 that is of 19th-century origin. Numbered record book 118, described in **MI.93.49.**, contains a few receipts for money disbursed by Hodgdon in May 1788. Another receipt book of Hodgdon's, filling the gap between numbered record books 77 and 78, is in the manuscript file described in **MI.93.10.** A receipt book of Hodgdon's for June-November 1781 is described in **MI.92.2.**

MI.93.47. Orders for payments and records of disbursements by the Commissary General for Military Stores' Department are in five volumes. The subseries "orders for pay, Commissary General of Military Stores' Department, March-October 1780" (Number 128, M853, roll 40), contains copies of orders for money payments to be made to officers and employees of the department, to suppliers, and to other persons for work performed and articles furnished. Each order gives the date, the payee, the amount, the purpose of the payment, and usually the name of the person certifying the order. Payments were made for various purposes including rent, enlisting soldiers, working in laboratories, making cartridges and buckles, repairing arms, cutting wood, blacksmithing, and furnishing and transporting supplies. The entries are arranged chronologically. The one-volume series **record of disbursements by the Commissary General of Military Stores' Department and orders for deliveries by the Superintendent of Military Stores, October 1780-June 1781 and July 1799-August 1801** (M927, 1 roll), contains copies of orders for money payments. The orders give the date, the purpose of payment, the payee, and the amount. Payments were for pay of department employees, purchase of supplies, travel expenses, and other purposes. Arrangement is chronological. At the beginning of the series are two unbound typewritten sheets, apparently prepared from secondary sources in the 1920s, that give a chronological summary of the use of Carpenters' Hall in Philadelphia by the Commissary General of Military Stores' Department during the Revolution and by Maj. Gen. Henry Knox for a time thereafter. The subseries "record of receipts and disbursements, Commissary General of Military Stores' Department, March 1780-October 1781" (Number 114, M853, roll 35), contains entries showing the name of the person to whom or from whom money was paid or received, the purpose, and the amount. Disbursements were made for tools, forage, clothing, transportation, pasturage, and other supplies, services, and expenses. Money was received from persons who bought sword blades, pistols, damaged cannon, and other articles from the department. Entries are arranged chronologically. "Record of disbursements by Samuel Hodgdon, Deputy Commissary General of Military Stores, March 1780-March 1781" (Number 117, M853, roll 35), shows for each disbursement the voucher number, the date, the payee, the purpose, and the amount. Disbursements were made for wire, iron, wood, paper, thread, rent, postage, chimney sweeping, advertisements, and other supplies, services, and expenses. Arrangement is chronological. A separate name index of 19th-century origin accompanies this volume. The transactions recorded in this volume are also recorded in numbered record book 114. "Record of cash received and of disbursements, October 1781-October 1788" (Number 96, M853, roll 36), appears to have been kept by Samuel Hodgdon as Commissary General of Military Stores, commissary of military stores, and assistant quartermaster. In addition to money received it shows disbursements for stores, transportation, salaries, provisions, rent, postage, forage, and other expenses of both departments. Entries show the names of persons from whom or to whom money was received or paid, the amounts, and the purposes. Some of the entries for money received concern individuals who purchased buildings and other items of public property from the government. Arrangement is chronological. A separate name index of 19th-century origin accompanies the volume. Many of the entries in this volume were posted to volume 144 of the numbered record books (**MI.93.46.**).

MI.93.48. Estimates of the quantities of military stores and other supplies needed for the army during and after the Revolutionary War; and of the funds needed by the Commissary General of Military Stores' and the Quartermaster General's Departments to procure the supplies and pay for salaries, rent, repair and construction costs; and of other expenses are found in "estimates of supplies and funds, 1780-93" (Number 148, M853, roll 29). Most of the estimates do not show to whom they were submitted, but some are addressed to the Secretary at War, the Board of War, and the Superintendent of Finance. Arrangement is chronological, and a separate name index of 19th-century origin accompanies the volume.

MI.93.49. Records of the Commissary General for Military Stores' Department—which account for military stores received by, delivered to, and on hand at various military units, governmental bodies, or locations—are found mostly among the numbered record books (**MI.93.8.**). They are presented here in tabular format. The descriptive pamphlets for relevant National Archives microfilm publications provide more complete descriptions of the records.

Nature of account(s)	Dates	Micro-film: Roll No.	Numbered Rec. Bk. Vol. No.
Various units in PA and 3 galleys	1776-80	M853:40	120
The Corps of Artillery in the Northern Dept.	1778-79	M853:40	119
Pluckemin, Albany, Farmington, New Hartford, East Hartford	1778-82	M853:40	118
Numerous places—includes captured stores at Yorktown, 1781	1777-83	M853:39	129-131, 151
Philadelphia	1780-84	M853:37-38	94, 122, 132, 133
The Main Army in the field	1780-83	M927:1	—
Accounts of the United States with PA, DE, MD, VA, NC, SC, GA, NJ	1780-83	M853:40	91, 113
Accounts for shot and shells	1780-85	M853:40	116
Returns of military stores purchased, on hand, and delivered	1781-82	M853:40	115

Commissary General of Stores and Provisions' Department and its successors

MI.93.50. One volume in the numbered record books (**MI.93.8.**), the subseries "record of rations issued in the Eastern Department, December 1776-November 1777" (Number 112, M853, roll 41), contains in its first part a record of provisions issued to Continental Army and state militia regiments, companies, and individuals. It shows dates of issuance, bill numbers, names of persons to whom provisions were delivered, and kinds and quantities of rations. The regiments listed are mainly from Massachusetts, Connecticut, and Rhode Island. The second part of the volume contains a record of rations received from military officers, personnel of the Commissary General of Stores and Provisions' Department, and other persons, and recapitulations of ration issued and received. The records in each of the two parts of the book are arranged by names of organizations and individuals, and thereunder chronologically.

MI.93.51. "Records of receipts and issuances of provisions and stores by Assistant Commissaries of Issues, 1776-83" (Number 121, M853, roll 41), consists mainly of accounts showing to whom provisions and related stores, such as soap and candles, were delivered or from whom they were received and the kinds and quantities of articles. There are also a few receipts, copies of letters, and other papers. Records kept by eight individuals who were Commissaries General, or assistant commissaries, of Issues are in the volume. It is arranged by records of particular individuals.

Other army staff departments

MI.93.52. "Letters sent by Brig. Gen. Edward Hand, Adjutant General of the Continental Army, March-July 1781, January-October 1782, and April-July 1783" (Number 162, M853, roll 17). The volume contains copies of letters sent by General Hand, mostly to officers commanding troops, relating to the movement of prisoners, courts-martial, assignments and details, and returns of personnel and equipment. The arrangement is chronological. Some copies of letters written by Hand in 1778, and copies of a few orders issued by him in 1776, are in volume 156 of the numbered record books, described in **MI.93.27.** See **MI.360.15.** for correspondence sent to Congress by Hand.

MI.93.53. "Letters sent by Gerrit H. Van Wagenen, Deputy Commissary of Prisoners, May-August 1779 and August 1780-June 1781" (Number 154, M853, roll 17), contains copies of letters sent by Van Wagenen to the Commissary General of Prisoners, justices of the peace, and army officers. The letters, arranged chronologically, pertain to the accommodation, movement, and escape of prisoners; exchange of prisoners with the enemy; and related matters.

COLONIAL AND STATE MILITARY RECORDS

MI.93.54. Colonial and state military records are intermixed with Continental Army records in series such as those described in **MI.93.10.** and **MI.93.14.**

Records pertaining to individual colonies and states

MI.93.55. The series **records pertaining to soldiers and activities in New Hampshire, 1629-1774,** consists of certified manuscript copies of letters to and from the Speaker and Committee of Correspondence of the New Hampshire House of Representatives, 1773-74; printed copies of records, 1629-1724, pertaining to such subjects as military pay, Indian troubles, subsistence and ordnance returns, colonial defense, construction of fortifications, and legislation; and printed copies of muster rolls and lists of New Hampshire officers and enlisted men who performed military service, 1709-73. The rolls usually give such information as the name, rank, and date of death or desertion of an individual, and sometimes the period of service and wages earned or due. The series seems to have been copied in 1895 from records in the custody of the New Hampshire Adjutant General and from publications of the New Hampshire Historical Society. The records have no discernible arrangement save the correspondence, which is in chronological order.

MI.93.56. Other records pertaining to individual states are among the numbered record books (**MI.93.8.**). "Miscellaneous records relating to soldiers and activities in New York State, 1781-82" (Number 161, M853, roll 17), includes records concerning supplies furnished or impressed, 1781; a petition seeking relief from prosecution for taking Tory property; a copy of an act of the New York legislature for raising militia and providing bounty land; and lists of men mustered for two and three years service in 1781-82. A more detailed statement concerning the records and their arrangement is given in the descriptive pamphlet for M853.

MI.93.57. "Record of clothing accounts of the 1st Virginia State Regiment kept by Lt. Charles Russell, 1779-80" (Number 99, M853, roll 22), consists of accounts that show the amounts debited and credited to individuals for clothing, the dates, and the kinds and quantities of clothing issued. It is arranged by the names of persons having accounts, all of whom appear to have been enlisted men, with a name index at the front of the volume. "Ledger of officers' accounts kept by Lt. Charles Russell, Paymaster, 1st Virginia State Regiment, 1779-80 and 1783" (Number 159, M853, roll 22), mainly shows amounts of money debited and credited to officers in 1779-80 for pay, repair of equipment, supplies, and other reasons. The few entries for 1783 appear to be accounts of a private nature relating to crops, plantation rent, and wages of free blacks. Arrangement is by name of account. There is a name index to the titles of accounts.

Records pertaining to several states

MI.93.58. Photographic copies of state records, ca. 1775-83, is a single series consisting of records that, at the time of copying, were in the custody of individuals and public and private institutions mainly in Virginia, North Carolina, and Massachusetts. They were copied pursuant to an act of Congress of March 2, 1913 (see **MI.93.4.** and **NA.45.1.**), and consist chiefly of letters and reports sent and received by state boards of war, governors, and military officers; minutes of boards of war; prize vessel accounts; accounts of the Westham Foundry, VA; rolls and returns; court records; and receipts for money and supplies. The series is arranged by states and thereunder mainly by numbers assigned to the records by the custodians of the originals or by the War Department. Numbers 35501-49983 of the manuscript file (**MI.93.10.**) were reserved for the photographic copies of state records, but not all of these numbers were used, and a significant number of Virginia records are numbered by schemes separate from that of the manuscript file.

MI.93.59. For name and subject indexes to the photographic copies of state records that are numbered as part of the manuscript file, see the first two indexes described in **MI.93.9.** Another series, **name index to Virginia records in series 9 [photographic copies of state records, ca. 1775-83]**, was prepared in the Adjutant General's Office sometime after 1913. It is an index to names of military personnel and civilians. In addition to a name and the number of a record, some of the entries give the rank and organization of the person indexed, the date of the record involved, and a brief summary of the nature and subject matter of the record. The series **subject index to Virginia records in series 9 [photographic copies of state records, ca. 1775-83]**, also prepared in the Adjutant General's Office sometime after 1913, is an index to names of vessels, places, organizations, and miscellaneous subjects such as counterfeiters, the Declaration of Independence, and prisoners of war. In addition to a subject and the number of the record, some of the entries give the date and a summary of the contents of the record. They are arranged alphabetically by subject. It appears that these two series, although they were never consolidated, were designed to complete the name and subject indexes mentioned first in this paragraph and in **MI.93.9.** There are also name and subject indexes to the Massachusetts records among the photographic copies of state records that seem to have the same origin and format. These Massachusetts indexes, however, were never completed, cover only a small part of the records, and are of only passing interest.

RECORDS OF BRITISH MILITARY ACTIVITIES

MI.93.60. Four volumes of British military records were received by the Record and Pension Office of the War Department from the Schuylkill Arsenal in Philadelphia in August 1903. They had been found there by a property clerk among "old records long stored away." All are in National Archives Microfilm Publication M922 (1 roll), which consists of three series:

1. **returns of the British Brigade of Foot Guards, March 1776-December 1779** (2 vols.);

2. **ledger of accounts, 1st Regiment of the British Brigade of Foot Guards, November 1777-January 1779** (1 vol.); and

3. **orderly book kept by a British soldier, October-December 1777** (1 vol.).

MI.93.61. Another orderly book is among the numbered record books (**MI.93.8.**)—"British orderly book, January-July 1779" (Number 163, M853, roll 17). It contains orders of British Commander in Chief in America Sir Henry Clinton, Maj. Gen. William Tryon, Maj. Gen. John Vaughan, and Lt. Col. Henry Johnson, as well as unidentified regimental and other orders. The regimental orders appear to be directed to the British 17th Regiment of Foot, the 44th and 57th British Regiments, the provincial "Loyal American Regiment," and various other British, provincial, and German regiments. The entries are arranged chronologically.

MI.93.62. British military and other correspondence intercepted during the Revolutionary War is among the records of the Continental Congress described in **CC.360.35.** (Item 51, M247, roll 65). Records concerning British evacuation of New York and misconduct of British troops toward civilians are described in **MI.360.36.-MI.360.37.** The series described in **MI.77.2.** and **MI.77.5.-MI.77.6.** contain British maps and plans relating to the war in America. Some of the wartime records of the government of British West Florida pertain to military affairs—see especially **LA.49.9.** A few fragmentary British military records antedating the Revolution are among the materials in the miscellaneous unnumbered records of the War Department Collection of Revolutionary War Records described in **MI.93.69.**

COMPILED MILITARY SERVICE RECORDS AND
RELATED LISTS

MI.93.63. The series **compiled military service records, 1894-ca. 1912** (M880, 4 rolls, and M881, 1,096 rolls), consists of abstracts of original and copied records, mainly military, prepared by the War Department as a means of consolidating information about individuals and preserving the source documents. A single service record is a letter-size envelope, called a jacket, in which are filed one or more cards containing information about a soldier, sailor, or employee of an army staff department copied from one or more original or copied records. The typical jacket is labeled with the name, the rank or other office or occupation of an individual, and the organization in which he served. Notations on the cards in the jacket often give the volume or other number of the record from which information was abstracted. Those originals and copies of Revolutionary War records on which the compiled service records are based are mainly among the muster rolls and other records described in **MI.93.14.-MI.93.16.** and the numbered record books (see **MI.93.8.-MI.93.9.**). If an individual served in two or more different organizations for which there are such records, there is a separate compiled service record for him pertaining to each relevant organization.

MI.93.64. The compiled service record jackets are divided into five subseries: continental troops not affiliated with particular states; troops affiliated with particular states, including continental units and purely state forces such as militia and state troops; Commissary General of Military Stores' Department personnel; Quartermaster General's Department personnel; and naval personnel. Most of the records are part of the first two subseries. Within the first (continental) subseries jackets are arranged in groups by organization, with regiments and other large units grouped before companies and other small independent units and miscellaneous bodies. Within each such grouping, arrangement is for the most part numerical by numbered units followed in alphabetical order by units with designations based on names of commanders. The second (state) subseries is arranged alphabetically by the names of states and thereunder in the same manner as the first subseries. Thereunder in these two subseries, and as the primary order in the other three subseries, arrangement of jackets is alphabetical by names of individuals for whom there are compiled records. Arrangement of cards within jackets is generally chronological by year. Included are empty jackets that serve as cross-references to variant spellings of the names of individuals. Frequently the jackets for all individuals in an organization are preceded by jackets containing cards on which are recorded the exact captions and certification parts of documents, such as muster rolls and payrolls used in preparing the compiled service records, the texts of general pay abstracts, and other information copied from documents pertaining to the unit rather than to individuals who were members of it. For more detailed information concerning the contents and arrangement of the compiled service records, including lists of the organizations for which there are records, see the introductions to National Archives Microfilm Publications M880 and M881.

MI.93.65. There are seven separate indexes to all or part of the compiled military service records. In all of them each entry shows an individual's name and his organization and often shows his rank or profession. There are entries for cross-references to variant spellings of names. The availability and arrangement of the indexes is listed in the following table.

Nature of Index	Arrangement	Microfilm Publication
General index	Alphabetical by surname	M860, 58 rolls
Continental troops unaffiliated with individual states	Alphabetical by surname	none
State troops	Alphabetical by state, thereunder by surname	
Connecticut		M920, 25 rolls
Georgia		M1051, 1 roll
North Carolina		M257, 2 rolls
Other states		None
Commissary General of Military Stores' Department personnel	Alphabetical by surname	none
Personnel in the Q'master General's Department	Alphabetical by surname	none
Major John Brown's detachment of NH, VT, and MA militia	Alphabetical by surname	none

It appears that all of the names in the indexes that have not been microfilmed are included in the general index (M860, 58 rolls). Because of the annotations on the cards in the compiled service records, these indexes may also serve as indirect indexes to the records from which the compiled service records were abstracted.

MI.93.66. The subseries "rosters of state and continental troops, 1775-83" (Numbers 1-11, M853, rolls 14-16), is made up of volumes 1-11 and one unnumbered volume in the numbered record books (**MI.93.8.**). According to citations in the compiled service records (**MI.93.63.-MI.93.64.**), these appear "to have been copied [from original rolls] in the Office of Army Accounts under the Paymaster General" at various times during the late 18th and early 19th centuries. There is at least one volume for each of the original states except Georgia, Maryland, Virginia, and New Hampshire, with two for New York records and two other volumes for continental troops unaffiliated with any state. Nearly all of the troops listed in the subseries were part of the Continental Army, although two volumes contain a few entries for state troops and militiamen. The volumes differ with respect to the amount of information provided about individuals. Generally rank and organization are shown for each officer and enlisted man, as well as dates of enlistment and appointment. Information may also be provided about dates of reenlistment, joining, muster, resignation, derangement, promotion, demotion, reduction, dismissal, discharge, desertion, capture, furlough, transfer, absence without leave, exchange, or death. More information about the records and their arrangement is in the descriptive pamphlet to National Archives Microfilm Publication M853.

MI.93.67. The series **lists and other reference materials relating to Revolutionary War records** consists of one volume, which begins with two typed lists entitled "A List of Organizations in the Revolutionary War Arranged as filed" and "Organizations of the Revolutionary War Alphabetically Arranged." Both were compiled in the Adjutant General's Office in 1930. The first is arranged the same as the compiled military service records (see **MI.93.64.**), but only down to the organization level, mainly regiments and companies. The second list is arranged alphabetically by the names of organizations, from "Abbot's (John) Regiment, Vermont Militia" to "York Militia, Pennsylvania, Andrew's Battalion," regardless of whether the unit was state or continental. The names of the organizations were derived from the names of their commanding officers or from places with which the units were associated. There are 17 other lists or sets of lists in this volume, which contains a table of contents with page references. The other lists include one related to Benedict Arnold and Major Andre, another of published Revolutionary War records, one of histories of Virginia counties, and a list of Massachusetts generals. Many lists refer to nongovernmental records and many give the location of records in RG 93. The series **lists of organizations** consists of carbon copies of the first two lists bound as one volume.

MI.93.68. The series **list of Revolutionary War officers** consists of alphabetically arranged lists of regimental and company officers of each of the states and the Continental Line, 1775-83, showing their names, ranks, and organizations; a list of organizations and their commanding officers named in the journals of the Continental Congress (**CC.360.10.-CC.360.14.**), arranged by volume and page numbers of the journals; and an unarranged list of aides to George Washington showing the states from which they came. Most of the lists were prepared, probably in the Records and Pension Office, from compiled military service records (**MI.93.63.-MI.93.64.**).

MI.93.69. There are five lists of uncertain administrative origin and date in RG 93. The first two are subseries; the other three are series:

1. "unidentified list of names, 1778-81" (Number 153, M853, roll 17);

2. "record of pay and service of officers and men of Virginia, New York, and Georgia, 1781-87" (Numbers 175-176, M853, roll 22).

3. **list of New Hampshire officers and men who received certificates for depreciation of pay [ca. 1857]** (1 vol.);

4. **Revolutionary War index to New York soldiers** (1 vol.); and

5. **list of certificates issued by the state of Pennsylvania for depreciation of pay** [ca. 1819] (1 vol.).

OTHER RECORDS

MI.93.70. **Miscellaneous unnumbered records, ca. 1709-1913**, is a series of a truly miscellaneous nature. It contains three groups of documents pertaining to the handling of Revolutionary War records in the late 19th and early 20th centuries, five registers and account books relating to the Quartermaster General's Department, loose title pages from formerly bound sets of records, an original undated letter from Jonathan Williams to Benjamin Franklin, and a few other documents. For more detailed descriptions of some of the records in this series, see **CO.93.3.-CO.93.4.**

MI.93.71. Among **miscellaneous printed records, 1774-1830**, are pamphlets from the 1780s concerning politics in Pennsylvania, copies of instructions and orders from the Board of Treasury to various officials, several newspaper clippings, and blank certificates of Revolutionary War scrip issued under an act of May 1830. Arrangement is generally chronological.

MI.93.72. The series **Revolutionary War stations** was compiled in the Old Records Division of the Adjutant General's Office in 1933, mainly from information obtained from compiled military service records (**MI.93.63.-MI.93.64.**). It shows the locations of regiments, companies, and other U.S. military organizations on various dates, 1775-83, and is arranged alphabetically by location.

MI.93.73. Included with the Revolutionary War records transferred by the War Department to the Department of State in 1888 was a body of letters from the period of the Revolution and later, numbered from 100 to 6311 and filed in numerical order. The series **wrappers to letters received, 1776-1814**, consists of the paper wrappers in which letters were encased. On each is written the file number, the date and sometimes the place of writing, the name of the writer and sometimes of the addressee, and a brief summary of the communication. The letters were removed from the wrappers when they were transferred from the Department of State to the War Department's Record and Pension Office in 1894. Those dated before 1784 were assigned new file numbers in the two series described in **MI.93.10.** and **MI.93.14.** The wrappers were kept together in numerical order. It is possible to locate a letter that was placed in the two files by looking up the name of the writer in the first index described in **MI.93.9.** and then using these wrappers to determine the new file number assigned in the Record and Pension Office. Another series, **registers of letters received, 1776-1814**, was created when the letters were received by the Department of State in 1888 from the War Department. The two volumes of registers are arranged alphabetically by the first two letters of writers' surnames or of subjects and thereunder generally numerically by file number. They thus serve as indexes to the series of wrappers.

MI.93.74. The series **register of army returns** (1 vol.) constitutes an index to records including rolls, personnel returns, and returns of military stores as they were arranged when in Department of State custody before 1894. The register thus is of only passing interest.

MI.93.75. **Card list of general information** (5 in.) consists of 3- by 5-inch cards prepared in the Old Records Division of the Adjutant General's Office, probably between 1928 and 1935. They contain information about persons, places, events, and other subjects such as "Hessians," "Negroes", and "Prisoners." Most of the cards concern subjects associated with the Revolutionary War, but some relate to the French and Indian wars and later wars through the Civil War. The majority of the cards give only bibliographic information about published works, but some contain references to records in RG 93. A similar series is **printed books relating to the Revolutionary War** (1 vol.), prepared in the same office at about the same time. It contains similar information about persons, places, events, and other subjects, but also present are newspaper clippings, copies of letters written in response to inquiries about the Revolutionary War, and a chronology of events, March 23, 1775-October 4, 1779. Arrangement after the initial chronology is alphabetical by subject.

Record Group 94
Records of the Adjutant General's Office

MI.94.1. The Continental Congress on June 17, 1775, appointed the Adjutant General of the Continental Army. From the disbanding of the army in 1783 until 1792, there was no such permanent position in the War Department. An act of March 5, 1792, created the position of U.S. Army Adjutant General, who was also to serve as Inspector General.

MI.94.2. The series **post-Revolutionary War papers, 1780-1815** (approx. 200 ft.), consists of bound and unbound records, about 6 inches of which are dated before March 4, 1789, and relate mainly to the Continental Army staff departments of the Commissary General of Military Stores, the Quartermaster General, and the Paymaster General and Commissioner of Army Accounts. Most of the pre-federal materials are bound volumes and are separately described in **CO.94.2.** and **MI.94.6.-MI.94.8.** A few documents at the beginning of some unbound records labeled "Hodgdon & Pickering Papers" are dated 1780-89 and include accounts and receipts for supplies and pay, returns of supplies and of work performed, pay and supply orders, and letters received by Commissary of Military Stores Samuel Hodgdon and Quartermaster General Timothy Pickering; drafts of letters written by Paymaster General and Commissioner for Army Accounts John Pierce; and registers of notes issued by Pierce in 1785 for the pay of troops "raised for the year 1784." Some of the records associated with Hodgdon concern private business rather than official matters. The pre-federal volumes and the "Hodgdon & Pickering Papers" are at the end of the larger body of records, which has no discernible overall arrangement.

MI.94.3. The National Archives Microfilm Publication *War Department Collection of Post-Revolutionary War Manuscripts* (M904, 4 rolls) includes letters, accounts, receipts, personnel and supply returns, powers of attorney, orders, and pay abstracts. Although the bulk of the records in the series filmed are from the period 1784-1811, most of them, including a few created in the 1850s, concern the supply and pay of militia of various states in the 1790s and the first decade of the 19th century. Among the two or three dozen items pertaining to the pre-federal period are copies of two letters sent in 1790 by the Office of Army Accounts to the auditor of Delaware concerning the service of Delaware troops in the Revolution (roll 3); an account between South Carolina and the United States for services rendered by the state in protecting the frontier, 1787-92 (roll 3); two returns of troops under Lt. Col. Josiah Harmar and Maj. Sebastian Bauman, 1784, and a return of clothing at Philadelphia, 1786 (roll 4); correspondence and accounts concerning the pay of officers and troops, including troops under the command of Josiah Harmar, 1784-87 (roll 4); and an order dated June 17, 1787, endorsed "Expedition against Colo. Daniel Shays" (roll 4). Arrangement of the series is numerical, mainly according to number assigned to the states and territories to which the records pertain. The microfilm includes a personal name index (rolls 1 and 2), which is arranged alphabetically by surname. Where the information is present in the records, an entry shows the rank and organization of the person indexed in addition to the location of the record. Some of the entries contain references to names in the record books described in **MI.98.3.-MI.98.4.**

MI.94.4. The series **muster rolls of volunteer organizations: war with northwest Indians, 1790-95**, contains two pre-federal documents. "Return of deserters since March 1, 1786, from a detachment of the First American Regiment Commanded by Lt. Josiah Harmar, April 16, 1786," gives the names of 14 deserters, their branch of service, age, height, complexion, birthplace, trade, clothing taken, date of enlistment, and date of desertion. "Pay abstract of the 'Corps of Artillery' Commanded by Capt.-Lt. William Johnston, June 1-November 1, 1785," is a certified copy, from 1790, of an original "filed in the War Office." It gives the names of 40 officers and enlisted men and shows their rank, period of service, rate of pay per month, total pay due, and date of discharge. Both documents were used to produce the compiled military service records (**MI.93.63.-MI.93.64.**).

MI.94.5. In the series **letters received**, in the subgroup Records of the Appointment, Commission, and Personal Branch of the Adjutant General's Office, 1863-94, is the portfolio "Forms of Army Commissions, 1775-1916." The commissions were gathered, apparently as a reference set, beginning in 1879 and include copies and originals, both blank and filled in. A few associated records, such as samples of transmittal letters for commissions, are also present. The pre-federal commissions in this file are all 19th- and 20th-century copies and consist of a typescript copy of Washington's commission as general and Commander in Chief of the Continental Army, June 19, 1775; a facsimile copy of John Paul Jones' commission as a captain in the Continental Navy, October 10, 1776; a typescript copy of a continental commission to an unnamed military officer, June 28, 1779; a photographic copy of a brevet commission as major general to Edward Hand, October 10, 1783; manuscript copies of a brevet commission and commission as major to Capt. Elnathan Haskell, September 30, 1783; a manuscript copy of a commission to Haskell as major in the "Second Regiment of Army of the United States," April 2, 1787; a photostatic copy of a commission to John Horton to be a "Leftenant" in the Morris County, NJ, militia, June 15, 1780; and a manuscript copy of a commission to Elnathan Haskell to be deputy adjutant general with the rank of colonel in the Massachusetts militia, April 24, 1786. Some of the copies of early commissions include the date of the copy and the location of the originals at the time of copying. The commissions as a whole are arranged in several sections according to general type, such as "Continental" and "Militia," and thereunder roughly by date or state.

MI.94.6. Four volumes among the **post-Revolutionary War papers, 1780-1815 (MI.94.2.),** contain records of pre-federal military affairs. The first three described here were used in producing the compiled service records (**MI.93.63.-MI.93.64.**). Volume 4 is "Payrolls and Pay Accounts for Capt. Henry Burbeck's Company, Capt. Joseph Savage's Company, and Ens. Francis Luse's Detachment, January 1, 1787-January 1, 1790." The payrolls are for Burbeck's and Savage's artillery companies, May 1, 1787-January 1, 1790, and for a detachment of the "United States Regiment" at West Point, January 1, 1787-December 5, 1789. Information given includes the names of individual officers and enlisted men and their ranks, periods of service, dates of commencement of pay, monthly pay rates, total pay earned, payments made to them, stoppages in pay for desertion, balances due, and dates of promotion, reduction, desertion, discharge, death, and other occurrences. The pay accounts are between the United States and the unit commanders. They summarize the data contained in each payroll. Arrangement is by organization, in the order mentioned. Volume 5 contains returns for the same units for approximately the same period. It also contains, in the following arrangement, a return of money paid soldiers discharged from the "1st United States Regiment . . . who have served in the Western Department"; a list of soldiers to whom payments were made by Capt. E. Beatty; a return of soldiers who sold their pay to Joseph Bindon of New York City; and a list of soldiers of the 1st U.S. Regiment to whom balances were due. Information given about the individuals named in the several returns and lists varies, but includes their rank, total amount of pay due, dates when installments of pay were to be made, dates of payments, names of persons paid, and dates of desertion, if applicable.

MI.94.7. Volume 3 is "Record of Clothing due to and Money Deducted from Pay of Enlisted Men of the First United States Regiment, 1788-89." It contains, in the following order, a "Return" of clothing due to the men "of the U States Regimt. and two Companies of Artillery, who were discharged and Died on the Ohio River in . . . 1788 and 1789." It shows the name of each soldier; his rank; the unit to which he belonged; the clothing due him in terms of kind, quantity, and total monetary value; the debit or credit status of his account; and, occasionally, the date of payment. The second part of the volume contains a list of accounts of individual soldiers, showing their companies, the form of their indebtedness, the name of the creditors and the amount due.

MI.94.8. An unnumbered volume in **post-Revolutionary War papers, 1784-1815**, is "Ledger of Military Stores Received and Delivered, March 1780-May 1795" (M927, roll 1). Begun during the Revolutionary War in the Commissary General of Military Stores' Department, presumably at Philadelphia, it was used through the 1780s and into the early years of the federal government. For the pre-federal period a great variety of accounts is present, including accounts for ordnance and related installations; military units, including the "Lines" of various states; several army staff departments; several warships and other vessels of the Continental Navy; several middle and southern states; the garrison at Fort Pitt; Indian commissioners; the Navy Board; and individual officers. The accounts generally show the kinds and quantities of military stores delivered to and received from the persons and other entities having accounts, the dates, and the names of specific persons to or from whom stores were delivered or received. The volume is arranged in two sections, from March 1780 to July 1781 and from July 1781 to May 1795, and thereunder chronologically by accounts. At the front of the volume are two indexes to the first section only; they are keyed to the names of the accounts.

MI.94.9. National Archives Microfilm Publication *Compiled Service Records of Veterans Who Served From 1784 to 1811* (M905, 32 rolls), contains records similar to those described in **MI.93.63.-MI.93.64.** The series was created in the Adjutant General's Office, beginning in 1912, from information found in the records described in **MI.94.4., MI.94.6.-MI.94.7.,** and **MI.98.2.** The records consist of envelopes (each showing the name of a soldier, his organization, and his rank) that contain a card or cards on which information relating to the individual is written. Occasionally an original pay account or other record pertaining to a specific soldier is also in his envelope. The series is arranged mainly into three groups for U.S., state, and territorial forces; thereunder by particular units; and thereunder alphabetically by surnames of individuals. Some unfiled original records are at the end of the series in alphabetical order by the names of the individual soldiers to whom they pertain. The index to these records makes up a separate series microfilmed as National Archives Microfilm Publication M694 (9 rolls). It is an index to the names of all persons for whom there are compiled records, regardless of organization. Each entry gives the name of a soldier, his rank, and the unit in which he served. There are cross-reference cards for variant spellings of names and for individuals who served in more than one unit.

MI.94.10. The records of the Appointment, Commission, and Personal Branch of the Adjutant General's Office contain the series **register of army commissions, 1792-1812** (1 vol.). Bound into the front of the volume is a manuscript containing three lists: two of Continental Army officers from Massachusetts and from New York who were disbanded at West Point in June 1783 and one of officers who served in the "third Regiment of Artillery Massachusetts Line" commanded by Col. John Crane. The lists contain information about whether the individuals named were still living in 1820 and, if so, their residences and sometimes their current government or other position or occupation. The Massachusetts and New York lists are arranged alphabetically by surnames; the list for Crane's regiment is in descending order of rank.

MI.94.11. The series **"Outline Index of Military Forts and Stations," n.d.**, consists of 27 volumes containing information and references to sources of information on military installations in the United States from ca. 1700 to 1900. Information provided for each post includes its location, the dates of its establishment and abandonment, the origin of its name, and references to published sources of information on it. Installations for which there are entries include U.S. posts, installations of foreign powers, fortified Indian towns, arsenals, redoubts, batteries, and civilian blockhouses. The entries are arranged in alphabetical order, mainly by the first two letters of the names of installations. There is a separate volume for each letter of the alphabet and one for "Mc." There are one or two indexes in each volume except "X." The volume for the letter "A," as an example, contains entries for the following types of installations for the pre-federal period: Spanish, French, Dutch, and English colonial forts; fortified towns of the Alabama Indians; a prehistoric defensive work along the Miami River; civilian blockhouses; and U.S. posts active during the Revolution, such as Fort Arnold, NY, and "Amboys Flying Camp," NJ. The series **reservation file, ca. 1800-1916**, is closely related to the outline index, but it consists of original records and references to other sources of information pertaining to military installations in the United States from the pre-federal period to 1916. The information, which concerns the establishment, maintenance, and abandonment of the installations, is in the form of correspondence, orders, and other records. The series is in two parts. The first is arranged alphabetically according to names of posts and the second by military departments and divisions.

MI.94.12. The series **vouchers, 1865-79**, records payments made from the Provost Fund, which included money belonging to deserters and Confederate prisoners of war and money acquired from other sources by U.S. military authorities during the Civil War. After the war the fund was in the custody of the Adjutant General, who disbursed sums from it for various purposes upon the order or approval of the Secretary of War. Among this series of vouchers, which consist mainly of receipts for payments and related correspondence, are several concerning the purchase and processing by the War Department of Revolutionary War records. The vouchers are arranged in numerical order.

MI.94.13. **"General Information Index," 1794-1918** (41 ft.), consisting of 3- by 8-inch cards alphabetically arranged, is a name and subject index compiled by clerks in the War Department to identify sources of information on subjects of frequent inquiry and subjects that required difficult searches. Index cards give file numbers for records now in the National Archives, including some in the War Department Collection of Revolutionary War Records (RG 93), and references to published records and secondary sources. Some original records are actually filed in the index, probably because they lack file numbers or other identifying information. Newspaper clippings and letters prepared in response to inquiries are also interfiled. Examples of index categories pertaining to the pre-federal period are "Col. Ethan Allen," "Maj. John Andre," "Brandywine," "Fort Niagara," "Fort Nonsense," "Negroes," "West Point," and "White Plains." No original pre-federal records are found in the index.

MI.94.14. **"Miscellaneous File," ca. 1800-1917**, consists of 300 envelopes, consecutively numbered, which contain original records, unofficial publications, newspaper clippings, copies of letters sent by the Adjutant General's Office in response to inquiries, copies of published maps, and other items brought together for reference use concerning military matters. The principal subjects of the materials in the series are indexed in the "General Information Index" described in MI.94.13.

MI.94.15. *The Negro in the Military Service of the United States, 1639-1886* (M858, 5 rolls), is part of the records of the Colored Troops Division of the Adjutant General's Office and was prepared by division head Elon A. Woodward. The first three chapters in volume 1 (roll 1) pertain to the period through 1789. Specific subjects include exemption and nonexemption of blacks from colonial militia service, the arming of colonial slaves in cases of invasion, the slave population in 1715 and 1775, enlistment of blacks in the Continental Army and in the British military service during the Revolution, George Washington's attitude toward the use of black troops, the raising of black troops by Lord Dunmore, plans for raising black troops in Rhode Island and South Carolina, naval service of blacks during the Revolution, the return to their owners of captured blacks and of blacks who enlisted in the Continental Army, and provision for the support of black veterans of the Continental Army after the Revolution. Many of the colonial laws cited also pertain to militia service by Indians.

Record Group 98
Records of U.S. Army Commands, 1784-1821

MI.98.1. In 1784 the U.S. Army consisted of one infantry regiment. Between then and 1789, additional units of infantry, artillery, and dragoons were added. During most of the period from 1784 to 1813, units and posts were under the direct command of the Chief of the Army, who was responsible to the Secretary of War. There were, however, several periods when field establishments were organized into one or more departments, each responsible to the Secretary of War. In 1813 such a division became a permanent concept with 9, and later 10, military districts. In 1815 the country was divided into Divisions of the North and South, with five military departments in each. In 1821 it was reorganized into the Eastern and Western Departments.

MI.98.2. The series **inspection return of the American Regiment of Foot under Col. Henry Jackson, May 1784**, is a slim volume in the subgroup Records of Units, Infantry. This return, on a printed form, gives such information as the number of officers and enlisted men of various ranks present and fit for duty, the number of men sick, the number of men "wanting" to complete the regiment, and the surnames of 11 absent officers and the reasons for their absence. Some of the officers and men are shown as being on duty at Fort Putnam and on command at Springfield.

MI.98.3. In the same subgroup is **orderly book for the company of Capt. Jonathan Heart, September 1785-May 1788**, which contains company, garrison, and detachment orders issued by Heart, Maj. John Doughty, and Lt. Col. Josiah Harmar at numerous places beginning at a tavern near New Windsor, NY, and ending at Fort Franklin, PA. Also in the orderly book is a statement of prices to be charged soldiers by women for making clothing, repairing shoes, and washing clothing; roll call regulations and regulations for examining arms; and garrison regulations for Fort Franklin. A 19th-century memorandum at the front of the volume states that Heart's company was raised in Connecticut. The book is arranged chronologically, with gaps of as much as 2 months between orders. Letters exchanged by Heart and Harmar during the establishment of Fort Franklin are in **letters sent and received by Capt. Jonathan Heart, company commander, 1787-88.** Besides Harmar, Heart wrote letters to Secretary at War Henry Knox; Col. William Butler; Capt. William Ferguson; James O'Hara, a contractor; Daniel Britt and Company; and a few other officers and civilians. Subjects include supply and construction problems, activities of hostile and friendly Indians, and British activity in the area. Indian tribes mentioned include Senecas, Munsees, Wyandots, Mohawks, Onondagas, and Shawnees. A 19th-century memorandum at the front of the volume gives a brief summary of the contents. Parts of many pages in the volume are missing. Both Heart's orderly book and letterbook are partially indexed by the index described in **MI.94.3.**

MI.98.4. In the subgroup Records of Departments, Districts, Divisions, and Posts is **orderly book for the garrison at Castle Island, Boston Harbor, 1786-87**, which contains copies of orders issued February 7-April 20, 1787. The troops commanded by the two officers were presumably the Massachusetts portion of troops authorized by Congress on October 20, 1786, to defend the western frontier from Indian attacks. Also in the volume are documents concerning the authorization, recruitment, training, and equiping of the troops at Castle Island. The records are arranged generally in chronological order. A separate, alphabetically arranged name and subject index compiled in the 19th century accompanies the records. The book is partially indexed in the index described in **MI.94.3. Records of the garrison at Fort Independence, Boston Harbor ("Castle Island Records"), 1803-28**, is a record book kept by later commanders of the post. At the beginning of the volume is a 25-page history of Castle Island, 1634-1803, containing detailed information about the first fort on the island (Castle William), the names of military organizations and commanding and other officers stationed there, the use of the fort by the British at the time of the Boston Massacre and in other disputes with the colonists, and activities there during the Revolution. Following this history is a register of the commanding officers at Castle Island under British, Massachusetts, and federal forces.

Record Group 107
Records of the Office of the Secretary of War

MI.107.1. The act of August 7, 1789, that created the Department of War entrusted to the Secretary of War responsibility for recruiting, provisioning, and regulating U.S. military and naval forces.

MI.107.2. The series **letters received by the Secretary of War, unregistered series, 1789-1861**, contains a few pre-federal appointments and related records.

Record Group 112
Records of the Office of the Surgeon General (Army)

MI.112.1. An act of April 14, 1818, regulating the staff of the army, provided for the establishment of the Office of the Surgeon General. Surgeons and mates had earlier served at posts or with regiments under the orders of the post or regimental commander, but they lacked a formalized common head or organization.

MI.112.2. The series **military service cards of Revolutionary War medical officers, 1775-1918**, consists of approximately 500 3- by 5-inch cards mostly for Revolutionary War officers; but some show service only after 1789. A card shows the individual's state of residence; the position or positions he held, such as surgeon, surgeon's mate, or hospital physician; the organization or organizations to which he was attached, such as continental, militia, and state regiments, army departments, and unidentified hospitals; the date of commencement of his service in each position; and the date of his resignation, retirement, or other service expiration. Many cards also show dates of death, and some have dates and places of capture. The sources of the information on the cards are not shown. The cards are arranged alphabetically by surname. **List of officers in the Medical Department, 1775-1892**, is a single-volume series similar to the military service cards. All of the information contained in the volume is also on the cards, which also convey additional information.

MI.112.3. Historical files of the Army Nurse Corps, 1900-47, contain a great variety of documents concerning the activities of the Army Nurse Corps in particular and nurses generally in American wars and in peacetime, from the colonial period through World War II. The few records that pertain to the pre-federal period include mimeographed and typed papers that contain some references to nursing during the Revolution, in a folder labeled "Miscellaneous"; reprints of articles in folders labeled "Barton, Clara" and "Nursing in the Civil War"; a typed paper titled "Historical Sources of Early Colonial and Revolutionary Care of the Sick" citing primary and secondary sources on such topics as kinds of diseases and medicines and the locations of Revolutionary War military hospitals; typed extracts from Continental Army hospital returns listing the names of some female nurses; and a paper titled "Organization of the Medical Department" concerning its history, 1775-1920.

Record Group 156

Records of the Office of the Chief of Ordnance

MI.156.1. The Ordnance Department was established as an independent bureau of the Department of War by an act of May 14, 1812. Its functions were to procure, maintain, develop, and test ordnance for the U.S. Army.

MI.156.2. In the series **letters received, 1812-94**, are some letters and related records received from Capt. David Hopkins pertaining to his Revolutionary War service. The documents are filed under the letter "H" for April 1816 and consist of original letters sent by Hopkins to Col. George Bomford, Chief of Ordnance, and other government officials in 1816, and copies of approximately a dozen letters and orders received by him as a captain of dragoons from Gens. George Washington and William Heath and their aides-de-camp, September 1777-August 1779, in an attempt to obtain an appointment as the superintendent of a government arsenal. There is also a copy of a letter to Hopkins from Return J. Meigs, March 15, 1816, recounting in detail their joint participation in the expedition to and attack on the city of Quebec in 1775.

MI.156.3. The series **history of Fort Monroe from 1607 to 1884, 1880-84**, is among the records of Fort Monroe (VA) Arsenal and appears to have been compiled in the Adjutant General's Office of the War Department. Although Fort Monroe as such did not exist until 1832, the study begins in 1609 and relates the pre-federal history of the area. The records also include several maps, newspaper clippings, printed military orders, and copies of legal documents and state and federal legislation pertaining to the fort and the surrounding area. They are in no discernible order.

Record Group 165
Records of the War Department
General and Special Staffs

MI.165.1. The War Department General Staff was authorized by Congress in 1903 and reorganized frequently thereafter. It was a separate and distinct staff organization with supervision over most military branches, both line and staff.

MI.165.2. The subgroup George Washington Atlas (Army War College) is a group of manuscript maps compiled in the 1930s by the historical section of the Army War College. They illustrate Washington's travels and campaigns during the French and Indian War and the Revolutionary War. Four of the 20 sheets were apparently compiled in connection with the establishment of Shenandoah National Park in Virginia. All of the maps are listed in National Archives Special List No. 26, *Pre-Federal Maps in the National Archives: An Annotated List* (1975). For more information on Special List No. 26, see the introduction.

MI.165.3. **Color lithographs of U.S. Army uniforms for the period 1774-1908, 1885-1908** (HOA, HOB, and HOC), are in portfolios and published volumes, consisting mainly of watercolors by Henry Alexander Ogden, that were copyrighted by the Quartermaster General of the U.S. Army, 1885-1908. One published volume, *Uniform of the Army of the United States Illustrated from 1774 to 1889* (1895), contains seven plates for the Continental Army, 1774-83, and extracts from documents pertaining to the uniforms. These include state legislative proceedings, George Washington's general orders, the journals of the Continental Congress, and historical publications.

Record Group 186
Records of the
Spanish Governors of Puerto Rico

MI.186.1. Spain ceded Puerto Rico to the United States by the Treaty of Paris of December 10, 1898. The cession included rights to the official archives and records on the island, which the United States agreed to preserve and make available for use. After inspection of the records at the Library of Congress in 1900-1901, many important administrative records were returned to San Juan, PR. Most of them were destroyed by a fire at the Archivo Historico in 1926. None of the records in this record group have been translated into English. Records from the 18th century are sparse and fragmentary; although the number of RG 186 records increases for each decade until the 1860s.

MI.186.2. Two series contain records related to military affairs in the period before March 1789:

1. **militar, asuntos generales [general records of military affairs], 1761-1858** (2 ft.); and

2. **presos [prisoners], 1767-1849** (1 ft.).

The records described in **CC.186.2.-CC.186.3.** also contain references to military affairs on the island.

Record Group 200
National Archives Gift Collection

MI.200.1. The National Archives Act of June 18, 1934, the Federal Property Administrative Services Act of 1949, as amended, and the National Archives and Records Administration Act of 1984 authorized the acceptance from private sources of material appropriate for preservation by the U.S. government as evidence of its functions, policies, decisions, procedures, and transactions. Records in RG 200 have been donated by a wide range of business and cultural organizations and institutions and by many individuals.

MI.200.2. The series **military correspondence and related papers, 1778-82**, contains two letters pertaining to pre-federal military affairs. A draft of a letter from Brig. Gen. Anthony Wayne to Maj. Joseph Lewis Finley is dated at "Head Quarters Savannah, June 25, 1782" and bears what appears to be Wayne's holographic signature.

An original letter received by Governor Thomas Johnson of Maryland from Governor Patrick Henry of Virginia, October 31, 1778, was written from Williamsburg.

Records of the Accounting Officers of the Department of the Treasury

MI.217.1. This record group contains records of officers responsible for settling federal and pre-federal accounts before 1921.

MI.217.2. Letters received by the Paymaster General and subordinate officers and related records, 1778-85, were addressed mostly to Paymasters General William Palfrey and John Pierce, especially the latter, but some were received by Pierce as Assistant and Deputy Paymaster General and Commissioner of Army Accounts. The principal writers are Joseph Carleton, Paymaster to the Board of War and Ordnance; Assistant Secretary at War William Jackson; Col. Robert H. Harrison, who often wrote on behalf of General Washington; Secretary at War Benjamin Lincoln; and George Washington. Subjects of the letters include payment of officers and men during the Revolution; payment of troops in 1784; the transportation of money for military pay; relocations of the Office of the Paymaster General and its records; settlement of accounts; claims for commutation; the service of foreign officers in the Continental Army; issuance of notes to troops for pay; and pay of U.S. Army officers who were prisoners of war. Some of Carleton's letters to Pierce concern the circumstance of mutual friends and the writer's relationship with a young lady in Maryland. Most of the letters are endorsed with the names of the writers and the dates written or received. They are arranged alphabetically by surnames of the writers, and thereunder chronologically. The records of the Third Auditor, described in **PE.217.3.**, contain some correspondence and receipts concerning supplies and services provided continental forces, including those sent to Canada under General Arnold in the winter of 1775-76.

MI.217.3. "Journals of expenditures relating to the Armies of the Continental and Confederation governments, June 25, 1776-May 24, 1786" (M1015, roll 1), consist of two volumes among the records of the Second Auditor of the Department of the Treasury. Headings at the tops of pages show that the first volume was kept mainly at the "Pay Office" at Philadelphia and for some periods at West Point, New Windsor, and "Camp," 1776-May 1784. The second volume was kept in New York City, November 1785-May 1786. Most of the entries are for transactions or services during the Revolutionary War. Among the matters to which they pertain are military pay and rations; the purchase of supplies, including arms, horses, clothing, forage, and medicine; recruiting expenses; dues of officers to the Society of the Cincinnati; and the issuance of final settlement certificates for pay, commutation, and other purposes. Information in each entry includes the date and nature of the transaction, the names and ranks of the person or persons involved, sums received or disbursed, the date of the entry in the journal, and the names of accounts presumed to be recorded in a related ledger. The record book to which the entries were posted has not been found. The entries are arranged generally in chronological order by date of entry.

MI.217.4. "Accounts of James Johnston, Paymaster of the 2nd Pennsylvania Regiment, March 1777-August 1779" (M1015, roll 4) consist mainly of entries showing money paid or due to officers and men of the regiment for pay and recruiting expenses. Entries include the names and ranks of officers and men, sums involved, dates of transactions, amounts of stoppages for clothing, and whether the persons due money were dead, deserters, prisoners, or otherwise absent. Dates of deaths and resignations are sometimes given. Also shown are sums of money received by Johnston from Paymaster General William Palfrey. Arrangement is mainly by companies and thereunder by names of individuals. For related and similar records, see **MI.59.2.-MI.59.3.**

MI.217.5. A 12-page document, signed at the end by "Jno Wright Clk. Office of Army Accots.," is titled "Account of Credits given to the State of Rhode Island in her account with the United States for Depreciation of Pay to sundry soldiers who are by Act of Congress of the 10 of April 1780 entitled to receive the same but for the payment of which no vouchers have been produc'd." It gives the names, ranks, and regiments of several dozen enlisted men, including noncommissioned officers, and shows the amount of money due each. It is arranged alphabetically by surnames.

MI.217.6. A document of apparent 19th-century origin, called "List of Revolutionary War Officers who received Final Settlement Certificates from Paymaster General and Commissioner of Army Accounts John Pierce," is among the records of the Claims Division of the Office of the Third Auditor of the Treasury Department. For each officer the information usually given is rank, state or organization for which he served, and the number of a single final settlement certificate. A penciled heading on the first page of the list refers to the certificates as being for commutation. For some officers, instead of a certificate number, a variety of notations (dated as late as 1852) include references to an unspecified "act of Cong.," to specific acts dating from 1792 to 1836, and to unidentified ledgers and journals. Most of the officers served in the Continental Army, but a few with Virginia state service are also listed. The purpose for which this volume was compiled has not been determined. It is arranged in alphabetical order by initial letters of surnames and thereunder mainly numerically by certificate number. For related records, see **MI.53.5.**

Record Group 391
Records of U.S. Regular Army Mobile Units, 1821-1942

MI.391.1.   U.S. Regular Army mobile units in 1821 consisted of seven infantry regiments and four artillery regiments. Such units varied greatly in number and type throughout the subsequent 120 years, usually as a reflection of conditions of war or peace and technological changes.

MI.391.2.   Among the records of the 5th Field Artillery are two original watercolors of an artilleryman of Capt. Alexander Hamilton's Provincial Company, New York Artillery, 1776. One is signed D. W. C. Falls, 1923, and is a full-length front view of the soldier. The other shows the detail of the back of his coat and bayonet holder.

CHAPTER NA
Records of Naval Affairs

NA.0.1. The Continental Congress established in succession four principal agencies for the administration of naval affairs. They were the Naval Committee, the Marine Committee, the Board of Admiralty, and the Agent of Marine. Subordinate navy boards and agents located in various states were supervised by these bodies.

NA.0.2. On October 13, 1775, Congress appointed three of its members to fit out two ships to intercept enemy transports. Expanded to seven members and given additional duties on October 30, this group came to be known as the Naval Committee. During its brief existence it purchased the first ships of the Continental Navy (converted merchantmen), drafted the first naval regulations and legislation concerning prize shares, appointed naval officers, and sent a small fleet to sea under Esek Hopkins.

NA.0.3. On December 13, 1775, Congress decided to build 13 warships and soon appointed a committee to superintend their construction and fitting out. The new committee, made up of one member of Congress from each colony, was soon designated the Marine Committee. The new group overshadowed and finally absorbed the Naval Committee when its four members remaining in January 1776 became members of the new committee. On January 25, 1776, the Marine Committee was empowered by Congress to direct the fleet that the Naval Committee had prepared and sent to sea. Other duties and powers exercised by the Marine Committee included the direction of ship movements by orders to naval officers, the appointment of officers, review of the findings of naval courts-martial, and the building and purchasing of ships. It also prepared and reported the larger part of the naval legislation of Congress.

NA.0.4. The increase and growing complexity of naval business led Congress nine months later to provide for the appointment of "three persons, well skilled in maritime affairs . . . to execute the business of the navy, under the direction of the Marine Committee." This body came to be referred to as the Navy Board of the Middle Department and was located most of the time in Philadelphia. On April 19, 1777, Congress established a similar board for the New England states, which became the Navy Board of the Eastern Department and was located in Boston. Both boards were composed of nonmembers of

Congress and were subject to the general direction of the Marine Committee and its successors. The duties of the boards included the immediate superintending of the building, manning, fitting out, provisioning, and repairing of ships in their respective geographical areas; notifying the Marine Committee of the arrival and departure of continental ships; and keeping accounts of disbursements. Because of its distance from the Marine Committee and the centering of shipbuilding and other naval activities in New England after 1776, the Boston board was more active and exercised greater powers than the one in Philadelphia. Both the Marine Committee and the navy boards exercised authority over prize agents appointed by Congress to receive and dispose of continental prizes in ports of various states. The prize agents generally were continental agents who served other administrative organs of Congress as well. Continental agents also assisted the Marine Committee in building, purchasing, refitting, provisioning, and manning naval ships.

NA.0.5. On October 28, 1779, Congress resolved "that a Board of Admiralty be established, to superintend the naval and marine affairs of these United States; to consist of three commissioners not members of Congress, and two members of Congress . . . to be subject in all cases to the control of Congress . . . ." The specific powers of the board included forming and laying before Congress "proper plans for increasing the naval force of the United States, and for . . . better regulating the same" and "ordering and directing the destination of all ships and vessels of war." They were also charged to "superintend and direct such navy boards as are now established or may at any time hereafter be established by Congress; examine the accounts of the several navy boards, and all agents and other persons who have transacted or may transact any business relative to the marine department, where such accounts have not been finally settled, . . . obtain regular and exact returns of all warlike stores, clothing, provisions and all other necessary articles belonging to the marine department; take the care and direction of all marine prisoners; execute all such matters as shall be directed, and give their opinion on all such subjects as shall be referred to them by Congress, or as they may think necessary for the better regulation and improvement of the navy of the United States; and in general to superintend and direct all the branches of the marine department . . . ." On December 8 Congress resolved that "all matters heretofore referred to the marine committee be transmitted to the Board of Admiralty." The board managed the dwindling naval activities of the continental government from December 1779 to mid-1781, served by the navy boards and individual agents of its predecessor. After 1779, the settlement of accounts became one of the principal tasks of the boards and agents.

NA.0.6. As part of the movement of 1780-81 for executive departments, each headed by a single official not a member of Congress, the legislators resolved on February 7, 1781, that there should be a "secretary of marine" and set forth his duties in detail. In general, the secretary was to "execute all the duties and powers specified in the act of Congress constituting the Board of Admiralty." After the person nominated to the newly created post declined to accept, Congress made no further choice, but provided instead, on August 19, 1781, for an "agent of marine" with authority to "direct, fit out, equip and employ the ships and vessels of war belonging to the United States, according to such instructions as he shall, from time to time, receive from Congress . . . ." As soon as such an agent should enter on duty, "the functions and appointments of the Board of Admiralty, the several navy-boards, and all civil officers appointed under them, shall cease and be determined . . . ." On September 7, 1781, Congress resolved that "until an agent of marine shall be appointed . . . all the duties, powers and authority assigned to the said agent, be devolved upon and executed by the superintendant [sic] of finance . . . ." Thus, in effect, Congress appointed Superintendent of Finance Robert Morris to serve also as Agent of Marine.

NA.0.7. Morris administered the naval concerns of the continental government, largely account settling, until he returned his commission as Superintendent of Finance to Congress on November 1, 1784. He was assisted in his capacity as Agent of Marine by a secretary, Joseph Read, and a paymaster, Joseph Pennell. The Navy Board of the Eastern Department and certain prize agents continued to function for a time under Morris. Although Congress proclaimed cessation of hostilities on land and sea in April 1783, the disposal of the few remaining continental warships had begun with the gift of the *America* to France in 1782. In August 1785 the last such ship, the *Alliance*, was sold. That, coupled with Morris' departure from the public service in 1784 and Congress' failure to name a replacement as Agent of Marine, brought the continental naval establishment to an end without any formal legislative act.

NA.0.8. From time to time continental bodies and individual officials other than those already mentioned played important roles in naval affairs. Special committees were appointed to deal with specific naval, as with other, matters despite the existence of more permanent administrative organs charged with the matters in question. The U.S. ministers in France and the Joint Commissioners to the Court of France rented, purchased, and built naval ships in Europe; manned and outfitted them for sea there; and directed naval operations such as those of John Paul Jones in the waters around the British Isles. Oliver Pollock, U.S. commercial agent at New Orleans, fitted out several ships for operation in that area during the Revolution. Both George Washington and Benedict Arnold fitted out, manned, and directed their own fleets in operations off the Massachusetts coast and on Lake Champlain in 1775-76, and the Executive Committee at Philadelphia performed naval functions in the winter of 1776-77.

NA.0.9. The holdings of the National Archives constitute a very small proportion of the extant records on continental naval affairs. Much of the collection consists of copies of records that reside elsewhere. Most of the documents have been published in the multivolume *Naval Documents of the American Revolution* (1964-   ).

NA.0.10. Many naval records related to the pre-federal period are described in *Guide to Genealogical Research in the National Archives* (revised 1985). That publication contains separate chapters on military, naval, and other categories of records, with thorough descriptions and directions on how to use them to develop genealogical information. Anyone planning to consult pre-federal records for genealogical information should use that guide.

Record Group 360
Records of the Continental and Confederation Congresses and the Constitutional Convention

NA.360.1. Record Group 360 consists primarily of PCC (M247, 204 rolls), and Miscellaneous PCC (M332, 10 rolls).* For additional information about those bodies of records and indexes thereto, see the introduction.

RECORDS OF THE MARINE COMMITTEE, THE BOARD OF ADMIRALTY, AND THE AGENT OF MARINE

NA.360.2. Marine Committee letterbook, 1776-80 (M332, roll 6), is part of Miscellaneous PCC. It consists of copies of letters sent by the Marine Committee through November 20, 1779, and the Board of Admiralty thereafter. Most of the documents, which include circular letters and orders, are addressed to the Navy Board of the Eastern Department, the Navy Board of the Middle Department, continental agents at various U.S. seaports, and individual Conti-

---

*For a complete list of National Archives Microfilm Publications cited in this guide, see Appendix A.

nental Navy officers. The records are arranged in generally chronological order. The specific correspondents, subjects, ships, and locations referred to in the letters are listed in *Index, PCC.* The letterbook itself also contains an index to names of persons and offices addressed. The volume has been published under the title *Out-Letters of the Continental Marine Committee and Board of Admiralty* (1914), which is also fully indexed.

NA.360.3.   Also part of Miscellaneous PCC is **reports of the Marine Committee, 1776-79** (M332, rolls 6 and 10). Many of the reports were made when letters, memorials, and petitions from the Navy Boards of the Eastern and Middle Departments, naval officers, and other persons to Congress were referred to the committee. Subjects vary greatly and are covered in *Index: PCC.* Most of the reports are endorsed, often in Charles Thomson's handwriting, with such information as the date, subject, and action taken by Congress. Arrangement is generally chronological.

NA.360.4.   Four additional Marine Committee reports made to Congress in 1779 are in the series **other reports of committees of Congress, 1776-88: reports of the Marine Committee and the Board of Admiralty, 1776-81** (Item 37, M247, roll 44). They are similarly endorsed and indexed, as well as reprinted in *JCC.* That series also contains 153 pages of letters received by the Marine Committee and its successors from the Navy Boards of the Eastern and Middle Departments. They date from August 6, 1777, to April 12, 1781. Only two are from the middle board.

NA.360.5.   The same series (Item 37, M247, roll 44) contains reports and letters received from the Board of Admiralty. Most of the reports were made on naval matters brought to the board's attention when motions, petitions, memorials, and letters of continental and state government officials and employees and private persons were referred to it by Congress. Also present are letters sent on behalf of the board by its secretary, John Brown, and by Francis Lewis, a member, to the President of Congress. These concern matters not specifically referred to the board by Congress or transmitted letters received directly by the board. Item 37 of PCC also contains Marine Committee correspondence with ship captains concerning diplomatic missions, foreign affairs, the establishment of foreign trade, and the outfitting of U.S. ships in foreign ports. All of the correspondence is in roughly chronological order.

NA.360.6.   For reports of other congressional committees on naval affairs, see **NA.360.14.** Letters and reports received by Congress from Robert Morris as Agent of Marine and a member of the Marine Committee are among the records described in **FI.360.4.**

RECORDS PERTAINING TO
PRIVATEER COMMISSIONS

NA.360.7. Ship bonds required for letters of marque and reprisal, 1776-83 (Item 196, M247, rolls 202-204), consist of original, executed bonds bound into volumes. They were transmitted to Congress by the states. Deposit of the bonds in the Office of the Secretary of Congress was required as part of the procedure whereby states could grant letters of marque and reprisal. A bond usually contains the names and residences of the bonders, the date and amount of the bond, the name and description of the ship, the name of the master or commander, the name or names of the owner or owners, and the names of the witnesses to the bond. Arrangement of the bonds is alphabetical by ship name. Lists of the commanders and the ships are at the end of the series. Alphabetically arranged abstracts of the bonds were published in *Naval Records of the American Revolution, 1775-1788* (1906), which also includes an index to names of ships and persons mentioned in the bonds.

NA.360.8. An account of commissions for private armed vessels received and forwarded to the several states, 1779-83 (M332, rolls 6 and 10), is a volume probably begun by Secretary of Congress Charles Thomson pursuant to Congress' order of July 27, 1780, that he keep such an account. It contains copies and memorandums of circulars and letters sent by Thomson to the chief executives of the states for the purpose of transmitting documents, calling for the return to his office of executed bonds (see **NA.360.7.**), and otherwise conducting the business of issuing, executing, and canceling commissions. The records are in roughly chronological order. They are followed by related ledger style nonfinancial accounts for the office of the secretary and for individual states. The entries show dates, quantities, kinds, and methods of delivery of documents (blank commissions, bonds, instructions) sent by the secretary's office to particular states and the receipt by the office of executed bonds sent in by those respective states. They are grouped into records of roughly half-year periods, which are arranged by state in geographical order from north to south. Multiple entries under each state are chronological.

NA.360.9. Some petitions to the Massachusetts government for privateer commissions are in the series described in **JU.45.2.** For a few journals kept aboard U.S. privateers, see **NA.45.23.-NA.45.24.** The records of colonial and state vice-admiralty courts and the Continental Court of Appeals in Cases of Capture and its predecessors contain much information about privateering and piracy. These are described in the chapter on records of judicial affairs (RGs 21, 267, and 360).

RECORDS PERTAINING TO THE CAREER OF
CAPTAIN JOHN PAUL JONES

NA.360.10. PCC contains four series with records relevant to the career of Capt. John Paul Jones. The largest is **letters and papers of John Paul Jones, 1777-91** (Item 168, M247, roll 185). Included in the two volumes are letters received from Jones by the President of Congress, the Board of Admiralty, Secretary for Foreign Affairs John Jay, and the Marine Committee. There is also correspondence of Jones with Benjamin Franklin, the Joint Commissioners to the Court of France, U.S. agents in France, and French officials and citizens. Subjects are wide ranging and include instructions to Jones concerning naval operations, the outfitting of ships, and disposition of prisoners. Enclosures include several documents concerning Jones' engagement with the *Serapis*, crew lists, and copies of Jones' correspondence with Russian officials. Many of the letters received by Jones are in French. Some are accompanied by English translations. A list giving the names of persons to or from whom letters were sent and received, dates of letters, and brief summaries of the subjects is found in the first volume of the series. The records are arranged in roughly chronological order.

NA.360.11. The series **transcripts of the letters from John Paul Jones, 1778-80** (Item 132, M247, roll 144), is a manuscript volume containing fair copies of letters sent and received by Jones and a few related documents. Following the last letter is an undated statement that the letters "are copied from letters in the Office of the Secy of Congress." The principal correspondents of Jones represented by the letters in this volume are Benjamin Franklin, Charles W. F. Dumas, Messers Gourlade and Moylan (prize agents), the Duc de la Vauguyon, Monsieur De Montplaisin, and Capt. Richard Pearson of the Royal Navy. Jones' letters were written mainly from L'Orient in France and Texel in the Netherlands, often from aboard the *Alliance* or the *Serapis*. Subjects of the copied correspondence include the payment of wages and prize money to officers and men, the transport of military supplies to the United States, the return by Jones to Lady Selkirk of plate taken in the course of a raid, Jones' suggestions for prosecuting the naval war against Great Britain, his movements in European waters, his disputes with Pierre Landais and Le Ray de Chaumont, the treatment of the wounded from the *Serapis*, and the exchange of naval prisoners. The series is arranged in no discernible order. For a number of the letters in this volume there are other contemporary copies bound in the series described in **NA.360.10.**

NA.360.12. The series **letters of John Hancock, and miscellaneous papers, 1774-85** (Item 58, M247, roll 71), is a bound volume containing some 120 pages of correspondence to and from Jones. Dated September 4, 1776, to February 22, 1778, and arranged in generally chronological order, these letters concern captures of prizes by Jones, his activities off the coasts of Newfoundland and Nova Scotia, the exchange of naval prisoners, and his suggestions for prosecuting the naval war. The series also contains a report of the Board of Admiralty of June 16, 1780, proposing that an "honorable Testimonial" be given Jones and the crew of the *Bonhomme Richard* for their exploits, especially the capture of the *Serapis*.

NA.360.13. Correspondence of Capt. John Paul Jones and letters and papers relative to the trials of Captain Landais and Lieutenant Degge, 1778-81 (Item 193, M247, roll 200), consists of two volumes. The first pertains mainly to problems connected with the prize money due officers and other crew members of the *Bonhomme Richard* and the *Alliance*, the acquisition of new ships for the U.S. Navy and funds for rerigging the *Alliance* and the *Ariel*, the procurement and shipment of supplies for the Continental Army, and the dispute between Jones and Capt. Pierre Landais over the command of the *Alliance*. Included are some letters from Benjamin Franklin to Landais. Volume 2 of the series contains the proceedings of the courts-martial of Landais and Lt. James Degge. The two were found guilty, broken in rank, and barred from future service in the Continental Navy. Other records concerning Jones' career are described in **NA.45.20., NA.45.22., NA.45.26., NA.45.28., NA.45.35., NA.59.2.,** and **FI.360.68.**

OTHER RECORDS

NA.360.14. Reports on naval affairs by bodies other than the Marine Committee and its successors are found in **other reports of committees of Congress, 1776-88: on the Prisoners' Department, the Admiralty and Agent of Marine, the executive departments, and other subjects, 1776-86** (Item 28, M247, roll 35). The reports, a number of which were responses to earlier reports by the Board of Admiralty, concern routine matters and are endorsed with such information as an assigned number, the subject, the names of committee members, the date delivered or read, and the nature and dates of subsequent action, such as passage or date assigned for consideration. The 75 pages are arranged in no particular order.

NA.360.15. Letters from general officers and the Count d'Estaing, 1777-86 (Item 164, M247, roll 181), include seven letters to the President of Congress, in French and English, from Count Charles d'Estaing, vice admiral of the French fleet. They concern routine naval and diplomatic affairs, including the coordination of naval and military operations, and are generally in chronological order.

NA.360.16. Letters received by the continental government from naval officers other than John Paul Jones are among the records found in **[miscellaneous] letters addressed to Congress, 1775-89** (Item 78, M247, rolls 90-104), described in **CC.360.26.** Communications received from the Joint Commissioners to the Court of France and other U.S. diplomatic and consular representatives abroad often concern naval matters. For example, see **letters from the Joint Commissioners for Negotiating Treaties with France and Great Britain, 1777-84** (Item 85, M247, roll 114), in **FO.360.30.**, and also **FO.360.11.-FO.360.13.** and **FO.360.31.** For letters received by Congress from French naval agent Jean Holker, see **letters from Holker, Barbe-Marbois, Forest, and Moustier, 1778-90** (Item 96, M247, roll 124). For records pertaining to the settlement of accounts of the Marine Department, see **FI.360.7.** and records interspersed in the series described in **FI.53.8.-FI.53.9.**

Record Group 19

Records of the Bureau of Ships

NA.19.1. The Bureau of Ships had its origin in the Bureau of Construction, Equipment, and Repairs established in the Navy Department by an act of August 31, 1842, to be responsible for the design, construction, conversion, procurement, maintenance, and repair of ships and other craft, and for shore facilities related to its mission. The functions existed under various organizational structures and names until the establishment of the Bureau of Ships in 1940. Although no agencies predating 1842 have records in RG 19, the Bureau of Construction, Equipment, and Repairs, or one of its successors, acquired some pre-federal records from the Offices of the Secretary of War and of the Secretary of the Navy and the Board of Navy Commissioners at some time during the 19th century.

NA.19.2. Plans of ships and shore establishments, 1794-1910, consist mainly of plans of U.S. naval ships. Three are for Continental Navy ships. One is for the 32-gun frigate *Randolph* built at Philadelphia by John Wharton and Joshua Humphreys in 1776. The other two are for a 74-gun ship, only one of which, the *America*, was built by the continental government at Portsmouth, NH, 1777-82.

The series is arranged numerically by file numbers and indexed by several files, including one arranged by names of ships.

Record Group 45

Naval Records Collection of the Office of Naval Records and Library

NA.45.1. The Naval Records Collection was begun in 1882 when the Librarian of the Navy Department, then in the Office of Naval Intelligence, began to collect for publication naval documents relating to the Civil War. In the early 1900s the office began collecting records of naval bureaus and records relating to naval personnel and operations before 1861. In 1906 an act (34 Stat. 579) required that all naval records in executive departments relating to public and private craft engaged in the Revolutionary War be transferred to the Secretary of the Navy. It was based on an earlier law with similar provisions regarding 1789-1860. It was found, however, that very few documents of the pre-1789 period were in federal custody. In 1913 an act (37 Stat. 723) authorized the collection of military and naval records of the Revolution. The funds that it allocated to the Navy Department were used to photocopy selected records, primarily in the state archives of Massachusetts, Virginia, and North Carolina.

THE AREA AND SUBJECT FILES

NA.45.2. Approximately one-fifth of the records in RG 45 are part of two series that were called the area file and the subject file when in navy custody. The **area file of the U.S. Navy, 1775-1910** (M625, 414 rolls), was established in 1924 for the deposit of unbound records pertaining mainly to naval operations, engagements, and related activities before 1911. It was believed that the records could be precisely arranged according to the places and dates of the records themselves or of the activities with which they were concerned. Thus they relate mostly to occurrences and conditions in definite places for periods of no more than a few days. The type of record, or its administrative origin, usually was not a factor in filing. Many different kinds of documents were placed in the file, including letters received and copies of letters and other communications sent by the Office of the Secretary of the Navy and the Bureau of Navigation, and originals and copies of records received by the Navy Department from other federal agencies, state governments, and private persons. Most of the documents date from 1775 to 1910, but some are from as early as 1648. The majority of the pre-federal documents are for the period of the Revolution and consist of photostatic copies, made in 1914-15, of records pertaining to naval affairs from several state archives and from papers in the possession of other state institutions and individuals. See **MI.93.4.** and **MI.93.58.-MI.93.59.** for a description of the project that produced those copies. Other photostatic and typewritten copies were made of articles in newspapers, letters and other documents published in Peter Force's *American Archives*, published and unpublished collections of the writings of Benjamin Franklin, naval records in the British Public Records Office, published records of New Hampshire, and correspondence of John Paul Jones in the Library of Congress. Also copied were manuscript and published letters and other documents found in the Yale University Library, the Public Archives of Canada, and autobiographical works of Revolutionary War figures. Copied records are often stamped or otherwise identified as to their source.

NA.45.3. A relatively small number of original records pertaining to the pre-federal period are also present in the series. Many were created decades after 1789 but were assigned to the pre-federal part of the area file because they related to events in that period. Among them are printed ordinances and similar issuances of the British government concerning naval matters, 1648-55; orders, discharges, and other Revolutionary War records of U.S. naval personnel removed from the series of pension application files described in **NA.45.29.**; depositions of witnesses, letters sent and received by the Commissioner of Pensions, and certified copies of Virginia Revolutionary War records made from the 1830s through the 1850s and pertaining to the service of officers in the Virginia State Navy (removed from the half-pay pension files described in **PE.15.8.-PE.15.10.**); records received from the Department of State and other sources by the Record and Pension Office of the War Department in the 1890s (many of these bear codes indicating that they were once part of the manuscript file described in **MI.93.10.-MI.93.12.**); and certificates prepared in 1833 by the Comptroller of the State of Connecticut concerning the service of individuals on the Connecticut State brig *Defence*. The original pre-federal records formerly in the custody of federal agencies other than the Navy Department were presumably received by the Navy under the act of 1906 referred to in **NA.45.1.** Some records bear stamps or other markings indicating the source from which the Navy Department obtained them.

NA.45.4. The area file is divided into eight sections or areas numbered 4-11, representing various parts of the globe. Four have been found to contain pre-federal and related records in quantities varying from a few inches to several feet. The records within each section are arranged chronologically by the dates of records or the dates of events or activities to which they pertain.

NA.45.5. Area 4 covers the entire North and South Atlantic Oceans eastward from longitude 50 degrees west—to longitude 80 degress east in the Arctic and longitude 20 degrees east to the south of Africa. It also includes contiguous inland bodies of water, such as the Black and Baltic Seas and navigable tributaries thereof. Pre-federal records of this area (M625, rolls 1-3) pertain mainly to events in France, England, and adjacent waters. Included are a few original printed ordinances, acts, and other issuances of the British government dated 1648-55; other British government records (apparently originals or contemporary copies) pertaining to naval ordnance and other subjects, 1716-50; letters and petitions received by the Massachusetts Council and the Board of War during the Revolution; extracts from the logs of the *Ranger* and the *Bonhomme Richard*; copies of correspondence of Lord Weymouth, Lord Storment, Lord Shuldham, Benjamin Franklin, Silas Deane, Arthur Lee, John Paul Jones, Lambert Wickes, Samuel Nicholson, the Committee of Secret Correspondence and the Marine Committee of the Continental Congress, and other British, French, and U.S. civil officials, naval officers, and government bodies during the Revolution; copies of petitions to the Massachusetts legislature from British subjects captured by U.S. privateers; extracts from newspapers concerning naval operations and engagements; and a few other documents.

NA.45.6. Area 7 covers the North Atlantic Ocean (including navigable rivers and certain lakes) west of longitude 50 degrees west and north of a line drawn from Cape Lookout, NC, to Bermuda and from there due east. Its pre-federal records (M625, rolls 61-74) mainly pertain to the eastern seaboard of the United States from North Carolina to New England. Included are a copy of a March 1709 order by Gov. Joseph Dudley of Massachusetts to British Capt. William Pickering; an original commission from the Governor of New York to Jacob Sherp to command a company of troops in Albany County, dated February 24, 1726; and a printed liquor license issued by the Mayor of New York City to Sherp in 1749. The remaining documents pertain to the Revolutionary period, mainly through 1781, and include copies of resolves and correspondence of the Massachusetts Provincial Congress; copied correspondence of the Committee of Safety of Cambridge, MA; copied minutes of the Pennsylvania Council of Safety; copies of proceedings of the Rhode Island General Assembly in June 1775; copies of correspondence of Esek Hopkins, George Washington, Gen. William Heath, Maj. Gen. Philip Schuyler, Gen. Israel Putnam, and Gen. Horatio Gates; extracts from *Town's*

Pennsylvania Evening Post; copies of Continental Congress resolutions; copies of correspondence of the Committee of Secret Correspondence; copies of letters and petitions received by the Massachusetts Council and the Board of War; copies of orders of the Massachusetts Board of War to state navy officers; copies of returns of Massachusetts militia who participated in the Penobscot expedition; and other documents.

NA.45.7. Area 8 includes the Atlantic Ocean south of a line due east from Cape Lookout and west of longitude 50 degrees west as it extends south to the coast of Brazil. Pre-federal records concerning the area (M625, roll 199) mainly cover events in the West Indies, North Carolina, South Carolina, and Georgia. Almost all of them are copies. Included for the period beginning in 1775 are correspondence and orders of U.S. and British naval officers; copies and extracts of correspondence of the War Office at Boston pertaining to naval affairs; copies of letters received by Maj. Gen. Benjamin Lincoln at Charleston, SC, in 1780 from Abraham Whipple; an account of James Allen with the United States for pay while aboard the galley *Washington* and while a prisoner of the British; copies of newspaper accounts of naval engagements; proceedings of British vice-admiralty courts in the West Indies; and material from the regimental book of Capt. James Bentham, town adjutant of Charleston, SC.

NA.45.8. Area 11 is a section of the area file set aside for records about the central administration of naval affairs rather than records related to a particular geographic area. Included for the pre-federal period (M625, roll 404) are copies of various records, beginning in 1775, including letters of Robert Morris dated at the "Office of Finance" (1781) and the "Marine Office" (1783); copies of letters sent to naval officers by the Naval and Marine Committees of Congress; copies of reports to Congress by Morris; copies of congressional resolutions, regulations, and ordinances pertaining to prizes, prisoners, and instructions for privateer commanders; a typewritten copy of proceedings at a conference between General Washington and Comte de Rochambeau at Hartford, CT; and a copy of a document submitted by Silas Deane to the government concerning expenses of fitting out warships in 1775.

NA.45.9. Unbound records that could not be fitted into the filing scheme of the area file (see **NA.45.2.-NA.45.8.**) were placed in **subject file of the U.S. Navy, 1775-1910**, by the staff of the Office of Naval Records and Library. General naval policy, strategy, and administration of forces are the principal topics of the series. It concerns not only operations of craft and naval commands, but also activities related to U.S. and foreign naval installations and merchant vessels and to domestic and foreign relationships affecting U.S. naval operation and the conduct of U.S. commerce. Files from executive departments of the U.S. government and private collections, published articles, copies of documents in print, newsclippings, maps, charts, broadsides, and ship plans were sources for the file, which is composed largely of copies. Some of the records pertaining to Virginia State Navy pensioners of the Revolutionary War that were once part of this file have become part of RG 15 (see **PE.15.8.-PE.15.10.**). The subject file is arranged in 17 subject categories, 7 of which contain pre-federal records. Each contains several divisions with alphabetic code designators. Descriptions of records in the subject file are listed in alphabetic order by these categories and division codes.

NA.45.10. H—Battles and Casualties to Ships

HM—Merchant ship engagements: contains a few documents, 1776-77, on British captures of U.S. merchant vessels.

HP— Privateer engagements (with or of enemy, no ship of war involved): contains information on the capture of the private sloop *Ranger* by the British ship *Jenny* in 1778, and a few other documents, including newspaper accounts, of similar engagements in 1776-77.

NA.45.11. N—Personnel

NA—Complements, rolls, lists of persons serving in or with vessels or stations: contains a paper on the experiences of sailors from Martha's Vineyard during the Revolution.

NJ— Discipline (minor) and minor delinquencies: includes papers relating to an alleged mutiny aboard the ship *Hazard* in April 1778.

NR— Recruiting and enlistments, shipping articles, etc: has information on recruiting crews for the sloop *Montgomery* in 1776 and the privateer *General Washington* in 1780.

NA.45.12. O—Operations of Naval Ships and Fleet Units

OC—Cruises and voyages (special): holds information on the expedition of the schooner *Charming Polly* to France in 1775 seeking munitions for the continental government. Also present are documents on James Willing's 1777 voyage to New Orleans and the activities of the brigantine *Tyrannicide* in 1779.

OJ— Joint military-naval operations: contains records on the Battle of Ticonderoga, operations around Lake Champlain in 1776-77, and a map and chart of Chesapeake Bay dated September 5, 1781.

OL— Mobilization—demobilization: has records concerning the fitting out of craft for war in 1775-76.

OM—Routine operations: contains approximately 15 pre-federal entries.

OO—Operations of large groups of vessels: contains a slightly larger number including information on naval operations on the Mississippi River, letters to the commissioners of the Rhode Island militia, and reports on supply vessels around Yorktown in 1781.

NA.45.13. R—Prisoners and Prisons (Including Prison Ships)

RB— Prisoners-of-war rolls and lists (hostile or foreign nationalities): contain information on British prisoners of war, 1775-83.

RL— Paroles (except lists): contains one document for the Revolutionary War period.

NA.45.14. S—Merchant Ships and Commerce

SP— Privateers and privateering (except HP): has nearly two feet of photostatic copies of documents from Massachusetts concerning the activities of "private armed vessels," 1775-83. They are arranged alphabetically by name of vessel.

SZ— Prizes (merchant ships and private property captured by U.S. ships and American captured by enemy), except legal and financial aspects: has about two inches of documents on subjects pertinent to the Revolution.

NA.45.15. V—Governmental Relationships—Domestic and Foreign

VC— National policy: holds information on peace commissions and the disposition of troops, war materials, and fortifications at the ends of wars from 1783 through 1897.

VD— Diplomatic negotiations, treaties, etc.: contains four general entries on that subject.

VI— International relations and politics: has a file on U.S. relations with Great Britain and Holland.

VL— Law, international: has records concerning the North Carolina legislature's provision for admiralty courts in 1777.

VN— Naval policy: contains statistics on manpower, vessels, and tonnage for as early as 1775. It also has files on the origins and development of the U.S. Navy, naval affairs in the American colonies before the Revolution (1636-1775), the building and outfitting of craft, and U.S. Navy regulations.

VR— Marine Corps, general policies: holds two files on marine troops during the Revolution.

NA.45.16. X—Supplies (Including Finance)

XN— Naval stores afloat: contains about five inches of documents on supplies provided to the Continental Navy and U.S. privateers by the Massachusetts Board of War, 1775-83.

XZ— Prizes, prize money, and prize sales (legal and financial aspects): has about a foot of records on prize money given to U.S. crews from Revolutionary War captures.

NA.45.17. Partial index to ships and persons named in the area file pertains mainly to records in the area file (**NA.45.2.-NA.45.8.**) from the period of the Revolutionary War through the War of 1812. Some references to records as early as 1745 and as late as 1855 have also been found. A few references to documents in the subject file (**NA.45.9.-NA.45.16.**) are also present. A typical entry includes the name of a ship, U.S. or foreign naval officer or other individual mentioned in the document; the file designation of the document; and its date. The 3- by 5-inch cards are arranged alphabetically by personal or ship name and thereunder chronologically. The index is incomplete and of limited usefulness.

CORRESPONDENCE

NA.45.18. The series **letters sent by Robert Morris as Agent of Marine, 1781-84**, consists of photostatic copies, in two volumes, of originals and handmade copies that are at the U.S. Naval Academy. They are addressed to the Continental Congress, commanders of ships, bankers, French officials, and other persons, and mainly pertain to finances or claims. Some relate to other naval matters, such as the exchange of prisoners. They are arranged chronologically. There is a name and subject index in each volume. The most complete set of letters sent by Morris in his dual capacity as Superintendent of Finance and Agent of Marine (Item 37, M247, rolls 148-150) is described in **FI.360.4.**

NA.45.19. The series **correspondence of Esek Hopkins, Commander in Chief of the Continental Navy, 1775-77**, is three volumes of negative photostatic copies of papers in the possession of the Rhode Island Historical Society. The first volume contains copies of communications received by Hopkins from the Continental Congress, letters from the Governors of Rhode Island and Connecticut, and communications from naval officers. The second volume contains copies of drafts of letters sent by Hopkins from January 1776 to April 1777, and copies of miscellaneous papers pertaining to the Continental Navy and other subjects. Included are an indenture dated March 13, 1677, transferring part of Maine to the colony of Massachusetts; an account of prize goods taken by Hopkins and sold at New London, CT, in 1757; U.S. naval signals; and a table of rations allowed to men serving on U.S. ships. The third volume is a copy of a letterbook, mainly for the period February 1776 to April 1777, containing fair copies of letters, reports, and orders. They are addressed mainly to the Marine Committee and to commanders of continental ships, with some letters to the Governors of Rhode Island and Connecticut, General Washington, and agents for the Continental Navy. They mainly relate to the activities of the continental fleet authorized by Congress in the fall of 1775. Documents are arranged within each volume in generally chronological order. The first and last volumes contain typed name and subject indexes covering all three volumes.

NA.45.20. The **letterbooks of officers of the U.S. Navy at sea, 1778-1908**, contain only one set of pre-federal records, the "Letterbook of Captain John Paul Jones, March 5, 1778-July 30, 1779." It is a one-volume negative photostatic copy of Jones' letterbook for the period indicated and three volumes containing typewritten copies of the letters in the letterbook, apparently prepared in 1905. The documents are principally fair copies of letters and orders written or issued by Jones at Brest, Passy, Nantes, and L'Orient in France, and from aboard the U.S. warships *Ranger* and *Bonhomme Richard*. Addressees include the Joint Commissioners to the Court of France (Franklin, Deane, and Lee); Minister of Marine Gabriel de Sartine and other French officials; Pierre Landais, Abraham Whipple, and other U.S. naval officers; and the Marine Committee. Subjects of the letters and orders vary greatly and are similar to those covered in other records pertaining to Jones (see **NA.360.10.-N.360.13.**). A few letters are partly or entirely in cipher. Enclosures referred to usually were not copied into the letterbooks. The letters are arranged chronologically and an alphabetical index to the names of addressees is included in both the photostatic and the typewritten volumes.

LOGS, JOURNALS, AND DIARIES

NA.45.21. In the subgroup Records of Citizens of the United States, 1776-1908, is the series **logs, journals, and diaries of officers of the U.S. Navy at sea, 1776-1908**, which contains a handful of pre-federal volumes. Many are not logs in the official sense, but are personal observations recorded by officers on board U.S. ships. Many are also copies of volumes held by organizations, such as historical societies, and by private citizens, which were made by the Office of Naval Records and Library.

NA.45.22. The brief "Log of the Continental Schooner *Wasp*" was kept on a voyage from the Bahamas to Philadelphia in March and April 1776. The photostatic copy contains an introduction and index. A diary was kept aboard the *Ranger* by Ezra Green from November 1777 to September 1778 and is in the collection as a typescript copy. A single-volume typescript copy of some 100 pages is of the logs of the *Ranger*, November 1777-May 1778, and the *Bonhomme Richard*, May-September 1779. Another photostatic copy of a log of the *Ranger*, August 1778-May 1780, contains a typed index. A single volume was used as a log on four ships: H.M.S. *Serapis*, September-November 1779; *Alliance*, November 1779-June 1780; *Ariel*, June-October 1780; and *Queen of France*, August-September 1782. The typescript copy also contains lists of officers, crew, and deserters from the *Bonhomme Richard* and officers and crew from the *Ariel*. A fragment of a log kept by Midshipman John Manley on the *General Washington* during a trans-Atlantic voyage of June-July 1783 is an original record submitted with a pension application in 1845. Manley's full file is in the series described in **PE.15.4.-PE.15.6.**

NA.45.23. Also in the subgroup Records of Citizens of the United States, 1775-1908, is the series **logs and journals of American privateers and merchant vessels, 1776-1867**, which contains six documents from the pre-federal period. "Log of the schooner *Active*, November-December 1776" was kept during activity between the West Indies and the east coast of North America. Many pages are missing, blank, or damaged. "Excerpts from the Journal of Jonathan Haskins, Jr., Surgeon on the Massachusetts Privateer Sloop Charming Sally, December 1776-October 1778" consists of photostatic copies of 13 pages from the original journal. Much of the volume pertains to the period of Haskins' imprisonment after the *Charming Sally* was captured by the British in January 1777.

NA.45.24. "Journal of the Rev. Medad Rogers on the Privateer *Hazard*, Cruising in and near Long Island Sound, July-September 1778," is a negative photostatic copy that seems mislabeled. Internal evidence suggests it was kept aboard the privateer *Revenge* of New London, CT. The journal includes observations recorded on land during preparation for the voyage. "Log of the Frigate *South Carolina* on a Voyage from Texel, the Netherlands, to Charleston, August 1781-May 1782," is misfiled in the series since the vessel was a warship hired out to the state of South Carolina by France. The voyage included visits to the Orkney and Shetland Islands, Spain, the Canary Islands, Havana, and the Bahamas. "Log of the Privateer *Hague* on a voyage from Boston to Martinique, September 1782-February 1783," is also misfiled since the *Hague* was a continental warship. The book was probably kept by the ship's surgeon. The sixth pre-federal item in the series, a journal kept on the *Alliance*, is described in **CO.45.3.**

NA.45.25. In **account books of vessels of the U.S. Navy, 1777-1879**, is "Papers of the Continental Brig *Lexington*, commanded by Henry Johnson, February 26-September 19, 1777." It is a photostatic copy of documents in the British Public Records Office that were taken during the *Lexington*'s capture in 1777. Included are lists of stores and expenditures, lists of crew members, fragments of a log, and a typed introduction and index.

PERSONNEL AND RELATED RECORDS

NA.45.26. **Lists concerning Revolutionary War service and imprisonment** (n.d.) consist of three sets of 3- by 5- inch cards produced by the Office of Naval Records and Library from information in four places: the "Journal of Fortin Prison," where many American captives were taken during the Revolution; *Senate Executive Document No. 11* (37th Cong., 2d sess., serial no. 1121), which contains a prize share statement for men who sailed under John Paul Jones; and volume 19 of the *New England Historical and Genealogical Register* and Charles Herbert's *A Relic of the Revolution* (1847), both of which provided names of persons sent to Old Mill Prison in England. Information on the cards varies, but generally includes the subject's name, rank, ship, and nationality or state of residence. Entries about prisoners often contain information on capture and release; those concerning prize shares reveal the amount paid to each individual. Each card is headed with a personal name, and they are arranged alphabetically by surname within each of the three sets.

NA.45.27. **Payroll of the continental ship *Confederacy*, 1780-81**, was found at Princeton University and presented to the U.S. Navy in 1930. Subjects of the entries, which are arranged by accounts and thereunder chronologically, are varied and include some payments to recipients other than individuals. A typewritten index to account names and personal names within accounts is inserted in the volume.

NA.45.28. The series **rosters of officers and crews of the *Bonhomme Richard*, the *Pallas*, and the *Vengeance*** (n.d.) is a photostatic copy of a manuscript sent by John Paul Jones to the Board of Treasury in 1786. It bears his signature certifying that it as "A true Copy from the Original in my Hands." A similar copy is bound in volume two of the records described in **NA.360.13.**, and another copy is the only pre-federal record in **muster rolls and payrolls of vessels, 1789-1885**, in RG 45.

NA.45.29. The series described in **MI.93.36.** (M853, roll 22) contains Virginia state officers, including naval officers, who received pay for service in the Revolutionary War. Similar information for the same state is in the files described in **PE.15.8.-PE.15.10.**

(M910). The files described in **PE.15.4.-PE.15.6.** (M804 and M805) contain similar pension data for naval veterans from throughout the 13 original states.

RECORDS PERTAINING TO THE BRITISH NAVY

NA.45.30. Logs and journals of British vessels, 1777-1899, contain excerpts from logs of five ships copied from originals in the Public Records Office. The ships are the *Fowey, Kingfisher, Liverpool, Orpheus*, and *Roebuck,* which were active in American waters from December 1775 to February 1777.

NA.45.31. Collection of autographs, letters, and miscellany pertaining to the British Navy, 1719-1849, is a volume, in the style of a scrapbook, of documents very likely collected for the signatures rather than for their content, which is of a routine nature concerning unrelated matters. An alphabetical index to the names of the signers of the documents is at the front of the volume and includes the naval rank or other position of those persons.

NA.45.32. Naval manuscripts copied for Capt. Alfred T. Mahan, 1807-15, primarily deal with the War of 1812, but the first of six volumes contains copies of a few documents, which are presently in the Public Records Office, related to the American Revolution. The pre-federal documents include a letter from one British officer to another, parts of a court-martial proceeding, and small fragments of logs of three British ships.

NA.45.33. Information on some applications for bounties, wages, and other allowances for naval service during the American Revolution is in **selected letters sent by Commissioners of the British Navy, 1784-90.** A few letters also concern transports used on the eastern coast of North America in 1782-84, payment of customs duties on prizes, and supplies used aboard British warships. The file described in **LA.49.9.** contains some documents relating to British naval activities in and around West Florida in the pre-federal period. Lists of prisoners taken by some British ships are among the records described in **NA.93.2.**

OTHER RECORDS

NA.45.34. History of the Boston navy yard, 1797-1875 (M118, 1 roll), is a three-volume manuscript history compiled by Commodore George Henry Preble from Navy Department records, published secondary works, and other sources. Most of the work pertains to the history of the yard from 1797, but an introduction starts with the year 1607 and contains information about shipbuilding in Massachusetts and Boston in the pre-federal period and about the site of the navy yard from 1629 to the Battle of Bunker Hill in 1775. Elsewhere in the work are a few references to subjects such as a visit to the yard by Lafayette in 1824 and the services as a naval storekeeper of Caleb Gibbs, who had served as the commander of General Washington's body guard during the Revolution. Included among a number of 19th-century plans, maps, photographs, and lithographic illustrations are an 1875 "Centennial Map" of Charlestown, MA, showing the British and U.S. military dispositions connected with the Battle of Bunker Hill, a second map of the battleground, and a view of Bunker Hill from the navy yard in about 1830. An index to personal names, names of ships, and subjects is in the last volume.

NA.45.35. Two items in RG 45 relate to the career of John Paul Jones. **Letters and documents formerly at St. Mary's Isle, Scotland, relating to Capt. John Paul Jones, 1778-91**, consist of letters and reminiscences of persons concerned with Jones' raids on St. Mary's Isle and Whitehaven, England. There are also extracts of logs of the *Ranger* and the *Bonhomme Richard*. The originals were destroyed by fire in 1938. The series **legal documents related to Capt. John Paul Jones ("Pieces Justificatives"), 1788-89**, consists of a negative photostatic copy of a collection of documents, written in French, concerning Jones' activities as a Russian rear admiral with a Black Sea command in a war between Russia and Turkey in 1788. Also present are copies of orders received by Jones, sworn declarations of naval officers who served under him as to his conduct, extracts of his remarks at councils of war, and a few other documents. They are arranged in generally chronological order. The originals are in the library of the Masonic Temple in Boston, MA. Other records related to Jones' career are described in **NA.360.10.-NA.360.13.**

NA.45.36. **List of American vessels captured during the American Revolution** (n.d.) consists of 3- by 5-inch cards containing information varying widely from card to card. Generally given are the name of the ship, its description, the date of capture, place of capture, and by what ship captured.

NA.45.37. For descriptions of other records in RG 45 which are primarily military, but have records of naval affairs intermixed, see **MI.45.2.-MI.45.6.**

Record Group 52
Records of the Bureau of Medicine and Surgery

NA.52.1. The Bureau of Medicine and Surgery was created in the Department of Navy by an act of August 31, 1842. Its mission was to administer hospitals and dispensaries; provide health care, including preventive medicine and site inspections; and conduct research and educational activities.

NA.52.2. Included at the beginning of **records pertaining to the history of naval medicine, 1775-1945,** is a copy of *Rules for the Regulation of the Navy of the United Colonies of North America*, first printed in 1775. Also present are data sheets containing excerpts from secondary sources on such topics as the history of naval medicine during the 17th and 18th centuries; diet and sanitary conditions on U.S. ships; uniforms, rank, and pay of naval officers; and naval boards and commissions during the Revolutionary War.

Record Group 59
General Records of the Department of State

NA.59.1. The Department of Foreign Affairs was established by an act of July 1789, and 2 months later it was designated the Department of State by the same Congress. It was assigned such functions as preserving and publishing laws and treaties, keeping the seal of the United States, and serving as custodian of the records of the United States previously held by the Secretary of Congress. The department was also in charge of territorial affairs from 1789 to 1873.

NA.59.2. "Photographs of the excavation for the remains of John Paul Jones in Paris, France, 1905," is a portfolio containing 13 mounted prints of the excavation site and concerned French and U.S. officials. It bears the number 144 and is marked with the stamp of the Bureau of Rolls and Library and the date June 6, 1905. Jones died in Paris on July 18, 1792. His remains were located in March 1905 and transported to the United States in 1906 for entombment at the U.S. Naval Academy at Annapolis, MD. This file was presumably received by the Department of State from U.S. diplomatic or consular officials in France. With the portfolio is a report by Dr. William Feldman on a trip he made to London and Paris in September 1955 for the Armed Forces Institute of Pathology to search for pathological materials removed from Jones' body.

NA.59.3. Part of **miscellaneous manuscripts, 1756-1918**, is "Record of French Naval Service, 1780-1817, of Marie Claude Francois Marrier d'Unienville, 1890," a document issued by the French government in 1890. It is based on information in the "Archives de la Marine" and shows that, in the course of his service, d'Unienville was a "Garde de la Marine" from 1780 to 1782. He served during that period aboard various ships, including the *Glorieux* in a squadron under Admiral de Grasse, the commander of the French fleet at Yorktown, and was present at the "Combat du 29 Avril 1781 devant la baie du For Royal (Martinique)" and the "Prise de Tabago, le 30 Mai 1781." There is no indication of when and how this document was acquired by the Department of State.

Record Group 93

War Department Collection of Revolutionary War Records

NA.93.1. The act of August 7, 1789, that established the War Department provided that the Secretary of War should have custody of all books and papers in the Office of the Secretary at War, who had headed the Department of War created in 1781 by the Continental Congress, including papers of the earlier Board of War. For a more detailed account, including loss of records by fire and accessions from other government and nongovernment sources, see **MI.93.1.**

NA.93.2. The War Department collected a few naval records but transferred most of them to the Navy Department in 1906 (see **NA.45.1.**). Before that time, however, 17 unbound naval records and one of the numbered record books (see **MI.93.8.**) were abstracted to form a part of the series **compiled military service records, 1894-ca. 1912** (M880, rolls 3 and 4). The numbered record book (Number 175, M853, roll 22) contains lists of soldiers and sailors from Virginia and New York who received after 1781 the balance of pay earned for service in state and continental units during the Revolution. The compiled naval service records include lists of U.S. sailors and vessels, payrolls, portage bills, and assignments of pay. They relate to ships of the continental and state navies and contain lists of prisoners taken by some British ships. For a fuller description of the compiled military service records see **MI.93.63.**

NA.93.3. The War Department created an index to personnel who served in state and continental naval forces during the Revolution (M879, 1 roll). Each of the approximately 1,000 cards gives the name of a sailor or civilian employee and sometimes his rank or profession, such as seaman, surgeon, quartermaster, pilot, carpenter, or landsman. Cards are arranged alphabetically by surname with cross-references for variant spellings.

Record Group 186
Records of the
Spanish Governors of Puerto Rico

NA.186.1. Spain ceded Puerto Rico to the United States by the Treaty of Paris of December 10, 1898. The cession included rights to the official archives and records on the island, which the United States agreed to preserve and make available for use. After inspection of the records at the Library of Congress in 1900-1901, many important administrative records were returned to San Juan, PR. Most of them were destroyed by a fire at the Archivo Historico in 1926. None of the records in this record group have been translated into English. Records from the 18th century are sparse and fragmentary; although the number of records in the record group increases for each decade until the 1860s.

NA.186.2. Two series in the governors' records contain a few documents from the period before 1789 related to naval affairs:

1. **abastos a navios [naval supplies], 1782, 1799** (1/4 in.); and
2. **marina (asuntos de) [naval affairs], 1782-1859** (2 ft.).

CHAPTER PE
Records of Pensions, Bounty-Land Grants, and Other Claims

PE.0.1. England's North American colonies provided pensions for disabled soldiers and sailors for more than a century before the Revolution. The first pension legislation enacted by the Continental Congress consisted of resolutions adopted on August 26, 1776. These promised half pay to both officers and enlisted men, including naval and marine personnel, who became disabled in the service of the United States and were thus rendered incapable of earning a living. On May 15, 1778, Congress offered to all officers who remained in the Continental service to the end of the war, half pay for seven years following the termination of hostilities. A one-time payment of $80 was offered to enlisted men who would serve for the duration. In October 1780 the 1778 legislation was amended to provide half pay to officers for life. In 1783 Congress, by "commutation," changed the promise of half pay for life to 5 years of full pay.

PE.0.2. During the entire pre-federal period pensions authorized by the Continental Congress for invalid servicemen generally were paid by the individual states. Only a few pensions granted directly by Congress to specified persons were paid by the central government. The first federal Congress acted on September 29, 1789, to provide that the central government would continue the pensions previously paid by the states. In March 1792 Congress acted to permit the addition of new names to the Revolutionary War pension list and provided for U.S. Circuit Court judges to receive claims. In 1793 the circuit courts were removed from the process and the Secretary of War was directed to send lists of claimants to Congress for final action.

PE.0.3. During the early 19th century most federal pension acts pertaining to Revolutionary War service were administered by the War Department. A unit for that purpose, generally referred to as the Pension Office, gradually evolved. On March 2, 1833, Congress formally provided for a Commissioner of Pensions to head the Pension Office and execute pension laws under the general direction of the Secretary of War. The office was transferred to the Department of the Interior upon its establishment in 1849 and became the Bureau of Pensions.

PE.0.4. The scope of earlier pension laws pertaining to Revolutionary War servicemen was expanded by an act of April 10, 1806, to include state troops and militia veterans in addition to those whose service had been with the Continental Army and Navy. Before 1818 all national pension laws concerning Revolutionary service, with the exception of the Continental Congress resolutions of May 15, 1778, required the disability or death of a serviceman as the basis for a pension award. Not until March 1818 did Congress authorize pensions to Revolutionary veterans for service alone. Officers and enlisted men were eligible under this act for lifetime pensions if they had served 9 months or until the end of the war in the Continental Army, Navy, or Marines.

PE.0.5. Other important federal pension legislation pertaining to service in the Revolution included the act of May 15, 1828, which granted full pay for life to surviving officers eligible for benefits under the May 15, 1778, enactments. An act of June 7, 1832, provided pensions for as little as 6 months continental, state, or militia duty, including naval service, as either an officer or an enlisted man. An act of July 5, 1832, directed the federal government to reimburse Virginia for half-pay payments the state had made to its Revolutionary War military and naval officers, and to make all future payments due them. Responsibility for administering all of these acts was initially placed with the Secretary of the Treasury, but was transferred to the Secretary of War by 1835. Except for a Continental Congress resolution of August 24, 1780, which provided 7 years of half pay to widows and orphans of certain officers, widows of Revolutionary War veterans were not eligible as a class for federal pensions until Congress acted on July 4, 1836. Eight acts from 1838 through 1878 continued and expanded widows' pensions. Before 1836 a few Revolutionary War widows received pensions pursuant to private acts of Congress.

PE.0.6. The practice of giving bounties of land to encourage and reward military service had its beginnings in the colonial period, and action by the Continental Congress to continue the practice actually preceded its resolutions on pensions. On September 16, 1776, the Congress resolved to grant land to Continental officers and enlisted men who served until the end of the war. "Representatives" of military personnel killed by the enemy were also to be eligible for land. The amount of land to be awarded was related to rank—from 100 acres for an enlisted man, up to 500 acres for a colonel. A later resolution provided bounty-land grants of 1,100 acres to general officers. The resolutions of September 1776 were the basic law under which Revolutionary War veterans were granted bounty land by the national government until 1855, but numerous acts were passed in the intervening years to implement the system and to provide claimants with additional time in which to apply for or locate land. In 1855 the government went beyond merely satisfying the basic provisions of the resolutions of 1776, and authorized grants of 160 acres to Revolutionary soldiers, regardless of rank, who had served for as few as 14 days or taken part in any battle. Widows and minor children of such veterans were also eligible. Persons who had already been granted land were awarded the difference between 160 acres and the amount already granted. An act of May 14, 1856, extended the benefits of the 1855 act to Revolutionary War naval and marine officers, enlisted men, and their widows and minor children.

PE.0.7. The process for claiming bounty land began with the issuance of a warrant for the land. The Continental Congress land ordinance of May 20, 1785, as supplemented on July 9, 1788, authorized the Secretary at War to issue such warrants to veterans and their "assigns or legal representatives." The 1789 act that established the War Department in the federal government provided that the Secretary of War issue bounty-land warrants. The responsibility of the department for receiving claims and issuing warrants was thereafter borne by various offices until 1841, when the function was placed under the Commissioner of Pensions. The bounty-land warrant system was administered by the Department of the Interior after the Pension Office was transferred to that department in 1849.

PE.0.8. Once a claimant received a warrant, he or she could then "locate" it, that is, obtain a specific piece of land in exchange for a warrant. The General Land Office, part of the Treasury Department from 1812 until 1849 and thereafter a unit of the Department of the Interior, accepted warrants in surrender for patents to land. Until 1830 warrants issued by the U.S. government were exchangeable only for land in the U.S. Military District in Ohio, which was established by Congress in June 1796. Warrants issued by Virginia for that state's Revolutionary War veterans were also received by the federal government in exchange for land, but in the separate Virginia Military District of Ohio. After 1830 the government allowed holders of unused U.S. and Virginia Revolutionary War bounty-land warrants to surrender them for scrip certificates. These could be used to secure warrants not limited to a particular geographical area within the public domain.

PE.0.9. The Continental Congress also promised land, to be provided at some unspecified future date, to "refugees" from Canada and Nova Scotia for military and other services rendered the American cause during the Revolution. Resolutions to provide for such grants were passed on April 23, 1783, and April 13, 1785. A provision in the land ordinance of 1785 reserved certain lands for the purpose, but it remained for an act of the U.S. Congress of April 7, 1798, to establish a systematic procedure for making claims of this nature.

Under that act, claims were presented for examination by the Secretary of War and the Secretary and the Comptroller of the Treasury. In 1801 various amounts of land were awarded to such refugee claimants. Subsequent acts extended the time in which claims could be made. Land was granted to claimants of this kind as late as 1834.

PE.0.10. Beginning in the pre-federal period, a wide variety of claims were submitted to the continental and confederation governments and the federal government seeking compensation other than pensions or bounty land for service rendered or losses incurred before March 4, 1789. These included claims for pay and salaries due to civilian employees and armed forces personnel of the pre-federal government, claims for additional pay because of the depreciation of continental currency, requests for payments due for supplies and services furnished the government by private persons, prize shares claims, and claims for losses suffered as a result of enemy actions during the war. These claims generally were made directly to the Continental Congress and the U.S. Congress. Both bodies typically assigned them to committees of their own members or to executive officers of the government for study and report.

PE.0.11. Many of the records of pensions, bounty-land grants, and other claims based on events in the pre-federal period are described in *Guide to Genealogical Research in the National Archives* (revised 1985). That publication contains separate chapters on pension, bounty-land, and claims records, as well as other categories of records, with thorough descriptions and directions on how to use them to develop genealogical information. Anyone planning to consult pre-federal records for genealogical information should use that guide.

PE.0.12. The scope of this guide is such that only those pension and claims records which bear information directly related to pre-federal times are described here. That usually means that records of applications and some case files are considered pre-federal records in this context. That is because they often contain documents or copies of documents from the pre-federal period, or attested statements concerning service rendered to the central or a state government before March 1789. Records that strictly concern later events, such as last and final payments on pensions, location of most bounty land, and settlement of accounts, often contain no information about events before March 4, 1789. Exceptions are noted, however, and an attempt has been made to indicate where one can easily find descriptions of 19th-century records whose only relation to the pre-federal period is that they were based on pre-federal claims.

Record Group 360
Records of the Continental and Confederation Congresses and the Constitutional Convention

PE.360.1. Record Group 360 consists primarily of PCC (M247, 204 rolls), and Miscellaneous PCC (M332, 10 rolls).* For additional information about those bodies of records and indexes thereto, see the introduction.

MEMORIALS, PETITIONS, AND SIMILAR COMMUNICATIONS RECEIVED

PE.360.2. Memorials addressed to Congress, 1775-88 (Item 41, M247, rolls 48-52), includes mostly documents addressed to Congress as a whole, but also some that were sent to delegations of particular states, the Board of War, the Marine Committee, and other subordinate bodies. Memorialists include active-duty and former military and naval personnel, other current and former government officials, private citizens, and groups of private citizens. The groups include inhabitants of particular localities, such as Bermuda, the Province of Quebec, and Philadelphia. The requests pertain to such matters as pay increases to compensate for currency depreciation, pay for services performed, and claims for wartime losses. Among the related records are reports of some committees of Congress to whom memorials were referred for consideration and documents submitted in support of the memorials. Most of the memorials are endorsed with such information as the name of the memorialist, the date read, the committee to which referred, the date of the committee report, and action taken. They are arranged in generally alphabetical order by the first letter of the surnames of individual memorialists or, in the case of groups, by the first letter of the surname of the first signer, the group's name, or the locality represented. Thereunder, arrangement is generally chronological by the dates of the memorials. An index to the names of memorialists and many subjects is included in the series. Reports of committees to which many of the memorials were referred are among the records described in **PE.360.6.-PE.360.7.**

PE.360.3. A very similar series is **petitions addressed to Congress, 1775-89** (Item 42, M247, rolls 53-56). The categories of

*For a complete list of National Archives Microfilm Publications cited in this guide, see Appendix A.

petitioners are quite like those of the memorialists, and the petitions relate to various matters, including final settlement of accounts and compensation for wartime losses. Most are endorsed in the same manner as the memorials, and the series is arranged in the same way as is the memorials. Reports of committees to which many of the petitions were referred are among the records described in **PE.360.6.-PE.360.7.**

PE.360.4. A series that is similar in origins, content, and arrangement to both the memorials and the petitions is **remonstrances and addresses to Congress, 1776-88** (Item 43, M247, roll 57). These various communications are also endorsed similarly.

PE.360.5. Other reports of committees of Congress, 1776-88: letters from the Comptroller of the Treasury and claims of Canadian refugees, with a few reports thereon, 1783-86 (Item 35, M247, roll 41), contain about 200 pages of memorials and petitions in French and English from Canadian refugees, and letters from their supporters. Usually the services performed by individuals or groups of claimants are described in detail and the object sought, such as payment for services or supplies, commutation pay, or land, is specified. Most of the petitions, memorials, and letters received by Congress are endorsed with such information as the writer's name, the date, and action taken. The records are in very rough chronological order.

REPORTS OF COMMITTEES OF CONGRESS

PE.360.6. The series **reports of committees on the application of individuals, 1775-89** (Item 19, M247, rolls 26-28), consists of reports made by committees to which Congress referred various claims, requests, and complaints for investigation and recommendations. Many were made on memorials and petitions described in **PE.360.2.-PE.360.3.** Most of the reports are endorsed with the names of committee members, the date delivered, the date read, an assigned number, and an indication of the action taken. They are arranged for the most part alphabetically by the first letter of the surnames of the persons to whom they pertain.

PE.360.7. Other reports of committees of Congress, 1776-88: on hospitals, on the Mustermaster's, Inspector's, Paymaster General's, and Quartermaster's Departments, on the Canadians, and on applications of invalids, 1776-88 (Item 22, M247, roll 30), contain about 20 pages of documents on Canadian affairs and about 30 pages on invalid veterans. The subjects of the reports related to Canada include provisions for aiding refugees from there and for providing them with land from the area ceded to the United States by New York. The other reports on claims deal with particular invalid veterans seeking aid, a plan for each state to support its own disabled veterans, the failure of states to send lists of invalids to the Secretary at War, and the cost of maintaining invalids. The reports are routinely endorsed and arranged into the subject categories indicated in the series title, and thereunder generally chronologically. The series is further described in **MI.360.33.**

PE.360.8. Letters and reports, 1781-88, from John Pierce, Paymaster General and Commissioner of Army Accounts, and records relating to investigations of Treasury offices, 1780-81 (Item 62, M247, roll 76), include many reports of claims for half pay and commutation. The series is described further in **MI.360.40.** and **FI.360.12.**

PE.360.9. Reports of the Board of Treasury, 1784-88 (Item 138, M247, roll 151), also contain many documents referring to claims, mostly for payment of debts incurred by the Continental Army during the war and for the settlement of claims for other goods and services provided the government. Further description of the series is in **FI.360.5.**

Record Group 15
Records of the Veterans Administration

PE.15.1. Although the Veterans Administration was not created until July 20, 1930, it was clearly the result of policies and programs dating back to the American Revolution. The pre-federal, and many early 19th-century, acts, bureaus, and administrative reorganizations pertaining to pensions are described in the introduction to this chapter. After 1840 the duties of the Commissioner of Pensions were under the direction of both the Secretaries of War and Navy. The office was transferred to the Department of the Interior in 1849, where it later became the Bureau of Pensions. In 1921 government functions involving war risk insurance, rehabilitation and vocational education, and veterans' activities in the Public Health Service were consolidated into the Veteran's Bureau. That bureau was merged by executive order in 1930 with the Bureau of Pensions, the National Home for Disabled Volunteer Soldiers, and functions of the Office of the Surgeon General to form the Veterans Administration.

CORRESPONDENCE AND RELATED RECORDS

PE.15.2. The correspondence of the Commissioner of Pensions and the Secretary of the Treasury that pertains to Revolutionary War pension claims consists of 14 series, mainly copies of letters sent, original letters received, and registers and indexes. The principal series, **letters sent, 1800-66** (496 vols.), contains copies of letters sent by the Commissioner of Pensions, and for the early years by the Secretary of War, to pensioners and pension claimants and their agents, members of Congress, the Secretaries of the Treasury and the Interior, Treasury Department auditors, and other persons. Subjects of the letters that relate to pre-federal service include notifications to claimants and to government officials that the claimants' names had been added to the pension rolls, the movement of pensioners from one state to another, deficiencies in evidence submitted in support of pension claims, criteria for qualifying for pensions under various acts, removal and restoration of names on the pension rolls, the loss of pension records in the War Department fires of 1800 and 1814, and the loyalty of pensioners in the southern states during the Civil War. Five series (44 vols.), 1828-36, consist of letters received and copies of letters sent by the Commissioner of Pensions and the Secretary of the Treasury pertaining to pension claims under an act of May 15, 1828. Seven series (13 vols.), 1832-61, consist of letters received and copies of letters sent by the Commissioner of Pensions and the Secretary of the Treasury, correspondence registers and indexes, and miscellaneous papers such as copies of Virginia records and published lists of officers, all of which pertain to federal payment of claims made against the state of Virginia (see **PE.15.8.-PE.15.10.**). There is one series (21 vols.) of copies of letters sent by the Commissioner of Pensions, 1853-56, pertaining to claims of widows of Revolutionary War veterans under an act of February 3, 1853. The records are arranged by series in the order described; most of the series are arranged chronologically. Some of the series are indexed completely or partially by indexes to names of addressees and writers of letters.

PE.15.3. Miscellaneous correspondence, reports, and copies of War Department records, 1812-1913, form a series consisting of a foot of records that are quite varied in form and subject matter. Among the most valuable of those relating to the Revolutionary War are several lists indicating which muster rolls, payrolls, orderly books, and other records and indexes thereto were sent by the Bureau of Pensions to the War Department, Navy Department, and the Library of Congress, 1892-1913 (see **MI.93.3.-MI.93.4.**). These include records removed from the pension and bounty-land warrant application files described in **PE.15.4.-PE.15.6.** Correspondence related to these transfers is dated as late as 1933. Other records that pertain to the Revolution include several items of correspondence, reports, and lists that were responses to inquiries concerning military service in that war. These include information on Negro troops and the Society of the Cincinnati. The series is in no discernible order.

RECORDS OF PENSION AND BOUNTY-LAND WARRANT APPLICATIONS

PE.15.4. **Case files of pension and bounty-land warrant application files based on Revolutionary War Service, 1800-1900** (M804, 2,670 rolls, and M805, 898 rolls), consist of some 80,000 claims submitted to the federal government on the basis of Revolutionary War, and occasionally later, military, naval, and marine service by officers and enlisted men. A file is typically a large envelope containing documents pertaining to one or more claims for pensions, land, or both, based on the service of a single veteran. Each file contains from one to more than 200 pages; but the average size is around 30 pages. Claims were made mainly by surviving veterans and by their widows and children. Some files are cards containing information about pension claims and bounty-land warrants destroyed by fires in the War Department in 1800 and 1814; cross-reference cards filed under the remarried names of former widows of veterans for whom there are files; and cross-reference cards for variant spellings of the names of veterans. A file is usually labeled with the name of the veteran upon whose service a claim or claims were made, the state or organization in which he served, and an alpha-numeric file designation. Many labels also include widow's names, the numbers of bounty-land warrants granted, and additional information as applicable.

PE.15.5. Most of the files contain the formal application or applications of one or more claimants, documents submitted as evidence of identity and qualifying service, and papers showing the actions taken by various federal offices in processing the claim or claims. The kinds of documents in each file depend on the nature and number of the claims involved, but may include affidavits of other veterans; copies and originals of family records; original military papers; briefs summarizing the service of veterans; property inventories of applicants; certified copies of veterans' service records provided by state governments; letters received by federal agencies from attorneys, U.S. Congressmen, and other third parties; copies of replies to such letters; powers of attorney; and notes describing original records removed from the files (see **PE.15.3.**). Most of the records removed from the files were sent, between 1894 and 1913, to the War Department, the Navy Department, and the Library of Congress (see **MI.93.3.-**

MI.93.4.). Those sent to the first two agencies may be in the numbered record books, manuscript file, and muster rolls described in **MI.93.8.-MI.93.15.** or the area and subject files described in **NA.45.2.-NA.45.16.** Some files contain final payment vouchers removed from the records referred to in **PE.217.2.** The varied documents in the files contain both historical and genealogical information. They reveal such matters as the composition and movements of military organizations, incidents in battles and campaigns, naval and privateer operations, civilian conditions, and the activities of individual officers and men during the Revolutionary War. Genealogical information may include, in addition to a man's rank, unit, and dates of service, his birthdate, birthplace, various residences, date of death, and sometimes similar information for his wife and children. The information in any one file varies with the nature of the claim or claims represented and the number of documents.

PE.15.6. The files are arranged, for the most part, alphabetically by the names of the veterans upon whose services claims were based. When two or more veterans have identical surnames and given names, further arrangement is alphabetical by the names of the states and organizations in which they served. Cards for remarried widows of veterans are arranged alphabetically by the surnames the women acquired upon remarriage. When a file consists of an envelope with more than 10 pages of documents, the more genealogically significant records are at the beginning of the file and are designated "selected" records. Every page of every file has been reproduced in the National Archives Microfilm Publication, *Revolutionary War Pension and Bounty-Land Warrant Application Files* (M804, 2,670 rolls). All files of 10 pages or less and the "selected" portions of all larger files are reproduced in the National Archives Microfilm Publication, *Selected Records From Revolutionary War Pension and Bounty-Land Application Files* (M805, 898 rolls). The descriptive pamphlets for both publications contain more detailed descriptions of the records than are given here. Several hundred of the files in this series contain references to the series described in **PE.15.8.** and **PE.15.11.**

PE.15.7. There are 25 volumes in the series **registers of bounty-land claims filed and warrants issued, 1800-1912,** making up 51 feet of records. These include registers of applications received and warrants issued that were based on Revolutionary War service. Information contained in the register varies from one volume to another. Kinds of facts recorded include dates of applications, names of the veterans on whose service they were based, the ranks and organizations of the veterans, names of applicants other than veterans, warrant numbers issued, dates of issue, acres granted, and actions taken other than issuance of warrants. The records are arranged generally chronologically by the acts of Congress under which bounty land was granted, and thereunder in various ways for individual volumes and groups of volumes. The series **stubs and duplicates of bounty-land warrant certificates and scrip certificates, 1803-97**, consisting of 1,739 volumes making up 200 feet of records, contains similar information arranged similarly.

PE.15.8. The National Archives Microfilm Publication *Virginia Half Pay and Other Pension Application Files* (M910, 18 rolls) consists of copies of 279 case files. A few records, originals and copies, date from as early as 1778, but most were created 1830-75. The majority of the files concern half-pay pension claims based on the service of officers with Virginia state military and naval forces during the Revolution. There are a few files related to pension claims based on other Revolutionary War service of officers and enlisted men of various states, and a few based on service as late as the Civil War. The Virginia pensions resulted from a state act of 1779 authorizing half pay for life for certain Virginia military and naval officers. The U.S. Congress directed the Secretary of the Treasury in 1832 to reimburse Virginia for half-pay pension payments already made and to make further payments to this class of pensioners.

PE.15.9. A typical file contains 50 pages of documents, similar in content to those described in **PE.15.4.-PE.15.6.** Most of the files for military veterans contain 3- by 8-inch cards on which genealogical and other information from the documents in the file is summarized. The information on these cards has been copied and consolidated in the volume described in **PE.93.4.** There are a few records in the series that are not identified with any one file. These have not been microfilmed. They include lists of Virginia military and naval officers and correspondence of the Commissioner of Pensions, the Third Auditor of the Treasury Department, Virginia officials, and the Secretary of War. Many case files in the series have a cross reference to files for the same individual among the records described in **PE.15.4.-PE.15.6.** That set of records, which is the main series of Revolutionary War pension and bounty-land warrant application files, also contains files based on Virginia half-pay claims for which there are not corresponding files in this series.

PE.15.10. The series of Virginia half-pay and other files is arranged mainly in two subseries of case files, one each for military and naval veterans. Within each subseries arrangement is alphabetical by the surnames of the servicemen. The few records unidentified with any one file are at the end of the series. Within files containing more than 10 pages of records, the more genealogically significant documents are at the beginning of the file and are labeled "selected records." A complete list of the files in this series, with cross references to the related files in the main series (**PE.15.4.-PE.15.6.**) is in the descriptive pamphlet to National Archives Microfilm Publication M910. The list is annotated to indicate Virginia veterans, and also identifies them as soldiers or sailors.

PE.15.11. Case files of pension applications based on death or disability incurred in service between 1783 and 1861, except in the War of 1812 and the Mexican War, consist of 111 feet of claims based mainly on military and naval service beginning with the Indian Wars of the early 1890s. However, a few files pertain to military service in the pre-federal period. For example, there are files based on the services of militiamen in campaigns against the Cherokee Indians in 1787-88 under Gen. Joseph Martin. Kinds of documents in the records include pension applications, affidavits of witnesses, and letters received by the Commissioner of Pensions. The series is arranged alphabetically by the surnames of the veterans for whom there are files. An alphabetically arranged name index to the series has been microfilmed as National Archives Microfilm Publication T316 (7 rolls).

PE.15.12. The series **case files of bounty-land warrant applications based on service between 1812 and 1855 and disapproved applications based on Revolutionary War service, 1800-1900**, consists of some 450,000 files. Only a small number are based on service in the Revolution. The series is arranged alphabetically by the surnames of servicemen.

REGISTERS, RECEIPT BOOKS, AND RELATED RECORDS

PE.15.13. The series **pension payment roll of veterans of the Revolutionary War and the regular army and navy, March 1801-September 1815**, is a single volume that gives the name and rank of a pensioner, the name of the state in which payments were made, and the amounts paid in March and September of each year. Most of the pensioners are Revolutionary War veterans. The information in the records relates to 19th-century events, such as the places of residence and deaths of the claimants. The records are described in *Guide to Genealogical Research in the National Archives*.

PE.15.14. Described in the same publication are the records kept by local pension offices, which make up the 2,430 volumes of the series **pension agency payment books, 1805-1909.** Information in these records is also related to 19th-century events.

PE.15.15. The series **miscellaneous registers and reference compilations, 1865-1900**, consists of 35 volumes (3 ft.) of records. The first three volumes relate entirely to Revolutionary War service. They were kept by Bureau of Pensions clerks for use in connection with the adjudication of claims. The first volume includes typewritten and manuscript copies of rolls and lists of military and naval personnel of the Revolution; originals and copies of correspondence of the War Department and Bureau of Pensions with state governments, 1836-89; and a few original Revolutionary War documents such as receipts for supplies and a personnel roll, apparently removed from one or more pension or bounty-land warrant application files. There are also a few unbound documents in the volume including copies of a list of prisoners on the ship *Torbay* and of a list of exiles to St. Augustine. The volumes contain lists of monthly or daily rates of pay established for various grades of Continental Army, Navy, and Marine officers and enlisted men, line and staff, and the dates of the establishment of those rates; information about two proclamations of George Washington concerning deserters; and a two-page listing of battles and other military actions. The first volume is arranged in no discernible order but has a table of contents; the second volume is arranged alphabetically by names of grades or positions.

PE.15.16. Among a subgroup of financial records and control registers and lists relating to pensioners is the series **list of widows and other dependents of veterans of early wars pensioned from 1831 to 1873, n.d.** It was prepared on printed forms designed for recording information about Indian war pensioners under an act of 1892. Claims on the basis of pre-federal service against Indians and in the Revolution are included. For each entry the following information is generally given: a certificate number, the full name of the serviceman, his rank, the organization in which he served, the first name of the widow and her last name if remarried, the pension agency, the date of issue, the rate of the pension, the commencement date of the pension, and the war in which service was performed. A few entries are for unnamed minor children of servicemen. The series is arranged numerically by the certificate numbers from 1 to 9458, most of which are actually the numbers of the corresponding pension application files for widows in the series described in **PE.15.4.-PE.15.6.**

OTHER RECORDS

PE.15.17. Four series in RG 15 consist of information compiled in various 20th-century federal pension offices for reference use. They contain excerpts and copies of legislation and statistical and other tables and lists that pertain to pension and bounty-land systems from the pre-federal period into the 20th century. They are:

1. **Reports and studies pertaining to the pension system of the United States from the colonial period to 1930, ca. 1926-34** (3 vols.);

2. **Synopses of pension legislation from 1776 to 1899, n.d.** (1 vol.);

3. **Scrapbook containing statutes and regulations pertaining to bounty-land grants and miscellaneous statutes relating to bounty lands, n.d.** (1 vol.); and

4. **"Men Engaged in Various Wars," n.d.** (1 vol.).

Record Group 21
Records of District Courts of the United States

PE.21.1. United States district and circuit courts were created by the Judiciary Act of 1789 under the constitutional provision that the judicial power of the United States be vested in a Supreme Court and in such inferior courts as the Congress may establish. This record group includes records of federal district and circuit courts and those of their predecessors, such as courts of U.S. territories and colonies that became states. Original records in this record group are generally located in the National Archives regional archives responsible for the region in which the respective court is or was located. All of the pre-federal records relating to pension claims are at the regional archives in Boston.

PE.21.2. Among the records of the U.S. Circuit Court for the District of Connecticut are **claims for Revolutionary War invalid pensions, 1792-95** (1 vol.). These are mainly minutes of proceedings on pension applications executed under the act of March 23, 1792, to "provide for the Settlement of Claims of Widows and Orphans Barred by the Limitations heretofore Established, and to Regulate the Claims of Invalid Pensions." The information present for each applicant includes his name, residence, and occupation; his rank in the service; and the recommendations of the court as to whether or not he should be placed on the pension list, the amount of arrearage he should receive, and the percentage of his former pay he should receive according to the degree of his disability. In 1793 special commissioners were appointed to examine the claims of veterans, and the records for 1793-95 give only the names and ranks of claimants. Their cases were referred to the War Department. A similar series, **petitions for pensions for Revolutionary War veterans, 1792** (1 vol.), is among the records of the U.S. Circuit Court for the District of Rhode Island.

PE.21.3. The series **journal and list of Revolutionary War pension applications, 1806-32** (1 vol.), is in the records of the U.S. District Court for the District of Massachusetts. It consists of chronological entries recording actions taken with regard to applicants for pensions, 1818-20, based on the act of Congress of March 18, 1818. The journal records the issuance of commissions authorizing doctors and others to take evidence in the cases of applicants for invalid pensions, and court orders directing the transmission of the papers of various claimants to the Secretary of War. The list of applicants for pensions includes the name and place of residence of each applicant, the length of his service, his rank at separation, the regiment or vessel in or on which he served, and a list of documents accompanying the application.

PE.21.4. Affidavits made before the U.S. District Court for the District of Maine as required by an act of Congress of May 1, 1820, are in the series **list of petitioners for Revolutionary War pensioners, 1820-32** (1 vol.). Information in these records, aside from the veteran's rank and the military unit in which he served, has very little to do with pre-federal affairs. The separate series **list of Revolutionary War pensioners making affidavits, 1820-36** (1 vol.), contains similar information differently arranged.

Record Group 39
Records of the Bureau of Accounts (Treasury)

PE.39.1. The Bureau of Accounts was created in the Department of Treasury in 1940 to succeed the Office of the Commissioner of Accounts and Deposits, which was established in 1920 to coordinate the work of divisions engaged in accounting transactions and the deposits of public funds, but some records of the bureau's predecessors date to the pre-federal period. Among the bureau's functions are maintaining a unified system of central accounts, producing central financial reports, and furnishing technical guidance and assistance to treasury bureaus.

PE.39.2. Two series among the records pertaining to the public debt consist of documents resulting from the claims of Silas

Deane's heirs against the federal government. They were seeking compensation for Deane's expenditures and services while he was in France as an agent and commissioner of the continental government, 1775-79. **Letters relating to the claim of Silas Deane for outfitting vessels for the Continental Congress, 1776-77**, consists of a volume of 19th-century copies of correspondence, appointments, and commissions related to Deane's activities. **Copies of Silas Deane's papers concerning settlement of his accounts, 1777-1835**, consists of manuscript copies of records dating mainly 1775-89, concerning Deane's appointments, services, and European expenses. Among the documents in this volume are accounts of Deane, Benjamin Franklin, Caron de Beaumarchais, Le Ray de Chaumont, and other persons; a report concerning Deane's accounts made by a Continental Congress committee chaired by Arther Lee on November 4, 1783; and correspondence of Deane with Robert Morris, Thomas Barclay, John Jay, and other persons concerning his accounts, private business, and other subjects. The first series is arranged by groups of related documents in roughly chronological order. The second is arranged mainly in numerical order according to numbers assigned to specific documents or groups of related documents. A table of contents is at the front of the volume. For related records see **CO.360.5.** and **FO.360.67.**

PE.39.3. The series **register of private claims paid under relief and appropriation acts, 1789-1858** (2 vols.), is also among the records pertaining to the public debt. Records related to the pre-federal period include claims made by the commissioners who supervised the British evacuation of New York; by Oliver Pollock for supplies of clothing and military stores provided the continental government during the Revolution; by the firm of Dunlap and Claypoole for printing done for the Constitutional Convention of 1787; by Pierre Landais for compensation for prizes taken in 1779; to the widow of John de Neufville for unspecified wartime services performed by him; and other similar records. Information given for each claim usually includes the claim number, the name or names of the claimants or other payees, the act of the U.S. Congress granting the claim, the date of payment, the payment warrant number, the title of the officers who settled the claim, the settlement number, the amount paid, the year and page number of the annual federal government publication where the payment was also recorded, and the nature of the claim. The entries are arranged by claim number, generally chronologically by date of settlement.

PE.39.4. The series **claims of heirs to prize money due their ancestors who fought in the American Revolution, ca. 1853-54**, is a small volume among the records of the public debt. It consists mainly of copies of petitions to Congress from heirs of officers and men who served aboard the continental warship *Franklin* during the Revolution. The petitioners claimed prize money allegedly due the servicemen because of their capture of the British transport *Hope* in 1776. A few other petitions and related documents in the volume concern pension and bounty-land claims based on naval service in the War of 1812. The series is in no discernible order.

Record Group 46
Records of the U.S. Senate

PE.46.1. The U.S. Senate and House of Representatives were established by article I, section 1, of the Constitution as the legislative branch of government. The Senate is empowered to try all impeachments and to judge the elections, returns, and qualifications of its members. It also shares executive responsibility with the President through the constitutional requirement for its advice and consent in the negotiation of treaties and the appointment of certain federal officials.

PE.46.2. The series **petitions and memorials, 1789-1970**, consists of those documents and supporting material received from individuals and organizations seeking relief through Senate action. They concern a wide variety of subjects, including private pension legislation for Revolutionary War service in cases where the service did not fall within the provisions of public pension acts. Others relate to commutation pay promised certain officers who served to the end of the war, or reimbursement for private funds allegedly spent for public purposes during the war. Supporting papers include affidavits about services performed, correspondence with state officials, and, occasionally, original records from the pre-federal period. The petitions and memorials in this series are arranged chronologically by Congress, and thereunder either alphabetically by names of petitioners and memorialists, or chronologically. For similar records of the U.S. House of Representatives see **PE.233.2.**

PE.46.3. **Committee records and reports, 1789-1973**, are records created or received by standing and select Senate committees. Among them are reports and papers of committees including select committees (beginning in 1789), the Committee on Claims and the Committee on Pensions (both beginning in 1815), and the Committee of Revolutionary Claims (beginning in 1831). Some of these reports and papers pertain to claims arising out of the pre-federal period. The records are arranged chronologically by Congress; thereunder the committee reports and papers are arranged by committees, and thereunder chronologically through the 29th Congress (1845-47). Beginning with the 30th Congress the reports are arranged in numerical order, and the papers by committee. For similar records of the U.S. House of Representatives see **PE.233.3.**

PE.46.4. Private pension and other claims cases brought before the Senate from 1815 to 1881 are indexed by the names of claimants in *Senate Miscellaneous Document 14* (46th Cong., 3d sess., serials 1945-1946). These volumes show the nature or object of each claim, the Congress and session before which it was brought, the committee to which referred, the nature and number or date of the report, and the bill number if any. Many petitions for claims submitted to Congress through 1823 are printed in *American State Papers, Class IX, Claims*, along with committee reports and other documents. Some petitions, as well as all committee reports, were published in the Congressional serial set, begun in 1817, as Senate and House Documents.

Record Group 48

Records of the Office of the Secretary of the Interior

PE.48.1. The Department of the Interior was established by an act of March 3, 1849, which provided that the Secretary of the Interior should assume powers previously exercised by the Secretary of War over the Commissioner of Indian Affairs, by the Secretary of the Treasury over the General Land Office, by the Secretaries of War and the Navy over the Commissioners of Pensions, by the Secretary of State over the Commissioner of Patents, and by the President over the Commissioner of Public Buildings.

PE.48.2. Among the records of the Patents and Miscellaneous Division of the Office of the Secretary of the Interior are two claims based on service in Virginia forces during the Revolution, both initially brought under the act of July 5, 1832. One concerns the claim of the heirs of Thomas Ewell for the difference between half pay for life, already collected, and commutation with interest. The other concerns a resubmission in 1862 of the claim of the heirs of James Monroe, whose initial application was rejected as not falling under the provisions of the 1832 act. Both claims were again rejected upon resubmission.

Record Group 49
Records of the Bureau of Land Management

PE.49.1. The Office of the Secretary of the Treasury and the Register of the Treasury handled disposition of the public domain until April 25, 1812, when the General Land Office was established in the Department of the Treasury. The General Land Office was moved to the Department of the Interior in 1849 and consolidated with other functions in 1946 to form the Bureau of Land Management.

PE.49.2. This record group contains a large volume of records that pertain to the granting of bounty lands to Revolutionary War veterans and their widows and children, the exchange of warrants for such land for scrip, and the location and registration of such land. The records consist of correspondence, registers and case files of warrants issued, location notices, treasury certificates for patents, and lists and indexes to the records. Even though the grants were based on pre-federal service, the information contained in these records reveals practically nothing about pre-federal matters. In the few cases in which it goes beyond administrative or accounting information, it has to do with 19th-century events. There is a smaller group of similar records concerning grants in Ohio to "refugees" from Canada and Nova Scotia who assisted or suffered losses in the Revolution because of their allegiance to the continental government. The records are described in *Guide to Genealogical Research in the National Archives* (revised 1985). Cartographic records related to those grants are among the records described in **LA.49.20.-LA.49.21.**

PE.49.3. There are a few records concerning the Virginia Military District of Ohio that document activity on land grants there that occurred late in the pre-federal period. The case files of the "Kendrick Cases," named for Eleazer P. Kendrick, Surveyor of the district at Chilicothe, OH, contain requests for patents, powers of attorney, warrant assignments, plats, notes, contracts, and copies of correspondence from as early as 1782. There are also two sets each, both of which are necessary to establish a complete record, of land entry books and of survey books. They date as early as 1784. The case files and the entry and survey books are also described in *Guide to Genealogical Research in the National Archives* (revised 1985). Cartographic records related to those grants are among the records described in **LA.49.20.-LA.49.21.**

PE.49.4. Part of **special acts series, n.d.**, are records relating to land granted to the Marquis de Lafayette for his service in the Revolutionary War. This was done on the basis of special acts of Congress of March 3, 1803, and December 28, 1824. The records, which total about 5 inches, include warrants, plats, surveys, correspondence, and printed materials pertaining to the decision in the U.S. Supreme Court case *Heirs of Lafayette v. Joseph Kenyon* (59 U.S. 197). They are arranged in folders according to subject.

PE.49.5. For records concerning land grants made by the government of British West Florida to veterans of the Seven Years War and to Americans who were Loyalists during the Revolution, see **LA.49.8.-LA.49.11.**

Record Group 53

Records of the Bureau of the Public Debt

PE.53.1. From 1776 to 1817 subscriptions to government loans were handled by offices of the commissioners of loans established in the states under supervision of the Continental Congress and continued under the federal government. In 1817 the duties of the loan offices passed to the Second Bank of the United States, and upon expiration of its charter to a succession of offices in the Department of the Treasury.

PE.53.2. In the subgroup Records Relating to Loans Made before 1837 is the two-volume series **registers of Revolutionary bounty-land scrip, 1832-70.** The series records and indexes scrip issued in exchange for warrants under the acts of May 30, 1830; July 13, 1832; March 2, 1833; and March 3, 1835. None of the information contained in the records relates directly to events in the pre-federal period. The records are described in *Guide to Genealogical Research in the National Archives* (revised 1985).

Record Group 59

General Records of the Department of State

PE.59.1. The Department of Foreign Affairs was established by an act of July 1789 and 2 months later was designated the Department of State by the same Congress. It was assigned such functions as preserving and publishing laws and treaties, keeping the seal of the United States, and serving as custodian of the records of the United States previously held by the Secretary of Congress. The department was also in charge of territorial affairs from 1789 to 1873.

PE.59.2. Among the records of the Bureau of Rolls and Library, in the series **miscellaneous manuscripts, ca. 1756-1918**, is a "Petition of James Boyd to the President and Congress of the United States Concerning His Land Holdings along the St. Croix River, with Related Papers, November 27, 1789." Boyd's petition, dated at Boston, MA, stated that the government of Nova Scotia had granted him land west of the St. Croix River in 1767, that he fled the area at the beginning of the Revolution because of his pro-American attitude, and that the lands were now part of the territory of the United States but still occupied by the British. He requested that the U.S. government put him in possession of his land. Among the related papers are copies of Massachusetts legislative proceedings pertaining to the case, copies of depositions made in 1784-85 concerning a 1764 survey made to determine the location of the St. Croix River, a 1789 copy of a map of part of the "Bay of Croix," and other documents mainly concerning the borders of Nova Scotia and the location of the river. The enclosures follow the petition and are arranged numerically by numbers assigned to them.

Record Group 76
Records of Boundary and Claims Commissions and Arbitrations

PE.76.1. This collective record group was established for segregated files relating to internal boundaries, claims, and arbitrations received from the Department of State and international commissions. Certain classes of spoliation claims of U.S. citizens against France, growing out of seizures of U.S. merchant vessels during the wars of the French Revolution, were assumed in 1800 by the U.S. government in consideration of release by France of certain treaty obligations. The State Department assisted claimants and the U.S. courts in gathering documentary evidence for settlements. For other records concerning French spoliation claims see **CO.123.2.-CO.123.5.**

PE.76.2. The series **miscellaneous records, ca. 1789-1804**, made up of documents related to claims under the Spoliation convention of April 30, 1803, between the United States and France, contains records pertaining to the claim of Pierre Augustin Caron de

Beaumarchais. Beaumarchais was a French dramatist who furnished military and other supplies to the United States during the Revolutionary War on behalf of the French government through the fictitious business firm of Roderigue Hortales and Company. Later he made a claim for a large personal payment which was opposed by Arthur Lee, one of the Joint Commissioners to the Court of France during the war and a member of the Continental Congress and the second Board of Treasury. The records, in English and French, consist chiefly of original reports of committees of the Continental Congress, 1779-88; original letters received by the President and committees of Congress and by the Joint Commissioners to the Court of France from Beaumarchais and others; copies of letters exchanged between Beaumarchais, the commissioners, the President of Congress, Benjamin Franklin, and Robert Morris, 1779-83; a single document containing copies and extracts of letters between Franklin, Morris, Charles Thomson, and others, 1781-87, with annotations by Arthur Lee; and a petition to the "Peuple Souverain d'Amerique" from Beaumarchais, April 10, 1795. The series is arranged in no discernible order. For related records see **CO.360.5.** and **FO.360.67.**

PE.76.3. Part of a series, **records relating to miscellaneous claims, ca. 1809**, associated with the spoliation convention of March 28, 1830, between the United States and Denmark, are records pertaining to claims based on the service of John Paul Jones. The claims were for prize money due Jones for vessels captured by a squadron under his command in 1779, but returned to the British by the government of Denmark. The prizes had been taken to Bergen (now in Norway). The records include petitions of heirs of Jones and heirs of Richard Dale, first lieutenant on the *Bonhomme Richard*, to the federal government; 19th-century copies of correspondence of Jones with Thomas Jefferson, the Board of Treasury, and others, 1778-87; and originals and copies of documents, 1779-85, received by Benjamin Franklin from the prize masters, the French consul at Bergen, and Jones. The records associated with Jones' and with Dales' claims are in separate folders, but there is no further discernible arrangement.

PE.76.4. Article VI of the Treaty of Amity, Commerce and Navigation between the United States and Great Britain, November 19, 1794 (Jay's Treaty), provided for a joint commission to receive claims and determine amounts of money due by U.S. citizens to British subjects for debts contracted before the definitive peace treaty of 1783. The commission disbanded in 1799 without settling the issue, but a convention of 1802 between the two countries provided for the United States to pay a lump sum to the British government to discharge the claims. Two of the three small series comprising the records related to that commission contain documents pertaining to pre-federal affairs. **List of claims, July 17, 1801**, includes the names of claimants, the nature of the debts claimed as being owed them, the amount of each claim, and the dates from or to which interest was claimed. **Miscellaneous records, ca. 1796-1800**, includes copies of memorials of claimants to the commissioners, copies and extracts of the proceedings of the commission, and copies of notes submitted by one of the British commissioners. The list of claimants is arranged alphabetically by their surnames; the miscellaneous records are arranged in roughly chronological order.

Record Group 93
War Department Collection of Revolutionary War Records

PE.93.1. The act of August 7, 1789, that established the War Department provided that the Secretary of War should have custody of all books and papers in the Office of the Secretary at War, who had headed the Department of War created in 1781 by the Continental Congress, including papers of the earlier Board of War. For a more detailed account, including loss of records by fire and accessions from other government and nongovernment sources, see **MI.93.1.**

PE.93.2. In the series **numbered record books, 1775-98** (M853, 41 rolls), see **MI.93.8.-MI.93.9.**, is "List of Pennsylvania Officers and Men Entitled to Donation Lands" (Number 173, M853, roll 21). This volume contains the names of those entitled to donation lands as a result of service in various Continental Army regiments and other organizations during the Revolutionary War. It gives, for each individual, his name, rank, and organization. The list was certified by the Secretary of the Land Office of Pennsylvania in 1830 as having been compiled from other lists in his office, but the dates of the original lists are not given. The entries are arranged alphabetically by surnames.

PE.93.3. The series **South Carolina legislative enactments, 1778-1836**, contains copies of acts and ordinances pertaining to the Revolutionary War and its pensioners. They consist of six acts concerning recruitment and financing of the war, 1778-83, and three pension acts, 1834-36. The series is arranged chronologically.

PE.93.4. **Record relating to pensions and claims for pay, [n.d.]**, is a single-volume series which consolidates the information on the 3- by 8-inch cards in the Virginia half-pay and other pension application files described in **PE.15.8.-PE.15.10.** Information given about individuals includes rank and organization, residence, period of service, date of death, and names of heirs. The entries are arranged alphabetically by surname. At the beginning of the volume is a separate list of names, similarly arranged, with the file numbers of the servicemen.

Record Group 107

Records of the Office of the Secretary of War

PE.107.1. The act of August 7, 1789, that created the Department of War entrusted to the Secretary of War the responsibility of recruiting, provisioning, and regulating U.S. military and naval forces.

PE.107.2. The one-volume series **letters sent and received, 1791-97**, contains contemporary fair copies of letters of the Secretary of War, with enclosures, most of which pertain to Indian affairs in the 1790s. Pages 526-612, however, are copies of letters and reports sent by the secretary to Congress pertaining to invalid pension claims based on Revolutionary War service, and copies of "statements" listing claimants that were also sent to Congress. The statements, dated at the War Department Accountant's Office, December 1794-January 1796, were based mainly on evidence forwarded to the Secretary of War by judges of the U.S. District Courts. Each statement lists one or more pension claimants for a particular state, including Vermont, Kentucky, and Maine. Information given for each person generally consists of his name, his rank, the military organization or naval vessel in or on which he served, the nature of his disability, the date and place disabled, his current residence, the amount of the pension to which he was entitled, and a comment on the quality of the evidence offered to support the claim. Claimants included officers and enlisted men who served in the Continental Army, the Continental Navy, and the militia. The volume is arranged in roughly chronological order; the statements for each state are arranged alphabetically by the surnames of claimants. Pension application files based upon the statements are in the series described in **PE.15.4.-PE.15.6.**

Record Group 123
Records of the U.S. Court of Claims

PE.123.1. The U.S. Court of Claims was established by an act of February 24, 1855, to hear claims against the United States based on any law of the Congress, regulation of an executive department, or contract with the government, including all claims referred to the court by Congress. Among the various classes of claims cases heard by the court are general jurisdiction cases, which concern claims brought directly under general provisions of law.

PE.123.2. The large series **case files, 1855-1939**, contains records of general jurisdiction cases, a few of which involve claims based on Revolutionary War property losses and personal services for which compensation was sought. Examples include the case of Jacob Bigelow (case file 1847), administrator of Francis Cazeau, a Montreal merchant whose heirs sought payment for supplies and intelligence he provided to U.S. forces in the early years of the Revolution. In the case of Nancy D. Holkar [sic], administratrix of John Holker (case file 1456), the claimant sought partial payment of the value of 37 loan office certificates destroyed in a fire in John Holker's Philadelphia residence in 1780. He was a French diplomatic official in the United States at the time. Jacques Charlant (case file 328), an heir of Revolutionary War Sgt. Peter Charlant of Moses Hazen's Regiment, sought arrearages and interest on a pension claimed by his ancestor. The case of Charles J. Davis (case file 1995) involved commutation allegedly due on the basis of Davis' Revolutionary service as a captain in the 9th Pennsylvania Regiment. Records found in the case files include petitions of claimant, powers of attorney, briefs on behalf of claimants and the government, depositions and affidavits, opinions of the court, and evidentiary materials entered as exhibits by both claimants and the government. The series is arranged numerically by numbers assigned to the cases.

PE.123.3. Case files and dockets pertaining to general jurisdiction cases heard by the U.S. Court of Claims are also among the records of the Court of Claims Section of the Department of Justice (RG 205), but are similar to those described in **PE.123.2.**, and are thus not described in this guide. For pre-federal records found among French Spoliation case files of the court see **CO.123.2.-CO.123.5.**

Record Group 217

Records of the Accounting Officers of the Department of the Treasury

PE.217.1. This record group contains the records of officers responsible for settling federal and pre-federal accounts before 1921.

PE.217.2. This record group contains a large volume of records that pertain to the payment of pensions to Revolutionary War veterans and their widows and children. They consist almost entirely of ledgers and registers of payments, and of account books recording final settlement of individual pension accounts. Even though the pensions are based on pre-federal service, the information contained in these records reveals practically nothing about pre-federal matters. In the few cases in which it goes beyond accounting information, it has to do with 19th-century events. The records are described in *Guide to Genealogical Research in the National Archives* (revised 1985).

PE.217.3. The Third Auditor of the Treasury Department was an office established in 1817 to settle subsistence accounts, Quartermaster General accounts, pension accounts, and claims for property destroyed in war. The subgroup Records of the Third Auditor, 1794-1921, contains **correspondence, 1812-1912**, that includes letters received from heirs, attorneys, and Congressmen, seeking to learn if commutation was due to particular Revolutionary War military officers. Information in the letters includes names of officers, their ranks and organizations, periods of service, and sometimes dates of death. Some letters inquire about more than one veteran, in which case they are filed under the name first mentioned. There are cross-reference cards to the other names. The letters and cards are arranged alphabetically by the surnames of the individuals about whom inquiries were made.

PE.217.4. Among the records of the Second Comptroller of the Treasury are **records relating to the payment of pensions, 1812-82.** Five volumes contain abstracts and other information about land claims based on Revolutionary War service and losses of Canadian and Nova Scotian refugees. Four of the volumes are abstracts, each differing somewhat in format and contents, but generally including the names of claimants, summaries of documents submitted in support of the claims, letter codes assigned to the documents, and statements specifying the nature of the claimants' service to the

United States, or the losses they incurred, during the Revolution. Other information present includes the dates the evidentiary documents were received by the federal government, the locations of the claimants' residences during and after the war, and the occupations of the claimants. The fifth volume contains several lists of quantities of land the claimants' named therein were entitled to, a list of claimants whose "proofs" were incomplete, and a list of claimants not entitled to land. Some of the lists also show amounts of land granted to claimants by states. There are also some unbound records, mainly files of documents submitted by the claimants and summarized in the abstract volumes. The abstract volumes are arranged chronologically in the order in which the claims were received; the files of unbound supporting documents are arranged mainly by the letter codes assigned to the summaries in the bound volumes.

PE.217.5. Also among the records of the Second Comptroller are a few documents pertaining to a claim for "indemnification" by Maj. Gen. Nathanael Greene's widow. They include a printed copy of a report of the Secretary of the Treasury that was read in the House of Representatives on December 26, 1791. It contains the text of Catherine Greene's petition to Congress seeking compensation for the effects of certain financial agreements entered into by her late husband while he commanded the Southern Department during the Revolution. There are also letters received by the comptroller concerning the claim, 1792-96; original mortgages for buildings and land in Portsmouth and Fredericksburg, VA, 1784; and original bonds entered into by Greene and other persons, 1782-84. The records are arranged in no discernible order.

PE.217.6. Federal government accounts of the First Auditor of the Treasury Department, which are described in **FI.217.13.**, contain some information on claims related to pre-federal events.

Record Group 233

Records of the
U.S. House of Representatives

PE.233.1. The U.S. House of Representatives was created by article I, section 1, of the Constitution. Although it shares legislative power with the Senate, the House originates all bills for raising revenue and, by custom, general appropriation bills. The House has sole

power to impeach U.S. civil officers, and judges elections, returns, and qualifications of its members.

PE.233.2.   Petitions and memorials, 1789-1972, are similar to the U.S. Senate records described in **PE.46.2.** They include petitions and related documents referred to select committees concerned with persons who had been disabled by wounds received in the Revolutionary War and with half pay for Revolutionary War military officers. There are also similar records that were referred to the Committee on Pensions and Revolutionary Claims (beginning in 1813), the Committee on Revolutionary Claims (beginning in 1825), and the Committee on Revolutionary Pensions (beginning in 1831). Some records of the Committee on Pensions and Revolutionary Claims were burned during the occupation of Washington, DC, by the British in 1814, as were certain petitions submitted before 1799. The pensions and memorials are arranged chronologically by Congress, thereunder mainly by the committees referred to, and thereunder in various ways, including alphabetically by names of petitioners.

PE.233.3.   Committee records, 1789-1974, are similar to the U.S. Senate records described in **PE.46.3.** Among them are reports and papers of committees including the Committee on Claims (beginning in 1793), the Committee on Pensions and Revolutionary Claims (beginning in 1813), the Committee on Revolutionary Claims (beginning in 1825), the Committee on Revolutionary Pensions (beginning in 1831), and select committees (beginning in 1789). The records are arranged chronologically by Congress. The committee reports and papers are arranged through the 36th Congress (1859-1861) by names of committees, and thereunder chronologically, alphabetically, or by subjects.

CHAPTER PO
Records of Postal Affairs

PO.0.1. A Post Office Department was established by Continental Congress resolutions of July 26, 1775, which provided for a Postmaster General, a comptroller, and local postmasters as necessary throughout the colonies from "Falmouth in New England" to Savannah, GA. Subsequent pre-federal enactments altered the organization, the number and kinds of personnel, and the responsibilities of the postal establishment. For example, resolutions passed on October 17, 1777, provided for three "surveyors of the post office" and an inspector of dead letters. In a letter to Congress of September 19, 1786, however, the Postmaster General complained that these offices and that of the comptroller all had been discontinued, leaving him with only an "assistant" in his immediate employ.

PO.0.2. Congress established several special and standing committees on postal affairs throughout the pre-federal period. Article 9 of the Articles of Confederation provided that the "united states in congress assembled shall . . . have the sole and exclusive right and power of . . . establishing and regulating post-offices from one state to another, throughout all the united states, and exacting such postage on the papers passing thro' the same as may be requisite to defray the expences of the said office." A continental ordinance of October 18, 1782, superceded all previous legislation and served as the basic law of the Postal Department until February 1792. As of August 1788 there were 69 postmasters serving throughout the 13 original states.

PO.0.3. Only three individuals served as Postmaster General during the pre-federal period. Benjamin Franklin was elected to the post by Congress on July 26, 1776, and served until he assumed his role as a diplomat for the new nation. Richard Bache was appointed by Congress on November 7, 1776, and served until the election of Ebenezear Hazard on January 28, 1782. Hazard served until the term of the first federal Postmaster General began.

Record Group 360
Records of the Continental and Confederation Congresses and the Constitutional Convention

PO.360.1. Record Group 360 consists primarily of PCC (M247, 204 rolls), and Miscellaneous PCC (M332, 10 rolls).* For additional information about those bodies of records and indexes thereto, see the introduction.

PO.360.2. Postal records of the Continental Congress are in the series **letters and papers of Richard Bache and Ebenezer Hazard, Postmasters General, 1777-88, and reports of committees of Congress on the Post Office, 1776-88** (Item 61, M247, roll 75). Most of the 440 pages of letters are from Hazard and are addressed to the President of Congress and to committees on postal affairs. Their subjects include the need for expansion of postal service, the financial condition of the department, accounts of the Postmaster General, the wartime dangers to post riders, the condition of roads and ferries, mail service to Canada and the Northwest Territory, plans for mail service to Europe, location of post routes, rates, memorials and petitions concerning postal matters (see **PE.360.2.-PE.360.4.**), and the appointment of personnel. The 170 pages of reports are chiefly the product of two committees—one to revise postal regulations and the other to inquire into the operation of the Post Office. Subjects include the financial condition of the department, establishment of routes, rates, contracts for carrying the mail, personnel practices, exemption of personnel from military duty, mail robberies, franking privileges, and the power of Congress to operate a postal system. Some of the reports were made on memorials and petitions and motions of members of Congress (see **PE.360.2.-PE.360.4.**); some were made on letters sent to Congress by the Postmaster General. Among the enclosures to these communications are letters received by the Postmaster General from subordinates and significant dead letters. Endorsements on letters and reports include such information as the date written, writer's name, subject, date read in Congress, and action taken. The records in the series are arranged in roughly chronological order.

---

*For a complete list of National Archives Microfilm Publications cited in this guide, see Appendix A.

Record Group 28
Records of the Post Office Department

PO.28.1. The Office of the Postmaster General was created by an act of September 22, 1789, which continued regulations that originated with the appointment of Benjamin Franklin as Postmaster General by the Continental Congress. The first act to provide in detail for a Post Office Department was passed on February 20, 1792, and subsequent legislation enlarged the duties of the department.

PO.28.2. The continental Postmaster General very likely maintained letterbooks as did other pre-federal executive officials, but no such volumes are extant. Most of the pre-federal postal records remaining are fiscal records, all of which are now among the records of the Division of Finance of the Bureau of the Third Assistant Postmaster General.

PO.28.3. Accounts of the General Post Office in Philadelphia and of the various deputy postmasters ("Ledger of Benjamin Franklin"), 1775-80 (T268, 1 roll) is a single volume begun when Franklin was Postmaster General. That explains the title on the spine, which is of a later date than the record, although there are very few entries involving Franklin. The first accounts in the volume are those of the General Post Office concerning the Postmaster General and other officials in the Philadelphia office. These are followed by accounts of the General Post Office with post offices in most of the states and at Montreal and Continental Army headquarters. At the end of the volume are a few accounts with surveyors in the middle and southern districts. The accounts in the first and last parts of the volume pertain to salaries, allowances, travel expenses, cash received from post offices, and other cash transactions not further specified. Those with post offices relate mainly to adjustments of their quarterly accounts. Some of the accounts refer to balances carried to "Book B," which is not among the records of the National Archives. A brief sketch of Benjamin Franklin's career as a postal official under the British and continental governments and of the U.S. postal service to 1802, and a contemporary document showing letters sent and received at "George Town," January-March 1778, are attached to the front of the volume. The book is arranged in three sections as described, thereunder by account, and thereunder chronologically. It contains an index to the accounts arranged according to the first vowel that occurs in the name of each post office. Thus both

Alexandria, VA, and Falmouth, ME, are indexed under "A", and Philadelphia under "I".

PO.28.4. The series **journals of the General Post Office, 1782-1801**, consists of two volumes, the first of which contains a general journal dated February 2, 1782-July 25, 1790. The accounts are for the General Post Office staff and for post offices in various states. They pertain to such matters in the General Post Office as office rent, purchase of supplies, printing expenditures, cash paid to and received from various persons, and salaries. The accounts for post offices relate mainly to adjustments of their quarterly accounts. There are also entries for quarterly salary payments to the Postmaster General and Assistant Postmaster General, and for the expenses of moving the General Post Office from Philadelphia to New York City. Arrangement of the entries is by accounts, which are in no discernible order, and thereunder chronologically. Numbers on the journal pages refer to page numbers in the ledger which is the first volume of the series **ledgers of the General Post Office, 1782-1803** (7 vols.), to which the entries were posted. Most of the accounts in it are for post office stage "proprietors" and post riders. It is arranged like the journal from which it was posted, and both are indexed like the volume described in **PO.28.3.**

PO.28.5. Another volume in the same series was begun in the early 1790s, but contains two accounts pertaining to the pre-federal period. One only concerns a bond dated 1788, but the other, a lengthy account for Thomas Hall, Postmaster at Charleston, SC, has entries for as early as July 1, 1783. There is an index in the volume which is arranged alphabetically by surnames of persons for whom there are accounts.

PO.28.6. The series **ledger of postal accounts of post offices with the General Post Office, 1785-86** (1 vol.), contains printed account forms, but only the first 16 pages have been filled out. They cover mainly single quarters for 17 post office locations, mostly in New England, and concern such matters as the postage on various kinds of letters, salaries, money paid to post riders, the purchase of supplies and repair of equipment, and balances of money due the General Post Office. The arrangement is by account, in roughly chronological order by quarter.

PO.28.7. Among the records of the Museum of the Post Office Department, under the supervision of the Chief Clerk, is the series **records of letters sent from the Wilmington, Del. post office to other post offices, 1786-92** (1 vol.). It shows the date each letter was sent and its destination, the number of unpaid and free letters, and sums paid and unpaid. Entries are arranged chronologically.

PO.28.8. Also among the museum's records is the **journal of Hugh Finlay, surveyor of the post roads and post offices, 1773-74** (T268, 1 roll). This series is a fair copy of the journal made at a time unknown. It was sent to an official in the Post Office Department by Frank H. Norton of New York City, whose firm had published 150 copies of the journal in 1867. Finlay was appointed surveyor by the British Postmaster General in December 1772. He explored the region between the Chaudiere River in Canada and the Kennebec River in Massachusetts in September 1773 for the purpose of establishing a new post route. The greater part of the volume, however, pertains to his subsequent inspection tour of post offices and roads from Falmouth, ME, south to Philadelphia, and from Savannah, GA, north to York, VA. His tour lasted from October 1773 through June 1774. Finlay gives information on the natural features and settlements in the territory through which he passed. Most of the volume concerns his inspection, with observations on the competence of postmasters, the adequacy of their records, the expenses and routes of post riders, schedules, irregularities in service, the condition of roads and ferries, the location and size of settlements, and suggestions for improving mail service. The volume contains a map of the post road from New London, CT, to Saybrook, CT; a small sketch of Wilmington, NC, showing buildings and roads; and a map of a post road from Canada to Massachusetts proposed on the basis of Finlay's explorations.

APPENDIX A

National Archives Microfilm Publications Cited in the Guide to Pre-Federal Records

(DP) indicates that a descriptive pamphlet is available for the microfilm publication.

The paragraph number citations under each entry are listed in the order in which they appear in the text.

M23   *Despatches From U.S. Consuls in Algiers, Algeria, 1785-1906.* 19 rolls
FO.59.17.

M28   *Diplomatic and Consular Instructions of the Department of State, 1791-1801.* 5 rolls (DP)
FO.59.10.

M30   *Despatches From U.S. Ministers to Great Britain, 1791-1906.* 200 rolls (DP)
FO.59.14.

M31   *Despatches From U.S. Ministers to Spain, 1792-1906.* 134 rolls (DP)
FO.59.14.

M34   *Despatches From U.S. Ministers to France, 1789-1906.* 128 rolls
FO.59.14.

M35   *Despatches From U.S. Ministers to Russia, 1808-1906.* 66 rolls
FO.59.14.

M40   *Domestic Letters of the Department of State, 1784-1906.* 171 rolls
FO.59.2.
LA.59.10.

M43   *Despatches From U.S. Ministers to Portugal, 1790-1906.* 41 rolls
FO.59.14.

M50   *Notes From the British Legation in the United States to the Department of State, 1791-1906.* 145 rolls
FO.59.16.

M56   Notes From the Netherlands Legation in the United States
       to the Department of State, 1784-1906. 13 rolls (DP)
       FO.59.16.

M59   Notes From the Spanish Legation in the United States to the
       Department of State, 1790-1906. 31 rolls (DP)
       FO.59.16.

M61   Foreign Letters of the Continental Congress and the
       Department of State, 1785-1790. 1 roll (DP)
       FO.59.4.
       FO.59.10.

M77   Diplomatic Instructions of the Department of State,
       1801-1906. 175 rolls (DP)
       FO.59.10.

M86   Journal of Charles Mason, Kept During the Survey of the
       Mason and Dixon Line, 1763-1768. 1 roll (DP)
       LA.59.9.

M116   State Department Territorial Papers, Florida, 1777-1824.
       11 rolls
       FI.59.2.
       FO.59.6.
       MI.59.8.

M118   History of the Boston Navy Yard, 1797-1874, by
       Commodore George Henry Preble, U.S.N., 1875. 1 roll (DP)
       NA.45.34.

M162   The Revolutionary War Prize Cases: Records of the Court
       of Appeal in Cases of Capture, 1776-1787. 15 rolls (DP)
       JU.267.2.-JU.267.6.

M179   Miscellaneous Letters of the Department of State,
       1789-1906. 1,310 rolls (DP)
       FO.59.12.
       IN.59.2.

M214   Appellate Case Files of the U.S. Supreme Court,
       1792-1831. 96 rolls (DP)
       JU.267.9.

M222   Letters Received by the Secretary of War, Unregistered
       Series, 1789-1861. 34 rolls (DP)
       CO.107.2.

M235   Miscellaneous Treasury Accounts of the First Auditor
       (Formerly the Auditor) of the Treasury Department,
       September 6, 1790-1840. 1,170 rolls
       FI.217.13.

M246   *Revolutionary War Rolls, 1775-1783.* 138 rolls (DP)
IN.93.4.
MI.93.5.
MI.93.14.-MI.93.15.

M247   *Papers of the Continental Congress, 1774-1789.*
204 rolls (DP)

See appendix B for a list of citations to PCC, arranged by
item number.

M332   *Miscellaneous Papers of the Continental Congress,*
1774-1789. 10 rolls (DP)
CC.360.1.
CC.360.4.
CC.360.7.
CC.360.12.
CC.360.29.
CC.360.32.
CN.360.1.-CN.360.2.
CN.360.4.-CN.360.5.
CO.360.1.
FI.360.1.
FI.360.7.
FI.360.14.
FO.360.1.
FO.360.7.
FO.360.14.
FO.360.16.-FO.360.17.
FO.360.19.-FO.360.27.
FO.360.30.-FO.360.32.
FO.360.34.-FO.360.35.
FO.360.37.
FO.360.43.-FO.360.44.
FO.360.50.
FO.360.52.-FO.360.53.
FO.360.55.
FO.360.57.
FO.360.69.
IN.360.1.
JU.360.1.
JU.360.7.
JU.360.9.
LA.360.1.
LA.360.5.
MI.360.1.
MI.360.36.
MI.360.39.
MI.360.42.
MI.360.44.

NA.360.1.-NA.360.3.
NA.360.8.
PE.360.1.
PO.360.1.

M338 *Certificates of Ratification of the Constitution and the Bill of Rights, Including Related Correspondence and Rejections of Proposed Amendments, 1787-1792.* 1 roll
CN.11.3.

M408 *Index to Appellate Case Files of the U.S. Supreme Court, 1792-1909.* 20 rolls (DP)
JU.267.9.

M470 *State Department Territorial Papers, Territory Northwest of the River Ohio, 1787-1801.* 1 roll (DP)
LA.59.2.

M471 *State Department Territorial Papers, Territory Southwest of the River Ohio, 1790-1795.* 1 roll (DP)
LA.59.3.

M521 *Card Index to "Old Loan" Ledgers of the Bureau of the Public Debt, 1790-1836.* 15 rolls (DP)
FI.53.11.

M570 *Copybooks of George Washington's Correspondence With Secretaries of State, 1789-1796.* 1 roll (DP)
FO.59.18.

M625 *Area File of the Naval Records Collection, 1775-1910.* 414 rolls (DP)
NA.45.2.
NA.45.5.-NA.45.8.

M668 *Ratified Indian Treaties, 1722-1869.* 16 rolls (DP)
IN.11.2.

M694 *Index to Compiled Service Records of Volunteer Soldiers Who Served From 1784-1811.* 9 rolls (DP)
MI.94.9.

M721 *The Territorial Papers of the United States.* 16 rolls (DP)
LA.59.2.

M804 *Revolutionary War Pension and Bounty-Land Warrant Application Files.* 2,670 rolls (DP)
CO.15.2.
NA.45.29.
PE.15.4.
PE.15.6.

M805   *Selected Records From Revolutionary War Pension and Bounty-Land Warrant Application Files.* 898 rolls (DP)
NA.45.29.
PE.15.4.
PE.15.6.

M847   *Special Index to Numbered Records in the War Department Collection of Revolutionary War Records, 1775-1783.* 39 rolls (DP)
MI.93.9.
MI.93.13.

M853   *Numbered Record Books Concerning Military Operations and Service, Pay and Settlement of Accounts, and Supplies in the War Department Collection of Revolutionary War Records.* 41 rolls (DP)
CO.93.2.
FI.93.3.
IN.93.2.
MI.93.5.
MI.93.8.-MI.93.9.
MI.93.17.-MI.93.21.
MI.93.24.-MI.93.27.
MI.93.29.
MI.93.31.-MI.93.32.
MI.93.36.-MI.93.53.
MI.93.56.-MI.93.57.
MI.93.61.
MI.93.66.
MI.93.69.
NA.45.29.
NA.93.2.
PE.93.2.

M858   *The Negro in the Military Service of the United States, 1639-1886.* 5 rolls (DP)
MI.94.15.

M859   *Miscellaneous Numbered Records (The Manuscript File) in the War Department Collection of Revolutionary War Records, 1775-1790s.* 125 rolls (DP)
IN.93.3.
MI.93.5.
MI.93.10.

M860   *General Index to Compiled Military Service Records of Revolutionary War Soldiers.* 58 rolls (DP)
MI.93.65.

M866   *Records of the Constitutional Convention of 1787.* 1 roll (DP)

CN.360.2.
CN.360.5.
CN.360.7.-CN.360.13.

M879   *Index to Compiled Service Records of American Naval Personnel Who Served During the Revolutionary War.* 1 roll (DP)
NA.93.3.

M880   *Compiled Service Records of American Naval Personnel and Members of the Departments of the Quartermaster General and the Commissary General of Military Stores Who Served During the Revolutionary War.* 4 rolls (DP)
MI.93.5.
MI.93.63.
NA.93.2.

M881   *Compiled Service Records of Soldiers Who Served in the American Army During the Revolutionary War.* 1,096 rolls (DP)
MI.93.5.
MI.93.63.

M904   *War Department Collection of Post-Revolutionary War Manuscripts.* 4 rolls (DP)
MI.94.3.

M905   *Compiled Service Records of Volunteer Soldiers Who Served From 1784 to 1811.* 32 rolls (DP)
MI.94.9.

M910   *Virginia Half Pay and Other Related Revolutionary War Pension Application Files.* 18 rolls (DP)
NA.45.29.
PE.15.8.

M913   *Personnel Returns of the 6th Massachusetts Battalion, 1779-1780, and Returns and Accounts of Military Stores for the 8th and 9th Massachusetts Regiments, 1779-1782.* 1 roll (DP)
MI.93.16.
MI.93.44.

M922   *Orders, Returns, Morning Reports, and Accounts of British Troops, 1776-1781.* 1 roll (DP)
MI.93.60.

M925   *Records of the Massachusetts Continental Loan Office, 1777-1791.* 4 rolls (DP)
FI.53.8.

M926   *Letters, Returns, Accounts, and Estimates of the Quartermaster General's Department, 1776-1783, in the*

War Department Collection of Revolutionary War Records.
1 roll (DP)
CO.93.3.-CO.93.4.
MI.93.39.
MI.93.42.
MI.93.47.

M927   *Letters, Orders for Pay, Accounts, Receipts, and Other Supply Records Concerning Weapons and Military Stores, 1776-1801.* 1 roll (DP)
MI.92.2.
MI.93.42.
MI.93.49.
MI.94.8.

M948   *Case Papers of the Court of Admiralty of the State of New York, 1784-1788.* 1 roll (DP)
JU.21.7.

M1004   *Central Treasury Records of the Continental and Confederation Governments Relating to Foreign Affairs, 1775-1787.* 3 rolls (DP)
FI.39.2.
FI.53.2.
FO.53.2.

M1005   *Records of the Connecticut, New Hampshire, and Rhode Island Continental Loan Offices, 1777-1791.* 2 rolls (DP)
FI.53.8.

M1006   *Records of the New Jersey and New York Continental Loan Offices, 1777-1790.* 2 rolls (DP)
FI.53.8.

M1007   *Records of the Pennsylvania Continental Loan Office, 1776-1788.* 3 rolls (DP)
FI.53.8.

M1008   *Records of the Delaware and Maryland Continental Loan Office, 1777-1790.* 1 roll (DP)
FI.53.8.

M1014   *Central Treasury Records of the Continental and Confederation Governments, 1775-1789.* 23 rolls (DP)
FI.39.3.
FI.53.13.-FI.53.14.
FI.53.25.
FI.53.27.
FI.217.2.
FI.217.4.
FI.217.5.
FI.217.7.

M1015   *Central Treasury Records of the Continental and Confederation Governments Relating to Military Affairs, 1775-1789.* 7 rolls (DP)
MI.39.2.
MI.53.2.
MI.53.5.
MI.217.3.-MI.217.4.

M1180   *Pre-Federal Admiralty Court Records, Province and State of South Carolina, 1716-1789.* 3 rolls (DP)
JU.21.8.-JU.21.9.

M1182   *Admiralty Final Record Books and Minutes for the U.S. District Court, District of South Carolina, 1790-1857.* 4 rolls (DP)
JU.21.9.

M1382   *Bound Records of the General Land Office Relating to Private Land Claims in Louisiana, 1767-1892.* 8 rolls (DP)
LA.49.14.
LA.49.16.-LA.49.17.

T20   *Despatches from U.S. Consuls in Havana, Cuba, 1783-1906.* 133 rolls
FO.59.17.

T39   *Customs Journals of the Danish Government of the Virgin Islands.* 22 rolls
CO.55.3.-CO.55.4.

T168   *Despatches from U.S. Consuls in London, England, 1790-1906.* 64 rolls
FO.59.17.

T180   *Despatched from U.S. Consuls in Lisbon, Portugal, 1791-1906.* 11 rolls
FO.59.17.

T211   *Despatches from U.S. Consuls in Hamburg, Germany, 1790-1906.* 35 rolls
FO.59.17.

T220   *Despatches from U.S. Consuls in Marseilles, France, 1790-1906.* 20 rolls
FO.59.17.

T260   *State Department Territorial Papers, Orleans, 1764-1823.* 13 rolls
LA.59.4.

T268   *Journal of Hugh Finlay, Surveyor of Post Roads and Post Offices, 1773-1774; and Accounts of the General Post Office in Philadelphia and of the Various Deputy*

Postmasters—"The Ledger of Benjamin Franklin"—Jan. 1775-Jan. 1780. 1 roll
PO.28.3.
PO.28.8.

T316 *Old War Index to Pension Files, 1815-1926.* 7 rolls
PE.15.11.

T357 *Despatches from U.S. Counsels in Alicante, Spain, 1788-1905.* 3 rolls
FO.59.17.

T631 *Records of the Bureau of the Public Debt: Pennsylvania Loan Office Records Relating to the Loan of 1790.* 8 rolls
FI.53.9.

T652 *Records of the Bureau of the Public Debt: New Hampshire Loan Office Records Relating to the Loan of 1790.* 6 rolls
FI.53.9.

T653 *Records of the Bureau of the Public Debt: Rhode Island Loan Office Records Relating to the Loan of 1790.* 13 rolls
FI.53.9.

T654 *Records of the Bureau of the Public Debt: Connecticut Loan Office Records Relating to the Loan of 1790.* 10 rolls
FI.53.9.

T694 *Records of the Bureau of the Public Debt: Georgia Loan Office Records Relating to the Loan of 1790.* 2 rolls
FI.53.9.

T695 *Records of the Bureau of the Public Debt: North Carolina Loan Office Records Relating to the Loan of 1790.* 4 rolls
FI.53.9.

T696 *Records of the Bureau of the Public Debt: Virginia Loan Office Records Relating to the Loan of 1790.* 12 rolls
FI.53.9.

T697 *Records of the Bureau of the Public Debt: Maryland Loan Office Records Relating to the Loan of 1790.* 9 rolls
FI.53.9.

T698 *Records of the Bureau of the Public Debt: New Jersey Loan Office Records Relating to the Loan of 1790.* 2 rolls
FI.53.9.

T719 *Records of the Bureau of the Public Debt: South Carolina Loan Office Records Relating to the Loan of 1790.* 3 rolls
FI.53.9.

T783 *Records of the Bureau of the Public Debt: Massachusetts Loan Office Records Relating to the Loan of 1790.* 7 rolls
FI.53.9.

T784   *Records of the Bureau of the Public Debt: Delaware Loan Office Records Relating to the Loan of 1790.* 1 roll
FI.53.9.

T786   *Records of the Bureau of the Public Debt: Central Treasury Records Relating to the Loan of 1790.* 1 roll
FI.53.10.

T787   *Records of the Bureau of the Public Debt: Old Loans Records Relating to Selected Loans of the Period 1795-1807.* 6 rolls
FI.53.10.

T899   *Register of Audits of "Miscellaneous Treasury Accounts" (First Auditor's Office).* 1 roll
FI.217.14.

T952   *Records Relating to the Danish West Indies, 1672-1860, Received From the Danish National Archives.* 19 rolls
CC.55.3.
CO.55.2.

T1122   *Reales ordenes, 1792-1793, y reales ordenes y decretos, 1767-1854 (Royal Orders and Decrees).* 1 roll
CC.186.2.

APPENDIX B

PCC Items Cited in the Guide to Pre-Federal Records

The paragraph number citations under each entry are listed in the order in which they appear in the text.

All of PCC is reproduced in National Archives Microfilm Publication M247, *Papers of the Continental Congress, 1774-1789*, 204 rolls (DP).

Item No.	Paragraph No. of Reference	Item No.	Paragraph No. of Reference
1	CC.360.10. FO.360.61.	18	CC.360.22.
2	CC.360.11. FO.360.61.	19	FI.360.9. PE.360.6.
3	CC.360.13. FO.360.61.	20	CC.360.28.
4	CC.360.13. FO.360.61.	21	MI.360.33.
5	CC.360.13. FO.360.61.	22	MI.360.33. PE.360.7.
6	CC.360.13. FO.360.61.	23	CC.360.28.
7	CC.360.13. FO.360.61.	24	CC.360.28.
8	FO.360.61.	25	FO.360.45.
9	CC.360.3.	26	FI.360.8.
10	CC.360.14.	27	MI.360.33.
11	MI.360.31.	28	CC.360.28. MI.360.33. NA.360.14.
12	FI.360.13.	29	FI.360.8. FO.360.46. JU.360.3. MI.360.33.
12A	CC.360.21.	30	IN.360.2. LA.360.4. MI.360.33.
13	CC.360.21.	31	CC.360.28. CO.360.2. FI.360.7. MI.360.33.
14	CC.360.21.	32	CC.360.15. C.360.28.
15	CC.360.21.		
16	CC.360.21.		
17	CC.360.22. LA.360.4.		

Item No.	Paragraph No. of Reference	Item No.	Paragraph No. of Reference
33	CO.360.3. MI.360.29.	56	IN.360.6.
34	FI.360.8.	57	MI.360.35.
35	FI.360.3. PE.360.5.	58	CC.360.25. IN.360.8. NA.360.12.
36	CC.360.15.	59	CC.360.37.
37	FO.360.2. NA.360.4.-NA.360.5. NA.45.18.	60	LA.360.3. MI.360.4. MI.360.43.
38	MI.360.33.	61	PO.360.2.
39	MI.360.31.	62	FI.360.12. MI.360.22. MI.360.40. MI.93.31. PE.360.8.
40	JU.360.8.		
41	IN.360.5. PE.360.2.		
42	IN.360.5. PE.360.3.	63	IN.360.9. MI.360.19. MI.360.37.
43	PE.360.4.		
44	JU.360.2.	64	CC.360.27. IN.360.10.
45	JU.360.4.		
46	CC.360.36. FO.360.41.	65	CC.360.27. IN.360.10.
47	CC.360.3. FO.360.49.	66	CC.360.27. IN.360.10.
48	LA.360.2.	67	CC.360.27. IN.360.10.
49	CC.360.30.		
50	CO.360.4.	68	CC.360.27. IN.360.10.
51	CC.360.35. IN.360.10. MI.93.62.	69	CC.360.27. IN.360.10.
52	MI.360.36.	70	CC.360.27. IN.360.10.
53	MI.360.33. MI.360.35.-MI.360.36.	71	CC.360.27. IN.360.10.
54	CO.360.5. FO.360.67.	72	CC.360.27. IN.360.10.
55	CC.360.30. FI.360.10. FO.360.42.	73	CC.360.27. IN.360.10.
		74	CC.360.27. IN.360.10.

Item No.	Paragraph No. of Reference	Item No.	Paragraph No. of Reference
75	CC.360.27. IN.360.10.		FO.360.21. FO.360.29. FO.360.32.
76	CC.360.27. IN.360.10.	92	FO.360.17. FO.360.19.
77	CC.360.27. CN.360.3. IN.360.10. JU.360.5.-JU.360.6.		FO.360.25.-FO.360.26. FO.360.39.
		93	FO.360.22.
78	CC.360.26. IN.360.10. MI.360.10. NA.360.16.	94	FO.360.34.
		95	FO.360.35.
		96	FO.360.36. NA.360.16.
79	FO.360.3. FO.360.5.	97	FO.360.37.
		98	FO.360.69.
80	FO.360.9.	99	FO.360.38.
81	FO.360.10.	100	FO.360.33.
82	FO.360.16. FO.360.30.-FO.360.31.	101	FO.360.63.
83	FO.360.24. FO.360.31.	102	FO.360.33. FO.360.62.
84	FO.360.19. FO.360.22. FO.360.30.-FO.360.32.	103	FO.360.33.
		104	FO.360.33. FO.59.7.
85	FO.360.30.-FO.360.31. NA.360.16.	105	FO.360.33.
		106	FO.360.33.
86	FO.360.32. FO.360.64.	107	FO.360.33.
87	FO.360.16. FO.360.32.	108	FO.360.33.
		109	FO.360.33.
88	FO.360.24.	110	FO.360.33.
89	FO.360.19. FO.360.22.-FO.360.24. FO.360.27. FO.360.30.	111	FO.360.34.-FO.360.35.
		112	FO.360.34.-FO.360.35.
		113	FO.360.34.-FO.360.35.
90	FO.360.15. FO.360.18. FO.360.20. FO.360.28.	114	FO.360.34.-FO.360.35.
		115	FO.360.22.
		115B	FO.360.33.
		116	FO.360.64.
91	FO.360.14. FO.360.16.	117	FO.360.65.

Item No.	Paragraph No. of Reference	Item No.	Paragraph No. of Reference
118	FO.360.4. FO.59.4.	146	CC.360.30.
		147	MI.360.2.
119	FO.360.4. FO.59.2.	148	MI.360.3.
		149	MI.360.5.
120	FO.59.2.	150	IN.360.10. MI.360.6.
121	FO.59.4.		
122	FO.360.58.	151	IN.360.10. MI.360.6.
123	CC.360.20.		
124	FO.360.6.	152	IN.360.10. MI.360.25.
125	FO.360.37.	153	IN.360.10. MI.360.23.
126	FO.360.54.		
127	FO.360.56.	154	IN.360.10. MI.360.14.
128	FO.360.40.		
129	FO.360.40. FO.360.59.	155	IN.360.10. MI.360.14.
		156	IN.360.10. MI.360.14. MI.360.16.
130	FO.360.60.		
131	FI.360.14.		
132	NA.360.11.	157	IN.360.10. MI.360.15.
133	CC.360.23.		
134	IN.360.7.	158	IN.360.10. MI.360.16.-MI.360.17. MI.360.19.
135	FO.360.48. IN.360.3.		
136	FI.360.2.	159	IN.360.10. MI.360.13. MI.360.15. MI.360.17.-MI.360.18. MI.360.22. MI.360.25.-MI.360.26.
137	FI.360.4.		
138	FI.360.5. PE.360.9.		
139	FI.360.6.		
140	FI.360.6.	160	IN.360.10. MI.360.15. MI.360.24.
141	FI.360.13.		
142	FI.360.9.		
143	FI.360.11. MI.360.41.	161	IN.360.10. MI.360.17.-MI.360.18. MI.360.20. MI.360.23. MI.360.25.-MI.360.26.
144	FI.360.13.		
145	FO.360.44. FO.360.47. FO.59.22.	162	IN.360.10. MI.360.12.-MI.360.13. MI.360.18. MI.360.24.

Item No.	Paragraph No. of Reference	Item No.	Paragraph No. of Reference
163	IN.360.10.	174	IN.360.3.
	MI.360.13.	175	CC.360.19.
	MI.360.15.	176	LA.360.6.
	MI.360.17.	177	CC.360.31.
	MI.360.19.-MI.360.21.		IN.360.11.
164	IN.360.10.		LA.360.8.
	MI.360.12.	178	CC.360.16.
	MI.360.14.	179	CC.360.7.
	MI.360.16.	180	CC.360.30.
	MI.360.22.	181	CC.360.18.
	MI.360.24.	182	CC.360.9.
	NA.360.15.	183	CC.360.17.
165	FO.360.16.	184	CC.360.8.
	IN.360.10.	185	CC.360.17.
	MI.360.13.	186	CC.360.17.
	MI.360.16.	187	CC.360.18.
	MI.360.20.	188	CC.360.28.
	MI.360.22.	189	CC.360.17.
166	IN.360.9.	190	CC.360.17.
	MI.360.30.	191	CC.360.17.
	MI.360.37.	192	MI.360.21.
167	MI.360.35.		MI.360.29.
168	NA.360.10.	193	NA.360.13.
169	IN.360.10.	194	MI.360.38.
	MI.360.27.	195	CC.360.8.
170	IN.360.10.		MI.93.17.
	MI.360.27.	196	NA.360.7.
171	IN.360.10.		
	MI.360.27.		
172	IN.360.10.		
	MI.360.27.		
173	IN.360.10.		
	MI.360.28.		

BIBLIOGRAPHY

Publications of the National Archives

Butler, John P., comp. *Index: The Papers of the Continental Congress, 1774-1789*, 5 vols. Washington, DC: National Archives and Records Service, 1978.

Hargett, Janet L., comp. *List of Selected Maps of States and Territories.* National Archives Special List No. 29. Washington, DC: National Archives and Records Service, 1971.

Harris, Kenneth and Steven D. Tilley, comps. *Index: Journals of the Continental Congress, 1774-1789.* Washington, DC: National Archives and Records Service, 1976.

Hill, Edward, comp. *Guide to Records in the National Archives of the United States Relating to American Indians.* Washington, DC: National Archives and Records Service, 1981.

Kelsay, Laura E., comp. *List of Cartographic Records of the Bureau of Indian Affairs.* National Archives Special List No. 13. Washington, DC: National Archives and Records Service, 1954.

_____. *List of Cartographic Records of the General Land Office.* National Archives Special List No. 19. Washington, DC: National Archives and Records Service, 1964.

McLaughlin, Patrick D., comp. *Pre-Federal Maps in the National Archives: An Annotated List.* Washington, DC: National Archives and Records Service, 1975.

National Archives and Records Administration. *Guide to Genealogical Research in the National Archives.* Washington, DC: National Archives and Records Administration, 1982; rev. 1985.

National Archives and Records Service. *The Formation of the Union.* National Archives Publication No. 70-13. Washington, DC: National Archives and Records Service, 1970.

Van Neste, W. Lane and Virgil E. Baugh. *Title Papers of the Public Buildings Service*. National Archives Special List No. 30. Washington, DC: National Archives and Records Service, 1972.

Other Publications of the U.S. Government

Carter, Clarence Edwin, comp. *The Territorial Papers of the United States*, 22 vols. Washington, DC: Government Printing Office, 1934.

Clarke, William Bell, William J. Morgan, and William J. Dudley, eds. *Naval Documents of the American Revolution*, vols. 1-9. Washington, DC: Government Printing Office, 1964-

Force, Peter, ed. *American Archives*. Washington, DC: U.S. Department of State, 1837-53.

Ford, Worthington Chauncey, Gaillard Hunt, John C. Fitzpatrick, and Roscoe R. Hill, eds. *Journals of the Continental Congress, 1774-1789; Edited from the Original Records in the Library of Congress*, 34 vols. Washington, DC: Government Printing Office, 1904-37.

Library of Congress, Manuscripts Division. *Naval Records of the American Revolution, 1775-1788. Prepared from the Originals in the Library of Congress by Charles Henry Lincoln of the Division of Manuscripts*. Washington, DC: Government Printing Office, 1906.

Martin, Lawrence, comp. and ed. *Constitution Sesquicentennial Atlas of the United States of America*. Washington, DC: U.S. Constitution Sesquicentennial Commission, 1937-38.

_____, ed. *The George Washington Atlas; A Collection of Eighty-five Maps Including Twenty-eight Made by George Washington, Seven Used and Annotated by Him, Eight Made at His Direction, or for His Use or Otherwise Associated with Him, and Forty-two New Maps Concerning His Activities in Peace and War and His Place in History*. Washington, DC: U.S. George Washington Bicentennial Commission, 1932.

Ogden, Henry Alexander. *Uniform of the Army of the United States Illustrated from 1774 to 1889; Authorized by the Secretary of War and Prepared under the Supervision of the Quartermaster General by Lieut. Colonel M. I. Lundington, Quartermaster's Department, U.S. Army*. Washington, DC: U.S. Quartermaster's Department, 1895.

Sparks, Jared, ed. *Diplomatic Correspondence of the American Revolution. Being the Letters of Benjamin Franklin, Silas Deane, John Adams, John Jay, Arthur Lee, William Lee, Ralph Izard, Francis Dana, William Carmichael, Henry Laurens, John Laurens, Marquis de Lafayette, M. Dumas, and Others, Concerning the Foreign Relations of the United States During the Whole Revo-*

lution; *Together with Letters of Reply from the Secret Committee of Congress, and the Secretary of Foreign Affairs. Also the Entire Correspondence of the French Ministers, Gerard and Luzerne, with Congress. Published Under the Direction of the President of the United States from the Original Manuscripts in the Department of State, Conforming to a Resolution of Congress on March 27th, 1818,* 6 vols. Washington, DC: U.S. Department of State, 1857.

U.S. Congress. *American State Papers, Documents, Legislative and Executive, of the Congress of the United States; Class IX, Claims.* Washington, DC: Gales and Seaton, 1832-61.

_____. *Journal, Acts and Proceedings, of the Convention, Assembled at Philadelphia, Monday, May 14, and Dissolved Monday, September 17, 1787, which formed the Constitution of the United States.* Boston: Thomas B. Wait, 1819.

U.S. Continental Congress. *Journals of Congress,* 11 vols. Various places: various printers, 1777-88.

_____. *Register of the Certificates, Issued by John Pierce, Esquire, Paymaster General, and Commissioner of the Army Accounts, for the United States.* New York City: Francis Child, 1786.

_____. *Rules for the Regulation of the Navy of the United Colonies of North America.* Philadelphia: William and Thomas Bradford, 1775.

U.S. Department of State. *Calendar of the Miscellaneous Letters Received by the Department of State. From the Organization of the Government to 1820.* Washington, DC: Government Printing Office, 1897.

_____. *Diplomatic Correspondence of the United States from the Definitive Treaty of Peace, 10th, September 1783, to the Adoption of the Constitution, March 4, 1789. Being the Letters of the Presidents of Congress, the Secretary for Foreign Affairs—American Ministers at Foreign Courts, Foreign Ministers Near Congress—Reports of Committees of Congress, and Reports of the Secretary for Foreign Affairs on Various Letters and Communications; Together with Letters from Individuals on Public Affairs. Published Under the Direction of the Secretary of State, from the Original Manuscripts in the Department of State Comformably to an Act of Congress, Approved May 5, 1832.* Washington, DC: F. P. Blair, 1833-34.

U.S. Quartermaster's Department. *A Sketch of the Organization of the Quartermasters' Department from 1774 to 1868.* Washington, DC: Government Printing Office, 1876.

U.S. Congress, Senate. *Annual Report of the National Society of Daughters of American Revolution, 1914.* S. Doc. 988. 63d Cong., 3d sess., 1914-15.

_____. *Payments, Under Act of Congress of March 28, 1848, for Relief of the Heirs of John Paul Jones.* S. Exec. Doc. 11. 37th Cong., 2d sess., 1861-62.

_____. *List of Private Claims, Senate, 14th-46th Congress, 2 Volumes.* S. Misc. Doc. 14. 46th Cong., 3d sess., 1880-81.

U.S. Superintendent of Finance. *A Statement of the Accounts of the United States of America, During the Administration of the Superintendant [sic] of Finance [Robert Morris] Commencing with His Appointment, on the 20th Day of February, 1781, and Ending with His Resignation, on the 1st Day of November, 1784.* Philadelphia: R. Aitken, 1785.

Non-Government Publications

Faden, William. *Atlas of Battles of the American Revolution, Together with Maps Showing the Routes of the British and American Armies, Plans of Cities, Surveys of Harbors, Etc., Taken During that Eventful Period by Officers Attached to the Royal Army.* New York: Bartlett and Welford, 1845.

Franklin, William Temple, ed. *Memoirs of the Life and Writings of Benjamin Franklin, Written by Himself to a Late Period, and Continued to the Time of His Death by His Grandson, William Temple Franklin. And His Select Political, Philosophical, and Miscellaneous Works, Published from the Original Manuscripts.* 6 vols. London: H. Colburn, 1818-19.

French, Benjamin F., comp. *Historical Collections of Louisiana; Embracing Translations of Many Rare and Valuable Documents Related to the National, Civil, and Political History of That State,* 5 vols. New York: Wiley and Putnam, 1846-53.

Herbert, Charles. *A Relic of the Revolution.* Boston: C. H. Pierce, 1847.

Paullin, Charles Oscar, ed. *Out-Letters of the Continental Marine Committee and Board of Admiralty,* 2 vols. New York: Naval Historical Society, 1914.

Sparks Jared, ed. *The Works of Benjamin Franklin; Containing Several Political, Philosophical, and Historical Tracts Not Included in Any Former Edition, and Many Letters, Official and Private, Not Hitherto Published; With Notes and a Life of the Author,* 10 vols. Boston: Hilliard, Gray, and Company, 1836-40.

Waldemaier, Nellie Protsman, ed. *Some of the Earliest Oaths of Allegiance to the United States of America.* Lancaster PA: Lancaster Press, 1944.

INDEX

The paragraph number citations under each entry are listed in the order in which they appear in the text.

Several entries will not be found in this index because they are pervasive throughout the text. These include Confederation and Continental Congresses, Continental Army, Revolutionary War. Please look for more specific entries.

Accounts, Chambers of, FI.0.3–5; FI.360.2–3, 12; FI.217.8
Accounts, Committee of, FI.0.1
Accounts (Treasury), Records of the Bureau of (RG39), FI.39.1–7; MI.39.1–2; PE.39.1–4
Active (schooner), NA.45.23
Adams, John, FI.360.14; FI.39.2; FI.53.26; FI.59.4; FI.217.8; FO.0.7, 9; FO.360.19, 22, 30, 31, 32, 33, 49, 51, 63, 65; FO.53.2; FO.59.7; LA.76.9
Adams, John Quincy, CN.59.3; FI.360.14
Adjutant General's Office, MI.93.67, 72, 75; MI.94.9,15
Adjutant Generals Office, Records of the (RG 94), CO.94.1–2; IN.94.1; MI.94.1–15
Admiralty, Board of, FO.360.2; NA.0.1, 5–6; NA.360.2, 4, 10, 12, 14
Agricultural products, CO.36.6, 11, 16, 18; CO.123.4–5; CO.181.2; MI.93.57
Aguada, PR, CC.186.3
Ainsworth, Fred C., MI.93.3
Alabama, LA.49.14
Albany, NY, CO.93.3; IN.360.7; MI.360.4, 41; MI.53.2; MI.93.49; NA.45.6
Alden, Roger, FI.217.8; LA.360.5
Alexander Nesbit & Co., CO.36.16
Alexandria, VA, CO.79.4; CO.181.2; LA.121.2
Algiers, FO.360.14, 65; FO.59.11, 14, 16, 17, 18
Alicante, Spain, FO.59.17
Allan, John, IN.0.4; IN.360.8
Allen, Ethan, MI.360.9, 12; MI.94.13
Allen, James, NA.45.7
Alliance (ship), CO.45.3; FI.217.8; JU.267.2; NA.0.7; NA.360.11, 13; NA.45.22,24
Amboys Flying Camp (NJ), MI.94.11
America (ship), NA.0.7; NA.19.2
American Indians, *see* all IN; CO.93.3; FI.360.7; FI.56.2; FI.217.8;

FO.59.10,12; LA.59.5; LA.233.2; LA.267.2; MI.0.6; MI.360.8, 30, 37; MI. 98.3

and the American Revolution, MI.94.15

and the British, IN.360.6–8, 9, 10; IN.75.2–3

Christians, LA.360.6

Military actions against, MI.360.2; MI.93.27; MI.98.4; PE.15.11, 16

Prisoners taken by, IN.360.6, 9

Problems with settlers, LA.360.2, 3, 6

Treaty negotiations with, MI.360.6

see also individual tribes

Amherst, Gen. Jeffrey, CO.93.3

Amsterdam, FI.39.2; FI.59.4; FO.360.41

Anderson, John, FI.39.5

Andre, John, MI.59.4; MI.93.67; MI.94.13

Annapolis, MD, CO.36.6; CO.41.2; LA.121.2; MI.59.4; MI.93.34, 36

Annapolis Convention, CN.0.1–2, CN.360.3–4

Anspach, Peter, CO.94.2; FI.53.21; MI.93.40, 41, 43

Antigua, FO.186.2

Appeals, Standing Committee on, JU.0.4; JU.360.3; JU.267.3

Ariel (ship), NA.360.13; NA.45.22

Arms and ammunition, FI.53.2; FO.0.2; MI.360.5; MI.45.2, 4; MI.53.2; MI.92.2; MI.93.23, 24, 42, 46, 47, 49, 55; MI.98.3; MI.217.3; NA.45.12

Armstrong, John, MI.360.12

Army engineers, MI.360.42

Army War College, MI.165.2

Arnold, Benedict, CO.36.4; FI.217.8; JU.267.2; MI.360.13; MI.53.2; MI.59.4; MI.77.4; MI.93.67; MI.217.2; NA.0.8

Association of the Freemen of Maryland, CC.59.3

Associated Loyalists, MI.360.38

Austin, Ebenezer, FI.56.2

Bache, Richard, PO.0.3; PO.360.2

Bahama Islands, NA.45.22, 24

Baltimore, MD, CC.360.23; CO.36.8–9; CO.41.2; CO.123.3; FI.360.11; LA.121.2; MI.59.4

Bank of North America, FI.217.8

Bankers, foreign, FI.360.14; FI.39.4; FI.360.44, 47; FO.11.2; NA.45.18

Bankson, Benjamin, CN.360.5, 11

Bankson, Benjamin Jr., LA.360.5

Barbados, CO.36.6

Barbary States, FO.0.9; FO.360.37, 51, 64, 69; FO.59.11

Barbe-Marbois, Francois de, FO.360.36

Barclay, Thomas, CO.76.2; FI.39.2; FI.53.2; FI.217.8; FO.360.16, 21, 29, 65; PE.39.2

Barrell, Joseph, CO.59.2

Barrell, William, CO.92.2

Barry, John, FI.217.8; JU.267.2

Bauman, Sebastian, MI.94.3
Bealle, Thomas, CO.79.6
Beatty, E., MI.94.6
Beaufort, SC, LA.58.2
Beaumarchais, Pierre Augustin Caron de, CO.360.5; FI.39.2; FI.217.8;
    FO.360.67; FO.59.10; PE.39.2; PE.76.2
Belknap, William, MI.93.2
Bellin, Jacques Nicolas, LA.92.2
Benard de La Harpe, Jean Baptiste, LA.59.5
Bentham, James, NA.45.7
Berckel, Franco Petrus van, FO.360.38
Berckel, Pieter Johan van, FO.360.38; FO.200.3
Beresford, Richard, IN.59.2
Bering Sea Claims Commission, LA.76.4
Bermuda, PE.360.2
Berlin, FO.0.8; FO.360.15
Bethlehem, PA, MI.93.18
Betsey (brig), FO.360.69
Betsy (sloop), CO.94.2
Beverly, MA, CO.36.10
Bigelow, Jacob, PE.123.2
Bilboa, Spain, FO.360.25
Bill of Rights, CN.11.3
Bindon, Joseph, MI.94.6
Bingham, William, CO.36.17; FI.39.2; FI.217.8; FO.360.20; FO.59.6
Bitters, Charles, CO.94.2
Black Americans, CO.79.6; MI.360.36; MI.93.57, 75; MI.94.13, 15; PE.15.3
Blaine, Ephraim, MI.360.13
Blair, John, MI.45.2
Blockhouses, MI.94.11
Blodget, William, LA.267.2
Bloomfield, Joseph, CN.360.12
Boats, purchase of, MI.45.6
Bombay, India, CO.45.3
Bomford, George, MI.156.2
Bond, George, FI.217.8
Bond, Phineas, FO.59.18
Bondfield, John, FI.39.2; FO.360.17
Bonhomme Richard (ship), NA.360.12, 13; NA.45.5, 20, 22, 28, 35; PE.76.3
Bonnecamps (Jesuit mathematician), LA.77.3
Boothbay, MA, CO.36.12
Bordeaux, France, FO.360.17
Boston, MA, CC.59.4; CO.36.6; CO.59.2; CO.123.5; FI.360.11, 41;
    JU.267.2; MI.0.8; MI.45.6; NA.0.4; NA.45.7, 24; PE.59.2
Boston Harbor, LA.77.3; MI.98.4
Boston Navy Yard, NA.45.34
Boston Tea Party, CC.59.3
Boudin, Nicholas, LA.49.6
Boudinot, Elias, CC.360.21; FI.53.20; JU.267.6

Boundary and Claims Commissions and Arbitrations, Records of
(RG 76), CO.76.1–2; LA.76.1–13; PE.76.1–4
Boundary disputes,
Between states, CC.360.27; JU.0.5; JU.360.5–8; JU.267.8;
LA.59.5, 9; LA.267.2
International, FO.0.11; FO.360.10; FO.59.14,15,16; IN.360.8;
LA.76.2, 9, 13
Boundary lines, surveying of, LA.360.3; LA.49.2–4, 21; LA.59.9
Bounty land grants, JU.267.7; LA.0.2, 4–5; LA.360.5, 7; LA.49.20;
MI.0.6; MI.360.6; MI.93.56; PE.0.6–12; PE.15.3–12, 15, 17;
PE.49.2–4; PE.93.2
Bounty money, MI.59.2; MI.93.23, 39
Bowen, Jabez, FI.217.12
Boyd, James, PE.59.2
Brandywine, PA, MI.94.13
Branford, CT, CO.36.5
Brearley, David, CN.360.12
British Army, CO.45.2; CO.93.3; LA.49.2
British colonies, CO.36.15; FO.0.1
British Navy, CO.45.2; NA.360.11; NA.45.7, 30–33
British property, confiscation of, FO.59.10; MI.93.56
British vice admiralty courts, JU.21.2–6, 8; NA.45.7
British West Florida, IN.75.3; LA.360.5; LA.49.8–11, 20; LA.59.3;
LA.76.5; MI.93.62; NA.45.33; PE.49.5
Broadsides, CC.360.32; CC.59.3; FI.360.14; FO.200.2; JU.267.6; NA.45.9
Broome, John, JU.360.9
Broome, Samuel, JU.360.9
Brown, John, MI.93.65; NA.360.5
Bullfinch, Charles, CO.59.2
Bunker Hill, Battle of, NA.45.34
Burbeck, Henry, MI.94.6
Burgoyne, John, MI.360.35
Burr, Aaron, JU.360.9
Burrall, Jonathan, FI.217.16
Butler, Richard, MI.360.6
Butler, William, MI.98.3

Cadiz, Spain, FO.360.26
Cahokia, LA.360.2
California, LA.11.2; LA.59.7
Cambridge, MA, CO.360.3; MI.360.29; NA.45.6
Canada, CC.0.2; IN.360.8, 9; MI.360.37; PE.360.7; PO.360.2;
PO.28.8
and the American Revolution, MI.0.8; MI.360.30; MI.53.2;
MI.217.2
Refugees from, FI.360.3; LA.0.4; LA.360.5, 6; LA.49.20,
21; PE.0.9; PE.360.5, 7; PE.49.2; PE.217.4
Canadian settlers, LA.360.5; LA.49.20
  see also Nova Scotia; French-Canadian settlers

Canals, CO.79.2
Canary Islands, NA. 45.24
Canton, China, CO.45.3
Cape Henlopen, DE, CO.26.2
Capital city, selection of, CC.360.36
Cargoes, ships, CO.360.2; CO.27.2; CO.36.2, 5, 6, 7, 8, 9, 11, 14–15, 16, 18; CO.55.4; JU.360.2
Caribbean islands, CO.78.2
Carleton, Joseph, LA.360.3; MI.360.4, 43; MI.217.2
Carleton, Sir Guy, MI.360.36, 38
Carmichael, William, CO.360.2; FO.360.24, 33; FO.53.2
Carpenters' Hall, MI.93.46, 47
Carroll, Daniel, CO.79.5
Carter, George, LA.59.8
Carter, John, CO.15.2
Castle Island, Boston Harbor, MI.98.4
Catawba Indians, IN.59.2
Catherine (ship), CO.123.2
Caverly, Richard, JU.21.4
Cayuga Indians, IN.360.9
Cazeau, Francis, PE.123.2
Census, Records of the Bureau of the (RG 29), IN. 29.1–2
Censuses, IN.360.11
Central America, LA.76.3
Certificates for depreciation of pay, MI.93.69; MI.217.5; PE.0.10
Certificates of indebtedness, FI.39.7; FI.53.8–11, 15, 17–19, 21–24, 27; FI.217.11–12, 16–18, 19; JU.267.6; MI.53.5
Chapelles, Le Breton des, FO.59.16
Charlant, Jacques, PE.123.2
Charlant, Peter, PE.123.2
Charles II, LA.60.2
Charleston, SC, LA.121.2; MI.93.34; NA.45.7, 24; PO.28.5
Charlestown, MA, MI.45.6; NA.45.34
Charming Polly (schooner), NA.45.12
Charming Sally (sloop), NA.45.23
Cherokee Nation, IN.0.4; IN.360.3; IN.15.1; IN.59.2, 3; IN.93.5; LA.360.3; PE.15.11
Chesapeake and Ohio Canal Company, CO.79.2
Chesapeake Bay, CN.0.1; CO.71.2; NA.45.12
Chickasaw Nation, IN.360.3; IN.59.2; IN.75.3; LA.49.20
Child, Francis, CO.59.3
Chilicothe, OH, PE.49.3
China, CO.27.2; CO.45.3; CO.59.2; FO.360.41
Chinn, Edward, FI.53.15
Chisholm, Alexander, JU.21.11
Chisholm v. Georgia, JU.21.11; JU.267.8
Chittenden, Thomas, JU.360.8
Choctaw Nation, IN.360.3; IN.59.2; IN.75.3; LA.49.20
Chippewa Nation, IN.360.3

Defence (brig), NA.45.3
Degge, James, NA.360.13
Delassus, Charles Dehault, LA.49.16
Delaware, CC.360.27; CN.0.1; CN.360.3; CO.26.2; FI.53.8, 9;
FO.360.36; LA.59.9; LA.60.2; MI.59.2; MI.93.49; MI.94.3
Delaware Bay and River, LA.77.3
Delaware Nation, IN.360.3, 6, 9; IN.59.3; LA.360.3; LA.59.9
Denmark, CO.55.4; FO.360.51; FO.55.2; JU.55.2; PE.76.3
Derby, CT, CO.36.5
Des Barves, J. F. W., LA.77.3
Deserters, MI.45.4; MI.53.3, 4; MI.59.2, 4, 6, 7; MI.93.14, 27, 29, 36, 55,
66; MI.94.4, 6; MI.217.4; NA.45.22; PE.15.15
Detail, Committee of, CN.0.4; CN.360.10, 12
Detroit, MI, LA.49.6, 13
Dickinson, John, CC.0.3; CN.360.4; LA.0.2
Dickinson College, FI.53.20
Digges, Dudley, MI.45.2
Dinwiddie, Robert, MI.59.6
Diplomatic communications, FO.0.1–2, 4; FO.360.2–7, 10–32, 33
Diplomats, foreign, FO.360.34–40, 59; FO.59.3, 8, 16; PE.123.2
Diplomats, U.S., FI.39.2; FI.53.2; FI.217.8; FO.0.7–11; FO.360.2, 4,
10–32, 62–66; FO.53.2; FO.59.4, 5, 10, 11, 14, 17, 18, 22;
FO.84.1–2; NA.360.5, 10, 16; NA.45.15
District of Columbia, LA.42.2–4
District Courts of the United States, Records of the
(RG 21), JU.21.1–11; PE.21.1–4
District land offices, LA.49.5, 13
Dixon, Jeremiah, LA.59.9
Dongan, Thomas, JU.21.2
Doughty, John, MI.98.3
Drayton, William, JU.21.8
Driver, Michael, CO.78.2
Du Coudray, Philippe Charles Tronson, MI.360.10, 14
Dublin newspapers, CC.45.2
Duck Creek Roads (Smyrna), DE, CO.181.2
Dudley, Joseph, NA.45.6
Dumas, Charles W. F., FI.39.2; FO.0.2, 7, 9; FO.360.22, 33, 63;
FO.53.2; NA.360.11
Dunham, Azariah, JU.267.6
Dunham, James, JU.267.6
d'Unienville, Marie Claude Francois Marrier, NA.59.2
Dunlap, John, CC.360.5; FI.59.2
Dunlap and Claypoole, PE.39.3
Dunscomb, Andrew, FI.39.5
Duportail, Louis L., MI.360.14

East Hartford, CT, MI.93.49
East Indies, FO.360.41
Edenton, NC, CO.36.14

Martha's Vineyard, MA, NA.45.11
Martin, Joseph, IN.0.4; PE.15.11
Martinique, FO.360.20; FO.59.6; NA.45.24; NA.59.3
Maryland, CC.360.27, 31; CN.0.1; CO.36.6–9, 12–13; CO.41.2;
    CO.79.2–3, 5; FI.53.8, 9; JU.360.5; LA.0.2; LA.59.9; LA.77.3;
    MI.59.2, 5; MI.93.36, 49; MI.200.2
Maryland Loan Office, FI.217.13
Mason, Charles, LA.59.9
Mason, George, CO.79.3–4; FI.360.7
Massachusetts, CC.360.27, 31; CN.360.3; CO.26.2; CO.36.10–11, 12;
    FI.53.8, 9; FO.360.53; FO.59.16; IN.360.10; JU.360.8; JU.45.2;
    LA.360.3, 5; LA.76.5; MI.45.3, 4, 6; MI.59.2; MI.93.36, 42, 44,
    50, 58, 59, 65, 67; MI.94.5, 10; MI.98.4; NA.0.8; NA.360.9;
    NA.45.1, 5, 6, 14, 19, 34; PE.21.3; PE.59.2; PO.28.8
Massachusetts Board of War, MI.45.3, 5; NA.45.16
Massachusetts Committee of Safety, MI.45.6
Massachusetts House of Representatives, CC.0.1
Mathews, John, MI.360.31
Maury, Matthew Fontaine, CO.78.2
Medical Department, MI.360.33; MI.112.2, 3
Medical officers, MI.112.2
Medical supplies, CO.79.3, 6; CO.181.2; FI.360.11; MI.360.41; MI.45.5;
    MI.59.2; MI.217.3
Medicine and Surgery, Records of the Bureau of (RG 52), NA.52.1–2
Meigs, Return J., MI.156.2
Mercer, Hugh, MI.360.18
Merchant ships, CO.36.4–18; CO.41.2; CO.45.2–3; NA.45.9, 10, 14,
    23; PE.76.1–3
Merchants, American, CO.0.3; CO.360.5; CO.15.2; CO.36.4, 9, 14;
    CO.41.2; CO.45.2; CO.59.3; CO.76.2; CO.92.2–4; CO.107.2;
    CO.123.2–5; IN.59.3; JU.59.2; MI.93.46
Merchants, foreign, FI.360.6; FI.39.2; FI.59.4; FO.360.2; FO.11.2; PE.123.2
Mercury (brig), CO.123.3
Meteorological records, CO.27.1–2; CO.45.3
Mexico, FO.186.2; LA.49.18; LA.59.7; LA.77.3
Miami Nation, LA.360.3
Middletown, CT, CO.36.12
Middletown, RI, MI.45.4
Mifflin, Thomas, CC.360.21; LA.59.10; MI.360.18; MI.93.39
Mighill, Thomas, MI.93.25
Milford, CT, CO.36.5
Military clothing and uniforms, MI.0.6; MI.360.5; MI.39.2; MI.45.4;
    MI.53.2; MI.59.3; MI.93.14, 24, 25, 26, 29, 36, 39, 42, 46, 47,
    56; MI.94.3, 4, 7; MI.98.3; MI.165.3; MI.217.3, 4; MI.391.2;
    NA.52.2; PE.39.3
Military commissions, MI.93.8, 11, 13, 17–19; MI.94.5, 10
Military expenditures, FI.360.2, 13; FI.39.4, FI.53.12; FI.56.2; FI.93.2;
    FI.217.8; MI.39.2; MI.45.2; MI.53.2; MI.59.3; MI.92.3;
    MI.93.28, 39, 45, 46, 57; MI.94.3

Military installations, MI.360.33; MI.77.2; MI.94.11
Military operations, MI.93.8, 11
Military pay and payrolls, FI.360.2; FI.56.2; FI.93.3; FI.217.13, 20;
    MI.15.2; MI.45.2; MI.53.2, 3, 5; MI.59.2, 3; MI.92.3; MI.93.5,
    11, 14, 15, 25, 28, 31, 32, 34–36, 39, 55, 57, 64; MI.94.2, 3,
    4, 6, 9; MI.217.2, 3, 4; NA.45.27–29; NA.52.2; NA.93.2;
    PE.0.10; PE.15.3,15
Military personnel,
    Promotions, MI.360.5; MI.93.20, 66; MI.94.6
    Recruitment and enlistment, MI.360.2, 33, 43; MI.39.2; MI.45.6;
      MI.53.2; MI.59.2; MI.93.11, 23, 28, 34, 39, 47, 66; MI.94.4,
      15; MI.98.4; MI.217.3, 4; PE.93.3; PE.107.1
Military service records, MI.93.63–69, 72; MI.94.4, 6; NA.93.2
Military Stores Department, Commissary General of, MI.92.2; MI.93.2,
    42, 45–49, 64, 65; MI.94.2, 8
Military supplies, CO.0.1–4; CO.360.2; CO.15.2; CO.45.2; CO.92.2;
    FI.360.2; FI.53.2; FI.93.2; FI.217.13; FO.0.11; JU.21.11;
    MI.360.2, 5, 33, 41; MI.45.2, 4, 5, 6; MI.53.4; MI.59.2, 5;
    MI.92.2; MI.93.8, 11, 20, 24, 25, 26, 28, 29, 37, 39, 40,
    41, 42, 44, 46, 47, 48, 50, 56, 57, 58, 74; MI.94.2, 3; MI.98.3;
    MI.217.2, 3; NA.360.11, 13; NA.186.2; PE.0.10; PE.39.3;
    PE.76.2; PE.123.2
Military training, MI.360.2; MI.98.4
Military Units, British,
    British Brigade of Foot Guards, MI.93.60
    Seventeenth Regiment of Foot, MI.93.61
    Forty-fourth Regiment, MI.93.61
    Fifty-seventh Regiment, MI.93.61
Military Units, U.S.
    Numerical designations:
    First American Regiment, MI.94.4
    First Massachusetts State Regiment of Foot, MI.45.4
    First New Jersey Regiment, MI.53.4
    First Pennsylvania Line Regiment, MI.53.3
    First Virginia State Regiment, MI.93.57
    First United States Regiment, MI.94.6, 7
    Second Connecticut Regiment, MI.93.26
    Second Pennsylvania Regiment, MI.93.24; MI.217.4
    Third Massachusetts Regiment, MI.93.44
    Third Regiment of Artillery, Massachusetts Line, MI.94.10
    Fourth Connecticut Regiment, MI.93.23
    Fourth New York Regiment, MI.93.28
    Sixth Massachusetts Battalion, MI.93.16
    Eighth Massachusetts Regiment, MI.93.44
    Ninth Massachusetts Regiment, MI.93.44
    Ninth Pennsylvania Regiment, PE.123.2
    Eleventh Pennsylvania Regiment, MI.93.29
    Twenty-sixth Continental Regiment, MI.93.25
      Nominal designations:

Cavendish Regiment, MI.45.4
Col. Samuel Gerrish's Massachusetts Regiment, MI.93.25
Moses Hazen's Regiment, PE.123.2
Col. John Lamb's Artillery Regiment, MI.93.36
Pulaski's Legion, FI.217.13
Vose's Regiment of Light Infantry, MI.93.43
    Miscellaneous:
American Regiment of Foot, MI.98.2
Artillery Brigade, The, MI.93.44
Artillery, Corps of (Northern Department), MI.93.49
Continental Line, MI.93.68
Convention Troops, MI.360.35
Illinois Regiment, MI.49.2
Independent Light Dragoons, MI.59.7
Loyal American Regiment, MI.93.61
New York Artillery, MI.391.2
North Carolina Line, MI.59.3, MI.93.36
Virginia Line, MI.93.36
Miller, Hunter, FO.11.3
Milligan, James, FI.360.3
Mingo Nation, LA.360.3; LA.59.9
Mississippi River, FO.360.10; FO.59.10, 11, 14, 16; LA.267.2; NA.45.12
Missouri River, LA.77.2
Mitchell, John, LA.76.9, 11
Mobile, AL, LA.49.6, 20
Mohawk Indians, IN.360.9; LA.59.9; MI.98.3
Mohawk Valley, IN.360.9; MI.360.37
Monroe, James, CN.59.2; PE.48.2
Montgomery (sloop), NA.45.11
Montgomery, Richard, MI.360.18; MI.53.2
Montgomery, Robert, FO.59.17
Montplaisir, _____, NA.360.11
Montreal, Quebec, PO.28.3
Moravian Society for propagating the Gospel among the Heathen, LA.360.6
Morgan, George, IN.0.4; IN.360.10; IN.93.2; MI.360.19; MI.93.27
Morgan, John, IN.360.9; MI.360.19, 37
Morocco, FO.360.21, 43, 65, 69; FO.11.4; FO.59.8, 15, 18
Morrel, Jonathan, JU.360.9
Morris, Richard, JU.21.5
Morris, Robert, CO.36.16, 17; CO.76.2; FI.0.5, 8; FI.360.4–5, 14; FI.39.2,
    3, 4, 5; FI.53.5; FI.59.2; FI.217.8, 20; MI.93.37; NA.0.6–7;
    NA.360.6; NA.45.8, 18; PE.39.2; PE.76.2
Morris, Thomas, CO.0.3
Morris County, NJ, MI.94.5
Morristown, NJ, FI.360.10
Moultrie, William, MI.360.19
Moustier, Comte de, FO.360.36
Moylan, Stephen, MI.93.39; NA.360.11
Muhlenberg, Peter, MI.360.19; MI.93.18

Pennsylvania Council of Safety, NA.45.6
Pennsylvania Loan Office, FI.53.11
Penobscot Bay, LA.77.3
Penobscot expedition, CO.45.2; MI.45.3; NA.45.6
Penobscot Nation, IN.360.8
Pensacola, FL, LA.49.10, 20; LA.77.3
Pension Office, PE.0.3, 7
Pensions, *see* all PE; CO.15.2; FI.53.9, 16; FI.217.8
    Invalid pensioners, MI.360.4; PE.0.1–2, 4; PE.360.7; PE.21.2–3;
        PE.107.2; PE.233.2
    Legislation, PE.0.1–6
Pensions and Revolutionary Claims, House Committee on, PE.233.2–3
Pensions, Bureau of, PE.15.3, 15
Pensions, Commissioner of, PE.0.7; PE.15.1–2, 9, 11
Pensions, Senate Committee on, PE.46.3
Peterson and Taylor, CO.71.2; CO.181.2
Pettit, Charles, MI.360.21
Philadelphia, CC.360.23, CN.360.7; CO.360.5; CO.26.2; CO.36.16–17;
    CO.76.2; CO.92.2; FI.360.11; FO.360.2, 41; LA.360.3;
    LA.121.2; MI.360.29, 41; MI.45.6; MI.59.8; MI.92.2;
    MI.93.32, 39, 47, 49, 60; MI.94.3, 8; MI.217.3; NA.0.4, 8;
    NA.19.2; NA.45.22; PE.360.2; PO.28.3, 4
Philadelphia Mutiny, MI.360.32, 33
Phillips, Benjamin H., CO.36.17; CO.93.2
Phillips, Jonas, CN.360.7
Pickens, Andrew, IN.59.2
Pickering, Henry G., MI.93.4
Pickering, Timothy, FI.53.21; IN.93.2; MI.360.21; MI.45.6; MI.93.2, 4, 8,
    37–38, 40–41, 45, 46; MI.94.2
Pickering, Thomas, CN.360.6, 10; CN.59.3; CO.94.2
Pickering, William, NA.45.6
Pierce, John, FI.360.12; FI.53.15; FI.217.16; MI.360.11, 22, 40; MI.15.2;
    MI.53.2, 5; MI.93.31, 33, 34, 35; MI.94.2; MI.217.2, 6; PE.360.8
Pinckney, Charles Cotesworth, JU.21.9
Pinckney's Treaty, FO.59.10, 14, 16
Piracy, JU.21.2–6, 8, 9; NA.360.9
Pittsburgh, PA, IN.59.3; LA.360.3
Pluckemin, NJ, MI.93.49
Pollock, Oliver, CO.0.3; CO.360.4; FO.59.16, 17; NA.0.8; PE.39.3
Poor, Enoch, MI.360.8, 22
Population data, CC. 360.30; CC.186.3; CN.360.12; FI.53.12; IN.360.11
Port-au-Prince, Haiti, FO.84.2
Port Royal Island, SC, LA.58.2
Portsmouth, NH, NA.19.2
Portugal, FO.59.14, 17
Post Office Department, Records of the (RG 28), PO.28.1–8
Post Vincennes, FO.59.11; LA.360.2; LA.49.20
Postal officials, FI.217.8; PO.0.1; PO.360.2; PO.28.3–6, 8
Postmaster General, PO.0.1, 3; PO.360.2; PO.28.1–4

Potomac Company, CO.79.2–6
Potomac River, CN.0.1; CO.79.2–3
Pots, Jonathan, MI.53.2
Preble, George Henry, NA.45.34
Prince Georges County, MD, LA.42.3
Printing costs, CC.360.36; CO.59.3; FI.39.4; FO.59.12; PE.39.3; PO.28.4
Prisoners' Department, NA.360.14
Prisoners of war
    American, FI.53.2; LA.49.2; MI.217.2; NA.45.7, 13, 23, 26, 33; NA.93.2
    British, FI.217.8; MI.360.38; NA.45.7, 13, 23, 26, 33
    Exchanges of, MI.360.35, 36; NA.360.12; NA.45.18; NA.93.2
    Taken by American Indians, IN.360.6, 9
    Taken by Americans, MI.0.6; MI.360.2, 5, 33, 35; MI.53.2;
        MI.59.5; MI.93, 27, 46, 52, 53, 59, 75; MI.217.4; NA.0.5;
        NA.360.10, 11; NA.45.8, 13; PE.15.15
Privateer commissions, NA.360.8–9
Privateers, foreign, CO. 123.2–5; FO.59.16; JU.360.4
Privateers, U.S., CO.0.2; CO.45.2–3; JU.360.4; JU.45.2; JU.267.9;
    NA.360.8–9; NA.45.5, 8, 10, 14, 16, 23; PE.15.5
Privy Council (VA), MI.45.2
Prize agents, NA.0.4, 7; NA.360.11
Prize cases, JU.0.2, 4; JU.360.2–4; JU.21.5–6, 8; JU.45.2; JU.267.2–6,
    9; NA.45.26
Prize money, FI.217.13; FO.360.66; MI.53.2; NA.360.11, 13; NA.45.16;
    PE.0.10; PE.39.3–4; PE.76.3
Prize vessels, MI.45.5; MI.93.58; NA.0.2; NA.360.12; NA.45.8, 14, 16,
    19, 33
    Sale of, CO.0.2; CO.360.2, 4
Providence, RI, FO.360.41; MI.45.4
Prussia, FO.0.8; FO.360.52; FO.11.4
Public Building Service (GSA), Records of the (RG 121), LA.121.1–2
**Public Buildings and Public Parks of the National Capital, Records of
    the Office of** (RG 42), LA.42.1–4
Public debt, PE.39.2–4
Public Debt, Commissioners of the, FI.53.12
Public Debt, Records of the Bureau of the (RG 53), FI.53.1–27;
    FO.53.1–2; MI.53.1–5; PE.53.1–2
Public debt certificates, FI.53.8, 16, 21, 22; FI.217.15–18
Public Debt Division (Treasury Department), FI.217.15–18
Public land states, LA.49.5–13
Puerto Rico, Records of the Spanish Governors of (RG 186),
    CC.186.1–3; FI.186.1–2; FO.186.1–2; JU.186.1–2; MI.186.1–2;
    NA.186.1–2
Pulaski, Casimir, MI.360.9, 22; MI.93.18
Putnam, Israel, MI.360.22; NA.45.6

Quartermaster General, Records of the Office of the (RG 92),
    CO.92.1–2; LA.92.1–2; MI.92.1–4
Quakers, MI.360.32, 33

Russia, FO.0.8; FO.360.23; FO.59.14; NA.360.10; NA.45.35

St. Augustine, FL, LA.77.3; PE.15.15
St. Clair, Arthur, CC.360.21; LA.360.6; MI.360.6, 23
St. Clair, John M., LA.49.6
St. Croix, Virgin Islands, CC.55.1, 3; CO.55.2–4; FI.55.1; JU.55.2
St. Croix (Virgin Islands) Burgher Council, CC.55.3
St. Croix River, FO.59.16; PE.59.2
St. Domingo, FO.59.19
St. Dominique (Haiti), CO.360.5
St. Genevieve, MO, LA.49.17
St. Helena Parish, SC, LA.58.2
St. John, Virgin Islands, CC.55.1; CO.55.2
St. Lawrence River, MI.53.2
St. Louis, LA.49.15, 16
St. Mary's Isle, Scotland, NA.45.35
St. Philipp, LA.360.2
St. Stephens, AL, LA.49.5
St. Thomas, Virgin Islands, CC.55.1, 3; CO.55.2
St. Vincents, FL, LA.360.5
Salaries and wages, CC.360.30; CO.36.18; CO.79.3; CO.93.2; CO.123.4;
        FI.360.2, 5; FI.39.4; FI.53.2; FI.56.2; FO.59.18; IN.360.2;
        JU.21.6, 7, 8, 9; LA.360.3; MI.45.5; MI.93.37, 39, 45, 46,
        47, 48; NA.360.11; PE.0.10; PO.28.3, 4, 6
    see also Military pay
Salem, MA, CO.36.10–11; CO.78.2
Salem, OH, LA.360.6
Saltonstall, Dudley, MI.45.3
San Diego, CA, LA.11.2
San Juan, PR, FI.186.2
San Juan (Puerto Rico) hospital, CC.186.2
Sandy Hook, NY, CO.26.2; LA.77.3
Santa Fe, NM, LA.49.18
Saratoga, Convention of, MI.360.35
Saratoga, NY, MI.360.35
Sargent, W., LA.49.20
Sartine, Gabriel de, NA.45.20
Sauthier, C. J., LA.77.3
Savage, Joseph, MI.94.6
Savannah, GA, MI.200.2
Schuyler, Philip, CO.93.3; IN.360.10; MI.360.23, 27, 30, 31; MI.53.2; NA.45.6
Schuylkill Arsenal, MI.93.60
Schweighauser, John Daniel, FI.39.2; FO.360.66
Scotland, NA.45.35
Scrip, bounty-land, PE.15.7; PE.53.2
Scull, William, MI.93.29
Seamen, FO.360.69; JU.21.6–9; JU.267.2
Secret Committee (of Congress), CO.0.1–4; CO.360.5; FI.360.11; FO.360.2
Secret Correspondence, Committee of, FO.0.1–3; FO.360.2–7; NA.45.5, 6

17; FO.186.2; JU.186.2; LA.360.5; LA.11.2; LA.59.4–6; LA.77.2; NA.45.24
   and American Indians, IN.93.2
   Debts owed, FI.360.8, 9
   Land grants, LA.49.5, 7, 14, 16–19
Spanish colonies, CC.186.1–3; FI.186.2; LA.76.3; LA.77.3
Spencer, Joseph, MI.360.23
Spoliation treaties, PE.76.2–4
Springfield, MA, MI.98.2
Squash Cutter (Delaware Indian), IN.360.6
Stafford County, VA, LA.42.3
Staphorst, Jacob van, FI.59.4; FI.217.8; FO.360.44
Staphorst, Nicholas, FI.59.4; FI.217.8; FO.360.44
Stark, John, IN.360.10; MI.360.24
State, Department of, FO.360.58; FO.11.3; FO.59.1–23;
   Records management (of old records), CC.360.34
State, General Records of the Department of (RG 59), CC.59.1–4;
   CO.59.1–3; FI.59.1–4; FO.59.1–23; IN.59.1–4; JU.59.1–2;
   LA.59.1–10; MI.59.1–8; NA.59.1–3; PE.59.1–2
State admiralty courts, JU.0.4; JU.360.2; JU.21.2–4; NA.45.15
State courts, JU.360.3, 9; JU.59.2
State debts, FI.53.16, 17, 19
State delegates to Congresses, FI.217.8
State loan officers, FI.0.2, 4; FI.360.6; FI.53.22; FI.217.8
State loan offices, FI.360.8; FI.53.1, 3, 5, 8–11, 16, 17, 18–20, 22, 23, 24;
   FI.217.11–12, 17
State maritime acts, JU.360.2
State militia, MI.0.10; MI.93.15, 20, 50, 54–59, 64–69; MI.94.3, 5, 8, 15;
   NA.45.6, 12; PE.0.4, 5; PE.15.8–10; PE.107.2
State Papers, CC.360.27, 34; CN.360.3
Staten Island, MI.360.37
States, Committee of the, CC.0.9, 14–15, 28; FI.360.4
Stephen, Adam, MI.360.24
Stephen Collins & Son, CO.92.2
Steuben, Friedrich von, MI.93.18, MI.360.24
Stevens, Henry, FO.59.21
Stirling, Lord William Alexander, MI.360.12
Stockley, Charles, MI.93.36
Stoddard, Amos, LA.49.17
Stone, William J., CC.59.2
Stretch, Joseph, FI.217.10
Stuart, John, LA.77.3
Success (sloop), CO.93.2
Sullivan, John, IN.360.9, 10; IN.93.2; MI.360.24, 30, 37; MI.45.4; MI.53.2
Supreme Court of the United States, Records of the (RG 267),
   IN.267.1; JU.267.1–9; LA.267.1–2
Surety bonds, FI.39.5
Surgeon General (Army), Records of the Office of the (RG 112),
   MI.112.1–3

Weedon, George, MI.360.26
West Florida, Council of the Province of, LA.49.9
West Indian government records, CC.55.3
West Indies, NA.45.7, 23
West Point, MI.0.11; MI.94.6, 10, 13; MI.217.3
Western land claims, LA.0.1
Western lands, cession of, LA.0.2–4; LA.360.5
Western Territory, IN.360.2; LA.360.4–6; LA.76.6; MI.360.33
Westham Foundry, VA, MI.93.58
Whampoa, China, CO.45.3
Wharton, John, NA.19.2
Wharton, Samuel, JU.360.5
Whipple, Abraham, NA.45.7, 20
White, John, MI.93.34–36
White Plains, NY, MI.93.18; MI.94.13
Whitehaven, England, NA.45.35
Whole House, Committee of the, CN.360.8, 9
Wickes, Lambert, NA.45.5
Wilkins, John, LA.49.6
Wilkinson, James, CO.107.2
Williams, Jonathan, FI.39.2; FO.360.18, 66; MI.93.70
Williamsburg, VA, MI.45.2; MI.93.39, 41; MI.200.2
Williamson, Hugh, FI.360.3
Willing, James, NA.45.12
Willink, Jan, FI.217.8; FO.360.4, 44
Willink, Wilhem, FI.217.8; FO.360.4, 44
Willink & Staphorst, FI.39.2; FI.59.4; FI.217.8
Wilmington, DE, PO.28.7
Wilmington, NC, PO.28.8
Women workers, MI.98.3
Woodward, Elon A., MI.94.15
Wooster, David, MI.360.26; MI.53.2
Worthington, Henry, CO.123.3
Worthington and Troup, CO.123.3
Wright, Jno., MI.217.5
Wyandot Nation, IN.360.3; LA.360.3; MI.98.3
Wynkoop, Jacobus, MI.53.2
Wyoming County, PA, JU.360.6
Wyoming Valley, IN.93.2

Yards and Docks, Records of the Bureau of (RG 71), CO.71.1–2;
York, Duke of, LA.60.2
York, PA, LA.121.2; MI.93.39, 41
Yorktown, VA, MI.360.42; MI.59.4–5; MI.77.4; MI.93.26, 49;
      NA.45.12; NA.59.3

The Propaganda Warriors

The Propaganda Warriors

America's Crusade Against Nazi Germany

Clayton D. Laurie

 University Press of Kansas

Published by the University Press of Kansas (Lawrence, Kansas 66049), which was organized by the Kansas Board of Regents and is operated and funded by Emporia State University, Fort Hays State University, Kansas State University, Pittsburg State University, the University of Kansas, and Wichita State University

Library of Congress Cataloging-in-Publication Data

Laurie, Clayton D. (Clayton David), 1954–
    The propaganda warriors : America's crusade against Nazi Germany /
by Clayton D. Laurie.
        p.   cm.   (Modern war studies)
    Includes bibliographical references and index.
    ISBN 0-7006-0765-X
    1. World War, 1939–1945—Propaganda.   2. Propaganda, American.
3. Propaganda, Anti-German.   I. Title.   II. Series.
D810.P7U395   1996
940.54'88673—dc20   95-26321

British Library Cataloguing in Publication Data is available.

Printed in the United States of America

10 9 8 7 6 5 4 3 2 1

The paper used in this publication meets the minimum requirements of the American National Standard for Permanence of Paper for Printed Library Materials Z39.48-1984.

To George, Donna, Sandra, Ian,
and Tyler James Laurie

. . . the public policy, foreign or domestic, in which a man believes, is the logical extension of the philosophy which governs his behavior as an individual toward the society in which he lives. . . . What we are, here at home, conditions and determines what we do as a nation outside of our own borders; and conversely, . . . our relationships abroad influence and to a large extent determine what sort of society we are able to create at home.

—*James P. Warburg*, Foreign Policy Begins at Home

Secret Agents rarely make history, but they frequently indicate its hidden trend. The amoral raison d'état that is their professional code is all too often the unacknowledged ethic of the governments that employ them. Officially controlled conspiracy, like illegally organized but tolerated prostitution, reveals the unsanctified needs, the secret cynicisms, and even to a certain degree the unavowed values, not only of the states, but of the societies on behalf of which it is conducted. Sometimes it may express the unconscious purposes of people themselves.

—*Edmond Taylor*, Awakening from History

Contents

Illustrations

xii *Illustrations*

Figures

Acknowledgments

No historical study can be completed without the substantial assistance and co-operation of other people. This work is certainly no exception. Foremost I want to acknowledge the significant contribution of Richard Breitman, professor of History at the American University, who first suggested in 1987 that I examine the recently declassified records of the OSS Morale Operations Branch at the National Archives in Washington, D.C. That initial inspection, benefiting from the guidance of John Taylor of the Modern Military Reference Branch, proved so exciting and fruitful that it prompted several years of research in the records of the COI, OSS, OWI, and associated agencies carried out in Washington, D.C., and elsewhere across the country.

The present book was developed from a Ph.D. dissertation completed at the American University in 1990 under the direction of Robert L. Beisner, Richard Breitman, and Ira Klein. These three historians read repeated drafts of that manuscript and offered numerous suggestions that improved the final product. Their dedication to their profession was in itself an inspiration, and their sustained support is greatly appreciated. In addition I want to thank Albert E. Cowdrey and David W. Hogan, Jr., of the U.S. Army Center of Military History in Washington, D.C., for taking time from their busy schedules to critique the book and to provide comments and suggestions. Dennis Showalter of Colorado College and Theodore Wilson of the University of Kansas read later drafts of the original manuscript, the latter discussing the work with me on many occasions during his tenure as a visiting scholar at the Center of Military History in 1989–1990. Dr. Wilson's continued interest in my study of psychological warfare after his return to the University of Kansas as well as that of Michael Briggs of the University Press of Kansas prompted me to pursue publication. A similar vast debt of appreciation is owed to the archivists of the Modern Military Reference

Branch of the National Archives and Records Administration in Washington, D.C., and to the staff of the National Archives Still Picture Branch, who provided invaluable assistance in finding the photographs that appear in this volume. Similar gratitude is due to the many employees of the Library of Congress in Washington, D.C., especially those in the Main Reading Room, Manuscript and Photographic Divisions, and Law Library, and to the employees of the Franklin D. Roosevelt Presidential Library in Hyde Park, New York, and the U.S. Army Military History Institute in Carlisle, Pennsylvania. Finally, I express my appreciation to my wife, Sandra, and two sons, Ian and Tyler James, whose patience, tolerance, and understanding ultimately allowed the completion of the book.

List of Abbreviations

ABSIE	American Broadcasting Station in Europe
AFHQ	Allied Force Headquarters
BEW	U.S. Bureau of Economic Warfare
CDAAA	Committee to Defend America by Aiding the Allies
CIAA	U.S. Office of the Coordinator of Inter-American Affairs
COI	U.S. Office of the Coordinator of Information
CPT	U.S. Army Combat Propaganda Team
ETO	European Theater of Operations
FBIS	U.S. Foreign Broadcast Intelligence Service
FFFC	Fight for Freedom Committee
FIS	COI Foreign Information Service
G-2	U.S. Army Military Intelligence
INC	Information, News, and Censorship Division/AFHQ
JCS	U.S. Joint Chiefs of Staff
JPWC	U.S. Joint Psychological Warfare Committee
JPWSC	U.S. Joint Psychological Warfare Subcommittee
JSP	U.S. Joint Staff Planners
MEDTO	Mediterranean Theater of Operations
MID/WDGS	Military Intelligence Division/War Department General Staff
MO	OSS Morale Operations Branch
MOI	British Ministry of Information
MRBC	U.S. Army Mobile Radio Broadcast Company
NATO	North African Theater of Operations
OCD	U.S. Office of Civil Defense
OEM	U.S. Office of Emergency Management

OFF	U.S. Office of Facts and Figures
OGR	U.S. Office of Government Reports
OKW	Oberkommando der Wehrmacht (High Command of the German Armed Forces)
OSI	U.S. Office of Strategic Information
OSS	U.S. Office of Strategic Services
OWI	U.S. Office of War Information
P&PW	Publicity and Psychological Warfare Branch
PWB	Psychological Warfare Branch
PWD/SHAEF	Psychological Warfare Division, Supreme Headquarters, Allied Expeditionary Force
PWE	British Political Warfare Executive
SIS	British Secret Intelligence Service
SOE	British Special Operations Executive
SSG/WDGS	Special Studies Group/War Department General Staff
USIA	U.S. Information Agency
VOA	Voice of America

Introduction

During World War II the United States conducted a propaganda campaign against Nazi Germany of a magnitude never before seen in American history. At least seven different federal organizations were involved in operations that were called either propaganda, psychological warfare, or information activities from 1939 to 1945, but three of them—the Overseas Office of War Information (OWI), the Office of Strategic Services Morale Operations Branch (OSS MO), and the U.S. Army—carried the brunt of the strategic and tactical propaganda offensive in Europe after 1941. This book describes the creation, operation, and guiding doctrine of each of these organizations.

The federal government never formulated an official propaganda policy during World War II. In retrospect this lack is not odd, as Pres. Franklin Roosevelt's wartime administration never enunciated specific war aims, beyond winning a total military victory over the Axis powers, or clearly defined specific postwar goals. As a result, many Americans believed that the Allied war effort lacked a clear moral or ideological foundation or any goal higher than a simple military victory. The overall lack of specific aims for war and peace also meant that the American propaganda agencies that were developed during the war lacked clear moral and ideological policies on which to formulate their propaganda. In lieu of guidance from the president, the nation's leading propagandists, William Donovan of the OSS and Robert Sherwood and Elmer Davis of the OWI, developed policies and strategies based largely on their personal views of what constituted effective propaganda. Their views became institutional doctrines followed by the thousands of people who joined the propagandists' respective organizations after 1941. The directors of the U.S. Army propaganda program pragmatically used the services of both civilian agencies while developing their own strat-

egies and doctrines to reflect a uniquely military viewpoint of propaganda and how it best met tactical needs.

Thus, the civilian and military leaders eventually controlled agencies that disseminated three very different forms of propaganda reflecting of three definable schools of thought concerning domestic politics and society, foreign policies and war aims, and the roles of propaganda, the federal government, and the United States in world affairs. Although their techniques and methods were similar—using radio, printed materials, loudspeakers, undercover agents, air-dropped and artillery-delivered leaflets, still photographs, and films—the propaganda messages and overarching goals were quite dissimilar. I describe and analyze the development of these different schools of propaganda thought beginning in the late 1930s when the majority of the future propagandists first became aware of the Nazi use of propaganda and of the potential value of propaganda for obtaining American political, diplomatic, and military goals.

This book focuses on those people who may aptly be described as the elites of the American psychological warfare campaign during World War II, a small number who created, shaped, and led propaganda agencies, who formulated theories and policies, and who conducted operations from the highest levels. Although the public was concerned about the effects of Nazi propaganda on the United States and generally favored a propaganda response and the defeat of the Axis, the ordinary citizen had little impact on the creation of American propaganda and none on the governing policies, content, and scope of subsequent operations. The psychological warfare campaign against Nazi Germany was organized and conducted by elite insiders in government, the military, media, and political circles who, unlike President Roosevelt and other elected leaders, did not have to pay such close attention to public opinion regarding their agencies and activities. The propaganda of the OSS MO Branch was always covert, and that of the U.S. Army was similarly conducted under heavy security. The operations of the OWI Overseas Branch were public, but its foreign propaganda targeted Axis populations, not Americans, and therefore elicited far less attention than OWI's domestic operations. Despite the fact that many Americans had an interest that bordered on fascination with propaganda, their impact on the operations of the OSS, OWI, and the U.S. Army was not great.

This is also a book about ideology and wartime bureaucratic empire-building and the effects of the ideologies and strong personalities on propaganda operations abroad and on the continual domestic political struggles for influence over American foreign policy. Clearly, peoples' views of propaganda, in all its aspects, were determined by their perceptions, their educational, professional, and political backgrounds, and their outlook and values concerning domestic politics and

foreign affairs. In the immediate prewar years and during the war itself, the Americans who became involved in propaganda tended to gravitate toward the organizations and leaders that most closely reflected their personal views. More often than not they were friends, schoolmates, and professional associates who had known each other years before they became engaged in propaganda affairs, as was certainly true of William Donovan and Robert Sherwood, who founded the COI and later the OSS and OWI. In turn, their perceptions determined the types of agencies that were created to fight the propaganda war against Germany, the organization and staffing of these agencies, and the planning and practice of the propaganda. Their battles over propaganda between 1941 and 1944 reflected ongoing domestic and foreign political and ideological conflicts, which in many cases had existed since the founding of the nation and which were intensely debated during the 1930s. To a large measure the conflicts centered on the question of whether Roosevelt's domestic and foreign policies were expressive of true and long-held American traditions, goals, and values that were worthy of being spread worldwide through wartime American propaganda or whether his policies were expressive merely of the views of narrow, liberal extremists who supported Roosevelt and the New Deal. To many critics, the extremists were nothing more than transitory figures dedicated to a passing political fad. A fundamental question that many propagandists were forced to ask themselves was whether the president's beliefs, however vaguely defined, were to provide the central themes for the moral and ideological foundations of American propaganda. The people in the OWI answered in the affirmative; the OSS and U.S. Army thought otherwise.

The struggle to influence the thoughts and behavior of friends and foes alike made World War II a contest of ideologies as well as of arms. The emphasis placed on winning the two contests, however, differed greatly. To the leadership of the OSS and the U.S. Army, the Anglo-American victory in May 1945, as intended by those leaders, was primarily a military victory over the Wehrmacht; all activities furthering this single goal received top priority. Second, the war was a triumph of the American ideals of democracy over Fascist totalitarianism. To many members of the OWI, however, the narrow Allied focus on a total military victory resulted in blotting out the objective that the OWI leadership deemed far more important: the ideological struggle against fascism, which they thought was (or should have been) Roosevelt's ultimate priority. The Allies had obtained a military victory but had not totally destroyed fascism or supplanted its reactionary philosophies in Europe or elsewhere with the ideas of liberal democracy as represented by the New Deal, the primary and tantamount goal of OWI prior to 1944. In a general sense the

ideological and political conflicts among propagandists concerning the content and goals of the propaganda campaign against Germany were similar to the conflicts experienced by American politicians, diplomats, and soldiers throughout the decade ending in 1945 as to the shape of foreign and domestic policies, war aims, and postwar goals. The conflicts experienced by propagandists while conducting their war against Germany, therefore, represented a microcosm of the larger conflicts in American domestic politics and foreign affairs that began long before World War II, came to the fore during the conflict, and, in many ways, continued well into the era of the cold war.

This book shows that the people who became propagandists during World War II did not enter such work by happenstance or through coincidence. Through personal experiences they came to see such service as a means not only to defeat fascism but also to spread their ideologies and beliefs worldwide as members of powerful propaganda organizations that had the capability to influence the direction of American foreign policy, the American image abroad, and the thoughts and beliefs of populations beyond North America. The propagandists were elites who had long histories of interaction with the Nazi regime; most were members of groups that studied propaganda, politics, and foreign affairs; most were active interventionists and internationalists; and many had professional backgrounds in the arts and letters, media, and communications or in social sciences where the power of the written and spoken word to inform and persuade was clearly understood.

Prominent among these individuals were men and women who had direct experience with propaganda, a group that included foreign correspondents, diplomats, and academics who had had contact with Fascists during the prewar years and who had developed both an interest in and a loathing for Nazi Germany. Many of them were witnesses to what they believed was the effective use of propaganda by the Nazis in Europe in the 1930s and early 1940s. Through their experiences they concluded at an early date that propaganda was a superweapon that the United States had to develop, and they sought to convince a skeptical Roosevelt administration of their views.

Many other Americans entered the propaganda trade through their longstanding interests in international affairs, public and private. They viewed propaganda as a useful tool of business and diplomacy in peacetime and as a valuable military weapon in wartime. It could be used to persuade other peoples of the justice of a cause or, as the Nazis had used it, to manipulate people and their governments to meet prescribed goals, consciously or unconsciously. Propaganda could ably serve the national interest, and within this category of believers were the traditional American elites, individuals who often were political,

economic, social, and cultural leaders. William J. Donovan was representative of this group. Ideologically conservative, ultranationalistic, Ivy-League, wealthy, and Republican, Donovan and others like him considered themselves the heirs of the political tradition in which elites determined the nation's foreign policies and domestic course. They held views of foreign policy similar to those of Theodore Roosevelt, who believed that a nation's rise to greatness was an unremitting Darwinian social struggle. In foreign policy, they were realists who favored a forward and dominant role for the United States in world events at all times. Preferring evolutionary change, they were antirevolutionary and found both the idea of the common man and mass-participatory democracy distasteful, especially when the latter was directed toward taking part in the determination of foreign policy. They viewed the Nazi threat as an attack on the nation and on their positions and their classical-liberal views of democracy. For reasons of expediency and practicality these individuals emulated Nazi subversive tactics to defend their interpretation of democracy. The majority were from business or from legal or financial professions and belonged to groups such as the Council on Foreign Relations. Most of them joined the OSS and emphasized limited government intervention in domestic affairs, opposing the New Deal although they haltingly supported FDR's foreign policy. They held strong beliefs about individual liberty—political, economic, and personal.

Also within the ranks of propagandists were those internationalists who espoused the domestic and foreign policy values of Woodrow Wilson and Franklin D. Roosevelt, who was perceived by many people as the heir to the more enlightened Wilsonian and progressive traditions. To a significant number of these people, such as Robert Sherwood and James P. Warburg, World War II was merely a resumption of the struggle undertaken by Wilson in 1917 to make the world safe for democracy—an idea defeated when America refused to embrace the Versailles Treaty and the League of Nations. Unlike their conservative counterparts in the OSS and the U.S. Army, they did not think the world was a field of constant struggle but a place where all nations and people could cooperate for the advancement of justice and for the good of all humanity—if only the nations could be educated and shown a better way to accomplish these ends. The goals sought, but not obtained, by Wilson, these individuals believed, could be reached in the new struggle if the United States was prepared to act. They viewed Nazi propaganda as a monstrous assault on the liberal democratic values of Western Civilization and placed a high value on individual liberty and democracy. But unlike their conservative, internationalist counterparts, they believed the proper response was a truthful, idealistic program of propaganda that expressed clear and egalitarian moral and ethical values for all people every-

where, ideas increasingly popular in the twentieth century. Idealistic internationalists stressed values that they believed were traditionally American in their propaganda. New Deal liberals and Democrats, they often followed left-wing political ideologies and were also frequently utopians who supported Franklin Roosevelt in his domestic and foreign policies as they understood them. They believed in massive government intervention in social and economic affairs and hoped for a globalization of the New Deal and the creation of a new postwar world order based on international organizations committed to reason and liberal democracy. The United States would assume a position of progressive leadership in world affairs without dominating other nations for selfish interests.

Many individuals who were to become propagandists were active in interventionist groups after September 1939 and were ardent Anglophiles who closely equated the survival of Britain with that of the United States. They believed in the value of aiding the Allies and warning against and combating Nazi propaganda directed toward the United States. Moreover, they wanted to mold American public and government opinion toward favoring an interventionist stance.

Responding to a lack of any concerted governmental effort to combat Nazi propaganda in the late 1930s and early 1940s, a sizable majority of interventionists and of people who sympathized with their values and goals undertook private efforts to counter Nazi propaganda. They sought to prevail upon the government through high-level contacts to become more actively involved in such activities. And they partially succeeded in summer 1941 when the Office of the Coordinator of Information (COI) was formed.

Within the COI, the differences among internationalists, interventionists, conservatives, New Dealers, liberals, Democrats, and Republicans became glaringly apparent, as evidenced by the conflicts between Robert Sherwood and William Donovan. A significant portion of the debate developed from differences in interpretation over the meaning of propaganda.

For the purposes of this book, propaganda is defined as any organized attempt by an individual, group, or government verbally, visually, or symbolically to persuade a population to adopt its views and repudiate the views of an opposing group. Psychological warfare is defined as propaganda, sometimes involving subversion, used in support of military operations against either an opposing military force or a civilian population before, during, or after hostilities. Subsequent clashes over definitions of propaganda, how it was organized and used, and for what ends, as well as the clashes over the American role in foreign affairs and the efficacy and morality of various types of propaganda, destroyed the COI. Its demise resulted in bitter internecine conflicts and the creation of two entirely different organizations, the OSS and the OWI.

Within the new agencies contrary doctrines were developed, each representing a different perspective on propaganda. The OSS drew the conservatives, realists, and Republicans who believed in emulating Nazi subversive propaganda. The group viewed the world as a brutal and ruthless place where democracy could not long survive if left to its own peaceful and slow-moving devices of high morals, truth, compromise, and consensus. The propaganda of the OSS reflected the conservative ethic of its members' own backgrounds and their belief that the end justifies the means. Conversely, the OWI drew liberals, New Dealers, and individuals involved in the media and arts and letters who believed that the truth, combined with Wilsonian ideals and values as expressed by Franklin Roosevelt, would win out through the sheer power of its message. They detested Nazi Germany and all it stood for and were loath to emulate Nazi tactics.

Each group, the OSS MO Branch, the OWI, and eventually the U.S. Army, claimed that its propaganda operations were the most effective, fueling a debate on the value of propaganda and on political ideologies that did not end with World War II but that still continues in works concerning propaganda. Judgments over the quality of the propaganda effort and its effectiveness in undermining the Axis powers are still highly subjective. In this book, therefore, I will play down such judgments and will instead describe the schools of propaganda as they developed and their proponents, how their views were institutionalized in the doctrines of the OSS MO Branch, the Overseas OWI, and the U.S. Army, and how their influence was broadly disseminated through American propaganda.

1 · American Perceptions of Nazi Propaganda, 1933–1941

In the 1930s Nazi Germany created an apparently comprehensive state bureaucracy for the use of propaganda as a weapon to gain national goals through the destruction of governments deemed unsympathetic to Nazi policies and through the subversion of populations targeted for attack or annexation. To spread their propaganda, the Nazis reputedly organized legions of Germans and foreign nationals into a worldwide "fifth column." The network's existence and successful operation were publicly acknowledged and promoted by Nazi leaders and affirmed by American journalists reporting from Europe.[1]

Propaganda was increasingly viewed by many people as a prelude to and adjunct of armed aggression, especially as Nazi rhetoric and diplomacy became more provocative in the late 1930s. Eyewitness accounts of dubious validity tended to feed the suspicions. The Nazi propaganda machine thus became the subject of extensive debate based on enormous amounts of myth and fiction and little fact. Yet the belief in the existence of the threat and the perceptions of the effectiveness of propaganda, no matter how baseless, became the reality to millions of people. Foreigners, especially American journalists working in Europe, became convinced through personal observation and Nazi revelations that the same psychological warfare tactics used by the Third Reich in Europe were being practiced against an unwary and unprepared United States. It became their goal, with the support of American diplomats, government officials, academics, businessmen, interventionists, and internationalists, to warn the public and to persuade the Roosevelt administration of the efficacy of propaganda as an offensive and a defensive weapon.

The use of propaganda as a prominent feature of statecraft was seen as a Nazi invention and a priority of Hitler's well before he took power in March 1933. According to American journalist Edmond Taylor, "Both the concept and tac-

8

tics of modern political warfare owe a great deal" to Hitler, who first demonstrated that "the strategic will of a nation can be broken without the direct use of force."[2]

Hitler, like many of his compatriots, was convinced that Germany's defeat in World War I was due to domestic defeatism, treachery, and subversion fomented by years of clever and insidious Allied propaganda. One result of the Nazi fixation on a propaganda-induced stab in the back was the idea that propaganda constituted a sort of superweapon. Nazi propaganda methods, therefore, were patterned after the approaches Hitler believed had been the most successful during World War I.[3]

Primarily, Nazi propaganda operated on the assumption that people have short memories and limited intellect. Appeals need not force thought but rather force acceptance of simple ideas, concentrating on unsophisticated emotional appeals that were decisively subjective, avoided abstractions, and allowed no equivocation. Themes were repeated endlessly and emphasized only a few crucial points cast in black and white terms. Nazi propaganda, therefore, was a negative, subversive, and an offensive weapon for destroying popular support for a world-view in preparation for its replacement by fascism.[4]

The knowledge that the Nazis intended to use psychological weapons against their enemies was a matter of public record. Hitler was reputed to have said that Germany's future wars would be fought "before military operations begin." Artillery would be replaced by propaganda "to break down the enemy psychologically before the armies begin to function at all." Enemy peoples "must be demoralized and ready to capitulate, driven into moral passivity, before military action can even be thought of." The goal was to create "mental confusion, contradiction of feeling, indecisiveness, panic." Once this was accomplished, "a single blow" consisting of "aerial attacks, . . . surprise, terror, sabotage, assassination from within, murder of leading men, overwhelming attacks on all weak points in the enemy's defense" would destroy Hitler's adversaries.[5]

The beliefs held by Hitler and Paul Joseph Goebbels concerning the effectiveness of propaganda were eagerly reported by journalists to a fascinated American public and allegedly were shared by an increasing number of German military and political theorists as well. The Wehrmacht thought propaganda so useful as an adjunct to military operations, observers wrote, that it was studied in the same way as conventional tactics.[5]

In reality Nazi propaganda theories were not infallible. It was mistakenly accepted, for example, that methods that had worked in Germany were equally applicable abroad without change. In fact, the Nazis made few attempts specifically to tailor propaganda themes for foreign use. Instead, the same stock meth-

ods and themes, centered on anti-Semitism, anticommunism, and antidemocracy, were endlessly repeated, sometimes clumsily, in each new situation. The Nazis themselves tended to exaggerate the potential of propaganda, believing it capable of extraordinary feats when combined with diplomatic threats or military force. Evidence suggests that Hitler relied, perhaps overly so, on a psychological "strategy of terror" and "war of nerves" to gain his goals without actual hostilities, seeking, in the words of one observer, to make opponents commit national suicide.[6] Surprisingly, these points were lost on observers of Germany, however, who in their hatred for the Nazi regime accepted Hitler's propaganda theories and accomplishments at face value. Few observers objectively analyzed Nazi propaganda or bothered to compare the exaggerated claims with the actual meager results. Yet the Nazis succeeded in convincing a gullible world that propaganda was indeed a superweapon.

Nazi psychological warfare allegedly involved active subversion in addition to mere rhetoric and study. Emigrés, foreign observers, and journalists charged that a vast Nazi subversive propaganda network operated worldwide as early as 1934.[7] Observers pointed to the large number of German cultural and informational organizations abroad as proof of the pervasiveness of the Nazi fifth column. The network allegedly included agencies that underwent nazification after 1933 and others created after the Nazi rise to power that were unlike any existing in the European democracies or in the United States.

Like the German intelligence network and armaments industry, however, the Nazi propaganda bureaucracy was large, diffuse, and prone to duplication of effort and internecine conflicts. These negative factors, most of which were not public knowledge, instead of indicating the existence of fundamental weaknesses in the Nazi system, were misinterpreted by foreigners to the opposite extreme. The existence of so many agencies allegedly devoted to subversion and propaganda indicated the value attached to psychological warfare by the Nazis and served as confirmation that they intended to use such weapons. Most observers never understood or realized that the Nazi propaganda services were racked with debilitating problems that hampered their effectiveness abroad. As a result, foreigners, who mistook the existence of multiple Nazi propaganda bureaus as a sign of sophistication rather than of weakness, fed a growing hysteria in Europe and the United States, leading many observers to believe unrealistically that Nazi activities, although threatening, were much more sinister and pervasive than they actually were. Indeed no German conquest was ever accomplished by using propaganda alone. Yet observers mistakenly accepted Nazi propaganda as a dangerous reality and readily ascribed Hitler's victories to invisible weapons wielded by a score of subversive agencies.[8]

The Nazi system for subversion did appear enormous. The most visible organization was Dr. Paul Joseph Goebbels's Ministry for Popular Enlightenment and Propaganda (RMVP), containing Foreign, Foreign Press, and Broadcasting Divisions and employing a total of 1,000 people in April 1939. Dealings with foreign correspondents, domestic news going abroad, and official interpretations of world events were the purview of the RMVP Foreign Press Division. Taken over from the Foreign Office in fall 1933, the division held news conferences and provided press releases through the Correspondence and Article Information Service (KAN) and private news agencies such as the Frankfurt-am-Main–based Transozean News Service and the Erfurt-based Weltdienst.[9]

The RMVP also trained propagandists for diplomatic outposts abroad after taking control of the Foreign Ministry's Institute for International Affairs. Critics claimed that German embassies were havens for subversives and that "in minor posts, where diplomatic experience and skill were not considered necessary, the minister was . . . most likely a propaganda trained rather than a diplomatically trained individual."[10]

Although the minister of propaganda, Goebbels constantly had to protect his domain from interlopers. After the 1939 nazification of the Foreign Office, Joachim von Ribbentrop proceeded to duplicate many RMVP functions, creating his own Foreign Press Division and broadcast-monitoring station at Berlin-Wannsee. Although these operations were ostensibly under RMVP oversight, Ribbentrop routinely evaded such control until Hitler issued a directive in September 1939 placing all propaganda under Goebbels. Ribbentrop ignored the directive and Nazi propaganda forever remained fragmented and disorganized.[11]

Ribbentrop was not Goebbels's only competitor. Observers claimed correctly that within the National Socialist German Workers' Party (NSDAP) itself there existed several propaganda agencies disseminating materials to "racial" Germans and Nazi sympathizers abroad. The two organizations most often accused of subversion were the totally ineffectual Foreign Political Office of the NSDAP, led by Alfred Rosenberg, and the Ausland or Foreign Organization (AO) of the NSDAP, under Ernst W. Bohle.[12]

Founded in 1931, the AO had an estimated annual budget of $100 million to support the activities of a reported 28,000 members in 1937. Critics claimed AO's membership was even larger than reported, however, roughly 3 million in forty-five countries in 1937, who were directed in their nefarious activities by 25,000 agents and 2,000 members of the Gestapo. The AO directed its efforts exclusively toward Reich nationals, recent German emigrés, and Nazi sympathizers abroad, who were lumped together by anti-Nazis and labeled the fifth column, all supposedly taking orders directly from Hitler to conduct sabotage, espionage, and subversion although little evidence of a connection ever existed.

Most German or pro-Nazi organizations overseas, however, were mistakenly suspected of being under Bohle's direction, and many American correspondents, Otto Tolischus and Dorothy Thompson among others, repeatedly warned their readers of AO plots. It was supposedly the "most aggressive of all agencies among German communities operating abroad during the Nazi period." It allegedly laid the foundation for the "Germanization" of Austria, Czechoslovakia, and Memel and had sent "veritable armies of Nazi provocateurs" throughout Europe, South America, and the United States where they "stirred up violence, spread anti-Semitic propaganda and fomented dissension."[13]

The AO allegedly carried out its mandate in league with the Abwehr, the military intelligence agency under Wilhelm Canaris, and, after 1939, with Reinhard Heydrich's Reichsicherheitshauptamt. The AO, according to Americans William J. Donovan and Edgar A. Mowrer, also received aid and advice from a military psychological laboratory in Berlin that "placed its findings and its trained saboteurs and Gestapo agents at the disposal of Bohle and the *Abwehr* for service abroad.[14]

Several older, private organizations were allegedly Nazi propaganda fronts, according to outside observers, including the Association or League for Germandom Abroad (VDA: Volksbund or Verein für das Deutschtum in Ausland), the German Institute of Foreign Countries (DAI: Deutsches Ausland Institut), the Deutsche Schutzbund, the Hamburg Deutscher Fichtebund, the German Academic Exchange Service (DAAD), the Munich Deutsche Akademie, the German Railway (Deutsches Reichsbahn) and tourist boards, and the Munich Goethe Institute.[15] Conclusive evidence proving that any of these agencies were actually engaged in subversion eluded contemporaries, but accusations were still made. The Fichtebund and the DAAD were especially singled out as notorious propaganda fronts. The Fichtebund, allegedly subsidized by the RMVP Foreign Division, published 208 pamphlets in foreign languages and 70 German language pamphlets in 1937 alone. Alfred Rosenberg controlled the DAAD, which critics described as one of the "most skillfully disguised agencies for carrying on this work." The DAAD director reportedly told one group of exchange students in 1937 that "they were an important element of Germany's foreign propaganda." By the late 1930s, critics were incorrectly accusing nearly every German organization overseas with spreading Nazi propaganda.[16]

Most German organizations overseas were not created specifically for propaganda purposes, yet many were used by the Nazis in any capacity deemed helpful to the state. Many organizations at home and abroad, although claiming independence and political neutrality, were unknowingly infiltrated and used for subversive purposes but never to the degree that anti-Nazis and emigrés alleged.

Yet American journalists claimed that in subverting the Weimar Republic the Nazis had used a carefully planned propaganda program to sell National Socialism to a gullible German people. Journalist Frederick Oechsner wrote that once this feat was accomplished, the propagandists were instructed "to sell National Socialism to the world . . . and to assist Hitler's expansionist schemes" by "facilitating the work of fifth columnists abroad."[17] The same correspondents, however, ignored more pertinent factors in the rise of Nazism such as the many internal weaknesses of the Weimar regime, its lack of popular support, the ill effects of economic depression, fears of communism, and German ultranationalism. Many observers claimed that the Nazi rise to power, rather than being an expression of the popular will of Germans, was a trick, the result of a nation being duped by clever propaganda.

The Nazis allegedly demonstrated the power of propaganda outside Germany for the first time in the Saar, a former German area, which in 1935 was under a League of Nations mandate pending a plebiscite to determine final sovereignty. Postwar evidence does exist to show that the Nazis attempted in limited ways to prepare the people of the Saar psychologically for reentry into the Reich, although contemporaries grossly exaggerated the scale of the effort. Special radio programs beamed from Germany did denounce everything connected with France and the League, as well as Marxists and Jews. To facilitate the spread of the message, Goebbels allegedly established an office to coordinate the Saar broadcasts with acts of terrorism and intimidation and distributed thousands of radio sets in the region. Critics were not surprised when the January 1935 plebiscite showed that 91 percent of Saar residents favored a return to German control, a result attributed by many individuals to clever Nazi propaganda. Contemporaries ignored the fact that the Saar had been a part of Germany prior to 1919 and that its population was German in language, culture, and heritage and genuinely favored a return to the Reich over the prospect of continued French rule.[18]

Nazi propagandists reputedly focused considerable attention during the 1930s on regions with ethnic German populations, such as Alsace-Lorraine, an area controlled by Germany between 1870 and 1919. Although the Nazis could not realistically hope to sway Alsace-Lorraine, which was predominantly French in culture and population, to National Socialism, they did seek to undermine French authority. To what extent Nazi agents were involved in subversion in the area is not clearly known, but contemporaries claimed that Germany orchestrated the distribution of millions of anti-Semitic leaflets, encouraged the painting of swastikas on Jewish homes, and helped form pro-Nazi groups to agitate for annexation. The Nazis beamed radio programs from Stuttgart and Saarbrucken

to Alsace-Lorraine consisting of attacks on the French government and leftists, broadcasts that gave weight to other more hysterical and baseless accusations by anti-Nazi critics. It was alleged, but not proven, for example, that over 50,000 propaganda publications were imported by the Nazis from Erfurt each week and offered at half price to ensure rapid sales. Although proof of direct Nazi subversion was not conclusively shown, the "Alsatian problem" was a constant Nazi propaganda theme through the 1930s.[19]

The Austrian *Anschluss* was interpreted by foreign observers as a classic example of the use of subversive propaganda to obtain Nazi goals. Many people believed that the Austrian republic was systematically undermined as early as 1934 by the Nazis, although the extensive German Nazi participation was more fiction than fact as observers overlooked the independent actions of indigenous Nazis and the public's pro-German feelings. Critics, however, charged that German Nazi propaganda was alone responsible for bringing about an outcome that most of them assumed was an impossibility. Austrian Nazis supposedly received unlimited funds from the NSDAP, which sponsored, approved, and abetted acts of terrorism. A May to July 1934 German campaign was said to have directly caused the assassination of Austrian chancellor Englebert Dollfuss and showed clear German efforts at "boring from within." Toward the end of 1937 the Nazis supposedly resumed their campaign of subversion, prompting German annexation in March 1938. As two American propaganda experts claimed, "For the first time, the radio was used by Nazism in a way which has become since a standard article of Nazi propaganda: 'the strategy of terror.'" Radio broadcasts whipped Germans and Austrians into a frenzy, showing "Austria disintegrating into anarchy, a prey to Bolshevik mobs . . . armed by Czechs, [who] ruled the streets and caused a terrible bloodbath among peaceful burghers."[20]

Concomitant with the Austrian *Anschluss*, Nazi propaganda attacks on Czechoslovakia attracted world attention. Only a few overt anti-Czech broadcasts, such as those to Alsace-Lorraine, were made prior to the Munich Crisis of September 1938, although one Czech complained in 1934 that "the Hitlerites are doing everything in their power to invade the borders of my land and to prejudice the people against Jews and Marxists." The fact that anti-Czech broadcasts were made by the Nazis in 1938 is not in doubt since journalists described them in detail. The programs were meant primarily for Sudeten Germans and world public opinion and consisted largely of overexcited, hysterical, and passionate references to atrocities committed by Czechs, Jews, and Bolsheviks against Sudetens.[21]

Radio broadcasts represented only the tip of the iceberg, according to propaganda watchers although they lacked concrete proof of other Nazi subversive ef-

forts. Nonetheless, the claims were made. The Nazis allegedly supported radio campaigns with covert broadcasts and an army of spies, saboteurs, and fifth columnists within Czechoslovakia. The network consisted of members of Konrad Henlein's Sudeten German Party (SDP) and Gestapo-trained Nazis who posed as industrialists, waiters, business travelers, barbers, or taxi drivers, all of whom crossed the frontier for the purposes of converting Sudeten Germans to the Nazi cause, creating demoralization and confusion, and conducting espionage and sabotage. The entire propaganda campaign, Goebbels was later reported to have said, had been carefully calculated to aid Hitler in obtaining his goal of dismembering Czechoslovakia. American journalist Edmond Taylor reported that after "studying the Nazi techniques of semi-overt conspiracy in the Saar and in Austria, the Sudeten pattern was unmistakable."[22] Propaganda attacks soon gave way to open threats of war, ending with the Munich Pact of 30 September 1938. The Nazi "'diplomacy of dramatic intimidation,'" one observer wrote, "used the war threat to its full value, with the result that Czechoslovakia surrendered the Sudetenland without a shot."[23]

Overt Nazi propaganda broadcasts continued into 1939, allegedly completing the conquest of Czechoslovakia through psychological weapons alone. Appeals were made to pro-Nazi groups in the rump Czech state—the Fascist-secessionist Hlinka faction—and to Slovaks. Atrocity stories mounted until Hitler was compelled in March 1939, as he had been in Austria, to occupy Czechoslovakia to prevent further depredations.[24] Although radio propaganda was used by the Nazis as an adjunct to diplomacy and the threat of military force, the exaggerated emphasis given by correspondents to propaganda and subversion as the sole factors for the ultimate demise of Czechoslovakia caused many people in Europe and America to ignore the more pertinent factors of Anglo-French appeasement as well as the unwillingness of the United States, the USSR, and other powers to defend Czechoslovakia.

By the time the Nazis began the war of nerves against Poland in summer 1939, their methods were allegedly clear. To many observers, propaganda was the single most important if not the sole factor for Nazi successes. Supposedly, as with previous campaigns, Nazi agents had "managed to worm their way into Polish life," undermining unity and gaining intelligence for the use of future invading armies. Other factors that caused or contributed to Polish instability or weakness were simply overlooked. The anti-Polish campaign allegedly began with Nazi propagandists demanding self-determination for Danzig. By August 1939 the campaign was extended to include Memel.[25] Radio broadcasts accused the Poles of anti-German designs, and for weeks Polish aggressiveness was played up as Nazi propaganda became more violent and emotional on all issues: atroci-

ties, mass arrests of ethnic Germans within Poland, and the plight of panic-stricken *Volkdeutsch*. The Poles were accused of outdoing the Czechs in depredations against ethnic Germans, and by 26 August the first border incidents were reported. Following a staged attack by Nazis in Polish uniforms on the radio station at Gleiwitz on 1 September 1939, Germany invaded Poland.[26]

Hitler's plan to gain *Lebensraum* to the east entirely through a strategy of terror and war of nerves had clearly failed, however, despite the claims and predictions of journalists and anti-Nazi propaganda watchers. Britain and France declared war on Germany on 3 September but did not move. Instead, for seven months a state of war existed in which both sides waited, preparing for a future clash. To some observers, however, the Phoney War or Sitzkrieg was not a period of total Nazi inactivity but merely a planned strategy to allow time for propaganda to undermine the will and determination of Allied troops. The propaganda campaign of 1939–1940, especially as directed toward France, was supposedly the result of a conspiracy of such scale that it dwarfed all previous efforts, allegedly proving the assertions journalists had made about the effectiveness of Nazi propaganda for years.[27]

France was apparently a fertile ground for Nazi propaganda because of inherent social, political, ideological, and economic divisions that were already causing the decay of its institutions; Germany intended to exploit and exacerbate the preexisting fissures. For six years, the Nazis supposedly conducted a comprehensive subversive campaign against the Third Republic using radio, written materials, and stories planted in the French press. Nazi propaganda sought "to demoralize the enemy, to destroy the cohesion, discipline, and collective morale" of the French, "to break the enemy's will to win or simply his will to resist." No segment of society was immune from attack, according to correspondent Edmond Taylor, and by the time of Munich in 1938, the Nazi war of nerves was under way and "counted heavily on propaganda and the social decomposition of the enemy."[28]

Evidence of subversion was perceived everywhere. The Nazis were reported to have sent propaganda to tens of thousands of randomly selected French citizens via hand-addressed letters containing cardboard swastikas or defeatist leaflets and pamphlets. Newspapers were allegedly corrupted, correspondents bribed, and publishers subsidized. Moreover, according to American ambassador William C. Bullitt, evidence existed that the Nazis had built a fifth column in France under Otto Abetz, a German diplomat stationed in Paris. Abetz was eventually expelled, but his subversive network was believed to have remained in full operation throughout spring 1940.[29]

As with other European nations, the French government was made aware of Nazi efforts but was unprepared to respond and unable to separate fact from fiction. Though many French suspected the danger, considerable controversy arose about the form counterpropaganda should take, if undertaken at all. Limited efforts were made to establish an office of information, but French propaganda from the outset only reacted to Nazi output and never took the offensive.[30]

Tantalizing but specious stories describing secret spy rings, mysterious communications, and covert radio broadcasts abounded in France during the Phoney War, but actual campaigns intended to demoralize and divide the Allied armies by emphasizing their differences and age-old enmities were confirmed fact. Leaflets dropped to British soldiers declared that "the French want you to fight for French domination of the European Continent" and that British blood should not "be spilt to satisfy unreasonable French ambitions," when Britain had more in common with the Germans. Similarly, the Nazis began campaigns directed toward French troops. One stunt attempted to convince French soldiers that while they were at the front, their British comrades were sleeping with their wives, sisters, and sweethearts. Another ploy informed French soldiers that "Britain, as usual, wants you to pull British imperial chestnuts out of the fire" and that "Britain, as usual, is willing to fight to the last Frenchman" and "will leave you in the lurch." As with British troops, the Nazis asked the French, "Haven't you more in common with Germany, your neighbor, than with Britain, which really does not belong to Europe at all?"[31] One leaflet, dropped by the millions over the Maginot line, contained a simple piece of poetry on a leaf-shaped piece of paper:

> Autumn, the leaves are falling.
> We will fall like them.
> The leaves die by the will of God,
> but we fall by the will of the English.
> Next spring nobody will remember
> either the dead leaves or the dead soldiers.[32]

Critics correctly asserted that little was done to counter Nazi propaganda attacks. Attempts by the Allies to decide on a joint counterpropaganda effort quickly came to nought amid interservice and nationalistic bickering. Consequently, each nation attempted to battle Nazi propaganda alone with dismal and counterproductive results. Radios provided to French troops for listening to government morale-building broadcasts, for example, were in fact tuned to pro-

grams beamed from Stuttgart. French troops claimed that Nazi programs were more entertaining, better directed to their audiences, and less boring and highbrow than French broadcasts. Conducted by two renegade French journalists, Andre Obrecht and Paul Ferdonnet, the Stuttgart broadcasts "in the course of the winter and early spring . . . succeeded in acquiring a considerable following across the Rhine" as French morale steadily declined.[33]

As the Allies waited, Nazi Germany invaded Scandinavia in April 1940. The rapid and successful offensive showed massive evidence, observers claimed, of years of subversive preparation. Alternative causes for Nazi victories, such as surprise and the military weakness of Norway and Denmark, were ignored. Instead, it was alleged that Nazi activities such as contacts with pro-Nazi groups, the spreading of Fichtebund and Weltdienst literature, and propaganda stressing Nordic-Aryan similarities so weakened the unity of the Scandinavian nations that they were unable to prepare any defense. As elsewhere, the actual Nazi activities were blown out of proportion in the attempt by propaganda watchers to show the existence of a subversive conspiracy. Nazi businessmen allegedly used Scandinavian contacts to spread propaganda while others cultivated connections in government circles, such as the link with former Norwegian minister of defense Vidkun Quisling. Reporter Leland Stowe, who covered the campaign for a shocked and incredulous American public, wrote sensational stories concluding that Norway was "seized with unparalleled speed by means of a gigantic conspiracy," in which the Nazis, through bribery, infiltration, and treason "built a Trojan Horse" inside Scandinavia.[34]

Before they were finished in Norway, the Nazis launched their blitzkrieg in the West on 10 May 1940. Almost immediately, rumors of fifth-column activities surfaced as did accusations of treasonous behavior by soldiers, politicians, and civilians. Setbacks were not due to Allied deficiencies materially, strategically, or tactically, stunned observers claimed, but to treason, sabotage, and subversion. The Allies and the world, shocked by the initial enemy successes, attributed the rising domestic defeatism and treachery to propaganda, much in the same way as the Nazis had attributed their defeat of 1918 to Allied propaganda. The conquest of the Netherlands, for example, resulted from subversion fomented by Dutch Nazis and their agents although military unpreparedness and surprise were more pertinent factors. Although it was true that pro-Nazi groups and the 120,000 Germans residing in the Netherlands published and read pamphlets for years before the war emphasizing the closeness of Germany and the Netherlands, it is doubtful that agents set up an enormous fifth-column network to aid invading forces as claimed. The same situation prevailed in Belgium, which contained 60,000 German residents. These people, allegedly working with indige-

nous Fascists, such as Leon Degrelle's Rex, systematically undermined morale, turned over vital locations to enemy troops, induced panic, and hindered defensive operations. The speed and force of the Nazi onslaught and the small size of the opposing military were factors overlooked in the Belgian defeat.[35]

The main Nazi propaganda effort was supposedly unleashed on France, and even though propaganda attacks were small in scale when compared to the conventional blitzkrieg, they were portrayed as a major factor in the Nazi victory. As the Wehrmacht wheeled toward Paris, Ferdonnet, the "traitor of Stuttgart," beamed programs predicting defeat and encouraging surrender. The sense of defeatism and betrayal that had long affected segments of French society soon permeated the French military, and panic gripped tens of thousands of civilians. In addition to radio programs, Section 4 of the Wehrmacht Propaganda Branch initiated tactical propaganda campaigns aimed at French troops. Millions of leaflets, developed in cooperation with the Foreign Ministry, were dropped by the Luftwaffe and distributed by artillery shell over enemy positions; loudspeakers, posters, and placards were used against surrounded and demoralized units manning the Maginot line. In less than six weeks, resistance collapsed.[36]

Stunned by the French defeat, observers searched for an explanation and found propaganda and fifth-column subversion. In a spate of articles and books published in the following year, largely in the United States, French and American authors provided lurid accounts of the Nazi propaganda that had defeated the French before the first shot was fired.[37] The successes attributed to propaganda in France initiated new and more hysterical concerns about the existence of a similar subversive threat in the United States, a likelihood that had been discussed for years in some circles. Although circumstances in the United States were different, distinctions were lost on most Americans. Supposedly no nation was immune from the devastating effects of Nazi propaganda. William Bullitt claimed that "the United States is in as great peril today as was France a year ago. Unless we act now, decisively, to meet the threat we shall be too late."[38]

To one particular group of Americans, the correspondents assigned to the capitals of Europe, getting the message to the public became a top priority. Most Americans who maintained an interest in world affairs received their information from this rather sizable corps of radio and press journalists who shared common characteristics that included long absences from American residence, a firm belief in internationalism and the power of the written and spoken word, a cosmopolitan outlook on social and political affairs, a firsthand knowledge of the negative aspects of European fascism and, as a result, an abiding hatred of its leaders and ideology.

The power of these journalists to influence government and public opinion

at home was enormous. In general, they were experienced, were well known to the public, and had reputations seemingly beyond reproach. Their reports were accepted as fact and their speculations as prophecy. Through articles, books, and radio, they became the first Americans systematically to warn their country of the Nazi propaganda threat as they perceived it, often grossly sensationalizing and exaggerating what they had seen and heard. Their efforts were successful, however, and their beliefs in the danger and in the efficacy of propaganda as a weapon were avidly accepted by their largely uncritical audiences. Their descriptions of the supposed propaganda-abetted Nazi conquests were heavily publicized, and according to some critics, created by them. Yet many correspondents later used their skills against fascism as members of propaganda agencies, and their perceptions, ideology, and professional backgrounds significantly influenced the anti-Nazi offensive and the course of American foreign policy.[39]

The foreign correspondents were eventually joined by thousands of other Americans who read their reports from abroad and supported their attempts to awaken the wider public to the existence of a Nazi fifth column in their midst. By early 1940 enough like-minded individuals were so convinced that they undertook private countermeasures and pressured the government to become more actively involved in filling what was then perceived as a propaganda gap. Yet when Americans accepted the presence of the threat, their concern tended to border on hysteria. As in Europe, many people totally accepted the sensational and exaggerated stories, despite a minority who counseled reason, and came to believe in the existence of a danger greater than any that ever actually existed. Their concern was heightened by many prominent Americans who were certain, because of events in Europe and disturbing signs in the United States, that there was no time to lose in combating Nazi attacks.[40]

There was seemingly no dearth of information concerning Nazi plans for America. Hitler and Goebbels reportedly believed it to be a fertile ground for subversion as it consisted of "a medley of races" undergoing "a process of decay." According to one writer, Nazi plans for world conquest could not be successful with anything "less than the annihilation of the military and economic power of the United States." But because of the nation's size and location behind a "geographic Maginot Line," wrote James P. Warburg, it "would have to be reduced by psychological rather than military weapons," weapons that William Bullitt claimed had doomed the French.[41]

The Nazi attack on America, experts claimed, apparently came from several sources: a fifth column of spies, saboteurs, and propagandists consisting of pro-Nazi, or isolationist groups; Reich citizens operating on orders from Berlin; or Nazi diplomatic, military, labor, academic, or business people.[42] Nazi goals were

as straightforward for North America as they had been for Europe. Subversives sought "to disrupt and disunite the American people" by furthering racial and religious hatred, destroying confidence in democratic forms of government, halting preparedness and isolating the nation physically and psychologically, and by building up pro-Nazi groups that could one day act as a fifth column.[43] In sum, as Edmond Taylor wrote, Nazi political warfare meant "all the roughest and shadiest tactics of politics such as bribery, blackmail, terrorism, assassination, and propaganda . . . to destroy the enemy from within."[44] The methods used, Taylor predicted, would be "very similar to those means by which they had conquered Germany" and by which they had forced their other victims to "dig their own psychological graves."[45]

American observers claimed that an omnipresent fifth column, either domestic or Nazi-trained and infiltrated, formed the vanguard. In times of peace, it supplied information on national morale and on commercial, industrial, and political activities. Fifth columnists trained as shock troops, reinforced by Nazis disguised as sportsmen, tourists, commercial agents, and cultural representatives, were prepared to level the first blow when war broke out by conducting sabotage attacks on strategic places. In addition, experts maintained, "the Fascist powers have developed another and even more deadly method of crippling their enemies. This is psychological sabotage." As perfected in Europe, fifth columnists in America used propaganda, rumors and lies, opposition movements, bribery, corruption, and intimidation to undermine the will of the people "to make them easy prey for . . . Gestapo hangmen."[46] To skeptics, William Donovan replied, "are we Americans . . . invulnerable to Nazi propaganda? . . . Our masses are strikingly susceptible; hundreds were quick to flee before columns of allegedly advancing invaders from Mars," a reference to the Orson Welles broadcast of Halloween 1938.[47]

To the supposedly astute observer it was evident that the Nazis did not lack potential recruits. The number of *Reichsdeutschen* (German nationals) in the United States, for example, was estimated at 264,000 by American officials although the exact number was never known. Moreover, the United States had one of the largest populations of German ancestry anywhere. At least 25 million Americans traced their roots to Germany, half a million of whom had emigrated during the Weimar years alone. Supposedly, according to Nazi officials, the ethnic Germans were open to ideological appeals and could be organized into bunds under AO control.[48]

In reality the situation in the United States fell far short of Nazi hopes and the worst American fears. Among Nazi officials, Joseph Goebbels knew the scope of anti-Fascist feelings in the United States and the extent to which Ger-

man-Americans had lost their race consciousness. He therefore favored the creation of a well-camouflaged propaganda network to give impetus to pro-Nazi groups to come together voluntarily, thereby avoiding any incriminating Nazi connection abroad. The groups could then be brought under Hitler's control. The debate over the role of the NSDAP in aiding American Nazi groups became embroiled in larger struggles within Germany, however, hampering propaganda efforts worldwide. As a result, the supposed fifth-column network was never as large, as efficient, or as threatening as Americans maintained. Public opinion polls, taken throughout the 1930s, consistently indicated that Americans despised Hitler and the Nazis and routinely ignored their appeals. Yet right-wing movements, at home and abroad, were unrealistically viewed as being monolithic, operating as a single entity on Hitler's command. Constant publicity raised American consciousness, and a July 1940 Roper Poll showed "that 71 percent of the respondents were persuaded that Germany had already started to organize a 'fifth column' in this country." Proof supposedly lay in the number of pro-Nazi movements nationwide.[49]

Nazi organizations existed in the United States before 1933, yet most of them were founded without NSDAP aid. Such groups included the small Teutonia Organization, founded in Detroit in 1924, and its successor, the Gauleitung-USA, formed in 1931. Yet the negative publicity surrounding the Nazi seizure of power and the inability of the groups to form viable cells renewed the debate within the NSDAP concerning the sort of ties that should be sought, if any. Sensing that the organizations did more harm than good, Goebbels overrode objections and ordered all Nazi groups with Reich national members in the United States to disband in 1933, thus severing all official ties. American Nazis ignored this unilateral break, however, and soon formed the independent Friends of the New Germany (BFND), which established informal contact with Nazi diplomats and businessmen.[50]

The repeated Nazi attempts to distance themselves from American groups were unsuccessful. Despite the belief of Ernst Bohle that "the dictates of German blood demanded that Berlin support its racial comrades in America," Goebbels renewed his efforts to break all ties with U.S. Nazi groups before they caused a crisis in German-American relations. He wanted propaganda to brighten the Nazi image abroad, a purpose not served by contentious American groups. Furthermore, he believed, if the BFND were to be of any use, it had to appear to be a homegrown product devoid of NSDAP connections. Thus in 1934 Rudolf Hess and Bohle, under pressure from Goebbels and Hitler, publicly ordered all nationals in the United States to resign from the BFND and to quit spreading propaganda among non-Germans. When Reich nationals, who

formed 60 percent of the BFND's membership, again ignored the NSDAP order, it was repeated, largely without result, twice in 1935 and again in 1937.[51]

The much-publicized efforts of the Nazis to break their foreign ties had no real effect on American attitudes and opinions, and Nazi pronouncements were routinely discounted. For example, William E. Dodd, the American ambassador to Germany, reported receiving Hitler's personal assurances "that [Hitler] would throw any German official into the North Sea if he sent propaganda to the United States." Dodd nonetheless remained convinced that NSDAP subversion continued.[52] Secretary of the Interior Harold Ickes had similar concerns and wrote that Secretary of Labor Frances Perkins told him a "long, circumstantial and lurid story of German intrigue" and that she had heard that Germany "had several hundred big men over here who have systematically joined the German societies, the control of which they are rapidly taking over."[53]

Despite Nazi efforts to minimize their contacts with American Nazi groups, independent-minded right-wingers maintained their organizations, created new groups, and publicized any and all contacts with Nazi Germany. The American Nazi movement, as Goebbels originally hoped, did come under indigenous control with the founding of the German-American Nazi Bund by Fritz Kuhn in 1936; however, it proved a major disappointment to Nazi officials. Although the largest, the most visible, and the most extreme of American Nazi cells, the Bund never enjoyed official NSDAP recognition or support but indeed was an embarrassing liability because of Kuhn's harsh rhetoric and combative style. Still, most Americans firmly believed, as did Texas Democratic congressman Martin Dies, that the 100,000 Bund members represented "the spearhead of Hitler's attempted penetration" of America.[54]

The Bund grew rapidly, even under Kuhn's bumbling leadership, counting sixty-six branches and paramilitary training and summer camps in ten states. Its 8,300 members, located wholly in the New York City area, held numerous rallies, dressed in Nazi-style uniforms, published their own newspaper, reprinted material received from NSDAP outlets, and sold Hitler's *Mein Kampf* on the streets of New York. Despite these highly publicized activities, the Bund failed to gain NSDAP recognition, even after Kuhn went to Berlin for the 1936 Olympics and was photographed with Adolf Hitler.[55] Yet Kuhn's actions strengthened American convictions that the Bund was a Nazi fifth-column force bent on the overthrow of the United States. One historian wrote that "Kuhn could not have appeared at a more auspicious time for the enemies of fascism and Nazism in the United States. . . . [He] represented the essence of un-Americanism," and inadvertently "made numerous Americans aware of the Fascist challenge."[56]

Other right-wing groups and individuals were also suspected of serving Nazi

ends. Journals, newspapers, and pulp magazines throughout the 1930s printed lurid and graphic stories describing an estimated 800 right-wing groups with ties to Nazi Germany. Among the larger American organizations were the Knights of the White Camellia and American Nationalist Confederation led by George Deatherage, the Crusader White Shirts led by George W. Christians, and the Silver Shirts led by William Dudley Pelley. Individuals as well as groups were alleged to have direct ties to Nazi propagandists, such as the Reverend Gerald Winrod of Wichita, Kansas, and Charles Coughlin, the "radio priest" of Detroit. Collectively these groups and individuals convinced Americans of the existence of a concerted propaganda and fifth-column attack on the nation where in reality none existed. When in late 1937 and early 1938 the Erfurt Weltdienst sponsored a well-publicized international conference attended by Deatherage and representatives of twenty-two nations, Coughlin, Pelley, Kuhn, and their cohorts were no longer seen by Americans as domestic lunatics but as foreign-controlled Nazi propagandists and fifth columnists. "It would be much easier," the Institute of Propaganda Analysis concluded, "to laugh at these little men if we did not remember Hitler in 1932. It was easy to laugh at him."[57]

The threat posed to the United States by domestic groups paled in comparison, many experts claimed, to that stemming from Nazi government representatives and shortwave radio broadcasts. As one journal reported, "Nazi propaganda is indubitably well-organized, well-financed and infinitely more clever than the stupid, bungling German propaganda of the World War." The alleged headquarters for Nazis in America were diplomatic outposts. In July 1941 the Institute for Propaganda Analysis hailed the deportation of 450 Italian and German consular officials, claiming that they were a major part of the propaganda apparatus of their two countries.[58]

The Nazis were similarly accused of orchestrating subversive activities through citizens living or traveling abroad. According to State Department commercial attaché Douglas Miller, the Nazis connived with German businessmen to subvert nations economically. They engaged in dumping, unfair subsidies, and high-pressure sales tactics; all German business aims, he claimed, had Nazi political overtones. Miller exposed the business trickery in a best-selling and sensational book, *You Can't Do Business with Hitler*, a warning to American businessmen that dealing with Nazi Germany was a clear threat to the nation's future.[59]

American scholars were supposedly among the chief hopes of the Nazis. Prof. Frederick E. F. Auhagen, formerly of Columbia University, was reputed to be "one of the leading apologists for Herr Hitler in the United States," who, with Prof. Paul K. Krueger of Wittenberg University, formed the American Fellow-

ship Forum. The group published two journals, *Today's Challenge* and *Forum's Observer*, edited by George S. Viereck, and published articles by isolationist congressmen and academics. The forum had only a few hundred members and collapsed from a lack of support in 1940, yet critics continued to claim that it was a "Nazi conspiracy to initiate a . . . campaign of psychological sabotage . . . [to] spread Axis appeasement propaganda, to encourage isolationism, and to promote opposition to defense preparations."[60]

German students in the United States were especially suspect, and according to one observer, they devoted most of their energy "to spreading Nazi ideology and meeting with secret agents and military spies." Exchange students were allegedly told to report immediately to the nearest cell of the German-American Nazi Bund. The State Department later claimed to possess information that the director of the German Student Exchange Agency required students to "prepare political reports on the prevailing attitudes of various colleges and universities at which they were enrolled." When threatened with public exposure, the agency shut down in January 1939.[61]

Nazi subversive propaganda often came from seemingly innocent ventures. The German National Railway, the Tourist Information Bureau, and the Library of Information, the latter two established in New York in 1920 and 1936, were accused of being propaganda fronts. The library allegedly worked with the Weltdienst, Fichtebund, and the tourist bureau in compiling an American mailing list of over 100,000 names. Its activities were deemed so threatening that it was closed by the federal government in June 1941. Despite this action, the Institute for Propaganda Analysis claimed there were still 178 German language publications in the country, in addition to 13 daily newspapers and 111 weeklies. All but a few supposedly gave favorable treatment to the Nazi Regime. Even well-known papers, such as the *New Yorker Staats-Zeitung*, the *New York Journal of Commerce*, the *St. Paul Dispatch*, and *St. Paul Pioneer Press*, favored the Nazis in news coverage and carried stories from the RMVP.[62]

The participation of American citizens in Nazi propaganda efforts was also highly publicized. Writer and publisher George S. Viereck was often mentioned as being a Nazi agent who was closely associated with the isolationist America First movement and who was also, according to the Justice Department, on the payroll of the German Library of Information and the *Munchener neueste Nachrichten*. As an unregistered agent, Viereck set up a pro-Nazi isolationist publishing house called Flanders Hall in Scotch Plains, New Jersey. "Flanders Hall," the Nazis were alleged to have claimed, could be presented "as an ostensibly legitimate and impartial enterprise" and could act as "the publishing outlet for the

America First movement." Under Viereck's leadership it published anti-British and proisolationist books, including works by twenty-four U.S. congressmen.[63]

The most overt Nazi propaganda attacks came over the shortwave radio from Germany. The RMVP controlled the official German news agency, the Deutsches Nachrichten Buro (DNB), and the overseas shortwave broadcasting system, Deutsche Kurzwellensender (DK), consisting in 1939 of one station and ten transmitters located at Naven and Zeesen, Germany. The shortwave service employed 250 people who produced and broadcast twelve hours of music, news, political commentaries, and economic reports for American consumption each day. One writer claimed, "It is a part of the most sinister movement in the world," and another drew the parallel between broadcasts to the United States and those to France and Britain: radio shattered French morale and "has become both the voice of destruction and the instrument of conquest."[64]

In addition to the propaganda broadcasts themselves, Nazi shortwave programming was supported by an extensive "zone service" that provided 75,000 bilingual programs to American patrons. Newspapers and radio magazines carried program schedules as well as features on programs and radio personalities. Efforts were made to find broadcasters familiar with Americans and their language, customs, and preferences, and the Nazis employed American expatriates to host programs for every segment of society. In response, it was alleged, the Nazi shortwave system received 50,000 fan letters annually from American listeners while WNBC in New York, one of the most popular stations in the nation, received only 20,000.[65]

The Nazis countered the charges of critics on several occasions and claimed that fifth-column stories were the result of rumormongering by British agents who hoped to drag the United States into war as they had in 1917. Instead of hunting for fifth columnists, the Nazis advised, Americans should scrutinize the actions of the English who had a direct interest in seeing America act again to save the British Empire.[66]

By 1940 many Americans, faced with daily evidence of Nazi propaganda allegedly abetted by indigenous traitors, began to sense a new danger in their fellow citizens who expressed isolationist opinions. Significant numbers of Americans held isolationist views in the interwar period, rooted in the disillusionment resulting from World War I. These sentiments, however, were not shared by all Americans. In spring 1940 several influential internationalists and interventionists formed pressure groups to encourage the Roosevelt administration to do more to combat Nazism by direct intervention. In response and opposition, isolationists organized their own pressure groups.[57]

By far the largest and most visible and powerful isolationist organization was

the America First Committee, founded in Chicago in September 1940 by Yale socialite and Quaker Oats heir R. Douglas Stuart, Jr. The goals of the movement, far from being pro-Nazi, were to keep the nation out of war, to counter interventionist groups, and to impede all government policies that could jeopardize neutrality. The movement claimed 800,000 members in 450 chapters nationwide by December 1941, although most of them were concentrated in the Chicago area and the Midwest.[58]

Isolationists were quick to attack the notion of a subversive threat to America. One journal claimed that fears of the fifth column were overblown by interventionists, internationalists, Jews, Democrats, liberals, Communists, and Socialists, all of whom were encouraged by President Roosevelt, to convince Americans of a fifth-column threat where none existed. Another writer, John T. Flynn, accused Roosevelt of demagoguery and warmongering. The president was abetted by a corps of reporters and commentators who "pumped away— hour after hour, day after day, on the strings that thrilled the hysteria."[69]

Isolationists' claims that the domestic Nazi threat was overblown had some validity, but individuals who made such charges, like isolationists in general, were accused of being in league with Hitler. Interventionists James P. Warburg and Edward Y. Hartshorne publicized the notion that isolationists and Nazi propagandists shared similar themes, methods, and goals in their campaigns. One Avedis Derounian, an undercover FBI agent who infiltrated the movement, wrote a book in 1942 under the pseudonym John Roy Carlson that confirmed the fears that people held—isolationists were conspiring with Nazis and anti-Semites. His book went through twenty-six printings in six months. Carlson's revelations, though sensationalized and exaggerated, fed hysterical beliefs that any person or group not supporting Roosevelt's foreign policy was a Nazi agent or sympathizer.[70]

Despite years of minimal successes, the Nazi propaganda campaign intensified with the outbreak of war in Europe and counted among its primary goals defeating Roosevelt's reelection bid in 1940. The Nazis hoped that isolationists would carry out propaganda work and sought to bolster the movement through covert, indirect contacts, such as giving support and literature to groups opposing HR 1776 (the Lend-Lease bill). The Nazis commissioned literary works by isolationists and other writers through front organizations such as Flanders Hall and gave aid to groups, including the Make Europe Pay War Debts Committee. The staffs of consulates sought to use right-wing domestic groups to conduct "anti-Semitic whispering campaigns," and isolationist speeches were distributed by the Transozean News Service and the German Library of Information to influence public opinion. The efforts largely came to naught, however, in a coun-

try more vigilant and sensitized to what many people termed "un-American" behavior.[71]

The Nazis avoided situations directly connecting them with isolationists, but many American organizations were not as discreet. At least sixteen groups with known Nazi ties allegedly supported the America First Movement with volunteers, propaganda, and money. The allegations concerning Nazi-isolationist ties became especially heated when it was discovered that an agent named Prescot Dennett had struck up a friendship with George Hill, a congressional staffer of Cong. Hamilton Fish (R-N.Y.). In cooperation with Hill, Dennett obtained franked envelopes in the names of eighteen senators and representatives, which were then used to send Nazi propaganda nationwide at taxpayer expense.[72]

By summer 1940 Americans who supported Britain, who detested fascism, and who believed that they had witnessed Nazi propaganda in action were reacting. They pointed to Nazi statements concerning the value of propaganda, to the score of domestic and foreign groups with Nazi ties, real and alleged, and to inexplicably effortless Nazi victories abroad. Usually without substantial evidence, a real public hysteria and a genuine phobia concerning fifth-column activities were created that convinced many people to search for concrete ways to combat the threat.

2 · The American Private Sector Mobilizes, 1938–1941

The private sector of American society was the first to react to the threat of Nazi propaganda and to call for defensive measures. The people in the forefront of these early efforts were the elites of society, and over the course of three years, they publicized the need for counterefforts while pressing the government to create a federal propaganda agency. They set the tone of the subsequent debate concerning propaganda, determined the ultimate nature of the American response, and in later years created, defined, and operated the American wartime propaganda agencies.

Few American elites had any formal training in propaganda. Just as the journalists in Europe, however, they believed that propaganda had "the power to capture men's hearts and bypass their natural processes" in such subtle ways that many people were entirely unaware of its subliminal influence. They analyzed propaganda, wrote widely circulated books and articles, delivered speeches, and shared their findings with a public that viewed the subject "with morbid fascination."[1]

Evidence that Americans at all levels of society were concerned about propaganda existed in the proliferation of materials on the subject.[2] The average number of citations in the *Reader's Guide* under "propaganda" in 1929, one author wrote, was about six per year. By 1935 the number had risen to forty, "while today, in 1939, it is running more than 50 titles a year." Likewise, the number of books went from "but a handful" in 1924 to over 5,000 titles in 1935, with hundreds added thereafter. Another author scanned the *Congressional Record* and found "literally scores of occasions" when propaganda and its relation to American policy had been discussed in Congress. Many popular films, such as *Confessions of a Nazi Spy* released in April 1939, drew throngs of intrigued moviegoers.[3]

The efforts of elite groups of interventionists and internationalists to focus

the public's attention on the Nazi threat succeeded because of their contacts with influential individuals, with organizations that studied propaganda and morale issues, and with important members of the Roosevelt administration. Many of these prominent individuals were actually members of the government or were on close terms with people who were. Their primary goals, before and after 1940, were to aid the Allies, silence isolationists, and push the federal government into world affairs and direct anti-Axis efforts, including propaganda action. Through their efforts, they managed to convince President Roosevelt and members of his administration to begin studying the Nazi threat in 1940. Although the public was widely (although tangentially) concerned about Nazi propaganda activities, it was these prominent individuals who succeeded in prompting government action. They pressured President Roosevelt to create agencies in 1941 to counter propaganda at home and to use it as an offensive weapon abroad. They directly influenced federal decisions and policy and later served in top posts in the Office of War Information and the Office of Strategic Services.[4]

Lesser-known groups and organizations played a key role in heightening public awareness although most of them did not have an impact on subsequent government actions. Yet the groups did catch the attention of Americans who had the ability, stature, and power to influence the president. One such group was the Institute for Propaganda Analysis, organized in New York City in 1937 with a grant from the late Boston merchant Edward Filene. The founders of the institute believed there were three ways to deal with propaganda: suppress it, meet it with counterpropaganda, or analyze it. They opted for the last approach. The purpose of their nonprofit, nonpartisan, educational organization was to show Americans how they could identify propaganda, analyze it, and thereby become virtually immune to its ill effects. Such a response was necessary because propaganda methods had "become more and more complex and insidious" since World War I and required "careful scientific analysis before they may be exposed." The group's chairman, educator Clyde R. Miller, directed an advisory council consisting of social scientists, several of whom had already devoted years to such work, for example, Harold D. Lasswell, Hadley Cantril, and Leonard Doob.[5]

Published studies were the primary medium used to heighten public awareness. The institute published a monthly newsletter with articles such as "Some ABC's of Propaganda Analysis," which consisted of seven rules that enabled readers to recognize propaganda in its most common forms. The institute's publications eventually reached 7,000 private and institutional subscribers, in addition to the people attending institute-sponsored seminars as part of some 300

study groups formed under its auspices. Further, 550 high schools and colleges offered its propaganda-analysis courses. Institute reports were widely distributed, and one, "Attack on Democracy," sold over 15,000 copies and was printed in *Look, Life,* and the *Milwaukee Journal.*[6]

Despite its seemingly nonpartisan appearance, the institute's activities attracted criticism from individuals claiming that its membership consisted primarily of left-wingers, New Dealers, or pro-Communists who were antibusiness and pro–New Deal. In fall 1941, therefore, the institute disbanded because it could not continue its "dispassionate analysis." Its directors wrote that they desired to maintain their nonpartisanship and feared that their work was being misunderstood and used against the government. Collectively, they wanted to prevent the institute from being drawn into the growing disputes between interventionists and isolationists.[7]

It is unlikely that the Institute's work directly affected later decisions to create a propaganda apparatus since its members had little immediate connection with members of the Roosevelt administration. The institute's work, however, was praised by interventionist and internationalist groups, future propagandists, and influential Americans, including U.S. Education commissioner John Studebaker, historian Henry Elmer Barnes, journalist Irving Pflaum of the *Chicago Times,* and other "persons of community or national prominence." The institute's primary contribution was in the publicity it gave to propaganda, a hitherto little-understood topic.[8]

Academics were always in the forefront of efforts to counter Nazi propaganda, as evidenced by the large number associated with the Institute of Propaganda Analysis. Other scholars were directly involved with groups such as the Princeton University Listening Center, founded in November 1939 with a Rockefeller Foundation grant. The staff of the center consisted of academics recruited by John R. Whitton, who, after speaking with CBS correspondent Edward R. Murrow, was "impressed by the increasing use of radio as a weapon of politics, particularly in the hands of Nazi propagandists." A committee of Whitton, Hadley Cantril, William S. Carpenter, all of Princeton, O. W. Riegel of Washington and Lee University, Brunson R. McCrutcheon, and Harold N. Graves established the center.[9] The men determined that 500 shortwave propaganda programs, which should be recorded and analyzed, reached an estimated 20 million receiving sets in America each week. With an initial staff of ten, they produced over 100 volumes of transcripts of 250 pages each, a total exceeding 8 million words of transmissions received from Berlin, London, Rome, Paris, and Moscow. Pamphlets summarizing their findings were sent to the government, newspaper editors, radio executives, commentators, and specialists in international rela-

tions, propaganda, public opinion, and radio research. Twenty such summaries were published between 15 December 1939 and 15 July 1941. Later, in conjunction with the American Institute of Public Opinion and the Columbia University Office of Radio Research, the Princeton Listening Center, with Harold Gosnell of the University of Chicago and Jerome Bruner of Harvard University, conducted surveys to ascertain the character, extent, and listening habits of the American audience.[10]

The center was the first operation of its kind. It did nothing, however, in the way of actively combating propaganda or increasing the general public's knowledge. It merely recorded and analyzed incoming broadcasts for a small segment of the population, who may or may not have passed the findings on to people with sufficient influence to act. The center operated for a total of twenty months, until July 1941, when the new Foreign Broadcast Intelligence Service (FBIS) of the Federal Communications Commission (FCC) superseded its efforts.[11]

Other private groups were similarly active in the study of morale and Nazi propaganda in the effort to counteract its perceived negative effects. Among the more prominent were the Committee on Morale of the Society for the Psychological Study of Social Issues, under Gardner Murphy; the Conference on Morale, directed by Edward L. Bernays; the Morale Committee of the American Library Association; the American Defense Morale Committee; and the National Solidarity Group affiliated with the Social Science Research Council, directed by Robert Crane. These groups shared a common perception of propaganda and appealed to patriotic and nationalistic sentiments to defend the nation from Nazi psychological attack.[12]

One group whose members were influential in later propaganda affairs was the Council for Democracy, founded in July 1940 by internationalist and *Time* vice-president C. D. Jackson, Archibald MacLeish, Cass Canfield, Raymond Gram Swing, and Carl Friedrich. The purpose of the council was to "convince the administration to exert a greater effort to explain the war and mobilization to the public in ideological terms" and "to cooperate as far as possible with all trade and professional groups, patriotic and civic organizations, women's clubs, . . . [in] extending their activity along pro-Democracy lines." To many interventionists, however, the group was of limited value as it "expressed its beliefs in lofty moral terms, and its studies of the freedoms guaranteed under the Bill of Rights were erudite." The council's membership, however, was well connected with the Roosevelt administration and in a position to influence future government actions.[13]

The vast majority of private groups were not especially interventionist or in-

ternationalist in outlook and most did not call for creation of a government-sponsored propaganda agency. Most smaller groups maintained that private citizens, properly educated and organized, could fight Nazi propaganda without government intervention. One author claimed that federal agencies were generally not desirable because they tended to monopolize power and that "the same service in the hands of the state . . . would carry with it the evils" of the Nazi system. Though civilian morale agencies had negative attributes, the commentator wrote, such as a tendency to restrict membership to people of a specific class, gender, race, religion, or ideological leaning, they were nonetheless a potent force in the defense of democracy.[14] Generally, the approach of many of the smaller groups tended to be amateurish, educational, and defensive, and their emphasis was domestic rather than international. The collective influences of such groups on government efforts were minimal although many of their members later joined larger internationalist and interventionist groups and served in propaganda agencies. Often they had gained their first knowledge of Nazi propaganda activities through their affiliations with small analysis groups.

A significant group of individuals interested in propaganda favored an alternative viewpoint requiring a more prominent government role and a different emphasis. They believed that the only viable defense was a propaganda offense with the goal of undermining enemy military and civil populations, using the truth if possible but if necessary the enemy's own subversive techniques. Propaganda was international in scope, ideological in content, and had to be conducted on a massive and highly organized scale, necessitating the funding, direction, and authority of the federal government.[15]

Beginning in early 1940 and continuing through the war years, the two opposing philosophies clashed. The differences of opinion on the proper role of propaganda mirrored the differences among Americans generally about the proper national response to events in Europe and about domestic politics and foreign policy. The dichotomy was especially evident following the advent of the interventionist movement, which itself was divided over the proper response to the Nazi threat.

The Committee on National Morale favored the aggressive use of propaganda. Its membership overlapped several interventionist and internationalist organizations, including the Council for Democracy, its parent organization. The committee was founded in July 1940 as a private, nonprofit body that believed "morale represents a decisive force in human affairs which needs to be thoroughly understood and intelligently utilized for the national safety and welfare." Its members, most of whom had professional and academic training, prepared studies on propaganda and morale, including by 1942 three books, scores

of research projects on the "penetration and intensity of Axis propaganda in the United States," studies of national groups, and "confidential projects, . . . for government and private agencies."[16] Members included capable and talented specialists in psychology, political science, psychiatry, physiology, propaganda and public opinion analysis, publicity, radio, and motion pictures and students of foreign affairs, military science, social work, and economics. Its more prominent and influential members included publisher, journalist, and broadcaster John Farrar; academic and Asian expert Owen Lattimore; academic, author, and business expert Douglas Miller; CBS executive, educator, and radio-psychology expert Frank Stanton; and soldier, military analyst, and author Maj. George Fielding Eliot. Twenty-six other members of the committee later filled top posts in the COI, OWI, and OSS. The committee was the first major organization to study propaganda with an eye toward using it as a weapon to combat the Axis powers. It was also the first to include prominent individuals capable of pushing and, more important, willing to press, the issue of government-sponsored defensive and offensive propaganda on President Roosevelt. As such, the committee's activities and policies represented a departure from the smaller-scale, more informal, and less intense activities of private groups that hesitated to undertake such actions.[17]

The committee had a distinct advantage over most smaller groups because many of its members were already familiar and recognized authorities who had produced several written works on Nazi Germany, propaganda, and military and international relations in the late 1930s and early 1940s. Most of their works received a wide circulation, including those by Pulitzer Prize–winner Edgar A. Mowrer, educator Edward Y. Hartshorne, and writers Morton Royse and Edmond Taylor.

Among the members of the Committee on National Morale, Edmond Taylor had perhaps the greatest effect on subsequent propaganda activities. The author of the well-received *Strategy of Terror*, detailing the fall of France, he later recalled that "having written about political warfare, I naturally qualified as an expert in the field, and . . . there were probably not many Americans whose visible qualifications were much higher." A largely self-educated journalist, his work consisted of finding means to undermine enemy morale, "of plotting the American counter-offensive." He soon became consumed by his new profession and began to believe in "the idea of fighting Hitlerism with Hitler's favorite weapons" while having to overcome "the ideological and moral scruples of the government officials and opinion leaders" in the process. He found himself being "carried along by my psychological momentum toward positions more extreme than some of

Foreign correspondent, author, Committee on National Morale member, and OSS agent Edmond Taylor upon his return to the United States in 1940. (Courtesy AP/Wide World Photos)

my colleagues approved or than any with which I would earlier have chosen to identify myself."[18]

For Taylor, "The only defense is attack, total attack, with emphasis where the enemy puts it, on political and psychological factors." He wanted Axis consulates closed, Nazi groups smashed and their leaders jailed, and the FBI turned loose to pick up the remaining spies and saboteurs. Any American guilty of seditious activities should also be locked up, including all followers of the Fascists, for the duration. Moreover, the government should be combed for anyone not 100 percent committed to democracy. All appeasers, isolationists, Roosevelt-

haters must go, before the nation went to war. Although such measures were contrary to constitutionally guaranteed civil rights, Taylor was convinced "that Nazi political warfare was a threat to American democracy calling for urgent measures to strengthen our defenses against subversion and demoralization." After all, he reasoned, "If defeatist propaganda is undermining public morale, the propaganda must be stopped. How does not make any difference." The goal "is to shut up the propagandists before they have a chance to do any undermining."[19]

Taylor outlined a plan for an American response to Nazi propaganda through several articles and in his work for the committee. He suggested creating a "foreign-propaganda service under government direction, working in close liaison with the State, Navy, and War Departments," with an annual budget of $10 million. The agency could direct the work of private groups, produce patriotic films, provide press information, distribute propaganda leaflets to businessmen for inclusion with all shipments abroad, and create "volunteer morale ambassadors"—citizens traveling in Europe to "carry American propaganda through personal contacts." The federal gold reserve at Fort Knox could be used to buy weapons for resistance groups and the support of friendly governments, newspapers, and individuals in order to convince foreigners that their interests lay with the United States, to feed unoccupied Europe, and to create an adequate military-political intelligence system. The organization, like the entire government, would be staffed by people who most passionately wanted to win. "These are the people," Taylor maintained, "who have never had any doubts about the need for fighting the war, and never will have, no matter what happens." Such a group, he believed, would be of different parties, different backgrounds, and different ideologies, but members would have the will to win without equivocation. The U.S. Army, U.S. Navy, and the State Department as well as other agencies "must be staffed with men who care nothing for politics in any narrow partisan sense of the word" and "who approach all problems from the viewpoint of self-conscious, militant American Democrats."[20]

Taylor's philosophy and his techniques, largely drawn from his perceptions and observations of supposedly similar Nazi actions in Europe, later appeared in reports reaching President Roosevelt and members of his cabinet and reflected the aggressive doctrine of the future COI and OSS of which Taylor was a founding member. Although many people considered his suggestions harsh and draconian in 1940, the time arrived when his views became the operational dicta of hundreds of OSS members. His views were certainly shared by many American interventionists who not only belonged to the Committee on National Morale but who also favored the immediate initiation of a counterpropaganda effort.

The main proponents of an offensive response to Nazi propaganda were interventionists and internationalists. These individuals, however, were not concerned exclusively with Nazi propaganda but viewed it as only one part of a larger threat to Western Civilization. They knew that the United States was protected by two oceans from direct Nazi aggression, but they also realized that a physical assault on North America was the least likely form of attack. Instead, the Nazis could defeat America only by sowing internal discord, by paralyzing governmental processes and defense efforts, by cutting the nation off from foreign markets and sources of raw materials, and by destroying its image abroad through propaganda. Therefore, propaganda became a potent weapon in the hands of the Nazis and perhaps the most dangerous and realistic threat to the nation.

In the months prior to Pearl Harbor the groups worked to pressure the president into aiding the Allies and into fighting perceived threats at home. Initially, the public showed no enthusiasm for direct intervention abroad, especially when compared to their enthusiasm for fighting internal subversion. The groups thus undertook the daunting task of molding public opinion and of prevailing upon Roosevelt to react to the Nazi menace in general and to the propaganda threat in particular. Roosevelt in turn came to rely on the groups to shape and monitor public opinion toward favoring intervention, a task he could not undertake himself without political risk.[21]

The Committee to Defend America by Aiding the Allies (CDAAA) was the largest interventionist group in the United States in 1940. Composed largely of liberal internationalists, it was founded by William Allen White, the Republican editor of the *Emporia Gazette*, from remnants of the Nonpartisan Committee for Peace Through Revision of the Neutrality Laws, formed in 1939. The CDAAA went public in May 1940 with 53 members, a number that grew to 350 by the end of that month and that peaked at 750,000 in 125 chapters nationwide by May 1941. Unlike the America First Committee, whose members were mainly from the Chicago area, the CDAAA was strongest in the Northeast. The organization was "committed to an Allied success because America and the American way of life will be gravely imperiled by an Axis victory." The committee thus advocated any measure to aid the Allies through the provision of weapons, money, and moral and diplomatic support. The group halted their endorsement of aid to a stance just short of war, a position that caused dissension within the group and an eventual defection of members who favored more aggressive measures. One clearly agreed-upon goal, however, was the support of "strenuous efforts to combat Nazi propaganda in the Americas with care to preserve civil liberties." From the outset, CDAAA members saw propaganda as a threat to be

countered, a threat many of its members did not see as diminishing after the United States entered the war in 1941. To them propaganda was a vital weapon needed to obtain a victory over the Nazis, and they devoted the war years to its development and use.[22]

The membership of the committee was a who's who of the nation's political, social, and economic elite concentrated in the northeastern United States. The majority were highly educated, white Anglo-Saxon Protestants from middle and upper-class business and professional groups. Most members were prominent and respected leaders in their fields, and over one-third were academics; labor and farm representation was absent. Initial members included future Secretary of War Henry Stimson, future Secretary of the Navy Frank Knox, serving and past governors of New York, Maine, Rhode Island, New Jersey, Kansas, and Florida, university presidents James B. Conant of Harvard, Charles Seymour of Yale, Frank Kingdon of Newark, and Frank P. Graham of North Carolina, Archibald MacLeish, librarian of Congress, and Rabbi Steven Wise.[23] As the organization grew and as the Nazis scored further victories, influential Americans flocked to the committee while operating funds poured in from some of the nation's wealthiest people, including J. P. Morgan, Robert Woods Bliss, Mrs. Dorothy Backer, newspaper owner Barry Bingham, and publisher Mrs. Dwight Morrow.[24]

Although called warmongers by isolationists, most CDAAA members simply believed that Nazi aggression, physical and psychological, was a clear danger to the nation that had been tolerated for too long. Playwright and CDAAA member Robert Sherwood informed William Allen White in December 1939 that the nation should actively intervene in Europe. He wrote that he had "consistently tried to plead the cause of pacifism and of the highest patriotism. . . . But the terrible truth is that when war comes to you, you have to fight it." "It is not enough," Sherwood felt, "to withdraw ambassadors, to utter noble protests against aggressors and extend sympathy to their victims." It was in the power of the United States "to save the human race from complete calamity," and Americans "should not hesitate any longer to assume our sacred responsibility."[25]

A significant number of CDAAA members shared Sherwood's sense of emergency and gathered petitions supporting Roosevelt's efforts to provide all aid short of war to France and Britain. Not content with mere petitions, however, Sherwood, writer George F. Kaufman, and publisher Henry Luce went directly to the public and bought a full-page newspaper ad that ran nationwide on 10 and 11 June 1940. Entitled "Stop Hitler Now," the ad, written by Sherwood, called for an immediate declaration of war against the Nazis. The nation had stood idly by long enough and must act now, it declared. If Britain and France

fell, the United States "will find itself alone in a barbaric world—a world ruled by Nazis." Americans had to devote themselves to a vast defense program as a united people. Anyone who argued the opposite or thought that the Nazis would wait until the United States was ready, "is either an imbecile or a traitor." The ad singled out the Nazi propaganda threat, asserting that "we have to guard night and day against the manifold enemies from within." Americans could not "ignore the fact that Trojan Horses are grazing in all the fertile fields of North and South America."

Appearing in newspapers with a total circulation of 8.5 million, the ad drew the attention of President Roosevelt, who was reported as having privately "endorsed it, saying it was 'a great piece of work.'" Although the president could not publicly embrace CDAAA positions for political reasons, the group clearly shared and expressed his foreign policy views as CDAAA members understood them, and they had close ties with the administration. White later commented that he "knew he had his [FDR's] private support. . . . I never did anything the president didn't ask for, and I always conferred with him on our program."[26]

Many committee members favored Sherwood's more aggressive approach. On the same day that his ad appeared, another, drafted by attorney and international businessman Whitney Shepardson and entitled "A Summons to Speak Out," also ran, calling for an immediate declaration of war on Germany. Its thirty signers belonged to the Century or Miller Group, comprising some of the most outspoken interventionists and CDAAA members in the country.[27] The driving force behind the Century Group was its founder Francis P. Miller, a liberal democrat, philanthropist, politician, and interventionist who advocated the adoption of an immediate anti-Nazi foreign policy. Miller recruited other individuals belonging to the New York City Century Club, including diplomat, journalist, and broadcaster William Hessler; banker, lawyer, and businessman George Watts Hill; banker James P. Warburg; *Foreign Affairs* editor, journalist, and self-described expert on international relations Hamilton Fish Armstrong; Allen Dulles; John J. McCloy; Dean Acheson; and Frank Polk, among many others.[28]

The fall of France was pivotal for interventionists. Many of them, especially those in the Century Group, felt that efforts to date had been too weak and were proving too little too late, an attitude that produced a schism within the CDAAA.[29] New York City Mayor Fiorello LaGuardia expressed his concerns to William Allen White in December 1940 when he wrote that CDAAA actions did not match its words and that the committee should divide into two groups, the one chaired by White called the Committee to Defend America by Aiding the Allies with Words and the other called the Committee to Defend America

by Aiding the Allies with Deeds.[30] Although White left the CDAAA in late 1940, the indecision over maintaining an all-aid-short-of-war policy versus adopting a policy calling for direct intervention continued. As the debate progressed, an organization much like the latter one suggested by LaGuardia was founded on 19 April 1941 by members of the Century Group, the Fight for Freedom Committee (FFFC).[31]

Its members believed that American survival, and civilization as it was then known, depended upon a total eradication of fascism. Unlike the CDAAA, FFFC members were more outspoken in their demands for the creation of a government propaganda agency and for stringent anti-Nazi actions. They were also zealously anti-isolationist, favoring "immediate, unrelenting and unceasing war on Hitler and the forces he has unloosed." They advocated an immediate break in diplomatic relations, the use of U.S. naval forces to clear the seas of U-boats, the military occupation of all strategic spots in any ocean, the immediate repeal of neutrality laws, and the election of congressmen who supported "militant, aggressive action dictated by common sense, decency and our self-interest to defeat the Nazi menace." They pledged to "support all steps necessary to defeat the enemies of our freedom both from within and without." Zealous in both word and deed, FFFC member Herbert Agar bluntly informed Secretary of the Interior Harold Ickes that the organization's "real object . . . was to agitate for an open declaration of war against Germany and Italy."[32]

Elites dominated the Fight for Freedom Committee. Although member Henry Hobson claimed that the group had "no political affiliation, no connection with any group or special interest in society," its founders and dominant members were drawn from a small and exclusive group consisting largely of white Anglo-Saxon Protestant business and professional people residing in the Northeast. The same profile held true even as the movement grew to include 372 local committees nationwide. In addition to enjoying an elite status in American society, most FFFC members were personal friends or social and business associates of many individuals serving in the Roosevelt administration and belonged to the same private clubs and internationalist groups, such as the Century Club, Council on Foreign Relations, the Foreign Policy Association, and the Council for Democracy. Therefore, although the FFFC claimed a membership of "individuals from all regions, all segments of society and all walks of life" who desired "to meet the present crisis with reality, courage, honesty and a loyalty to those ideals upon which the future existence of our nation depends," such was not the case. The committee was always more representative of several narrow interests held by small numbers of wealthy, prominent, and influential easterners.[33]

Thus, the early membership of the FFFC suggested a virtual who's who of the eastern establishment and of the nation's financial, industrial, commercial, communications, and academic elite among whom New Yorkers predominated. It was also a who's who of the top policymakers of the future COI, OSS, and OWI, including thirty-one individuals who later served in those organizations. The FFFC Executive Committee, for example, the group directing programs and campaigns, consisted of twelve individuals, of whom eight held later leadership positions in either the OSS or the OWI. The FFFC policy committee of twenty-four people contained five future OSS or OWI leaders and policymakers. Substantial funds were provided to the FFFC by members later associated with the OSS and the OWI, including Darryl Zanuck, Jack and Harry Warner, Marshall Field, Max Ascoli, and Frank Altschul. Mellon family member David K. E. Bruce donated $10,000, a sum matched by the Rockefellers.[34]

Contacts between FFFC members and the Roosevelt administration always had been close but became even closer during 1941. According to FFFC member F. H. Peter Cusick, the group's New York office was in contact several times a day with presidential advisers Steve Early and Gen. Edwin M. (Pa) Watson, and members such as Robert Sherwood, one of Roosevelt's speechwriters, had daily direct access to the White House. Cusick and fellow FFFC member Ulric Bell were asked to advise Fiorello LaGuardia about organizing the Office of Civil Defense (OCD), and Office of Government Reports (OGR) director Lowell Mellett and administration members Steve Early and David K. Niles "suggested people to fill key positions on the Committee's staff and administration officials to speak at its rallies." Furthermore, Vice-President Henry A. Wallace spoke at several FFFC gatherings and "invited Ulric Bell to take part in informal, private discussions [Wallace] was conducting on war aims." Eleanor Roosevelt, Frank Knox, William Knudson, and Sidney Hillman, the latter two of the federal Office of Production Management, gave speeches on behalf of the FFFC; others, such as W. Averill Harriman, who felt his position precluded membership, asked his wife to join in his place. William J. Donovan, William H. Standley, and James B. Conant, although employed by the federal government in 1941, were nonetheless active FFFC members.[35]

The committee had many goals that were avidly pursued in public and private. Members made contacts with individuals in the Roosevelt administration and gave speeches, drafted petitions, and otherwise worked to influence public opinion and the actions of the president. They wrote prolifically, especially on the subjects of Nazi Germany, propaganda, and foreign and military affairs. Although many members did not actively participate in CDAAA and FFFC campaigns and programs, their writings on similar subjects gained a wide audience

and convinced Americans of the existence of a Nazi threat and of the need for a more forward foreign policy. Their writings influenced members of the Roosevelt administration, and the president perused many of their works.[36]

Significant numbers of interventionists, in addition to people belonging to the CDAAA and FFFC, had spent years engaging in such public and private activities as members of existing internationalist organizations of high repute and influential standing. The groups, some of which had been in existence for decades to keep Americans informed about world and European events, opposed appeasement and neutrality policies. One movement, Union Now, attracted many internationalists, interventionists, and Anglophiles. Founded in 1939 by Geneva-based *New York Times* correspondent Clarence K. Streit, the group hoped to "marshal the opinion of the democratic world to combat the grandiose plans for a Hitlerian world order."[37] Streit outlined his ideas in a book published in 1940, *On Freedom and Union Now*, and attracted a wide and influential following.[38]

Two of the most prominent internationalist organizations were the Foreign Policy Association and the Council on Foreign Relations, both of which favored a forward foreign policy and advanced antiappeasement and antineutrality policies. After 1939 the two groups supported direct military, economic, and diplomatic aid to the Allies. The Foreign Policy Association, founded in 1921, had 14,000 members in 1937. Three of its members, John T. Whitaker, Charles A. H. Thomson, and James Phinney Baxter III, told President Roosevelt on one occasion that the organization's purpose was informational and that it did not "advance any propaganda program or given line of policy." After September 1939, however, the association favored, and publicly advocated, an interventionist policy.[39]

A more elite group that was similar in philosophy, outlook, and purpose to the Foreign Policy Association was the Council on Foreign Relations, founded as a New York social club by businessmen, attorneys, and academic experts on diplomacy after the Versailles Peace Conference in 1919. The council, through its publication *Foreign Affairs*, sought to influence foreign relations and opposed isolationist and neutrality policies while advocating aid to the Allies. As the nation drew closer to war, and during the war itself, council members filled the ranks of the Century Group, FFFC, CDAAA, and top leadership positions in government agencies, most notably the State Department. Council members helped draft the Atlantic Charter, and one member, Francis P. Miller, initiated the idea of the destroyer-for-bases deal implemented by Roosevelt in fall 1940.[40] Of the active membership between 1938 and 1947, seventy-eight council members were involved with interventionist groups, the OWI, or the OSS.[41]

As with the larger groups, the council's 650 members had impeccable reputations, and their advice was respected throughout the United States, in Europe, and by the Roosevelt administration. Similarly, its members were overwhelmingly white Anglo-Saxon Protestant males. They were almost exclusively Republicans who lived in the Northeast, had attended private or Ivy League schools, had traveled widely in Europe, and who practiced corporate law or were involved in business or finance. Their values, like those of the interventionist groups and especially the later OSS, were instilled by elite social circles, exclusive schools, and establishment clubs and organizations.[42]

As a group, the council's membership held elitist and narrow ideological views; they had "developed a weary contempt for the public's inability to understand international relations," thinking the public was "always stupid and usually wrong."[43] The council, in contrast, was "comprised of a group of men in America best qualified to give counsel and assistance in the study of America's proper course." They envisioned a future in which the United States dominated world affairs according to a foreign policy determined by a narrow elite of experts such as themselves. Council members represented "a very special internationalism" that recognized the rights of other nations but that always put American interests first. Although many of them advocated a postwar world organization to maintain the peace, it had to be one in which the United States predominated. Council member Hamilton F. Armstrong wrote a fellow member soon after the war began that the "measure of [America's] victory will be the measure of our domination after victory," and member Maj. Gen. George V. Strong advocated that the U.S. "cultivate a mental view toward world settlement . . . which will enable us to impose our terms, amounting to a Pax Americana." The Council on Foreign Relations was not a propaganda agency, per se, but its philosophy was heavily represented in the wartime propaganda of the OSS and, to a lesser extent, in that of the OWI.[44]

Clearly by late 1940 many Americans believed in the existence of a Nazi propaganda threat, however exaggerated that belief might have been. More important, they realized the value of propaganda as a weapon, perceptions that resulted from the work of scores of small private groups who recorded, examined, and analyzed Axis propaganda and its supposed effects. Only after the creation of larger groups, such as the Committee on National Morale, however, did prominent, powerful, and influential individuals become involved. The establishment of this organization was a crucial and significant first step in the development of the American propaganda effort against Nazi Germany. Its membership, which overlapped that of several interventionist groups, brought propaganda issues to the attention of organizations whose elite members were

not hesitant to press their opinions on the Roosevelt administration. Increasingly these individuals spoke out publicly, while meeting with members of the Roosevelt administration, on the need for a government-sponsored propaganda agency and for more active measures against the Nazis. Although support for the Allies and eventual American military participation were the primary goals of interventionist groups, the need to counter Nazi propaganda and to develop a counterpropaganda capability was also a high priority. The later OWI and OSS service of many interventionists and internationalists is indicative of the importance the groups' members attached to propaganda as a weapon of war and as a tool of diplomacy.

Interventionist and internationalist groups pressured the administration to act, yet executive office responses were barely perceptible although Roosevelt never totally ignored their advice or their efforts. The first anti-Nazi actions, however, came from the one branch of government least positively involved in wartime propaganda activities: the U.S. Congress.

3 · The Federal Government Defines a Propaganda Role, 1939–1941

Government leaders, prominent citizens, and the American public believed that Nazi propaganda threatened the nation, but no one had accurate or detailed information on the extent of the nature of the threat or specific plans to counter propaganda attacks. Everyone relied on exaggerated and anecdotal media accounts and on reports of varying quality and validity from Congress, interventionist groups, and propaganda analysts. Nonetheless, the dominant American perception concerning propaganda was that it always preceded armed Nazi aggression. Accepting this view, many Americans believed the nation was already at war by the late 1930s.[1]

American assumptions concerning Nazi propaganda presented the Roosevelt administration with both an opportunity and a dilemma. The idea of a fifth-column threat bolstered the president's appeals for national unity and for faith in his leadership as well as the aims of his domestic and foreign policies. Conversely, Roosevelt was the elected leader of a democratic nation where political opposition was taken for granted and where public opinion mattered. Popular support was especially crucial to the president as he sought an unprecedented third term of office in 1940 in an arena where Republican charges of his alleged dictatorial tendencies and criticisms of his domestic and foreign policies were frequently leveled.[2]

In this uncertain political climate, the administration, under considerable pressure from internationalist and interventionist groups, began to study the problem of Nazi propaganda attacks on the United States and the difficulties associated with the activities of domestic right-wing and isolationist groups. The first steps were undertaken as well to examine the efficacy of creating a federal agency to counter the attacks and to use propaganda as an offensive weapon. Private groups and individuals were responsible for the initial moves to convince

members of the administration that creation of a federal agency for such activities was both prudent and warranted. Once influential members of the government, such as Harold Ickes, John J. McCloy, and Frank Knox, became convinced of the interventionist argument they prevailed upon the president. Evidence suggests that Roosevelt initially did not know how to react. Yet apparently he knew that propaganda agencies were needed and would one day be created, just as he knew that the nation's involvement in another world war was virtually inevitable. Secure in the knowledge, the president moved slowly toward defining a federal propaganda role and in creating a single, comprehensive organization but only after he had considered all options and the level of public support for each. Roosevelt, however, relied primarily upon private groups to educate the public and to garner support for his policies regarding both intervention and propaganda. The president, according to one historian, "was by nature and experience disposed to flexibility, and the absence of pat solutions to problems that were at once complex and evolving reinforced his penchant for improvisation." He was aware that hasty federal reactions could increase public fears of Nazi propaganda and both public and Republican suspicions of his motives. Over the course of two years, he constantly tested the waters of public opinion, the depth of interventionist support, and the extent of isolationist and Republican opposition to all matters pertaining to propaganda.[3]

The president's knowledge of propaganda was sketchy. He therefore delegated leadership to private groups and cabinet members who attempted to devise, largely through trial and error, a viable federal agency that could effectively combat subversive propaganda. Yet Roosevelt never formulated a coherent federal propaganda policy. During this period, from mid-1940 until mid-1941, the president seemed uninvolved and detached, taking small actions when necessary but avoiding the large, potentially risky political step of creating a suitable federal agency. Thus he remained generally immune from the opposition's criticism leveled at individuals in his administration who were working at his behest toward creating a propaganda organization. Subordinates consequently bore the brunt of the attacks on the idea of a propaganda bureau controlled by the executive branch. Only when he came under strong pressure from members of his cabinet, who in turn were influenced by interventionist groups, did the president create the first agencies in spring and summer 1941. Although they did not meet all the goals of interventionists, the agencies did at least provide an opportunity for initial study and organization until more definitive action could attract solid public and political support. In retrospect, the president's actions were astute. But as he waited for public opinion to swing toward his own views and for a practical agency with workable methods and techniques to emerge,

considerable time and effort were expended with few tangible results. While the executive branch stalled, Congress took the lead in exposing and countering Nazi subversion.

Congressional interest in propaganda during the 1930s always seemed to increase or decrease in relation to public fears or apathy. In one instance, the chair of the House Immigration Committee, Samuel Dickstein, a Democrat from New York City's heavily Jewish lower East Side, shocked the nation in 1933 when he claimed that Nazi propaganda, money, and arms were being smuggled into the nation with the intent "to establish their principle of government here."[4] Although he had no concrete proof, his charges prompted the House "to investigate 'the extent, character, and objects of Nazi propaganda activities' " in March 1934. The committee took Dickstein's name and was chaired by Cong. John McCormack (D-Mass.).[5]

The Dickstein Committee conducted a year of sensational hearings that brought detailed findings of Nazi subversion to public attention for the first time. In its report of 15 February 1935 the House Special Committee on un-American Activities claimed that the Nazis had a pervasive propaganda program in the United States that used Fascist right-wing groups and foreign agents for fomenting subversion and disseminating propaganda. The report warned the Nazi government that "any spread of the organization of the NSDAP to American soil, even in limited form, would be ill regarded by a great number of American citizens." The committee then suggested legislation to shorten or terminate the visas of any person who engaged in subversive propaganda activity. Although the resulting Dickstein bill became law, it was assailed by many critics as a violation of constitutionally guaranteed rights and liberties.[6]

The Dickstein hearings heightened public interest and prompted a new investigation by Cong. Martin Dies (D-Tex.). In the first of many annual reports, Dies claimed to have uncovered new evidence that the Nazis, described as "archetypal enemies," were active and posed "unequivocal threats to American Civilization." "Unless checked immediately, [they] may cause great unrest and serious repercussions in the United States."[7] Dies's committee, however, like its predecessor, was immediately criticized by civil libertarians for conducting a politicized witch-hunt, for making gross exaggerations, and for accepting at face value the statements of Fritz Kuhn and his cohorts. Yet Dies was undaunted by criticism and claimed that polls showed that most Americans approved of his efforts to expose Communist and Nazi subversion. His work had already produced results, Dies said, by exposing subversives to "the spotlight of publicity," which caused many of them to curtail their activities. In true partisan fashion, Dies deflected further criticism by invoking the administration, stating that

President Roosevelt had "joked at one time about [the Committee's] revelations" as did secretaries Ickes and Perkins, but that "the president no longer views . . . the Committee as ridiculous or unfounded or inconsequential." Had Roosevelt and the Justice Department acted two years earlier, Dies asserted, thousands of fifth columnists who had now gone underground could easily have been picked up. Nonetheless, the congressman assured the public and law-enforcement agencies that he possessed twenty volumes of "names, addresses, identities, methods, and plans of many of the Fifth Columnists" for future reference.[8]

Dies's work was conducted without administration support even though he had written the president in June 1940 to make "an earnest and sincere plea" for action "with reference to the 'fifth column.'" Roosevelt agreed that such groups were dangerous, but he showed relief that Dies felt "there is no occasion for hysterical alarm and no justification to resort to repressive or undemocratic measures." Dies, however, suggested just this course in August 1940 and urged Roosevelt's support for legislation outlawing the Communist party, the German-American Bund, and "all political organizations that are shown to be under control of foreign governments" or who acted as their agents. Roosevelt doubted this solution was consistent with preserving the rights of the citizens of a democracy or with constitutional principles and told the congressman so in a September 1940 White House meeting. Dies remained convinced that subversive conspiracies existed and that the president was doing nothing to combat them.[9]

Congress undertook additional efforts as more and more Americans became aware of the alleged Nazi threat. In 1938 both houses passed the Foreign Agents Registration Act requiring all persons working for a foreign government to register with the Justice Department. The law was strengthened in June 1940 by the Federal Alien Registration Act requiring all foreigners to make their whereabouts and residence known annually to federal authorities. Perhaps the strictest piece of legislation intended to control the activities of foreign agents was the Voorhis Act, passed into law on 17 October 1940, which required compulsory registration of groups seeking the overthrow of any government, be it that of the United States or of any other nation.[10]

Except for restrictive legislation, congressional actions to create some sort of propaganda agency brought dismal results. In 1937 Cong. Emmanuel Celler (D-N.Y.) introduced legislation to establish a government shortwave station to combat Axis propaganda, but the bill failed in committee. Similar bills were introduced in 1939 but also failed because of opposition from Republicans, isolationists, and private broadcasters who claimed such activities constituted un-

warranted government meddling in foreign affairs and with privately held communication companies. Unknown to most congressmen, however, the executive branch, publicly silent about the entire subject, was studying the problem and was seeking possible solutions.[11]

Roosevelt's hesitancy to create a propaganda agency stemmed in large measure from negative World War I experiences with information output. In 1917 the government had created the Committee on Public Information (CPI) under George Creel. Its task was to build support for the war effort from its news bureau in Washington and through publicity missions in nine nations abroad. It focused the heaviest effort, however, on America. The CPI produced films, cartoons, posters, and syndicated features and sponsored patriotic speakers, information bureaus, and programs for ethnic and racial minorities. The programs were simplistic, heavily nationalistic and ultrapatriotic, and prone to hysterical, lurid, and crude exaggeration.

The CPI wed ideology and propaganda, and its overzealous activities created a negative backlash that contributed to postwar American dislike for anything that smacked of propaganda, slick promotion, or manipulation. Creel recognized that the CPI might have been extreme in its work but maintained that such an approach was necessary to protect the nation during a time of danger. Nonetheless, the CPI became a model for the sort of agency that Roosevelt sought to avoid.[12]

Except for the dismal lessons of the CPI, the administration lacked any applicable knowledge of propaganda, and "thinking on the kind of organization required for effective operations . . . was neither clear nor consistent." Roosevelt, however, a clever manager of the press, was aware of the political value of information and the maintenance of good public relations. As early as 1933 the Division of Information of the Office of Emergency Management (OEM) and the National Emergency Council were created to provide favorable information to the media and the public on the domestic programs of the New Deal. Critics of the administration charged that these offices were little more than propaganda agencies intended to further the president's political fortunes and to silence opposition, despite administration denials.[13]

Dealing with the Nazi propaganda threat required a more sophisticated approach than mere public relations as conducted by early New Deal information agencies. In November 1938, as more Nazi propaganda successes were pointed out abroad, a committee was appointed to study "affirmative propaganda." The group concluded that the nation "needed to counter foreign propaganda, especially Axis propaganda," a job not being done by private broadcasters. In response, Roosevelt drafted an executive order in April 1939 to create an office of

home defense within OEM, directed by the Republican mayor of New York City, Fiorello LaGuardia. Supporters claimed that involving citizens, and Republicans, in the defense program would intensify their enthusiasm and determination, thereby building national morale in the face of Nazi threats. The executive order was not issued for another two years, however, because Roosevelt considered both the Congress and the American public unprepared for such a move.[14]

With the outbreak of war in Europe, the president did sense the need for some sort of agency to explain government defense preparations to the public and thereby boost national morale. On 8 September 1939 he issued Executive Order 8284, creating the Office of Government Reports, an agency doing essentially the same job Roosevelt had intended LaGuardia to do. Directed by *Washington Daily News* correspondent Lowell Mellett, the OGR was to be a "low-key informational and coordinating service," acting as a clearinghouse for information concerning government activities. It was not intended as a propaganda agency, despite the claims of its critics, and merely took over the functions performed by the U.S. Information Service. Mellett feared that any "high-powered government propaganda" would alienate rather than positively influence public opinion and would be counterproductive: nonetheless, he repeatedly was forced to answer charges that OGR was just a New Deal propaganda agency. The OGR was actually a cautious organization under Mellett, and his refusal to advertise Roosevelt's defense policies aggressively, to advocate interventionist themes, or to counter Nazi propaganda created intense disappointment among proponents of a more active response such as Harold Ickes, Henry Stimson, Dean Acheson, William Bullitt, Archibald MacLeish, and Frank Knox.[15]

The president did consider the possibility of establishing a federal agency for morale and propaganda as Nazi efforts seemed to intensify at home and abroad, discussing the matter with advisers Harry Hopkins, Wayne Coy, William Bullitt, and Budget Director Harold Smith. Instructions were given in March 1940 for drafting a new executive order, based on a letter Roosevelt had received from interventionist journalist, historian, and government consultant George F. Milton, but nothing was subsequently done. Similarly, the president neglected to act on a report written in fall 1939 (delivered in June 1940) by a joint Army-Navy Board that called for the appointment of a public relations administrator to maintain national morale.[16]

Such considerations were too indecisive and bureaucratic to make public, but Roosevelt had other means of stirring the populace on the subject of propaganda. The president began speaking publicly of the fifth-column threat as well as of the damage being done to national unity and preparedness by isolationists.

In a May 1940 speech to Congress, he referred to "the treacherous 'fifth column' in which . . . visitors were actually part of an enemy unit of occupation."[17] Within days, in a fireside chat, he said that the threat to the nation was "not a matter of military weapons alone. We know of new methods of attack" such as "the Trojan Horse . . . the Fifth Column . . . spies, saboteurs and traitors," who disseminate discord, "create confusion of counsel, public indecision, political paralysis and . . . a state of panic." Their purpose, Roosevelt warned, was to delay preparedness, to create "a new and unreasoning skepticism," and to undermine unity. "It has happened time after time, in nation after nation, during the last two years" and should not be allowed to spread in the New World as it had in the Old. "Our morale, and our mental defenses, must be raised as never before against those who would cast a smoke screen across our vision."[18] Through such speeches, Roosevelt raised propaganda consciousness within his administration and among the public, but he took no firm stance regarding the creation of a propaganda agency. By spring 1940, however, administration members, cued by the president's rhetoric and by interventionist and internationalist pressures, took the initiative.

While Roosevelt spoke publicly about the fifth-column threat, he discussed privately the creation of a national morale agency with adviser Louis Brownlow. In September 1940, on Roosevelt's suggestion, Brownlow submitted a report recommending for the first time that government information services be organized in a threefold manner to meet public and government needs: ordinary government information services, a service for dissemination of defense-related information, and a counterpropaganda agency to defend against attacks from the totalitarian states.[19] Although Roosevelt did not immediately act on Brownlow's report, it was one of an increasing number of suggestions from cabinet members and private groups reaching the Oval Office in summer and fall 1940.

Spurred by the collapse of France and frightened by the alleged role of propaganda in the Nazi victory, other groups and individuals were aggressively demanding federal action. Archibald MacLeish, the librarian of Congress, urged President Roosevelt to appoint a coordinator of civilian volunteer activities for defense, a position to include morale building and counterpropaganda responsibilities. MacLeish was not alone; the activities of interventionist groups and the large number of letters from citizens imploring the government to respond to Nazi propaganda in some fashion lent support to his proposal. One delegation with ties to the administration that included Herbert Agar, Grenville Clark, William J. Donovan, Clarence Dykstra, Ernest K. Lindley, Leo Rosten, and William Y. Elliott met with Harry Hopkins in August 1940. They impressed upon

him that much of the public shared Roosevelt's views of foreign affairs but that they lacked any coordination or encouragement. The men then asked that the president be urged to support some sort of federally sponsored "citizens council for national unity" to coordinate "patriotic ventures."[20]

With pressure building for the president to take some sort of action on the entire issue, Roosevelt made the first of many small steps toward creating a propaganda agency. At a November 1940 cabinet meeting, according to Interior Secretary Harold Ickes, the president "expressed concern about the attitude and influence of certain Americans who seem to be Fascist sympathizers," meaning right-wing and isolationist groups. In response, Ickes suggested setting up "some machinery for propaganda." As he later recalled, he had "introduced a very interesting subject." Frank Knox, secretary of the navy since July, supported the idea as did Roosevelt and others. The president, clearly interested, "suggested that a group of us . . . discuss ways and means." The Ickes Committee, at the president's suggestion, would consist of Secretary of War Henry L. Stimson, Postmaster General Frank Walker, Secretary of the Navy Knox, Attorney General Robert H. Jackson, Labor Secretary Perkins, Federal Security Agency administrator Paul McNutt, Selective Service director Clarence Dykstra, OGR director Lowell Mellett, and Louis Brownlow, with Ickes as chair.[21]

This committee was the first government group charged with considering the creation of a propaganda agency. During its brief life members discussed a host of controversial issues, many of which plagued propagandists for the remainder of the war. Its meetings covered the gamut of viewpoints of what propaganda was, how it had been and should be used, who should control and use it, and what (and whose) political and ideological message it should convey.

The first Ickes Committee meeting "to consider . . . setting up some machinery to combat subversive propaganda" was attended by most of the members suggested by the president. Ickes, on the advice of Stimson, invited Assistant Secretary of War John J. McCloy. A newcomer to Washington, McCloy possessed recent and detailed knowledge of Nazi subversion, having spent the period between 1930 and 1939 prosecuting Germans involved in the Black Tom munitions-supply depot sabotage case. The affirmation that the 1916 explosion was indeed the work of German saboteurs only confirmed in his mind that what had been done once could be done again. In October 1940, largely because of his work on the case, he was asked by Stimson to accept a position with the War Department. One month later, he was before the committee.[22]

From the first meeting a wide divergence of opinion existed concerning the role of propaganda in a democracy and whether the American response to Nazi efforts should be defensive or offensive. Ickes's viewpoint, later implemented by the Office

John J. McCloy, assistant secretary of war and a key member of the Ickes Committee on National Morale, in 1941. (U.S. Army, OWI Photo PRD-HICOG, no. 322; reproduced at the National Archives)

of Civil Defense, emphasized a defensive and domestic program enabling organizations with federal financial aid to disseminate patriotic propaganda through speakers and local study groups. McCloy, who dominated the meeting, quickly interjected that more efforts were needed than just educating the public. Propaganda to McCloy was an offensive "military weapon in this day and age . . . an extension of a military concept . . . the idea of a super barrage to precede the artillery barrage—the barrage of ideas." Hitler was sold on the concept long before coming to power, McCloy claimed, and had built the AO accordingly. "It seems . . . silly," he concluded, "to sit back and just take that and build up only what constitutes a sort of anti-aircraft fire against it. . . . You have to have counter methods." McCloy suggested a military-controlled propaganda agency to build morale at home while simultaneously undermining enemy morale abroad.[23]

McCloy had well-developed views concerning propaganda and the correct methods of implementation. He also had ideas on making this course of action palpable to the American people. As propaganda agencies were by nature controversial and prone to raise suspicions, especially if controlled by the federal government or the military, McCloy suggested that a man of broad gauge should lead the agency, a man seemingly above politics with solid civilian credentials, such as Frank Knox, Edgar Mowrer, Henry Luce, Edward Bernays, or Charles Taft. Candidates for director should be knowledgeable about international politics and public relations and have press contacts and firm leadership skills. His staff should consist of scientists, radio specialists, perhaps a high official of the FBI, and, of course, military personnel. The Germans had set up their propaganda machine based on such a pattern.[24]

McCloy's assessment indicated that he saw propaganda from a perspective that most committee members had not considered, as something more than public relations work. He envisioned using German citizens to spread propaganda within the Third Reich in the same manner as Bohle's AO was supposedly operating in the Americas and Europe. Building domestic morale and educating the public were not his concerns; he was intent on stopping subversive activities in the United States while using the same methods against enemies abroad. Since propaganda was so closely related to national policy and military strategy it had to be under government rather than under private control.[25]

Faced with McCloy's new, unexpected, and novel ideas, Ickes and Clarence Dykstra expressed partial approval, but Frances Perkins strongly objected. Nonetheless, the committee agreed that McCloy was definitely knowledgeable about Nazi techniques. One historian has claimed that although McCloy's "remarks were somewhat off the mark," his admiration for the Nazi propaganda machine, which he viewed as the most effective system in the world, was shared by the other committee members. Its future report reflected much of McCloy's thinking, ideas that were also held by men such as Edmond Taylor and William Donovan.[26]

McCloy's idea of creating a government propaganda agency for offensive military purposes represented an evolution in American thought. Most committee members hesitated to endorse such a step, agreeing only on the need for some sort of foreign counterpropaganda and domestic morale-building agency under civilian control. Among the members favoring the latter idea was Clarence Dykstra, who commented that he had been approached by C. D. Jackson of the Council for Democracy with a plan to create "a private organization for the stimulation of American and democratic propaganda" that could be of use to the government. Louis Brownlow, who also balked at McCloy's suggestions, in-

formed the committee of the contents of his 9 September 1940 memo to the president. Members in attendance focused immediately on Brownlow's proposed counterpropaganda agency, deemed crucial by committeemen affiliated with the military, McCloy, Knox, and Stimson. McCloy noted that Stimson was "very interested in the counter-subversive activities and the offensive character of propaganda," adding, however, that propaganda was a poor word to describe such activities. Brownlow elaborated on his idea that any activity must be conducted by a federal agency that worked closely with private groups to avoid the expected charges of political partisanship. It would be a coordinating agency, not an investigative one, pulling together information from many groups, providing it to the public, and indicating an avenue of attack against the Axis. The agency could be financed from the president's emergency funds, thereby avoiding undue publicity and congressional oversight.[27]

Although Brownlow recognized that charges would be made that the government was creating a propaganda agency to enhance administration powers and to perpetuate itself, the current danger was great enough to warrant such a risk. His proposal prompted Ickes to appoint a subcommittee of McNutt, Brownlow, and McCoy to prepare a report for the president.[28]

Considering the divergence of opinion among committee members regarding propaganda, the completed report was relatively simple. The subcommittee recommended the creation of an agency to work with the FBI, Justice, State, Navy, and War Departments to analyze and combat propaganda, "to fortify national morale," to create positive propaganda informing people of "the nature and direction of the American way of life," and to make known to all "the nature and sources of the present threats to their liberties, civil, economic, and political." The proposed federal agency, which closely resembled the later Office of War Information, was to consist of a committee of cabinet members to develop policies and programs, an advisory council of distinguished citizens, and a director. It was not, however, to interfere with or overlap the functions of any existing agency and was strictly informational. The report repeated McCloy's suggestion that the director should be a person with proven executive ability and experience in public relations and foreign affairs but without active partisan affiliations. Possible candidates included academics James B. Conant and James P. Baxter III and former New Hampshire governor John G. Winant. While pondering this report, Ickes received similar suggestions from Saul Padover, his assistant at the Interior Department.[29]

Although the committee members favored the creation of a federal morale and propaganda agency, their differences were by no means settled. The men associated with the military firmly believed that propaganda had more of an offen-

sive military function than a defensive domestic-morale role. Knox said that Americans were "the victims of constant propaganda from abroad" and should respond in kind. Every "totalitarian power has found one of its most effective weapons in . . . a 'ministry of information,'" and the United States needed "a formal, thoroughly organized, well-implemented bureau of public information [and] counterpropaganda." Brownlow and Ickes agreed but still emphasized domestic morale, Ickes adding that the lack of such an agency was like meeting "an attack without having an air defense." The issue of domestic versus foreign emphasis remained unresolved, however, as did the issue of military versus civilian control.[30]

Questions concerning the themes, ideology, and content of the proposed propaganda programs were largely ignored during the early meetings. Henry Stimson was the first person to raise these matters when he commented that "what we do and what we say must be nothing that is not true." The thorny issues of morality, ideology, and politics then entered the discussion. To Stimson the coming struggle was "a war between truthful methods supported by freedom of discussion . . . and the sinister kind of propaganda . . . supported by falsehood and terrorism." He reminded his colleagues that "our defense is the freedom of the press and freedom of discussion" and that in combating the Axis powers they had to avoid Nazi methods and "stand upon a spirit of aggressive truth on our side." Despite the tantamount importance of the issues to subsequent propagandists and to the agencies they created and operated, the committee failed to define any specific policy. Its only substantive accomplishment was the report forwarded to Roosevelt suggesting the creation of some sort of propaganda and morale agency.[31]

Having recently been reelected to a third term, Roosevelt was devoting considerable energy toward obtaining material and financial aid for Britain when the Ickes Committee report reached him on 28 November 1940. Thus with more important problems at hand, he did nothing in the way of implementation, much to the chagrin of Ickes, who felt there was no time for delay. Unbeknownst to Ickes, the president and Secretary of State Cordell Hull were carrying on negotiations with the British Broadcasting Corporation (BBC) to rebroadcast U.S. commercial programs to counter Nazi propaganda. Roosevelt agreed to such an arrangement, but the British found the CBS and NBC programs too neutral to serve their purposes. They did offer suggestions, however, on how American radio could serve their cause. Ickes's report meanwhile remained unread for weeks.[32]

The continued inaction of the president led to further private initiatives. In January 1941 adviser Ben Cohen delivered to Ickes a number of memorandums

prepared by the Committee on National Morale. The group, its work, and its membership were discussed at a 23 January cabinet meeting, where it was decided that $5,000 in unvouchered funds should go to the committee to prepare a plan for a proposed federal propaganda and morale agency. Ickes met the committee's leader Arthur Upham Pope in Washington, D.C., and commissioned the report, which was delivered on 21 February 1941.[33]

The lengthy study, *A Plan for a National Morale Service*, confirmed many of Ickes's fears regarding Nazi propaganda and again raised many of the same issues that had been discussed in the fall. The report claimed that through a coordinated program the Axis powers were already conducting "psychological warfare against America" and were counting on that weapon for victory. In face of such an attack, American morale was unsatisfactory. The experiences of Britain and France clearly showed that "routine and homespun morale policies" were "ineffective and even damaging to morale." France, for example, could have been saved had a morale service been created in 1938. The committee believed "that America is in this position, that already the American people are being to some extent undermined by propaganda." Lacking a propaganda service, the United States was bound for defeat "before the continuous, insidious, and highly skilled morale offensive which is being and will continue to be directed against us."[34]

The committee suggested avoiding Nazi methods, which were deemed "inappropriate to American character and . . . political ideas." The United States could not "profitably imitate the techniques of Nazi Germany"; they had to fight such methods, not adopt them. The committee also warned that the propaganda legacy of World War I—the cynicism and apathy of large numbers of Americans—meant that "a return to the propaganda techniques of the last war would precipitate a morale crisis." The nation needed a service that was "loyally and consistently democratic," that sought "to preserve, extend and realize the full implications of the democratic ideal," and that defended "essential freedoms" and "a dynamic interpretation of the ideal of democracy as a goal to be progressively realized." It should not control morale, as was the case in the dictatorships, but offer a free flow of information and ideas. Only military information should be restricted and then only temporarily. The service could provide a defense against enemy propaganda by strengthening "the foundations of confidence in free institutions."[35]

The committee report focused primarily on domestic morale issues but did stress that "a morale counter-offensive abroad" could be directed against the enemies of democracy although no indication of military participation was given. The campaigns could offer encouragement to neutrals and the victims of fascism

as well as hopes of "a just and permanent peace." To implement the program, the committee urged using the nation's psychologists and social scientists, historians, linguists, and specialists in foreign literature, drama, art, and folkways. The report closed by suggesting the creation of a National Morale Service.[36]

Many individuals within the administration who had different views on propaganda expressed them in criticisms of the committee plan, provoking an internal debate that continued until Roosevelt intervened months later. Opposition attacks indicated the depth of confusion and the lack of knowledge concerning propaganda, the stark lack of consensus, the ongoing fear of adverse public reaction, and the hesitancy to create or to give control of information to any agency, public or private.

Lowell Mellett of OGR, who initially believed that the Committee on National Morale was going to run the government propaganda program, was the harshest critic around whom additional opponents soon rallied. Mellett's views were known well in advance, and he quickly voiced opposition to anything that smacked of government propaganda because, as he told the president, there could be no "government propaganda operation on behalf of national policy" until such a policy was created. When the Committee on National Morale report began to circulate, Mellett was the first to warn of the potentially damaging consequences that the agency could have for the administration, the nation, and democracy in general. He simultaneously admitted he had no direct knowledge of the plan or of the work of the Ickes Committee, yet he told Ickes that he had visited with Pope "and from him obtained the impression of impracticality."[37] Furthermore, Mellett forwarded a note from an anonymous yet knowledgeable person who claimed that the plan could "lead to most unfortunate consequences for national morale and would reflect badly on any persons who might be responsible for supporting this committee." The entire group, the author wrote, "is composed largely of academicians, psychiatrists, market research people" and although it contained good names and people, most of its work, including the plan, was done by "second or third rate individuals who have nothing better to do." Mellett fully agreed with the assessment and bluntly informed Ickes of his opinion.[38]

Fearing that the entire idea of a federal morale and propaganda agency was in jeopardy because of criticism that could not fail to reach and influence the president, Ickes called two meetings to discuss opposition to the plan. The acrimonious sessions, and the correspondence that surrounded them, evidenced the broad gulf regarding propaganda. Mellett was asked to attend the meetings because of his influence with the president, but he balked. Ickes later described Mellett's attitude as one of "astounding indifference" toward propaganda based

on a lack of "any conception of what had been done along the same lines by the Germans or of what ought to be done here." He recalled that Mellett claimed that Americans, unlike Germans, "would not be told what to think" and that Hitler's methods were "no pattern for America."[39]

After reading the committee plan Mellett was still convinced that any operation should be only of "an advisory character"; nothing but confusion would result otherwise. He concluded that the entire concept was ill-timed, ill-conceived, and a recipe for political disaster, especially when considering the unclear state of foreign policy, strong isolationist and Republican opposition, and the unsettled nature of public opinion.[40] His response led Ickes to conclude that Mellett believed that "we do not need to either build up morale in our own people or do anything in the way of countering propaganda either at home or in the Americas." Ickes later wrote regarding Mellett that "it was all I could do to keep my temper and be reasonably courteous."[41]

Other government critics of the committee plan did not hesitate to express their views. Justice Department Solicitor General Francis Biddle, originally a supporter of the concept, wrote Ickes, after meeting with Mellett, that the proposed agency was superfluous, that it would create a negative impression with both the press and public, would be expensive, and would be difficult to coordinate and control. He doubted the need for a centralized federal agency in peacetime because the extent and the effect of propaganda was unknown. Furthermore, Biddle claimed, the most serious problem was not foreign propaganda but Congress and the isolationists. A "Morale Service would . . . smother and suppress this opposition," which though odious and troublesome, was legal and necessary. Biddle could not advocate such a course, nor could Attorney General Robert Jackson.[42]

Ickes was the government official most closely associated with the committee plan, but others heard criticisms as well. Secretary Knox received a letter from William Allen White questioning committee capabilities and warning Knox to "beware of psychologists."[43] John J. McCloy, previously the most ardent advocate of an offensive propaganda agency, was now ambivalent about the plan. He did write Biddle that something had to be done and done soon, as the nation was under attack. Yet he admitted that the plan was "so slight a step in the right direction (if that) as scarcely to be worth while."[44]

Ickes had attempted to rally support to defend the plan, and McCloy's defection must have counted as one of many heavy blows, especially given his early advocacy and his initial spirited defense of the committee plan. The assistant secretary of war was heavily involved in the early meetings because, in Ickes's words, "he knows more . . . and has better ideas than anyone else in the War

Department." In one stormy session when critics claimed that scarce national resources were needed to build conventional defenses and could not be diverted to morale agencies, McCloy had quickly responded that he shared that view but also strongly believed that the nation needed a propaganda agency as badly as it did airplanes. The loss of McCloy's support, and, by implication, that of the War Department, seriously hurt Ickes's cause.[45]

Ickes counterattacked as best he could with diminishing support. One steadfast ally was Arthur Pope. Sensing that critics of the plan were exaggerating both the scope and the scale of the agency, Pope attempted to clarify the committee's suggestions in a letter to Ickes, claiming that merely a morale service was proposed and that he "opposes vigorously and for specific reasons . . . any form of propaganda bureau." Despite the clarification the opposition remained unmoved.[46]

Among the individuals involved with the Ickes Committee and the morale-agency plan, none received more criticism or was more committed to the idea at the time than Ickes himself. Like McCloy, he was certain that Mellett's criticism was the most damaging. The OGR director had to be won over or silenced, and it was up to Ickes either to enlighten or convince him that his input and interference were unwarranted and unneeded. With diminishing enthusiasm, Ickes attempted to sway him over to his views on both the Committee on National Morale and propaganda in general. Concerning the former, Ickes contacted Mellett after receiving a strange, although positive, letter from Dr. Carl J. Friedrich of the Council for Democracy. Friedrich, Ickes told Mellett, had offered the full cooperation and support of the council and of the Committee on National Morale to the government, had endorsed the idea of a federal morale agency, and in a reversal of his earlier anonymous and critical appraisal of the plan that he had sent to Mellett, had now spoken highly of both groups to Ickes.[47]

On other issues, Ickes fully agreed with Mellett that Hitler's domestic propaganda methods were not applicable to the United States. Nonetheless, it seemed that Mellett had overlooked "the fact that Hitler's method of breaking down the morale of other people had proved to be pretty effective in Austria and Czechoslovakia, and Belgium and France." It was obvious, Ickes declared, that Mellett had not "understood the suggestions that have been made to the president" about a propaganda and morale agency and that it was never suggested by the Ickes Committee or anyone else that the Committee on National Morale run a propaganda program. In the attempt to convey the impression that the plan had wide administrative support, to which Mellett was the sole dissenter, Ickes explained that "a cabinet committee had met and drafted a report long before it had even heard of the Committee," a fact Mellett would have known had

he attended the November meetings. Ben Cohen, Ickes added, introduced him and Knox to Pope, and both men had been impressed by his work. A report from Pope's committee was commissioned by a second cabinet group set up by the president and, following its submission, the group made a recommendation similar to the first. "There the matter rests and apparently there the matter is going to rest," Ickes closed, "until we pay the same cost that France and other countries have paid for stupidity and inertia."[48]

With the various factions deadlocked, Roosevelt intervened to break the impasse. The president, who had just successfully orchestrated the passage of the Lend-Lease bill, approved the Ickes Committee November report in principle and asked the interior secretary to "go a bit further" and submit a plan of organization, a budget, and a list of names for a possible morale director and advisory committee. Ickes enthusiastically responded, suggesting that Ralph Ingersoll of *PM* or John J. McCloy serve as director. He then listed names of interventionists, internationalists, and members of the Committee on National Morale for an advisory council, adding that he "avoided putting on representatives of business to be balanced by representatives of labor." In addition, he wrote, "Religious and racial groups have not been taken into consideration. Politics have been entirely ignored."[49] Strangely, the president did not respond to the suggestions, and as the weeks passed it became apparent to Ickes that Roosevelt had changed his mind, probably because of the controversy that continued to swirl around the Committee on National Morale's plan. In utter frustration, Ickes requested that he be relieved from any further responsibility in the matter, a request that the president promptly approved.[50]

Although Pope continued to urge Ickes and Roosevelt to use the services of the Committee on National Morale and to create a morale agency, the influence of both Ickes and the committee gradually evaporated.[51] Ickes later complained to interventionist Herbert Swope that the military had not killed the concept, as Knox, Stimson, and McCloy favored it or some variation of it. "Lowell Mellett," he wrote, "was one obstacle, but I wouldn't have thought that he would be influential enough to defeat the formidable crowd of us who pressed upon the president for action." Although Ickes had first broached the topic with Roosevelt two years earlier and had "never worked on him with more determination in my life," he "got precisely nowhere at all." He made a vain appeal to the president in April to create a morale agency because "the isolationists were carrying on a planned campaign of defeatism" with "the administration . . . doing nothing to tell its side of the story." But his final plea, coming in September 1941, was a gloomy assessment of the state of American morale, in which he revealed his belief that the nation had waited too long. Ickes's work on propa-

ganda matters brought the topic to Roosevelt's attention but ended there. Sub-sequent developments were undertaken without Ickes's input.[52]

Strangely, OGR director Lowell Mellett subsequently came under attack for heading the office that many people thought was the very government propaganda agency he had so vehemently opposed. The criticism became so intense that he responded publicly in September 1941 that he was "weary of being charged with engaging in propaganda on the one hand, and weary of being urged to engage in propaganda on the other." Many people insisted "that we take up the tactics of Hitler and turn them to our own purpose," that we "out-Hitler-Hitler or out-gabble-Goebbels," but such tactics always failed. "The American people have been freely exposed to . . . every trick in the Berlin bag . . . and the net result . . . is nothing to make Berlin happy."[53]

Roosevelt did act between March and May 1941 to resolve the controversy, despite his earlier silence regarding Ickes's efforts. The president had publicly indicated his awareness of the fifth-column threat in a March radio address to nationwide Jackson Day dinners and again when proclaiming an unlimited national emergency on 27 May 1941.[54]

Moreover, even before the demise of Ickes's concept, the president had met with a new group of individuals and as a result had instructed William Bullitt, Harold Smith, and Wayne Coy, who in turn sought out McCloy, to draw up an executive order creating a bureau of civil defense. The decision followed similar suggestions made by Frances Perkins, Frank Knox, Henry Stimson, and Henry Wallace. Although Roosevelt had expressed renewed interest in a civil defense agency, he planned to delay a formal announcement until a suitable director was found, one acceptable both to the public and to the political opposition.

Wallace was put in charge of the search as well as the task of drafting an appropriate executive order. After speaking with Arthur Pope, Wallace sought out Coy, Smith, and McCloy and, much to his surprise, found that the trio had already written an order based on the unissued April 1939 draft executive order. Wallace also discovered the old differences concerning propaganda that had been encountered but left unresolved by the Ickes Committee. Wallace himself favored a blatant propaganda effort along the lines of the Nazi RMVP, as did McCloy and Knox, but Smith and Coy wanted a less extreme approach and pointed out that an agency on the Nazi model would not be possible, even if desirable, because it would require government direction of privately owned media. Roosevelt, after weighing both options, approved the latter view as more acceptable to the public and more politically expedient and offered the directorship of the office of civil defense to Fiorello LaGuardia as planned two years before. Even after this decision was made, however, the president delayed

issuing the executive order. Ickes recalled hearing him remark at a 4 May 1941 cabinet meeting that "the matter should be allowed to rest for two or three weeks longer," causing him to reflect that whoever was blocking action was "doing a thoroughly good job."[55]

Sensing that the political timing was correct and that his actions had public support, President Roosevelt issued Executive Order 8757 on 20 May 1941 creating the Office of Civil Defense under Mayor LaGuardia. He then asked Mellett, Ickes, and FFFC–member Ulric Bell to meet with LaGuardia "in regard to the whole subject of effective publicity to offset the propaganda of the Wheelers, Nyes and Lindberghs." Ickes refused, both because of Mellett's involvement and because he believed it was a mistake to put morale, civil defense, and propaganda activities together in one agency. Reflecting on past events, he hoped that some day he would "know why the president has so set his face against anything in the way of straightforward propaganda."[56]

The new OCD was to facilitate constructive civilian participation in the defense program and to sustain national morale. It was not to have a role in foreign propaganda. Roosevelt instructed LaGuardia to coordinate the hundreds of state, local, and nongovernmental volunteer civil defense organizations in their morale-building activities. The mayor favored the assignment as he was more interested in domestic morale than in propaganda, a task he intended to delegate to some as yet unnamed appointee.[57]

The president's creation of the Office of Civil Defense seemed to be a step in the right direction to many observers, yet LaGuardia's lack of interest in foreign propaganda immediately elicited criticism, most notably from columnists Drew Pearson and Robert Allen, who blasted OCD in their Washington Merry-go-Round newspaper column. Additional criticism came from cabinet members and from Eleanor Roosevelt. It soon became obvious to the president that OCD was not interpreted by many interventionists as an adequate response. To stem further criticism, Roosevelt created a separate Bureau of Facts and Figures (BFF) within OCD in July 1941. He disagreed, however, with LaGuardia's plan for dividing the bureau into three branches consisting of a speaker's bureau, an office to collect and analyze information and opinion from the news media, and a Foreign Information Service (FIS) to disseminate propaganda abroad. Roosevelt instead decided to separate domestic and foreign functions by removing the FIS from OCD, giving it to the new Office of the Coordinator of Information (COI) under William J. Donovan. From that point domestic and foreign propaganda diverged although each branch experienced similar difficulties from the same opposition, and each in turn failed to deal with fundamental political and ideological differences. Perhaps most important at the time, however, was that the

Bureau of Facts and Figures was not provided with any clear policy to direct its functions.[58]

Dissatisfaction over LaGuardia's performance as director of Civil Defense grew during the summer and fall, and he was unable to find a director for the new Bureau of Facts and Figures. James Conant, Frank Graham, and Archibald MacLeish, his early choices, initially declined although MacLeish later agreed to serve if the bureau were fully independent of OCD and if he were allowed direct access to the president. Under increased public scrutiny, Roosevelt was now willing to follow the lead of the people most intimately involved in propaganda matters. Listening to MacLeish, LaGuardia, and Samuel Rosenman, who in turn were influenced by journalist Robert Kintner, the president issued Executive Order 8922 on 24 October 1941 creating the Office of Facts and Figures (OFF) within OEM.[59] The OFF was to coordinate domestic radio broadcasts and provide the media with information on government departments, programs, and defense matters. In reality it was the domestic propaganda agency that President Roosevelt had always hesitated to create, and despite MacLeish's belief that OFF was to be comparable to Britain's Ministry of Information (MOI), Roosevelt always considered it little more than an advisory agency.[60]

Roosevelt's opinion regarding the role of the Office of Facts and Figures ultimately prevailed. The OFF was never comparable to Britain's MOI, nor was it an official propaganda agency despite such charges by critics, which were hotly denied by both MacLeish and LaGuardia. MacLeish stated that OFF confined its activities to the dissemination of accurate facts and figures, sought "increased public understanding of administration policy," and attempted "to ascertain the subjects on which the public appears misinformed" for prompt remedial action. In addition, and more important, OFF always followed the policy of "the 'strategy of truth' rather than the 'strategy of terror' . . . followed by the propaganda offices of the totalitarian states." If OFF did not imitate the Nazis, MacLeish and many like-minded individuals reasoned, it was therefore not a propaganda agency. What the Nazis did was propaganda; OFF did something else. According to OFF's Henry Pringle, "The Nazis employ psychological warfare to consolidate their own people, to divide proposed victims of aggression, and to destroy their will to resist." The Nazi " 'strategy of terror' must be combatted just as carefully as enemy tanks and planes," but with a strategy of truth.[61]

The philosophy of truth was the hallmark of OFF, and the later Office of War Information, and came to form the basis of one of three fundamental schools of thought governing American propaganda during World War II. Despite the presence of competing propaganda philosophies and doctrines and the lack of an official federal policy, the emphasis on the truth, as interpreted by the

leadership of the OFF and later of the OWI, was always claimed as the official American propaganda policy.

The membership, philosophy, and organization of the OFF reflected a particular ideological bent from the top levels down. Librarian of Congress, interventionist, liberal idealist, and poet Archibald MacLeish represented the ideology and was well suited for the directorship. He saw the war "as a revolution aimed at the destruction of the whole system of ideas, the whole respect for the truth, the whole authority of excellence which places law above force, beauty above cruelty, singleness above numbers." As an interventionist, he spent considerable time after 1938 advocating a response to the Nazis in defense of liberal democracy and civilization. To him the conflict was a moral crusade, a simple contest of good against evil, and he constantly encouraged Americans, Europeans, and Asians to fight the Axis powers and all perpetrators of inhumanity and aggression.[62]

When MacLeish began recruiting a staff, his idealism served as a beacon to individuals who wanted to fight Nazi ideology; the OFF provided the first opportunity for them to put their knowledge of the written and spoken word to effective use in government service. Henry Pringle later wrote that the effort was made to obtain people who were "highly skilled and experienced in the press, radio, and magazine fields." Although the OFF never totaled more than 291 employees before its abolition in July 1942, the stature of its membership was impressive and included interventionists and internationalists, liberals and conservatives, academics, businessmen, lawyers, journalists, publishers, and media and communications people. Over thirty-five OFF members later served in top positions in the OWI or the OSS.[63]

The OFF existed for barely nine months and accomplished little, due to a lack of direction and a coherent policy defining its functions. As a result, many of its members left for the COI and the FCC. An added factor in OFF's decline was its status as a defensive, morale-building propaganda agency: in McCloy's analogy, an antiaircraft gun of propaganda that reacted to attacks rather than launching its own. Yet the government did possess a foreign propaganda apparatus as of 15 July 1941 in the Office of the Coordinator of Information.[64]

In the eighteen months prior to American entry into the war, the government reacted to interventionist and isolationist pressures and moved toward creating an agency capable of using propaganda as a weapon. President Roosevelt had determined a need for some sort of federal organization to build domestic morale and to combat Nazi propaganda, yet fearing adverse public and political reaction, he hesitated to create such an agency. Instead, he encouraged two groups of government officials to study the issues, and although neither group,

nor the one private agency involved, developed an entirely satisfactory solution, they succeeded in bringing opinions concerning the dangers and usefulness of propaganda to the president's attention. Furthermore, their efforts succeeded in defining a government role, no matter how small and halting it was initially. The work of the various executive branch committees constituted the first serious federal venture into propaganda since World War I. While these groups debated the merits of defensive versus offensive propaganda, other groups labored to create a propaganda program directed solely toward Germany, using the methods they deemed most successful when used by the Nazis themselves.

4 · Taking the Offensive: The COI, 1941

President Franklin D. Roosevelt issued an executive order creating the Office of the Coordinator of Information and designating William J. Donovan as its director on 11 July 1941. The COI was a unique entity charged with two functions. The first was intelligence collection and analysis from all sources, including the armed forces, and dissemination of the information to the president and federal agencies. This practice in itself was not new, as many agencies, including the military services, the OGR, and the OFF, performed some of the same tasks. The second function was not explicitly spelled out, but it made COI distinct; it was to disseminate propaganda created from the intelligence to areas outside the Americas. Yet COI propaganda activities largely resulted from the broad interpretations given the executive order by Donovan, Robert Sherwood, and other top COI policymakers. Although forbidden to interfere with the duties of the military services or other government offices, the COI under Donovan's leadership took advantage of the vague wording of the order and broadly expanded its missions. By the time of Pearl Harbor, it was the only agency performing both propaganda and intelligence duties.[1]

The tasks performed by COI came under the vast rubric of unconventional or psychological warfare as defined in 1941. None of the activities had ever been used systematically before by the United States, yet to many COI members they were not only necessary but similar to the methods used by the Nazis with great success between 1933 and 1941. The emulation of alleged Nazi tactics, and indeed the very existence of COI, intensified the controversies within the nation, within the Roosevelt administration, and within the military over the role of government propaganda, over whether the activities should be overt, covert, or both, and over whether they should be conducted by military or civilian agencies, if practiced at all. Many people in COI, the military, and other agencies

such as OGR and OFF, although they were anti-Fascists, interventionists, and internationalists, realized that the activities proposed by Donovan and his agency represented a moral and ethical departure into territory Americans had never deliberately entered for long. Furthermore, many observers soon realized that great perceptual, political, and ideological gulfs existed between members of the various information and intelligence services and even among members within the individual services. The differences resulted in controversy and internecine conflicts that retarded American efforts for three years.

Donovan fully intended that the COI be the federal agency that practiced the psychological warfare techniques he believed were successfully used by the Nazis, methods that in summer 1941 the United States was wholly unprepared to perform. He created the COI with the cooperation of like-minded friends in the administration, in interventionist and internationalist circles, and in the British intelligence and propaganda services. Donovan apparently was not widely known as an interventionist-minded anti-Fascist prior to 1940, nor was he closely associated with propaganda affairs. As later critics pointed out, the opposite seemed to be true: he opposed the Nazis, but he appeared to be an admirer of their strength and efficient military organizations. Donovan's past, though revealing his political, philosophical, and ideological beliefs, provided only a few indications of the importance he later attached to psychological warfare.[2]

Born in Buffalo, New York, Donovan was an Irish Catholic, a lawyer, soldier, and politician who had received his education from Catholic Niagara University and Columbia University, graduating from the latter in 1908. Soon after entering private law practice as a partner in John Lord O'Brian's Buffalo firm, he joined the New York National Guard. In February 1916, as a representative of the Rockefeller Foundation, he traveled to London, Berlin, and Belgium, ostensibly to help arrange Belgian relief services although some people have speculated that he used the opportunity to make important intelligence contacts in Britain, France, Germany, and Belgium. Returning to the United States in June, Donovan answered the call for National Guard troops to help track down the Mexican bandit Pancho Villa. Shortly after the United States entered World War I, Donovan's unit, the New York Sixty-ninth Fighting Irish National Guard Regiment, was made a part of the famed Forty-second Rainbow Division and was sent to France in November 1917. The Fighting Irish suffered heavy casualties there, and Donovan was repeatedly decorated for bravery, eventually winning the Congressional Medal. By the time of the armistice, he was commanding the regiment as a full colonel.[3]

While on occupation duty in Germany after the armistice, he and Col. The-

Maj. Gen. William J. Donovan: *war hero, Wall Street lawyer, coordinator of information, and director of the Office of Strategic Services, 1942–1945. (U.S. Army, OWI Photo; reproduced at the National Archives)*

odore Roosevelt, Jr., a longtime friend, indicated an interest in intelligence and morale matters, discussing the creation of a patriotic, morale-boosting veterans' organization with the head of army intelligence, Maj. Gen. Ralph van Deman. The proposed organization later became the American Legion, which Donovan cofounded.[4]

Donovan was an avid and inquisitive traveler. After discharge from active duty in early 1919, he left for a year-long trip to Eastern Europe, Japan, and elsewhere in the Far East as a private investigator for Thomas Lamont, president of the New York–based J. P. Morgan banking firm. During his travels he visited Siberia, allegedly at the behest of Secretary of State Robert Lansing, where he observed White Russian forces in their struggle against the Bolsheviks in the Far East. He later submitted a written report to Lansing that was sent to Pres. Woodrow Wilson. After a further six months in Europe, he returned to New York City in 1920 to establish a law practice, counting Standard Oil of New Jersey and the Morgan and Hambrow banks as clients. In 1922 he entered politics, running unsuccessfully as the Republican candidate for lieutenant governor of New York. On the rebound, Donovan became the U.S. attorney for the Western District of New York. The following year he traveled abroad again, this time to Germany, where he met Adolf Hitler.[5]

As a capable attorney earning an estimated $500,000 per year and as a staunch Republican conservative and war hero, Donovan was a logical choice for public office and was appointed assistant U.S. attorney general by Pres. Calvin Coolidge in August 1924. He served one year on criminal cases before transferring to the antitrust division. Although controversy exists over how hard the wealthy corporate lawyer worked to bust trusts, apparently Donovan conscientiously did his job.[6]

Heavily involved in Republican party politics, Donovan wrote Herbert Hoover's speech accepting the 1928 nomination, revealing much of his conservative, laissez-faire ideology. He wanted the job of attorney general or secretary of war in the Hoover administration but was denied both posts, allegedly because he was an Irish Catholic. Embittered, he refused to take any job in the new administration and resigned from the Justice Department in December 1929 although he did support Hoover's candidacy in 1932. Throughout the 1930s Donovan practiced at his Wall Street firm, Donovan, Leisure, Newton and Irving, founded in 1929, representing many influential and wealthy clients on both sides of the Atlantic, including Winston Churchill. Yet according to one colleague, Donovan "devoted the minimum time to law practice, since he had no interest in accumulating a fortune, in making money for money itself. His interest was in world affairs." In 1932 Donovan again ran unsuccessfully for public

office, this time for governor of New York, becoming one of the many Republican victims of the Democratic political sweep that year.[7]

Donovan resumed traveling in the 1930s, largely on his own accord but often at the behest of business associates, legal clients, government leaders, and friends. In 1931 he visited war-ravaged Manchuria, recently conquered by Imperial Japan. Then in 1935 he sailed to Rome to visit Fascist dictator Benito Mussolini and the combat zone in Abyssinia, probably prompted by legal clients Standard Oil of New Jersey and Thomas Lamont, director of the Morgan Bank, the latter anxious about his institution's large investments in Fascist Italy and American public opinion regarding the Ethiopian war. Donovan met with Il Duce in December and discussed a wide range of topics, including American domestic politics and public opinion on the war in Ethiopia, volunteering that he agreed with Mussolini that neither Americans nor their government fully understood the Abyssinian situation. Donovan told the Fascist dictator that he could not "tell whether Roosevelt will be reelected [in 1936] but that the election will be decided on domestic issues unless something unusual happens in the foreign field." Personally unsympathetic to Roosevelt's domestic policies, Donovan told Mussolini that the president was popular among "the Left of Labor, the Left of the farmers and the great masses of those who want something for nothing," but economic recovery was coming "in spite" of the New Deal.[8]

Following his audience with Mussolini, Donovan was granted permission to enter both Libya and Abyssinia for fifteen days to examine the Italian military. He first met with Field Marshal Italo Balbo in Libya and then with Field Marshal Pietro Badoglio, who commanded Italian forces in Abyssinia; Donovan had met Badoglio during his visit to Buffalo in 1921. After a three-hour meeting Donovan returned to Rome, where he offered a flattered Il Duce his favorable impressions of the technical proficiency and health of Italian troops. According to his travel log, he immediately set sail for New York, arriving on 16 January 1936, but he probably stopped for further interviews elsewhere in Europe and in Great Britain although he left no written record.[9]

During the remainder of the decade Donovan practiced law, served as president of the American Bar Association, and took annual trips abroad. In May 1937 he visited Germany, in fall 1938 he toured the Sudetenland, Czechoslovakia, the Balkans, and Italy, visited the Fourth Army front on the Ebro River in Spain, and then returned to Germany as a guest of the Wehrmacht to watch army maneuvers in Nuremburg. On his return to America, he briefed U.S. Army Chief of Staff Gen. Malin Craig on what he had seen, in particular the new 88-mm antiaircraft gun.[10]

By early 1939 Donovan was coming into more direct contact with key inter-

ventionists and with people later involved in the COI, the OSS, and Britain's Secret Intelligence Service (SIS) and Political Warfare Executive (PWE), including, among others, Vincent Astor, Kermit Roosevelt, Nelson Doubleday, James P. Warburg, and David K. E. Bruce. On 28 January 1939, lawyer and international businessman Whitney Shepardson, a Century Club member and ardent interventionist, received a telegram from Lord Lothian, the future British ambassador to the United States. Lothian was visiting the country to examine American reactions to the recent Munich Pact and to meet with President Roosevelt. Lothian wired, "Reach NY eight o'clock Thursday evening on my way to Washington. Is there any chance of our dining together to discuss international situation?" Shepardson replied on 3 February and telegraphed Lothian again five days later:

> Regarding lunch tomorrow. It will be at the Broad Street Club at one o'clock in private room no. 7. . . . I have asked the following, . . . Allen Dulles—whom you do know. Geoffrey Parsons—Chief Editorial writer for the *New York Herald Tribune*; . . . Col. W. J. Donovan—formerly candidate for governor of New York. Also a lawyer. His personal record during the war was remarkable. Received every imaginable decoration for personal performance, and has since traveled to Europe almost every year, keeping in intimate touch with military people in the important countries. He came back from such a trip about four months ago.[11]

Although what transpired at this meeting is unknown, by March 1939, within thirty days of the luncheon, Donovan was again abroad, visiting civil-war-ravaged Spain. He made contact with Fascist forces and observed their weapons, tactics, and doctrine, probably at the request of Lord Lothian and British intelligence. Immediately following his Spanish tour, Donovan traveled to Nazi Germany, where he was again the guest of the Wehrmacht during annual army maneuvers in Nuremberg. In June and July he met with Ambassador Hugh Wilson in Berlin before going to France, Belgium, Holland, Scandinavia, and Britain. Whom he saw or spoke with once back in the United States is uncertain, but shortly after his return, war broke out in Europe.[12]

Seemingly eligible for government office because of his knowledge and contacts, Donovan nonetheless lacked a mission in September 1939. With reliable evidence scarce, he remains an enigmatic figure during this time. Although maintaining close contacts in British government and in legal and business circles, he was not an Anglophile. And while a member of several interventionist groups and a supporter of aid to Britain he was a friend of Robert E. Wood, the

leader of the America First Movement. In one area, however, it was certain that Donovan's ideas concerning intelligence and propaganda were reaching a higher degree of sophistication, especially after his return from Europe in 1939. He later told one historian that "the idea [of the COI] had been in the back of his mind for some years. . . . It was something the government should have recognized long before it did." Allen Dulles also later wrote that "in the thirties Donovan was convinced . . . that what we now call 'unconventional' or psychological warfare would have a major place in the battles of the future." Yet despite these claims, Donovan was not obviously or closely involved in such activities until at least mid-1940.[13]

President Roosevelt and *Chicago Daily News* publisher Frank Knox, who frequently corresponded with the president, did have Donovan on their minds during late 1939, both men thinking he possessed a special knowledge and an ability that could be of use to the administration. The two men discussed the possibility of placing Donovan in some post as early as December 1939. It is probable that Knox and Donovan, friends since the former's unsuccessful Republican candidacy for vice-president in 1936, were considering some type of psychological warfare organization prior to that time, perhaps in league with British officials. Knox wrote Roosevelt in December concerning the president's suggestion that a Republican be brought into the cabinet to make it more bipartisan, thereby blunting the opposition's criticism that Roosevelt was leading the nation toward a New Deal war. Knox was flattered that the president was considering him for the post of secretary of the navy, despite his past criticism of Roosevelt's domestic policies, and he suggested that the president name William Donovan secretary of war, an idea Knox had long entertained. Roosevelt responded that Donovan was an old friend from law school and that he wanted him in the cabinet "for his own ability" and "to repair . . . the great injustice done him by President Hoover in the winter of 1929," but he added that "two Republicans in charge of the armed forces might be misunderstood in both parties" and that the decision should wait until summer. In June 1940 Knox accepted the post of secretary of the navy, and Republican Henry Stimson became secretary of war.[14]

Knox did not forget Donovan, and their relationship became much closer in early July 1940, when the secretary-designate arrived in Washington, D.C., for Senate confirmation hearings. He later wrote his wife that Donovan was waiting for him when he arrived and acted as his legal adviser while he lived at Donovan's Georgetown townhouse for several weeks. During this time the two men spent considerable time together at luncheons, dinners, and receptions on

Secretary of the Navy Frank Knox. (Official U.S. Navy photograph; reproduced at the National Archives)

the yacht *Sequoia*, where members of the administration and the British government mingled freely.[15]

Donovan had other influential contacts in government and in Allied circles in addition to Knox, the most important at this stage being the head of the British Security Coordination (BSC), William Stephenson. Donovan had met Stephenson at New York City's St. Regis Hotel in June 1940, where the latter had suggested that Donovan visit England to study British intelligence and military establishments. Stephenson had many American contacts at this time, including President Roosevelt, with whom he had discussed intelligence matters in May; Nelson Rockefeller, the coordinator of Inter-American Affairs; and more important, Knox, who probably orchestrated the meeting between Stephenson and Donovan. Strangely, Stephenson later maintained that Donovan helped convince Roosevelt, Stimson, and Knox "of the 'possibilities of economic warfare,'" indicating that Donovan was "preparing 'far-reaching plans that would give him control over the administration of economic-warfare, secret service, and political and psychological warfare.'" Most evidence suggests, however, that it was Knox who contrived with Stephenson to introduce Donovan to Roosevelt.[16]

Knox's ever deeper involvement in psychological warfare matters came to the attention of other individuals in the government, in particular the president and Secretary of State Cordell Hull. Hull had expressed his concern to Knox about Nazi fifth-column activity in Latin America and suggested that a study be made of British anti–fifth-column methods as a way to stymie Axis subversion. Knox quickly put forward his friend's name, and soon after, Donovan was "unexpectedly called to the White House," where he met Roosevelt, Hull, Stimson, and Knox and was asked to travel secretly to England to "learn about Britain's handling of the Fifth Column problem." His further task was to determine whether British military strength and civil morale could withstand an expected Nazi invasion in the fall, as the president had been receiving increasingly pessimistic reports from his representatives in Britain.[17]

Donovan was to act as Roosevelt's secret eyes and ears, gathering information and establishing contacts with British psychological warfare and intelligence experts. His itinerary was carefully arranged by Knox and Lord Lothian to ensure that he not only learned as much as possible but that he also was introduced to all the right people. Donovan boarded an air clipper for England on 14 July 1940 and completed a whirlwind two-week series of meetings with the king and queen, Prime Minister Churchill, SIS/MI-6 chief Stewart Menzies, Royal Navy intelligence chief Rear Adm. John H. Godfrey, and scores of other officials. Topics discussed included intelligence, propaganda, and Nazi fifth-column

activities. At Knox's behest as editor and owner of the *Chicago Daily News*, Donovan was joined in London by journalist Edgar A. Mowrer before returning to the United States.[18]

Donovan learned much from his travels and integrated the knowledge with his own developing ideas concerning the value of psychological warfare. After meeting with members of both houses of Congress and with several cabinet members, he reported to Roosevelt and Knox at Hyde Park on 9 August that fifth-column activities were an "important factor in modern warfare" and that the Allies should take steps to combat it and "develop it as an offensive weapon." He turned his findings over to Mowrer, who wrote a series of articles on the fifth column for the *New York Times* later that month. The articles were later printed in pamphlet form at Roosevelt's request as *Fifth Column Lessons for America*, with an introduction by Knox and with Donovan as coauthor. During a later rail trip through New England with Roosevelt, Donovan elaborated on his earlier reports and told the president that he was certain the British would hold out, despite pessimistic reports from Ambassador Joseph Kennedy, and that the United States must help, at least with supplies. Thoroughly convinced of the seriousness of the Nazi threat, Donovan began to speak out publicly for rearmament, the destroyer-for-bases deal, aid to Britain, and for combating the Nazi fifth column.[19]

Roosevelt's high opinions of Donovan's knowledge and usefulness as an unofficial government envoy were more than confirmed, and Donovan was again asked by the president in November 1940, after urging by Lord Lothian and other British officials, to undertake another fact-finding trip to the Balkans and the Mediterranean. Donovan left Baltimore for Bermuda on 17 December 1940 where he met Stephenson, who accompanied him to London for a meeting with Churchill. Donovan then began a four-month tour with sixteen stops where he met a score of monarchs, soldiers, and statesmen.[20]

Donovan returned with a wealth of new information that, when combined with the intelligence gathered the previous summer, confirmed his belief in the value and efficacy of psychological warfare and the need for the United States to respond immediately to Axis propaganda. He forcefully pressed his views on Roosevelt, Knox, and Harry Hopkins, expressing "the extraordinary importance of psychological and political elements in planning and executing national policies," having seen the results of Axis methods in Europe. The Nazis, he explained, "were making the fullest use of threats and promises, of subversion and sabotage, and of special intelligence." He claimed that "they sowed dissension, confusion and despair among their victims and aggravated any lack of faith and hope." The Allies, he continued, were not "fighting this new and im-

portant type of war on more than the smallest scale. . . . Defenses . . . were feeble," and efforts toward "carrying the fight to the enemy were pitifully inadequate." He dwelt on successful Nazi techniques and emphasized that Americans should "fight with the same weapons." Donovan then suggested the creation of an agency to carry out "five special functions: open or white propaganda; secret or black psychological warfare; sabotage and guerrilla warfare; special intelligence; and strategic planning." President Roosevelt listened intently but "neither definitely endorsed or definitely rejected" his proposals.[21]

Word of Donovan's increasing stature as an authority on psychological warfare matters and as an administration insider who had the ear of Roosevelt, Knox, and Stimson soon became grist for the Washington rumor mill. Moreover, his suggestions for a comprehensive psychological warfare agency with military aspects began to alarm members of the U.S. Army. Gen. Sherman Miles, chief of the Military Intelligence Division, War Department General Staff, wrote to Chief of Staff Gen. George C. Marshall in April that such "a super-agency controlling all intelligence would appear to be very disadvantageous, if not calamitous," in the War Department's view.[22]

Despite the military's uneasiness with his activities and the lack of movement on Roosevelt's part, Donovan pushed his ideas about psychological warfare. He viewed Knox as one of his strongest supporters and as a man capable of impressing Roosevelt with the importance of his theories. Donovan took great pains to keep the secretary of the navy informed of the evolution of his thinking, writing Knox that intelligence operations were one of the "most vital means of national defense and should be directed by a presidential appointee responsible only to the commander-in-chief. The operations should be financed through a secret fund with expenditures "made solely at the discretion of the President." Donovan continued, "Modern war operates on more fronts than battle fronts," and the nation should intercept mail, cables, and radio communications and use "propaganda to penetrate behind enemy lines" to actively conduct "subversive operations in enemy countries."[23]

Knowledge of Donovan's ideas and expertise spread quickly among other members of the Roosevelt administration involved in propaganda issues. In May 1941, for example, Donovan was introduced to a committee established in March and consisting of Stimson, Knox, and Jackson to examine morale and propaganda matters. After discussing with them the idea of creating an intelligence agency with propaganda and subversive functions and after considerable contact with John J. McCloy, Robert Sherwood, John G. Winant, Vincent Astor, and the director of Royal Navy Intelligence Rear Adm. John H. Godfrey, Donovan expanded his ideas to stress "the psychological warfare element in

modern warfare and the vital importance of radio as a weapon." Winant, in concurrence with the committee, urged Roosevelt to accept the plans, prompting the president to encourage Donovan to outline his proposal in more detail. Donovan's subsequent report, "Memorandum of Establishment of Service of Strategic Information," reached the president in early June.[24]

Donovan's memorandum formed the philosophical foundation for the Office of the Coordinator of Information and the later Office of Strategic Services. It was written with the aid of his British supporters, William Stephenson, David Eccles, Rex Benson, John Godfrey, and Ian Fleming, a group that underestimated Donovan's knowledge of psychological warfare and overestimated his influence with President Roosevelt. The memorandum, nonetheless, though showing British input, encapsulated Donovan's thoughts to that date.[25]

Primarily, Donovan stressed that the United States lacked a capable intelligence organization, a characterization that included the military intelligence agencies, which to date had demonstrated that they were too small and parochial to obtain the amounts of "accurate, comprehensive, long-range information needed for strategic planning." He therefore proposed creating a new, comprehensive, and centralized intelligence agency to include military personnel and "specialized trained research officials in the relative scientific fields." In addition to emphasizing the need for intelligence gathering, Donovan identified a threat that the nation had to meet: "the psychological attack against the moral and spiritual defenses of a nation," in which "the most powerful weapon is radio." It had been "effectively employed by Germany" and could be perfected by the United States. Aware of the latent bureaucratic jealousy within the military services and the government, Donovan suggested that the agency be configured so as not to encroach on services performed by other agencies and that it should be responsible directly to the president. To ensure that the new office met everyone's needs, it would be assisted in its work by an advisory panel of representatives from the federal departments and military services with whom it shared major concerns.[26]

The early June delivery of Donovan's memorandum to the president was fortuitous. Roosevelt had just created the Office of Civil Defense weeks before and was now facing increased criticism because that agency lacked a propaganda capability. As he mulled over the idea of a Foreign Information Service as part of a Bureau of Facts and Figures within OCD, Donovan's memorandum surfaced, providing him with a timely solution. The FIS could fit neatly within Donovan's proposed psychological warfare agency. Roosevelt moved rapidly and arranged a conference between Donovan and adviser Ben Cohen to draft an executive order to create an agency to implement Donovan's ideas. At this 15 June 1941

meeting, Donovan first proposed that Roosevelt's speechwriter, Robert E. Sherwood, head the overseas propaganda branch of the organization since he was reportedly anxious to be on Donovan's staff. Pressures to name Donovan head of the new agency came from all sides, including Roosevelt's cabinet, and from Stephenson, Fleming, Godfrey, and Sir William Wiseman, the former British intelligence chief in the United States during World War I and a close friend of Donovan's. Despite signs of growing opposition from within the State Department and from the military services, the executive order creating the Office of the Coordinator of Information was issued on 11 July.[27]

The general wording of the order enabled Donovan to implement his ideas fully and to create a powerful psychological warfare agency. He proposed initiating "an effective psychological counterattack . . . against the Axis" through a comprehensive and self-sufficient psychological warfare agency. His "basic idea was to beat the Germans at their own game." As successfully demonstrated by the Nazis, the first step was to demoralize the enemy prior to armed attack. Vast quantities of intelligence would show enemy strengths, weaknesses, and vulnerabilities. Following analysis, the information would be used against the enemy in "a continuous propaganda counter offensive" combined "with a covertly-conducted campaign of subversion and sabotage." Finally, commandos would be unleashed "raiding, seizing or destroying as a prelude to . . . invasion." Donovan planned to implement the strategy with an agency consisting of intelligence, counterespionage, research and analysis, sabotage, commando, and propaganda sections.[28]

The COI needed a full complement of talented and capable people to accomplish its unique mission; during summer 1941, therefore, staffing the agency took top priority. One of the first recruits was playwright and White House speechwriter Robert E. Sherwood, a man suggested to Donovan by both Harry Hopkins and President Roosevelt to lead the Foreign Information Service. Donovan and Sherwood had already communicated about possible recruits in mid-June. Within a year, however, the two men, with such different perceptions and backgrounds, changed being close colleagues to bitter enemies, largely over the ideological issues surrounding propaganda. Sherwood proved a controversial appointee, who, according to his critics, was a poor choice for the FIS director because of his strong, almost blinding admiration for Franklin Roosevelt and for the New Deal. He was further chided for his idealism, liberalism, simple patriotism, and, to some critics, astoundingly naive view of America's position in the world.[29]

Born in 1896 to a New York family known for its artistic abilities, Sherwood attended Harvard University. During his senior year the country entered World

Robert E. Sherwood, interventionist, renowned playwright, Roosevelt's speechwriter, and director of the Overseas Branch, OWI, 1942–1944. (OWI Photo; reproduced at the National Archives)

War I and, having been declared unfit by the U.S. Army due to his height, he went to Canada and joined the Black Watch Regiment. He fought at Arras and Amiens, was gassed at Vimy Ridge, and was severely wounded in both legs. After his recovery and return to the United States he began a career as a journalist and playwright, writing nine plays in ten years, the most successful being *Abe Lincoln in Illinois*, which opened to critical acclaim in 1936.[30]

During the mid-1930s Sherwood became increasingly concerned with European events, especially the perceived threat to the peace posed by Nazi Germany and the Soviet Union. He was profoundly affected by events in Austria and Czechoslovakia in 1938 as described in G. E. R. Gedye's *Fallen Bastions*, which filled him "with such desire for retribution" that he could not rest until he helped "bring the . . . criminals to justice." He was more convinced by September 1939 that "Hitlerism was as great a menace to the United States as it was to

any free country of Europe" and that "if we failed to help . . . we should be helpless to oppose it." That fall he joined William Allen White's committee seeking repeal of the Neutrality Acts and, as president of the Dramatists Guild, "urged that writers use their pens as a means for propaganda against Hitler." The combined shocks of the Nazi-Soviet Pact, the Polish invasion, and Charles Lindbergh's isolationist speeches proved to him "that Hitlerism was already powerfully and persuasively represented in our own midst." Like many people, Sherwood had viewed the Soviet Union as a bulwark against fascism, a role abdicated by the Western democracies bent on appeasement. The Nazi-Soviet Non-Aggression Pact of August 1939 shattered his illusions, however, and the Russo-Finnish war that winter convinced him that there was no significant difference between the two totalitarian powers.[31]

Sherwood rapidly sought out the individuals on both sides of the Atlantic who were organizing themselves to battle the dictatorships. He became an interventionist and an advocate of Clarence Streit's Union Now movement and offered his services to President Roosevelt, through Harry Hopkins, in January 1940, the night after attending a White House screening of the film version of *Abe Lincoln in Illinois*. Sherwood had long admired Roosevelt and had written journalist Walter Winchell during the Munich Crisis that "we now have a President who has more strength, more wisdom, more political skill and down-right sense than all the 'statesmen' of Europe and Asia put together." Imagine, he wrote, how different events in Munich would have turned out if "the voice of democracy (and civilization) had been Roosevelt's instead of Chamberlain's. . . . People everywhere look to the United States and Roosevelt as the sole hope of the human race."[32]

A passionate man, Sherwood soon committed his literary talents to the cause of freedom. His first effort, *There Shall Be No Night*, was a play describing the Soviet war against Finland. It opened in New York's Alvin Theater in late April 1940 and was the greatest critical and financial success of his career. Many noted luminaries attended the opening night festivities, including William Donovan, who met Sherwood for the first time. Thereafter, Sherwood devoted his energy and talents solely to interventionist activities.[33]

The success of Sherwood's play, his literary talents, and his high public profile as an interventionist ensured his inclusion in groups formed by people concerned about Axis aggression. In May 1940 William Allen White asked Sherwood to join the Committee to Defend America by Aiding the Allies, which he did, but he later found the philosophy of Francis P. Miller's Century Group, the forerunner of the Fight for Freedom Committee, more to his liking, joining that group in April 1941. Following the publication of his "Stop Hitler Now" ad in

June 1940 and after the publication of a newspaper article in the *New York Times* in July, Roosevelt sought him out. During a meeting with Hopkins, Sherwood agreed to help with the president's upcoming reelection campaign. In October he wrote a well-received Columbus Day address for the president and from that point on became a White House speechwriter. He was serving in this capacity when his name was suggested to Donovan by Roosevelt and Hopkins as a possible leader for FIS. The president was convinced of his writing talents and of his suitability for propaganda work, later writing Gen. Douglas MacArthur that "my old friend, Robert Sherwood . . . was largely responsible for the organization of our psychological warfare activities in this war."[34]

In his capacity as the director of FIS and as a deputy director of COI, Sherwood suggested many recruits for both his branch and for the agency as a whole. Donovan allowed Sherwood an amazing degree of latitude and independence to hire his own people, preferring to concentrate his own efforts on filling other COI positions concerned with intelligence gathering, commando work, and research and analysis. Because the COI was new and had been created in great haste, both men quickly sought people from their own immediate social and professional circles whom they trusted, largely from outside the federal civil service. They employed friends, friends of friends, business and professional associates, and people who through their prior writing, speaking, interventionist, internationalist, and professional activities had indicated a dislike of the Nazis and a proclivity for propaganda work. Perhaps most striking, the membership of the COI drew heavily from the rolls of the internationalist and interventionist groups active since the late 1930s. People were hired for all levels of the agency on referral or on the basis of brief five-minute interviews. Although the process was later criticized, it did result in the gathering of an amazing group of talented people in a very short time. The recruits included idea men and creative men, individuals with a background in business, advertising, broadcasting, or journalism; researchers, writers, journalists, foreign correspondents, and academics knowledgeable about world affairs, politics, psychology, economics, and history; administrators with financial, legal, or business backgrounds; managers with the ability to operate large organizations; and technicians who had the know-how to work the equipment necessary for dissemination of propaganda.

Donovan's earliest recruits came from his large circle of social, professional, and political acquaintances and generally were wealthy Ivy League–educated males—lawyers, intellectuals, academics, businessmen, or financiers. Most of them were internationalists and interventionists long before the war started, had been active in such affairs for years, and were Republicans and Protestants, usually Episcopalians.[35]

Robert Sherwood, like Donovan, began recruiting for the Foreign Information Service before the executive order creating COI was even issued. As Thomas Troy has written, however, many people inherently distrusted propaganda and initially declined FIS employment until the United States entered the war, preferring to leave such work to "eager interventionists and those especially affected by Nazism," such as the people derisively referred to as "Jewish scribblers" by the Nazis. Sherwood was aware of such an attitude, but he did not consider participation in an interventionist group or alien status to be a liability; on the contrary, he considered it one of many important prerequisites. He was also not averse to hiring Jewish refugees, adherents to left-wing philosophies, or other emigrés, not only because they harbored a fanatical hatred of fascism but also because they had the language, literary, political, and cultural skills the FIS needed.

Unlike Donovan, Sherwood purposely avoided hiring people from the foreign service, the military, the civil service, and individuals with elite academic, legal, financial, and business credentials. Instead he hired the foreign correspondents who had written of Nazi propaganda successes in Europe, other film and print media people, and writers, "men who were both comfortable with words, and well acquainted with foreign languages and European governments." Thus the FIS came to include a significant number of people who possessed the necessary literary and communications skills to produce and project American propaganda abroad.[36]

Sherwood realized that emigrés had a rich source of knowledge of European culture and events and that often they were fanatically anti-Nazi. He therefore readily took advantage of the abundant supply of refugees in the United States, enlisting the services of Raoul de Sales and Eve Curie of France, Max Ascoli of Italy, and Carl J. Friedrich, Hans J. Meyer, and Hermann Rauschning of Germany. In order to find qualified personnel and to skirt civil service hiring criteria that required federal employees to be citizens, a dummy corporation called Shortwave Research was created in October 1941. Its employees, although doing propaganda work for the FIS, were not civil servants. John Houseman, like Sherwood, was especially adept at hiring alien media people, eventually recruiting Ascoli; German-born actor Stefan Schnabel of the Mercury Theater; Lewis Galantiere; Franz Hollering; French surrealist, Communist and poet Andre Breton; and the former editor of *Paris Soir*, Pierre Lazareff.[37]

Their efforts paid off handsomely. By January 1942 Sherwood had recruited 260 people for the FIS and had made requests for funds to employ 928 more. The flurry of COI recruitment, although not widely publicized, did catch the attention of the nation. Houseman wrote that "personnel were being recruited in

such numbers and of such quality that newspapers began to write about the most mysterious office in Washington" and "surmised that a propaganda bureau was being prepared." By 5 September 1941 COI employed 71 people, a number that grew to 152 by the end of the month and to 224 by mid-October. COI asked the Bureau of the Budget, which had originally earmarked funds for 70 people, for appropriations to pay a projected 1,131 employees by mid-1942.[38]

As the initial recruits were obtained and assimilated, Donovan and Sherwood set out to form a workable structure. The COI, according to Donovan's scheme, reflected his penchant for military organization, strict compartmentalization, and rigid chains of command. His most trusted personal associates were placed in control of the five mutually supporting branches: Foreign Nationalities, Special Activities (subdivided into SA/B and SA/G sections), Visual Presentation, and Research and Analysis (R&A). The services rendered by these branches were crucial, Donovan believed, for the proper functioning of the fifth branch, the FIS.[39]

Donovan and Sherwood agreed on the potential of propaganda and made the operations of the Foreign Information Service a top COI priority. The branch received more funds than any other in COI's first budget and was fully entrusted to Sherwood's abilities, oversight, and judgment. Yet this loose administrative control later became a primary cause of friction between the two men and one of many factors leading to the demise of COI.[40]

The FIS had multiple functions. It prepared and implemented programs for the dissemination of information to foreign countries through radio and print media, analyzed foreign propaganda, and prepared counterpropaganda in the form of facts for countries abroad. It was charged with the American program for the truthful dissemination of propaganda, or "information services" as Sherwood euphemistically called them, worldwide.[41]

Radio was the primary and most effective means of dissemination for FIS, capable of reaching a wide audience at low cost. According to Sherwood, "Shortwave radio is a vital strategic weapon, political and military in character," which must be used "with emphasis on the fact that the U.S.A. is speaking to the world with unanimity." Yet the Foreign Information Service, until the founding of the Voice of America (VOA) in January 1942, lacked transmitters to broadcast propaganda except through private companies who used FIS materials on a take-it-or-leave-it basis. Although such an arrangement calmed private fears of government censorship, it was unsatisfactory to Donovan, who wrote President Roosevelt in early 1942 requesting permission to purchase or lease all shortwave transmitters for the duration of the war and to build thirty more. Roosevelt con-

curred, and by fall 1942 the federal government controlled the fourteen stations capable of shortwave broadcasting for the use of VOA.[42]

The FIS organization resembled a radio and film studio that had been combined with newspaper, printing, and advertising agencies. By November 1941 the office had the basic form it kept for the remainder of the war, consisting of five divisions and a Planning Board. The largest section was the Radio News and Features Division, under Joseph Barnes in New York City, Irving Pflaum in Washington, D.C., and Morris Gilbert in London. The group monitored enemy broadcasts, processed news, and prepared feature materials and commentaries on the American view of world events for private radio, Morse broadcasters, and the VOA.[43]

The Radio Production Division, under John Houseman in New York City, supported the Radio News and Features Division, creating foreign language programs based on information it provided. Its first broadcast was made in October 1941 in Czech, and by mid-November 1941 the division was producing programs in fifteen languages.

The Radio Technical Division, under Murray Brophy, provided assistance to private radio companies and set up the physical facilities to link FIS to broadcasters through land lines and the FIS Bronze Network.

The Pictures and Publications Division, under Edward Stanley, was established in October 1941 to spread propaganda in eighteen languages via pamphlets, leaflets, posters, paintings, cartoons, books, magazines, newsreels, letters, stickers, labels, phonograph records, films, and photographs. It printed propaganda messages on everything from paper cups, notebooks, cards, blotters, and paper matches to packets of cigarettes, seeds, needles and thread, soap, chocolate, and vitamin pills.[44]

The Outpost Division, established in early 1942 under Viking Press owners Harold Guinzburg and James Linen, collected intelligence, distributed propaganda, and performed troop morale-building activities from fourteen locations worldwide. The majority of outpost activities consisted of public relations and information programs directed toward U.S. service personnel, neutrals, and Allies.[45]

An organization such as FIS that performed so many different functions needed skilled coordination and coherent plans. All operations were organized by a Planning Board in Washington, D.C., which created directives for each region served. Sherwood originally intended that the individuals who made the plans would implement them; however, it was soon apparent that policy formulation was a full-time and difficult job, as was executing the policy. Furthermore, FIS lacked cooperation from other agencies and a separate intelligence-gathering

section. As a result, plans made in Washington were rarely followed by the New York City operations center, and, by May 1942, the Planning Board collapsed in one of the first of many administrative debacles that plagued the agency.[46]

The COI was fully operational by the time of the Japanese attack on Pearl Harbor in December 1941. It was becoming increasingly apparent by that time, however, that major operational difficulties remained to be ironed out and that major philosophical differences existed within the organization and between COI members and other government agencies. The differences, stemming from a variety of factors, were not only hampering the effectiveness of COI but also were threatening its very existence just months after its formation.

Despite ominous signs on the horizon, several factors held the COI together for nearly a year, by which time the foundations of the American propaganda apparatus were firmly established. Although enormous differences existed, the top-level COI leaders shared some outlooks and opinions regarding democracy, the United States, and American society as well as the proper role of individuals in government and of government in the lives of its citizens.

Despite personal ideologies and beliefs, the top COI members were patriots, singularly devoted to the defense of the nation and its system of government and to the values, traditions, and processes they believed it represented. Although many critics later claimed that propaganda agencies harbored Fascists, Communists, and other political extremists, the views of the COI membership did not initially interfere with the main goal of defending the United States through the use of propaganda as a defensive and offensive weapon. COI members were clearly anti-Fascists who, while exhibiting varying degrees of anti-Nazi fervor, realized the seriousness of the danger and the probable ramifications of a Nazi victory. Although some members admired aspects of German military efficiency and organization and although most considered the Nazi propaganda machine the model of an effective psychological warfare system, they despised the Nazis and all they stood for.

Moreover, the vast majority of the top COI policymakers were well-known internationalists and interventionists, people who maintained an active, public, and private interest in world affairs throughout their adult and professional lives. As such, and for years in some cases, they staunchly opposed policies favoring isolation, neutrality, and appeasement. They favored providing economic, diplomatic, or military aid to the Allies between 1939 and 1941, a more forward American role in foreign affairs, and an increased and permanent leadership role for the United States before, during, and after the war.

COI members shared the belief in the mass use of propaganda, either as a military weapon or as a diplomatic tool. Most of them had witnessed Nazi prop-

aganda in action and perceived that American efforts were unsophisticated by comparison. Convinced that propaganda had enormous potential, many members also realized that it could not alone produce a victory. A mammoth effort was necessary to reach all audiences, at the right times and with the right methods. Regardless of their individual beliefs on the role of government in human affairs, COI members saw the government as the only entity with the resources to run such an operation successfully, if only temporarily. Finally, they felt that efforts to date had failed to produce an agency capable of meeting the threat. At that point, however, the agreement ended, and despite the attitudes shared by the majority of COI members, far more crucial differences separated them.[47]

5 · The Self-destruction of COI, 1941–1942

Within weeks of the formation of the COI and through fall and winter 1941 and 1942, top policymakers began to perceive significant differences among members concerning the agency's guiding philosophy and the best methods to organize and operate an American psychological warfare program. During the prewar years, as future propagandists watched the Nazi system and worked frantically to raise consciousness and compel federal actions, the political and ideological dissimilarities seemed unimportant. The difficult task of establishing a capability to meet the Nazi threat was the top priority. Hammering out a coherent doctrine and propaganda policy was interpreted by many people as a secondary task that would solve itself; in any event, it could wait. The longstanding unresolved issues resurfaced after the creation of COI, however, causing rifts at all levels and alienating many members, especially those belonging to the FIS. As Edmond Taylor pointed out, "The internal conflicts . . . prevented the emergence of any clear doctrines or ideology." "One group," he later wrote, "was horrified at the crude way of the other groups. Sometimes we wouldn't admit we were doing propaganda at all."[1]

Already beset by internal divisions, the COI also faced numerous attacks from the outside. Critics who had been waiting in the background now stepped forward from the military services, the State Department, the FBI, the Bureau of the Budget, and the Office of the Coordinator of Inter-American Affairs (CIAA) to charge in unison that Donovan's agency was a dangerous rival, an unnecessary duplication of effort, and simply superfluous. President Roosevelt failed to provide a clear federal propaganda policy and took no new actions concerning the matter until spring 1942 when the impasse threatened to create damaging political scandals and public outrage. COI did not survive the neglect by the chief executive or the assaults of its rivals. Although the foundations for

a psychological warfare campaign against the Axis powers were established by mid-1942, an actual offensive capable of producing results had yet to start.

The internal COI disputes were evident at the top levels, particularly between Donovan and his deputy director Robert Sherwood. The two men not only had fundamentally opposing definitions of propaganda but also differed in their basic philosophical and political outlooks. The employment policies followed by COI, which emphasized recruiting friends, professional associates, and acquaintances, meant that Sherwood's philosophy was shared by the majority in the FIS while Donovan's was supported by those in the remaining COI branches. The differences eventually developed into fundamental and irreconcilable incompatibilities that prevented COI members from working together smoothly.

The backgrounds and ideologies shared by the majority of the people in the Donovan-controlled COI branches led them to favor using propaganda in either covert or overt forms to support military operations as part of a comprehensive psychological warfare campaign. Such activities needed strict regulation and control, which they believed was possible only under a military- or paramilitary-styled organization. Total war, and the necessity of defending democracy against the most powerful antidemocratic forces yet seen in world history, demanded that the openness as well as the ethical and moral considerations characteristic of liberal democracies needed to be temporarily relaxed or even suspended to ensure an ultimate victory. Donovan's faction was heavily influenced by their perception of Nazi expertise, demonstrated during the previous decade in Europe and America; they fully intended to use the same tactics against the Nazis. Although many members admired Nazi efficiency, their intended emulation of enemy methods and techniques did not stem from pro-Fascist sympathies but from the realization that the United States was far behind in all propaganda-related matters and needed to catch up quickly. Therefore, enemy methods, which they perceived as the most advanced, became the guide.

Republican and politically conservative, Donovan's recruits tended not to support Roosevelt's views of the role of government or his New Deal domestic policies and viewed the programs as antibusiness, antiwealth, and socialistic, boosting the common man over traditional elites. They favored ordered, clearly established, closely controlled, secure, and well-defined organizations and aggressive and activist methods of operation as found in the military and in commerce and believed in the concept of an overriding and steadfast loyalty to the leader and the organization. Donovan was the COI to these individuals, and his philosophy was the only one by which to conduct the nation's psychological warfare program. Although Donovan had once said that "the war was a global

struggle for liberation. . . . A people's war, a fight for freedom against slavery, and [for] freedom," these views did not accurately reflect his hard-bitten proposals on how that war should be fought and victory obtained, especially after he had received Roosevelt's approval to form the COI.[2]

Overwhelmingly Republican and politically conservative, Donovan's philosophy had not changed since he had written "Memorandum for Strategic Service Information." To him propaganda was one part of a comprehensive psychological warfare program that "consisted of *all means*, physical as well as moral, which could be used to break the will of the enemy." Rather than being just an educational device "to condition the minds of peoples to democracy," or "preaching the American way of life." Donovan considered propaganda foremost to be a weapon, "an instrument to baffle and bother the enemy" as an adjunct to military operations." One critic later claimed, as did many FIS officials, that Donovan had no real interest in propaganda beyond this narrow role and that he was always more interested in intelligence gathering and in espionage and sabotage operations. He never gave the FIS the proper attention or emphasis that it deserved; and, as Sherwood and his staff frequently complained, he merely wanted to use the activities of FIS as a front to mask covert COI endeavors.[3]

The doubts harbored by FIS members concerning Donovan's beliefs were largely exaggerated and incorrect. From Donovan's perspective, the COI performed many duties in which propaganda was a small, yet crucial, part. His interest in psychological warfare in general stemmed not from his seeming fixation on intelligence gathering and sabotage activities but from his longstanding interest in propaganda and morale matters. He frequently repeated his operational plans, which began with the gathering and analysis of intelligence. "Propaganda, as the 'arrow of initial penetration,' " was the first operational phase, followed by "special operations in the form of sabotage, fifth column work and other types of subversion." Next came "the commando raids and the harassing guerrilla tactics and uprisings behind the lines," serving as part of the "softening-up" process for invasion by conventional forces. The processes were interdependent; none could be entirely effective alone. As for using FIS activities as a screen for covert activities, Donovan admitted as much to Roosevelt in October 1941, believing this tactic to be legitimate according to his overall psychological warfare theory. Such revelations, however, only tended to confirm FIS suspicions.[4]

Propaganda was simply a tool, one of many means to obtain a particular end. To Donovan it had specific goals, such as fomenting revolt and directing anti-Nazi opposition. The FIS, he believed, should incite rebellion by whatever

means available, subversion included. The end was more important than the truth or the means used to obtain one's goals. Edmond Taylor shared Donovan's view although he worked for Sherwood's FIS. Taylor "wanted to take off the gloves and emulate Goebbels . . . without troubling much about morality or civil liberties." He believed that "an open society" could not defend itself "against subversive attacks of a closed one without in some measure adopting the latter's tactics and operational code." Taylor later described FIS reaction to his suggestion that the United States emulate the hard-hitting tactics of Britain's Political Warfare Executive, which used many Nazi methods. He admitted that Robert Sherwood accepted the necessity of sometimes engaging in such tactics, but many of his colleagues "seemed baffled, and some were horrified" by Taylor's attitude, which by his own admission "appeared cynical and reactionary." Yet Taylor stated that it was not a lack of ideological conviction that led him to "advocate fighting the enemy with his own weapons" but the feeling "that democracy was in imminent danger" and that "to save it, all means were democratic."[5]

Thus, like most of the COI, Taylor implied that democratic ideals could not compete or ultimately prevail over well-entrenched totalitarian regimes. The traditional American elites, individuals who had the power, influence, education, and expertise, had to rescue the American system and guide the nation's destiny as they had done so frequently in the past. Desperate times required desperate measures, mandating that Americans fight fire with fire.

Yet the type of propaganda used to facilitate victory, either overt, official, and white or covert, unofficial, and black, was of little consequence to Donovan. Covert propaganda always figured in his program for psychological warfare, but he believed that both types, white and black, could condition people's minds or could obtain a particular political or military goal when used as a strategic weapon, a purpose he favored. His subsequent emphasis on subversive "morale operations" appears to have come about not because he thought it was the only effective means of propaganda but because official propaganda was monopolized by the Office of War Information and the U.S. Army. This system left only a small, covert, black propaganda niche that was later filled by the Office of Strategic Services (OSS). Donovan was often accused of attempting to infringe upon the mandates of other agencies and of duplicating their activities. Yet more correctly, the COI, and later the OSS, filled a vacuum in the American psychological warfare campaign, taking on roles, mandates, and missions that were not performed by others or likely to be taken up. Many COI critics simply missed the unique nature and intent of Donovan's ideas.[6]

Tight operational control was deemed vital for success, and the entire pro-

gram of psychological warfare, including deception, guerrilla warfare, intelligence, subversion, and propaganda, according to Donovan, had to be coordinated by the military so that once war started all unconventional and propaganda resources could be effectively coupled with military strategy. He further recognized that such operations could not escape eventual military control at home or abroad in a nation devoting all its resources toward winning a total war.[7]

During fall 1941 Donovan became convinced that the FIS and the rest of COI should conduct psychological warfare under the direction of the military services, with propaganda being just one of many COI-controlled programs. He also knew that by attaching COI to the military he could guarantee its survival in a government inundated with information and intelligence agencies. A lifelong student of military affairs who had spent a considerable portion of his life in uniform, Donovan was untroubled by the prospect of putting COI under the control of soldiers, a goal he actually sought with increasing vigor. Such affiliation was anathema, however, to the members of the FIS, especially to Robert Sherwood.

The operational ways and means of the Foreign Information Service provided the clearest indication of the COI's need for military control and discipline. The badly overcrowded FIS Madison Avenue offices in New York City were populated by workers in shirtsleeves, operating "with considerable bustle" at "stop watch speed against many deadlines," with the informality of a big-city newspaper newsroom. To those people in the more homogenous and less crowded COI branches, "the FIS appeared to betoken a Babel, not only of bustle, but also of positively raffish confusion." Many critics referred to it as the Syrian Village. The confusion and frenetic activity was attributed to a combination of poor administration, amateurish leadership, little discipline, and a lack of organization, all of which had military solutions. Donovan's increasing closeness to the Joint Chiefs of Staff (JCS) therefore convinced FIS members that their branch should leave COI or face being overwhelmed by people whose philosophies they found repugnant.[8]

In other matters beyond psychological warfare Donovan had fundamental differences with Sherwood and many members of the FIS. As a Republican and a Wall Street corporate lawyer Donovan was not in sympathy with the domestic policies of Roosevelt's New Deal, nor was he a personal admirer or friend of the president. Although a patriotic soldier, he made a "fundamental distinction" between Roosevelt "as Chief Magistrate and Commander-in-Chief" and as "a party leader and the proponent of a political and economic outlook on life," an outlook he opposed. Many members of the FIS, however, Sherwood included,

did not make this distinction concerning Roosevelt and his politics and "were so fervent in their devotion that . . . they suspected of disloyalty on all scores men who were only of other views on certain of them." Many FIS members harbored such suspicions toward Donovan personally.[9]

The FIS school of thought represented a second political and propaganda philosophy that reflected Sherwood's views. Adherents favored an overt propaganda program unfettered and unsullied by clandestine operations, an information program conducted and controlled entirely by civilians according to the philosophy and under the direction of President Roosevelt as FIS policymakers understood it. Such an independent program, while meeting military needs, was based on the truth, on liberal and Wilsonian ideals and principles, and on the as-yet vague and undefined presidential aims for war and peace. It would spread American liberalism worldwide, globalize the New Deal, and cause dramatic changes in world institutions and philosophies in the same way that Roosevelt and other New Deal liberals had effected similar changes at home between 1933 and 1941. To Sherwood, the wartime and postwar goals of the United States were synonymous and should seek to obtain the kind of world that had been denied to its citizens through the repudiation of Wilson's ideals, represented by the Fourteen Points and the League of Nations twenty years earlier.

Sherwood and his lieutenants knew of the dangers they faced and the obstacles FIS had to overcome. Nonetheless, although they recognized the Nazi's propaganda advantage and the ramifications of an enemy victory, they did not believe in a victory obtained at the expense of democracy, nor were they willing to subvert democratic processes and ethical and moral standards to ensure victory, as Donovan and Taylor were willing to do. Great consideration was given to the postwar era and to the future of the world and of the United States if Americans stooped to Nazi methods to maintain their existence. FIS members recoiled at the thought that any portion or process of democracy should be perverted or destroyed in order to save it. Yet the FIS never believed that defeat was the alternative. To the contrary, they believed so strongly in the message of the United States, in the inherent worth of American values, institutions, and traditions as embodied by Roosevelt in the New Deal that they thought these factors alone when juxtaposed with Nazi philosophies, would be enough to persuade the world of the justice and worthiness of the American cause. There was no need for secrecy, blackmail, intimidation, or other immoral or unorthodox practices. Liberal democracy itself was the ultimate war-winning ideology, and its strength lay in its content.

Foreign Information Service members differed in many other respects from their COI counterparts. Most of them were involved in communications and

the media as writers, poets, filmmakers, journalists, broadcasters, actors, and publishers. They were not representative of the nation's eastern, Protestant, Ivy League–educated establishment, nor were they wealthy. They were liberal humanists and Democrats or, in some cases, independents who had supported the New Deal and Roosevelt's perceived political philosophy, sharing what they believed to be the president's outlook on the role of the United States in the world and the role of government in people's lives. They did not fear the power of centralized government; to the contrary, they welcomed it as a benevolent engine of human progress. Most FIS members were highly individualistic and independent and accustomed to flexible hours, loose chains of command, and a high degree of personal freedom in both word and deed. Although in general they were steadfastly loyal to Sherwood and the FIS, the loyalties were secondary to spreading the word about the virtues of the American political, social, and economic systems.

Sherwood exemplified the humanistic, zealously ideological, and moralistic ideas institutionalized in the FIS. As John Houseman later wrote, "He made no secret of his ideological basis" for recruiting FIS members and excluded "anti-New Dealers," "Roosevelt-haters," and individuals whose philosophy was not "expressive of the President's." "It was Sherwood," Houseman claimed, "individually and through the personalities of the men he chose . . . who gave the FIS the humane and civilized quality that distinguished . . . its work." He determined branch goals and created the impression that FIS was fighting "a people's war, a gallant crusade against the forces of reaction that could make the world a better place to live."[10] Wallace Deuel wrote that Sherwood "was a great idealist," a "passionate believer in the necessity, not only of winning the war, but also of making a better world afterward."[11] As a result of his beliefs and efforts, the FIS came to be "staffed by men who . . . were loners by nature, individuals who had chosen their profession accordingly." Few were team players. They sincerely believed, "almost in their bones," that wars were made and won in the minds of men and that they could win, but success required ingenuity, resourcefulness, and money.[12]

Committed to the moral high road, most FIS members did not believe that a democratic country could practice an immoral or "a Goebbels-deception type of foreign propaganda." Instead, the truth, as they defined it, was the key and the "only effective base on which to build an American information program." Black operations, to most FIS people, were unacceptable in any form. The reporting of the news would shape the basis of each day's programming. This policy was the only sound one, and the work of FIS took on the trappings of a white versus black crusade of good against evil, of light against darkness, with

critics in the rest of COI and the military often being included by FIS members in the second category. This simple perception disturbed many of Donovan's followers, who viewed the FIS outlook with growing misgivings, finding it "liberal to the point of being radical, and, in at least a few cases, dangerously close to the political and economic philosophy of fellow-travelers of Communism." Edmond Taylor held this view and scorned "the moderation of earnest and somewhat doctrinaire American Liberals in the organization who desired to be mere informationalists and tell the story of America." To FIS members, psychological warfare consisted of "sermons" on Roosevelt's Four Freedoms and "folksy chats about the neighborhood drugstore as a national cultural institution." "This Chautauqua outlook," Taylor believed, "seemed naive and anachronistic."[13]

Propaganda, to people in the FIS, had a positive rather than a negative purpose and goal. Sherwood believed propaganda was a tool capable of uplifting, of educating, of enlightening the world to the high ideals, virtues, and aims of Americans. He thought it should purvey the truth, not mislead the enemy, and "should stick scrupulously to the facts, and let the truth eventually prevail." "The American image overseas would suffer," he believed, "if we emulated Axis methods and resorted to lies and deceit."[14] Propaganda "may employ truth instead of falsehood in its operation . . . be directed to worthy instead of unworthy purposes" as "democracies have a good story to tell. We stick to the truth," he said, "for we believe the truth is on our side."[15]

Although the information that FIS disseminated was allegedly the truth, "truths" were carefully selected and defined. Potentially damaging information was generally withheld, a tactic that did not seem to bother Sherwood or his colleagues, who actually believed that the United States had little to hide or to regret. As he told Donovan in October 1941,

> There is not the slightest doubt that we . . . can be an immediate and incalculably valuable force. . . . The words of our president and . . . national leaders—the very facts of our tremendous national effort—must be broadcast. That is the most effective answer to Hitler's propaganda and the most effective message of hope to his victims—past, present, or future.[16]

Unashamedly, the branch "spread the gospel of democracy" and the cause of the united nations. It set out to tell the people of the world of the American war effort, to describe how democracy works, and to publicize Roosevelt's policies. Archibald MacLeish shared Sherwood's views and maintained that "government information . . . should be employed to strengthen, if not develop, emo-

tions in . . . people, either hatred towards the Axis or idealistic love of the Atlantic Charter and the Four Freedoms."[17]

The proper course and strategy for propaganda was thus self-evident. Sherwood once said that America's enemies "knew that words and ideas weaken nations and render them defenseless even before a single shot was fired," yet "we paid but little attention to the possibilities." The enemy was far ahead "in poisoning the airwaves of the world with their propaganda of deception, corruption, and demoralization." Nonetheless, "our own voice . . . had been sincere and honest." The Americans had one great strength the Nazis lacked, "the power of truth." The FIS was committed to telling the world "the essential truth about this war" and "the substance of our democratic faith—that the truth is mighty and shall prevail—the truth shall set you free."[18]

Sherwood set the ideological tone of his service. His views were zealously shared and expressed by many other members, including Joseph Barnes, James Warburg, and Edd Johnson—the three top FIS executives under Sherwood—as well as Harwood Childs, Wallace Deuel, George F. Eliot, and Percy Winner. Although Sherwood's philosophy ultimately won out with the creation of the OWI, the victory was obtained at the expense of Donovan's regard and the organizational integrity of the COI.[19]

Central to Sherwood's notion was the idea that propaganda should remain under civilian control. A few FIS members were willing to accept State Department guidance, but they were opposed to any form of military involvement. The war was just as much a contest of political ideologies as a contest of arms. The military services, though capable of fighting a conventional war, were too unsophisticated and conservative to undertake an ideological struggle successfully, especially one espousing liberal and progressive philosophies. The military's operational methods, doctrines, and institutional thought troubled the liberals in the FIS. In regard to Donovan's ability to develop and operate a comprehensive agency under military control, "both President Roosevelt and Sherwood, found certain of Col. Donovan's plans . . . so unorthodox as to verge on the bizarre," and they questioned his management skills. On the latter point a critic noted, "as an administrator, Donovan tended to be uneven, at the very best." He was "much like the checker-playing dog, the wonder wasn't really how erratically he played, but that he managed to play at all."[20]

Despite being a combat veteran of World War I, Sherwood did not share Donovan's fascination with the military. The FIS director believed in the concept of a people's struggle, as it was the "great masses of the people everywhere, not the generals, who would determine the course and conduct of the war." The FIS, therefore, would "talk as civilians to civilians." It became apparent to him,

by early 1942, that Donovan had sold out to the generals at the expense of FIS and that the COI director's acceptance of a military philosophy, and of the military itself, was indicative of his conservative, if not reactionary, views. After all, FIS members claimed, had Donovan not served in one Republican administration and offered his services to another? Had he not been the president of the conservative American Bar Association? Had he not traveled to Nazi Germany as a guest of the Wehrmacht? Had he not observed Fascist forces in Spain, sympathized with Franco, and congratulated Mussolini on his conquest of Abyssinia? Had he not been a Wall Street corporate lawyer for twenty years?[21]

Sherwood's suspicions of Donovan's ideology tended to be automatically extended to the other non-FIS members of COI. They might have had useful talents and abilities, but Sherwood would not have them in top FIS positions, and he told Donovan so in January 1942.[22] Calvin B. Hoover, who worked for COI R&A Branch, the most liberal-minded section after the FIS, agreed with Sherwood's assessment, commenting that the COI "sheltered screwballs, crackpots, and adventurers, professors from Ivy League universities, ex-soldiers and an unprecedented number of heirs to great fortunes."[23] Furthermore, Sherwood rejected Donovan's concept of psychological warfare, and, like other FIS members, was "inclined to be skeptical and irreverent" in his views toward the rest of COI. As journalists, media, and communications people, FIS members were "by temperament and training apt to suspect sawdust behind every stiff shirtfront and a swindle behind every secret." They were suspicious of elaborate COI security measures "and were more than half-persuaded that these mysteries, like so many others in a naughty world were frauds." They derisively referred to the rest of COI as "the Cloak and Dagger Departments."[24]

The unity created during the prewar years by the perceived need to combat Axis propaganda quickly dissipated after the primary goal of establishing a federal propaganda agency was obtained. There were many early indications that the dissimilar personalities and political viewpoints contained within COI would cause significant and debilitating problems, such as the differences of opinion over organizational matters that raged between Donovan and James P. Warburg in 1941.[25]

One incident providing clear evidence of the preexisting and ever-widening philosophical gulf between Donovan and Sherwood occurred in late 1941, revealing their views on the role of psychology in psychological warfare. Harvard University psychologist Walter C. Langer, the brother of COI R&A member William Langer, having served overseas in World War I, recalled being unimpressed with Allied propaganda efforts and thought they should consist of more than "a constant repetition of fabricated atrocity stories." Thus, in November

1941, he sent Donovan a memorandum describing a proposed Psychoanalytical Field Unit (PFU) to be included in COI to formulate "a comprehensive conception of the basic psychology of Germany," to conduct "an analysis and appraisal of German morale and the psychological condition of the German people at the present time," and to "frame a sound psychological offensive." Donovan liked the idea, William Langer later wrote, because he was "ever groping for new solutions to old problems" and "had enormous respect for scholarship and was always ready to listen to those who had specialized knowledge."[26]

The Foreign Information Service, the intended recipient of the PFU's output, shared neither Donovan's enthusiasm nor his respect for Langer's ideas. Sherwood was categorically and unequivocally opposed to the entire concept, writing Donovan of "the alarm" he felt "at having a staff of psychoanalysts mixing in our work." "COI will become a target of ridicule if there are any grounds for the suggestion that our operations are being guided by psychoanalysts," who in the public mind were little better than "astrologists or palmists." "I do not want any group of psychoanalysts in the FIS," Sherwood declared, as he had already "heard some derisive murmurings about this in Washington." Sherwood's colleagues concurred, as did Budget Director Harold Smith, who refused to fund the unit on the grounds that a similar agency already existed within the R&A branch. Although Walter Langer submitted his resignation in December, Donovan was convinced that psychoanalysis played an important role in psychological warfare. Langer was kept on as a freelance psychoanalytic consultant although little evidence exists to show that psychology provided any solid foundation for subsequent campaigns.[27]

The differences between Sherwood and Donovan and their followers prompted both groups to conclude that something had to be done to settle the internal philosophical contradictions. Sherwood wrote Donovan in October 1941 that COI could not "afford to lose invaluable time through childish bickerings, puny jealousies or backstairs intrigue" when the agency's entire effort was necessary for "winning first the war and then the peace." His solution, unannounced to Donovan, was to remove FIS from COI before it was turned into a military unit totally reflecting Donovan's ideology. Donovan, meanwhile, was working to attach COI firmly to the military to protect the agency from external attack while simultaneously attempting an internal reorganization to decrease the size and influence of FIS, thus regaining control of the branch from Sherwood.[28]

By early 1942 both sets of plans were under way. The basic differences in ideologies regarding propaganda and foreign affairs, in lieu of an official federal policy, resulted in a long and debilitating period of bureaucratic infighting between

opposing factions seeking to monopolize psychological warfare activities for the purposes of advancing their own philosophies while simultaneously defeating the Axis. The bureaucratic struggles clearly reflected the political, ideological, and social schisms that had marked American politics since the beginning of the New Deal and in many ways since the founding of the nation.

The opening salvos took place in January 1942 when COI's London representative, William D. Whitney, after talking with other COI members, wrote Donovan of their increased frustration. He pointed out that until the war started COI had been a flourishing agency, but because all agencies had been placed on a war footing, COI, which had been a valued source of information for the president, was being overshadowed by other agencies, particularly by the army and navy military intelligence offices (G-2 and ONI). Unless something was done, Whitney reasoned, the COI could be abolished or broken up. The office, with its intelligence, special operations, and propaganda programs, was trying to do too much and needed to regroup and concentrate on one area. Whitney wrote that "already our toe-hold is precarious on all of them, except for the last one." Because COI had no specific mandate, "others in the circus are clutching at our togas, and they will soon be appealing to the circus-master to put us out of the ring altogether." Whitney suggested that COI "get on one horse" and drop other functions; the agency needed to fill a niche and to create a unique role and mission or face extinction. Another COI member, Atherton Richards, saw a similar problem, noting that Donovan's organizational methods were comparable to "pouring molasses from a barrel onto a table. It will ooze in every direction." Still wed to the idea of a comprehensive psychological warfare agency, Donovan dismissed Whitney's view.[29]

The Whitney memorandum raised a significant issue that was widely perceived as a growing dilemma within government circles: the glut of overlapping agencies. In December 1941, for example, there existed at least twenty-six federal propaganda, intelligence, and information agencies employing more than 3,000 people. Most of the groups were small and mutually hostile, and few were satisfied with the arrangement, least of all Budget Director Harold Smith. John Houseman concluded that the "vague assignment of powers was typical of Roosevelt's method of government," and critics charged that the president's usual solution to any given problem was to create a new federal agency. Yet Roosevelt was hesitant to move too quickly, even with the nation at war. Although he had discussed a sweeping propaganda reorganization with former secretary of the navy Josephus Daniels in October 1941 and had considered creating a unified agency at that time, he was waiting for events to play out, a position entailing far less political risk.[30]

Regardless of Roosevelt's intentions, the troubles plaguing the myriad propaganda and information agencies were becoming a national scandal that many administration insiders feared would draw an inordinate amount of public attention and congressional criticism. The problem had now even come to the attention of the Bureau of the Budget, an office already straining to fund a burgeoning wartime bureaucracy.

Previously uninvolved in propaganda matters, the Bureau of the Budget, for fiscal reasons, placed itself in the forefront of efforts to create a single propaganda agency. Soon after the Whitney memorandum reached Donovan, the bureau released its own report based on a fall 1941 study which stated that the "time has come . . . to unify the domestic and foreign propaganda and psychological warfare agencies," implying that FIS be split from COI. Though it is not known whether Sherwood prompted the report, he did request a meeting with Budget Director Smith in mid-January 1942 to discuss the report and "the larger organizational problems in the entire propaganda field" as well as policy. Prior to the release of the report Sherwood apparently had discussed the same issues with other people in the Budget Bureau, with Nelson A. Rockefeller of the CIAA, and with OFF director Archibald MacLeish.[31]

Sherwood continued to write Smith and to meet with Rockefeller and MacLeish, Treasury Secretary Henry Morgenthau, and presidential advisers Harry Hopkins and Samuel Rosenman. In all probability they discussed the removal of the FIS from the COI and the amalgamation of the former with the OFF. Archibald MacLeish, whom Sherwood described as a "kindred spirit," informed both Smith and Roosevelt of his ideas in late February. Smith then suggested that OFF and OEM's Division of Information be abolished and that the propaganda and information functions of COI and CIAA be combined in a new office of war information, a name coined by MacLeish. The discussions took place without Donovan's knowledge and although not privy to exact events, the COI director was aware that something was afoot.[32]

In wake of the Bureau of the Budget's report, Donovan gave new consideration to the Whitney memorandum. To stave off attempts to whittle away COI, Donovan in February 1942 circulated a memorandum to all branch chiefs encouraging them to look at each branch and "see how they all tie into one whole" and to "examine our potentialities, limitations and errors." Donovan then appointed a committee of Elmo Roper, William Langer, Atherton Richards, "Ned" Buxton, Thomas Early, and Robert Sherwood to look at several issues, including work that COI could do that was not being done and work that it was doing but that was not useful or that should not be a COI responsibility. The committee promised to devise a new organizational chart and to compile a list of past

Harold D. Smith, President Roosevelt's director of the Bureau of the Budget. (OWI Photo; reproduced at the National Archives)

mistakes. Committee chairman Roper concluded, however, that "our no. I problem is to go thoroughly into FIS," a task assigned to Buxton, Early, Langer, and Richards. Sherwood's name was conspicuously absent, an indication to FIS members that the deputy COI director was rapidly losing favor. Just as the Roper committee began its internal examination, however, the COI was threatened from the outside.[33]

Donovan was aware of efforts to consolidate federal propaganda agencies and viewed the move as a veiled attempt to destroy his budding empire. He wrote Roosevelt that he had not heard the source of the proposals, nor had he been consulted about consolidation, but he asked the president to keep several vital considerations in mind. Propaganda must be employed as a military weapon, Donovan wrote, and domestic and foreign propaganda under all circumstances must be kept separate, as in reality they were different in aims, purpose, and method. Furthermore, propaganda was a secret-attack weapon and as such should be blanketed in security and closely tied to the military services. The COI was devoted to just this end: the creation of a comprehensive, secret, psychological warfare agency capable of supporting military operations. Donovan reminded the president that he had deemed it prudent to separate domestic and foreign propaganda in July 1941, thereby successfully keeping the people involved with operations abroad "free from domestic issues" so that they could "carry out the military purpose and function of our work." Donovan's statements clearly revealed his belief in the offensive and military nature of propaganda and his conviction that creeping New Deal philosophies had no place in American propaganda.[34]

Budget Director Harold Smith represented the views of COI's many critics and dealt a blow to Donovan's concept of a military-controlled psychological warfare service in early March 1942 when he urged Roosevelt to create a single civilian agency. Smith's memorandum, "Reorganization of War Information Services," contained a proposed executive order for "consolidating a number of existing war informational services into an Office of War Information," ostensibly for reasons of economic efficiency. The proposal, Smith claimed, was the result of three months of study by staffer Milton Eisenhower, which gave credence to the idea that he and Eisenhower had been heavily influenced by Sherwood and MacLeish.

Smith pointed out the similarities and resulting "conflict and duplication" between the six civilian and two military information agencies, stressing the overemphasis on short-term results and the lack of long-range planning. He did not suggest combining every function performed by each agency, but he did propose the consolidation of OFF, the Division of Information, the media and film divisions of CIAA, and the entire FIS into one unit. Smith said he had dis-

cussed the proposal with Lowell Mellett, Sherwood, MacLeish, Samuel Rosenman, and Wayne Coy, all of whom he claimed approved his suggestion. Although CIAA director Nelson Rockefeller was not in total agreement with the scheme, believing that the CIAA should be left under the control of the State Department, he was, Smith reported, "willing to cooperate under any arrangement agreed upon." Donovan was not initially apprised of Smith's work.[35]

Convinced that consolidation was key to creating an effective psychological warfare program, Smith met with President Roosevelt and Samuel Rosenman to discuss an executive order. The president was concerned about Donovan's reaction, to which Smith replied that "the order did just what the president had in mind so far as Donovan was concerned." When Roosevelt inquired about a possible director for the new agency, Smith proposed MacLeish as chairman and Sherwood as director, a suggestion to which the president demurred as he "did not think that Sherwood had very much administrative ability" although he did not object to either man's politics. The conference ended without a decision, however, as Roosevelt chose to observe the course of events and allow matters to play themselves out with a minimum of executive input.[36]

Having failed to get the president to resolve the crisis quickly, Smith and Rosenman met with Sherwood and Rockefeller to discuss further action. After the meetings, which failed to produce an agreement, Rosenman, who had little patience with the thirty-four-year-old Rockefeller, complained that the CIAA director "was trying to maintain his show at all odds" and that "Donovan had been lying to the president about what he had been doing" with COI. Both Rosenman and Smith concluded, however, that the ultimate decision and responsibility rested with Roosevelt, who "would not take any action to clear up the mess until forced to do so, probably by a Congressional inquiry."[37]

The president's initial lack of interest in the Bureau of the Budget's proposal prompted Sherwood and Smith to undertake unilateral steps to force executive action. Sherwood, for example, sent Roosevelt a confidential memorandum in March, in which he "presumed to speak for Bill Donovan," suggesting the abolition of COI and the distribution of its branches to various civilian and military agencies. At the same time, Smith, knowing of the impasse and of the increased curiosity and rising ire of Congress, prepared a memorandum that listed several recent developments "which make early actions on the proposed War Information Executive Order extremely urgent." These developments concerned the fiscal 1943 budget and manpower projections submitted by the war information services, with estimated spending rising from $24 million to $38 million and personnel needs increasing from 3,400 people to nearly 4,300. Smith hoped that probable congressional inquiries over the amount of money and number of em-

ployees involved in similar work would force Roosevelt to issue the executive order before Donovan or the State Department could take any steps to stymie the consolidation. Smith's gambit failed, however. On 26 March 1942, Donovan and the JCS announced a scheme that upset the budget director's plans.[38]

In keeping with his psychological warfare theories and to save COI from dissolution in a struggle that was becoming an all-out war for control, Donovan sought to attach his agency to the military in late February and March. Initially, the military services did not view such a relationship with any enthusiasm, as most soldiers held views concerning psychological warfare contrary to both Sherwood's and Donovan's. The military thus came to represent the third school of propaganda thought evident during the war.

Previously silent on most propaganda matters, and totally uninvolved in the creation of the COI, the higher-level officers of the U.S. Army were initially uninterested in psychological warfare. In time they came to view it expeditiously and pragmatically as strictly a nonpolitical, tactical tool, one of many weapons for military use under U.S. Army control. Although members of a politically and socially conservative institution, U.S. Army personnel were supposedly not at liberty to inject their personal political beliefs into the rancorous disputes overwhelming the civilian agencies.

Furthermore, the military was slow to grasp the value and impact of this untested, somewhat vague and ill-defined form of unconventional warfare. Having struggled through two decades of retrenchments, the U.S. Army, now facing a threat of enormous proportions and unprecedented mobilization demands, was more concerned with conventional rearmament than with propaganda, which seemed to have too many political and ideological strings attached and few practical or proven uses. Increasingly, due to the insistence of both the British military services and the American civilian propaganda agencies, top army planners came to see psychological warfare as an enhancer in conventional operations. The military, however, had a longstanding suspicion of civilian agencies, especially those that could interfere with military operations. From the outset of their involvement, the army sought to control and coordinate civilian propaganda operations and to direct them toward strictly nonpolitical, tactical uses.

The military's involvement with psychological warfare was an outcome of the Anglo-American alliance. After France fell, the British gave considerable thought to psychological or "political" warfare, eventually designating it as the fourth arm of modern war. Theorists in Britain succeeded in convincing their military services that such activities could play an independent strategic role, largely because British conventional military capabilities were then at an all-time low and little else remained in their arsenal to contest the Nazi domination of Europe actively.

During Anglo-American staff talks in June 1941, the British Joint Planning Staff strongly emphasized the importance of subversion and propaganda and its coordination with other forms of offensive warfare. Again, in August 1941 at the Argentia Conference, the meeting that produced the Atlantic Charter, the British emphasized the triple theme of bombing, blockade, and subversion as the scenario that must precede any Allied invasion of Axis-occupied Europe. By then political warfare had become an integral part of the British strategic program. The reactions of American military leaders to these ideas were "dominantly negative"; they favored a continental invasion at the earliest possible date and paid little regard to British fears of another bloody war of attrition as experienced between 1914 and 1918. Unconventional warfare on the scale the British proposed would not substantially aid efforts to mount an invasion and would certainly divert scarce manpower and material resources from the main offensive. The British, nonetheless, continued to emphasize the need for the United States to adopt unconventional warfare as part of their strategy. They also stressed that the United States needed to develop a joint military staff system similar to the British Chiefs of Staff to coordinate American planning and to meet on an equal footing with their British counterparts.[39]

In deference to their allies, the U.S. military acquiesced and accepted psychological warfare as a feature of grand strategy during the Arcadia Conference in December 1941 and January 1942. At the same time, the two allies created the Combined Chiefs of Staff (CCS), consisting of the British Chiefs of Staff and the soon to be created American JCS, to act as the principal military advisers, coordinators, and strategic directors of the military forces of the two nations.[40]

Because of British influences, psychological warfare thus became an interest of the JCS. Seeking to gain control rapidly, the JCS, at its first meeting on 9 February 1942, adopted a plan developed by the Joint Staff Planners (JSP) that recommended tying "Col. Donovan's office into the high command of the Army and Navy," thereby putting psychological warfare under joint military control. The JCS recognized that the existing COI could adequately fill the psychological warfare role that the British insisted the United States needed if it were properly organized and controlled. The Joint Chiefs then issued JCS 12, which officially recognized the existence of psychological warfare, thus meeting the desires of their British counterparts while simultaneously and inadvertently provided a military niche for the COI. The directive also defined psychological warfare as

the integrated use of all means, moral and physical—other than those of recognized military actions—which tend to destroy the will of the enemy to achieve victory and to damage his political and economic capacity to

do so; which tend to deprive the enemy of the support, assistance, or sympathy of his allies or associates or neutrals . . . or which tend to maintain, increase, or acquire the support, assistance and sympathy of neutrals.[41]

Although Donovan was not responsible for the JCS definition, it matched his own and gave him reason to believe that the COI could be transferred intact to military control.

Although the JCS was interested in aspects of the COI, skepticism about Donovan and about psychological warfare in general was still prevalent in the military. Many officers, including Brig. Gen. Walter Bedell Smith, JCS secretary, considered Donovan, as a National Guard officer, to be essentially "a civilian dabbling in a military preserve." Smith further thought Donovan to be "an inexperienced interloper whose schemes were a threat to security, efficiency, and military success." Other military men thought so as well. In a March 1942 report prepared for the JCS by Capt. Francis J. Denebrink, USN, who had worked with James P. Baxter III in the COI R&A Branch, the naval officer suggested that the office as configured should be dismantled. He had an especially "low opinion of FIS, which was not well organized or well disciplined," and he suggested it be controlled by the War Department Psychological Warfare Branch (PWB) under Col. Percy Black. It is likely that Denebrink shared the assessment of most COI members that FIS was unmilitary. He concluded that absorption of some COI functions by the armed services was an option, but without Donovan.

Other soldiers, however, thought poorly of the entire COI organization. One officer who happened to visit the COI offices at Twenty-fifth and E Streets in Washington, D.C., claimed that "the hard-bargaining corporation lawyers and insurance brokers and random academics from every part of the haute-bourgeois forest" had turned the headquarters "into something which closely resembled a cat house in Laredo on a Saturday night, with rivalries, jealousies, mad schemes and everyone trying to get the ear of the director." However reluctantly, the JCS decided to make the entire COI a supporting agency of the Joint Chiefs, not wanting to lose the talent thus far assembled to other agencies. Moreover, the JCS considered many of Donovan's branches and some of his proposals as having potential, if properly managed.[42]

But the apparent general lack of understanding and support for his ideas prompted Donovan to undertake a bold initiative to put the entire agency firmly under the JCS. Appealing to the president, who originally seemed to appreciate the idea of a comprehensive psychological warfare agency, Donovan wrote that the four COI branches, Special Intelligence, R&A, FIS, and Special

Operations, worked in close cooperation with the military and performed unique functions that in Britain required six different organizations. If the branches were put under a single authority, "an economy of force, a vital principle of warfare," would be obtained, and he suggested that Roosevelt issue a military order creating a JCS–COI affiliation.[43]

Once Donovan made his desires known to the commander-in-chief, he turned to the military. Sensing that his military allies were in effect not allies at all, Donovan sought out General Smith, the harshest JCS critic, to win him and thus the military over to his plan. Donovan gave Smith a draft of a military order he had proposed to Roosevelt creating an Office of Strategic Information (OSI). The proposed agency included the COI functions of planning and execution of foreign propaganda, psychological warfare, and special service units. General Smith forwarded the plan to the JCS without recommendation, but many members of the military, who previously had watched the civilian propaganda conflicts from afar and had seen little use for propaganda, now agreed with Donovan that the military had to take some action or risk losing influence and control over a potentially useful weapon. Seeking to correct their past position of dealing with propaganda matters only when forced to by their Allies and the president, the JCS created the Joint Psychological Warfare Committee (JPWC) on 18 March to coordinate the activities of the COI, CIAA, the State Department, and the Bureau of Economic Warfare (BEW) for military purposes. It was suggested that Donovan be made its chair. Soon after, Donovan's OSI proposal was accepted and forwarded to Roosevelt with the suggestion that COI be put under JCS control.[44]

Sensing that victory over his rivals was near, and having firmer military support, Donovan again urged Roosevelt to sign the order creating the OSI, an action, Donovan believed, which would be a step that "exactly conforms to your original directive to me, both in name and function." The president, however, forwarded Donovan's proposal to Harold Smith, telling him that he now believed FIS should not be connected with the military, indicating a belief that propaganda was not just a military domain. At this point, 1 April 1942, President Roosevelt had on his desk an order creating a military-controlled psychological warfare agency out of Donovan's COI and Smith's executive order creating a civilian-controlled propaganda agency by consolidating the civilian agencies, including the FIS. Yet he did not act on either, and for the next two months a race ensued between soldiers and civilians to get Roosevelt to move first on their respective orders.[45]

In the meantime, Donovan was injured in an automobile accident in front of Washington, D.C.'s Union Station. Although assured of a full recovery, he was

ordered to undergo complete bed rest, and for several weeks his activities were severely limited. During his prolonged absence his rivals attempted to move the OWI executive order forward. During an early April meeting at the White House, Smith encouraged the president to sign the order without delay, an action Roosevelt refused to take while Donovan was recovering. Although both Rosenman and Smith felt the delay was unnecessary, they also realized that the decision was one of many matters on the president's mind and that in characteristic fashion he had to "take some little time . . . to face up the issues" and "make sure in his own mind just what he wanted to do, as he would have to fight for the program from here on out." In the interim Roosevelt asked Francis Biddle to get the parties together to solve the problem.[46]

Having been uninvolved in propaganda matters since the Ickes Committee's controversies the previous year, Biddle had a great deal to catch up on in a limited time. After learning as much about the situation as he could, he gave the president a series of options. He suggested that Elmer Davis, originally proposed for director of a new office of war information by E. B. White, Archibald MacLeish, and Felix Frankfurter in February, be asked to create an organization containing a domestic division consisting of the OFF, the OGR, and the Division of Information and a foreign branch consisting of the FIS and the CIAA. Unbeknownst to the other individuals involved, Biddle's plan impressed Roosevelt as the best possible solution.

While the president pondered Biddle's suggestions, Donovan returned to work, finding to his chagrin that Roosevelt had not acted on the JCS order. He wrote the president that "if this war has taught us anything, it has taught us the need for unification of all the efforts—some new—which play a part in modern warfare." He restated the main points of his earlier memorandum concerning the importance of a comprehensive psychological warfare agency. Concurring with the JCS suggestions, he denied that the COI had encroached in any way on military functions and implored the president to keep the agency from being "disturbed" before it had a chance to prove itself. Sensing that his gains were slipping away, Donovan forwarded a copy of the letter to General Smith, along with a further letter emphasizing the value of the COI to the JCS and the need to act quickly. The JCS wanted portions of the COI, excluding the FIS, yet as late as May Donovan could still count few military allies. Indeed, General Smith, Harold Smith, Rosenman, and Biddle were still toying with the idea of breaking up the COI and unconditionally terminating Donovan.[47]

To improve the attractiveness of the agency to the JCS, Donovan acted on the internal COI reorganization study completed in April. Considering the ideological preferences of the committee, it is not surprising that the report al-

leged that the main COI problems stemmed from the FIS. The committee argued that it was of little use for the FIS to conduct operations if the people making the plans were not knowledgeable about "the major achievements desired from political warfare activity," implying that FIS ideologies and political ideas were contrary to the purpose of the COI as defined by Donovan. The committee further believed that the FIS could not operate effectively without being held strictly accountable to overall COI goals. The members recommended the establishment of a planning board consisting of people from COI, BEW, OFF, CIAA, and the War and Navy Departments and including only one member from the FIS to determine the broad goals of political warfare. Reorganized into radio and publication departments, FIS would no longer be in charge of policy development but would follow the direction set for them by COI members, adhering to Donovan's and not to Sherwood's philosophy.[48]

Donovan agreed with the committee findings, and without consulting Sherwood, whose opinions were of the opposite extreme, used their suggestions to reorganize the COI. In a clear attempt to curry military favor, the FIS Planning Board and Board of Analysts were eliminated and replaced with a Washington, D.C.–based Planning Board directly responsible to Donovan. The Pictures and Publications and the Outpost divisions were taken from the FIS and were made independent COI branches. Finally, Donovan offered new and somewhat vague assignments to Edmond Taylor and to James Warburg, which promoted them from the FIS and put them under his closer supervision instead of Sherwood's. The changes were made, Donovan declared, because the COI branches had grown too big to be administered properly. In reaction, Sherwood wrote Donovan twice in early April explaining why he and Harold Guinzburg thought that the FIS, despite the committee findings, should be left intact, operating from New York City. His reasoning fell on deaf ears.[49]

In the attempt to further cement his position with both the JCS and the president, Donovan prepared a five-page memorandum pressing his views. He wrote Roosevelt and Rosenman that a breakup of the COI at that time "would be a serious impairment of the whole war effort." The branches of the COI, including the FIS, could not operate independently: "There was such an interplay of functions that to rip this out now would tear the tissue of our whole organization." Donovan suggested a trial period to see if a single domestic and foreign propaganda agency under one director could work, putting off either a complete breakup or a consolidation, believing as he did that a domestic agency on its own would not prove successful. He closed by again urging that the JCS order be signed to "break the log jam."[50]

Despite Donovan's machinations and memos, at the end of May Roosevelt

moved in the direction Donovan opposed and expressed his willingness to sign the executive order creating an Office of War Information. The president did not immediately implement the order, however, prompting Harold Smith again to raise the issues of unwieldy budgets, public confusion, and congressional ire. By the first week of June 1942, the president informed Smith that he would sign the order creating the OWI, with newsman Elmer Davis as director, Archibald MacLeish as domestic chief, and Robert Sherwood as foreign propaganda head. Nelson Rockefeller's CIAA would be left intact, and the COI, without the FIS, would become a JCS supporting agency. When Smith informed Donovan of the impending orders, Donovan again wrote Roosevelt, hoping to persuade him at the eleventh hour to transfer the COI intact to the JCS, claiming that his comprehensive psychological warfare agency required the "distribution of public information abroad."[51]

Donovan's appeals were ignored, however, and the JCS prepared to integrate the COI, without the FIS, into the military. On 13 June 1942, Roosevelt issued the executive order favored by Sherwood, MacLeish, Rosenman, and Smith creating the Office of War Information. At the same time, however, the president unexpectedly issued the JCS order creating the Office of Strategic Services. Roosevelt wrote Sherwood that he had decided to take FIS out of COI, believing that its work was "essentially information and not espionage or subversive activity among individuals and groups in enemy nations." In the memorandum the president indicated his view that information was propaganda and vice versa and should be disseminated by a civilian agency. He wrote that Donovan did not agree, "but the rest of COI, including himself, belongs under JCS," minus propaganda functions. Roosevelt concluded by predicting that Elmer Davis "with his long experience and his genuine popularity in press and radio circles, will be able to tie together the many factors of information in the broadest sense of the term" and that he and Davis definitely wanted Sherwood and MacLeish to continue.[52]

The choice that remained for COI members was to establish which agency, the OWI or the OSS, they would join. The agency numbered 1,852 people by June 1942, half of whom worked for the FIS. Although all COI branches, except for the FIS, had transferred intact to the OSS, losing few members, the same was not true for the FIS. Since the OWI was charged with the official government program of propaganda at home and overseas, it appeared that the OSS was not to perform the function that FIS members had trained for; thus the OWI seemed the logical choice for propagandists. Nonetheless, many FIS members faced a difficult decision. Edmond Taylor wrote that he had "grown fond of the fumbling, slow-speaking, but sensitive and witty Sherwood," whose "Lincoln-

esque" political views were ironically closer to his own as opposed to "Donovan's blend of Wall Street orthodoxy and sophisticated American nationalism." Yet Donovan's "personal charisma had proved overpowering," and Taylor joined the OSS. Wallace Deuel, close to both men, decided to remain with Donovan. Ultimately, Deuel and Taylor proved exceptions, as 816 FIS members, including the directors and the division and branch chiefs, joined the OWI.[53] Sherwood was gratified by FIS loyalty and was convinced the branch could now practice the type of propaganda the members saw as best serving the needs of the nation without interference. In July 1942 the OWI began a new round of organization and recruiting under a new leader.

The demise of the COI again brought to the fore the issues that had plagued American propaganda theorists since the 1930s. The conflicts manifested themselves in bitter bureaucratic struggles, which, though appearing to be nothing more than rivalries for power, actually represented struggles for political and ideological hegemony and control of American propaganda, whose practitioners believed reflected the very ideals and values of the nation. Whoever controlled the propaganda apparatus determined the course of the word war against Nazi Germany and also controlled a powerful information system that could advance political ideologies everywhere in the postwar world. By summer 1942, after nearly a year of internecine conflict, it seemed that a solution had been found in the OWI, a civilian-controlled agency charged with the official U.S. government program of information. It appeared to the people who supported a government program espousing the views of President Roosevelt that they had won out over Americans who favored a conservative, military-controlled subversive program. The triumph, however, was short-lived, and in reality the settlement of July 1942 was not a true victory for either side.

6 • The Menagerie of the Old Guard of the New Deal: The OWI Overseas Branch

The creation of the Office of War Information was a personal and ideological victory for Robert Sherwood and the members of the Foreign Information Service who favored a civilian-controlled propaganda program emphasizing the truth and projecting their perceptions of President Roosevelt's philosophies. Without an overall federal policy to guide them, OWI members thought they were free to practice the type of propaganda they favored without the necessity of spending time and money engaged in a variety of activities they deemed of dubious morality and effectiveness. For the first eighteen months of its existence the Overseas Branch of the OWI expressed the idealism and ideology of Deputy Director Sherwood and the former members of the FIS in its propaganda. Although a triumph for the people favoring a strategy of truth based on the assumed ideals of FDR, the period of operational and ideological independence was short-lived and masked several negative aspects that complicated future operations, in effect hiding the many issues left unresolved by the lack of a clear federal propaganda policy.

The first major problem faced by OWI was organizational and was attributable to the abolition of the COI. Although many individuals in OWI claimed that their agency could operate independently, they soon found that without the intelligence and research-and-analysis units that were not transferred in the breakup of COI they were unable to operate efficiently or as effectively as possible. It was necessary, therefore, to re-create a new propaganda organization around the skeleton that existed in June 1942.

Another apparent difficulty concerned the type, content, and scope of OWI propaganda, both foreign and domestic. The former FIS members of the OWI Overseas Branch found that even though their new agency was committed to an overall strategy of truth, subject to various definitions, the entire leadership was

not necessarily committed to projecting Roosevelt's worldview as Sherwood felt it should or to the sort of propaganda work Sherwood and his closest associates considered the most effective. The people who entered OWI after June 1942, thus beginning propaganda work much later than the old guard, did not share Sherwood's liberal, internationalist, and idealistic zeal. Increasingly, the more ardent and fanatical liberals and New Dealers within the Overseas OWI came under attack, not only from the less political and zealous members of their own branch and organization but from Congress and other federal agencies who had always distrusted the notion of government-sponsored propaganda that purported to be the sole font of truth.

The Overseas OWI formed but one portion of the larger OWI agency, and its goals often did not match those of Sherwood and his lieutenants. The OWI was thus divided internally, just as the entire community was divided over definitions of propaganda and its use. In lieu of a clear federal policy, the Overseas OWI operated according to self-defined rules that tended to conflict with the rest of OWI. As a result, the Overseas Branch encountered internal and external resistance and criticism on a scale far beyond the level it had experienced while under Donovan's control.

The propaganda mandate of OWI seemed explicit to the people joining the new organization. The June 1942 Executive Order 9182 gave OWI the authority by using press, radio, and motion pictures to create and conduct "information programs" to facilitate "an informed and intelligent understanding, at home and abroad," of the war effort, government policies, combat activities, and war aims, however vaguely defined. The OWI was to coordinate all information activities; dispense information to other federal, state, and local agencies; review, clear, and approve all public and private radio and motion picture programs; and maintain liaison with information services of the united nations. Nowhere in the order was the word "propaganda" used, nor did it give any hint as to federal policy on propaganda, other than recognizing "the right of the American people and all other peoples opposing the Axis aggressors to be truthfully informed."[1]

The Office of War Information had been created from the remnants of the OFF, the OGR, and the FIS, Outpost, Publications, and Pictorial divisions of COI as well as the OEM Division of Information. As a highly visible public agency, touching nearly every American's life during the war either at home or overseas, the OWI was the constant focus of a great amount of popular attention. On the day the executive order was signed, the White House issued a press statement explaining that the OWI was divided into two sections dealing with domestic information for the United States and foreign information for the rest

of the world except Latin America, an area that remained the exclusive preserve of Nelson Rockefeller's CIAA. The OWI was empowered "to eliminate all overlapping and duplication" and to discontinue any "informational activity not necessary or useful to the war effort." Any information services that did remain had to "conform to the directives issued by the Director of the Office of War Information." The statement explained that the COI, now renamed the Office of Strategic Services and minus the FIS, had been transferred to the JCS but had no function dealing with the dissemination of information. The new director of the OWI was Elmer Davis.[2]

President Roosevelt's appointment of Davis initially appeared to be a wise decision. In 1942 he was an enormously popular and well-known CBS radio commentator with a nationwide following who admired him for his common-man attributes, his strong character, and his personal integrity. His selection also was approved by the OWI membership, most members of the government, and the press.[3] An Indiana native, Davis was a Rhodes scholar at Oxford before joining the *New York Times* in 1914. After leaving the *Times* ten years later, he became a successful freelance writer, producing several novels and short stories. In 1939, at the urging of CBS executive Edward Klauber, Davis replaced H. V. Kaltenborn as a news analyst and commentator and within two years had a nightly radio audience of 12.5 million. Known for his dry humor and calm and even delivery, Davis had a "gift for expressing his thoughts pithily." It was said that he had an "incisive, analytical mind" and "loved facts, unadorned facts."[4]

Davis's personal and professional background gave little indication of the political and ideological convictions he held in the early 1940s. Although from the Midwest, an area considered by many people as bucolic, backward, and isolationist, Davis, since 1939, was a well-known although not an outspoken internationalist, Anglophile, and interventionist, like many of the other members of the Century Group, the Committee on National Morale, and the Century Club, to which he belonged. Politically a Democrat, he was once vaguely defined as "a horse-sense liberal . . . neither given to hysterical hand-wringing nor to fuzzy optimism." He was working for CBS at an annual salary of $53,000 when Roosevelt approached him in May 1942 to become the OWI director for $12,000 per year, as a patriotic gesture. Davis's popularity, his lack of prior involvement in the propaganda debacle, and his views on the war and the role of information convinced the president of his suitability for the new OWI post.[5]

Davis did have notable shortcomings that were not apparent at the time, shortcomings that subsequently interfered with OWI's success. Although he was a popular and respected radio personality noted for his political neutrality, his skills as a diplomat, socializer, and politician were dismal. Like Sherwood,

and to a lesser degree Donovan, Davis lacked administrative ability and experience, especially the kind needed to run a federal agency eventually employing 10,000 people worldwide. From the outset he proved to be a poor leader and a poorer bureaucratic infighter. Repeatedly the OWI emerged as the bloody loser from conflicts with the military services, Congress, and other federal departments because Davis failed to press his views forcefully and to exercise his authority over subordinates or other agencies that were not fulfilling mandates or who were overstepping their bounds and interfering with OWI functions. Repeatedly he missed opportunities to resolve small problems tactfully before they became larger and much more serious and damaging crises. An indication of his failing was his indifference to a July 1942 offer to have a daily, scheduled, fifteen-minute conference with the president to discuss government information problems and OWI's work. "By this one naive action," one historian has written, "Davis threw away his best source of bureaucratic power." Other propaganda chiefs, most notably in Nazi Germany and Great Britain, had easy and regular access to chiefs of state. Davis refused such access and the support it could have provided.[6]

Strangely, Davis, who was the director of the largest propaganda organization ever created, exercised little control over OWI foreign activities. Like Donovan, he allowed Robert Sherwood and the Overseas OWI leadership to chart their own course for over a year according to their perceptions of what the as yet nonexistent federal propaganda policy should be. On the other hand, Davis became overinvolved in domestic OWI activities at the expense of the proper management of the entire office, having always maintained that the agency's most important task was to tell the American people why the country was at war. His perspectives and goals remained domestically oriented, clearly indicating that he believed more strongly in a domestic, defensive, morale-boosting mission than in the use of propaganda as an offensive strategic and tactical weapon directed against Axis populations. Davis's narrow focus on domestic objectives and his lack of leadership qualities were evident from the outset and seriously jeopardized OWI's work and indeed its very survival.[7]

The initial task before Davis and the OWI staff was to organize an efficient federal propaganda agency that could begin the tasks of fighting the propaganda war against Nazi Germany and bolstering home front morale. Months were devoted to developing a new organizational scheme and to recruiting personnel to fill the many expanded posts in OWI's domestic and foreign branches. Davis sought, and received, a great deal of advice on these matters from Robert Sherwood, former CPI director George Creel, and Budget Director Harold Smith, who now had a personal stake in OWI's success.[8]

Staffing the new agency was less difficult than creating an efficient organizational structure. It was apparent that no successful model had ever existed. The World War I–era Committee on Public Information, despite Creel's enthusiastic and positive but exaggerated anecdotes, was not deemed a suitable model. Therefore, the designers of OWI created a new agency by adapting to propaganda work the organizational models they knew best: newspaper newsrooms and editorial offices, radio and film studios, printing and publishing houses, theaters, and university committee rooms and research libraries. The structure of OWI thus reflected a mixture representative of these professional locales, loosely organized and informally managed. An outsider could tour the OWI offices and see journalists, radio broadcasters, film directors, printers, advertisers, playwrights, actors, business managers, administrators, and academics working in adjacent offices in the same building: a colorful and diverse group of people with similar professional, political, and ideological backgrounds.

Although opponents criticized both the seemingly haphazard organization of OWI and the unusual makeup of its staff, the diversity probably was crucial to OWI's effective, although not always efficient, operation. It is unlikely that the agency, considering its unusual mission and its equally unusual mixture of personnel, could have succeeded had it been organized or staffed in any other manner. Davis thus made the best of a less than optimum situation and gathered together people from defunct organizations, abolishing some divisions, combining others that were similar, and generally grafting the new onto the old. He eventually established a unique agency where none had existed before.

The OWI's personnel and its organizational structure reflected the agency's unique nature. At the top was the Director's Office, operating out of Washington, D.C., consisting of Davis as agency head and former Agriculture Department officials George Barnes as assistant director and Milton Eisenhower as associate director. Archibald MacLeish, formerly head of OFF, took a post as assistant director, with interventionist Tristram Coffin and former BBC broadcaster and Harvard University lecturer Charles Siepmann as his assistants. *Des Moines Register* publisher Gardner Cowles became the Domestic OWI director with midwestern newsman Robert J. Blakely as his assistant. Sherwood remained as Overseas director.[9]

The Director's Office controlled the activities of the two main OWI Branches: Domestic and Overseas. Davis's control of the former was always concrete; his control of the latter before 1944 was merely theoretical. The Domestic Branch, which was always under fire, monopolized Davis's time and thoughts through 1943, as it did the attention of Congress and the Republican opposition. Moreover, it had little direct influence on the propaganda war against the

Axis. To find personnel to fill the many positions in the Domestic OWI bureaus, divisions, and subdivisions, Davis, Eisenhower, and MacLeish drew heavily on the pool of talent belonging to the defunct OGR, OFF, COI, and Division of Information. Most individuals selected for employment had significant and long experience in the study of propaganda and public opinion or in anti-Fascist, internationalist, and interventionist activities. At least fifty-five individuals from the older agencies took top positions in the Domestic OWI.[10]

The Overseas Branch, concerned solely with foreign propaganda, initially consisted overwhelmingly of former FIS members. Below the policymaking levels, however, the agency was quickly and significantly augmented after July 1942, making the original founders of the OWI a distinct yet still dominant minority within a few months. New recruits were obtained as the OWI conducted national searches focusing on influential persons from academe, from the media and communications industry, and from the field of arts and letters. Just as in the FIS, however, personal and professional contacts with employees of the OWI remained a primary means of identifying suitable hires.[11]

In several respects the new personnel coming to the OWI were dissimilar from the FIS veterans. The vast majority were not as overtly or zealously idealistic, ideological, or fervent in their attitudes toward Roosevelt's political philosophy and his world outlook as were the founders of the OWI, even though all of them despised the Nazis. The new recruits simply did not display the ultrapatriotic zeal, the ardent adherence to the New Deal liberalism of the FIS old guard, nor did they believe that propaganda could remake the world in America's image. Instead they were more realistic, although still overwhelmingly liberal, in their perceptions of propaganda and the job to be done.

Director Davis and Associate Director Milton Eisenhower were certainly representative of the new type of propagandist. They believed that OWI's job was to present the American perspective of the war in a clear, factual, truthful, and nonpartisan, nonideological, and overt fashion, using carefully selected news to convey the right message. Individuals who joined the OWI after June 1942 shared their outlook. The new recruits were highly skilled media and communications professionals who benefited OWI operations by bringing to the agency the technical and managerial skills they had practiced daily in their civilian careers, tending to leave behind personal political preferences and extremist ideologies. Though exhibiting a loyalty to the organization, their allegiance stemmed from the belief that the OWI was useful to the war effort and that its message had value in that context alone. They sought to win the war with words, not to remake the world.

Talented and highly qualified, the people employed by the OWI were from di-

verse professional backgrounds yet were still remarkably similar, both politically and ideologically. Davis, Sherwood, Eisenhower, and MacLeish, despite efforts to do otherwise, created a staff that was overwhelmingly liberal. As a result the agency had "one of the highest percentages of interventionist New Dealers of any wartime agency." The perception was widely held by friends and foes alike, including the military, Republicans in Congress, most federal departments, the public, and America's Allies, especially the British.[12] Perhaps the situation was unavoidable since the media and communications industry tended toward liberalism and the political left wing, but it was not coincidental that liberals, independent-minded, and even eccentric and colorful individuals were attracted to the OWI. In his diary James Rogers described the group:

> OWI is the menagerie of the Old Guard of the New Deal—the reformer-intellectuals. There is Sherwood, the playwright who does the President's speeches, lean, ragged, impulsive and a zealot. Archie MacLeish, the poet, Librarian of Congress but really a dreamer. Edgar Mowrer to whom men are black or white, "fascists" or "liberals." Barnes—"Joe"—whom I do not know. A barrel full of Jews, Communists or as the phrase goes, "fellow travelers." I enjoy nearly all of them. They fight "evil." They are the political guerrillas pricking Satan with words for needles, like the Salem witches but on God's side. At the head a Hoosier writer and politician, Elmer Davis.[13]

Director Davis was painfully aware of OWI's leftist tilt. From the outset he made an effort to play down extreme and overt expressions of ideology and politics or any activities that could be perceived as partisan by Congress, the public, and the president's critics and political opponents. He admitted that the OWI membership was often "described as . . . something out of this world . . . a band of dreamers and theorists" who ran "an uncontrolled propaganda mill grinding out promises, threats and cajolery." Thus Davis sought, but with limited success, a politically and ideologically balanced membership and enlisted at least one conservative Republican, Gardner Cowles, Jr., for the high-level post of Domestic Branch director, hoping to avoid the lunatic-liberal label. Davis's efforts eventually proved too little too late, however, although he was ultimately successful in removing the most outspoken liberals from OWI leadership positions, it was not before the agency had been permanently and indelibly branded a leftist, New Deal propaganda agency.[14]

Davis's efforts to infuse nonpolitical and nonideological blood into the OWI had little effect on the Overseas Branch. Its leadership, from its creation until

February 1944, was firmly and totally under the control of Robert Sherwood, Edd Johnson, Joseph Barnes, James Warburg, and like-minded individuals from the old FIS. They brought with them and maintained intact their liberal idealism, their personal political ideologies, and their contempt for anybody or any ideas right of the political center. They despised conservative elitists and the people they considered enemies of the New Deal, Wilsonian internationalism, and Franklin Roosevelt. To the OWI they brought their beliefs in the concept of fighting a people's war with propaganda to save civilization from a monstrous Fascist evil. They bristled at the accusations, in the words of Joseph Barnes, that "our propaganda . . . has been too simple, too provincially American, and too deeply committed to using truth as a weapon." The OWI's mandate forbade the "technique of falsehood" and "the strategy of terror." To the critics who claimed that the OWI had no guiding policy, Barnes retorted that their only policies were the ideals of the Four Freedoms and the Atlantic Charter.[15]

The views of the former FIS members became more extreme after the creation of the Overseas OWI. James P. Warburg, one of the most zealous OWI leaders, wrote that the war was an ideological struggle against fascism at home and abroad and not just a military contest between the Allies and the Axis. The war was "between those who want freedom for mankind and those who want freedom for themselves" at others' expense, "between those who believe in the equal rights of human beings . . . and those who believe in the divine right of power and privilege." The struggle had been going on for centuries. In both Europe and North America, Warburg believed, "a century of runaway capitalism" had "prepared the ground for fascism" by creating powerful groups of elites and special interest groups. The New Deal had shown the special interests at home and throughout the world that "American democracy had once more become dynamic . . . that the American people had once more regained their momentum as champions of human freedom." "The forgotten man," Warburg wrote, "had been once more remembered" and was on the rebound everywhere. "Modern economic man could throw off his chains . . . runaway capitalism did not have to lead to fascism." Through the Four Freedoms and the Atlantic Charter, Americans had pledged their support to "freedom for all everywhere and a just peace and establishment of a world order based on human freedom and justice." The threat of Fascist domination, however, was not just from abroad. Warburg believed that "what we are, here at home, conditions and determines what we do as a nation outside our own borders." "Conversely," he claimed, "our relationships abroad influence and to a large extent determine what sort of society we are able to create at home." The public and foreign policy that a person be-

OWI's James P. Warburg (left), with Archibald MacLeish and Murray Brophy in London, 1942. (Courtesy AP/Wide World Photos)

lieves in, according to Warburg, was the logical extension of the philosophy that governs the behavior of each individual toward the society in which he lives.[16]

Warburg's theories, which became part of the institutional thought of the Overseas OWI, applied not only to the Nazis but also to domestic enemies and rivals. The emphasis of the OSS on black propaganda and subversion, Warburg thought, was a worldwide extension of the personal philosophies held by OSS members. Likewise, Nazi behavior reflected the individual views of its followers, just as Warburg's own philosophies, shared with other OWI members, determined the ideological cast of their propaganda output. Not until late 1943 and early 1944 did their grip on the OWI loosen, bringing to the fore the newer, less extreme propagandists who had received formal instruction in one of OWI's new training centers rather than through years of political and ideological confrontation. Yet in many ways, the Wilsonian idealism and philosophies and the nostalgia for Roosevelt and the New Deal that was inserted into OWI propaganda output by Sherwood, Johnson, Barnes, Warburg, and their colleagues, although purged in 1944, remained a guid-

ing philosophy for many people involved in American domestic politics and international relations well into the postwar era.[17]

The similar backgrounds of OWI personnel were nowhere more apparent than in the Overseas Branch, where individuals from many related civilian professions held leadership positions in the various bureaus and offices. The traits and characteristics they commonly held were in turn reflected in policies, structure, and operations. The Overseas OWI eventually played the central role in U.S. propaganda efforts abroad, received three-quarters of the total OWI budget, and employed two-thirds of the agency's staff, although personnel turnover was always high and a persistent problem. As reorganized by Sherwood in December 1942, the branch was larger than the FIS but contained the same components that remained established for the duration.[18]

Sherwood dominated the Overseas OWI as director, assisted by deputies Joseph Barnes, Louis Cowan, Philip Hamblet, and James Warburg. In the director's office were the Regional Divisions, consisting of seven units of specialists, who produced specific studies and programs. Regional Division chiefs dealing with Europe included Edgar Mowrer, Ferdinand Kuhn, Douglas Miller, Bjarne Braatoy, and Percy Winner. A new R&A section was formed in fall 1942 under Eugene Katz. The OWI foreign outposts, as in the FIS, were entrusted to Harold Guinzburg and later to James Linen. In June 1942 the COI had had twelve outposts overseas, a number that under the OWI grew to twenty-one by September, to thirty-four by March 1943, and to thirty-eight in twenty-five countries by May 1945. Wallace Carroll was chief of the London outpost, correspondent Richard Watts, Jr., ran the outpost in Dublin, and NBC employee Gerald Mayer directed the outpost in Bern, Switzerland. The old FIS Radio Technical Division became the Communication Facilities Bureau (CFB) in the new OWI under Murray Brophy.[19]

The heart of the Overseas Branch was in New York City. The chief of the New York office, Joseph Barnes, was assisted by Edd Johnson, who directed the control office, which monitored OWI's output for accuracy and adherence to directives. Barnes in turn was assisted by James Warburg, who divided his time between New York City and OWI headquarters in Washington, D.C., as liaison between the overall policymaking and planning boards and the operational people in New York. The New York City office consisted of a Planning Board that developed and distributed weekly directives drafted by Warburg, containing instructions for propaganda to Europe, and the operational divisions that concentrated on radio activities. After December 1942 the New York City OWI office consisted of the Overseas Motion Pictures, Overseas Radio Programs, Overseas Publications, and Overseas News and Features bureaus.[20]

The Radio Program Bureau, under John Houseman and later under Lawrence

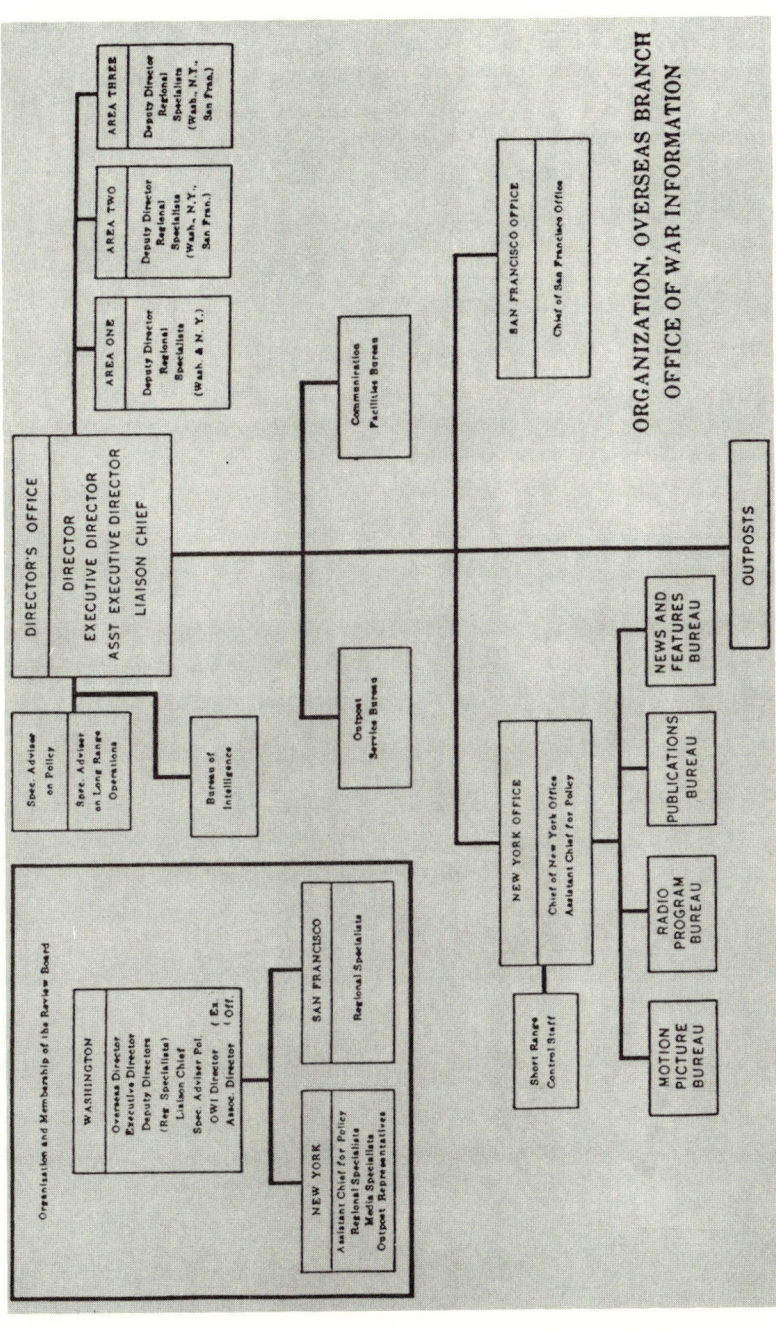

Figure 6.1. Organization of the Overseas Branch, U.S. Office of War Information, 1942. (Courtesy the National Archives)

Blochman, was the dominant branch of the East Coast OWI and controlled the shortwave Voice of America, located on West Fifty-seventh Street. The bureau contained a Programming Division, a Language Division, and, the largest of the three, a Broadcast Division, producing VOA material for Europe, Africa, and the Middle East. By the end of the war the VOA controlled thirty-six shortwave transmitters in the continental United States and fourteen overseas. The Broadcast Division contained national desks whose members developed programs and broadcast them for their particular national audience in unaccented native tongues.[21]

The Voice of America was the premiere OWI service. It expanded as rapidly as the American war effort and by 1 September 1942 employed 3,000 people, producing its own programs and material for rebroadcast by the BBC as well as recording domestic transmissions for overseas dissemination. It broadcast in twenty-two languages at the rate of 253 fifteen-minute shows per day, or a total of 443 hours per week. OWI officials confidently claimed in fall 1942 that the VOA was finally competing "on more nearly equal terms with the Axis radio." Although by no means the only VOA focus, Nazi Germany was a daily target.[22]

The remaining branches of the Overseas OWI were transferred directly from the FIS and included the Overseas Publications Bureau, originally under Edward Stanley, and the Overseas News and Features Bureau, first directed by Joseph Barnes and then by Edward Barrett. The latter bureau, like the others, had subdivisions, including a Basic News Division consisting of a Central News Desk, Press Review Desk, Cable Wireless unit, and a Features Desk.[23]

Policy formulation and the coordination of OWI's many divisions quickly proved a daunting problem seemingly devoid of solutions. To create policy guidelines Elmer Davis created a Committee on War Information Policy. The group, composed of representatives of several government agencies, was meant to develop policies for both OWI branches, but it soon became known as the Overseas Planning Board as most of its meetings involved overseas propaganda. The board met bimonthly in Washington to create plans in accordance with vague government propaganda policies that were then supplemented with the suggestions of individual board members.[24] The goal was not to dominate the process or even to produce propaganda "but to control propaganda along lines which are determined by basic policy and the decisions of appropriate federal agencies." The State Department representative, for example, could in theory veto any campaign deemed inconsistent with American foreign policy, and the military representatives could do likewise with propaganda dealing with military matters abroad. The end result was a program that was supposedly consistent with federal military, foreign, and propaganda policies even though the policies were vague and prone to broad interpreta-

tion. Board meetings were often the scene of acrimonious debates between members who held opposing views on propaganda and foreign policy.[25]

Working to form OWI policy and to control operations in league with the Overseas Planning Board was the Washington Review Board, a group that coordinated the plans created by the larger body with the overseas operational bureaus. The review board drafted weekly, periodic, and central directives that interpreted and refined the planning board's overall objectives. The directives provided background material on military and political issues in the target area and instructed bureaus on the best treatment of the issues in all output. During Sherwood's tenure the directives contained a politically oriented, highly ideological, and therefore controversial section, "Projection of America," which dealt with some aspect of U.S. life and culture from a liberal democratic view.[26]

The entire process of creating and implementing directives was complex and time-consuming. The central directive was usually completed on Thursday before being sent to the New York City office, where a regional directive was produced, tying the central themes into a plan for each of the seven geographical regions the OWI targeted just in Europe, a process that took place on Friday. The regional directive modified the general instructions of the central directive while adapting its emphasis and themes to fit the assumed characteristics of the audience. Drafts of the directives were then cleared after consultation with regional specialists and were checked for contradictions with federal policies. The plans were then returned to Washington where they were reviewed, usually on Saturday, and if approved, were implemented on Monday.[27]

The entire planning and review process, while satisfactory on paper, quickly broke down. The system of planning and review boards, multilevel directives, and complex checks and balances failed to account for rapidly changing events or to provide for the delineation of any long-range plans. To overcome one difficulty, daily directives or guides were produced, first in Washington and later in New York City, to govern output for each twenty-four-hour period. They took into account any last-minute news gathered by the OWI or intelligence services. Drafts were usually developed in a 9:15 A.M. meeting of regional specialists in Washington, who then forwarded their work to the review board in New York at 11:00 A.M., which in turn issued a guide for broadcasters at 6:00 P.M. Though the OWI was engaged in what many referred to as psychological warfare, no psychological theory was applied to any aspect of OWI planning and none appeared in the directives. As one member said, "One is justified in saying that any use of psychological principles by OWI was purely accidental." Whether Sherwood's known antipathy to psychology was responsible for the omission is unknown, but the number and influence of so-

cial scientists, including psychologists, did increase dramatically in the OWI as the war went on, especially after Sherwood's ouster.[28]

The early efforts to improve the OWI planning process, which many members quickly regarded as totally unworkable, only made a bad situation worse. Within a short period of time the system had collapsed to the point that James Warburg, as OWI deputy director of Psychological Warfare, had assumed almost total responsibility for drafting propaganda plans. He wrote much of the central directive after meeting briefly with the planning board in Washington and after the most cursory discussion with individuals outside OWI. In fairness to Warburg, who was later sharply criticized for his actions, most of the outsiders he consulted were uninterested in OWI's work and gave only passing thought to propaganda matters. Though Warburg's arbitrary acceptance of responsibility for OWI planning solved most of the problems associated with trying to create policy by committee, it meant that OWI policy was almost entirely his personal policy, reflecting his philosophy. Overseas OWI doctrine was thus created without the constraints or controls of other agencies. The New York City offices, as a result, became nearly autonomous and were wholly under the control of Warburg, Barnes, and Johnson by late 1942.[29]

Elmer Davis later was chagrined to discover that even when up-to-date directives were sent to the field they often were not followed. As late as July 1944 complaints were being received that the directives, often sixteen typewritten pages in length, were simply too long and detailed to allow harried and overworked field operators time to study or to follow their contents closely. To solve the additional problem of a lack of overall long-range propaganda planning, the OWI eventually created basic directives, one for each nation or region. The permanent, standing directives contained broad objectives for each area and served as a guide for writing central, regional, and daily directives.[30]

The diffusion of authority and control worsened as OWI operations proliferated overseas. Just as the Washington planning activities became remote from those in New York, the directors there realized that effective coordination of European operations mandated the creation of offices closer to target areas, thereby increasing the importance of OWI outposts in the months after June 1942. Although they varied in size, they had information and media facilities and other separate bureaus to disseminate propaganda, either as independent OWI operations or as an adjunct to tactical operations under Allied military control. The outposts also became the main centers for gathering intelligence and monitoring enemy propaganda. Such information was then forwarded to OWI planners in the United States.[31]

The closeness of the Anglo-American alliance and Britain's close physical proximity to the European continent ensured London's importance as the center for OWI overseas activities. The London Outpost was created by Robert Sherwood

and Edmond Taylor in September 1941, when both men still worked for the COI, and was transferred to the OWI intact in June 1942. The office provided liaison between New York City and the outposts in Europe, the Middle East, and North Africa and became a major production and intelligence-gathering center. Overseeing the entire operation was a policy and planning section that created leaflets, set radio policy, worked with the U.S. Army in creating combat propaganda campaigns, and coordinated American propaganda with that of the British Political Warfare Executive and Ministry of Information. Wallace Carroll was director of the London OWI office, which also had regional bureaus like those in New York City. Richard C. Hottelett of CBS directed the propaganda bureau targeting Nazi Germany. The London Outpost gained an importance and prestige unknown elsewhere, due mainly to a close relationship with its British counterparts and its distance from the deleterious interservice rivalries and ideological bickering in the stateside OWI centers. By August 1944 the London OWI office employed over 2,500 people and helped formulate the American military psychological warfare program in Europe, producing the bulk of the publications, leaflets, films and pictures used in the European theater.[32]

Radio, as with the Voice of America in New York City, came to account for the largest measure of London OWI's time and funds. To better reach European audiences who either lacked shortwave sets or who could not receive VOA broadcasts, London OWI, in cooperation with the U.S. Army and the BBC, established the American Broadcasting Station in Europe (ABSIE) in April 1944. Its first director was Brewster Morgan, who was later replaced by Philip H. Cohen. The staff of ABSIE, although under OWI's immediate control, ultimately was directed by the Psychological Warfare Division of Supreme Headquarters, Allied Expeditionary Force (SHAEF) and the U.S. Army. By 1945 ABSIE employed 248 people, of whom all but ten were OWI civilians. During an average month ABSIE broadcast eight hours daily and originated 682 programs in seven languages; 620 programs were fed through ABSIE transmitters and 62 through the VOA transmitters in New York, for a total on-air time of 232.5 hours. News made up most of the output, supplemented by longer features, as in the VOA programs. Rebroadcasts of both VOA and BBC programs filled out the ABSIE schedule. Policy guidance was forwarded by the Washington OWI headquarters, but, unlike VOA, ABSIE worked in close cooperation with Allied military officials in determining both audiences and broadcast content.[33]

Cooperation between the OWI and British psychological warfare agencies was close and increased as the war progressed. All OWI overseas planning for Europe was eventually done in conjunction with Britain's PWE. The OWI operatives received directives from Washington OWI headquarters, central, regional, and daily

guidance from New York City and London, and individual British directives. By 1943 OWI and PWE were producing "married directives" combining Allied plans, objectives, and themes for a more coordinated effort against Nazi Germany.[34]

The close Anglo-American cooperation troubled some of the more Anglophobic members of the OWI, primarily among the people joining after 1942, who feared British domination of American propaganda. Though Sherwood, Philip Hamblet, and C. D. Jackson favored such cooperation, Elmer Davis and Edward Barrett distrusted British influence and suspected British motives. Efforts were made to have propaganda more closely reflect American rather than British foreign policy objectives, but the OWI as a rule followed British propaganda plans. According to one scholar, "The British participated in American propaganda on the most intimate level" and helped in the production, format, style, and organization of American propaganda agencies, attended planning and production meetings, and helped in the production of propaganda directives and guidance at all levels in the United States and Europe.[35]

By late 1942 the Overseas OWI was beginning to conduct propaganda operations in Europe and North Africa and was expanding the activities of the VOA. Elmer Davis and Robert Sherwood had succeeded in staffing and organizing an agency to fill what they believed was President Roosevelt's mandate regarding propaganda. Although the OWI resembled a menagerie to its critics, its staff was one of the most talented, literate, and technically proficient groups of propagandists ever assembled.

From the time of its creation, differences of opinion existed on how the OWI should operate and what messages its propaganda should convey. The differences were based partly on the timing of OWI recruitment, which inadvertently collected two different categories of individuals. Most of the people with experience in propaganda matters prior to July 1942 were more zealous and more politically and ideologically motivated than the individuals who joined after 1942. The differences did not appear to cause debilitating problems at the outset or to reflect fundamental flaws of organization or leadership. Left unsettled, however, they resurfaced in 1943 as major disputes that dramatically altered the OWI. The conflicts occurred at a time when the OWI's propaganda was most vital to the Allied war effort and when the agency's monopoly was being seriously challenged by the psychological warfare programs of the OSS and the U.S. Army.

7 · The Bargain Basement of the Military: The OSS MO Branch

William Donovan did not agree with President Roosevelt's decision to separate propaganda activities from the new Office of Strategic Services, and he continued to advance the concept of a comprehensive military-controlled psychological warfare agency. Within seven months of its inception, the OSS reentered the propaganda field by filling a self-defined gap in the U.S. psychological warfare campaign, calling its new activities "morale operations." By Donovan's definition morale operations consisted of subversive or "black" propaganda, which he had always thought more effective than the OWI's strict dissemination of overt and truthful information. Donovan steadfastly maintained, with some accuracy, that subversive propaganda was a form that the OWI did not recognize or practice. The OSS, therefore, supplied a service that no other civilian or military agency accepted or performed. Nonetheless, when the existence of the OSS Morale Operations Branch became known to people in the OWI, a bitter interagency conflict resulted that had a debilitating effect on the operations of both agencies for several months during the height of World War II.

Continued military skepticism of both the OSS and of Donovan personally compounded his difficulties with the OWI. Even though the OSS was under the control of the JCS, its very existence and mission were not fully accepted, appreciated, or understood by that body or by the U.S. Army, the service that worked most closely with the OSS in North Africa, Europe, and the Mediterranean. The unorthodox nature of the OSS and its civilian personnel, with their overall outlook on warfare and foreign policy, caused apprehension among many officers. For six months following June 1942 Donovan struggled to create a firm niche for the OSS within the military establishment. During the following year he continued to battle enemies in the military and in the OWI to defend that niche, especially the place reserved for morale operations.

The military order creating the OSS was brief and vague. Beyond stating that the COI, including the FIS, was abolished, it did not provide any significant direction. The OSS was only to "collect and analyze . . . strategic information" and "plan and operate . . . special services" as directed by the JCS.[1] Donovan interpreted the latter duty as a mandate to conduct morale operations, but nothing in the order explicitly charged the OSS with this function. Yet neither Roosevelt nor the military attempted to define the OSS mission further.

The vagueness of the military order was deliberate and was directly attributable to political and ideological factors. The OSS was a controversial organization from the outset, with many well-placed and influential opponents. Its covert nature and implicit mandate to conduct subversive operations troubled many people, including OWI's Robert Sherwood and Elmer Davis as well as Maj. Gen. George V. Strong, chief of the Military Intelligence Division, War Department General Staff (MID/WDGS). These men exemplified the individuals who believed such unorthodox activities were unnecessary, unworthy of a democracy, and dangerous to military security and to America's image abroad. The president, however, was anxious to end internecine conflicts while establishing the agencies necessary to win the war: hence a vague military order that created a covert agency whose existence and true activities and doctrine were known to but a few.

An even more significant factor in the order's lack of specificity was Roosevelt's hesitancy to endorse publicly any agency that could become a domestic political or foreign diplomatic liability if its operations went awry. The OSS, a secret agency designed to engage in all manner of unsavory subversive activities that when practiced by the Nazis had caused American outrage and disgust, certainly had the potential to place Roosevelt in an embarrassing position amid a renewed controversy over federal propaganda programs. The vague military order thus provided the president with political security and insulation from adverse public reaction should OSS activities become known. Whatever the OSS did, President Roosevelt's personal reputation and political position would not be affected since the order did not delineate any directives that could be construed as an executive mandate for the agency to conduct unethical or immoral operations. As he had done on previous occasions, Roosevelt prudently allowed the responsibility for defining the OSS mission to the individuals directly responsible for the agency.

Following the shadowy mandate of the president's military order and in lieu of a federal propaganda policy, the OSS and the military created their version of a sound doctrine tailored to military needs. Within ten days of the order, the

Joint Chiefs issued JCS 67, a document that formally put the OSS under military control and broadened the scope of its activities to include providing intelligence and research to MID/WDGS and to the Office of Naval Intelligence as well as preparing plans and executing "subversive activities." The document marked the first time such missions were formally mentioned in connection with the OSS. Further, JCS 67 directed the OSS "to operate and train an organization for the collection of information through espionage," another task not specified in the original order. The OSS was now under the authority of JCS but was still beyond the direct control of its critics in the top command of the army and navy. Although the latter could, and did, interfere with the OSS at home and abroad, the agency was not in danger of abolition as long as it kept in the Joint Chiefs' good graces. Thus with a clear JCS mandate, Donovan began forming the OSS, largely without the help or enthusiastic cooperation of the federal government or the military. Nonetheless, he moved ahead to organize the psychological warfare office he had first proposed in 1941.[2]

Donovan's first task was to recruit additional personnel. Since the JCS controlled the OSS, and in consideration of Donovan's psychological warfare philosophy, a substantial number of military men were sought out. Moreover, many of the new civilian recruits, like those civilians who had joined earlier, took commissions in one of the military services on entering the agency to better enable them to operate in a military environment with its strict chain of command, hierarchical organization, and protocol. Consequently, the OSS showed increasing signs of militarization in terms of ideology and personnel as early as fall 1942.

The OWI's recruitment process was duplicated by the OSS. Donovan drew on experienced personnel from defunct federal agencies and then sought new people from the private sector. The former COI was heavily represented in the OSS; the entire membership, except for most FIS members, transferred en masse. Donovan then began recruiting outside the military and civil service by selecting individuals from his wide social and professional circles and from a pool of candidates suggested by his COI colleagues. Recognizing the recruiting mistakes associated with the FIS, Donovan became adept at identifying and then hiring people who shared his political and ideological views. People were selected for top positions after only a brief interview with the director to determine whether they agreed with the OSS ideals that Donovan had institutionalized. As one observer wrote, one of Donovan's "great gifts" was the ability "to read a man's character in a flash and get the best out of him." Perhaps 90 percent of the people in the OSS "would never have done much with their lives but spend their money," but Donovan was able to give them a purpose and to en-

gage their loyalties. His employment policy was to "hire a talented man and then let him, the organization, and the developing situation conspire to find the proper niche for him."[3]

The top OSS people were a select yet similar group. Largely a men's club, they not only shared Donovan's personal viewpoints and educational and professional background but also had demonstrated their beliefs through business, politics, and in prewar interventionist and internationalist activities. In recruiting, Donovan first turned "to men whom he knew and trusted, and this gave the . . . agency its tinge of well-to-do, Ivy League, often Republican, socially prominent men and women." This approach was necessary because of the covert nature of OSS activities and because of the notion that people who were financially and socially comfortable in life, who went to the same schools, belonged to the same political party, clubs, and professions, and whose fathers knew each other were least "likely to commit treason." Critics maintained that such criteria did not always result in the most effective personnel policy. Columnist Drew Pearson referred to the OSS as "one of the fanciest groups of dilettante diplomats, Wall Street bankers, and amateur detectives ever seen in Washington." Austin Cassini, a reporter for the *Washington Times Herald*, claimed that if a person entered OSS headquarters they found the blue-bloods of democracy, "ex-polo players, millionaires, Russian princes, society gambol boys, scientists, and dilettante detectives" and "the prettiest, best-born, snappiest girls who used to graduate from debutantedom to boredom." Agency member William Casey recounted that one recruit, Naval Lt. Comdr. Raymond Guest, later chief of the London Maritime Unit, like so many others, came to the OSS "fresh from the polo fields of Long Island and Virginia."[4]

A number of Donovan's supporters publicly contradicted the negative characterizations of the OSS staff. Columnist Arthur Krock, for one, took exception to the idea that the OSS was dominated by conservative Republicans, Wall Street bankers, corporate executives, millionaires, or individuals with Fascist leanings. He chided critics who claimed that the OSS stood for "Oh So Social" because of the "number of prominent members of old and established families who have gone to work there." Indeed Krock praised Donovan's recruitment policies, showing that OSS members came from diverse backgrounds, citing the example of the academics in the liberal-minded (but atypical) OSS R&A Branch. Krock, a critic of Roosevelt and the New Deal, wrote little about the status that other members held in business and society, however, and said nothing about the positions the same individuals held within the policymaking apparatus of the OSS. His *New York Times* article further neglected to mention that these people were friends and business acquaintances and that they shared

political and social beliefs stemming from prewar contacts. Despite Krock's assessment, the OSS was a bastion of the American conservative, legal, political, social, and business elite: the rich, the well educated, the well connected, and the powerful. It became a personal empire created and staffed solely by William Donovan without any input or interference from groups of liberal political or professional persuasions or from the president, the civil service, or, ironically, the U.S. military.[5]

Left to his own devices, Donovan exercised considerable latitude as to whom he recruited. The government and public knew little about the covert OSS or who worked for it although the vast majority of its members were prominent. In the final analysis, the professional, political, and social lives of the recruits contradict Krock's claim that the OSS was representative of a cross-section of society. The people in policymaking or supervisory positions were individually and collectively an extraordinarily successful and powerful group. Most of them were responsible for policy creation and implementation and, as is often the case in wartime, they frequently made crucial and important decisions at the front without higher approval or guidance. Their decisions were consistent with agency doctrine, either from knowledge of Donovan's intentions, or, more likely, because their own beliefs about the practices that constituted effective psychological warfare were the same as the director's.[6]

As new recruits were obtained, Donovan organized the covert and comprehensive psychological warfare agency he had envisioned years before. Like the OWI during the same period, the OSS underwent frequent changes, many of which were mandated by the JCS to militarize the OSS, but others were undertaken to maintain the security of the agency's clandestine tasks. A final factor for change grew from the need to establish a flexible framework that allowed expansion if further activities, propaganda for example, were deemed necessary to support military operations. Unlike the OWI, the OSS had a military structure, a strict hierarchy, and a clear chain of command. In many ways it reflected the corporate styles of organization that its members knew in civilian life and in the military services. The well-defined structure, at the outset, allowed a small group of men closely connected to Donovan to guide OSS operations effectively.

As part of a continuing process to mold the OSS into an agency fitting military needs the JCS continued to issue directives reorganizing the unit and expanding its role as demands arose. On 23 December 1942, for example, the Joint Chiefs issued JCS 155/4/D, revamping the OSS and putting it on equal status with the military services. The order took effect in early January 1943 and was issued without Roosevelt's input or the approval of Elmer Davis because it was interpreted by the people involved as a routine military administrative matter.

The document established the OSS as an agency performing a wide variety of unconventional military operations. The agency's activities were vastly expanded in all areas, except the Western Hemisphere, and it gained the responsibility for "the planning, development, coordination, and execution of the military program of psychological warfare." The program included propaganda, economic and guerrilla warfare, sabotage, partisan contacts, espionage and counterespionage in enemy-occupied or -controlled territory, and research and analysis, virtually all the duties Donovan envisioned. The propaganda mandate denied to Donovan and the OSS by Roosevelt and to the civilians in the OWI was now granted by the military, wholly without the president's knowledge or input. In the attempt to avoid or deflect conflicts with potential rivals, the order forbade the OSS from duplicating the functions of other agencies and ordered them to work with these groups under the control of theater commanders.[7]

The JCS order necessitated a revamping of the entire military program of psychological warfare to accommodate the new structure and role of the OSS. Donovan was instructed to form a new planning group that was to include nine civilians from the State Department and representatives of the OSS and the military. It would replace the atrophied Joint Psychological Warfare Committee created in March 1942, which had included the uncooperative OWI, CIAA, and BEW representatives who viewed propaganda as strictly a civilian concern. Donovan appointed the OSS members to the new planning group and approved or vetoed the membership from the other agencies. The appointment of a new planning unit caused the abolition of other JCS committees dealing with propaganda matters, including the Joint Psychological Warfare Sub-Committee and the Joint Psychological Warfare Advisory Committee. Future OSS plans were to be approved by the director of Strategic Services (Donovan's title), the JCS, and Joint Staff planners before being sent to field operatives. Abroad, OSS operations were theoretically subject to approval of the theater commanders.[8]

Convinced that propaganda would be of greater use to the military as the war progressed and sure of the need for closer supervision, the JCS mandated another OSS reorganization through General Order 9 on 3 January 1943, which provided the shape of the agency for the duration and made it a true military organization. Under Director Donovan, now a brigadier general, and the assistant director, Col. Edward Buxton, were an Executive Committee and support units responsible for administration, liaison, and planning. The operational branches, each under a deputy director, were the heart of the OSS. First in status and importance were the Secret Intelligence (SI), Research and Analysis and Foreign Nationalities (FN) branches. These unique services later expanded to include Counterintelligence (X-2) and Censorship and Documents (CD). The second

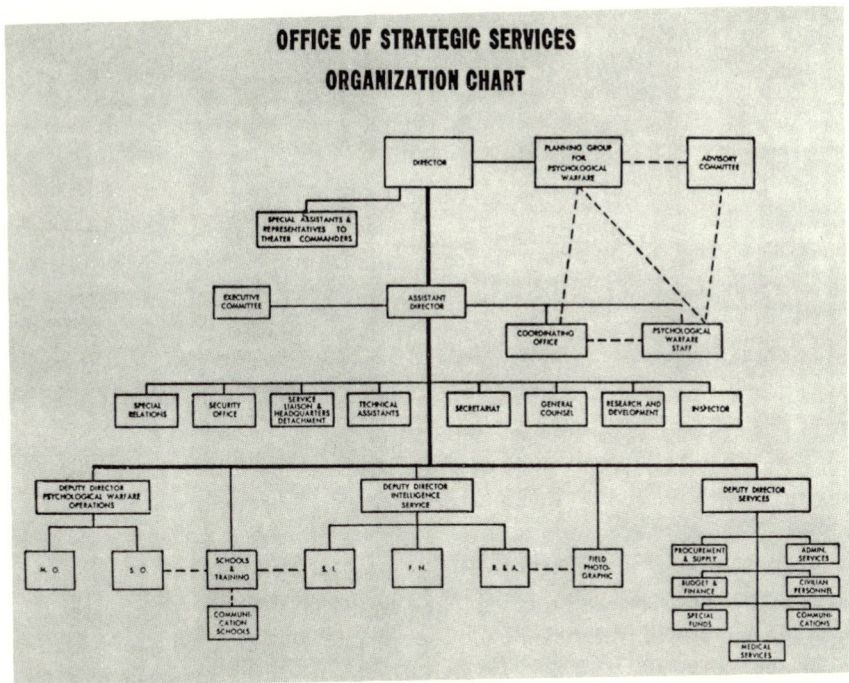

Figure 7.1. Organization of the Office of Strategic Services, 2 January 1943. (Courtesy the National Archives)

branch under a yet-to-be-appointed deputy director of Psychological Warfare Operations included Special Operations (SO), a new subversive black propaganda unit, the Morale Operations Branch (MO), and in 1944 a Maritime Unit (MU), Operations Group (OG), and Special Projects (SP) section.[9]

The capstone of JCS efforts to ensure that OSS plans and doctrine met military needs came with JCS 155/11/D, a seminal document that required all OSS programs be coordinated by a Planning Group for Psychological Warfare under Dr. James G. Rogers. It was responsible directly to Donovan and, through him, to the JCS. The group met daily to create basic plans for psychological warfare for OSS branches and to formulate the agency's guiding doctrine. Operational details were left to field operatives. Basic plans were developed by regions, one or more for each, depending on a region's importance in overall strategy, and were to include special and basic programs and detailed operational plans. The plans were to be updated with the most recent intelligence, provided by a Secret Intelligence Branch weekly summary covering political, economic, and military events. The plans drew from studies prepared by R&A experts familiar with

each targeted country or subject. In theory, the OSS could now operate as a self-contained, self-sufficient, and comprehensive military psychological warfare unit.[10]

Adjusting an essentially civilian organization to a military mode of operation and thinking proved a difficult task. In many ways, planning, coordination, and control within the OSS was just as haphazard, complex, and inefficient as it was in the OWI, despite Donovan's insistence on the close monitoring of processes and the agency's military-style organization. Once the planning group developed a basic plan, often with Donovan's personal input and always with his approval, it went to the JCS for review. If they passed it, which rarely happened without substantial revision, it went to the OSS Planning Staff and then to branch planning sections for transmittal to field operatives, who often made substantive last-minute and unannounced changes. The campaigns were then implemented after supposedly obtaining the approval of the theater's military commander.

The branches, with increased strictness, were required to file monthly reports detailing conformity with the plan, including operational successes and failures, the number of personnel on duty, and ideas for future operations or for improvements on existing campaigns. The entire process was time-consuming, complicated, and frustrating, especially considering the obstacles placed in the way of the OSS by the military services, the OWI, the State Department, and by actual field conditions. Planning Group chairman Rogers often expressed his frustration over the group's lack of achievements, complaining in late 1943 that "we are accomplishing little in getting OSS as an effective force. It remains a plaything and amusement . . . for Bill Donovan." The OSS, Rogers concluded, is "'the bargain basement" of the military services. It is full of remnants and novelties, all underground.'"[11]

The process of making the OSS an effective force was complicated by clashes with the OWI at home and with the U.S. Army abroad. Many of the conflicts were caused by Donovan's stubborn insistence that the OSS be the sole psychological warfare agency supporting the military. As a result, some OSS branches did indeed duplicate functions performed by other civilian and military agencies, including the OWI and the U.S. Army.

The OSS branch that was most deeply resented and seen as a direct encroachment on OWI's mandate was the Morale Operations Branch, a unit whose primary function the OSS defined as attacking "the morale and the political unity of the enemy through . . . psychological means operating or purporting to operate within the enemy or occupied territories." Donovan had always considered subversive propaganda an essential element of psychological warfare.

It was something "he had not been able to develop in the old COI, where the adepts of black propaganda were badly outnumbered by the 'truth-will-win-out' believers." The splitting of the COI, with its denial of any definable OSS propaganda function, had dealt a blow to Donovan's concept of a centralized and comprehensive agency that employed "all moral and physical means, other than orthodox military operations."[12]

The OWI practiced only official or overt propaganda; indeed, black, covert, or subversive propaganda was not being conducted by any federal agency. Donovan, therefore, sought to fill the void by creating an OSS propaganda function. He had Edmond Taylor draw up a complete morale operations program that supposedly did not infringe on the OWI's mandate, a mandate that, according to the OSS, allowed the OWI to oversee official "propaganda and publicity, including the dissemination of information, arguments, appeals, and instructions by mass means of communication." Given Donovan's fascination with Nazi practices and his psychological warfare philosophy, which referred to propaganda as "the initial arrow of penetration," it is not surprising he directed his energies toward covert operations.[13]

The American concept of morale operations was wholly defined by William Donovan and Edmond Taylor. It emulated Nazi tactics as supposedly used in Europe and was intended "to incite and spread dissension, confusion and disorder within enemy countries" and to promote "subversive activities against enemy governments." Donovan believed that MO "coaxes the minds of those it wishes to manipulate with the confidential voice of an accepted friend." Thus, "It can be far more effective than direct appeals or the stern commands, threats or promises of a stranger," practices conducted by the OWI. In enemy-occupied countries, MO sought to encourage resistance by means of field agents, native residents, rumors, printed matter, radio, "contacts with underground movements," bribery and subsidies, blackmail, counterfeiting of currency, ration cards, passports, personal papers of enemy prisoners or the dead, abduction, chain letters, poisoning, distribution of toy gadgets, assassinations, and other "divers manipulations."[14]

The suggestion that the United States conduct a campaign of subversive morale operations against the Axis countries was both innovative and controversial. No distinction had been made by Americans between white and black propaganda during World War I, nor had they drawn a clear distinction since 1941, despite the work of early agencies. The proposed MO Branch, as a result, produced immediate critics within the OSS, the military, and especially the OWI. The critics, one MO proponent stated, had forgotten German efforts such as "the crepe-hung war widows paid to weep in public places," or "the coffin-

shaped leaflets," or "the balmusette jingles blared toward the French trenches by German loudspeakers," or the "traitor of Stuttgart broadcasts." Yet after the fall of France, "even the most conservative had to recognize that here was a new and powerful offensive weapon" that the Allies had to match. The Axis powers had psychological warfare agencies practicing subversive morale operations long before the war; the Allies did not. It was not surprising that "England, and after her the United States, had to learn their lessons from the Germans." Edmond Taylor did not minimize the origin or the devious nature of morale operations, saying that "black propaganda is essentially calumny and provocation, the age-old crafts of tyrant and conspirator, spread with twentieth-century technology." He proposed that MO follow Britain's PWE, whose campaigns were "more imaginative and frequently more ruthless than any Nazi psychological warfare."[15]

In defining and developing the methods used by the OSS, Donovan and Taylor borrowed heavily from the British. They eventually refined PWE techniques, which included the production of leaflets, posters, stickers, stencils, newspapers, and magazine articles disguised as enemy publications or as materials of fake enemy dissident or resistance groups in enemy-occupied countries. Distributed by air, by partisan, or by agent, the printed materials were delivered in ever-increasing quantities. MO developed forgeries of commercial, civilian, and military documents, Nazi party and business stationary, ration cards, and postage stamps, all of which were used to intimidate collaborators, to implicate enemy officials, soldiers, or civilians in subversive plots against the state, and to harass the Gestapo. One form of forgery, the poison-pen letter, was used to incriminate or intimidate business firms, soldiers, or collaborators.[16]

Radio was another medium used by MO to disseminate propaganda to broad audiences. Clandestine transmitters, posing as "freedom stations" of a resistance or dissident group within an enemy or enemy-occupied nation, spread propaganda not otherwise easily distributed by agents or in print form. Morale Operations used other broadcasts to give false instructions to Nazi party officials, military commanders, and civil leaders. Another technique, despite the lack of MO agents in enemy territory until late in the war, was rumors, slogans, jokes, and planted witticisms that OSS Special Operations and Secret Intelligence agents were encouraged to pass when in Germany or in enemy-occupied areas. Until sufficient MO people reached the front, rumors were a main propaganda method.[17]

Although Donovan and Taylor had little difficulty in creating suitable plans for morale operations, they had few people to implement them. Their first obstacle after General Order 9 was issued was finding qualified individuals. According to one OSS member, "Most of the celebrities in the field had long since

been snapped up by other agencies" or already worked for the OSS so that "MO had to be content with too many unknown people," a factor that "contributed largely to its low standing in the [OSS] organization." Donovan transferred personnel from other branches, but such methods produced little more than a high turnover, as many people sent to MO quickly sought transfers to the more glamorous and seemingly effective SI and SO branches. Members of these branches in turn had a low opinion of MO and "disapproved of its mission . . . did not believe in it, and in general harbored much the same feeling" toward MO that "they had toward FIS." As a result MO always remained small and, to its critics, ineffectual.[18]

Internal agency transfers failed to fill MO personnel needs, and Donovan sought in vain to lure people from other agencies. He immediately focused on the Overseas OWI. John Houseman recalled an episode in 1942 when he and a dozen senior OWI members were asked to an elegant private lunch at the St. Regis Hotel in New York City, during which Donovan "wooed" them "with a glowing account of the attractions and excitements of his own expanding 'black' operations." The attempt to lure OWI people failed, Houseman recounted, because Donovan ignored "the deep, personal loyalty we all felt for Robert Sherwood and the pride" each member took in their work under him. Although Donovan did obtain a small number of the OWI people, such as Paul West, Jack Crutcher, Harold Peters, and Roland Dulin, he was again forced to turn to prewar business, legal, social, and media contacts. And OSS recruiters turned increasingly to refugees and foreigners in the United States and in the combat theaters.[19]

Surprisingly, considering the intensive recruiting efforts of the COI, the OSS, and the OWI during the previous two years, Donovan's efforts to attract propagandists were successful. In the new round of hiring he sought people "who were not only outstanding in initiative, resourcefulness, and intelligence" but who also had experience in writing, graphics, printing, and radio, or a special knowledge of a foreign area, its people, and its language.[20]

Although it was true that most of the celebrities in their respective fields had already been recruited or had selected the OWI as their first choice as a propaganda employer, the OSS did find many qualified and talented individuals. Many of them were young and inexperienced, far more so than earlier recruits, and generally they were not prominent in internationalist, business, media, academic, or interventionist circles as earlier COI and OSS people had been. The later recruits, who shared most of the ideological and political beliefs of earlier OSS recruits, however, formed the core of the first American agency specifically charged with conducting subversive propaganda.[21]

Frederick Oechsner, prewar foreign correspondent and the first chief of the Office of Strategic Services Morale Operations Branch in 1943. (U.S. Army Photo; reproduced at the National Archives)

Donovan was always personally involved in every major decision concerning the OSS, and he directly selected the head of the new Morale Operations Branch. The first director, and the man deemed most suited for the task during the war, was veteran foreign correspondent Frederick Oechsner; he was replaced by steel executive Kenneth D. Mann in May 1944, when Oechsner left to represent MO-OSS within PWD/SHAEF. During MO's brief history it had a series

of chiefs in addition to Oechsner and Mann, including Charles P. Healy, Patrick Dolan, Morton Bodfish, and Herbert S. Little.[22]

Despite having a talented and capable staff, the MO Branch was always considered the poor relation and never contained a large number of people relative to the other OSS branches. Yet its small size became a significant factor in its ultimate success and continued existence. The Morale Operations Branch survived its disputes with the U.S. Army and the OWI and the internal disputes within the OSS because it was simply too small to merit a great deal of attention by institutions containing thousands, if not millions, of members. Had MO been more ubiquitous and had its campaigns proved a serious enough threat to U.S. Army combat operations or to the OWI campaigns, it is likely that the branch would have been demolished by its larger rivals through any available means. Yet MO filled a small but vital niche, one that was ultimately deemed of insufficient importance to either the OWI or the U.S. Army. Nonetheless, MO's effect on psychological warfare theory and doctrine and on propaganda operations abroad was significant. It introduced an unexplored and untried form of warfare into the campaign against Nazi Germany.[23]

Although small, the Morale Operations Branch, like the remainder of the OSS, was divided into several divisions performing specific tasks as originally conceived by Donovan and Taylor. The divisions included the Special Communications Detachment, which conducted combat propaganda operations in cooperation with the U.S. Army in Europe; a Radio Division, which conducted all black or clandestine radio campaigns; a Special Contacts Division, which distributed propaganda to partisan groups; a Foreign Division, which conducted miscellaneous MO activities abroad; and a Publications and Campaigns Division, which produced leaflets, pamphlets, and whispering campaigns.[24]

To implement its programs, small MO outposts were set up throughout Europe, North Africa, and the Mediterranean, usually in close proximity to U.S. Army combat or intelligence outfits, at times being integrated into the headquarters staff of the latter. By 1945 MO had base operations in Algiers, Algeria; Cairo, Egypt; Bari, Caserta, Siena, Naples, Rome, and Brindisi, Italy; Paris, Bern, Stockholm, and London. From these bases MO personnel conducted subversive propaganda campaigns against the Axis throughout Eastern and Western Europe, North Africa, and the Middle East. The branch targeted enemy civil and military audiences, seeking to create distrust, suspicion, resentment, civil strife, and friction by playing up social, national, and ethnic rivalries and differences as well as by turning people against their governments, leaders against leaders, social and economic class against class, soldiers against officers, unit against unit, service against service, ally against ally, and civilians against the military.[25]

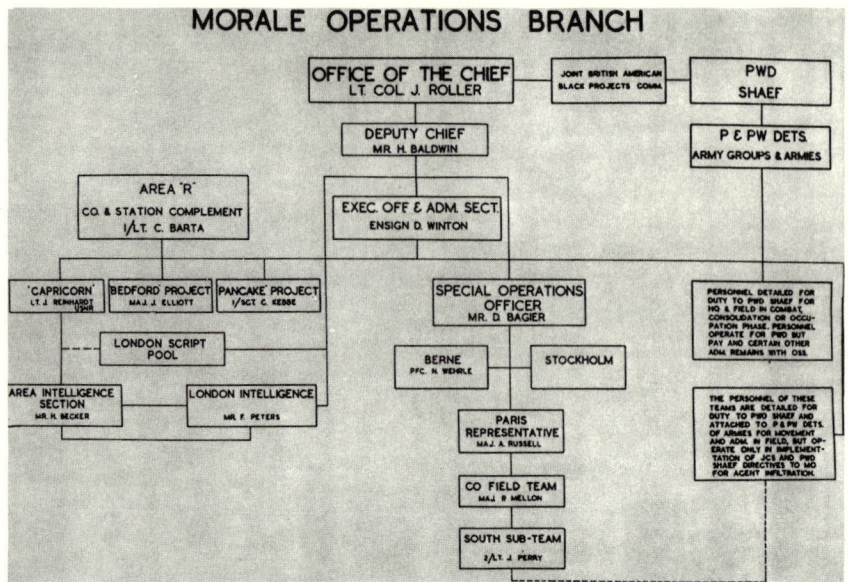

Figure 7.2. Organization of the Office of Strategic Services Morale Operations Branch, European Theater of Operations, February 1945. (Courtesy the National Archives)

The most important foreign MO base was in London. Established in early 1943, much later than its Overseas OWI counterpart, the London OSS grew rapidly after MO was given sole responsibility for conducting all subversive propaganda for the Psychological Warfare Division of SHAEF. In this capacity MO worked in close cooperation with the other Allied military and psychological warfare services, especially Britain's PWE. Soon after the Normandy landings MO was allowed to conduct operations independently of PWD although the branch was still under military control.[26]

To coordinate and control OSS morale operations, a complex system was created in Washington that stretched to the combat theaters. It largely failed to meet expectations, and by late 1943 all MO planning was transferred to the OSS Planning Group. Like the OWI's system, the OSS procedure looked good on paper but was increasingly cumbersome and divorced from actual field events. By May 1944 the Washington headquarters had little direct control over actual MO operations, which were planned and implemented at regional outposts.[27]

By March 1943 the MO Branch, following the other branches of the OSS, was ready for action in Europe. Doctrine was created, techniques were being developed, and personnel had been recruited and trained.[28] Before MO could be-

come operational abroad, however, the branch came under increasing attack from many people within the OSS, from the U.S. Army, and from the OWI who considered it superfluous, dangerous, immoral, and unethical. Surprisingly, even OSS Planning Group Chair James Rogers derided MO, claiming it "is a silly performance," consisting of "rumor mongering, clandestine 'Freedom Station' radio pretenses and not at all in its real field of intrigue against the enemy."[29]

Thus instead of being accepted and well on its way to undermining the Nazis in conjunction with the OWI and the U.S. Army in the European theater, the MO Branch found itself increasingly questioned, poked, and prodded by numerous critics at home. General Donovan still considered morale operations vital to the war effort, however, and continued to support the branch against a rising tide of skeptics. Morale operations were a crucial part of his overall concept of psychological warfare and had to be preserved. Although Donovan had succeeded in creating the organization he had earlier envisioned by late 1942, the ability of the OSS in general and of the MO Branch in particular to perform their missions without interference from rivals and to remain viable abroad was still very much in doubt.

8 · Controlling a Rear Echelon Insanity: The U.S. Army and Psychological Warfare, 1941–1943

The soldiers of the U.S. Army entered the field of psychological warfare much later than civilians did. Ultimately, however, the military came to oversee that aspect of the offensive against Germany and succeeded in fashioning a campaign that made propaganda a valued weapon. Their eventual military domination of the American psychological warfare campaign did not occur by happenstance but was the result of a concerted effort by U.S. Army leaders to harness propaganda for military purposes and to gain absolute control over all operations in the combat theaters.

Of the groups involved with psychological warfare during World War II, only the U.S. Army had had any practical experience of it, dating from World War I.[1] The brief use of tactical propaganda against the Central Powers in 1918, however, failed to convince postwar army theorists of its utility as an offensive weapon. Thus, the U.S. Army's propaganda capability deteriorated completely during the interwar years. It was not until the OSS and the OWI became active at home and abroad, until army leaders became concerned about draftee morale, and until public hysteria about Nazi propaganda peaked that civilians in the War Department began to press the issue of propaganda for military purposes. At that point, soldiers began to accept the idea that unconventional weapons could perhaps help shorten the war.

The army was slow in realizing the negative ramifications stemming from their years of neglecting propaganda. When they did recognize them, army officials also discovered that the lead held by civilian propaganda agencies had substantially outpaced their own feeble efforts. In a realm of warfare increasingly seen by civilians and a few soldiers as a necessary ingredient for the success of modern armies, the U.S. Army lacked doctrine, organizations, personnel, and

perhaps most significantly any real voice in propaganda matters that could directly affect future operations overseas.

Complicating the problems caused by the lack of an army capability was the presence of significant numbers of civilian propagandists in the combat theaters who were largely beyond army control. The heavily political and ideological nature of civilian operations, both OSS and OWI, and the lack of a federal propaganda policy raised troubling new issues about civil-military relations, ideology, military security, and overall control of propaganda. It was apparent by late 1942, however, that propaganda and the civilians who practiced it were well entrenched and unlikely to cease operations or disappear from the combat theaters just because the army was uncomfortable with their activities.

Faced with difficulties and with organizations not of their own creation and choosing, the U.S. Army aggressively pursued a solution to propaganda-related problems for two years, a solution that was relatively simple—the imposition of a strict and complete control of propaganda activities in the combat theaters— regardless of whether they were military or civilian in origin or whether civilian agencies desired or welcomed such control. To the U.S. Army, the primary national goal was the total military defeat of the Axis powers; all energies should be devoted to this end alone. Political and ideological agendas that complicated or delayed the victory were to be avoided. Winning the war was an immediate army priority; constructing the peace was a postwar job for diplomats and politicians. The observations of army officials between 1940 and 1943 led many people to the conclusion that national priorities were becoming confused and perhaps inextricably connected with combat operations, especially in the realm of psychological warfare. The U.S. Army, the largest western Allied military service in Europe, therefore purposely assumed a leadership role in psychological warfare matters involving American civilians and set out in 1942 to gain control of civilian propaganda activities overseas through the top Allied military headquarters in the Mediterranean and in northwest Europe.

Taking over the civilian propaganda programs abroad did not resolve the difficulties associated with the fact that the army lacked its own propaganda capability. Thus, to meet specific tactical or combat propaganda needs, the U.S. Army began to co-opt OWI and OSS civilians and to develop U.S. Army psychological warfare units, which, though relying on civilian expertise, were organized as military formations and were largely apolitical and which used personnel and equipment under army control.

The drawn-out and massive transition was characterized by contention, confrontation, and turmoil. To many civilians, army intervention was interpreted as a dangerous and unwelcome development. Soldiers supposedly lacked the politi-

cal and ideological zeal of civilian propagandists and the knowledge and experience in propaganda matters acquired by civilians through decades of study and observation. Between the wars, when Germany exerted considerable efforts to study propaganda, no comparable War Department psychological warfare office existed so that the lessons learned during World War I were lost. The emphasis of the small, conservative-minded interwar U.S. Army was on "pragmatic concerns . . . away from psychological warfare [and] toward consideration of things that were more 'practical, immediate, tangible.'"

American foreign policy stressed a defensive military posture, and when combined with the distrust of propaganda, the lack of adequate funding, and the U.S. Army's conservative outlook on politics, strategy, tactics, and doctrine, propaganda received little consideration. The situation was worsened by an army leadership that "grew increasingly narrow and strictly professional. No high officer . . . wanted to stick out his neck on any subject and everyone was desirous of avoiding responsibility," especially in propaganda matters. Only one officer with propaganda experience remained with the Military Intelligence Division of the War Department General Staff by 1941.[2]

The U.S. Army, like the government and much of the public, did come to regard Nazi propaganda as a major threat. In fall 1939 a joint service report was prepared on the necessity of bolstering morale defenses in the armed forces. Yet even when such slight interest was exhibited, military theorists showed a clear predilection to view propaganda as a defensive tool, not as an offensive weapon. The 1940 fall of France prompted startled U.S. Army leaders seriously to notice offensive psychological warfare for the first time, believing, as did most Americans, that Nazi propaganda was primarily responsible for the French defeat.[3]

Motivating the army to create a propaganda capability was an arduous task undertaken by both soldiers and civilians, the latter predominating. The two most active individuals in the War Department in this regard were Assistant Secretary of War John J. McCloy and Brig. Gen. Sherman Miles, the acting assistant chief of staff, G-2. At their behest, Chief of Staff Gen. George C. Marshall ordered the General Staff intelligence section to prepare an estimate of Axis propaganda in the Americas, indicative of the belief that the greatest propaganda threat to the nation was in South and Central America and that propaganda had some connection to intelligence activities. The latter assumption caused a great deal of confusion within the army and was not corrected until intelligence and psychological warfare functions were formally separated in 1944. As a result of Marshall's order, G-2 prepared two studies, submitted in July and November 1940, suggesting that the War Department undertake some form of counterpropaganda and morale-building activities. At the same time, the War

Department began to prepare a field manual on propaganda, which appeared in December 1940 but subsequently received limited circulation in a service concerned overwhelmingly with conventional rearmament.[4]

Assistant Secretary McCloy, who was heavily involved in the work of the Ickes Committee, knew that the support of the General Staff and chief of staff was crucial in getting results. He therefore wrote Marshall in spring 1941 suggesting that a propaganda section be developed within the War Department Military Intelligence Division, but the chief of staff refused, thinking such a group would not meet with congressional approval. Further, Marshall appeared to have little regard for intelligence officers in general at this time, including the headstrong Maj. Gen. George V. Strong, who was later appointed chief of MID in June 1942.[5]

Marshall was similarly unreceptive to the ideas of General Miles, who had written him in January 1941 suggesting that the army act to refute the enemy's psychological attacks and to take "the offensive . . . to instill into the enemy's masses discontent with their leaders, defeatism, and even belief and hope in our ideals and our successes." Miles was convinced of the effectiveness of propaganda, his convictions based on the German success in France and on the work of the Ickes Committee. Thinking of the day when propaganda could play a major role in military operations, he concluded that "the War Department should assume an initial interest and, eventually a paramount one" in government propaganda operations. Marshall, however, remained impervious to the efforts of both McCloy and Miles.[6]

Blocked by a military hierarchy focused on more pressing matters of mobilization and disappointed by the work of the Ickes Committee, McCloy continued to push the idea of an army propaganda program on lower-level military officers and civilians within the War Department. He acted on the suggestion of the former military attaché to Berlin, Lt. Col. Percy G. Black and urged General Miles to gather a small group of officers unofficially to study "the psychology of our own people and forces" and "that of neutral and enemy nations." McCloy then turned to his mentor, Secretary of War Henry L. Stimson, who, though known to find both propaganda and intelligence activities distasteful in the extreme, was sympathetic to McCloy's efforts. Stimson broke the impasse by ordering Marshall to create a Special Study Group (SSG) to examine propaganda matters for the army. Marshall complied, and the group was formed in June 1941; by the end of the summer, it included six officers and eleven civilians.[7]

Although the Special Study Group constituted an important first step by the War Department, it was largely ignored by the army and fell far short of McCloy's expectations. The group's primary functions were to act as liaison with ci-

Secretary of War Henry Stimson with U.S. Army chief of staff Gen. George C. Marshall in January 1942. (U.S. Army, OWI Photo; reproduced at the National Archives)

vilian propaganda agencies, to obtain weekly and daily summaries of foreign propaganda broadcasts, to complete surveys for private groups, such as the Council for Democracy, to initiate a weekly telegram service reporting defense-related developments to military missions abroad, and to counteract the effects of German propaganda by distributing issues of *Newsweek* and *Life* within the army. The secret group quickly proved a complete failure as its members discovered that they lacked high-level support in the ever-growing, ever more crowded psychological warfare field. Moreover, "Many senior personnel regarded psychological warfare with downright suspicion." To add insult to injury, SSG was even refused meeting places in the War Department and ended up gathering in an empty classroom at nearby George Washington University. The snub by the War Department meant in turn that the U.S. Army failed to establish early control of propaganda and let it slip to the COI, OWI, and OSS, all of whom were unwilling to cooperate with the military services if it threatened their institutional independence or organizational integrity.[8]

Many of the SSG's troubles were caused by Colonel Black, described by crit-

ics as a poor leader who committed the group to so many sorts of propaganda work that it could not cover any area well. He sought advice only from academic psychologists rather than from journalists or radio broadcasters who had more expertise in media, public relations, and propaganda matters and who were flocking to the civilian agencies that largely duplicated SSG's efforts in a far more competent way. Finally, he failed to mobilize or garner any high-placed, effective military support as Donovan had done. Throughout the war, the U.S. Army lacked any military figure of sufficient stature to champion psychological warfare within the service. Support always remained halfhearted, and propaganda efforts, even when successful, were viewed with skepticism. During Black's tenure, no "government agency, military or civilian, made use of [SSG] work for policy planning." In the absence of any military or corresponding federal policy, the civilian services developed their own doctrines and clung to them long after the army began trying to assert control, causing debilitating interservice and ideological conflicts. By late 1942 the civilian agencies simply realized that they could ignore the U.S. Army with impunity.[9]

The army's initial indifference diminished as the Allied war effort expanded. Soon after Pearl Harbor, during the Arcadia Conference, the JCS took responsibility for psychological warfare matters. General Miles was soon replaced by Brig. Gen. Raymond E. Lee, who suggested the creation of a JCS committee of two army and navy representatives, with one SSG member "to coordinate psychological warfare of other U.S. government agencies." The resulting Joint Psychological Warfare Committee, formed in February 1942, ended any need for SSG's independent existence, and in the following month, when the War Department Military Intelligence Division was reorganized, the SSG was redesignated the Psychological Warfare Branch, G-2. Although it was officially charged with carrying out War Department psychological warfare functions, a somewhat vague and empty assignment, it had no operational role and served as little more than a liaison agency. Its chief, Col. Oscar Solbert, represented the War Department at OWI, CIAA, and OSS policy-planning meetings and handled messages to U.S. Army propaganda units abroad. Yet PWB G-2 was also viewed as powerless, and, despite the efforts of Solbert and others to save the office, it was abolished in December 1942 following the issuance of JCS 155/4/D. The directive also abolished the JPWC and named the OSS as the sole agency responsible for planning, coordinating, and executing the military program of psychological warfare.[10]

Many soldiers were uncomfortable with the idea of the largely civilian OSS being in charge of psychological warfare. Since Allied propaganda operations abroad were proving to be in need of centralized control, Maj. Gen. T. T.

Handy, assistant chief of staff for Operations (G-3), and Maj. Gen. George V. Strong (G-2) decided to reverse the December 1942 decision. Acting on the suggestion of OWI's C. D. Jackson, the civilian deputy of PWB/Allied Force Headquarters (AFHQ), and AFHQ's chief of Information, News, and Censorship (INC), Brig. Gen. Robert A. McClure, Handy, and Strong recommended to Secretary Stimson that a central propaganda authority be reestablished within the War Department. Thus, in late October 1943, a new PWB G-2 was created. Its primary purposes were to ensure that the civilian agencies met army needs and provided adequate liaison with the JCS, the Combined Chiefs of Staff, and theater commanders abroad.[11]

War Department accomplishments fell far short of expectations. Even after PWB was reestablished, most tactical propaganda work involving planning, coordination, and implementation was still carried out at the theater level. The War Department PWB quickly shrank into insignificance, while the theater PWBs flourished worldwide. By degrees, however, the U.S. Army had started to establish a military-controlled, civilian-operated psychological warfare system that was to operate in the combat zones with the approval of the theater commanders.[12]

Perhaps not surprisingly, the first military propaganda organizations in the combat zones overseas were formed by civilians. The individuals making up the Psychological Warfare Service, Allied Force Headquarters (PWS/AFHQ), assembled in London in October 1942 under OWI's Percy Winner. The original army membership of the infant organization consisted of only six officers and enlisted men from PWB G-2 and OWI. The entire service, which numbered just fifty people, was dominated at the time by thirty-five Britons. Simultaneously, two other groups, largely from OWI and under OWI's Jay Allen and Oliver H. P. Garrett, were formed in the United States for the purpose of landing with American troops in North Africa. According to Robert Sherwood, who was unaware of PWS's existence until after the TORCH landings, there were no formal Allied agreements founding PWS, only the realization that psychological warfare "was an Allied problem and that we must work closely together."[13]

The army quickly moved to assert some sort of control over the PWS. On 27 October 1942, as the invasion forces formed, Gen. Dwight D. Eisenhower, the Allied TORCH commander, appointed a cavalry officer, Col. Charles B. Hazeltine, to command the group. Although Eisenhower had admitted to OWI's Wallace Carroll early in the summer that he knew little about psychological warfare, he was willing to give it every chance. His attitude appeared to be more enlightened than the army norm, and it was shared by the new PWS chief. Hazeltine, who described himself as "the senior Colonel in the U.S. Army," lacked any

Col. Charles B. Hazeltine (center), *chief of the Psychological Warfare Branch, Allied Force Headquarters, at a meeting with his staff in North Africa in early 1943. (U.S. Army, OWI Photo; reproduced at the National Archives)*

knowledge of psychological warfare but professed a willingness to try it after attempting to duck his new assignment during a conference with Gen. Walter Bedell Smith. Hazeltine was joined in Gibraltar in early November by Percy Winner. Together, Hazeltine, Winner, Edmond Taylor, and C. D. Jackson organized the unit for the scheduled 8 November invasion. No one realized that the unresolved propaganda issues that had caused conflicts at home for over two years were about to spread to the combat zone with disastrous diplomatic and political consequences. Two days prior to TORCH, PWS was officially activated.[14]

As Allied forces gathered for the largest amphibious landing to date, the OWI began the first full-scale U.S. propaganda operations of the war in support of military operations. On 7 November the Voice of America, independent of military control, delivered radio broadcasts from New York City and London announcing that the liberation phase of the war was soon to begin. The next day, 8 November 1942, D-Day in North Africa, the strategic propaganda programs were supplemented by tactical broadcasts by Jay Allen from the USS *Texas* off Morocco. Radio appeals were followed by a speech in French from President Roosevelt to the people of North Africa, by two appeals from General Eisenhower to the Vichy French not to resist the landings, and by leaflets at-

tempting to split the French and Italians from the Germans. All Allied propaganda operations were produced and carried out by civilians, with only minimal army input despite orders that all such operations needed prior military approval.[15]

Amid the backdrop of large-scale military operations, the small PWS operated unfettered and unassisted by the AFHQ command. Their heavily political and extremely ideological activities, however, did not go unnoticed for long. The first major clash was only weeks in coming and involved behavior that was perceived by U.S. Army commanders as gross insubordination from OWI members over the policy of working with the Vichy French leader, Adm. Jean Darlan, rather than with Gen. Henri Giraud, a figure whom Americans mistakenly thought more acceptable to the French. When it was discovered that Giraud was indeed unpopular as well as weak and bumbling, in spite of American propaganda efforts to portray him otherwise, the decision was made to work out a deal with Darlan.[16]

American cooperation with Darlan was meant to facilitate army operations, yet it contradicted the primary OWI propaganda theme that liberation from fascism was at hand. The policy was also contrary to the personal philosophies of most OWI propagandists, individuals "who viewed the war as a crusade for a better world [and] felt that principle had been sacrificed for expediency," the first of many such examples. Robert Sherwood believed the deal gave ammunition to Axis propagandists and served to reinforce European suspicions that although Americans "talked big" about the Four Freedoms and the Atlantic Charter, "they actually knew nothing about Europe and could be hoodwinked by any treacherous gangster who offered them collaboration." To Sherwood, the values Americans stood for "constitute the one ideology that men of freedom and goodwill can turn to." If that ideology was unknown or misunderstood, Sherwood declared, "we betray not only the people of America, but all people everywhere." James Warburg thought the policy destroyed beliefs "in the good faith of the United States and the sincerity of our war and peace aims." It indicated that when Americans liberated a country, they put friends in jail and surrendered nations "to the enemies of democracy." Warburg warned that if this impression took root, the North African campaign would be a "political defeat irrespective of any military success."[17]

In their statements regarding the Darlan deal, the top OWI leaders clearly indicated their belief that the war was an ideological crusade in which high-minded principles should not be scrapped for short-term tactical goals. Rather than throw Vichyites out of power, the government had ordered the OWI to support Darlan's civil structure and to play down his more odious tactics and

questionable sympathies. President Roosevelt unflinchingly adhered to the deal, despite a plea from Sherwood, Hopkins, and Rosenman to make clear that it was only temporary and carried with it certain stipulations. OWI directives in late November 1942 explicitly stated that the president had set a clear policy line "which should be considered a directive . . . the best was going to have to be made of a bad situation. Further discussion of Darlan should be dropped."[18]

Outraged OWI–PWS propagandists did not end their criticisms and took unilateral and unauthorized steps to subvert Darlan. Ignoring their instructions and official policy, they formed an anti-Darlan resistance group that gathered intelligence on Vichy atrocities and gave the stories to Allied war correspondents who slipped them by army censors to outraged newspaper editors and citizens at home. The actions, implicitly criticizing Allied diplomatic policies and the U.S. Army, created an even greater furor than the initial Darlan agreement. Accordingly, "Some of the news dispatches that cast the greatest discredit on the United States were inspired by Americans who had gone to North Africa to make propaganda capital for America."[19]

Darlan's December 1942 assassination ended the immediate diplomatic dilemma, yet the damage to army–OWI relations was practically irreversible. Not only did OWI members appear to be more loyal to a philosophy contrary to that of the U.S. Army, but they also appeared willing to put personal beliefs, and Sherwood's and Warburg's conception of propaganda and morality, above official policies. They had interfered with U.S. Army and State Department matters, had openly criticized Darlan and Vichy, had destroyed materials and radio and press facilities that belonged to Vichy supporters, and covertly had undermined and subverted U.S. Army censorship and propaganda-control efforts. Military reaction was swift and negative. Gen. Walter B. Smith exclusively blamed OWI civilians for the public-relations debacle and claimed that "Europe and Africa together were too small to hold [Percy] Winner and the U.S. Army." Secretary Stimson complained that "Eisenhower was harassed at the very time when he should be devoting all his strength to the war in Tunisia." As a result, Associate OWI Director Milton Eisenhower went to North Africa and met with his brother to smooth over the rift and to prevent the planned expulsion of OWI personnel from the theater.[20]

The Darlan incident demonstrated to the army that closer supervision of civilian propagandists was definitely in order. On 1 February 1943, Brig. Gen. Robert A. McClure, who had figured in the London organization conferences on psychological warfare in October 1942 but who otherwise lacked propaganda experience, became the Information, News and Censorship Division chief (INC) of Allied Force Headquarters. The PWS was placed under his supervision and

Brig. Gen. Robert A. McClure, chief of the Information, News, and Censorship Division of Allied Force Headquarters in 1943 and of the Psychological Warfare Division of the Supreme Headquarters Allied Expeditionary Forces in 1944–1945. (U.S. Army Photo; reproduced at the National Archives)

renamed the Psychological Warfare Branch. The U.S. Army now considered PWB to be part of a larger, comprehensive special staff section of AFHQ dealing with a wide variety of communications functions, indicating continued army indecision over what propaganda was and where this largely civilian bureau belonged in the military hierarchy.[21]

The difficulties surrounding PWB prompted a close army examination of the group for the first time. The soldiers found that the hitherto unnoticed branch was actually a combined Allied, joint-service, military and civilian operation manned overwhelmingly by civilians from the OWI, OSS, Britain's PWE and Ministry of Information. The top leadership positions, however, entirely lacked British or U.S. Army representation even though officers were supposed to be in command. Operationally, PWB was a loosely controlled affair, run on an ad hoc basis, according to a relatively simple and informal organizational structure. Civilians performed most of the propaganda tasks; Allied military personnel provided only technical and administrative support services and operated vehicles and equipment. Allied military leaders were determined to control PWB, which had grown unnoticed in their midst, but they provided little direction until late 1943 because an overall propaganda policy was lacking. Despite later army input, PWB, in the words of General McClure, remained "primarily an administrative clearing house and support depot between headquarters and the OWI-OSS personnel conducting psychological warfare operations at remote stations."[22]

The U.S. Army thus attempted to steer PWB toward fulfilling more combat propaganda needs, deeming heavily political or ideological propaganda unnecessary, although most civilian propagandists practiced it and believed in its value. What was needed, according to army commanders who were still skeptical of propaganda in general, were campaigns of tactical use. PWB did respond by dispatching combat propaganda teams to the front as army commanders requested, where they were temporarily attached to the headquarters unit. The general propaganda policy of each team was controlled by PWB, but individual campaigns were developed by civilians after theoretically gaining the approval of the local commander. This system allowed great latitude in the type of operations undertaken as well as for individual politics and ideology to creep into propaganda output, setting a precedent for the duration.[23]

The independence shown by civilians was partly a reaction triggered by their perception of years of military indifference or hostility to their activities and of the army's niggardly physical support. PWB, though a part of AFHQ, lacked an official table of organization and equipment (TO&E). Consequently, the largely civilian PWB was not recognized as a part of the nation's armed forces by the

U.S. Army and received no funding, personnel, or equipment through regular channels, a strong indication of the continued skepticism toward and lack of importance attached to psychological warfare and of the army's general distrust of civilians. PWB, at all levels, virtually had to beg, steal, or borrow every additional member as well as the necessary equipment and supplies. Considerable time and effort were expended on such matters at the cost of operational effectiveness, and only after receiving the grudging help of other AFHQ staff sections were a number of specialists and administrative officers made available as were a few vehicles and a limited number of other supplies. Rented civilian vehicles provided by OWI funds were often the only ones available for use by PWB units in North Africa.[24]

Psychological Warfare Branch civilians found adjustment to the army way of doing things a slow and frustrating ordeal when compared with the less formal manner in which both the OSS and the OWI operated, especially in seeking additional personnel and equipment. Even when TO&Es were formulated, the rapid pace and expansion of combat operations rendered them obsolete before they were acted upon. Throughout its history, PWB never received an official U.S. Army TO&E. All PWB units, in the field and at headquarters, were stitched together from a wide variety of Allied and indigenous personnel, using a similar array of military and civilian vehicles and equipment. During the latter part of the war in North Africa, however, a considerable number of U.S. Army personnel were drawn to the organization as increasing numbers of troops reached the fighting fronts, but generally they were linguists, drivers, radio technicians, and other specialists relegated to support roles who did not actively participate in the planning, creation, and dissemination of propaganda.[25]

Despite army indifference, the propagandists attached to PWB forged ahead, conducting as many operations as they could with the available resources. One of the most successful combat propaganda teams at the time was commanded by Capt. Con O'Neill, a British officer. O'Neill was responsible for producing propaganda and for acquiring the necessary personnel, equipment, and supplies for operations in the British First Army area. Like his American counterparts, he found that one of his biggest problems was convincing skeptical soldiers of the uses of propaganda, having literally "to peddle its leaflets to artillery units, praying that they would be fired."[26]

As the U.S. Army sought to gain control of the PWB in North Africa, army leaders at home began to develop their own tactical propaganda capability without troublesome civilian participation. The first steps toward this end were taken in December 1942 when the War Department PWB created the First and Second Broadcast Station Operating Detachments (BSODs) at Camp Ritchie,

PWB/AFHQ *propaganda materials printed in Florence, Italy, for use in the Mediterranean Theater of Operations on display in* 1945. *Notice the issue of* Frontpost *and the safe conduct surrender pass leaflet at lower-left center.* (U.S. Army Photo; *reproduced at the National Archives*)

Maryland. Each group contained three officers and thirty-nine enlisted men who together formed the First Combat Propaganda Company, the prototype for later units that were attached to each army overseas. The company, however, left army control within weeks when JCS 155/4/D ended any direct military involvement in propaganda. It was then run by the OSS until the army realized the mistake of placing all military propaganda operations under that agency and brought the unit back under its own authority in February 1943. Soon thereafter it was shipped abroad and joined PWB.[27]

The army continued to improve its psychological warfare capability by creating even more new units. In spring 1943, PWB/AFHQ took possession of the U.S. Army First Mobile Radio Broadcast Company (MRBC). An improvement on the original army propaganda detachments, it was unlike anything seen before. It contained complete public address systems, radios, monitoring sets, loudspeakers, typewriters, printing presses, and leaflet bombs and was intended to be a self-contained, army-controlled mobile unit that could be dispatched on a moment's notice to the front for the purpose of conducting tactical propaganda in direct support of military operations. Although the detachments were army units with TO&Es, the U.S. Army soon discovered that it lacked trained, uniformed propagandists. Civilians from the OWI and the OSS were grudgingly recruited to fill most of the slots in the MRBCs, with soldiers, as before, performing only technical, administrative, and support functions and having little if any role in determining propaganda content. The creation of the First MRBC, which served in the Mediterranean Theater for the duration, was the beginning of a concerted and deliberate U.S. Army program that eventually created five MRBCs.[28]

Army leaders, despite their efforts to create an independent propaganda capability, were clearly frustrated by the knowledge that the major American propaganda efforts abroad were civilian-dominated. The OSS was becoming an ever-stronger presence in the Mediterranean, and OWI's New York City–based Voice of America remained under the exclusive control of the independent-minded and highly ideological triumvirate of Robert Sherwood, James Warburg, and Joseph Barnes. Yet both organizations had spent months establishing a presence in the future combat zones, long before the U.S. Army arrived.

Of the American agencies, the OSS could legitimately claim the earliest foreign presence. Its North African operations began under the COI when William Eddy made contact with Robert Murphy's State Department North African vice-consuls in fall 1941. In March 1942 Eddy, at Donovan's behest and in league with Britain's PWE, set up clandestine radio stations in Tangier, Casablanca, Algiers, Tunis, and Oran. The stations attempted to counteract Nazi anti-Semitic

propaganda among Arab populations by providing pro-American materials, such as President Roosevelt's speeches and U.S. magazines.[29]

The OSS expanded after the TORCH landings, but because the morale-operations mission was not fully delineated until March 1943, members of the branch played only a small role in North African combat operations. Even though they considered their black propaganda to be different from the white operations of PWB and OWI, they quickly found that Colonel Hazeltine, like most soldiers, "would have no truck with what he called alphabetical organizations." He never recognized MO as an independent unit, and its personnel were attached to PWB and "set to work where there was work to be done, regardless of MO's exclusively subversive mission." The original three-man MO contingent arrived in North Africa in March and grew slowly to seven people by mid-1943. As a result of this slight participation, Donovan took steps to create a separate MO mission within AFHQ, a goal realized in September 1943. Yet it was not until March 1944 that OSS MO became autonomous within PWB under OSS member and U.S. Army Lt. Col. John Whitaker.[30]

The army attitude toward the OSS in general was similar to that shown toward MO in particular. Agency personnel were considered a threat to security, efficiency, and military success, and their independence in the military theaters caused concern among the "traditionalists in the armed forces," especially when confronted with "the irreverent individuals . . . who constantly flouted both authority and standard operating procedures." OSS members in turn believed that the U.S. Army in North Africa purposely hindered their efforts because of age-old prejudices against civilians and for selfish professional reasons. James G. Rogers of the OSS Planning Group wrote in March that the army "resists, fights stubbornly, partly ashamed that civilians should stain nice, clean, old-fashioned warfare by secret and devious information, subversion and sabotage." The jealous behavior stemmed from a "legitimate suspicion of an impetuous and disorderly group." The outspoken Rogers saw the old professional army as being inadequate and hostile to the new psychological warfare activities, wanting only to engage in "'boom-boom' warfare."[31]

The mutual enmity was not peculiar to the War Department and the OSS headquarters in Washington, D.C., but was also evident in North Africa. Edmond Taylor wrote Donovan in early 1943 that "the Army . . . dislikes all civilian agencies about equally [and] does not believe that psychological warfare can accomplish anything useful, but suspects that it can be dangerous." Because of this suspicion, propagandists were not given the opportunity to support army operations adequately. If the situation did not improve, Taylor predicted, it was unlikely that propagandists could render "any real assistance during the conti-

nental offensive." Although the OSS still consisted largely of civilians with a clear political and ideological agenda, its wholly conservative outlook more closely matched the views of most army officers than the opinions of the highly suspect OWI. Yet the OSS could take little comfort in the knowledge that the U.S. Army disapproved of OWI even more than it did of the OSS.[32]

The tenor of OWI's message made the army more anxious because the office's output was heavily political from the time of the first FIS–VOA broadcasts from New York City in January 1942. Furthermore, OWI operations were conducted without military input in any real sense. Between the time of the creation of the FIS and fall 1943, the period when Sherwood, Barnes, Warburg, and Johnson controlled planning and operations, the directives emphasized the virtues of democracy and stressed American war and peace aims, however vaguely defined.[33]

Nearly every OWI directive of the period contained a section "Projection of America," which revealed the personal philosophy of Sherwood's triumvirate most clearly. In one early VOA program series, "United America Fights," beamed to friend and foe alike, the OWI portrayed the United States as "a diverse country devoted to democracy, imbued with the principles of equality and dedicated to social mobility." Accordingly, "the scripts read like a textbook on the great principles of American ideology and mythology." Postwar goals were a staple of the broadcasts rather than more immediate wartime tactical goals and were put in "aggressively democratic terms—ridding the world of oppression and tyranny and giving the world peace and freedom." The programs mirrored FDR's Four Freedoms and claimed that the United States "was fighting 'for all men, not only for one generation but for all generations' " and was seeking "the objective of liberating the subjugated nations . . . establishing and securing freedoms of speech, freedom of religion, freedom from want and freedom from fear everywhere in the world."[34]

These ideas colored all OWI output, to the dismay of Allied leaders, and increasingly, in 1943, to the chagrin of the U.S. Army, which loathed politics and expressions of liberal ideologies. Such themes were still evident in OWI output well after the TORCH landings, and even after the Darlan deal, the declaration of the unconditional surrender policy, and the issues surrounding the Italian surrender made such themes impractical, unrealistic, and overly idealistic. The politicized and idealized campaigns of the OWI were frequently at odds with accepted Allied military and diplomatic policies. Thus, the very philosophical foundations of the OWI made its continuing operations a lighting rod for criticism.

Even before the controversy and ill-feelings surrounding the Darlan deal had

faded away, the OWI was faced with yet another more serious dilemma posed by the unconditional surrender policy proclaimed at the January 1943 Casablanca Conference. At this first wartime meeting between British Prime Minister Winston Churchill and President Roosevelt, the latter had announced at a post-summit press conference, in a clearly off-the-cuff manner, that the Axis powers would be forced to surrender unconditionally and that such a demand would henceforth be adopted as an Allied war aim. Although the announcement supposedly took Churchill by complete surprise, such a policy had been discussed and the prime minister was convinced of its moral value.[35]

The American president had several aims. First, Roosevelt wanted to generate "awe in the enemy" and to "develop confidence and a sense of solidarity among the United Nations." Second, he wanted to make clear to the Axis, especially to the Nazis, that no compromise peace, only total Allied victory, would take place, thereby avoiding the stab-in-the-back mentality of World War I. Third, the president wanted to dispel Soviet suspicions by showing that the Western Allies were fully committed to the destruction of fascism and to assure the Russians that the Allies would not take the first opportunity to abandon the war and the Soviets, in favor of a separate peace. Finally, Roosevelt wanted to impress upon the members of the Grand Alliance as well as upon the Nazis that the United States was not going to settle for a continuation of the Fascist regime or its philosophy after the war but was intent on its total eradication.[36]

Nobody in the Office of War Information was consulted about the unconditional surrender policy, nor was their advice sought concerning its implications for propaganda. Although it seemed at face value to be a statement of moral principle of a type that the membership of the OWI would normally favor and had even pursued through years of internationalist and interventionist activity, in reality the policy complicated the agency's job. It provided the Nazis with superb propaganda, and they cited it in efforts to push Germans on to greater sacrifices, predicting that defeat meant the dismemberment of the Reich and the annihilation, if not the outright extermination, of the German race.[37]

American propagandists, like their British counterparts, had always given the Germans what the OWI had termed a "hope clause" in its propaganda as part of an overall policy intended to create a mood of acceptance for defeat that could end the war sooner. Although the OWI never made specific promises about the future, its propaganda implicitly spoke of a new and better postwar world where victor and vanquished coexisted in equality and peace. Americans fought savagely for victory, the agency claimed on one occasion, but they were capable of treating defeated enemies with humanity and justice. The Allies merely intended to demilitarize Germany, end the Nazi regime, and punish any-

one responsible for war crimes. The enunciation of a policy implying an all-out struggle to the death contradicted this view. Although Robert Sherwood considered the policy ill-advised, he personally favored it from a moral standpoint but also realized that it was "very deeply deliberated" by FDR and was "a true statement of Roosevelt's considered policy" that had to be accepted by the OWI.[38]

After Casablanca the OWI started to temper its propaganda, keeping in mind that the war was ultimately one of total victory or defeat. They concentrated on convincing Germans that their defeat was inevitable and that further resistance would only prolong their misery. Unconditional surrender was a fact, and there could be no armistice as in 1918. Considerable time and effort were expended by OWI in indirectly refuting the charges of Nazi propagandists that unconditional surrender meant the annihilation of the German people, although it did mean that the guilty would be punished and National Socialism ended. Nazi attempts to push Germans to greater resistance because of the unconditional surrender policy was only a ploy, according to the OWI, to maintain the Nazi regime. Regardless of how the agency attempted to play down or evade the negative ramifications of the policy in its propaganda, it continued to hamper Allied efforts. Nevertheless, the OWI adhered to the policy for the duration.[39]

Although a testing ground for American propaganda, North African operations failed to make the case for either the civilian or the military propaganda units. More time was needed to organize and refine the weapon, and the pending operations in Sicily and Italy were anticipated as the next testing ground. By summer 1943, just prior to the landings in Sicily, PWB had expanded to approximately 400 Allied civilian and military personnel and was growing at a rapid pace. C. D. Jackson was the top PWB civilian, PWE's Richard Crossman controlled propaganda planning, Edmond Taylor directed PWB intelligence, and William S. Paley directed PWB radio operations.

Propaganda operations during the Sicilian campaign showed that many of the problems preventing effective cooperation between soldiers and civilians in North Africa had been worked out, although not to everyone's satisfaction. In July 1943, over 35.5 million leaflets, both strategic and tactical, were disseminated, supplemented by radio operations conducted by OSS MO, OWI, and PWB. One of the first stations, Radio Hippo, began both overt and clandestine broadcasts to France, Italy, and Germany in March 1943; Radio Tunis, heavily damaged by the retreating Germans, was repaired and began broadcasts in May. The stations conducted their own operations within PWB directives although staffed entirely by OWI and OSS civilians. A further station, Radio Swindle, was set up eighteen miles outside Algiers in November 1943 for broadcasts to the Balkans.[40]

Civilians were crucial to the establishment and success of the first Allied radio propaganda operations. OWI's Oliver Garrett, for example, in cooperation with OSS MO, was instrumental in establishing a clandestine radio station near Tunis in late July 1943. Radio Italo Balbo, named after the popular Italian field marshal who was killed when his plane was mistakenly downed by Italian anti-aircraft gunners near Tripoli in 1940, was a mobile unit so secret it was unknown to the rest of PWB. The OSS, which actually ran the station, claimed that Balbo's death was a Fascist ruse to disguise his defection to the Allies. According to Garrett, the station's broadcasts, which were intended to create friction between the Italian population and the Fascists and the Nazis, were jammed on five occasions to minimize their effect. Nonetheless, the programs gained a wide and gullible audience who believed the station was located on the Italian mainland. Garrett later said, "We had almost more to do with the downfall of Mussolini than any other political influence and we have some corroboration from within Italy itself." The station closed after the invasion of Italy in September 1943.[41]

The Morale Operations Branch of OSS, perhaps more than any other group, had much to prove during the Sicilian operations. Although the U.S. Army was anxious about the content of OWI's output, the operations of the highly secret OSS MO detachments initially caused even greater concern because few field commanders knew when these operations were taking place or what they entailed. As a result, MO personnel became increasingly active and vocal promoters of subversive propaganda with PWB, making certain that both the presence of MO teams and their modes of operation were known to local commanders.[42]

Prior to the campaigns in Sicily and Italy, OSS MO had been primarily concerned with the creation and dissemination of rumors, patterned after the Nazi *Mundpropaganda* perceived as having been so successful between 1933 and 1940. Despite pervasive army opinions that such projects were a ludicrous waste of time, the majority of early MO efforts were expended on rumor production. Approximately ten to fifteen rumors of six different types were developed weekly by a Washington, D.C., OSS rumor committee. Approved rumors were sent to London, where they were reviewed by a joint OSS-PWE committee before being distributed by agents through Europe.[43]

Drawing further examples from the Nazi bag of subversive and dirty tricks, the OSS MO branch began creating black propaganda newspapers just prior to the invasion of Sicily. One such newspaper, measuring 2.5-by-4 inches, was dropped to German troops and purported to originate with Italian Fascists in Rome. Printed in North Africa, it consisted of 1,200 words spread over five

pages that contained jokes, rumors, sabotage instructions, excerpts from prisoners' mail, and news stories. The front page was truthful news, but the remaining pages contained subtle anti-Fascist and anti-German information. The first issues of the paper, *Marc Aurelio,* were air-dropped over the Italian mainland in May 1943 by Allied aircraft returning from bombing missions. The black newspaper was thought to be a perfect medium for covering large audiences without access to radio, but the OSS, like the OWI, soon discovered that the U.S. Army, always leery of civilian operations, was hesitant to provide personnel and supplies for any scheme not having direct tactical results.[44]

Despite its misgivings concerning psychological warfare, which continued well into 1944, the U.S. Army began providing more facilities, supplies, and vehicles to PWB but not in quantities deemed necessary by its civilian members. When the Allies landed at Salerno in early September 1943, and after Naples was captured in October, PWB was granted permission to use the media facilities of a major urban area for producing propaganda for Italy. Moreover, the 1,400 Allied members of PWB began to take advantage of the large numbers of Italians who were willing to work for the branch, eventually employing over 3,000. Meanwhile, Allied specialists, mostly OWI and OSS civilians, were rushed from North Africa to the new propaganda center and the Italian PWB headquarters at Naples. Bari, Italy, then became the OWI and OSS center for radio and leaflet operations directed at the Balkans.[45]

Seeking to expand the role of propaganda at a level commensurate with increases in conventional operations in Sicily and Italy, PWB combat teams, consisting of Allied military and civilian personnel, unilaterally and arbitrarily attached themselves to the U.S. Fifth and British Eighth armies. Each group dispatched ever greater numbers of smaller teams consisting of three to five men who were provided with jeeps and trailers and enough food, equipment, and supplies to allow self-subsistence, protection, and relatively independent operations for a period of five days to a week. According to John Whitaker, "Their duties were manifold," including intelligence gathering, the conducting of psychological warfare, and " 'selling' . . . propaganda and psychological warfare to field commanders."[46]

The increased activity and visibility of the combat teams at the front disturbed many local commanders and again raised larger questions of who controlled the propaganda, thus affecting operations. The autonomy and the heavy preponderance of OSS and OWI personnel in the teams, especially in leadership and operational roles, led to a situation the PWB official history referred to as "empire building." Clearly, by 1943, civilians, with their political and ideological beliefs concerning the war and propaganda, came to dominate all aspects of psy-

chological warfare in the Mediterranean theater. PWE and OWI representatives in the policy control groups of PWB were stronger than ever in pressing their views while the positions of the local army commanders, who sought to play down politics and ideology, as well as the position of Colonel Hazeltine at AFHQ, were growing steadily weaker, a direct reflection of similar events in the United States.[47]

The military's slight control of propaganda in the combat theaters was a problem of their own creation. Army difficulties stemmed from past neglect of propaganda matters, from the tendency to post unqualified officers to psychological warfare command positions where they acted as caretakers rather than as leaders, and from a general lack of aggressiveness in asserting military authority. The majority of people involved in propaganda in the Mediterranean were civilians, who, though in uniform and holding military ranks, still thought of themselves as civilians and acted accordingly, often at the expense of military efficiency, discipline, and protocol. The army was correctly viewed as having nothing to offer in the propaganda war except personnel and equipment, as most of the expense of propaganda operations as well as of equipment and personnel, native and Allied, throughout the theater was routinely provided almost entirely from the budgets of the OWI and OSS MO. This fact alone caused many civilians to take army efforts at command and control less than seriously.

Though the U.S. Army provided overall coordination and administration and maintained the right in theory to grant or deny final approval to all propaganda activities, civilians increasingly disregarded the military's efforts. Furthermore, the civilian-dominated PWB rather than the Allied military commanders directed the largely autonomous combat propaganda teams in Italian combat zones, which compounded friction. Military leaders were soon convinced that the large number of civilians in the theater made overall army control less than a reality and left crucial tactical propaganda needs unfulfilled as political and ideological views permeated propaganda output. Increasingly, open friction between soldiers and civilians was evident on all levels, from PWB to the combat teams in the field.[48]

Through its contact with civilian propaganda agencies in the combat theaters, the U.S. Army discovered three fundamental and disturbing facts by summer 1943. First, most civilians did not fully or willingly accept the principle of military control of propaganda or the idea that the primary goal of the war was to obtain a military rather than a political or ideological victory. Second, most civilians did not entirely agree with the army's view of propaganda or that it should be used only for nonpolitical tactical purposes. Third, civilians could not find common agreement even among themselves on the same issues.

The army discovered itself bogged down in a morass of differing and conflicting political and ideological views concerning propaganda that had existed for years and that were spilling over into the combat theaters, unnecessarily politicizing the war and complicating the military's mission. Army personnel had little desire to become involved in the conflicts, but as they were charged with bringing about a military victory over the Axis, it was necessary for them to intervene to bring order out of chaos. During the North African operations the U.S. Army discovered that instead of having one propaganda program in the Mediterranean, united in purpose, outlook, and intent, three fundamentally different programs practiced by three different groups—two civilian and one military, each with a different ideology, with different means and methods, and with different goals—were in simultaneous operation. And these did not even include the propaganda programs of America's Allies. The performances of OSS and OWI were unsatisfactory by army standards, and the agencies' operations were still perceived as dangerous, not only to tactical operations but also to foreign diplomatic initiatives. The situation had already caused acrimonious confrontations, exemplified by the Darlan incident, and showed no signs of abating unless dramatic changes were implemented. The differences and mutual suspicions, according to both soldiers and civilians, had hampered effective operations; most important, from the army standpoint, they had totally negated efforts to harness energies for use against Axis military forces.

The army's dissatisfaction with the American psychological warfare campaign was shared by many members of the OWI and the OSS. The former sensed a developing tendency to sacrifice moral principle for quick military gain, and the latter smarted from continued military skepticism toward its morale operations and from OWI criticism of its involvement in any type of activity remotely resembling propaganda. Thus by late 1942 major transformations were beginning to occur that would dramatically change the civilian agencies, their doctrines, and their memberships during 1943 and 1944.[49]

9 · The Final Ideological Clash, 1944

The growing tensions between military and civilian propagandists overseas paled in comparison to the ongoing home-front disputes between the OWI and the OSS and the many detractors of government-sponsored and civilian-directed propaganda. The need for a federal propaganda policy to determine ultimate goals or the content, methods, and direction of American propaganda became paramount in 1943. The differences over policy that had remained unresolved since 1940 and that were now complicated by the U.S. Army's involvement eventually destroyed the civilian agencies as they had existed. The conflicts resulted in the complete militarization of the American psychological warfare campaign so that by early 1944 the major efforts were conducted under military control. Militarization affected doctrine, agency membership, and the type of operations implemented. The propaganda empires of Sherwood and Donovan were either modified or co-opted as pragmatic Allied military and civilian personnel muted the rivalries, halted all campaigns using political and ideological themes, ended internal conflicts, drove out the ideologues, and refused to sanction operations that did not have a direct and immediate impact on the Axis.

Although the U.S. Army ultimately came to dominate psychological warfare, not all the changes were mandated by soldiers. Internal modifications in the OWI, initiated by Elmer Davis, followed the attacks on his organization by the military, the U.S. Congress, and OWI members, who, much like him, favored more factual, less politically extreme, and less ideological propaganda than that practiced by Sherwood, Warburg, Johnson, and Barnes. Davis realized in 1943 that if the OWI were to survive and accomplish any part of its mission it must decrease the overt ideological appeals that characterized its output under Robert Sherwood. Davis's reforms resulted in many of the most able and quali-

fied propagandists leaving the OWI in disgust over what they viewed as a sellout of American ideals for the sake of military expediency.

The OSS Morale Operations Branch experienced similar troubles. Not only did Donovan have to fend off OWI attacks for over eighteen months, but he also had to counter internal resistance to his psychological warfare theories as well as continued army skepticism. Donovan, unlike Sherwood, persevered and maintained the OSS as it was originally configured.[1]

The interagency clash that had the greatest effect on the American psychological campaign was that between the OSS and the OWI. Even after the breakup of the COI, the controversy over propaganda domains continued. The OWI was firmly committed to a strategy of truthful propaganda that neither hid sources nor sought to deceive audiences with atrocity stories or false news.[2] Its intent was to deliver information and clearly state the policies of the government, meet Nazi propaganda with truth, aid the military, and sustain anti-Nazi morale everywhere. Most OWI members held OSS operations in disdain, and although efforts were made at informal collaboration abroad and the two agencies did cooperate on occasion, Donovan favored Nazi-like propaganda tactics used in direct support of military operations and set up the OSS Morale Operations Branch accordingly. In doing so he put the agency into direct conflict with the OWI.[3]

The disputes that had destroyed the COI were not forgotten by the OSS and OWI leadership. The spark that renewed the conflict came in December 1942 when JCS 155/4/D reorganized the OSS and created the Morale Operations Branch. Possible OWI reactions were not considered, and the document reopened old wounds, according to one critic, by giving "too little emphasis to the prevailing American philosophy that propaganda is first and foremost a civilian and not . . . a military responsibility."[4]

Elmer Davis immediately protested the JCS action, claiming that the OSS was seeking to duplicate the OWI functions in a deliberate violation of the presidential orders creating the two agencies. Loosely interpreting the directive, he alleged that "it was possible to define psychological warfare as to include 'propaganda' as one of its constituent elements." Such activity was "an absolute OWI monopoly." Receiving no OSS response, Davis and Sherwood asked Roosevelt on Christmas Eve 1942 to revoke the JCS order or to accept their resignations.[5]

Members of the OSS knew of the dissatisfaction among OWI's leadership, James Rogers writing that Davis, Sherwood, MacLeish, and Cowles were threatening to resign, as "they fear subordination to the military, hate Bill Donovan," and "think they are alone saviors of idealism, and the soldiers and we reactionaries." Rogers thought the OWI did nothing more than preach "democracy,

New Deal, Liberty to the people of Europe hour after hour"; it was, he concluded, a useless and silly performance. Rogers also knew, however, that the president supported Davis and Sherwood for political and ideological reasons and that he saw the OSS "as Republican, aligned with the Republican-Military Congress side . . . as contrasted with the White House–Democratic–New Deal–Civilian Reformer Army."[6]

President Roosevelt did not welcome the reappearance of the old bickering but took no action until February 1943 when Davis and Sherwood again pressed for action. The president acquiesced and directed Gen. George V. Strong, a confirmed enemy of the OSS, to rescind the JCS directive and to put the OSS, minus the soon-to-be abolished MO, under U.S. Army Military Intelligence Division control. Rogers, on hearing of this, wrote, "Today the President's axe fell on OSS," as the idea of "military psych war" was rejected for that controlled by civilians. Roosevelt's decision was due to his "reluctance to have any policy in Republican hands, his fears of [Donovan's] ambitions," and "his support of [Davis's] insistence on civilian control." George Milton and Harold Smith made similar suggestions and "repudiated 'military psychological warfare' as an idea," though agreeing with Davis that "[Donovan] is too grasping and uncontrollable."[7]

Individuals who had consistently favored the idea of propaganda to support military operations were not prepared to watch silently as their hard-won gains were demolished. This attitude was especially true of the military, who, while not enamored of the OSS, were unwilling to turn over propaganda to the OWI with its promises that combat needs would be met. Army memories of the Darlan deal were still fresh. The JCS therefore rescued the OSS at its 23 February meeting after several members "denounced the OWI as 'a nuisance'" and claimed they "got less help from OWI than from any other agency." Furthermore, the JCS established that it would set a bad precedent for them to "submit to Mr. Davis' views." Adm. William D. Leahy concurred and prevented action on Strong's order.[8]

Donovan, with JCS support, dismissed the OWI complaints. He admitted that most propaganda was not an OSS responsibility but claimed that rumors, whispering campaigns, deception, black leaflets, and radio were more akin to subversion, to psychological warfare and special services, than to propaganda as he and the military services defined it. These methods were more "clearly an OSS area than the 'information' and 'war information' that belonged to OWI." As before, Donovan argued that where tactical operations were involved, psychological warfare, which, depending on one's definition, could or could not include propaganda, had to be integrated with the military.[9]

Seeking to depreciate Davis's case and to defuse the controversy, Donovan told Roosevelt that despite news reports, neither he nor the OSS had any quarrel with the OWI. He suspected that confusion had arisen "because the word 'psychological' has been given different meanings by different . . . agencies." "The JCS," Donovan explained, "used the word in the general sense employed by the Germans and other continental armies as applying to all unorthodox methods." It was psychological "because of the effect produced rather than as a description of the means employed."[10]

Yet the dispute did not end just because Donovan and the JCS refused to recognize OWI's definitions or the validity of Davis's complaints. The OWI director was still disgruntled and, in an uncharacteristic display, pressed noisily for a resolution. Thus on 9 March 1943 President Roosevelt again intervened to prevent the conflict from becoming a major public controversy by issuing Executive Order 9312, "Defining the Foreign Information Activities of the Office of War Information." In one of the few instances in which the president took a stand on propaganda issues, he directed that "OWI will plan, develop, and execute all phases of the federal program of . . . foreign propaganda activities involving the dissemination of information." As a sop to the military and to prevent the OWI from running amok overseas, the president directed that in "areas of actual or projected military operations" the OWI was required to coordinate plans with the JCS, the War and Navy Departments, to work under their control, and to gain theater commanders' approval prior to any operation. The order appeared a clear victory for Davis and Sherwood in that it seemed to ensure civilian control of propaganda activities. To stave off future troubles and to mend fences with the military, Davis wrote Stimson, promising to do all that he could to maintain effective relations with the U.S. Army and to guarantee that propaganda abroad was "in harmony with military plans." Davis ignored Donovan.[11]

The victory that Davis and Sherwood savored was not total. The OSS could still perform its morale operations, and still had a JCS mandate to conduct military psychological warfare. In actual fact, the OSS had lost nothing while the OWI had come firmly under military control abroad, a major loss of operational independence. Davis further learned that the OSS director considered the new executive order inapplicable to MO, which Donovan denied was a euphemism for propaganda, claiming it was altogether different. Believing that the OSS, with military connivance, was using semantics to encroach on the OWI's turf, Davis wrote that his mandate "covered *all* kinds of propaganda."[12]

Crucial decisions defining propaganda and questions of control were left unresolved by the March 1943 executive order. Although negotiations aimed at settling differences continued between Edmond Taylor of the OSS and OWI's

Milton Eisenhower, the JCS escalated the conflict by issuing JCS 155/7/D on 4 April 1943, redefining the OSS mission in line with the new executive order. Psychological warfare included "all measures, except propaganda, taken to enforce our will upon the enemy by means other than military action," and the OSS was declared as the agency responsible for the execution of military psychological warfare.[13]

Even then, Davis and Donovan failed to reach agreement on propaganda definitions and domains, and the new documents only fueled the debate. Davis maintained that the OWI had an "absolute monopoly on government activities employing radio, press, leaflets and related media," that no difference existed between "official and clandestine, or between black and white propaganda," that "the term federal meant not official but on behalf of all federal agencies, and that dissemination of information also included misinformation." According to Frederick Oechsner of the OSS, "Davis . . . took the attitude that propaganda was propaganda, whatever form it took," no matter how defined. Psychological warfare was just another vague term, like information services, war information, and propaganda, all of which were used by the OWI to describe their activities. Davis insisted that he retain control over black propaganda and over any other form. The OWI director, Oechsner said, told him that "OWI was not doing black, might never do it, but would not relinquish the right to do it." In turn, Donovan refused to accept Davis's definitions and claimed that the OSS had neither the means nor the desire to carry on propaganda and did not wish to. The OSS practiced morale operations as part of a comprehensive, military-controlled program of psychological warfare in support of combat operations. The only OSS method that even remotely resembled propaganda, according to Donovan, was falsification of material through use of the radio and the printing press.[14]

As on other occasions, the main figures involved failed to find common ground. OSS member Wallace Deuel wrote that a settlement would be miraculous and that it was a shame that the agencies did not work together. The trouble, Deuel claimed, lay with the loose organization of the OWI and "the personal elements involved," including "the President's dislike of careful definitions of functions, authority, and responsibility."[15]

In the midst of the dispute the JCS received the official OSS statement of doctrine, which exacerbated tensions by again raising the question of the role moral values played in American propaganda. General Strong immediately blasted the new OSS doctrine as being "devoid of reference to moral considerations or standards" and for assuming that the "United States had to take on the ethical color of its enemies in all particulars." Nonetheless, by the time the

OSS manual reached the JCS, the agency was already implementing the described operations. The Joint Staff Planners therefore requested a new directive in late August 1943 that reflected OSS activities as they were then being performed. Donovan, taking into account the ongoing dispute with the OWI, wrote a draft that defined OSS operations in such a way that Davis could not claim a duplication of effort. Donovan's description of OSS psychological warfare included

> all measures (except those pertaining to the federal program of radio press, publication and related propaganda activities involving the dissemination of information) taken to enforce our will upon the enemy by means other than military action, . . . in support of actual or planned military operations.

The OWI did not know the specific contents of Donovan's draft definition, but Wallace Carroll had written to Sherwood that the OSS was seeking a new propaganda role.[16]

The Joint Chiefs delivered the expected mandate to the OSS in JCS 155/11/D, which indicated their firm belief in the value of Donovan's morale operations as an adjunct to conventional warfare and their acceptance of the OSS definitions. The new directive, issued on 27 October 1943, contained no references to propaganda but did formally introduce "morale subversion" as a new and distinct OSS activity that included false rumors, leaflets, documents, freedom stations, and the organization and support of fifth-column activities to undermine enemy morale. The directive was a verbatim restatement of Donovan's draft. An MO field manual followed and was approved on 1 December 1943. Although Davis was still suspicious of the OSS, the MO Branch did not conduct propaganda even by OWI's definition, and the army assured Davis that the OSS was unlikely to affect OWI's work abroad.[17]

Sensing that military guarantees might not translate into concrete policies protecting OWI's mandate, Davis finally obtained Donovan's approval of an eight-point declaration in April 1944. Hereafter, the agreement stated, the OWI was responsible for propaganda from official sources; the OSS would conduct black propaganda. The OSS would not run black radio stations outside enemy territory without OWI's consent and the OWI would not dispatch agents or place outposts in enemy territory. Each man agreed to inform the other of operations affecting his agency, and both recognized that the OSS, in meeting military requirements, might have to undertake propaganda not reflecting official government policies. Two weeks later, Davis sent a copy of the agreement to

Samuel Rosenman. A final exchange of letters between Davis and Donovan in June 1944 ended two years of turmoil. The final details were worked out overseas by MO's K. D. Mann and the OWI's Edward Barrett.[18]

The ultimate solution was not as much a final settling of differences as it was a mutual recognition that two opposing schools of propaganda existed, a situation in part due to Roosevelt's consistent refusal to define a specific propaganda policy. Yet Elmer Davis had accepted the fact that the OSS Morale Operations Branch did not involve a great number of people, was not prevalent overseas, was under strict military control, and was not as threatening to the OWI as Sherwood, Warburg, Barnes, and Johnson claimed. The branch was not going to disappear, Davis realized, and coexistence was a practical necessity, preferable to the continued internecine conflict that jeopardized the effectiveness of the entire American propaganda effort. Davis determined that the OWI had a major job to do both independently of and in cooperation with the military; the task could not be delayed by conflicts with a group that in reality was a minor rival. Finally, Davis, like Donovan and his military supporters, realized that the origins of many of the conflicts lay in the political and ideological beliefs of the Overseas OWI's leadership. According to the OSS history, interagency problems did not end until Davis purged his ranks. Thereafter, "much of the bitterness had . . . gone out of this old feud" as the main protagonists were gone.[19]

The interagency squabbles between Davis and Donovan were complicated by OWI's concomitant feuds with Congress. Republicans viewed the OWI as a pro-Roosevelt propaganda agency seeking to globalize the New Deal. To one journalist, however, such attacks originated from "friendships for Fascism and dislike for Democracy," but another interpretation more correctly attributed them to "overheated American partisan politics."[20]

One of the first congressional flaps over the OWI occurred in early 1943 and concerned the glossy eight-page OWI magazine *Victory*, sent periodically to 500,000 foreign nationals. Sen. Rufus C. Holman (R-Oreg.) blasted the publication, claiming it was mere "window dressing" for a personal political campaign for a fourth term by FDR. Similar charges were leveled by Cong. John Taber (R-N.Y.), who claimed that the space taken to ship *Victory* to Europe prevented tons of munitions from reaching American forces. Republican congressmen were especially incensed by articles in *Victory* claiming that former Republican president Herbert Hoover had lost the 1932 election because he was the candidate of reactionaries and that FDR's New Deal had saved the nation from ruin and chaos. Another article quoted Vice-President Henry Wallace's "Century of the Common Man" speech, claiming that "the American war effort and the

Bolshevik revolution were linked as part of the fight for the 'people's revolution,' whose first shots had been fired in the American War of Independence."[21]

Initially seeing the criticism as mere partisan politics, Davis facetiously defended *Victory* and its companion magazine *USA*, supported by many liberal journalists. Though he admitted that some features were regrettable, he also testified that Taber had seen the first issue of *Victory* and voted appropriations without complaint. Davis professed ignorance of any plans of Roosevelt to run for a fourth term but doubted he could be reelected by votes cast in South Africa, Australia, Portugal, Egypt, France, England, and Spain, all destinations of *Victory*. He denied that the OWI consisted only of New Dealers, leftists, and liberals, and pointed out, inaccurately, that half of the OWI staff were Republicans. "If I were going to try to build up an organization for partisan propaganda," Davis testified, "I think I would have sense enough not to build it so half of it could always neutralize the other half."[22]

These first acrimonious confrontations between Davis and congressional Republicans set the stage for future clashes when OWI officials appeared before increasingly hostile House committees to seek appropriations. The OWI's difficulties with Congress resumed in full force in May 1943 during budget hearings for fiscal 1944, when the agency's foreign propaganda was criticized for allegedly favoring Communist policies toward Poland.[23]

The charge raised the entire troublesome issue of OWI's treatment of the USSR and its relations with Eastern Europe. Communism had never been popular in the United States, and traditional anti-Communist prejudices were heightened during the Spanish Civil War and the Phoney War. Following the Nazi-Soviet Non-Aggression Pact and the Russo-Finnish War, many Americans, liberals and conservatives alike, clearly considered Stalin the evil equivalent of Hitler. Exacerbating the negative Soviet image was the Communist Party USA, which adopted isolationist views in keeping with the Nazi-Soviet alliance, thereby making itself part of the perceived fifth-column threat to America.[24]

Despite negative prewar opinions of the USSR, the official American view changed with the Nazi invasion of the Soviet Union in June 1941. The federal government then accepted the Soviets as allies against fascism with little obvious equivocation. The OWI thus began to repeat the official view that although Stalin had appeared to be an ally of Hitler prior to 1941, the Soviet dictator was only cleverly buying time to build his defenses for the war he knew was coming. OWI directives stated that the Soviets were a bulwark against fascism, just as domestic pro-Nazi groups had made similar claims against communism in the prewar years. VOA broadcasts and the OWI-sponsored films were full of features

describing the sacrifices of the Soviet people and of news bulletins extolling the courage of the Red Army. Great strides were made to play down past Soviet perfidy and indirectly to refute Goebbels's propaganda about the Communist threat to Western Civilization. A significant number of specific OWI features made up a concerted campaign to show the closeness of the Anglo-American–Soviet Grand Alliance.[25]

Government attempts to change the negative image of the Soviet Union, including a number of books by the OWI officials, were not entirely successful. Complicating OWI's dilemma was the Katyn Forest massacre, made public in spring 1943 just before OWI budget hearings. When Germany invaded the Soviet Union in 1941, the USSR recognized the Polish government-in-exile in London, which in turn immediately made inquiries as to the whereabouts of some 15,000 missing Polish Army officers taken prisoner during the Nazi-Soviet conquest of Poland two years earlier. The USSR denied any knowledge of the men and continued its denials, despite the increasing doubts of the Polish government regarding Soviet veracity. Private Polish attempts to persuade the United States and Great Britain to intercede on their country's behalf failed, as neither nation wanted to jeopardize the Grand Alliance. The situation rested until April 1943 when the Wehrmacht announced the discovery of a mass grave of 10,000 Polish Army officers executed in the Katyn Forest near Smolensk in Byelorussia.

The announcement presented the OWI with a potentially major problem. Initially unperturbed, OWI's Wallace Carroll claimed that the Katyn massacre was an obvious attempt by the Nazis to disturb if not destroy Allied unity, especially the fragile Soviet-Polish relationship, and he believed that the OWI should state the case thus in its output. Yet the U.S. government and the OWI could not conceivably profit from any publicity concerning the incident, nor could they ignore the story without appearing to be participating in a cover-up. Admitting the truth of the Nazi charges could destroy the Allies' moral standing and perhaps the alliance itself. Denying the charges could place the OWI and the United States in a position in direct contradiction to the growing evidence of Soviet guilt.

To complicate matters further, the Polish government-in-exile, following a Red Cross investigation, unilaterally and publicly confirmed the Nazi charges and pronounced the Soviets guilty, even as the USSR continued to blame Nazi Germany. Faced with a no-win situation, the OWI meekly reported the charges and countercharges without comment, emphasis, or analysis. In the growing dispute between the USSR and the Polish government-in-exile, the OWI, like the U.S. government, did not take a clear position. The OWI did not refute

Nazi charges, did not support the Poles, and appeared to condone the Soviets' actions by their own inaction, outraging American conservatives. In the wake of the incident, the USSR broke off relations with the London Poles, accomplishing one Nazi goal, and established a parallel pro-Soviet Polish government. The incident not only showed American vacillation but also OWI's inability to criticize the USSR, prompting the congressional charges that the agency was pro-Communist.[26]

The OWI's weak response to the Katyn massacre heightened congressional interest in the agency's employees, and charges were leveled during budget hearings that pro-Left sympathies colored all OWI propaganda. Many congressmen further alleged that the OWI sheltered aliens, radicals, and subversives who had access to secret intelligence and were thus security risks. Davis freely testified that 6 of 2,000 employees investigated by MID, ONI, the OWI, the FBI, and the Civil Service had been recommended for dismissal as Communists, but his candor, rather than deflating suspicions, only confirmed the worst fears of critics and spurred further attacks.[27]

The OSS leadership watched the OWI's difficulties with considerable interest and seemed to share the Republican congressional view that the agency harbored radicals and Communists and was heavily influenced by "international Jewry." James Rogers wrote that some OSS members "insist OWI [is] full of Communist spies," but he claimed, "it is really full of international left-wing Jews," not real spies. Rogers wrote that OWI's problems were due to "its wretched foreign propaganda, its Jewish saturation which makes its voice un-American in the Western ear, [and] its availability for political campaign purposes."[28]

Although congressional criticism did not affect OWI's overseas operations, a mid-1943 incident involving Italian events prompted a dramatic purge of the OWI and fundamental changes in the entire American propaganda program. After four disastrous years of war that brought Allied armies to Italy and demonstrated the bankruptcy of the Fascist regime, Benito Mussolini was ousted by the Fascist Grand Council on 25 July 1943, and was replaced by Field Marshall Pietro Badoglio, appointed by King Victor Emmanuel III. Badoglio quickly and publicly reaffirmed Italy's alliance with Nazi Germany, even though he had approached General Eisenhower as early as January 1943 about a separate peace with the Allies, having been encouraged by the Darlan deal.

Badoglio continued his clandestine efforts during the early summer, as PWE and OWI continued broadcasts aimed at winning Italian goodwill and separating the populace from the Fascists. Furthermore, the OWI strictly monitored output to ensure adherence to the unconditional surrender policy, despite the

earlier misgivings of its leadership. Shortly before Mussolini's ouster, however, on 16 July Churchill and Roosevelt decided to attempt a negotiated peace short of unconditional surrender to end Italian belligerency and prepared a joint statement "declaring that Italy's sole hope of survival lay in 'honorable capitulation to the overwhelming power of the military forces of the United Nations,'" implying the possibility of an armistice. Neither Davis, Sherwood, nor any other OWI members were informed that the announcement constituted a top-level policy change.[29]

British propagandists, unlike their American counterparts, had access to top government officials and quickly changed their propaganda tack when the shift in Allied policy took place. As a result, on 25 July Britain optimistically hailed Mussolini's downfall as the end of both fascism and Italian belligerency in radio broadcasts heard worldwide, hinting that a compromise peace was in the offing. The members of the OWI were more circumspect in accord with standing directives that insisted they stick with the unconditional surrender policy and "continue and increase . . . attacks on the tyranny, incompetence and corruption of the Fascist regime and its groveling subservience to Hitler." The policy was based on a February 1943 directive and on guidance given to C. D. Jackson by General Eisenhower that stated "fascism includes not only Mussolini and his political accomplices but also the Royal House of Savoy."[30]

The sudden shift in Britain's propaganda troubled top OWI leaders such as James Warburg and Percy Winner, who considered the British broadcasts premature and indicative of yet another impending sacrifice of democratic values for the sake of military expediency. Winner wrote Sherwood that he perceived a softening of the OWI's propaganda and the playing down of "the ideological aspect" for the "specifically military aspect." Winner was not the only one who feared OWI's message was being eroded by people with a different agenda. The belief that the government and military were once again preparing to sell out American values for quick tactical gain was particularly acute following the recent Darlan deal, the debacle over Katyn, and congressional charges that the OWI was a left-wing New Deal agency. Increasingly, OWI members sensed that they were losing ground to the forces of conservatism and reaction.[31]

Mussolini's fall required an immediate official American statement, but as the ouster occurred on Sunday no senior public figures were available. OWI writers thus wrote a script for a broadcast that was forwarded for approval to the only high-level OWI official in New York City that weekend: Deputy Overseas Director James Warburg. He obtained clearance for the broadcasts from a low-level JCS official and from Robert Sherwood, who was visiting Roosevelt at Shangri-La. The program's contents were written according to OWI policy,

and Warburg instructed the VOA to treat the event coldly and without any jubilation. The final English-language broadcast that Warburg put together contained a commentary from *New York Post* columnist Samuel Grafton and was approved by Joseph Barnes of the OWI New York Control Desk. Because of the time factor, the program did not receive the approval of the OWI Washington Planning Board. In Warburg's words, however, it took "precisely the desired attitude."[32]

The program regarding Mussolini's ouster was approved for one broadcast as notice that Americans did not share Britain's excessive and premature optimism regarding Italian events. By error, however, it was delivered six times. Under the pseudonym John Durfee, Warburg broadcast news of Mussolini's ouster and Badoglio's appointment and then read Grafton's commentary, quoting that "the moronic little king who has stood behind Mussolini's shoulder for twenty-one years has moved forward one pace." Yet the events in Italy were a "political minuet and not the revolution we have been waiting for." Badoglio was "a kind of a Goering-like character, who has been considered by pro-Fascists to be one of the best fascists." The only significance of the week's events, Durfee sadly concluded, was that so little had actually changed. American attitudes were unchanged by Mussolini's ouster, and the battle would continue "whether Mussolini, Badoglio, or the Fascist King himself led the fight for Hitler."[33]

The broadcast created a political firestorm. Warburg was heard throughout Britain and by *New York Times* reporter Arthur Krock, who picked up the program from a monitoring station in New York City. His reaction, like that of others, was swift and scathingly anti–OWI. James Rogers wrote of the "hurricane" the OWI had caused "by attacking the king as 'moronic' and Badoglio as 'fascist'—contrary to every plan and policy," fulfilling Rogers's prediction that the OWI "would sooner or later trip" because of its "internal clumsiness." His comments underestimated the domestic controversy. Krock blasted the OWI in a front-page *New York Times* article for deliberately flouting government policy, for following the personal ideology of its members, for serving the interests of Communists, and for endangering American soldiers' lives. Other papers echoed the charges. The Hearst syndicate branded Grafton a Communist, and former New Dealer Raymond Moley wrote that "Europe must be getting the impression that the United States is two countries," one holding "American lives and military necessity above ideology" and "the other, voicing an irreconcilable, amateurish and bungling insistence that its beliefs come first, whatever the cost."[34]

The furor reopened the public debate concerning propaganda and gave additional ammunition to Roosevelt's critics, who claimed that the nation lacked

not only a federal propaganda policy but also cogent war aims. The president was again forced to reemphasize the Allied commitment to the unconditional-surrender policy and declared that the nation "will have no truck with fascism in any way, shape or manner." During a news conference the day after the broadcast, the president declared in good faith that neither he nor Sherwood had approved of the broadcast, although Sherwood had approved it but never informed FDR. Caught in a public controversy concerning propaganda that he had ceaselessly sought to avoid, Roosevelt declared that OWI's actions were out of line with government policy.[35]

The president's disapproval of the actions and his desire to avoid being embroiled in propaganda controversies were apparent from his refusal to support OWI's activities, even when the agency was assaulted by politically motivated critics. The attacks continued as Krock charged that administration employees had again made and carried out an individual foreign policy created "according to the personal and ideological preferences of Communists and their fellow travelers." George R. Brown, writing in the *New York Journal American*, declared that "as long as OWI follows the policies of nitwits, its half-baked international politicians, and its Communist lunatic fringe . . . innumerable opportunities [will] be presented for mischief."[36]

Virtually abandoned by the president, OWI's leadership attempted to defend itself and to fend off calls for its abolition. In early August, in the hope of gaining Roosevelt's support, Davis sent a memorandum to the White House with Sherwood's investigation of the incident. In his report, Sherwood admitted an error in judgment even though he had not violated any OWI, State, War, or Navy department policies. He praised the work of the Overseas OWI, criticized gratuitous and malicious press charges, and denied the negative characteristics attributed to the agency. He closed by stating that of the thousands of words broadcast by the OWI on Mussolini's ouster, an error had been made only in the use of the one quotation in the six broadcasts. Davis then sent a further letter to the president suggesting that he publicize a letter Davis himself had composed in Roosevelt's name, stating his approval of the broadcast, suggesting that the incident was blown out of proportion by antiadministration critics and the partisan press, and then praising the OWI for performing a valuable service that had his full support. Roosevelt did not respond.[37]

Interagency clashes had occurred over propaganda for years out of public view, but the moronic-little-king episode was interpreted as being a far more serious one. It provided a target for U.S. Army critics of civilian propagandists and also for OWI director Elmer Davis, who, along with the army, thought that the Overseas OWI was too ideologically motivated and politically independent for

its own good. The incident provided the OSS an opportunity to advance its own schemes emphasizing covert, subversive morale operations over the idealistic and liberal propaganda emanating from Sherwood's Overseas branch. The incident was the major wartime OWI crisis; it signaled the beginning of the end of the influence of Sherwood and his lieutenants. Many OWI members recalled later that the 1943 attacks destroyed the agency's effectiveness. Warburg wrote that despite later praise, "OWI never fully recovered here at home from the damage done to its prestige by Congress and by certain elements of the Press."[38]

The problems facing the OWI from external sources were exacerbated by internal difficulties. James Rogers wrote during this period that "OWI was in turmoil, facing assaults from Congress, with rebellion inside." The internal upheaval, starting in early 1943, led to the greatest changes in the OWI and revolved around the differing ideologies and definitions of the agency's mission held by supporters of Davis, on the one hand, and of Sherwood on the other. Although both men believed in an overall strategy of truth, Sherwood thought truth could be used effectively as political and ideological propaganda not only to change men's beliefs and motivate them to action during the war but also to influence their beliefs after it.[39]

As defined by James Warburg, an information agency disseminated only the truth, providing only fact and opinion to enable people to form their own judgments without outside interpretation. The function of a propaganda agency such as the OWI was to persuade, however, not to inform. It disseminated "only such fact, such opinion, and such fiction masquerading as fact as will serve to make people act, or fail to act in a certain way." The inability of the OWI to make the distinction, Warburg believed, caused its information to be tainted with propaganda and limited the effectiveness of its propaganda by making it conform to strict moral principles. The "purpose of spreading information is to promote the functioning of man's reason," but "the purpose of propaganda," he claimed, "is to mobilize certain of man's emotions in such a way that they will dominate his reason." Elmer Davis's "timid indifference," Warburg charged, was the cause of the philosophical dilemma, and the director considered the OWI nothing more than a "high class international news service." Davis failed to "understand that he was being entrusted with the management of an important branch of modern warfare."[40]

Davis, and the people who joined the OWI after 1942, publicly proclaimed that pure information was the key. "America should tell the truth, tell it intelligently, and tell it everywhere" in the form of plain, unadulterated facts that could "educate . . . listeners in a true interpretation of the enemy's designs, create a distrust of the enemy, and diminish their prestige."[41] Wallace Carroll

agreed, recalling that "many of us in OWI," including Davis, Edward Klauber, Edward Barrett, Ferdinand Kuhn, and himself, "were strongly predisposed by our previous training in favor of a program of information." The inclination of these journalists "was to put the facts of the war before the world." The difficulty was in choosing between providing news or suppressing it, "between the practices of journalism and the dictates of war, between the urge to inform and the passion to save lives, between common honesty and plain humanity." The conflicts were most apparent during planning sessions in which Davis and his supporters pushed their view, to the disgust of Sherwood, Warburg, Johnson, and Barnes.[42]

The internal conflicts over definition and content reflected deeper issues. The choice to use straight information was not just a matter of politics, morality, and ideology but of pragmatism. According to C. A. H. Thomson, "Any propaganda must choose to emphasize either factual material or ideology," but because American ideology was so diffuse, because it had an "absence of centrally agreed or imposed doctrine," the dissemination of Davis's straight facts as plain information had to prevail. Davis believed that if OWI's output "takes the form of news rather than ideological argument or debate, it will be more widely heard and circulated." Despite his views, the Overseas OWI people continued to practice a highly ideological propaganda based on Sherwood's political preferences and their own.[43]

The ideological indifference claimed by Elmer Davis and his followers, however, only masked a simpler, less politicized ideology. Despite public pronouncements that the OWI did the best it could to provide as much information as possible to audiences without jeopardizing military security, Davis did not believe in telling audiences all the story. He was not beyond withholding information he personally thought damaging to American interests, or to the Roosevelt administration, or to the OWI's reputation for reliable, factual reporting. Unverified stories and fantastic rumors that could serve only to inflame blind emotions and fuel hatreds were suppressed.[44]

Davis's assertion that not all news was fit for dissemination was most evident when applied to information that was termed World War I–style "atrocity propaganda," a definition extended to include news associated with the Holocaust. Until 1945, both Sherwood and Davis avoided or played down reports of atrocities perpetrated against the Jews of Europe. In late 1944, for example, the War Refugee Board made public a report on the Auschwitz extermination camp. Davis, whose propagandists had to pass on the information to audiences at home and abroad, was "angry about the publicity" and pressed to have the release squelched as too incredible. Davis believed the news of the Holocaust

would irreparably damage OWI's reputation for veracity and its credibility at a crucial juncture of the war. The audiences built up at home and abroad over two years could be lost permanently in an instant if presented with reports too fantastic to be believed. Arthur Sweetser reportedly told Leo Rosten that such stories would "be confused and misleading" and should be "contained and suppressed." Although the OWI took the lead in the last several months of the war in getting the news of the Holocaust out once the first extermination camps were liberated, such was not the case until it was clear the war was won. Thus while Davis and his followers maintained a policy of disseminating straight facts and the truth as they interpreted it, information had to be deemed plausible to audiences and harmless to OWI's reputation for sober truthfulness.[45]

The propaganda-versus-information debate and the struggle for ideological control of foreign propaganda were the true, although unacknowledged, reasons for the internal disputes that eventually led to a purge of the Overseas OWI in 1944. These fundamental issues were resolved in the context of seemingly unrelated organizational changes. In the rush to create a viable agency during summer 1942 many OWI members overlooked organizational weaknesses or treated them as unimportant secondary issues. One result of the neglect was the location of the Overseas Planning Board in Washington, D.C., and of the operational centers in New York City. Sherwood had always believed that all policies should be made and implemented in New York, where his authority was greatest, a goal realized by Warburg in the late 1942 OWI reorganizations.

Thus the OWI increasingly became a divided agency with two centers of power, two sets of leaders, and two different philosophies. Despite reforms implemented by Milton Eisenhower after the Darlan affair to strengthen Davis's control, and despite Davis's presence on the planning board and his responsibility for reviewing all material before dissemination, his attention was always focused domestically. Eisenhower expressed his concerns about this development in January 1943 when he told Gardner Cowles that neither he nor Davis had any idea what the Overseas OWI was doing, and if it supported "federal policy, it is almost accidental." He declared that "if we oppose some federal policy, I shall not be surprised." Following the exposure of the flaws in philosophy, organization, and control exemplified by the moronic-little-king incident and after the failure of the Overseas OWI to provide satisfactory explanations, Davis "recognized that the organization had . . . drifted out of his hands" and operated as a "closed corporation he could not penetrate." This development he believed was the work of Sherwood's New York lieutenants, James Warburg, Joseph Barnes, and Edd Johnson, who disagreed with Davis's philosophy and evaded his control whenever possible.[46]

The independence displayed by the New York City OWI office, physically and philosophically, was causing difficulties with the U.S. Army and the OWI abroad. In fall 1943, Wallace Carroll became irritated at the methods of the New York triumvirate and, being uncertain of his own authority and the competence of some New York officials, resigned as head of OWI London. He was followed by several others. Having already weathered mass resignations in the Domestic Branch earlier in 1943, Davis saw Carroll's resignation as the final straw and began a reorganization meant to place the entire OWI more firmly under his control.[47]

Internal differences of opinion regarding the most fundamental OWI policies were the main cause of instability, according to Davis. To regain stability he had to reorganize the agency and replace the people whose philosophy was contrary to his own. First, Davis appointed former CBS executive Edward Klauber to replace the outgoing Milton Eisenhower and, in early 1944, named Sherwood director of Propaganda and Information, with Edward Barrett as executive director and Thurman L. Barnard as his assistant. Barrett and Bernard were known for their businesslike ways and moderate political views. In this reorganization, which demoted Sherwood, there was no place for James Warburg, Joseph Barnes, and Edd Johnson, and Davis asked for their resignations. Sherwood's response was immediate and negative, terming the reorganization "irrational and irresponsible" and a change "which would seriously damage the war effort." He vowed to block any changes by going directly to the president.[48]

Both men recognized that Davis was attempting to gain clear dominance of the Overseas OWI and with it the power to control the ideological and political content and thrust of foreign propaganda. Both men also believed they had certain advantages and moved quickly to use them. Davis acted first by writing Roosevelt on 4 January 1944. He made no mention of the philosophical or personal differences between himself and Sherwood, but merely wrote that he was "convinced that certain changes must be made in the Overseas Branch." Though "Sherwood is an able propagandist," Davis wrote, his "administration has led to confusion and ineffectiveness," a problem Roosevelt himself had alluded to on occasion. Therefore, Davis continued, he had relieved Sherwood of all operating duties. He had also concluded that the OWI would benefit by the removal of Warburg, Johnson, and Barnes, "whose activities are . . . directed more toward getting and keeping power for themselves than to furthering the purposes of this organization." Davis referred to them as part of the "COI-before-Pearl-Harbor-Clique," who so dominated their branch that the "morale of the organization has been vitiated by the widespread belief that tenure of office depends on retaining the favor of this group." Davis admitted that Sherwood

disagreed with his conclusions, denied Davis's right to make personnel or organizational changes, and had threatened to persuade the president to split the Overseas Branch from the OWI, making it a separate entity under Sherwood's control. The director claimed that he would usually terminate such a mutinous subordinate but since Sherwood was willing to defer to the president's wishes, Davis thought he should keep Sherwood on as long as he "recognizes the full authority of the head of this office and behaves accordingly."[49]

Davis's letter convinced Roosevelt that yet another potentially damaging dispute was forming, but he did not act. Roosevelt had known and worked with Sherwood for four years, counted him as a friend, and knew that Sherwood's political and ideological views were closer to his own than were Davis's, a man who had never described himself as a New Dealer. In probable deference to Sherwood and to avoid yet another debilitating public scandal involving propaganda, Roosevelt wrote Davis that he had seen the draft reorganization order and that implementation should wait until the president received all the facts, meaning Sherwood's side.

Davis was aware of Sherwood's favorable position at the White House but also of the power of public opinion should the newest dispute become public. He was also confident of his power as OWI director, and he was determined not to be put off. Davis pressed the issue, responding that as director he should have full authority to run the OWI according to his own best judgment. It was evident that the Overseas OWI was "so confusingly organized, and so shot through with intrigue and office politics, that it can never operate . . . effectively . . . as long as Mr. Sherwood is its . . . head." Davis claimed that an effort had existed from the outset, and had increased in recent months, to prevent him from "exercising the authority . . . with which you charged me." He was unsure of Sherwood's role, as he often gave the impression of being "the victim of a small group of fast-thinking office politicians who shelter themselves behind his authority." Referring to Warburg, Barnes, and Johnson, Davis claimed "these men . . . have endeavored by double-talk and devious operation to maintain an artificial and arbitrary separation between Washington and New York" so that they could run the OWI to suit themselves. He argued that Sherwood "permitted this small inner circle to retain the actual control of the . . . Branch, for whose work I am responsible," and that Warburg and others, at Sherwood's behest, had so interfered with the workings of the Overseas Branch that many members had resigned. Davis's efforts to communicate directly with Sherwood had been blocked "due to the clique operation . . . and to Sherwood's reticence." He placed the blame for the current troubles on Sherwood's bad administrative skills and then offered to resign if the president wished, a move that

would definitely attract prompt and unwanted public attention and congressional interest. In short, Davis concluded, he could not "be responsible for actions undertaken against my wishes, and sometimes against my orders, by subordinates in whom I have lost confidence."[50]

The significant but unmentioned philosophical differences between the two OWI leaders were apparent to the president. Nonetheless, Sherwood's defense, laid out in a 13 January letter to the president, did not dwell on the differences. Instead, Sherwood wrote that the charges were blown out of proportion and that problems were due to Davis's own vacillation and neglect of foreign propaganda. Sherwood admitted that office politics were a fact but that they did not interfere with the quality of operations, which were praised by Generals Marshall and Eisenhower. Further, Sherwood wrote, the attacks on Warburg and Barnes were based not on the quality of their work but on Warburg's unpopularity at the White House in the 1930s and on Barnes's controversial world tour with Wendell Willkie in 1942. Warburg, Sherwood claimed, was "ardent and active" and "has done an exceptionally skilful job." Barnes was "one of the very best men in our organization," and he, like Warburg, was 100 percent loyal to FDR.[51]

Although the nature of the dispute, involving the top two propaganda officials in the nation, sent a strong signal that decisive executive intervention was necessary, Roosevelt stalled in characteristic fashion. His delay prompted Davis to write again, asking the president to settle the dispute; Roosevelt in turn refused to take sides or to become personally involved. The president's response was to order Sherwood and Davis to meet, as often as necessary, to effect an immediate, final, and complete solution. Suddenly without clear presidential support, Sherwood acquiesced to Davis's demands. The result was a February 1944 agreement that proved a clear victory for Davis at Sherwood's expense. "In order to promote harmony of operation," it was agreed that Davis was responsible for the policies and operations of the Overseas OWI and had complete authority over it and the right to initiate any policy or operation for implementation by the Overseas director, who thereafter would keep him informed in advance of any undertakings. Any personnel appointments or transfers had to be submitted to Davis for approval and were not valid without his consent. Sherwood's signature amounted to a capitulation of his political and ideological control over the Overseas OWI.[52]

The agreement served as a mandate for Davis to rid the OWI of the members who had exposed the agency to over two years of criticism. The forced resignations of Warburg, Barnes, and Johnson were an implicit part of the agreement and were accepted, although the trio "were at a loss, they told the press, to un-

derstand why." Their resignations followed those of many other veterans who could not abide the changed OWI philosophy and the increasing military control. Davis later wrote that OWI's one major problem was the "brilliant and zealous individual who cannot work as part of a team," a description that seemed to fit the pre–Pearl Harbor clique who were leaving. Davis realized that his agency, involved in a war with political and ideological overtones, "attracted many free-lance writers and others who had been used to working by themselves and had always jealously cherished their personal integrity and freedom of expression." Such individuals were apt to insist on proclaiming the truth as they saw it, and if told they must "proclaim the truth as the President and the Secretary of State see it," they "may feel . . . this is an intolerable limitation on . . . freedom of thought and speech." To Davis, such individuals were no longer welcome.[53]

With a virtual free hand to reorganize and realign the OWI as he saw fit, Davis moved quickly. Within two days he publicly announced Sherwood's departure for London where he was to assist with Allied propaganda planning. Edward Barrett, the new executive director of the Overseas OWI, was to serve Sherwood but in reality assumed his authority. The internal OWI tensions quickly dissipated. Wallace Carroll, who had accepted John Winant's advice to "stick with Elmer," wrote the ambassador that "OWI is a much stronger organization since the purge" and that "the old rivalry between the New York and Washington staffs is dying down." Soon thereafter, the OWI recruited an additional 400 people, most of whom were sent to London, the new OWI nerve center where they served with PWD/SHAEF, leaving the New York City office to become an administrative backwater.[54]

By early 1944 the OWI had become a unified organization reflecting Davis's ideology and propaganda philosophy. Although Sherwood remained in his post as Overseas director, operations were now conducted directly from London under Philip Hamblet, Edward Barrett, Thurman Barnard, Louis Cowan, Wallace Carroll, and Ferdinand Kuhn. None of the men shared Sherwood's extreme idealism or believed as he did "that Mr. Roosevelt and the New Deal are so fundamental that they cannot be separated from news and propaganda" or that "Roosevelt is America and his policies are the formula for the postwar world." Removed to an unimportant advisory position, Sherwood wrote Samuel Rosenman in March 1944 that "OWI has suffered a lot more than you would imagine by the publicity about the internal disputes." He acknowledged the perception that his philosophies had been repudiated and that he had been forced out by Davis and sent to London "as merely a face-saving device." He implied that his OWI career was over as he could not "go back to OWI Washington with Davis

OWI director Elmer Davis (center left) with OWI Overseas Branch members Cass Canfield (far left), Wallace Carroll (center right), and Philip Hamblet (far right), in Paris, 1944. (OWI Photo; reproduced at the National Archives)

and Klauber" and work "with two men for whom I have so little respect and so much distrust." On his return to the United States in late September 1944, realizing the organization he had helped found no longer existed or practiced the type of propaganda in which he believed, he tendered his resignation as director of the 5,000 Overseas Branch employees. Roosevelt and Davis accepted the resignation with "great regret."[55]

The U.S. Army was the main beneficiary of the dispute between the OWI and the OSS; the internal troubles both agencies experienced during 1943 and 1944 collectively facilitated the goal of militarizing the civilian agencies. This development was first demonstrated in the Mediterranean when military leaders took advantage of command changes and the stateside upheavals to reassert their control of propaganda. Col. Charles Hazeltine, PWB/AFHQ's commander, now seen as an ineffectual leader whose tenure brought increased civilian domination, was relieved of command in December 1943. OWI's Percy Winner and Oliver Garrett, part of the former COI pre–Pearl Harbor clique, were recalled to the states. The overall INC/AFHQ chief, General McClure, also

soon left PWB to assume command of the new PWD/SHAEF, taking along C. D. Jackson, his civilian deputy.[56]

With the leadership changes came increased military control and acceptance of propaganda. PWB/AFHQ remained the final authority on all propaganda matters, and the autonomy of the combat propaganda teams was tightened as military-civilian coordination improved. In December 1943, for example, the Fifth U.S. Army Combat Propaganda Team (CPT) was established as the official PWB of the Fifth Army. The team was essentially an expanded MRBC attached to military headquarters, and its commander became a full and theoretically equal staff member who received direction from PWB/AFHQ and OWI directives. Team members had access to military and civilian printing and radio facilities in Naples and Rome where they created, planned, and disseminated white tactical leaflets, pamphlets, and newspapers on demand of Allied commanders. The overall favorable response to the new PWB/AFHQ, and the Fifth Army CPT prompted the INC to relinquish its control of psychological warfare in October 1944. Thereafter, PWB was a special staff section under a civilian director, OWI's Russell Barnes, who reported directly to the chief of staff of the Supreme Allied Commander–Mediterranean. The branch then operated smoothly and effectively for the duration before being officially abolished on 15 July 1945.[57]

The U.S. Army learned a great deal about the value of propaganda and the difficulties of working with civilians through its experiences with PWB/AFHQ, lessons they applied when planners met in London in mid-1943 to begin creating a new psychological warfare agency for use in Northwest Europe. Seeking to avoid past mistakes, the planners decided at the outset to create a separate staff division for Publicity and Psychological Warfare (P&PW), totally divorcing it from intelligence work and thereby removing a main source of confusion. They then established the framework for a combined civilian and military agency to control all propaganda policy and planning, to coordinate all operations, and to conduct both strategic and consolidation propaganda. The new agency would not become involved in tactical propaganda operations but would allow each subordinate army group to form its own P&PW branches for such purposes. The army-group PWBs would control flexibly organized civilian and military CPTs, thus meeting the needs of army corps, divisions, and smaller units.[58]

Confident that the Allies now had a formula for a workable, military-controlled propaganda organization, Allied leaders turned plans into reality. In November 1943 General McClure arrived in London to meet with Wallace Carroll and C. D. Jackson of the OWI, Frederick Oechsner of OSS MO, and Richard Crossman of PWE about implementing the plans for a new psychological war-

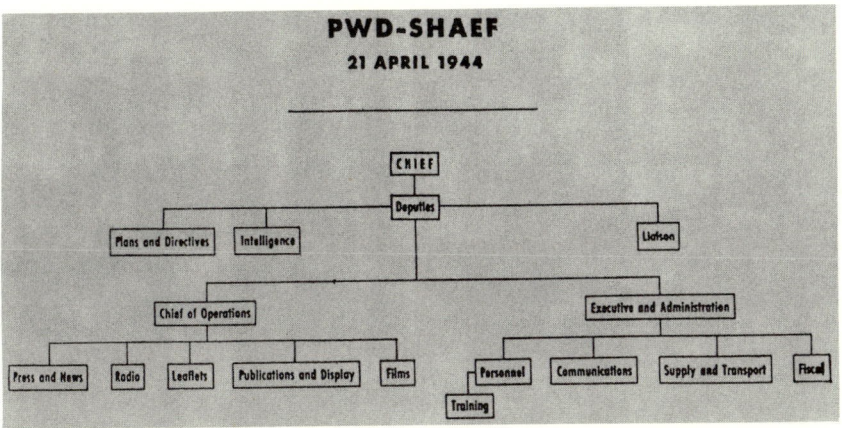

Figure 9.1. Organization of the Psychological Warfare Division, Supreme Headquarters, Allied Expeditionary Force, 21 April 1944. (Courtesy the National Archives)

fare agency. McClure was convinced that "psychological warfare must be in harmony with that carried out from the home bases" and that "policies must be closely coordinated." As a result, in April 1944 the Psychological Warfare Division (PWD/SHAEF) was created as part of the staff of the Supreme Allied Command.[59]

The unique PWD required a similarly distinctive form of organization. From the time of its creation, McClure was assisted by four civilian deputies, one representing each of the four Allied civilian propaganda agencies (OWI, OSS, PWE, MOI), and two military advisers, one British and one American. PWD had subdivisions including Plans and Directives, Intelligence, Radio, Leaflets, Press, Films, Publications and Display, Training, and Special Operations.[60]

Prior to the Normandy landings, to avoid repeating the error of failing to spell out roles, SHAEF issued Operation Memorandum 8 on 11 March 1944. Known as the PWD Charter, it delineated functions, defined psychological warfare, divided it into three types—combat, strategic, and consolidation—and established the authority of PWD over Allied propaganda operations in Northwest Europe. The primary duties of PWD consisted of top-level coordination of themes and policies among civilian and military agencies, the planning of operations and campaigns, the issuance of theater directives, the formulation of combat propaganda policy, the supply of personnel and equipment to CPTs, the supervision and training of military propaganda personnel, the production and dissemination of leaflets and other printed materials by strategic aircraft, the op-

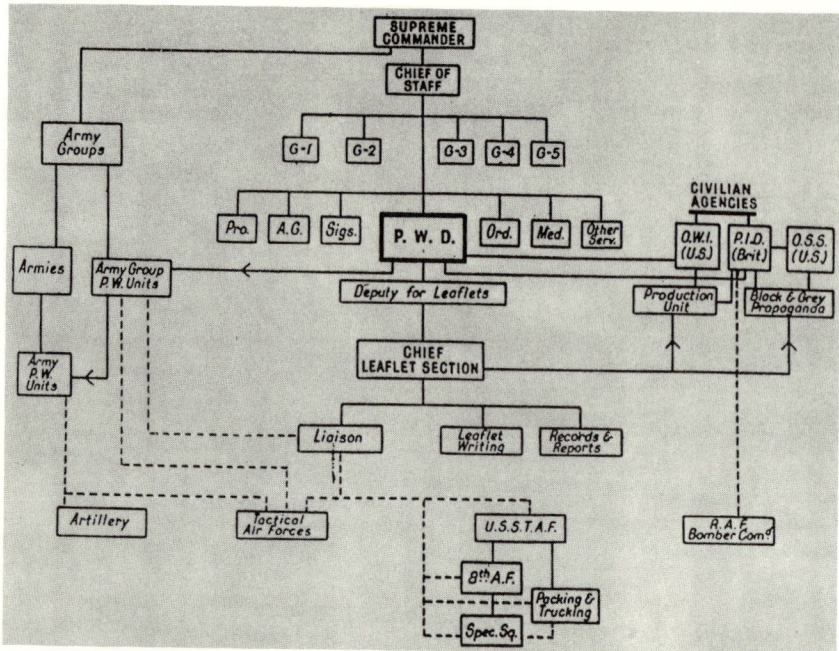

Figure 9.2. Propaganda Organization, European Theater of Operations, 1944–1945. (Courtesy the National Archives)

eration of strategic radio transmitters, and the conduct, coordination, and control of consolidation propaganda in liberated areas.[61]

As with PWB, the four civilian agencies provided the majority of PWD personnel and equipment, the OWI providing the most. In July 1944 PWD consisted of 361 military and civilian personnel with future estimates predicting a November 1944 complement of 1,500, most of them civilians. PWD leaders were determined to prevent the divided loyalties that had led to civilian domination of PWB, and in Memorandum 8 they made it explicit that PWD was the overall coordinating agency for all civilian and military psychological warfare campaigns in Northwest Europe. All personnel, regardless of agency affiliation, were under military authority and discipline and owed their first allegiance to PWD.[62]

The PWD Charter gave combat propaganda responsibilities to the army groups that administered and controlled CPTs, just as in PWB. Therefore, propaganda plans, once approved by PWD, were implemented by lower echelons that gathered intelligence, conducted mobile radio, printing, and loudspeaker operations, and otherwise performed tactical functions. In both the British Twenty-first and American Twelfth Army groups, PWB was part of a combined

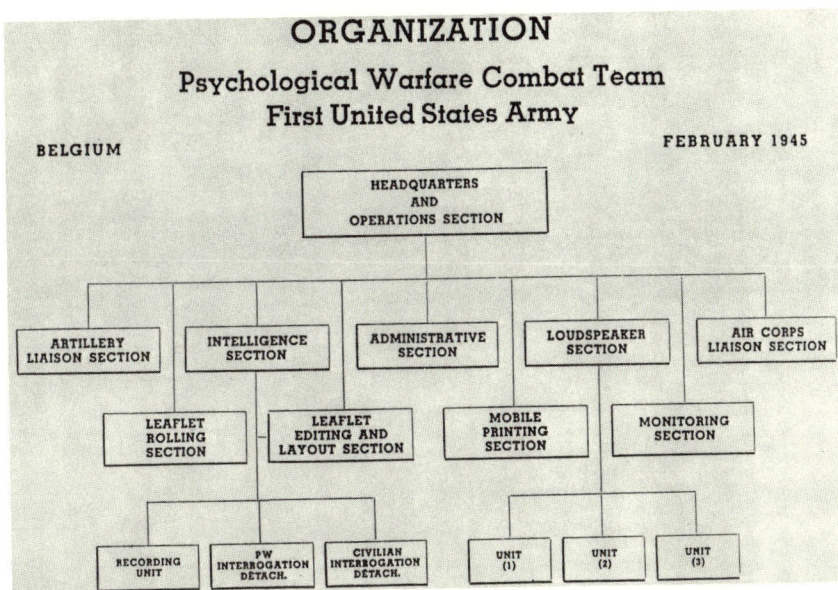

ORGANIZATION

Psychological Warfare Combat Team
First United States Army

BELGIUM   FEBRUARY 1945

Figure 9.3. Organization of the Combat Propaganda Team, First U.S. Army, European Theater of Operations, February 1945. (Courtesy the National Archives)

P&PW Division. Its senior member, the psychological warfare officer, was usually a full colonel on the special staff of the army group commander.[63]

The majority of tactical propaganda operations were conducted by teams consisting of five or six officers and fifty to sixty enlisted men who were usually part of a larger MRBC. The CPTs served armies, corps, and divisions and were dispatched to units at the request of local commanders after consulting psychological warfare liaison officers at the corps or army level. At lower echelons PWBs followed one of several configurations. In the Third U.S. Army, for example, a PWB consisting of two officers, two civilians, and eleven enlisted men was attached to headquarters and existed as a subsection of the G-2, despite the separation of these functions at the SHAEF level. The unit was charged with obtaining intelligence, maintaining communications with higher and lower echelons, preparing propaganda for use at lower levels, supervising the distribution of leaflets, monitoring enemy radio, and conducting consolidation operations. Further down the organizational scale, at the corps level, psychological warfare liaison officers were attached to the G-2 section and maintained contact with and met requests of PWB, corps, and lower divisional and regimental commanders. In the First U.S. Army the headquarters unit included a P&PW Divi-

sion and had a separate staff for the two divisions not connected to G-2. The intelligence functions of the division were performed instead by the OSS, and propaganda was conducted by the OWI. By February 1945 the First U.S. Army had organized its own CPT consisting of eight officers, fifty-one enlisted men, one civilian, and seven Belgian civilians.[64]

According to Memorandum 8, the Twelfth Army Group controlled the Mobile Radio Broadcast Companies that by fall 1944 included the Second, Third, Fourth, and Fifth MRBCs. The first MRBC arrived in France on 25 June 1944. As with the First MRBC in Italy, the combined civilian and military units bore the brunt of the tactical propaganda campaign after 6 June 1944.[65]

By mid-1944, after two-and-a-half years of turmoil at home and abroad, the U.S. Army had developed a useful military propaganda organization. The structure was not entirely an army creation, nor was it battle tested. It was, however, far less politicized than its civilian counterparts and was relatively well staffed and equipped and anxious to prove that psychological warfare could aid in destroying the Axis powers.

10 · The OSS Morale Operations Branch in Action, 1943–1945

The OSS Morale Operations Branch, unlike the U.S. Army or the OWI, practiced covert strategic and tactical morale operations based on deception and subversion. The types of campaigns conducted and the methods used supposedly closely resembled Nazi fifth-column activities of the 1930s and early 1940s. The OSS used whatever means gained results, and its members believed that Nazi psychological warfare had been extremely successful. The belief in the efficacy of Nazi methods indicated how firmly OSS policymakers supported a propaganda of realpolitik in which, as in Nazi Germany, scruples, ethics, and universally accepted agreements and decencies were morally relative if not totally discarded to obtain national goals. As MO output was covert, it could act without fear of damaging America's reputation or moral standing.

The MO Branch commenced operations relatively late in the war. Yet between 1943 and V-E Day it implemented campaigns of a scope and level of sophistication beyond any propaganda ever practiced by the Nazis. MO output was unofficial and disclaimed by federal authorities and was covertly disseminated to make it appear to be of enemy origin. The members of the branch hoped not only to aid the U.S. Army by demoralizing the Wehrmacht but also to undermine the Germans' beliefs in Hitler and Nazism and their faith in political and social institutions. They sought to unravel the very fabric of German society by creating the impression that a fifth column was at work within the Reich.

In July 1944 PWD's Gen. Robert A. McClure instructed OSS's David Bruce that MO was to create the impression in Germany "that internal rot has set in . . . that effective controls are breaking down. . . . That others . . . accept defeat as in the best interests of the nation." MO was to use all means available to encourage desertion, dereliction of duty, and surrender within the Wehrmacht and

to create divisions, frictions, and suspicion within the German civil administration and population.[1]

Although the primary mission of MO was to attack Germany, it also attacked Nazi allies. The branch had a job wherever Axis military and civilian populations were found, and its personnel eventually participated in all PWD campaigns after D-Day.[2]

In the early days rumors were used to disseminate MO propaganda which consisted of simple, brief, concrete, and vivid stories, purporting to come from inside sources concerning familiar persons and events. Successful examples were easy to remember, had a plot, concerned current events, and appealed to emotion and sentiment. Rumors were intended to subvert and deceive, to promote fear, anxiety, confusion, overconfidence, distrust, and panic. Once created and cleared by the OSS and PWE, up to twenty rumors were disseminated each week by agent, radio, and leaflet and through plants in enemy and neutral newspapers. Success was gauged by a "comeback," or mention of the rumor in the foreign, neutral, or Allied press or by Allied or enemy intelligence services. According to OSS tallies of comebacks, rumors were extraordinarily effective.[3]

Rumors were more strategic than tactical in nature, and pains were taken to hide their origin to make them appear homegrown. As a covert service, however, MO was not required to adhere to official U.S. policies; thus MO rumors in June 1944 included stories that British paratroopers had landed in Berlin, German sailors in Wilhelmshaven had shot their officers, Field Marshals Rommel and von Rundstedt had been captured, Luftwaffe pilots were refusing to fly, foreign workers had taken over the Krupp factory in Essen, former Nazi leader Rudolf Hess was leading a detachment of Allied troops in France, and Wehrmacht rations had been found to have been poisoned.[4]

Even after MO developed more sophisticated distribution methods and grander subversive schemes, rumors continued to be a favored means of attacking enemy morale. Post-D-Day rumors stressed tensions between the SS and the army and between Nazi Germany and her allies. Anti-Nazi rumors were a staple and included stories claiming that Nazi leaders were making plans to flee to South America, were enjoying foods and luxuries other Germans could not obtain, and were intentionally ordering the military to kill refugees because adequate food, housing, and evacuation areas could not be found. MO created stories about Wehrmacht generals martyred for their actions in the plot against Hitler and emphasized the selfishness of the Nazis who intended to make the people fight to the death while they fled to Japan. When V-weapons began to appear, MO started the rumor that launch crews were soldiers undergoing punishment who were required to fire a quota of the unstable and explosion-prone

missiles. Rumors concerning anarchy in Germany were a favorite and were passed with stories about the Nazi-controlled black market.[5]

Although most rumors fit the criterion of being plausible, on occasion some were deemed incredible. Such was the case when MO agents in Stockholm were told not to spread atrocity stories about human sausage, human skin decorations, and canned human meat because they were too fantastic to be believed. MO however, unlike the OWI, did not have to avoid atrocity stories and considered any rumor for dissemination—the more heinous examples were deemed most memorable and therefore more likely to be passed on. Rumor operations were halted in late April 1945 because OSS planners concluded that their highly volatile rumors were impossible to control in areas under Allied occupation and could do as much damage to friends as they had to Nazis.[6]

The MO Branch made use of leaflets, news sheets, and newspapers, but unlike the materials of their overt counterparts, theirs purported to originate from enemy sources. MO-printed materials were crudely designed and hurriedly produced with cheap paper and ink to create the impression that they were made by clandestine groups with small budgets and scarce supplies, operating one step ahead of the Gestapo.

The first major black-leaflet undertaking was the "Wie lange noch?" or "How much longer?" campaign, an operation consisting of sixteen different leaflets implying origins from an anti-Nazi resistance group. The leaflets, stickers, and posters, delivered by agents, were identified by a red circle and three extended fingers forming a W. Each one consisted of a captioned cartoon asking how much longer Germans were going to tolerate a certain situation before rebelling or quitting the war. Examples included cartoons showing crosses or other appropriate drawings and such captions as "How much longer will they deny that the East Front is a common grave?" or "How much longer shall our soldiers be forced to fight side by side with the dregs of Europe?" or "How much longer are we left behind while the party bosses flee the bombs?"[7]

One success toward the end of the war in Italy, according to MO, involved the dropping of safe-conduct passes allegedly from partisan groups in the vicinity of Italy's Fascist Monte Rosa Division, which held a vital sector of the front. Within one week over 1,000 Fascists deserted, carrying MO leaflets ensuring good partisan treatment. Further desertions were limited only by partisan refusal to accept the mobs of surrendering Fascists.[8]

Black leaflets covered a variety of situations adapted to local circumstances. Leaflets distributed to the Wehrmacht in Italy, for example, contained lists of bombed streets in German cities, instructions on how to desert to Switzerland or fake an illness, and false proclamations and orders from Wehrmacht officers

"How much longer shall our soldiers be forced to fight side by side with the dregs of Europe?"

"How much longer will they deny that the East Front is a common grave?"

"How much longer are we left behind while the party bosses flee the bombs?"

OSS Morale Operations Branch "Wie lange noch" propaganda leaflets disseminated in the Mediterranean Theater of Operations in 1943. (RG 226; reproduced at the National Archives)

as well as counterfeit leave passes or leaflets claiming that the wives, sisters, and sweethearts of soldiers were at the sexual mercies of foreign workers and Nazi party members at home. Other clearly pornographic materials were dropped to enemy soldiers to reinforce themes suggesting that women, boys, and girls were being forced to submit to all sorts of Nazi sexual perversions.[9]

The MO Branch developed the League of Lonely German Women campaign to heighten the anxieties of enemy soldiers over the women left behind. A leaflet instructed soldiers to place a small red heart on their lapel or glass the next time they were on leave or in a restaurant or tavern. The badge identified them to the League of Lonely German Women who were eager to do their part in boosting morale through sexual promiscuity. The leaflet continued, "Don't be shy. Your wife, sister, and sweetheart is one of us. We think of you, but we also think of Germany." Widely distributed, the leaflets were picked up by Allied intelligence agents and mentioned in the neutral media and in *Stars and Stripes*, Toronto's *Canadian Tribune*, and *Time* magazine. Many captured soldiers possessed both the leaflet and the heart-shaped lapel badge.[10]

Considerable effort was expended undermining the morale of Axis allies and enemy forces in occupied nations. Frequently the OSS air-dropped MO kits to partisan groups in Yugoslavia, France, Greece, and Italy containing leaflets, pamphlets, stickers, rubber stamps, and posters. Special aid was given to Tito's partisans by a two-man MO team dispatched to the island of Vis. Between June 1944 and April 1945 the team distributed over 3 million pieces of propaganda. Other MO agents disseminated leaflets and rumors seeking to undermine the pro-Nazi governments of Hungary, Bulgaria, and Rumania.[11]

Teams of agents, in addition to spreading propaganda, organized distribution networks and gathered intelligence behind enemy lines. The first such OSS MO operation, code-named Apple, consisted of six men who were delivered by British torpedo boat to enemy-occupied Crete. Their mission, lasting from May to July 1944, sought to confirm reports of low German morale and increasingly strong partisan activity. After landing, the team successfully accomplished their missions and determined in the process that enemy morale on the island was so low that only 3,000 of the 15,000 troops there were likely to resist an Allied attack.[12]

A further Greek mission, code-named Ulysses, was launched in June 1944 after reports were received that guerrillas on the island of Evvia and in Thessaly were willing to help Allied agents. MO thus decided to establish a local base to take advantage of the situation, sending a four-man team from Cairo to Evvia on 13 June 1944; due to enemy activity, however, the group went to the island of Volos. Once ashore, they distributed their stocks of newspapers, pamphlets, and

poison-pen letters, printed nearly 37,000 leaflets, sabotaged bridges, trucks, and locomotives, and avoided detection until Greece was liberated in October 1944.[13]

The OSS conducted similar operations in Northwest Europe. Leaflets informing German troops of the creation of soldiers' committees such as those of November 1918 were MO favorites in 1944. The most famous such committee was Soldatengruppe West, the subject of a score of MO leaflets. Other leaflets were dropped to Austrian divisions informing them of anti-Nazi groups such as the Democratic United Austrian Front.[14]

One operation, undertaken in 1944, was based on the 1918 incident of Field Marshal Erich Ludendorff's flight to Sweden to avoid capture following the armistice. Bogus leaflets of Ludendorff's explanation for his actions, addressed to officers on Wehrmacht High Command (OKW) stationery, were re-created in which officers were instructed to convince themselves, and then their troops, "that it is more important to save officer personnel for future wars than to die in a battle already lost. Soldiers are easily found, but officers are a rarer commodity." Enlisted men were to fight to the last because without the officer corps, the text read, Germany was kaput.

The purpose of the five-page pamphlet was to foment disobedience and suspicion among enlisted men and to facilitate mutiny and the creation of soldiers' committees. As similar incidents had actually already taken place, most notably at Cherbourg in July 1944, it was believed that the Ludendorff campaign could have a devastating effect on morale and discipline. The materials were distributed in summer and early fall by MO infiltration teams and fighter aircraft of the Ninth Tactical Air Force. Comebacks of the campaign's effectiveness came via the British House of Commons, where the pamphlet was introduced as a genuine OKW document, and in *Time* magazine. The story was also picked up by *New York Herald Tribune* reporter Joseph Driscoll and reported in September 1944, thereby making the story available for use by the OWI and BBC official broadcasters.[15]

Perhaps the most successful MO–Twelfth Army Group campaign, according to MO, was the Skorpion West operation, named after the Wehrmacht military propaganda unit created by Field Marshal Walter Model to bolster troop morale following the 1944 Normandy campaign. The Skorpion West unit attempted through a series of leaflets to appraise the mistakes of the summer and to encourage troops with morale-boosting descriptions of secret weapons, additional drafts of manpower, and Nazi Germany's adoption of total war. The leaflets, however, did not receive the wide distribution desired and Skorpion West began to air-drop them over the lines. MO quickly obtained copies of the leaflets and

began making black facsimiles that were distributed as the genuine article. The first MO leaflet claimed that Nazi leaders doubted Wehrmacht resolve to hold against Allied attacks and encouraged soldiers to scorch the earth before dying in a last stand for National Socialism. The second encouraged enemy soldiers to eliminate defeatist officers who attempted to surrender or retreat; they were to question all orders and shoot suspected officers without hesitation. A third leaflet ordered troops to aid civilian evacuation of every village, by force if necessary. This move, MO hoped, would clog roads and slow the movement of enemy supplies and troops as well as harry already overburdened civilian authorities. In rage and desperation, Model and OKW denounced all Skorpion West leaflets as forgeries, ordering troops to ignore the contents of any leaflet they found. To MO their response "was the crowning admission of defeat, since it was denouncing the whore from the pulpit and thus trebling her business." Skorpion West, having denounced their own campaign in order to stop MO's, soon halted leaflet production.[16]

Forged documents, letters, and poison-pen letters were MO staples and were used to create dissatisfaction, anxiety, and confusion, to intimidate collaborators, to terrorize soldiers and civilians, and to harass the Gestapo. In one operation, based on the 1944 capture of Generalmajor Karl Kreipe by British commandos, MO hoped to convince enemy soldiers that their officers were surrendering to save themselves. When Kreipe, the German commander of Crete, was captured, MO began a rumor, leaflet, and radio campaign claiming he had given up to prevent further useless slaughters resulting from Hitler's last-stand orders. Later, when Generalmajor Franz Krech was killed by Andartes guerrillas near Sparta, MO spread stories via the media that his death came at the hands of the Gestapo, who had allegedly shot him as he attempted to escape aboard a British submarine. Krech, according to MO, left a letter declaring that the war was lost and that further sacrifices were futile. The letter was distributed in cafes and taverns throughout Greece and the Balkans.[17]

Concomitant with the Kreipe and Krech campaigns, MO began Operation Hemlock, which involved poison-pen letters. The Greek operation was later repeated throughout Europe and consisted of anonymous letters that were sent to the Gestapo implicating collaborators in pro-Allied behavior or threatening traitors with assassination or other dire consequences. Other poison-pen letters in the form of death notices were sent to the families of German servicemen, as were letters informing them that their recently deceased loved ones were victims of mercy killings by army doctors or that wounded soldiers were robbed of valuables by Nazi party officials while they lay dying in hospitals.[18]

One novel poison-pen letter, created in December 1944, was sent to soldiers

from Lichtenau, Germany. Allegedly a Christmas greeting from the Nazi mayor, it informed the troops of local events. Although meant to boost morale, the letter contained many none-too-subtle indications that disaster was striking the community on a daily basis. The mayor cheerfully wrote that civilians had been armed and drafted into the Volkssturm, that youngsters aged fifteen to seventeen were being trained as pilots and would be in combat after only a few weeks of training, excepting three who had crashed on the town itself, killing themselves and five others, that several specifically named streets had been bombed without Luftwaffe opposition and with heavy loss of life, that wives, sisters, and sweethearts were sacrificing their health, lives, and beauty for the cause and were working overtime denouncing traitors to the Gestapo, that food, water, and electricity were not to be had, and that five births had been reported among town residents, one to a women whose husband had disappeared in France twelve months before. The letter closed with a Merry Christmas and a Heil Hitler.[19]

MO excelled at producing black newspapers and developed *La Ricossa Italiana* and *Marc Aurelio* for Italians, *Das neue Deutschland* and *Nachrichten für die Truppe* for Germans, and *Der Oesterreicher* for Austrians. Forged copies of the SS paper *Das Schwarze Korps* were printed as were issues of the *Berliner Illustrierte Zeitung*. By March 1945 MO was printing black versions of Wehrmacht unit papers, but the speed of the Allied advance made delivery haphazard.[20]

One paper, *Der Oesterreicher*, purported to represent a resistance group and sought to split Austria from Germany by portraying the former country as a Nazi-occupied nation. The paper was produced in Washington, printed in Rome, and delivered after October 1944 by agents and air-drops.[21]

Supposedly the most successful MO newspaper operation in Europe was *Das neue Deutschland* (DND), a campaign initiated by MO in Italy. DND was a fictitious, clandestine peace party, allegedly organized in Germany in April 1944 whose goal was an anti-Nazi revolution and the re-creation of a liberal democratic Germany. MO created DND to offer the widest appeal, promising everything to everybody in its political platform, and membership applications were dropped to enemy soldiers and civilians throughout Europe. Its official organ, the newspaper *Das neue Deutschland*, had an initial average run of 75,000 copies and later increased to 1 million per issue. It was printed in Algiers and later in Rome and Caserta, Italy.[22]

Nazi reactions and Allied comments indicated DND's success. Himmler's *Das Schwarze Korps* denounced the movement in December 1944 and February 1945, as did the DNB, and Wehrmacht bulletins warned that troops found in possession of DND literature were liable to court-martial or even execution. Nu-

merous soldiers possessed DND newspapers when captured and copies were found in Berlin, Pilsen, the Rhineland, and the Dachau concentration camp. DND's news was reported by the *Washington Times Herald* (12 April 1945), the *Washington Post* (9 August 1944), and surprisingly, by members of the OSS R&A Branch, who thought DND genuine. It was even the subject of correspondence among top OWI members, who instructed OWI outposts to watch "for any material published about the German underground, especially the Neues Deutschland." Once DND's existence was picked up in Allied circles, MO had help in spreading its message through the official news reports of the BBC, ABSIE, and VOA.[23]

MO produced scores of black magazines and newsletters for delivery to the Reich itself after determining that even the most educated Germans were familiar with no more than thirty or so publications and were unlikely to recognize a fake journal. In addition, special issues of *Time* and *Life* were printed for Axis forces, many of whom eagerly sought English publications. These magazines contained feature stories by fictitious POWs describing the luxuries of American captivity and encouraging others to quit the war and join them in Canada and America.[24]

One other unique operation, the Harvard Project, was started by Lt. (jg) William Casey, USN, for implementation by the MO Sioux Mission in Stockholm, Sweden. The clandestine two-man team was one of the first MO units to begin operations abroad in March 1944. Under State Department cover and with OWI–supplied equipment, the Sioux Mission began producing rumors and more than 250,000 pamphlets, leaflets, stickers, and letters subsequently disseminated by OSS–SO agents throughout Europe.[25]

The Harvard Project itself consisted of a four-page, letter-sized, weekly business publication, *Handel und Wandel*, that purported to be a factual analysis of world economic news of European interest. Its purpose was to convince German businessmen that if they threw out the Nazis, Allied business interests would cooperate with them in creating a capitalist bulwark against bolshevism. The operation aimed at splitting industrialists from the Nazis and pushing business groups to press the army to surrender before everything was destroyed. Limited distribution of the newsletter, about 1,000 copies each, was carried out by SO agents or was sent through the mails.[26]

The weight and bulk of printed materials always made agent distribution risky. MO's solution was to produce pregummed stickers and precut stencils that looked handwritten. Agents could quickly attach stickers to any surface with little risk, and stencils came with an easy-to-use paint pen specially developed by the OSS R&D Branch. Stickers and stencils consisted of simple anti-Nazi or de-

featist slogans such as "When Hitler dies—Germany lives," "We quit," "Capitulate," and "Must you be the last one to die?"[27]

MO produced posters as well, but their weight and bulk limited their use. Examples included a depiction of cemetery crosses, one bearing the epitaph "Killed on the last day of World War II. Will you be the last one to die?" Another showed a view from the bottom of an open grave with the caption, " 'Where the German soldier sets his foot, from there he never leaves.' A. Hitler, 7 Oct. 1942." Other posters relied on symbolism: a German soldier crucified on a swastika or Hitler's face superimposed on a skull and crossbones.[28]

Distribution problems spurred MO to develop new methods. Two operations in Italy, code-named Sauerkraut and Ravioli, used uniformed and armed German and Italian POWs who were provided fake identity papers and who then infiltrated the lines to gather intelligence and distribute propaganda. The first operation involved fourteen POWs who crossed the line near Siena on 21 and 25 July 1944 to distribute 3,000 pieces of material about the 20 July assassination attempt on Hitler. The initial foray was so successful that twelve more missions, involving a total of fifty POWs, were undertaken in and around Bologna before May 1945.[29]

The Sauerkraut and Ravioli missions exemplified perfectly the willingness of the OSS leadership to use whatever means were necessary to defeat the Nazis since these operations were in violation of the 1929 Geneva Convention and the U.S. Army Rules of Land Warfare, both of which applied to the OSS. William Casey was a major proponent of using expendable POWs for MO work and for equally dangerous SO and SI missions. He assured OSS member J. Russell Forgan of the full cooperation of the U.S. Army's provost marshal's office, which had guaranteed the OSS an unending supply of POWs.[30]

The idea of using POWs, partisans, and Allied agents for OSS work spread to Northwest Europe after D-Day. The most famous infiltration teams there were commanded by Maj. Paul Mellon, a relative of OSS leader David Bruce and heir to the Mellon family fortune, and Maj. Stacey Lloyd; both men were U.S. Army officers attached to the OSS. MO field teams operated in France after August 1944 and initially consisted entirely of Americans divided into three teams of eight officers, seven enlisted men, and six civilians. One team was eventually attached to each army of the Twelfth Army Group. The teams conducted sixty operations behind the lines, disseminating rumors, leaflets, stickers, stencils, and forged letters in mailboxes, under the doors of dwellings, in railroad cars and stations, in taverns, and by word of mouth. On one mission, eighty agents delivered over 15,000 pamphlets.[31]

Major Lloyd later reported to General Donovan that teams of the French re-

sistance had also delivered MO materials near Chartres and Rheims. One group actually secured a truck, filled its spare tires with MO propaganda, and drove to Paris two weeks before the August 1944 liberation, distributing Ludendorff leaflets along the way. Another team was sent to Metz and Nancy to operate with the U.S. Third Army, and a further twenty agents were sent into Germany and Belgium after Luxembourg City was liberated. A third MO team assisted Dutch resistance forces. In ten months, teams attached to the Twelfth Army Group infiltrated enemy lines with 150 agents; of this number, one was killed by U.S. troops, fifteen disappeared, and one was captured.[32]

The Morale Operations Branch was constantly on the lookout for new ways to deliver propaganda, and one method was adapted from a Hungarian operation conducted by MO's John Fistere. Code-named Cornflakes, it was developed by branch members Jan Libich and Jack Daniels in late 1944 and involved the participation of twenty-one MO members. After Libich investigated the workings of the German postal system, replicas of mailbags were made, complete with official markings. The bags were then stuffed with propaganda: poison-pen letters, black newspapers, leaflets, and posters bearing forged and canceled postage stamps and actual addresses gleaned from prewar German telephone directories. Aircraft of the Fifteenth AAF and Fourteenth Fighter Group then dropped the bags during the course of routine bombing and strafing missions of rail yards and trains in Germany between February and April 1945. Care was taken to ensure that the targeted areas were on the actual routes where the mail was addressed, and postage stamps were canceled to coincide with the date of the raids. The planners reasoned that Germans finding the bags would assume they were from destroyed mail cars and return them to postal authorities, where their contents would be distributed with the 15 million other pieces of mail handled daily, solving MO's distribution problems.[33]

The operation was described as a stunning success. MO personnel claimed that Cornflakes weakened civilian and military morale, added more confusion to an already chaotic communication and transportation network, and convinced many Germans, through MO material on their doorsteps, of the existence of bold and brazen anti-Nazi groups within Germany. Twenty such missions were conducted, delivering 320 bags of propaganda materials. Postwar POW interrogations revealed that many soldiers received copies of *Das neue Deutschland* via Cornflakes mail, resulting in Gestapo investigations and prosecutions.[34]

Air dissemination was key to MO's distribution problems, but air corps cooperation was not always forthcoming. Late in the war, MO decided to drop millions of issues of *Das neue Deutschland* from strategic aircraft to supplement

the normal 75,000 copies distributed through agents. PWB/AFHQ immediately protested that if MO's material was found in the same proximity to PWB's white propaganda, it would have a deteriorating effect on both. MO's solution, revealed in Operation Pig Iron, was to miniaturize the newspaper and label each with the message that it was a reprinted issue of the original product captured by Allied troops. This 10-by-6.5-inch version was initially dropped over Germany at the rate of 1 million copies per month, later increasing to 1 million per week. Over 10 million such small newspapers were eventually disseminated.[35]

Forgeries were always a staple of OSS black propaganda. MO developed postage stamps bearing the likeness of Himmler rather than Hitler, to give Germans the impression that der Führer had been ousted in a secret coup d'etat. In conjunction with PWE, MO produced counterfeit ration cards and forged civil certificates, forms, vouchers, military travel orders, and sick leave and furlough passes. The OSS Planning Group even considered counterfeiting German currency to destroy the Reich's economy. In another plan, to increase the likelihood of troops picking up MO material, it was suggested that propaganda be printed on the back of counterfeit banknotes or that special offers of rations or privileges be guaranteed to a person bearing the note when surrendering.[36]

In cooperation with the OSS R&D Branch and Britain's PWE, MO developed a variety of unusual gadgets intended to lower morale, such as the exploding ink pen. At one point, Jack Daniels suggested producing ammunition in enemy calibers that contained high explosives rather than smokeless powder, which could then be smuggled into the Wehrmacht supply system. When the device was fired, the resulting explosion would destroy both weapon and owner.[37]

Another operation, code-named Braddock II, allegedly caused untold problems for Nazi security forces. It involved dropping 4 to 5 million small, powerful time-fuse incendiaries in areas where heavy concentrations of foreign workers were found. Planners hoped the recipients of the devices would use them to set fires and sabotage enemy industry as well as keep already harried police busy. Intelligence reports, rumors from neutral capitals, and DNB press releases suggested that police units had devoted considerable time to monitoring foreign workers and tracking down arsonists responsible for a rash of suspicious fires blazing through the Reich in spring 1945.[38]

The value of radio was clearly recognized, and it became the primary medium for disseminating OSS propaganda. The first MO radio campaign was Station Italo Balbo in spring 1943, but operations began in earnest in January 1944 when seven MO members began a black radio station code-named Morse. The 250-watt facility broadcast four times nightly in clear Morse code, in German to

Germans, from Cairo to the Balkans. The purported source of the transmissions was a Wehrmacht radioman in Greece who gossiped with other radiomen between 10:45 and 11:00 P.M., discussing news and the latest rumors. The method introduced propaganda in an easily disguised form that did not require genuine German-accented broadcasters, program scripts, news bulletins, or features. Between May and October 1944 Radio Morse conducted 169 broadcasts and was thought so successful by MO personnel that its audience was expanded to include partisan groups and anti-Nazi civilians in Greece, Hungary, Bulgaria, and Rumania. The broadcasts carried news and stories to bolster partisan morale while demoralizing Germans and collaborators.[39]

Initial radio successes in the Mediterranean prompted the OSS Planning Group to order the development of a further station, code-named Boston, that broadcast from neutral Turkey near Izmir. Once Turkish permission was obtained in August 1944, Boston was on the air in ten days. The 100-watt voice transmitter broadcast to enemy garrisons and collaborators in the Balkans, claiming to be a group of deserters and contrite traitors who stressed the hopeless German military situation and who encouraged resistance. Its six ten-minute daily broadcasts ran from 8:00 to 9:30 P.M., seven days a week, and consisted of commentaries by former traitors and enemy soldiers, news broadcasts, highlights of the day in Germany, and underground reports, closing with late news at 9:15. The broadcasts were frequently jammed, and MO reported that the station was the target of repeated enemy sabotage attacks before it closed in October 1944.[40]

Radio operations conducted by MO in Northwest Europe were even more sophisticated. The most popular gray propaganda station of the war, Soldatensender Calais, was a joint MO-PWE venture that began in 1943 and for which the OSS provided twelve writers and six musicians. The program, supposedly coming from Calais, France, actually was beamed from a PWE radio transmitter in Woburn, England. The station broadcast news, music, nostalgic stories, and anti-Nazi propaganda to enemy troops and civilians, many of whom suspected the broadcasts were of Allied origin but whose suspicions were never confirmed.[41]

By April 1944 PWE had expanded to the point that they lacked the personnel to produce the quality entertainment thought necessary to hold an audience. MO therefore agreed to produce entertainment in an operation codenamed the Muzac Project. MO recruited Hollywood writers, an eight-piece orchestra, and big-name talent such as Marlene Dietrich. The branch opened a music department in New York City, used the services of the J. Walter Thompson advertising agency, and wrote and recorded black lyrics for 312 German and

American songs as well as specially written pieces. A typical twelve-hour broadcast day included news from the fronts, air-raid warnings and bomb damage reports, POW political commentaries, and German domestic news.[42]

The RMVP and OKW issued repeated warnings to civilians and soldiers not to listen to Soldatensender. Even Joseph Goebbels recognized its potentially negative effects, acknowledging that its clever job of propaganda was a cause for worry. Soldatensender did not just provide good music, however. After the 20 July 1944 attempt on Hitler's life, it broadcast the names of hundreds of Germans supposedly involved in the plot, seeking to implicate both the guilty and the innocent in order to eliminate Germany's leadership and intelligentsia. Postwar reports indicate that the Gestapo took Soldatensender's reports seriously. The Twelfth Army Group claimed that the station "was especially popular and that 90 percent of POWs taken in the summer of 1944 listened regularly," and similar testimonials were obtained from officers "driven to distraction" trying to prevent soldiers from tuning in the broadcasts, which continued until May 1945. Postwar interrogations revealed that even enemy civilians regularly followed Soldatensender West.[43]

An outgrowth of Soldatensender was the Joker campaign conducted in 1944 after the fall of Aachen. MO resurrected Gen. Ludwig Beck, former German Army chief of staff, who was killed following the failed 20 July plot against Hitler but whose death was never officially acknowledged. Beamed by mediumwave transmitter from England, Joker used a broadcaster with a voice like Beck's that shrilly claimed that Nazi amateurism had lost the war and demanded that Germans rise up, kill Hitler, overthrow the Nazis, and sue for peace, thus saving Germany from total annihilation. Rumors planted in advance of the broadcasts reinforced the idea that Beck was still alive. The first broadcast, made in October 1944, was picked up in Sweden and reported in other neutral nations. The Nazis, caught completely off guard, jammed Joker's second broadcast and continued jamming that frequency and many others every night for three weeks to prevent Joker's return.[44]

The Joker broadcasts not only produced consternation among the Nazis but also within PWD as well. Nazi jamming prevented Joker's return, but it also interfered with the transmissions of other Allied propaganda programming. This development caused a major row, especially when it appeared the Joker broadcasts did not have prior PWD authorization. General McClure told David Bruce that although he had been assured by OSS members Oechsner and McLachlen that the Joker broadcasts had been cleared in principle, he could find no such approval. He warned Bruce that MO had better adhere scrupulously to SHAEF directives and gain prior approval of all operations. MO chief

Howard Baldwin, McClure maintained, was responsible for the actions of his subordinates and was to ensure their compliance with PWD directives.[45]

Following the liberation of Paris and Luxembourg City, twenty-six MO agents took black radio to the Continent. The *Volkssender Drei* programs, approved by PWD in September 1944, came from a station at Villebon, near Paris, and broadcast between 10:00 and 11:00 P.M.. The programs purported to come from an anti-Nazi garrison commander named Hoffmann, allegedly the son of the general who had signed the Brest-Litovsk Treaty in 1918. Hoffmann, who lived in a mountainous region of Germany, had liberated his town from the Nazis and was waiting to turn it over to the Allies.

Capitalizing on civilian fears of Nazi scorched-earth policies, Hoffmann's actions were meant to offer hope and encouragement. Indeed, he asked other German leaders to follow his example and establish anti-Nazi civil administrations. *Volkssender Drei* programs consisted of talks by deserters, workers, housewives, youth leaders, and trade unionists, all citizens of Hoffmann's village. These people, as well as Hoffmann and his colleagues, a junior officer named Weber and a trade unionist called Karl, provided sabotage instructions, read the text of leaflets, stickers, and pamphlets, and gave faked coded messages to underground groups. Hoffmann and crew, who claimed to be a part of a German Freedom Party, provided advice to civilians on subverting the war effort, gave information from the fronts, and as time went on, reported brief and exaggerated news. The *Volkssender Drei* programs continued until late October 1944 when the Allies supposedly liberated the city.[46]

The programs were reported in French newspapers and were known to at least 2,000 POWs, who, in the words of one, "believed it meant the end of Germany." The Nazis repeatedly jammed the broadcasts, yet *Volkssender Drei* was so secret and convincing that Twelfth Army Group radio-monitoring personnel, unaware of the operation, awakened Gen. Omar Bradley on the night of the first broadcast to give him the news of Hoffmann's actions. Bradley put a parachute regiment on alert to aid with the liberation and ordered around-the-clock monitoring of the frequency in hopes of pinpointing Hoffmann's location.[47]

A similar program, Operation Capricorn, broadcast from England, repeated the *Volkssender Drei* theme in March 1945. The sixty-one broadcasts were created by nineteen MO members and ran until 27 April 1945. The program purported to originate with a German underground group led by a man named Hagedorn, who appealed to his compatriots to abandon the Nazis and avoid annihilation. He called for mass surrenders and a nationwide revolt and encouraged officials to rid their villages of the Nazis as he had done in a small, undisclosed Bavarian town. After the first broadcasts, a Swedish newspaper reported

Hagedorn's existence. In June 1945 MO interrogated three former Wehrmacht officers who were members of the anti-Nazi Bavarian Freedom Movement and who had listened to the BBC, ABSIE, and Soldatensender West. They admitted listening to Hagedorn as well and informed their interrogators of the differences between the genuine Capricorn station and the obviously faked Soldatensender West. Hagedorn, whom they quoted verbatim, accurately reflected their views and the feelings of all anti-Nazis. As far as they knew, he had not been captured by the Nazis, and they asked that the OSS find him since he could be of postwar use to Germany.[48]

The capture of Radio Luxembourg in September 1944 gave MO access to the most powerful radio transmitter in continental Europe. The radio facilities at Luxembourg City were used by the Nazis until just before their capture and no preparations had been made either to destroy the station or to jam its broadcasts. Thus, the station was not only left intact but was also outfitted with the most up-to-date equipment then available.

In cooperation with the Twelfth Army Group, MO received approval in early December 1944 to run a black campaign from Luxembourg code-named Operation Annie or Radio 1212. Annie broadcast from the same station, although on a different frequency, that was used for PWD-OWI daytime white broadcasts and special care was exercised to prevent any connection being made between the two. Radio 1212 ran nightly from 12:00 to 6:30 A.M. and purported to come from a Rhineland anti-Nazi group. Its news and information were addressed primarily to Rhinelanders, who were then in the immediate path of the Allied advance. Programs consisted of Rhenish music, news, and emotional features using speakers with Rhenish accents. Its chief announcer, MO's Benno Frank, addressed both enemy soldiers and civilians, talked of military events and air raids, gave extracts from OKW communiques, and read news on ways to evade Nazi party orders. Instructions and addresses were given to fictitious underground groups as well as information on how Germans were faring under the benevolent Allied occupation.[49]

Operation Annie had a subtle and clearly subversive mission. Although a black operation, Radio 1212 was not entirely subversive at the outset and concentrated on providing truthful, factual information to build trust. The station even claimed that its news was accurate enough for Wehrmacht commanders to maintain their positional maps. Once trust had been established, however, and after the Allied breakthrough in the Moselle region, Radio 1212 began inserting false reports, evacuation and mobilization orders, rumors, and exaggerated information, thereby creating chaos. After the Rhine defenses were breached, Ra-

dio 1212 invented a resistance movement within Germany and encouraged everyone to join.[50]

Reports from POWs, civilians, and the Swedish press indicated that Annie's audience was large for the 125 nights that it aired, ending on 25 April 1945. Even members of the Nazi party, who did not listen to the VOA, BBC, or ABSIE, allegedly listened to Radio 1212. One Swedish newspaper reported that the organization responsible for 1212 had branches in all towns and villages west of the line Hamburg-Bremen and Braunschweig-Jena-Munich and was organized to prevent scorched-earth policies. Other sources also maintained that 1212 was a legitimate station, one man believing it was run by renegade Nazi Otto Strasser. Overall Nazi reactions to 1212 indicated to MO that it was among the most successful campaigns of the war.[51]

MO planners anticipated further clandestine radio operations in spring 1945, but the rapid Allied advance and the chronic shortage of personnel, who were now being transferred to the Pacific and Far Eastern theaters, led to the deferment of plans for future campaigns.[52]

A final operation in which MO personnel took part, in cooperation with PWE, was the "ghost voicing" of German radio broadcasts. The project involved using the 600,000-watt Aspidistra transmitter at Woburn, England, literally to overpower radio signals and break into German broadcasts with anti-Nazi slogans, satirical comments, or sarcastic replies. Such an operation was carried out on 27 January 1945 when the Koenigsberg German Home Service was interrupted and a speech by Nazi Hans Fritzsche was heckled. Later, between 24 and 25 March and again on 30 March 1945, Aspidistra broke into broadcasts heard in Cologne, Berlin, Frankfurt, and Hamburg. During the Frankfurt broadcast the ghost voice announced the approach of a fictitious Allied tank force, ordered mobilizations of Red Cross and women's auxiliary groups in areas surrounding Frankfurt, and ordered police, Volkssturm, and other security personnel to detain the occupants of a gray car containing four uniformed impostors near the city. Goebbels recorded the operations in his diary, noting that the Americans were "trying to play the same game with the German people as we played with the French during our western offensive in the summer of 1940." "Almost hourly," Goebbels wrote, "they put out false reports of the capture of towns and villages, thus creating the greatest confusion among the German public."[53]

The Nazis quickly denounced the interruptions but could not jam the airwaves without ending their own programs carried on the same frequencies. They found themselves at the mercy of Allied propagandists, uncertain as to when and where the next intruder operation would take place. It was admitted

by one official that "considerable misunderstandings and great unrest were caused among the population by the intrusion of enemy wireless announcements on the German wireless." The success of the operations convinced General McClure that they had "caused the enemy considerable anxiety which should be exploited to the full." The broadcasts continued until April 1945.[54] As with other MO covert activities, black radio operations ceased in late April and early May 1945, just before Nazi Germany fell. PWD sent word to the OSS that all operations would cease on 1 May 1945.[55]

It is difficult to assess the effectiveness of OSS Morale Operations accurately. The relatively small scale of branch activities, when compared with propaganda campaigns carried out by the U.S. Army and the OWI and with the United Nations' conventional warfare efforts, seems insignificant. MO, unlike the army, lacked the personnel to conduct major postwar studies, and few surveys were completed describing the number of Germans who were exposed to or influenced by MO work. Perhaps the best indication of success is found in the official OSS history, which reported that MO carried on its efforts despite great handicaps at home and abroad and that by the war's end Allied military and political agencies had accepted the principle of morale operations. Most significantly, the branch

> had brought to the attention of American authorities a weapon which the United States had not heretofore systematically and effectively employed. It drew attention to the advantages of a specialized type of intelligence—information on the morale, social cleavages and underlying worries of foreign peoples, and how these could be used for national advantage.[56]

The Morale Operations Branch eventually became just the type of organization that Edmond Taylor and William Donovan had envisioned in 1941, and it clearly succeeded in its mission of fighting fire with fire, attaining a degree of sophistication never before imagined.

II · White Propaganda Operations, 1942–1945

The American propaganda offensive against Nazi Germany began in earnest relatively late in the war. Yet within months of its launching, propagandists were inundating the airwaves with radio programs and covering Europe with billions of leaflets and other printed materials. The OWI held undisputed responsibility for the official, or white, strategic propaganda assault on the Nazis after early 1944, having finally loosened the grip of the OSS and of the ideologues within its own ranks. Likewise, the U.S. Army, using large numbers of OWI and OSS personnel, exercised complete control over white tactical or combat propaganda designed to meet military needs.

The end of the disputes between Robert Sherwood and Elmer Davis saw the ideological tenor of overseas strategic propaganda diminish dramatically after early 1944. The entire agency at last adhered to a policy of disseminating carefully selected information to provide the fundamental and significant facts concerning the war, the United States, and the United Nations as interpreted by Elmer Davis. Yet OWI output still showed a clear bias, although not as strident, and continued proudly to trumpet the merits of the democratic way, displaying the values, ideals, and norms of most Americans at the time.

The agency's flagship service, the Voice of America, clearly contained an ideological bent from the time announcer William Harlan Hale began broadcasting fifteen-minute programs daily from New York City to Nazi Germany on 26 February 1942. Air time steadily increased until 1945 when over 280 minutes of German programming was broadcast each week. Two hundred three minutes were devoted to spot-news bulletins and eyewitness reports from the front, forty-six minutes to news commentaries, and thirty-three minutes to music. The information given to Nazi Germany was the same as that delivered by air in the form of leaflets, newspapers, and magazines, an example of the latter being Rich-

ard C. Hottelet's *Sternenbanner*. OWI personnel were convinced that news, focused on "the plain facts of the war, forcefully brought to the eyes and ears" of Germans, "would in the long run be more corrosive to Nazi morale than any amount of agitational propaganda."[1]

The agency's propaganda became more sober and factual as the war progressed. Through the central, regional, and weekly directives, the new emphasis on providing straight and significant facts is readily apparent. Planners set out specific themes for broadcasts that they believed furthered the goal of crushing enemy military and civilian morale and then presented facts and figures in the form of news by radio broadcast, maps, pamphlets, newspapers, magazines, and charts. As themes became outdated due to rapidly changing events, more current themes, or those needed to support a particular Allied goal, were developed. All themes had the aim of destroying morale by stating truthful information that even the most jingoistic and stubborn Nazis could grasp.

After the moronic-little-king incident, the first broadcasts in October, November, and December 1943 contained themes stressing the inevitability of Germany's defeat, its military and political weaknesses, its isolation, and the Allied superiority in men and equipment. Constant broadcasts sought to increase civilian defeatism and passive resistance and to raise distrust and resentment of the Nazis by quoting their past unfulfilled promises or by publicizing their numerous privileges and excesses. The air war, the Allied operation most visible to enemy civilians before Normandy, was a constant broadcast topic. Repeated programs discussed growing Allied air strength relative to the decline of the Luftwaffe and stressed Allied industrial production figures, especially fighter and bomber output, that were juxtaposed with much smaller German figures. Programs emphasizing Allied production figures for food, munitions, clothing, vehicles, petroleum, and consumer goods became staples of OWI media.

As in earlier periods, the VOA emphasized Allied successes against U-boats in the North Atlantic and Germany's inability to stop or even to slow the flood of men and supplies pouring into Europe. Nearly every story and feature sought to convey the impression that Germany had already lost the war, that defeat was inevitable, and that continued resistance only prolonged the final outcome. In early broadcasts when good military news was sparse, OWI's victory predictions seemed premature, so emphasis was placed on the Russian front where the Germans had already suffered major setbacks.[2]

Deducing the proper time for propaganda broadcasts in order to ensure the maximum effect on the audience was always a goal of American propagandists. The New Years' programs of the VOA and the American Broadcasting Station in Europe were usually reserved for retrospectives providing contrasts between

Allied and Axis gains and comparisons of Allied and Axis performance. Stories on the shrinking Axis world map and on production figures needed no exaggeration. One broadcast triumphantly reported that 77 percent of the world's population and 82 percent of the world's area were aligned against the Axis powers, and the 1944 New Year's Day broadcast emphasized the end of the U-boat menace, Allied mastery of the seas and skies, the extent of liberated territory, and the increases in Allied soldiers, supplies, and equipment.

New United Nations agreements on political and military goals and strategies were announced to reinforce the themes that Germany was surrounded, besieged, and isolated. The OWI intended through its New Years' Day broadcasts "to heighten the feeling of doom and collapse which is in store for Germany." Indeed, the 1944 OWI theme, which provided the thread tying together all broadcasts, was that this was "the Year of Doom for Germany and Japan." The first central directive of the year ordered OWI propagandists to use the media to "drive this line home" in order to "create a picture of absolutely overmastering United Nations military might" and "unity of organization and purpose . . . planned, equipped, coordinated, and directed to deliver a devastating attack."[3]

American propaganda efforts were redoubled during the six months prior to D-Day, with the intent of softening the enemy psychologically for the conventional Allied assault in June. The OWI reinforced the year-of-doom theme by emphasizing subthemes to convince Germans that an invasion and an Allied beachhead on the Continent were inevitable. All air, land, and sea efforts, Germans were told, were preparations for the invasion, which would take place when and where the Allies chose. The idea of the Maginot line mentality, used by the Germans in 1940 against the French, was now declared to be affecting the Wehrmacht in its most negative ramifications. Grim war news from the fronts continued, and additional themes emphasizing Nazi war guilt, broken promises, political, military, and economic mistakes, and criminal excesses were introduced to increase civilian doubts about the Nazi leadership.[4]

The OWI always painted the most dire portrait possible of the Axis situation. Yet a glimmer of hope was usually offered to the Germans to impress upon them that the Allied policy of unconditional surrender did not mean total annihilation or enslavement, as Nazi propagandists predicted, but "peace and an opportunity for all nations, large and small, to take part ultimately in a better world." Further resistance in the hopes of gaining an eleventh-hour victory, a negotiated settlement, or soft peace only forestalled the inevitable.[5]

In keeping with OWI's policy of recognizing Allied mistakes or weaknesses, tactical setbacks such as the 1944 Anzio invasion were treated cautiously but not pessimistically. Anzio, for example, though nearly a defeat, was portrayed as

a demonstration of American martial and material strength and as a sign of German weakness because Axis military forces neither prevented nor ultimately repelled the landing, despite inflicting heavy casualties. Nor did OWI propagandists gloss over Allied differences of political or strategic opinion, especially with the USSR, but presented them as indicative of United Nations openness and strength, an environment in which settlements were democratically negotiated and compromises effected for the common goal of defeating the Axis powers. These democratic processes, the OWI claimed, were to be established worldwide following the Nazi defeat. When Nazi propagandists emphasized Allied weaknesses or disagreements, the OWI gave them slight and indirect coverage in order not to appear to be responding to Nazi output and quickly moved on to news in other areas demonstrating Allied strengths.[6]

As Allied power grew, and as final preparations were made for the Normandy landings, the OWI broadcasters concentrated on themes seeking to undermine Wehrmacht morale. Repeated programs emphasized the prior stand-and-die orders of Nazi leaders, implying that the Wehrmacht was again being committed to the impossible task of preventing or repelling the enemy at all costs, regardless of the odds and despite good military strategy. Hitler "never cuts his losses," the OWI declared, and as a result of his stubbornness and lack of military acumen the invasion was sure to produce the same senseless and heavy casualties experienced in Tunisia and at Stalingrad.[7]

Concomitant with the stand-or-die theme, the failings and weaknesses of the Luftwaffe were included in every directive during March, April, and May 1944. The campaign sought to erode military and civilian morale and to goad the Luftwaffe's high command into an attempt to refute OWI's charges that they were finished as an effective fighting force by putting their remaining aircraft into the air where they could be destroyed by superior Allied air power before D-Day. Simultaneously, the OSS MO Branch ran a covert operation in support of OWI's campaign.[8]

The output of the VOA was supplemented by broadcasts of the new OWI American Broadcasting Station in Europe, which opened five weeks before D-Day. With the aid of Morgan Brewster, William Paley, Robert Sherwood, and later, Philip Cohen, Richard Condon, and Robert Saudek, ABSIE operated twelve transmitters in England eight hours daily. The station followed OWI central and regional directives and devoted one-third of its air time to German programs that included news and musical features such as "Music for the Wehrmacht," starring Bing Crosby and Dinah Shore. Although it rebroadcast BBC and VOA programs, ABSIE was more than a relay station and produced its own

features, interviews, and commentaries by exiles such as Jan Masaryk, Charles de Gaulle, and Norwegian King Haakon VII.

ABSIE became the primary broadcaster of "Voice of SHAEF," messages and coded instructions for the underground after D-Day. It always geared its output more closely to the needs of PWD than the independent VOA because it was closer to the front and more dependent on military support, equipment, and personnel. By war's end, ABSIE was said to be the "brightest feather in OWI's cap," having broadcast over 34 million words between April 1944 and July 1945.[9]

The D-Day reports of the OWI were handled in a matter-of-fact manner in keeping with Davis's policy of delivering only sober, factual information. Broadcasts during summer 1944 continued to emphasize Allied military strength and the fact that German defenses in France were irrevocably breached. The theme of how many more Normandies would Germany endure was repeated in nearly every OWI broadcast. When Nazi propagandists described enormous Allied losses, the OWI responded indirectly, as always, that casualties were lower than expected and could quickly be replaced. The OWI then cited the large numbers of men and machines arriving daily and announced that German losses in France, some of the highest of the war, were irreplaceable.

Providing news of Allied casualties never posed a major problem. One OWI directive stated that "our casualties should be reported fully and frankly" in order to maintain the agency's reliability, the main concern of Elmer Davis. Whenever possible Allied casualties were linked with news of German losses, the lack of German reserves, the dilemma of fighting a two-front war, and the unreliability of Germany's allies.[10]

American propagandists constantly attacked the quality of Nazi and Wehrmacht leadership as a means to undermine enemy morale. The battles in Normandy, directives stated, were to be highlighted as prime examples of the superiority of Allied arms and planning over that of the OKW to give weight to the idea that Germany's defeat resulted from top-level mismanagement despite the sacrifices and efforts of the common soldier or civilian. The inability of the Wehrmacht to slow the enemy advance and the many failed promises to repel the invasion were blamed on the stupidity, tactical blunders, and general incompetence of OKW and the Nazis.

Thus, German troops were never held accountable for defeats, nor were they ridiculed; instead, they were portrayed as victims of bumbling and ignorant superiors whose orders they were compelled to follow. The enemy's fighting spirit, loyalty, and devotion to comrades were never questioned. To do so, the OWI believed, alienated the very audience the agency sought to influence and was actu-

ally counterproductive as it strengthened enemy morale. The Wehrmacht, therefore, was often said to be valiantly defending a lost cause against overwhelming odds. The OWI suggested that an officer "who, in the face of . . . [such] odds and possibly against explicit orders from reckless superiors, surrenders in order to save his men shows responsible leadership." It was not dishonorable or cowardly to surrender to prevent further bloodshed, especially when certain death and defeat for a cause already lost were the only other options.[11]

Themes drawing on past German experiences were common in American broadcasts during 1944. One example was an OWI campaign running for several months comparing the two world wars, showing similarities between the current situation and that of the Hohenzollern Empire in 1918. The OWI was confident that this campaign, dealing as it did with events within living memory where the message was obvious, would devastate morale as German civilians themselves found similarities between the home-front conditions of 1918 and 1944, thus doing OWI's job.[12]

The rapid pace of the Allied advance in Western Europe during summer 1944, and the significant changes that had occurred in the leadership, philosophy, personnel, and organization of propaganda agencies at home and abroad, prompted a major shift in the psychological warfare offensive against Germany. On the day of the U.S. Army breakout from Normandy, an event causing great Allied optimism, the Overseas OWI restated its philosophy in "Special Guidance on Long-Range Media for Europe."[13]

In the document, Europeans, including Germans, were described as being wary of propaganda because of Nazi tactics; the OWI, therefore, should refrain from high-pressure propaganda. Without precise knowledge of the audience, such tactics could alienate or go beyond the understanding of most listeners. The only option was "to do a straight-forward information job." Europe was "hungry for facts," and the OWI was to provide just that, "good solid facts, not facile re-writes or generalities." The facts, however, were to be objective and delivered "without condescension or sermonizing." Propagandists were not to boast about the United States since Europeans, especially Germans, had basic fears and suspicions about Americans, whom they expected to be boastful, brash, and superficial. Broadcasts were to be modest, restrained, and thoughtful, the goals being to "create a favorable and friendly mind" toward America by talking about the U.S. Army, the American nation, its people, and their social, political, and diplomatic traditions. The aims were to show how much Americans and Europeans had in common, to clean up the ill effects of fascism, to help Europeans catch up on missed news, and constantly to push the idea of the

United Nations as a real entity for ending the war and securing the peace for all people.[14]

Learning from their past mistakes and omissions, the OWI leadership encouraged propagandists to cater to the needs of the military. Broadcasters were warned not to allow their propaganda to lag behind the military offensive, which by midsummer 1944 was exceeding all expectations in speed and success. The agency therefore adopted a diplomatically risky policy based on the assumption that the war would end by December 1944. Propagandists were to "purge" from their output all "vestiges of the long-war mentality" and were not to worry that information given on a particular day would "be quoted back by Goebbels six months from now." "The simple fact," the guidance pointed out, "was that they had been beaten." They "can fight on tenaciously and bravely but without any hope of changing the issue." For the remainder of the European war OWI propaganda was cast in terms that the Third Reich was crumbling and nothing could stop the trend.[15]

American propagandists steadfastly adhered to the new OWI emphasis despite signs that it was overly optimistic and premature. Although an ultimate Allied victory was certain, it was increasingly obvious that Germany still had sufficient reserves of morale and material to keep fighting for months. Nonetheless, through the use of sober fact, the OWI disparaged Nazi successes by asserting they had little effect on the final outcome of the war. It was flatly admitted that German V-weapons had created some damage, for example, but propagandists instead emphasized the significant fact that such secret weapons failed to obtain the goals the Nazis sought and had no effect on the Allied offensive. Similarly, the late October creation of the Volkssturm, hailed by the Nazis as an indication of the depth of the people's commitment to total war, was portrayed by the OWI as an ineffective, poorly trained and equipped, last-ditch militia consisting of the old, the infirm, and the class of 1928—youngsters sixteen years old. Considering the inexperienced draftees the Volkssturm took into its ranks, the OWI claimed, it could never become an effective fighting force. It only added to the Wehrmacht's burden by denying it equipment and could do nothing more than increase the bloodshed and prolong the war.[16]

The Second German Ardennes offensive indicated all too clearly that Allied optimism was indeed premature. Quickly rebounding, however, the OWI treated the December 1944 Battle of the Bulge routinely through its reporting of "straight news." Initial German successes and Allied setbacks were reported in a calm tone, within the context of the ongoing themes that the push could not produce a Nazi victory, that it was the last gasp of a failing Wehrmacht, the final desperate act of panic-stricken leaders who were "buying time" to save them-

selves by sacrificing precious men and machines. After the German drive stalled in January 1945, the OWI hammered home the futility of the offensive and pointed out that thousands of lives had been expended for nothing since lost territory had been retaken and more had been liberated and that the Reich was worse off than before.[17]

With the new year the OWI increasingly emphasized the themes that Nazi miscalculations and mistakes had put Germany in a no-win situation and that cowards were continuing a lost war merely to save themselves. The Nazis acted thus even though their actions brought increased death, misery, and destruction to Germany and to the people the Reich was supposedly defending. The OWI had reported the 20 July 1944 assassination plot against Hitler as an indication that the military no longer agreed with the Nazis about the prosecution of the war or in the inevitability of German victory, but such themes multiplied after New Year's 1945 as real opportunities existed to separate the German people from the Nazis. To reinforce the split, the OWI warned all Germans that their compatriots who committed war crimes at Nazi bidding, although such crimes were never defined or reported in detail, or who needlessly prolonged the war were liable to punishment, no matter who they were or where they tried to hide.

Germans were continually told that the Nazis had embarked on a policy of national suicide, taking innocent lives with them, and that individuals must do what they could to save their own lives through resistance, passive or direct. They were encouraged to save as much as possible for the future Germany.[18]

According to the OWI, the Germans had only two alternatives: "Surrender now or . . . precipitate a disaster unparalleled in history," a pre-1943 theme that had caused considerable internal OWI dissension but that was nonetheless constantly stressed. War news from all fronts, intended to show a steady Axis decline worldwide, was a consistent feature of 1945 OWI broadcasts as were increasing references to Allied conferences and the unity of the United Nations.[19]

When the OWI was not devoting broadcast time to long-term strategic themes meant to wear down enemy morale, the agency aided the OSS and the U.S. Army with campaigns. A 1944 operation, carried out in conjunction with the OSS, intended to give Germans the impression that Hitler was either dead or no longer in control of the Reich. The campaign sought to undermine faith in Hitler and to increase internal instability.[20]

The rapid advance of the Allied armies into Germany itself prompted another shift in American propaganda. By late March 1945 the OWI began broadcasts on the theme that the final battles of the European war had begun. Information was directed toward civilians rather than toward military units since the

latter had become so dispersed and disorganized they no longer constituted a cohesive audience. Programs concentrated on messages from the Voice of SHAEF telling Germans how to evacuate to safe areas and how to live under Allied occupation. By April 1945, the OWI and army tactical units performed most propaganda tasks. Even after the death of Hitler, however, the VOA did not decrease its anti-Nazi attacks and continued its verbal assaults on the Doenitz government. On 11 May, the OWI directives announced victory, stating that with V-E Day, psychological warfare against Germany had ended and that future operations would concentrate on winning the peace. Although radio broadcasts continued, ABSIE ceased operations on 4 July and VOA ceased broadcasting on 15 July 1945.[21]

Gauging the effectiveness of OWI strategic propaganda is difficult because VOA assessments are overwhelmingly positive, anecdotal, and subjective. The VOA conducted thousands of wartime POW, refugee, and partisan interviews seeking to establish whether the message was being heard. One survey found that 10.3 percent of POWs listened to VOA broadcasts, but such statistics indicated only that German soldiers occasionally listened to the radio. By and large the OWI broadcast in a vacuum and had little reliable information on audiences.[22]

One alleged indicator of propaganda's effectiveness was the frequency of Nazi jamming. The OWI claimed in April 1942 that over 40 percent of VOA French-language programs were jammed, a figure that grew substantially in the fall. Although the jamming speaks to effectiveness, it also indicates that fewer people were getting the OWI message than American propagandists had hoped. Moreover, jamming required a great deal of equipment and massive amounts of electrical power that the Germans simply did not have as the war progressed. The process further tended to interfere with Nazi broadcasts as well. Since the Nazis lacked the capability to jam all the Allied broadcasts, the process really showed only their technical capabilities rather than the effectiveness of OWI output. The OWI therefore monitored the number of times Nazi propagandists mentioned or responded to VOA output. In two months during spring 1942, for example, the Nazis mentioned VOA broadcasts 300 times in their own programs.[23]

The OWI had its critics and supporters, including among the former James P. Warburg, a Washington pariah after his ouster from the agency, who claimed that after September 1943 the OWI accomplished nothing. Yet the agency was praised by Generals Marshall, MacArthur, and Eisenhower, by Secretary of State Cordell Hull, Secretary of War Stimson, British Foreign Minister Anthony Eden, and Cong. Everett Dirksen (R-Ill.), who claimed that the OWI had done an effective and efficient job that hastened the Axis defeat everywhere, thus saving lives,

resources, and money. It was generally accepted that the OWI played a major part in the Allied victory and was important to American military successes.[24]

Although the impact of strategic radio operations was not clearly visible, OWI and U.S. Army tactical propaganda had definite and verifiable results. Unlike OWI strategic propagandists, U.S. Army and PWD–OWI personnel confined their post-1943 operations to tactical propaganda, which they deemed more suitable for winning the war. Like the OWI, the military practiced white propaganda and spent the months prior to D-Day refining it through extensive study of the effectiveness of various appeals, why they were effective, and how they were best disseminated. The activities grew from continued U.S. Army skepticism concerning propaganda, even as late as 1944. Military leaders reasoned that if time, effort, and personnel were going to be devoted to such unorthodox and unproven weapons, then as much as possible should be known about them before their use.

Relying on previous combat experiences as well as on information gained through POW interrogations, the U.S. Army determined that overt, nonpolitical, commonsense, and straightforward appeals to reason and to the intellect of German civil and military populations offered the greatest likelihood of success. Although many people, such as Robert Sherwood, claimed that Germans were so brainwashed by years of Nazi propaganda that they had lost all objective reasoning ability and must be lambasted by overwhelming ideological arguments, the army clearly rejected this view.[25]

The straightforward appeal permeated U.S. Army tactical propaganda, especially leaflets, which had little use for "sophisticated political propaganda appeals" because the soldier's horizon was limited and ideological considerations were secondary to survival. The leaflets that spoke "plain soldier-to-soldier language" and that appealed to enemy martial honor were deemed the most effective and could afford to be truthful and objective. The army's message was one of simple and sound advice spelled out in a specific and sober manner to enemies who were also military professionals.[26]

Army propaganda at all levels had the basic goal of convincing the enemy to quit the fight. It sought to persuade enemy soldiers to think about the war, their role in it, and their future. Leaflets, the medium used most frequently, indicated that the German soldier's future was bleak and likely to be very short if he did not capitulate. Leaflets at PWD and army levels reinforced the theme by providing news intended to further negative ideas, reduce morale and esprit de corps, and stimulate hopes of survival. Specific information on surrendering safely was also provided. Other leaflets were intended to influence enemy strategy, tactics, and deployments or to induce troops to surrender or desert rather than to en-

T-1 leaflet propaganda bombs dropping over Merseberg, Germany, from heavy bombers of the Eighth USAAF in July 1944. (USAF Photo; reproduced at the National Archives)

OWI-produced propaganda materials used by PWD/SHAEF in Western Europe in 1944 and 1945. Visible in the bottom center is the agency's version of the surrender pass leaflet. Also visible at the bottom and at right center is the "Eine Minute die Dir das Leben retten kann" ("One minute can save your life") leaflet. (OWI Photo; reproduced at the National Archives)

gage in last-ditch stands. As the U.S. Army propaganda network grew in size and sophistication, additional leaflets were developed to encourage resistance groups, to harass enemy intelligence and security forces, to create cleavages in enemy ranks or between services, to disrupt communications, and to induce panic among enemy populations.[27]

The leaflet was foremost a tactical weapon, although strategic leaflets of a standard 5.5-by-9.5 inches were developed by PWD for air dissemination over Germany and front-line areas. Examples of the latter included leaflets dealing with German reverses on the Eastern front and elsewhere on the "four front war," the Allied around-the-clock shuttle bombing of Germany and the resulting hardships at home, the failures of the Luftwaffe, news of the 20 July plot and its aftermath, including the increased friction between the party and OKW, and the lack of public visibility of Hitler and the top Nazis. Other leaflets proclaimed the inevitability of defeat or contained messages and instructions for foreign workers or German women, laborers, doctors, policemen, peasants, farmers, and other civilian groups. Beginning on D-Day, millions of Voice of SHAEF leaflets were dropped to civilians in occupied Europe and later in Germany itself, giving instructions on evacuations and the upcoming Allied occupation. Other messages explained ways Germans could ensure their own safety and prevent further destruction.[28]

Within a year of its creation, PWD had developed an efficient system for answering the increasing Allied demands for leaflets. By September 1944 the division was producing fifty-six different strategic leaflets, requiring about 80 percent of the offset printing capacity of Great Britain. They were primarily delivered by air, 90 percent by heavy strategic bomber, the remainder by tactical air forces. The demand for air-dropped propaganda became so great that PWD obtained the exclusive services of the British-based 442d AAF B-17 heavy bomber squadron, which began operations on D-Day when its aircraft followed Allied paratroopers with 9 million leaflets for German soldiers and French civilians. By late September 1944 over 800 million leaflets had been distributed by PWD, 300 million to German troops in Western Europe, 250 million to German civilians, and the rest to civilians in enemy-occupied Europe.[29]

Mediterranean leaflet operations were also extensive, but less so than in Western Europe. In PWB/AFHQ's area during the first two weeks of June 1943, for example, over 39 million German-, Italian-, and French-language leaflets were dropped over Italy and southern France, in addition to leaflets in Arabic for distribution in North Africa and the Middle East. Over 15 million leaflets, a record at that time, were dropped over Sicily in one week alone.[30]

To avoid delays in delivering their materials, PWD developed stock tactical

Soldiers of the U.S. Army Forty-fifth Division examine safe conduct passes before loading them into artillery shells for delivery to Nazi SS mountain troops near Hochberg, France, February 1945. (U.S. Army Photo; reproduced at the National Archives)

leaflets for distribution to individual army groups on request; though periodically updated, the leaflets were basically the same for the duration. The stock included leaflets showing how POWs were treated after surrender (leaflet ZG 54), instructions on how to capitulate safely once an attack began (ZG 74k), leaflets encouraging desertion, capture, and retreat (ZG 70, 44, 53, 56), and the three most successful: the safe-conduct surrender pass (ZG 61), the "Ei Sorrender" leaflet (ZG 45), informing enemy soldiers how to surrender using phonetic English, and the "One minute can save your life" leaflet (ZG 23 and ZG 73K), which instructed Germans to take a minute, read the leaflet, follow its instructions, surrender, and survive.[31]

U.S. Army leaflet operations increased in number and sophistication in northwestern Europe after D-Day. Not only did units have stocks of PWD leaflets to disseminate, but each army group and army also had a CPT or an MRBC to develop specially tailored materials. The need to cover a small area or to inun-

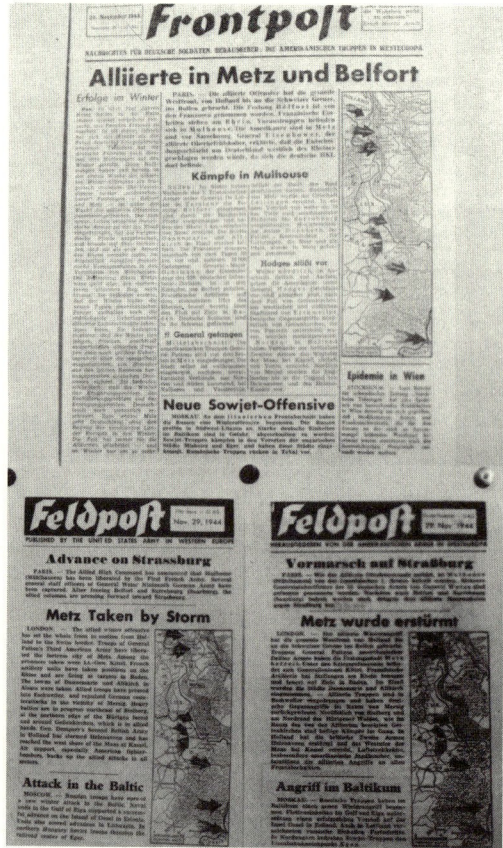

(left) *Issues of* Frontpost, *dropped by aircraft, and* Feldpost, *delivered by artillery shell, as produced by the Twelfth Army Group Publicity and Psychological Warfare Branch in November 1944.* (above) *A field near Bitberg, Germany, littered with leaflets dropped by the U.S. Army Air Forces informing German soldiers that further resistance was futile, February 1945. (U.S. Army Photos; reproduced at the National Archives)*

date a specific enemy unit meant that artillery and tactical fighter bombers were usually the main mode of delivery.[32]

Newspapers became a primary medium for distributing propaganda to German forces by 1944. The Twelfth Army Group created its own tactical newspapers, which were dropped over enemy forces weekly and then daily between August 1944 and V-E Day. The first newspaper, *Frontpost*, was a "well-edited, well-written and attractively made-up publication" created for "weakening the enemy's will to resist, emphasizing the hopelessness of his situation, undermining his own faith in his cause and leaders," and "bringing about a mental attitude conducive to surrender." Following the format of *Stars and Stripes*, *Frontpost*, and later, similar publications, contained information of interest to enemy troops such as short features, photographs, sports news, and jokes. It was originally a single sheet but was expanded in November 1944 to four pages and

11,000 words. In October 1944, for example, despite bad weather that hindered air operations, over 5 million issues of *Frontpost* were delivered. By the end of the war the paper had obtained a "circulation" of 2 million copies per issue.[33]

The size of Twelfth Army Group newspapers, which were delivered by strategic and tactical aircraft, often prevented them from reaching a satisfactory number of enemy troops. Propagandists therefore developed a small-scale version, *Feldpost*, for artillery delivery. Both newspapers were deemed so successful by U.S. Army observers that a newspaper for German civilians was started in November 1944. *Die Mitteilungen* was originally a single news sheet containing Voice of SHAEF information, which was dropped over German cities in the line of Allied advance.[34]

The U.S. First and Third Armies, like PWD and the Twelfth Army Group, developed and distributed their own MRBC–created tactical leaflets designed for specific enemy units and situations, for example, units that were cut off, surrounded, or especially steadfast. Depending on the quality of intelligence work, leaflets often were addressed to specific enemy commanders and their units, even down to the regimental or battalion level. Between D-Day in 1944 and February 1945, the U.S. First Army had disseminated by heavy bomber over 65 million strategic leaflets in the area of its front, 7 million by tactical aircraft, and 9 million via artillery. Dissemination of leaflets by the U.S. Third Army was even more extensive. In January 1945, for example, high level bombers dropped 8.7 million issues of *Nachrichten für die Truppen*, a PWE–OSS gray newspaper like *Frontpost*, and 47.6 million strategic leaflets; tactical aircraft delivered 210,000 issues of *Frontpost* and 1.68 million leaflets. Artillery units fired shells containing over 250,000 *Feldpost* newspapers and 1.29 million leaflets.[35]

Printed materials were the most common form of tactical propaganda, but they represented only one medium. In the area of strategic propaganda, PWD conducted radio programs to support field units and developed tactical radio and loudspeaker capabilities. Even though the U.S. Army had shown little interest in radio for supporting combat operations before 1944, the capture of the intact Radio Luxembourg by the OWI's Morrie R. Pierce and components of the First Army in late September 1944 changed their views. Put into immediate operation, Radio Luxembourg relayed SHAEF messages to enemy military and civilian populations and later supported Allied tactical operations. The staff of Radio Luxembourg consisted of a combined PWD Anglo-American military and civilian team with the OWI supplying the greatest number of people under the leadership of CBS owner William S. Paley.[36]

For seventeen hours daily, Radio Luxembourg was an official and overt Allied station disseminating white propaganda. It signed on each morning at 7:45

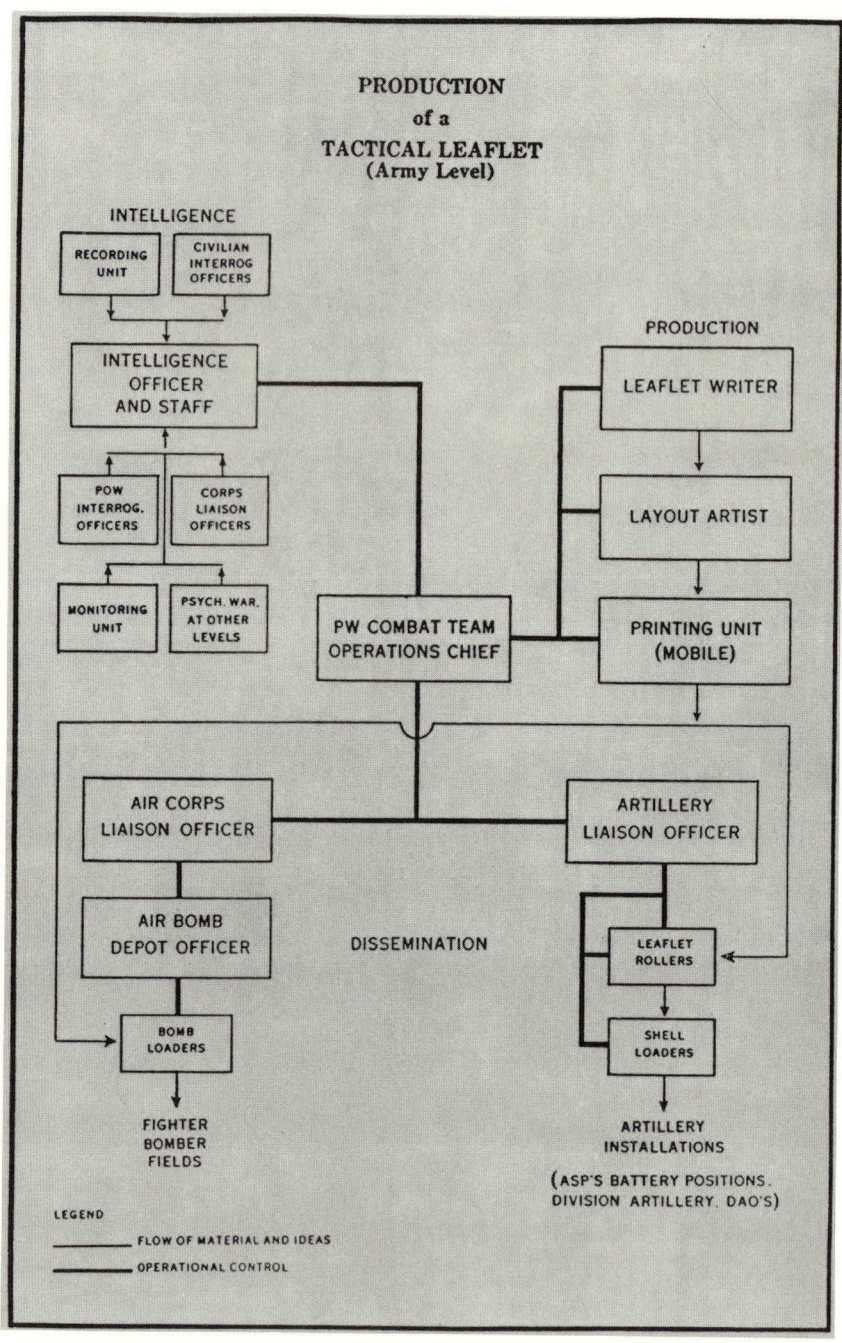

Figure II.I. *Production of a tactical leaflet (army level), European Theater of Operations.* (Courtesy the National Archives)

and signed off each evening at midnight. Each programming day opened with music, a German army show delivering news of the war, and features in nine languages. In the afternoon, the latest issue of *Frontpost* was read, as were POW letters. Symphonic music was played in the evening; and special programs and features, such as a program on the negative effects of the war on German youth, were played for both civilian and military audiences in the Reich. In addition to programs specially created for Radio Luxembourg, the station rebroadcast pertinent BBC, ABSIE, and VOA programs. Each program, especially those for Germany, had specific and subtle propaganda themes and goals even though much of Radio Luxembourg's output seemed to be pure entertainment. The broadcasts continued until V-E Day.[37]

The U.S. Army developed a tactical radio capability to support combat units, but major problems quickly arose because the army lacked portable radio transmitters and equipment. Even when such equipment was developed, it proved costly to operate, ponderous to move and use, prone to breakage, and of limited broadcasting range. Moreover, the rapid rate of advance and the lack of radio receiving sets in the hands of individual enemy soldiers meant that audiences had little time to listen and lacked the means to do so. Radio, therefore, was deemed "an instrument ill adapted for tactical use."[38]

Tactical radio did have one notable and highly publicized success during the siege of Lorient, France. The "radio siege" began in mid-August 1944 and was conducted by a nine–man combined U.S. Army, OSS MO, and OWI team under the control of the U.S. Third and later Ninth Army. A mobile 400-hundred-watt radio transmitter was set up overlooking the 30,000-man enemy garrison by Benno Frank, a former professor of German literature who had been a boyhood boarder in the home of Field Marshall Ewald von Kleist. Radio Lorient conducted two one-half-hour broadcasts daily, at 2:00 and 7:00 P.M., consisting of a letter-reading program, news, and factual reports. After the first prisoners were taken and interrogated, the broadcasts became more specific and included the reading of names of dead German soldiers, quotes of great Germans, letters from home, jokes, limericks, surrender appeals, and guest appearances by POWs. "Der Amerikanische Feld Funk vor Lorient" was deemed a success by the U.S. Army, largely because it had a captive and bored audience with access to radio sets and with no hope of relief or escape. Radio Lorient conducted 104 broadcasts during the sixty-two days of its operation and claimed direct responsibility for inducing 1,800 surrenders. In October 1944 its personnel were transferred to Radio Luxembourg.[39]

Tactical loudspeakers provided several operational successes as well. The army units, referred to as "hogcallers," were usually part of an MRBC. Each

consisted of a three-man civilian and military team operating from a panel truck. On request they went to the front where they placed loudspeakers from 30 to 500 yards from enemy positions and broadcast surrender appeals, information about the benefits and conditions of surrendering, and the hopelessness of the enemy situation. Such operations were deemed so useful for both tactical and consolidation propaganda purposes that plans were made to have one such unit attached to each division. By January 1945, however, only fifty-four units were available on the western front.[40]

Loudspeaker units were first used in the Normandy and Brittany campaigns in August 1944. It was found they were the most successful, and were therefore most often used, in cases where the enemy was cut off or surrounded. Their early success led to the frequent use of loudspeaker systems throughout the Twelfth Army Group, with some units eventually conducting up to 200 tactical and consolidation missions per month.[41]

The propagandists of the hogcalling units claimed many notable successes. The most famous occurred during the June 1944 efforts to reduce the German garrison of Cherbourg. On 27 June Maj. Gen. J. Lawton Collins, commander of the Seventy-ninth Division besieging the city, approved a plan by MO's Patrick Dolan to talk the garrison into surrendering by using loudspeakers, even though earlier surrender demands had failed. According to Dolan, it had taken considerable persuasion as "everyone thought the thing was ludicrous, the biggest goddamned joke of all time." He later wrote that "the West Point colonels could not find a cup of coffee for us before we started work." Following heavy bombardments, which convinced 10,000 men of the garrison to surrender immediately, Dolan and his team set to work. A loudspeaker truck pulled to within 250 yards of the enemy and began delivering two-minute-long surrender appeals in German, English, and Polish. Within minutes, over 600 more troops had surrendered. The next day the appeals were repeated, emphasizing the hopelessness of the situation and the fact that over 10,000 men had already surrendered and describing the honor of capitulating rather than dying for a lost cause. The appeals prompted the remaining soldiers to surrender, a major triumph for Dolan and his team. In less than twenty-four hours they had induced the surrender of over 2,100 of the enemy.[42]

Following the success of the team at Cherbourg, loudspeakers were used more frequently and were placed on a wide variety of vehicles including jeeps, half-tracks, trucks, ambulances, and, in one of the most heavily publicized successes, on tanks. The idea of tank-mounted loudspeakers originated in February 1945 during the Third Army's Ruhr operations, where three light tanks of the Fourth Armored Division were responsible for the surrender of 5,000 enemy

soldiers during the first month of use. Thereafter, the idea quickly spread to the U.S. Third, Fifth, Seventh, and Ninth Armored Divisions.[43]

During the battles for Magdeburg and other areas of eastern Germany in mid- to late April 1945, the loudspeaker tanks of the Second Armored Division were in constant use and brought about the surrender of 2,500 enemy soldiers. During an operation east of Wolfenbüttel, for example, 3,000 Waffen SS men of the Clausewitz Division, supported by several heavy tanks, self-propelled guns, and forty to fifty half-tracks, broke through U.S. Army lines in their attempt to link up with German forces surrounded in the Harz Mountains. Between 20 and 22 April a loudspeaker tank of the U.S. Second Armored Division broadcast seven surrender appeals and managed to convince 2,000 men of this force to capitulate.[44]

Although many soldiers were convinced of the utility of loudspeaker tanks, and of loudspeakers in general, even referring to them as weapons with a future, others thought they were not only ineffective but dangerous. One constant complaint was the frequent equipment failures, which occurred as often as the failures of tactical radio units. In addition, low amplifier power made many broadcasts inaudible over the noise of battle. The primary objection, however, was over the danger the units themselves posed: they drew enemy fire wherever they operated. One veteran complained, "loudspeakers had to be placed as close as 100 or 150 feet from the German line," and "enemy fire easily zeroed in on the blaring speakers," which "was likely to destroy, not only the amplifying equipment, but the announcer as well." Commanders refused to allow such units in many areas, as Patrick Dolan found, because they doubted their effectiveness and did not want to draw enemy fire that could produce more American casualties than enemy surrenders. By V-E Day, however, the U.S. Army had managed to convince most soldiers that psychological warfare was a viable weapon that had contributed to victory.[45]

The U.S. Army devoted substantial effort and personnel to determining the effect of tactical propaganda on German civilians and military personnel. The studies were done at PWD, army group, and army levels for the purpose of establishing whether propaganda could "pay its passage" in future conflicts. U.S. Army experts determined that several factors indicated effectiveness: the number of POWs taken after an operation, the quantity of leaflets found on POWs, their opinions and recollections of them, the favorable and detailed comments made about different campaigns by troops behind the lines as POWs recalled them, the preoccupation of German commanders or propagandists with counteracting leaflets, and reports from neutral observers or Allied agents.[46]

Enemy countermeasures were the best indicators of effectiveness. Experts

A light, loudspeaker-equipped tank of the U.S. Fifth Armored Division, Ninth Army, broadcasts to civilians in Peine, Germany, instructing them to lay down their arms and stay off the streets, 14 April 1945. (U.S. Army Photo; reproduced at the National Archives)

maintained that no enemy commander would waste time and effort counteracting material that was not affecting morale and performance, and substantial intelligence showed that Wehrmacht commanders at all levels were going to great lengths to combat the negative effects of propaganda on their troops. OKW, for example, issued repeated bulletins informing commanders of the presence of propaganda or of specific campaigns in progress. Furthermore, they issued explicit orders and decrees forbidding soldiers to read leaflets or to listen to propaganda broadcasts. Soldiers violating these orders were liable to court-martial and in extreme cases death. Such prohibitions, however, proved useless and impossible to enforce. At many points during the war enemy commanders were instructed to gather their troops for informal discussions about propaganda and its insidious nature and goals while simultaneously indoctrinating them with the tenets of National Socialism.[47]

In June 1944, realizing their measures to date were only stopgaps, OKW formed a special section of the Wehrmacht Propaganda Branch specifically to counteract enemy propaganda. The branch published newspapers and pamphlets, led informational courses for officers and enlisted men, conducted front-line tours informing troops of propaganda, and distributed counterpropaganda leaflets over Allied lines, seeking to negate the harmful effects of American output. The level of Wehrmacht counterpropaganda activity alone convinced many people in the U.S. Army and the OWI that their efforts were having the desired effect.[48]

The Nazis had always taken steps to ensure that civilians were exposed only to information the party wanted known, and a decree was issued in September 1939 forbidding Germans to listen to enemy broadcasts. Frequent lists of acceptable stations, meaning those under Nazi control in Europe, were distributed as a listener service as were warnings not to read leaflets. Nonetheless, as the Allied propaganda offensive geared up after D-Day, harsher measures were implemented by the Nazis to halt widespread clandestine listening. Allied radio monitors recorded frequent DNB radio broadcasts describing cases where Germans were imprisoned or executed for either spreading or listening to Allied propaganda. Despite these measures, Goebbels wrote, "enemy propaganda is beginning to have an uncomfortably noticeable effect on the German people. Anglo-American leaflets are now no longer carelessly thrown away but are read attentively."[49]

The success of leaflet operations was most easily quantified by U.S. Army experts, and numerous reports on enemy troop morale were conducted. Most reports, somewhat surprisingly, found that Wehrmacht morale stayed relatively intact until the end despite propaganda. Other reports merely stated figures of

the number of POWs who possessed or had seen certain leaflets, using the statistics as indicators of success. One SHAEF study concluded that over 90 percent of POWs had at least seen leaflets of various sorts and that 75 percent were in some way affected by them. A further study in summer 1944 determined that 77 percent of POWs taken between 26 and 28 June 1944 at Cherbourg had seen U.S. Army leaflets, that 69 percent captured during operations between 1 and 17 July between Carentan and St. Lo recognized specific leaflets, and that 84 percent of POWs taken at St. Lo had seen leaflets. Based on information gleaned by intelligence personnel and interrogators of the Army P&PW sections, it was clear that propaganda was at least on the minds of enemy soldiers.[50]

Propaganda's effectiveness was further judged by the quantity of safe conduct passes and other leaflets found on POWs. The U.S. Army discovered that 75 percent of POWs taken at Le Havre had leaflets, a figure reported by British Foreign Minister Anthony Eden to the House of Commons in July 1944. Similar reports came from the U.S. First Army, which found that 70 percent of the POWs interrogated between October 1943 and August 1944 were aware of strategic and tactical leaflets and that 40 percent had copies when captured. Of leaflets POWs had seen, the most memorable were the ones describing treatment in American captivity, the notices about the fall of Cherbourg, the attempt on Hitler's life, and the ubiquitous "One minute may save your life." The Fifth Army CPT in Italy claimed similar recognition rates, where interrogators reported that 50 percent of POWs had seen leaflets and 37 percent believed them.[51]

Critics questioned the reliability of the statistics, however. Many observers claimed that enemy soldiers often picked up leaflets as souvenirs or as insurance against the day when they might be captured. Furthermore, it was argued that interrogations were notoriously unreliable as POWs said whatever they believed interrogators wanted out of fear or in the hopes of gaining better treatment. Moreover, critics pointed out that the Germans who surrendered, especially before the military disasters of 1944–1945, were often not the best troops, nor did they represent mainline thoughts or morale. One observer maintained that Germany had withstood the full impact of "psychological warfare to the very end and yielded only to crushing material defeat. . . . The most fruitful psychological effects are produced . . . by material weapons."[52]

To counter criticism, propagandists claimed that their work had a cumulative effect on enemy morale and was incapable of producing rapid results. Propaganda could not be weighed or measured with precision. According to General McClure, "Except on the rarest occasions and under ideal circumstances, [propaganda] can never start or reverse a trend—it can only accelerate or retard one."

Effectively used, propaganda "does weaken the enemy's morale; does make him give up more easily; does cause him to fire fewer bullets," and "on occasions, does persuade him to cross the lines and quit the fight altogether." To the people concerned, propaganda saved Allied lives. As General Eisenhower concluded: "The exact contribution of psychological warfare toward the final victory cannot . . . be measured in terms of towns destroyed or barriers passed. . . . The expenditure of men and money in wielding the spoken and written word was an important contributing factor in undermining the enemy's will to resist and supporting the fighting morale of our . . . Allies in the occupied countries. Psychological warfare has proved its right to a place of dignity in our military arsenal."[53]

Conclusion

Nazi Germany was defeated by a combined Allied conventional military assault whose effects were enhanced by the propaganda and the unconventional warfare activities of the Overseas OWI, the OSS MO Branch, and the U.S. Army. Although the cumulative effects of conventional weapons provided the most obvious reason for the Allied victory, evidence does support the assertion that American psychological attacks also played a role in the final Axis defeat. Propaganda helped weaken Axis morale, convincing less dedicated enemy soldiers, civilians, and allies to quit the fight or to lessen their support of the Nazi regime and its war effort. American psychological warfare placed doubts in the minds of many Germans about the justice of their cause and the Nazi philosophy.

As a weapon of modern warfare, propaganda had recognizable shortcomings. Alone it could not produce a total military victory, as both soldiers and civilian propagandists realized and admitted. Despite the early and exaggerated predictions of prewar observers and self-proclaimed experts, no nation fell, and no battles were lost, solely because of Nazi or Allied propaganda. As it was practiced during World War II, propaganda was a relatively new phenomenon, and the fact that it did aid in the final Allied victory to any extent is an accomplishment in itself.

The assessments of American propagandists concerning the degree to which their psychological warfare campaigns contributed to the final victory are anecdotal and subjective. Published accounts focus almost exclusively on successful operations, but unpublished reports and documents recount the many failed campaigns or focus on those that were marginally successful. Some ideas were extremely successful, such as the U.S. Army surrender pass leaflet campaigns, the MO Branch clandestine radio broadcasts, and OWI's daily Voice of America and American Broadcasting Station in Europe programs. Other campaigns were

dismal and embarrassing failures, including those associated with the army's mobile radio transmitters, the OSS MO League of Lonely Women Campaign, and the OWI's much criticized moronic-little-king broadcast of 1943. The majority of the campaigns, however, fell somewhere in between, being neither overwhelming successes nor abject failures.

Each agency succeeded to some extent in developing campaigns and delivering propaganda suited to its particular notion of propaganda and the message it should convey. Success was achieved in spite of opposition from politicians, soldiers, civilians, other members of the Grand Alliance, and often from each other. The agencies developed planning mechanisms and used the same techniques of dissemination, including a variety of print and broadcast media, but each one developed a different propaganda message and approach based on the philosophies of its members.

The views of OSS members, and of the MO Branch, were reflected in a propaganda and foreign policy of realpolitik and grounded in a nineteenth-century conservative or classical-liberal philosophy that temporarily welcomed government involvement yet recognized that government had the potential for oppression. The members favored a foreign policy determined and implemented by elites, as was traditionally the case in American history, a policy that put the United States in a clear and dominant world position economically, politically, and ideologically. To them it was a given that at times the delicate framework of compromise and the rights and liberties enjoyed under democracy had to be deferred temporarily to fight a greater evil. At times democracy had to be manipulated in order to save it. In their propaganda the end justified the means, and because Nazi propaganda was viewed as the most successful to date, they did not hesitate to duplicate Nazi tactics.

The OSS MO Branch demonstrated that Americans could outdo and defeat the Nazis with their own techniques and methods, using the same tools to further the ends of democracy as opposed to totalitarianism. OSS work was secret, negative, and subversive but also successful in undermining enemy morale by creating the impression that a fifth column existed within the Reich. When considering the size of the MO Branch, compared to its rivals at home and to the opposition abroad, its accomplishments appear to be even greater than the surviving documents convey.

The propaganda message of the Foreign Information Service of the COI and later of the Overseas OWI represented the opposite ideological and political extreme from that of the OSS. Yet despite their size and resources, they initially failed in their attempt to propagate a highly moralistic, liberal message to Axis civil and military populations. The people in the OWI favored a truthful yet heavily ideolog-

ical program of persuasive propaganda meant to educate and to inform Europeans about traditional American values and ideals as the planners perceived them and to influence Europeans, including Germans, to accept a world shaped on Wilsonian principles. Their programs, taking a moral high road and emphasizing the good of America versus the bad of Nazi Germany, reflected the personal philosophy of President Franklin Roosevelt, as they understood it, and promoted a global manifestation of his domestic New Deal with heavy government involvement for the benefit of people everywhere. Ideas and practices that had worked in the United States during the past 150 years and that had rescued America in the 1930s could now save a war-ravaged world in the 1940s. Heavily represented in the Overseas OWI, the group included idealists, leftists, liberals, Democrats, journalists, individuals in the arts and letters, New Dealers, and people otherwise described as internationalists in the Wilsonian tradition.

Although OWI members thought their propaganda campaigns reflected the best of American traditions and values as expressed by President Roosevelt, many critics regarded their message as naive, abstract, and difficult for peoples living in totalitarian nations to grasp. The failure of the OWI to convey their idealistic message abroad successfully, however, was due not only to its lack of potential appeal but also to political and bureaucratic opposition at home, a result of the lack of political and ideological consensus among Americans. The strict adherence to a narrow ideological viewpoint hampered OWI efforts, making it perhaps the least successful American propaganda agency until midwar reforms changed its doctrine and ideological complexion.

Elmer Davis shared many of the critics' concerns regarding OWI's ideological, politically laden propaganda as disseminated before 1944. Sensitive of the need to avoid upsetting the Allies and to prevent stiffening the enemy's resistance through outright ideological appeals, Davis also wanted to avoid offending OWI's many political enemies at home. Ideologically motivated propaganda could and did raise such a domestic political furor on several occasions that it threatened the very existence of the OWI. To Davis it was far better to have a depoliticized, less ideological OWI, even if it meant losing the services of its most able and dedicated propagandists, than to risk the abolition of the agency. The purpose of the OWI was to defeat the Axis powers abroad, not to fight Roosevelt's political and ideological battles at home.

Davis's ultimate goal was to maintain OWI's credibility and reputation for honesty and truthfulness without harming President Roosevelt's political or diplomatic position or the unity of the United Nations. A propaganda agency widely perceived as playing politics, of boosting partisan interests, of sugarcoating bad news or exaggerating good would lose its credibility, soon thereafter its

audience, and eventually its usefulness. Although Davis publicly stated that he was for full disclosure of truthful information and that the OWI told all the news, good and bad, he was not beyond suppressing information that could raise doubts about OWI's veracity.

During the war the OWI had two different leaders, each creating propaganda with a different message. Before 1944 Robert Sherwood was the driving force of the agency and determined its ideological course. Elmer Davis, however, was the leader who was responsible for the majority of the agency's successes following Sherwood's ouster. By 1944 Davis had made internal adjustments and succeeded in showing friend and foe alike that a campaign of carefully and selectively chosen facts, centered clearly on the truth, could undermine enemy morale and cement nations into a Grand Alliance capable of defeating fascism. Nonetheless, in reshaping the OWI to better enable it to survive political criticism at home and military criticism abroad, Davis removed the ideological force that had attracted the majority of highly skilled propagandists to the agency to take up the war of words against the Nazis.

The military propaganda message was far less political than that of either civilian agency. The U.S. Army was the service responsible for actually fighting the war and, though ready to accept civilian aid, it was nonetheless suspicious of the ideological nature of civilian propagandists, viewing civilians as potentially dangerous to military success. Ideological propaganda, if handled poorly, could only increase the enemy's will to resist and the difficulty of the army's job as well as raise the cost in lives and resources.

Thus, the army expected civilian propagandists to adhere to military discipline, to clear all operations with the local theater and field commanders, and to follow military plans and orders. The U.S. Army believed so strongly in the need for military control of civilian propagandists abroad that by early 1944 all propaganda directed toward the Nazis was under army control, or its influence, and theoretically was carried out only with military approval.

The military approach, although developed far later than its civilian counterparts, ultimately produced the winning weapon in psychological warfare. U.S. Army propaganda was pragmatic and designed to appeal to the intelligence and common sense of the enemy's civil and military populations rather than to their political or ideological fears or preferences. Military campaigns were based on practical and honest messages that were known to have worked in the past. Such messages appeared on millions of leaflets and were heard in scores of radio and loudspeaker broadcasts. If the success of a psychological warfare message is based on the number of surrenders attributed to individual campaigns, then the

U.S. Army's approach was clearly the most successful undertaken during the war.

Scores of Americans played significant roles in the psychological warfare offensive against Germany. The four top leaders, Franklin Roosevelt, William Donovan, Robert Sherwood, and Elmer Davis, however, were most closely connected with propaganda matters. Their views and attitudes, with minor variations, were representative of those held by the vast majority of Americans who became involved with propaganda during World War II.

President Roosevelt normally remained aloof from propaganda affairs until the consequences of his continued inaction presented risks of greater controversy and political damage than his belated involvement. The largely amateur and partisan makeup of the groups involved with interventionist, internationalist, and propaganda matters and the initial public apathy concerning intervention convinced Roosevelt to move slowly toward creating any sort of federally sponsored propaganda agency. He was aware of the power of propaganda but was also mindful of the clout of isolationists groups and the depth of the public's loathing for anything that resembled slick promotion or propaganda. Not until it was evident that private groups were effecting slight but perceptibly favorable changes in the American public's attitudes toward intervention did the president create the Office of Facts and Figures and the COI.

Although Roosevelt played a role in the establishment of all the American propaganda agencies, his input was after the fact and largely confined to settling inter- and intraagency disputes. He never formulated a federal propaganda policy, and he never clearly defined war aims or postwar goals beyond the Four Freedoms and the Atlantic Charter. When the policy of unconditional surrender was announced as a wartime Allied goal, it complicated rather than aided the work of American propagandists. Despite OWI's pleas that Roosevelt formulate clear war policies that could serve as a basis for propaganda to Nazi Germany, no such policies were developed.

The president's role in the creation, organization, and operation of the American propaganda campaign was less than that played by other world leaders, both Allied and Axis. Other national leaders closely shaped and directed propaganda policy, but Roosevelt, in refusing to do so, failed to aid the propaganda effort substantially. As a result of his proclivity for creating multiple agencies to perform similar functions, the president actually seemed to hinder the activities of American psychological warfare organizations.

Yet Roosevelt's aloof leadership style did provide the American propaganda agencies with several advantages not enjoyed by Allied and Axis propagandists. The president was adept in choosing capable people, in allowing each propa-

ganda agency the latitude to develop methods, ideas, doctrines, and organizations, and in supporting the agencies at critical times during their early histories. He created both military and civilian propaganda agencies and tolerated all three regardless of their liberal, moderate, or conservative philosophies. He selected Donovan's ideas over those of Harold Ickes, he favored a civilian-controlled rather than a military-controlled OWI, he deferred to Republican critics of the OWI following the moronic-little-king incident in 1943, and he backed Elmer Davis over the more ideological Robert Sherwood in 1944, even though the latter's political and ideological views were closer to his own. Roosevelt's seemingly slight involvement in propaganda matters allowed interested Americans to organize and develop agencies that were capable of waging psychological warfare against the Axis powers without raising the suspicions of a skeptical and propaganda-weary American public. Although his role may appear slight at times, the president was responsible for creating the environment that allowed the three agencies to develop and to operate with varying degrees of success.

William Donovan was perhaps the most successful American propaganda leader of the war, given his devotion, his organizational skills and concepts, his ability to operate in Washington's wartime bureaucratic environment, and his determination. He developed two unique organizations, the COI and later the OSS, each with a mission that no other agency was capable of duplicating. Donovan gathered well-placed supporters for his ideas in the United States and in Britain, convinced an uninitiated president of the need for and utility of a subversive agency, and at the most critical moments succeeded in gaining the support of the Joint Chiefs of Staff to enable him to attach his organization to the powerful military bureaucracy, where it survived and thrived. The OSS was Donovan's personal creation, and it reflected his personal ideology, and, in many ways, his very personality. Through the careful selection of personnel, through strict operational secrecy that hid the OSS from public view and political controversy, and by rigid adherence to his original concepts, Donovan managed to wage psychological warfare against the Nazis while maintaining the ideological foundations and organizational integrity of the OSS in a manner unequaled by his contemporaries.

The leaders of the OWI were perhaps the most unfortunate American propagandists. Both Robert Sherwood and Elmer Davis worked for an agency that was perceived as openly political, pro–New Deal, and zealously ideological. Both men were public figures, whose backgrounds were well known prior to their OWI involvement. They were outspoken and temperamental to different degrees, but neither had the necessary diplomatic or political skills to fend off attacks from critics successfully. The OWI suffered as a result, and much of the or-

ganization's time and energy was devoted to survival rather than to attacking the Axis powers.

Sherwood is the tragic hero of the wartime American propaganda campaign. Dedicated, impassioned, and zealous, he lacked Donovan's ability to muster strong support for his propaganda philosophy from Congress, the military, and ultimately from his own superiors, Elmer Davis and Franklin Roosevelt. Sherwood's unshakable and moralistic beliefs in the value of American ideals and institutions and his belief in the ability of mankind to respond to reason eventually caused his own downfall and the reshaping of the OWI around doctrines and beliefs that were other than his own. His views of humanity and of the world were unrealistic and ultimately failed to compete against the more realistic views held by Donovan and the military. Although Sherwood may have been correct in his belief that the conflict was a "people's war" fought by and for people everywhere, he failed to understand that it was the elites who determined the policies and strategies needed to win wars and to shape the postwar world.

In most respects Elmer Davis, although surviving the war as director of the OWI, was hardly more successful than Sherwood. He clearly lacked Sherwood's drive, idealism, and devotion to Wilsonian principles. Davis was forced to compromise with OWI's critics to ensure the agency's survival, and thus he allowed its message to become diluted. By the end of the war, because of Davis's leadership, the OWI had become little more than an international news agency operating in support of Allied military forces.

Several years of bureaucratic infighting at home and rivalries abroad resulted in a coordinated and diverse American psychological warfare program. In the final years of the war, the OWI conducted informational activities, OSS MO practiced Nazi-like subversive actions, and the U.S. Army, in cooperation with the Overseas OWI, confined its use of propaganda to tactical exercises in support of military operations. The activities of each agency during the last two years of the war displayed a new nonpolitical, less ideological approach concentrating on military victory rather than on waging ideological warfare.

The American psychological warfare campaign against Nazi Germany before 1943 was a political and ideological campaign designed to root out fascism and to replace it with either the conservative ideology and worldview of the top members of the OSS or the liberal, New Deal ideology of the leaders of the OWI. After 1943 the U.S. Army controlled all American propaganda output for military purposes and refused to sanction any operation containing ideological or political themes that did not meet specific military goals.

Although they were successful wartime bureaucracies, neither the OSS, the OWI, nor the U.S. Army PWD survived V-J Day. The various propaganda agen-

cies were rapidly disbanded by executive order, yet they later reappeared in different forms. The OSS was re-created as the Central Intelligence Agency (CIA) in 1947. And although the new organization did not contain a specific branch charged with the conduct of morale operations, the CIA did emphasize covert operations and subversion as viable political and diplomatic weapons. The OWI also returned in the late 1940s as the United States Information Agency (USIA) attached to the Department of State. Just as in World War II, the Voice of America was its flagship service, and truthful news and information permeated its output. Both the CIA and the USIA maintained their basic ideological bent well into the cold war era, passing agency values, morals, and means first adopted during World War II to a new generation of agents and propagandists. Ironically, it was the U.S. Army, the skeptical latecomer to psychological warfare, that developed a prominent niche, a comprehensive doctrine, and a formal military school for psychological warfare and special operations by 1950–1951. Psychological operations by then had come to be recognized as an integral part of modern warfare.

Notes

Chapter 1. American Perceptions of Nazi Propaganda

1. The term "fifth column" originated during the Spanish Civil War when rebel Gen. Emilio Mola remarked that as his four columns attacked Madrid, a fifth column of sympathizers was attacking the city from within; see William Donovan and Edgar Mowrer, *Fifth Column Lessons for America* (Washington, D.C.: American Council on Public Affairs, 1941), 5–6; Hans Speier, *Treachery in War* (New York: New School for Social Research, 1940), 1; and Ray Cline, "U.S. Foreign Intelligence, 1939–1945," *Foreign Service Journal* 53 (1976): 17–18.

2. Taylor quoted in Edmond Taylor, *Awakening from History* (Boston: Gambit, 1969), 246. For Hitler's theories, see Hideya Kumata and Wilbur Schramm, "The Propaganda Theory of the German Nazis," in *A Psychological Warfare Casebook*, ed. William E. Daugherty and Morris Janowitz (Baltimore: Johns Hopkins University Press, 1958), 53; Adolf Hitler, *Mein Kampf* (Boston: Houghton Mifflin, 1971), 176–79, 579; and Gerhardt Niemeyer, *Commentary on Hitler's Theories on Propaganda*, Technical Memorandum ORO T-135 (Baltimore: Johns Hopkins University Press, 1951), 2, 14, 16–24 passim. For Goebbels's theories, see Leonard Doob, "Goebbels's Principles of Propaganda," *Public Opinion Quarterly* 14 (Fall 1950): 422–24; E. Bramsted, "Joseph Goebbels and National Socialist Propaganda: Some Aspects, 1926–1939," *Australian Outlook* 8 (June 1954): 69–70, 90–91; Derrick Singleton and Arthur Weidenfeld, *The Goebbels Experiment: A Study of the Nazi Propaganda Machine* (New Haven: Yale University Press, 1943), 74; Michael Balfour, *Propaganda in War, 1939–1945* (London: Routledge and Kegan Paul, 1979), 12; and Gorham Munson, *Twelve Decisive Battles of the Mind: The Story of Propaganda During the Christian Era* (New York: Greystone, 1942), 265–66.

3. For World War I propaganda, see George G. Bruntz, "Allied Propaganda and the Collapse of German Morale in 1918," *Public Opinion Quarterly* 2 (1938): 61–76; and Harold Lasswell, "Organization of Psychological Warfare Agencies in World War I," 122–25, both in Daugherty and Janowitz, eds., *Psychological Warfare Casebook*; Paul M. A. Linebarger, *Psychological Warfare* (Washington, DC: Combat Forces Press, 1954), 66; and

Harold Lasswell and James Wechsler, *Propaganda Technique in the World War* (London: Kegan Paul, Trench, Trubner and Company, 1927).

4. Quote from Hermann Rauschning, *The Voices of Destruction* (New York: G. P. Putnam, 1940), 4, 8–10.

5. Ladislas Farago, ed., *German Psychological Warfare: Survey and Bibliography* (New York: U.S. Committee for National Morale, 1942; reprint, New York: Arno Press, 1972), 131–32, 160–64, 181–296; James P. Warburg, *Unwritten Treaty* (New York: Harcourt Brace Jovanovich, 1946), 16; Leo Margolin, *Paper Bullets: A Brief History of Psychological Warfare in World War II* (New York: Froeben, 1946), 31; Hermann Franke, "Psychological Warfare and How to Wage It," *Current History* 51 (January 1940): 52–53; and Edmond Taylor, "How America Can Take the Offensive," *Fortune*, 23 May 1941, 64–65.

6. Kumata and Schramm, "Propaganda Theory," 49–50; F. Elwyn Jones, "The Modern Technique of Aggression," *Fortnightly* 151 (April 1939): 378–85; Joseph Bornstein and Paul R. Milton, *Action Against the Enemy's Mind* (Indianapolis: Bobbs-Merrill, 1942), 5–6, 9.

7. Albert Brandt, "Nazi International," *Catholic World* 138 (January 1934): 394, 398, 402–3. For activities in India, see Khawaja Ahmed Abbas, "India Listens," *Living Age* 357 (September 1939): 55, 58.

8. For the disorganized nature of German intelligence and war production, see Thomas H. Etzold, "The Futility Factor: German Information Gathering in the United States, 1933–1945," *Military Affairs* 39 (April 1975): 77–82; Michael Geyer, "National Socialist Germany: The Politics of Information," in *Knowing One's Enemies: Intelligence Assessment Before the Two World Wars*, ed. Ernest May (Princeton: Princeton University Press, 1986), 310–46; and Alan Milward, *The German Economy at War* (London: Athlone, 1965).

9. Alton Frye, *Nazi Germany and the American Hemisphere, 1933–1945* (New Haven: Yale University Press, 1967), 25–26; Balfour, *Propaganda in War* 35–37; Singleton and Weidenfeld, *Goebbels Experiment*, 81–85, 90–92.

10. Quote from Brandt, "Nazi International," 394; see also Kumata and Schramm, "Propaganda Theory," 53.

11. Z. A. B. Zeman, *Nazi Propaganda* (London: Oxford University Press, 1973), 67–71; Frye, *Nazi Germany*, 96; Jay W. Baird, *The Mythical World of Nazi Propaganda, 1939–1945* (Minneapolis: University of Minnesota Press, 1975), 36.

12. Frye, *Nazi Germany*, 20; Louis De Jong, *The German Fifth Column in the Second World War* (Chicago: University of Chicago Press, 1956), 278–88, 298–99.

13. Otto Tolischus, *They Wanted War* (New York: Reynal and Hitchcock, 1940), 176–78; Dorothy Thompson, "Nazi Foreign Missions," *Vital Speeches* 3 (15 September 1937): 713; Michael Sayers and Albert E. Kahn, *Sabotage: The Secret War Against America* (New York: Harper Brothers, 1942), 138; Frederick Oechsner et al., *This Is the Enemy* (Boston: Little, Brown, 1942), 359; Frye, *Nazi Germany*, 19; and Zeman, *Nazi Propaganda*, 76–81.

14. Quote from Donovan and Mowrer, *Fifth Column*, 12; see also Sayers and Kahn, *Sabotage*, 139, and Jeffrey R. Willis, "The Wehrmacht Propaganda Branch: German Military Propaganda and Censorship During World War II," Ph.D. diss., University of Virginia, 1964, 8–9, 16, 24, 29–30.

15. De Jong, *German Fifth Column*, 298–99; Frye, *Nazi Germany*, 16–18; Farago, ed.,

German Psychological Warfare, 141–44; and Sayers and Kahn, *Sabotage*, 137. For the early history of these organizations, see Zeman, *Nazi Propaganda*, 72–73.

16. Singleton and Weidenfeld, *Goebbels Experiment*, 85–88.

17. Quote from Oechsner, *This Is the Enemy*, 52; see also Farago, *German Psychological Warfare*, 135–36; Harold Lavine and James Wechsler, *War Propaganda and the United States* (New Haven: Yale University Press, 1940), 37; and Roger B. Nelson, "Hitler's Propaganda Machine," *Current History* 38 (June 1933): 287–89.

18. Julian A. S. Hale, *Radio Power: Propaganda and Internal Broadcasting* (Philadelphia: Temple University Press, 1975), 2; Harwood Childs and John Whitton, eds., *Propaganda by Shortwave* (Princeton: Princeton University Press, 1942), 11–13; and Oliver Thomson, *Mass Persuasion in History: An Historical Analysis of the Development of Propaganda Techniques* (Edinburgh, Scotland: Paul Harris, 1977), 115.

19. R. A. Friedman, "Alsatian Unrest," *Contemporary Review* 155 (February 1939): 214–17, 221, and Edmond Taylor, *The Strategy of Terror* (New York: Houghton Mifflin, 1942), 65.

20. Quote from Childs and Whitton, eds., *Propaganda by Shortwave*, 15–18; and Harold Graves, Jr., "European Radio and the War," *Annals of the American Academy of Political and Social Science* 213 (January 1941): 76.

21. Quote from Brandt, "Nazi International," 401; see also Childs and Whitton, eds., *Propaganda by Shortwave*, 35–37; Donovan and Mowrer, *Fifth Column*, 3–4; and Taylor, *Awakening from History*, 243–44, 249–50.

22. Quote from Taylor, *Awakening from History*, 244–50.

23. Quote from Graves, "European Radio," 76.

24. Ernest Albert, "The Press in Nazi Germany," *Contemporary Review* 154 (December 1938): 699, and Childs and Whitton, eds., *Propaganda by Shortwave*, 38–39.

25. Quote from Donovan and Mowrer, *Fifth Column*, 3; see also Edwin Muller, "Waging War with Words," *Current History* 50 (August 1939): 25, and George Glasgow, "Nazi Methods in Memel," *Contemporary Review* 146 (November 1934): 623–24.

26. Childs and Whitton, eds., *Propaganda by Shortwave*, 43–44, and "The War Comes," in Institute for Propaganda Analysis, *Propaganda Analysis*, 4 vols. (New York: Institute for Propaganda Analysis, 1941), 2:4.

27. Taylor, *Strategy of Terror*, 170–72, 90–94, 193; idem, "Strategy of Terror," *Reader's Digest*, September 1940, 89–92.

28. Quotes from Taylor, *Strategy of Terror*, 62–63, 65, 91; see also Margolin, *Paper Bullets*, 56–57; Robert de Saint-Jean, "Battle of Words," *Atlantic* 166 (November 1940): 612; Operations Research Office, *The Nature of Psychological Warfare*, ORO T-214, (Baltimore: Johns Hopkins University Press, 5 January 1953), 5–6.

29. Donovan and Mowrer, *Fifth Column*, 8–9; see also "Paris Press," *Newsweek*, 24 July 1939, 20.

30. "Paris Press," 20; Richard de Rochemont, "France and Propaganda," *Life*, 25 March 1940, 9–10; Taylor, *Strategy of Terror*, 61–62, 86; Childs and Whitton, eds., *Propaganda by Shortwave*, 184–86; and de Saint-Jean, "Battle of Words," 163, 612–15.

31. Warburg, *Unwritten Treaty*, 32, 33.

32. Charles Roetter, *Psychological Warfare, 1914–1945* (New York: Stein and Day, 1974), 98.

33. de Saint-Jean, "Battle of Words," 614–15; Charles Rolo, "The Strategy of War by

Radio," *Harper's* 181 (November 1940): 640–41, 643; Paul Blackstock, "The German Use of Psychological Warfare in 1940," in Daugherty and Janowitz, eds., *Psychological Warfare Casebook,* 418; Edward T. Lean, *Voices in the Darkness: The Story of the European Radio War* (London: Secker and Warburg, 1943), 104–42.

34. Quote from Paul Olberg, "Scandinavia and the Nazis," *Contemporary Review* 156 (July 1939): 28–30; Harold Lavine, *The Fifth Column in America* (New York: Doubleday, Doran, 1940), 3–9. For an overview that thoroughly debunks Nazi fifth-column efforts, see Alistair Horne, *To Lose a Battle: France 1940* (Boston: Little, Brown, 1969), 446–54.

35. Donovan and Mowrer, *Fifth Column,* 4–5, 7.

36. Lean, *Voices,* 104–42 passim; Hans Speier and Margaret Otis, "German Radio Propaganda to France During the Battle of France," in *Propaganda in War and Crisis,* ed. Daniel Lerner (New York: Stewart, 1951), 209–41; for German tactical propaganda see Willis, "Wehrmacht Propaganda Branch," 183–89, 192–200.

37. Robert Strausz-Hupe, *Axis America: Hitler Plans Our Future* (New York: G. P. Putnam's Sons, 1941), xi, xvii; Andre Maurois, "What Happened to France," *Collier's,* 21 September 1940, 17, 51–54; Taylor, *Awakening from History,* 284–85; and "Fall of France," in *Propaganda Analysis,* 3:iii.

38. Quote from William C. Bullitt, "America Is in Danger." *Vital Speeches* 6 (1 September 1940): 683–84; for a similar view, see Sketch of Radio Plan Suggested to Combat Subversive Activities in this Country by Marion Dix, 1–2, Box 379, Harold Ickes Papers, Library of Congress (LC), Washington, D.C.

39. Among notable correspondents were Edgar Ansel Mowrer and John Whitaker (*Chicago Daily News*), Edmond Taylor (*Chicago Tribune,* CBS), Frederick C. Oechsner (United Press), Jay Allen (*Chicago Tribune*), Sigrid Schultz (*Chicago Tribune,* Mutual Broadcasting System), Joseph C. Harsh (*Christian Science Monitor*), and Pierre J. Huss (International News Service). For a list of journalists, see Appendix 1 in Clayton D. Laurie, "Ideology and American Propaganda: The Psychological Warfare Campaign Against Nazi Germany, 1941–1945," Ph.D. diss., American University, 1990. For the White House Press Corps, which included future OGR, COI, OWI, and OSS members, see Betty H. Winfield, *FDR and the News Media* (New York: Columbia University Press, 1994), 242–251. For further information, see biographical sketch, Box 109, Edgar A. Mowrer Papers, LC; "Edgar Ansel Mowrer Dies at 84," *New York Times,* 4 March 1977; and *Current Biography,* 1941, 597–600. Mowrer's memoirs are entitled *Triumph and Turmoil: A Personal History of Our Times* (New York: Weybright and Talley, 1968). For Taylor, see *Awakening from History.* For Oechsner, see *This Is the Enemy,* 362, and *Current Biography, 1943,* 564–66. Oechsner was interned with 100 other Americans at Bad Nauheim, Germany, between December 1941 and March 1942. During this time he wrote *This Is the Enemy* and a report on propaganda; see Charles B. Burdick, *An American Island in Hitler's Reich: The Bad Nauheim Internment* (Menlo Park, Calif.: Markgraff, 1987). For Whitaker, see "J. T. Whitaker Dies; War Reporter, 40," *New York Times,* 13 September 1946, and "Transition," *Newsweek,* 23 September 1946. For Allen, see *Eyewitnesses: The Views of Americans Who Have Watched the Totalitarian Form of Government Rise All Over the World* (New York: FFFC, 1941), in Box 1, POF 4461: FFFC, 1941–42, FDR Library, Hyde Park, N.Y.; "Jay Allen, News Correspondent in Trench Coat Tradition, Dead," *New York Times Biographical Edition,* 22 December 1972, 2097; and *Current Biography, 1941,* 20–22.

For Schultz, see "Sigrid Schultz Is Dead; Reported from Berlin About Nazi Movement," *New York Times Biographical Service*, 17 May 1980; *Who's Who Among American Women*, 1972–1973, 7: 798; and "Sigrid L. Schultz, Reporter Who Covered Rise of Nazism, Is Dead," *New York Times*, 17 May 1980, 5. For Huss, see "Pierre J. Huss, 59; Reporter, Is Dead," *New York Times*, 23 March 1966, 3.

40. Childs and Whitton, eds., *Propaganda by Shortwave*, 45; Herbert Seligmann, "The New Barbarian Invasion," *New Republic* 95 (22 June 1938): 175; and James B. Conant, "Defenses Against Propaganda," *Vital Speeches* 4 (15 June 1938): 543.

41. First quote from Rauschning, *Voices of Destruction*, 4, 70–71; second quote from Strausz-Hupe, *Axis America*, 197; third quote from Warburg, *Unwritten Treaty*, 62; see also Bullitt, "America," 684, and Edward Y. Hartshorne, "Reactions to the Nazi Threat: A Study of Propaganda and Culture Conflict," *Public Opinion Quarterly* 5 (Winter 1941): 631.

42. Sander A. Diamond, *The Nazi Movement in the United States, 1924–1941* (Ithaca, N.Y.: Cornell University Press, 1974), 194–96, and Donald McKale, *The Swastika Outside Germany* (Kent, Ohio: Kent State University Press, 1977), 143.

43. Quote from Margolin, *Paper Bullets*, 73; see also Max Lerner, "Propaganda in Our Time," *New Republic* 103 (26 August 1940): 281; and Sayers and Kahn, *Sabotage*, 135–38. For Goebbels's alleged plans for the Western Hemisphere, see Ernst Kris, "German Propaganda Instructions of 1933," *Social Research* 9 (February 1942): 46–81, and Stanley E. Hilton, *Hitler's Secret War in South America* (Baton Rouge: Louisiana State University Press, 1981).

44. Quote from Edmond Taylor, *Smash Hitler's International* (New York: Greystone, 1941), 32, 34–35; see also idem, "How America," 64–65, 170–71.

45. Quote from Warburg, *Unwritten Treaty*, 28–29.

46. First quote from Tolischus, *They Wanted War*, 52–53, 57–59; second and third quotes from Sayers and Kahn, *Sabotage*, 132.

47. Donovan and Mowrer, *Fifth Column*, 5–7; see also Thomas R. Maddux, "Red Fascism and Brown Bolshevism: The American Image of Totalitarianism in the 1930s," *Historian* 40 (November 1977): 85–103.

48. For varying figures, see De Jong, *German Fifth Column*, 218–19; Diamond, *Nazi Movement*, 126–27; McKale, *Swastika Outside Germany*, 13; and Frye, *Nazi Germany*, 15.

49. Philip E. Jacob, "Influences of World Events on U.S. 'Neutrality' Opinion," *Public Opinion Quarterly* 4 (March 1940): 48–65; and Richard Breitman and Alan Kraut, *American Refugee Policy and European Jewry, 1933–1945* (Bloomington: Indiana University Press, 1987), 117–18.

50. McKale, *Swastika Outside Germany*, 14–16; Frye, *Nazi Germany*, 32–35; Diamond, *Nazi Movement*, 8, 32–33, 111; Geoffrey Smith, *To Save a Nation: American Countersubversives, the New Deal, and the Coming of World War II* (New York: Basic Books, 1974), 87; and Ludwig Lore, "Nazi Politics in America," *Nation* 137 (29 November 1933): 615–16.

51. For efforts to sever relations, see Frye, *Nazi Germany*, 38–39, 62–63; Diamond, *Nazi Movement*, 8, 30, 109, 115, 170; McKale, *Swastika Outside Germany*, 89–94; and Smith, *Save a Nation*, 93–94, 117.

52. William E. Dodd, *Ambassador Dodd's Diary, 1933–1938* (New York: Harcourt, Brace, 1941), 162, 340; Dodd claimed that Dr. Otto Vollbehr, who sold the Gutenberg Bible to the U.S. Library of Congress, was a notorious Nazi agent.

53. Harold Ickes, *The Secret Diary of Harold Ickes*, 2 vols. (New York: Simon and Schuster, 1954), I:III–12.

54. Diamond, *Nazi Movement*, 176, 192–93, 258; Frye, *Nazi Germany*, 80–82; and Morris Schonback, *Native American Fascism During the* 1930s *and* 1940s (New York: Garland, 1985).

55. Diamond, *Nazi Movement*, 204–9, 221–22, 257–64, and Alfred M. Lee, *The Fine Art of Propaganda* (New York: Institute for Propaganda Analysis, 1939, reprint; New York: Octagon Books, 1972), 120.

56. "The Vanishing Un-American," *New Republic* 103 (26 August 1940): 264.

57. Quote from "The Attack on Democracy," in *Propaganda Analysis*, 4:13–14; see also Johan T. Smertenko, "Hitlerism Comes to America," *Harper's*, November 1933, 662–64; "American Fascists," *New Republic* 98 (8 March 1939): 117–18. For Winrod, see "Voices of Defeat," *Life*, 13 April 1942, 98–99; "Attack on Democracy," 4:20; and Roy Campbell, "Gerald B. Winrod Versus the "Educated Devils," *Midwest Quarterly* 16 (Winter 1975): 187–98. For Coughlin, see "Voices of Defeat," 92–93; "American Fascists," 118; and Alan Brinkley, *Voices of Protest: Huey Long, Father Coughlin, and the Great Depression* (New York: Knopf, 1982).

58. Quote from "Whitewashing Hitlerism," *World Tomorrow* 17 (15 February 1934): 78; see also "Axis Voices Among the Foreign Born," in *Propaganda Analysis*, 4:1, and James E. Miller, "A Question of Loyalty: American Liberals, Propaganda, and the Italian-American Community, 1939–1943," *Maryland Historian* 9 (1978): 49–71.

59. Douglas Miller, *You Can't Do Business with Hitler* (Boston: Little, Brown, 1941).

60. First quote from John L. Spivak, *Secret Armies: The New Technique of Nazi Warfare* (New York: Modern Age Books, 1939), 119–20; second quote from Sayers and Kahn, *Sabotage*, 158–59.

61. Quote from Spivak, *Secret Armies*, 119–20.

62. Diamond, *Nazi Movement*, 194; McKale, *Swastika Outside Germany*, 143; Sayers and Kahn, *Sabotage*, 173, 180–81; see also Harold Lavine, "The Propagandists Open Fire," *New Republic* 100 (1 November 1939): 361.

63. Quote from "Flanders Hall Investigated by Grand Jury," *Publisher's Weekly* 140 (4 October 1941): 1385–86; see also Norman Cousins, "Books and Propaganda," *Saturday Review of Literature* 25 (21 February 1942): 10; and Frye, *Nazi Germany*, 162n.

64. First quote from Daniel Lang, "Berlin Sends Radio Greeting," *New Republic* 97 (11 January 1939): 281; second quote from Rolo, "Strategy of War by Radio," 641, 649; see also Graves, "European Radio," 80, and Childs and Whitton, eds., *Propaganda by Shortwave*, 19–21, 65.

65. Jerome Bruner, "The Dimensions of Propaganda: German Shortwave Broadcasts," *Journal of Abnormal Psychology* 36 (July 1941): 313, 330–34; Charles Rolo, *Radio Goes to War: The Fourth Front* (New York: G. P. Putnam's Sons, 1942), 124–26; and Floyd H. Allport and Mary Mathes Simpson, "Broadcasting to an Enemy Country: What Appeals Are Effective, and Why," *Journal of Social Psychology* 23 (May 1946): 217–24, 224. For the size of the U.S. audience, see Childs and Whitton, eds., *Propaganda by Shortwave*, 307–8. For Americans working for the RMVP, see William L. Shirer, "American Radio Traitors," *Harper's*, October 1943, 397–404; John C. Edwards, *Berlin Calling: American Broadcasters in Service to the Third Reich* (New York: Praeger, 1991); Clayton D. Laurie,

"Goebbels's Iowan: Frederick W. Kaltenbach and Nazi Short-Wave Radio Broadcasts to America, 1939–45," *Annals of Iowa* 53 (Summer 1994): 219–45.

66. Albert Jay Nock, "A New Dose of British Propaganda," *American Mercury* 42 (December 1937): 482–486.

67. On the isolationists, see Wayne S. Cole, *Roosevelt and the Isolationists, 1932–1945* (Lincoln: University of Nebraska Press, 1983); Gloria J. Barron, *Leadership in Crisis: FDR and the Path to Intervention* (Port Washington, N.Y.: Kennikat Press, 1973); and William L. Langer and S. Everett Gleason, *The Challenge to Isolation: The World Crisis of 1937–1940 and American Foreign Policy* (Gloucester, Mass.: Peter Smith, 1970).

68. Stuart, a future ambassador to Norway, was aided by future ambassador to Britain and Yale University president Kingman Brewster and future U.S. president Gerald R. Ford. See J. Garry Clifford, "Both Ends of the Telescope: New Perspectives on FDR and American Entry into World War II," *Diplomatic History* 13 (Spring 1989): 229; for contemporary views of the isolationists, see Sayers and Kahn, *Sabotage*, 157–65, 232–33; 239n; and 241–44.

69. Quote from John T. Flynn, "Mr. Flynn on War Hysteria," *New Republic* 103 (11 November 1940): 660; see also "Noise over the Nazis," *Current History* 46 (May 1937): 29–30.

70. For interventionist critiques, see Warburg, *Unwritten Treaty*, 28–29; Hartshorne, "Reaction to Nazi Threat," 628, 634–36; Cole, *Roosevelt and Isolationists*, 536–37; Deborah E. Lipstadt, *Beyond Belief: The American Press and the Coming of the Holocaust, 1933–1945* (New York: Free Press, 1986), 125; and John R. Carlson [Arthur Derounian], *Undercover: My Four Years in the Nazi Underground of America* (New York: E. P. Dutton, 1943).

71. Frye, *Nazi Germany*, 132–41, 155–56, and Hans S. Trefousse, *Germany and American Neutrality, 1939–1941* (New York: Bookman Associates, 1951), 103–11.

72. The sixteen groups are listed in Sayers and Kahn, *Sabotage*, 193–94, 208–9, 215–19; see also Frye, *Nazi Germany*, 160–63; and Cole, *Roosevelt and Isolationists*, 470–73.

Chapter 2. The American Private Sector Mobilizes

1. Allan Winkler, *The Politics of Propaganda: The Office of War Information, 1942–1945* (New Haven: Yale University Press, 1978), 4.

2. Edward Y. Hartshorne, "Reactions to the Nazi Threat," *Public Opinion Quarterly* 5 (Winter 1941): 637–38, and Edmond Taylor, *The Strategy of Terror* (New York: Houghton Mifflin, 1942), 187.

3. James Squires, "The Problem of Propaganda Today," *Vital Speeches* 5 (15 July 1939): 589; see also Eric J. Sandeen, "Anti-Nazi Sentiment in Film: Confessions of a Nazi Spy and the German-American Bund," *American Studies* 20 (1979): 69–81.

4. Thomas F. Troy, *Donovan and the CIA: A History of the Establishment of the CIA* (Frederick, Md.: University Publications of America, 1981), 95.

5. Quote from Alfred M. Lee, *The Fine Art of Propaganda* (New York: Institute for Propaganda Analysis, 1939; reprint, New York: Octagon Books, 1972), vii–viii, ix; "The Problem of Propaganda," *Collier's*, 23 December 1939, 62; Institute for Propaganda Anal-

ysis, *Propaganda Analysis*, 4 vols. (New York: Institute for Propaganda Analysis, 1941), 1:iv; "Analysis of Propaganda," *Newsweek*, 3 April 1939, 32; and Edward L. Bernays, "Does Propaganda Menace Democracy?" *Forum* 99 (June 1938), 341–42.

6. "Problem of Propaganda," *Propaganda Analysis*, 1:iv; see also "Let's Talk About Ourselves," in *Propaganda Analysis*, 2:106–7, and Clyde R. Miller and Louis Minsky, "Propaganda—Good and Bad—for Democracy," *Survey Graphic* 28 (November 1939): 709. For the "Seven ABC's," see Lee, *Fine Art*, 16–18.

7. "Let's Talk About Ourselves" and "We Say au Revoir," in *Propaganda Analysis*, 2:106–7 and 4:1–6.

8. "We Say Au Revoir," 4:1–6.

9. Harwood Childs and John Whitton, eds., *Propaganda by Shortwave* (Princeton: Princeton University Press, 1942), vii.

10. Edward Teale, "America Listens In," *Popular Science Monthly* (June 1941), 74–75; Childs and Whitton, eds., *Propaganda by Shortwave*, vii–ix; for survey results see 310–14. The American Institute of Public Opinion, founded in 1936, is now the Gallup Poll.

11. Childs and Whitton, eds., *Propaganda by Shortwave*, viii–ix, and Teale, "America Listens," 74–75. For the FBIS, see Ray Cline, "U.S. Foreign Intelligence, 1939–1945," *Foreign Service Journal* 53 (1976): 18.

12. Groups interested in morale, 24 November 1940, Box 68a, William J. Donovan Papers, U.S. Army Military History Institute (MHI), Carlisle, Pa.; see also Ernest Angell, "The Civilian Morale Agency," *Annals of the American Academy of the Political and Social Sciences* 220 (March 1942): 160–67; "Ten Commandments for Propaganda Protection," *Science News Letter* 36 (14 October 1939): 250; "Footprints of the Trojan Horse," *Scholastic* 37 (4 November 1940): 12–13; and the National Committee on the Cause and Cure of War, Box 1, William H. Standley Papers, LC. Other groups included the War Communications Research Office at the Library of Congress, the Kris Project at the New School of Social Research, and the American Film Center; see R. Keith Kane, "The OFF," *Public Opinion Quarterly* 6 (Summer 1942): 208–9.

13. Quote from Jane H. Schwar, "Interventionist Propaganda and Pressure Groups in the United States, 1937–1941" (Ph.D. diss., Ohio State University, 1973), 265–66; War Committee for National Morale, Box 379, Harold Ickes Papers; Mark L. Chadwin, *The Warhawks: American Interventionists Before Pearl Harbor* (New York: W. W. Norton, 1968), 157; and Sydney S. Weinberg, "Wartime Propaganda in a Democracy: America's Twentieth-Century Information Agencies" (Ph.D. diss., Columbia University, 1969), 154–55.

14. Angell, "Civilian Morale Agency," 166–67.

15. Letter, Maloney to FDR, 12 June 1941, POF 4453: Prop., 1933–41; letter, Drago to FDR, 26 Dec. 1942, POF 4453: Prop. 1942–45; letter, von Hentig to E. Roosevelt, 16 Nov. 1937, PPF 5774: Fascism; letter, Lazarus to FDR, 3 July 1940, POF 1661a: Fifth Column, 1940; letter, Tinker to McIntyre, 2 Jan. 1941, POF 1661a: Fifth Column, 1941–45; FDR Papers.

16. Ladislas Farago, ed., *German Psychological Warfare: Survey and Bibliography* (New York: U.S. Committee for National Morale, 1942, reprint, New York: Arno Press, 1972), 297–98. One recipient of fifteen committee monographs and reports was William J. Donovan; see German Psychological Warfare, Boxes 68a and 83a, Donovan Papers.

17. For a partial list of the membership of the Committee on National Morale, see Appendix 2, in Clayton D. Laurie, "Ideology and American Propaganda: The Psycho-

logical Warfare Campaign Against Nazi Germany, 1941–1945" (Ph.D. diss., American University, 1990); see also Farago, ed., *German Psychological Warfare*, 297–302, and Committee for National Morale, *A Plan for a National Morale Service, Submitted by the Committee for National Morale* (New York: Committee for National Morale, 1941). For biographical information, see "John C. Farrar, Publisher, Editor and Writer, Is Dead," *New York Times*, 7 November 1974, sec. 2, p. 48, and *Current Biography, 1954*, 268–70. For Lattimore, see *Current Biography, 1945*, 336–38, and *Current Biography, 1964*, 246–48. For Miller, see *Current Biography, 1941*, 581–83, and *Eyewitnesses: The Views of Americans Who Have Watched the Totalitarian Form of Government Rise All over the World* (New York: FFFC, 1941), 21, POF 4461: FFFC, 1941–42, FDR Papers (hereafter *Eyewitnesses*). For Stanton, see *Current Biography, 1945*, 571–72. For Eliot, see "George Fielding Eliot, 76, Dies; Military Writer of WW II," *New York Times*, 22 April 1971, 44, and sketch, George F. Eliot Papers, LC.

18. Edmond Taylor, *Awakening from History* (Boston: Gambit, 1969), 306–8.

19. Quotes from Taylor, "How America Can Take the Offensive," *Fortune* 23 (May 1941): 172, 174, 272–75; see also idem, *Awakening from History*, 306–8.

20. Taylor, "How America," 176–77, 272–75.

21. Philip E. Jacob, "Influences of World Events on U.S. 'Neutrality' Opinion," *Public Opinion Quarterly* 4 (March 1940): 48–65; and Michael Leigh, *Mobilizing Consent: Public Opinion and American Foreign Policy, 1937–1947* (Westport, Conn.: Greenwood Press, 1976), 43, 48.

22. Quotes from Official Statement of Policy Issued 17 Mar. 1941, POF 4230: CDAAA, FDR Papers; see also Schwar, "Interventionist Propaganda," 175–76.

23. Memo, Mrs. K. Roosevelt to Watson, 1 May 1941, Advisory Policy Committee, CDAAA, POF 4230: CDAAA, FDRL. The CDAAA advisory committee, chaired by White, included Conant, Graham, Seymour, Kingdon, Fiorello LaGuardia, Freda Kirchway, Thomas Lamont, Mrs. Lewis Mumford, Kermit Roosevelt, Robert E. Sherwood, James T. Shotwell, Herbert Bayard Swope, Henry P. Van Dusen, Douglas Miller, and Clark Eichelberger.

24. By March 1941 the CDAAA membership included Dean Acheson, Jay and Robert G. Allen, James Phinney Baxter III, Henry S. Canby, Ward Cheney, John Farrar, Herbert Agar, George and Marshall Field, Calvin B. Hoover, T. Walter Johnson, Helen Hayes, Max Lerner, John J. McCloy, Eugene O'Neill, Frank Polk, Conyers Read, William H. Vanderbilt, and James P. Warburg. For more membership lists, see letter, Clark to Early, 17 Mar. 1941; report, 15 Apr. 1942, Largest Contributors of CDAAA; and membership, CDAAA, 14 Mar. 1941, all in POF 4230: CDAAA, Jan. to May 1941, FDR Papers. For individual background, see Biographical Sketch, Frank Knox Papers, LC. For Baxter, see *Current Biography, 1947*, 36–38; and *Who's Who in the World*, 82. For Agar, see POF 4461, FFFC, 1941–42, *Eyewitnesses*, 9, FDR Papers; "Herbert Agar Dies; Author and Editor," *New York Times Biographical Service*, 25 November 1980, 1509; and *The National Cyclopedia of American Biography*, 237–38. For Read, see "Dr. Conyers Read, Educator, 78, Dies," *New York Times*, 25 December 1959, 21. For Vanderbilt, see "William H. Vanderbilt, 79, Dead; Former Governor of Rhode Island," *New York Times Biographical Service*, 16 April 1981, 571.

25. John Mason Brown, *The Ordeal of a Playwright: Robert E. Sherwood and the Challenge of War* (New York: Harper and Row, 1970), 26–29.

26. Ad and FDR quoted in Brown, *Ordeal*, 86–87; see also T. Walter Johnson, *The Battle Against Isolation* (Chicago: University of Chicago Press, 1944), 85; White quoted in Leigh, *Mobilizing Consent*, 48.

27. Chadwin, *Warhawks*, 34–40, 57 passim.

28. For members of the Century Club, see Appendix 3, Laurie, "Ideology and American Propaganda"; Allen Nevins, "The Centurions Survey a Century," *New York Times Magazine*, 27 April 1947, 16; and Johnson, *Battle Against Isolation*, 115–17, 249. For biographical information, see "Francis Miller Dies; Virginia Politician," *New York Times Biographical Service*, 5 August 1978, 969. For Hessler, see *National Cyclopedia of American Biography*, 51:523–24. For Hill, see *Who's Who in America, 1976–1977*, 1442. For Armstrong, see "Hamilton Fish Armstrong Dies at 80; *Foreign Affairs Quarterly* Ex-Editor," *New York Times*, 25 April 1973, 46; "Transition," *Newsweek*, 7 May 1973, 61; and *Current Biography, 1948*, 24–26.

29. Chadwin, *Warhawks*, 156–57.

30. Letter, LaGuardia to White, 26 Dec. 1940, PPF 1376: Fiorello LaGuardia, 1940–45, FDR Papers; see also Richard W. Steele, "Preparing the Public for War: Efforts to Establish a National Propaganda Agency, 1940–1941," *American Historical Review* 75 (October 1970): 1640; and William M. Tuttle, Jr., "Aid to the Allies Short-of-War versus American Intervention: A Reappraisal of William Allen White's Leadership," *Journal of American History* 56 (December 1970): 840–58.

31. Chadwin, *Warhawks*, 156–57, 160–67 passim.

32. Statement of Purpose quoted from *Eyewitnesses*, POF 4461, FFFC, 1941–42, FDR Papers; Agar's comments quoted in Harold Ickes, *The Secret Diary of Harold Ickes*, 2 vols. (New York: Simon and Schuster, 1954), 1:498.

33. Chadwin, *Warhawks*, 167–69, 171.

34. For a partial listing of the members of the FFFC, see Appendix 4, Laurie, "Ideology and American Propaganda"; see also Chadwin, *Warhawks*, 166, 168, and Ickes, *Secret Diary*, 1:497–98. FFFC members who later served in the COI, OSS, and OWI included Whitney Shepardson, Calvin Hoover, Allen Dulles, James Warburg, Harold Guinzburg, Corey Ford, Robert Woods Bliss, Richard Watts, and William H. Standley. The Executive Committee of the FFFC included Ulric Bell, Ward Cheney, Harold Guinzburg, Conyers Read, James Warburg, Herbert Agar, Allen Dulles, and Katherine Gauss Jackson, all of whom later held top positions in the COI, OSS, and OWI. The FFFC policy committee included Herbert Agar, William J. Donovan, Allen Dulles, Harold Guinzburg, and Conyers Read, also COI, OSS, and OWI leaders. For biographical information on Shepardson, see "Whitney Shepardson, 75, Dies; International Relations Expert," *New York Times*, 1 June 1966, 47. For Hoover, see "Calvin B. Hoover, Was Duke Dean," *New York Times Biographical Service*, 12 July 1974, 970, and Calvin B. Hoover, *Memoirs of Capitalism, Communism, and Nazism* (Durham, N.C.: Duke University Press, 1965), 179, 191, 193–95. For Dulles, *Current Biography, 1949*, 178–80; *New York Times Biographical Edition*, 31 January 1969, 725–29; and Robin Winks, *Cloak and Gown: Scholars in the Secret War, 1939–1961* (New York: William Morrow and Company, 1987), 274–75. For Warburg, see Ron Chernow, *The Warburgs: The Twentieth Century Odyssey of a Remarkable Jewish Family* (New York: Random House, 1993), 491–92; *National Cyclopedia of American Biography*, 231–33; *Current Biography, 1948*, 654–56; and "James Warburg, a Financier and Writer on US Policy, Dies," *New York Times*, 4 June 1969, 47. Warburg wrote a letter of

reconciliation to FDR on 19 June 1940 offering his apologies for his criticisms of the president and the New Deal in 1936. Roosevelt accepted the apology on 20 June (see letter, Warburg to FDR, 19 June 1940; and letter, FDR to Warburg, 20 June 1940, PPF 540: Warburg, James P., FDR Papers). For Guinzburg, see *Current Biography, 1957,* 223-25. For Ford, see "Corey Ford, Humorist, Is Dead; Writer of Literary Parodies, 67," *New York Times Biographical Service,* 28 July 1969, 903. For Bliss, see OSS Prominent People, Box 97, Entry 99 RG 226, NARA; and "Robert Woods Bliss Dead at 86; Former US Envoy to Argentina," *New York Times,* 20 April 1962, 27. For Watts, see "Richard Watts, Drama Critic at Tribune and Post," *New York Times,* 3 January 1981, 26. For Standley, see OSS Prominent People, Box 97, Entry 99, RG 226; and Biographical Sketch, Standley Papers. For Bell, see "Ulric Bell Dead; Film Official, 68. Executive Aide to Skouras; Had Served the *Louisville Courier-Journal,* 1910-1941," *New York Times,* 17 January 1960, 27, and *National Cyclopedia of American Biography,* 267. For Bruce, see *Current Biography, 1949,* 80–81; *Political Profiles: New York, Facts on File,* 73–74; *International Who's Who,* 230; *Who's Who in the World,* 153; *New York Times Biographical Service,* December 1977, 1595-97; OSS Prominent People, Box 97, Entry 99, RG 226; and David K. E. Bruce, OSS *Against the Reich: The World War II Diaries of Colonel David K. E. Bruce,* ed. Nelson D. Lankford (Kent, Ohio: Kent State University Press, 1990).

35. Chadwin, *Warhawks,* 202–6 passim.

36. Hamilton Fish Armstrong, for example, was a regular correspondent of FDR's and sent copies of his books to him in 1934, 1936, 1937, and 1940 (see PPF 6011: Armstrong, Hamilton; Maj. George Fielding Eliot did likewise, see PPF 8386: Eliot, Maj. G. F., FDR Papers).

37. Angell, "Civilian Morale Agency," 161.

38. PPF 1974: Clarence Streit, FDR Papers; and Chadwin, *Warhawks,* 19-20. Members of the Union Now movement included Grenville Clark, Gardner Cowles, Jr., John F. Dulles, Harold Ickes, Max Lerner, Robert Sherwood, William H. Standley, Lewis Mumford, George V. Strong, Betty Gram Swing, Edmond Taylor, H. E. Yarnell, William A. Eddy, Frank Kingdon, Henry Hobson, Carl J. Friedrich, Stringfellow Barr, and Andre Maurois.

39. Quote from Chadwin, *Warhawks,* 17; see also PPF 5684: Foreign Policy Association, 1933-41, FDR Papers.

40. Committee on Foreign Relations in John Winant Papers, FDR Papers; Douglas Miller, *Some Regional Views on Our Foreign Policy* (New York: Council on Foreign Relations, 1939), 195-212 passim; Lawrence Shoup and William Minter, *Imperial Brain Trust: The Council on Foreign Relations and United States Foreign Policy* (New York: Monthly Review Press, 1977), 26-28, 163.

41. For membership, see Appendix 5, Laurie, "Ideology and American Propaganda"; see also Council on Foreign Relations, *By-Laws and List of Officers and Members* (New York: CFR, 1938); idem, *Annual Report of the Executive Director* (New York: CFR, 1943); idem, *War and Peace Studies of the Council on Foreign Relations, 1939-1945* (New York: CFR, 1946), 121; idem, *The Council on Foreign Relations: A Record of Twenty-Five Years, 1921-1946* (New York: CFR, 1947), 64-75; Shoup and Minter, *Imperial Brain Trust,* 300-301.

42. Michael H. Hunt, *Ideology and United States Foreign Policy* (New Haven: Yale University Press, 1987), 136-37.

43. Robert D. Schulzinger, "What Ever Happened to the Council on Foreign Relations?" *Diplomatic History* 5 (1981): 278, 282–83.

44. Quotes from Shoup and Minter, *Imperial Brain Trust*, 26–28, 163, 165.

*Chapter 3. The Federal Government Defines a
Propaganda Role*

1. Richard W. Steele, *Propaganda in an Open Society: The Roosevelt Administration and the Media, 1933–1941* (Westport, Conn.: Greenwood Press, 1985), 71–72.

2. For an example, see Frank Knox's criticisms of the New Deal and FDR in *We Planned It That Way* (Toronto: Longmans, Green and Company, 1938). For FDR's interest in public opinion, see Michael Leigh, *Mobilizing Consent: Public Opinion and American Foreign Policy, 1937–1947* (Westport, Conn.: Greenwood Press, 1976), xiii, 21–22, 33; Richard W. Steele, "The Pulse of the People: Franklin D. Roosevelt and the Gauging of American Public Opinion," *Journal of Contemporary History* 9 (October 1974): 195, 208; and Philip E. Jacob, "Influences of World Events on U.S. 'Neutrality' Opinion," *Public Opinion Quarterly* 4 (March 1940): 48, 63–65.

3. Quote from Steele, *Propaganda in an Open Society*, ix–x; see also Sydney S. Weinberg, "Wartime Propaganda in a Democracy: America's Twentieth-Century Information Agencies" (Ph.D. diss., Columbia University, 1969), 139, 174; Leigh, *Mobilizing Consent*, 21–22; and Warren Kimball, *The Juggler: Franklin Roosevelt as Wartime Statesman* (Princeton: Princeton University Press, 1991).

4. "Propaganda by German Nazis in the United States," *New Republic* 4 (18 October 1933): 264.

5. Quote from "House Will Make Nazi Inquiry," *Newsweek*, 31 March 1934, 12; see also Sander A. Diamond, *The Nazi Movement in the United States, 1924–1941* (Ithaca, N.Y.: Cornell University Press, 1974), 158, 169, and Geoffrey Smith, *To Save A Nation: American Countersubversives, the New Deal, and the Coming of World War II* (New York: Basic Books, 1974), 96–97.

6. Alton Frye, *Nazi Germany and the American Hemisphere, 1933–1945* (New Haven: Yale University Press, 1967), 50–54, 58, 88–92, and "Should Congress Pass the Dickstein Bill?" *Congressional Digest* 14 (November 1935): 284–85.

7. Smith, *Save a Nation*, 150–51, and Diamond, *Nazi Movement*, 281, 323–24.

8. Quotes from "Mr. Dies Goes to Town," in Institute for Propaganda Analysis, *Propaganda Analysis*, 4 vols. (New York: Institute for Propaganda Analysis, 1942), 3:40, and "The Vanishing un-American," *New Republic* 103 (26 August 1940): 264. For the report, see U.S. Congress, House, Special Committee to Investigate un-American Activities in the U.S., *Investigation of un-American Activities in the United States*, 76th Cong., 3d sess., H. Rept. 2, 3 January 1939. For polls, see George Gallup, *The Gallup Poll: Public Opinion, 1935–1971*, vol. 1: *1935–1948* (New York: Random House, 1972), 11 December 1938, 1:128; 1 November 1939, 1:188; 15 December 1939, 1:195; 5 January 1940, 1:199; 4 December 1940, 1:252. Dies wrote a book about subversion devoting twenty-three of twenty-eight chapters to Communist groups (see Martin Dies, *The Trojan Horse in America* [New York: Dodd, Mead, 1940]).

9. Letter, Dies to FDR, 1 June 1940, and reply, 10 June 1940, PPF 3458: Dies, Mar-

tin, and letter, Dies to FDR, 27 Aug. 1940, and reply, 12 Sept. 1940, POF 1661a, FDR Papers.

10. Outlined in R. Keith Kane, "The OFF," *Public Opinion Quarterly* 6 (Summer 1942): 204–5.

11. Holly Shulman, "The Voice of Victory: The Development of American Propaganda and the Voice of America, 1920–1942" (Ph.D. diss., University of Maryland, 1984), 131.

12. Harold Lasswell, "The Organization of Psychological Warfare Agencies in World War I," in *A Psychological Warfare Casebook*, ed. William E. Daugherty and Morris Janowitz (Baltimore: Johns Hopkins University Press, 1958), 122, and Paul M. A. Linebarger, *Psychological Warfare* (Washington, D.C.: Combat Forces Press, 1954), 67–68.

13. Quote from William E. Daugherty, "United States Psychological Warfare Organizations in World War II," in Daugherty and Janowitz, eds., *Psychological Warfare Casebook*, 157. For earlier agencies, see Betty H. Winfield, *FDR and the News Media* (New York: Columbia University Press, 1994), chap. 5; E. Pendleton Herring, "Official Propaganda Under the New Deal," *Annals of the American Academy of Political and Social Science* 179 (May 1935): 167–75; Steele, *Propaganda in an Open Society*, 72–74; and idem, "Pulse of the People," 195–216.

14. Shulman, "Voice of Victory," 131, and Richard W. Steele, "Preparing the Public for War: Efforts to Establish a National Propaganda Agency, 1940–1941," *American Historical Review* 75 (October 1970): 1643–44.

15. On OGR, see Statement of Lowell Mellett Before the Committee on Expenditures in the Executive Departments, 11 February 1942, Lowell Mellett Papers, FDRL; and Thomas F. Troy, *Donovan and the CIA: A History of the Establishment of the CIA* (Frederick, Md.: University Publications of America, 1981), 121.

16. Steele, "Preparing the Public for War," 1642–43, and Troy, *Donovan and CIA*, 95.

17. Samuel I. Rosenman, com, *The Public Papers and Addresses of Franklin D. Roosevelt*, 13 vols. (New York: Random House, Macmillan Company, Harper and Brothers, 1938–1950), 9:198. Roosevelt's 16 May speech to Congress was reported by the *New York Times* on 17 May 1940.

18. Quotes from Rosenman, *Public Papers*, 9:38–39, and Robert F. Dallek, *Franklin D. Roosevelt and American Foreign Policy, 1932–1945* (New York: Oxford University Press, 1979), 225–26. See also FDR's references to the fifth column reported by the *New York Times* on 23 and 27 May and by the *New York Journal American* on 24 May. FDR's chat of 27 May was heard by an estimated 65 million people, a record to that time (see Winfield, *FDR and the Media*, 109).

19. Quote from Shulman, "Voice of Victory," 214; Steele, *Propaganda in an Open Society*, 83, 86–87; Minutes 2nd Meeting—Ickes Committee, Box 247, Ickes Papers.

20. Steele, "Preparing the Public for War," 1642–43, and idem, *Propaganda in an Open Society*, 85–86. A similar request was made by LaGuardia in October 1940.

21. Harold Ickes, *The Secret Diary of Harold Ickes*, 2 vols. (New York: Simon and Schuster, 1954), 1:368.

22. Letters, Ickes to Dykstra, Brownlow, Jackson, Mellett, Knox, Perkins, Stimson, McNutt, Walker, McCloy, 12 Nov. 1940, Box 379, Ickes Papers; see also Steele, *Propaganda in an Open Society*, 87–88, and Kai Bird, *The Chairman: John J. McCloy and the Making of the American Establishment* (New York: Simon and Schuster, 1992), 113–19, 126–

27. For biographical information, see "Statesman and Banker John J. McCloy, 93, Dies," *Washington Post*, 12 March 1989, 7, and *Current Biography, 1947*, 408–11. For the Black Tom Case, see Jules Witcover, *Sabotage at Black Tom: Imperial Germany's Secret War in America, 1914–1917* (Chapel Hill, N.C.: Algonquin Books, 1989).

23. Minutes of 1st Meeting—Ickes Committee, Box 247, Ickes Papers.

24. Ibid.

25. Ibid.

26. Steele, *Propaganda in an Open Society*, 87–89.

27. Minutes of 2nd Meeting—Ickes Committee, Box 247, Ickes Papers.

28. Ibid.

29. Tentative Draft: Report of Subcommittee, 20 Nov. 1940, pp. 1–4; and Memo, Padover to Ickes, 28 Nov. 1940, both in Box 379, Ickes Papers, LC.

30. Minutes of 3rd Meeting—Ickes Committee, 28 Nov. 1940, Box 247, Ickes Papers.

31. Ibid.

32. Report of Ickes to FDR, 28 Nov. 1940, POF 1661a: Fifth Column, 1941–45, FDR Papers; and Shulman, "Voice of Victory," 211–12, 234–36.

33. Memo, Cohen to Ickes, 17 Jan. 1941; memo, Ickes to Perkins and Wallace, 24 Jan. 1941; letter, Ickes to Cohen, 24 Jan. 1941; memo, Ickes to Biddle, Knox, McCloy; letter, Pope to Ickes, 21 Feb. 1941, all in Box 379, Ickes Papers; see also Ickes, *Secret Diary*, 1:419.

34. Committee on National Morale, *A Plan for a National Morale Service* (New York: Committee on National Morale, 1941), 1–2, explanatory index, 3ei, 5ei, 10ei.

35. Quotes from Committee on National Morale, *Plan for National Morale Service*, 3, 2ei, 12ei; see also "Dangerous for Democracies to Imitate Dictator Propaganda," *Science News Letter* 39 (18 January 1941): 39.

36. Ibid., 1–3.

37. First quote from Weinberg, "Wartime Propaganda," 163; see also letter, Ickes to Mellett, 29 Nov. 1940; and second quote in memo, Mellett to Ickes, 15 February 1941, Box 4, Mellett Papers.

38. Unsigned, undated letter given Ickes by Mellett, sub: Memo on Committee on National Morale, 15 February 1941, Box 379, Ickes Papers; for the same, see Memo, Mellett to Ickes, re: Committee on National Morale, 15 Feb. 1941, Box 4, Mellett Papers. Dr. Carl Friedrich of the Harvard School of Government, himself a member of the Committee on National Morale, was the author of the letter to Mellett (see Ickes, *Secret Diary*, 1:444–45).

39. Quotes from Ickes, *Secret Diary*, 1:419; see also Steele, *Propaganda in an Open Society*, 90–92, and letter, Ickes to Mellett, 18 Mar. 1941, Box 379, Ickes Papers.

40. Letter, Mellett to Ickes, 13 Mar. 1941, Box 4; and letter, Ickes to Mellett, 20 Feb. 1941, Box 379, both in Ickes Papers.

41. Quote from Ickes, *Secret Diary*, 1:444–45, 419.

42. Memo, Biddle to Ickes, 3 Mar. 1941, Box 379, Ickes Papers; and memo on the "Plan for a National Morale Service," Biddle to Mellett, 3 Mar. 1941, Box 4, Mellett Papers. For other critics see memo, Onslow to Ickes, 24 Mar. 1941, and memo, Straus to Ickes, 22 Mar. 1941, Box 379, Ickes Papers.

43. Letter, Knox to White, 3 Mar. 1941; letter, White to Knox, 14 Mar. 1941; letter, Knox to White, 22 Mar. 1941, Box 4, Knox Papers, LC.

44. Letter, McCloy to Biddle, 4 Mar. 1941, Box 379, Ickes Papers, LC.

45. Quotes from Ickes, *Secret Diary*, 1:419, 444–45; Steele, *Propaganda in an Open Society*, 90–92.

46. Letter, Pope to Ickes, 4 Mar. 1941, Box 379, Ickes Papers, LC.

47. Letter, Friedrich to Ickes, 8 Mar. 1941; letter, Ickes to Mellett, 8 Mar. 1941, Box 4, Mellett Papers; Ickes, *Secret Diary*, 2:518–21, 589.

48. Ickes, *Secret Diary*, 1:444–45.

49. Letter, FDR to Ickes, 3 Mar. 1941, and letter, Ickes to FDR, 6 Mar. 1941, POF 1661a: Fifth Column, 1941–45, FDR Papers. Ickes's list included James Baxter III, William C. Bullitt, Alfred Cohn, Elmer Davis, Marion Dix, George F. Eliot, Frank Graham, George Gallup, John Gunther, Thomas Huntington, Frank Kingdon, Ernest Kris, Henry Kingman, Henry Luce, Edgar A. Mowrer, Mrs. Dwight Morrow, Reinhold Niebuhr, Arthur Pope, Ralph Perry, Floyd Ruch, Charles Taft, and Dorothy Thompson.

50. Ickes, *Secret Diary*, 1:419; see also letter, Ickes to Mellett, 18 Mar. 1941, Box 4, Mellett Papers.

51. Letter, Pope to Ickes, 11 Apr. 1941, and letter, Pope to FDR, 11 May 1940, Box 379, Ickes Papers.

52. Letter, Ickes to Swope, 11 Aug. 1941; letter, Ickes to Swope, 9 Aug. 1941; letter, Swope to Ickes, 12 Aug. 1941; and letter, Ickes to FDR, 17 Sept. 1941, all in Box 379, Ickes Papers.

53. Quotes from Lowell Mellett, "Government Propaganda," *Atlantic* 168 (September 1941): 311–13. The OGR was abolished in June 1942. Mellett joined OWI and served as FDR's administrative assistant until returning to the *Washington Daily News*. See Letter of Resignation, Mellett to FDR, 22 Mar. 1944, POF 5659: L. Mellett, Mellett Papers.

54. Rosenman, *Public Papers*, 10:86–87, 191–92; Steele, "Preparing the Public for War," 1644–47; and memo for Gen. Watson, 19 Apr. 1941, POF 6095: Marshall Field, FDR Papers.

55. Quote from Ickes, *Secret Diary*, 1:505.

56. Steele, "Preparing the Public for War," 1649, and Ickes, *Secret Diary*, 2:518–21, 589.

57. Rosenman, *Public Papers*, 10:162–65; for OCD responsibilities, see 10:162–72.

58. Steele, "Preparing the Public for War," 1649–51; see also Kermit Roosevelt, *War Report of the OSS*, 2 vols. (New York: Walker, 1976), 1:10, 17.

59. Memo, Kintner to Rosenman, 26 Aug. 1941; letter, LaGuardia to Rosenman, 22 Aug. 1941, Samuel Rosenman Papers, FDRL; James P. Warburg, *Unwritten Treaty* (New York: Harcourt Brace Jovanovich, 1946), 90–91; Kane, "OFF," 204–20, 219; and Harold F. Gosnell, Bureau of the Budget, OFF, Box 12, Entry 6E, RG 208, NARA. LaGuardia remained OCD director until replaced by James M. Landis in January 1942.

60. Executive Order Establishing OFF Within OEM, Sept. 1941; Press Release Announcing OFF and its Functions, Rosenman Papers; Rosenman, *Public Papers*, 10:425–29; OFF—Statement of Functions and History, Box 6, Henry Pringle Papers, LC.

61. First quote from "Morale Defense: Its Nature and Organization," by R. R., 17 June 1941, Box 12, Rosenman Papers; Pringle quoted in OFF—Statement of Functions and History, Box 6, Pringle Papers.

62. Sydney Weinberg, "What to Tell America: The Writer's Quarrel in the Office of War Information," *Journal of American History* 55 (June 1968): 75.

63. Pringle quoted in OFF—Statement of Functions and History, Box 6, Pringle Papers. For members of OFF, see Appendix 6 in Laurie, "Ideology and American Propaganda" (Ph.D.) diss., American University, 1990); see also memo, Lewis to Pringle, 9 Jan. 1942, and Members of the BFF (OFF), 27 Jan. 1942, OEM–OFF Orders and General Memo, in Pringle Papers; OFF People; Description of Organizational Background, OFF, 11 Mar. 1942; Personnel and Administration Personnel OFF, 21 Jan. 1942, all in Box 12, Entry 6E, RG 208; OFF tel. dir., 21 Apr. 1942, Box 37, Arthur Sweetser Papers, LC; and U.S. Civil Service Commission, *Official Register of the United States, 1942* (Washington, D.C.: Government Printing Office, 1942), 20-21.

64. MacLeish wrote Samuel Rosenman that morale was so bad he had accepted thirty-eight resignations in six weeks, including those of Christian Herter, Henry Furst, and Dorothea Peters, who joined COI, and Vaughn Flannery, Philip Wylie, and Edward Shils, who joined FCC (see letter, MacLeish to Rosenman, 4 June 1942, re: Resignations, Rosenman Papers).

Chapter 4. Taking the Offensive

1. See Order Designating a COI, 11 July 1941, Box 80, Entry 99, RG 226; Kermit Roosevelt, *War Report of the OSS*, 2 vols. (New York: Walker, 1976), 1:8; Thomas Troy, *Donovan and the CIA: A History of the Establishment of the CIA* (Frederick, Md.: University Publications of America, 1981), 423; Samuel I. Rosenman, comp., *The Public Papers and Addresses of FDR*, 13 vols. (New York: Random House, Macmillan Company, Harper and Brothers, 1938-1950), 10:264-66; and William E. Daugherty, "United States Psychological Warfare Organizations in World War II," in *A Psychological Warfare Casebook*, ed. William E. Daugherty and Morris Janowitz (Baltimore: Johns Hopkins University Press, 1958), 127.

2. For interventionist admiration of some aspects of Nazi Germany, see Stephen J. Sniegoski, "Unified Democracy: An Aspect of American World War II Interventionist Thought, 1939-1941," *Maryland Historian* 9 (Spring 1978): 33-48.

3. OSS Prominent People, Box 97, Entry 99, RG 226, and Troy, *Donovan and CIA*, 24; see also Burton Hersh, *The Old Boys: The American Elite and the Origins of the CIA* (New York: Charles Scribners' Sons, 1982), 30-31. Donovan is alleged to have met future British SIS agent William Stephenson during this 1916 trip.

4. Robin Winks, *Cloak and Gown: Scholars in the Secret War, 1939-1961* (New York: William Morrow and Company, 1987), 64-65, and Ralph H. van Deman, *The Final Memoranda: Major General Ralph H. van Deman, USA, Ret., 1865-1952, Father of Military Intelligence* (Wilmington, Del.: Scholarly Resources, 1988), entries for 31 January 1919, 88; 8 February 1919, 88; and 17 March 1919, 89.

5. Anthony Cave-Brown, *The Last Hero: Wild Bill Donovan* (New York: Time-Life Books, 1982), 73-75, 77, 94-95, 97, 103, 115-16, 125; see also Ron Chernow, *The House of Morgan: An American Banking Dynasty and the Rise of Modern Finance* (New York: Atlantic Monthly Press, 1990), 211, and Hersh, *Old Boys*, 34, 55.

6. Troy, *Donovan and CIA*, 25-26.

7. Hersh, *Old Boys*, 55.

8. Entries for 15, 26 Dec. 1935, Ethiopian diary, Box 96A, and Ethiopian trip, 1935–36, Box 89 (1), Donovan Papers.

9. Entry for 16 Jan. 1936, Ethiopian diary, 1935–36, Box 96A; memo for Adj. Gen. from Simonds, 20 February 1936, Box 89 (1), Donovan Papers. American ambassador Hugh R. Wilson wrote that he received a telephone call from Donovan in Paris in January 1936 seeking Wilson's aid in setting up a meeting with British Foreign Secretary Anthony Eden. Wilson contacted Eden, who was most eager to see Donovan and arranged a London meeting that was canceled at the last minute due to the death of Britain's King George V; see Hugh R. Wilson, *Diplomat Between Wars* (New York: Longmans, Green and Company, 1941), 322. Burton Hersh claims Donovan did meet British intelligence chief William Wiseman at this time and provided him with information on the Italian military (see *Old Boys*, 55–56).

10. Hersh, *Old Boys*, 56–57.

11. Telegram, Lothian to Shepardson, 28 Jan. 1939; telegram, Shepardson to Lothian, 3 February 1939; telegram, Shepardson to Lothian, 8 February 1939, Box 7, Whitney Shepardson Papers, FDR Library. For Lothian see J. R. M. Butler, *Lord Lothian, Philip Kerr, 1882–1940* (New York: St. Martin's Press, 1960), 226–27.

12. Cave-Brown, *Last Hero*, 132–33; see also Hersh, *Old Boys*, 55–56.

13. Quotes from Troy, *Donovan and CIA*, 52–53; see also Cave-Brown, *Last Hero*, 133–39, 148.

14. Quotes from letter, Knox to FDR, 15 Dec. 1939, and reply, FDR to Knox, 29 Dec. 1939; see also letter, Knox to T. Roosevelt National Republican Club, 23 February 1935; letter, Frank to Annie Knox, 7 Aug. 1939, 1938–39, Box 4, Knox Papers; and Troy, *Donovan and CIA*, 30–31. For the popularity of FDR's decision, see George H. Gallup, *The Gallup Poll: Public Opinion, 1935–1971*, vol. 1: *1935–1948* (New York: Random House, 1972), 23.

15. Letter, Frank to Annie Knox, 6 July 1940, and letter, Frank to Annie Knox, 14 July 1940, Box 3, Knox Papers.

16. Quotes from Troy, *Donovan and CIA*, 54–55; see also William Stevenson, *A Man Called Intrepid* (New York: Ballantine Books, 1976), 84, and Paul Kramer, "Nelson Rockefeller and British Security Coordination," *Journal of Contemporary History* 16 (January 1981): 78–79, 82.

17. W. Deuel, "The COI as Originally Constituted," Box 70, Entry 99, RG 226; see also letter, Frank to Annie Knox, Box 3, Knox Papers.

18. Conyers Read Draft Hist.—OSS, Box 121A, Donovan Papers; see also Conyers Read Pre-COI Hist., Box 70, Entry 99, RG 226; Troy, *Donovan and CIA*, 31–33; Anthony Cave-Brown, *The Secret War Report of the OSS* (New York: Berkeley/Medallion Books, 1976), 42–43; and idem, *"C": The Secret Life of Sir Stewart Menzies, Spymaster to Winston Churchill* (New York: Macmillan, 1987), 264–69.

19. Read Pre-COI Hist., Box 70, Entry 99, RG 226; Cave-Brown, *The Last Hero*, 150–51; and Roosevelt, *War Report OSS*, 1:5–7. For the radio address, see remarks by Donovan on "National Defense Demands Conscription" over Station WGN, Chicago, 17 Aug. 1940, Box 2A, Donovan Papers. For Kennedy's role, see Jane Kardine Vieth, "The Donkey and the Lion: The Ambassadorship of Joseph Kennedy at the Court of St. James's, 1938–1940," *Michigan Academy of Science, Arts, and Letters* 10 (1978): 279–80, 279 n.15.

20. Cave-Brown, *"C,"* 264–69; idem, *Secret War Report,* 44; and idem, *Last Hero,* 150–51; see also Troy, *Donovan and CIA,* 38–39.

21. Quotes from Troy, *Donovan and CIA,* 38–39; see also Read Pre-COI Hist., and W. Deuel, "The COI as Originally Constituted," both in Box 70, Entry 99, RG 226, and "President On Way to Florida Vacation; Hears Donovan Report on Europe's Trend," *New York Times,* in Box 119A, Read Pre-COI no. 22, Donovan Papers.

22. Cave-Brown, *Last Hero,* 159.

23. Cave-Brown, *Last Hero,* 161; see also Troy, *Donovan and CIA,* 147, and letter, Knox to Felix Frankfurter, 22 May 1941, Box 4, Knox Papers, in which Knox complains that the president was not taking full advantage of Donovan's abilities.

24. Read Draft Hist., Box 122a, Donovan Papers; Cave-Brown, *Secret War Report,* 45; Roosevelt, *War Report OSS,* 1:7; and Troy, *Donovan and CIA,* 59, 61. For McCloy's role, see Kai Bird, *The Chairman: John J. McCloy and the Making of the American Establishment* (New York: Simon and Schuster, 1992), 54, 126–27, 129–30. McCloy first met Donovan at Pershing's AEF Headquarters in France in 1919. He suggested to Donovan the name "Office of the Coordinator of Information" in spring 1941 and gave him ideas for selling the concept to the president.

25. Troy, *Donovan and CIA,* 75, 81–83, and Cave-Brown, *Last Hero,* 162–63. The Secret Intelligence Service was the American Branch of Britain's BSC.

26. Quotes from Cave-Brown, *Last Hero,* 162–65; see also Memo of Establishment of Service of Strategic Information, Box 80, Entry 99, RG 226, and Roosevelt, *War Report OSS,* 1:7.

27. Cave-Brown, *Last Hero,* 162–65; James Warburg, *The Long Road Home: The Autobiography of a Maverick* (New York: Doubleday and Company, 1964), 189–91; for opposition, see letter, Knox to FDR, 25 June 1941, POF 4485: OSS, 1940–Oct. 1941, FDR Papers. For the order, see COI Documentation, Designating COI, 11 July 1941, Read Hist., Box 70, Entry 99, RG 226. The State Department had its own intelligence gathering unit at the time (see Ray Cline, "U.S. Foreign Intelligence, 1939–1945," *Foreign Service Journal* 53 [1976]: 18–19).

28. Quotes from Troy, *Donovan and CIA,* 75, 105; see also W. Deuel, "The COI as Originally Constituted," Box 70, Entry 99, RG 226.

29. Memo, Sherwood to Donovan, 16 June 1941, re: Personnel for FIS, Box 99B, Donovan Papers.

30. Robert E. Sherwood, Nov. 1942, Box 1, Entry 6E, RG 208.

31. Quotes from John Mason Brown, *The Ordeal of a Playwright: Robert E. Sherwood and the Challenge of War* (New York: Harper and Row, 1970), 46–47, and Robert E. Sherwood, Nov. 1942, Box 1, Entry 6E, RG 208. The book that so influenced Sherwood was G. E. R. Gedye, *Fallen Bastions: The Central European Tragedy* (London: Victor Gollancz, 1939).

32. Letter, Sherwood to Winchell, 2 Oct. 1938, PPF 7356: R. E. Sherwood, FDR Papers. Winchell sent this letter to FDR, bringing Sherwood to FDR's attention for the first time (see Sydney S. Weinberg, "Wartime Propaganda in a Democracy: America's Twentieth-Century Information Agencies" [Ph.D. diss., Columbia University, 1969], 147); see also Brown, *Ordeal,* 77–79, 82, and Walter J. Meserve, *Robert E. Sherwood: Reluctant Moralist* (New York: Pegasus, 1970), 144–45, 147–54.

33. Robert E. Sherwood, Nov. 1942, Box 1, Entry 6E, RG 208; Brown, *Ordeal,* 46–

47, 70–71, 77–79, 82; and Meserve, *Reluctant Moralist*, 144–45, 147–54. See also Robert Sherwood, *There Shall Be No Night* (New York: Charles Scribner's Sons, 1940).

34. Troy, *Donovan and CIA*, 78; Operations Research Office, *Views of World War II Psychological Warfare Personnel*, Technical Memorandum ORO-T-141 (Baltimore: Johns Hopkins University Press, 23 Nov. 1951), 21–59 passim, and Cave-Brown, *Last Hero*, 170–71; see also Brown, *Ordeal*, 91, 101–5; Meserve, *Reluctant Moralist*, 156, 159–60; and letter of intro., FDR to MacArthur, 20 Jan. 1945, PSF: R. E. Sherwood, FDR Papers.

35. The group included Donovan's former Justice Department law clerk James R. Murphy and New York lawyer William D. Whitney. Donovan recruited textile producer and World War I comrade Col. G. Edward "Ned" Buxton, who in turn recruited another army comrade, reporter John O'Keeffe. Donovan's law partners Richard Heppner and Otto Doering, Jr., joined, and recruited six others, including Edwin Putzell. Lawyer Allen Dulles joined and recruited Murray Gurfein, Arthur Goldberg, and Spencer Phenix. By August Donovan had hired John Magruder and Adm. William Standley, Williams College president James Baxter III, who recruited fellow academics Dewitt Poole of Princeton, University of California psychologist Robert C. Tryon, historians John Wheeler-Bennett, William Langer, and Donald C. McKay of Harvard, Conyers Read of Pennsylvania, and Walter L. Dorn of Ohio State, psychologists Donald T. Campbell and Joseph A. Gengerelli of the University of California, geographer Preston James and political scientist Joseph R. Hayden of the University of Michigan, John King Fairbank, economist Edward S. Mason and anthropologist Carleton S. Coons of Harvard, geographers Geroid Robinson of Columbia, James Preston of Michigan, Arthur H. Robinson of Ohio State, and Richard Hartshorne of Wisconsin, economist Calvin B. Hoover of North Carolina, Robert K. Gooch, Arthur Marder, Yale's Sherman Kent, Walter L. Wright, Jr., and Edward Mead Earle. Pollster Elmo Roper was recruited, as was Roper's friend Leslie T. Fossel. Donovan signed on foreign service officers David Williamson and John C. Wiley, former ambassador to Germany Hugh R. Wilson, lawyer Russell B. Livermore, New England textile manufacturer Howland Weston, publisher Victor Weybright, Assistant U.S. Attorney Malcolm Crusius, Sperry Corporation president Thomas A. Morgan, President Roosevelt's son James, Felix Frankfurter's sister Estelle, movie producers John Ford and Merian C. Cooper, writer Wilmarth Lewis, businessmen Atherton C. Richards, David K. E. Bruce, Whitney Shepardson, M. Preston Goodfellow, and William A. Kimbel. Thomas G. Early was recruited from the Civil Aeronautics Board and became COI's first executive officer, and William Phillips was hired from the State Department. Other early recruits included banker Malcolm Lovell and journalist Paul West, educator Hamilton Warren, journalist Arthur Eggleston, Jack Crutcher of NBC, economist Hubert C. Barton, Ralph Bunche, Kermit Roosevelt, Jr., Chandler Morse, writer Selden C. Menefee, Buford Junker, Edward Arluck, business consultant Frank L. Sweetser, Thomas Whitney, David K. Pinckney, and journalists Richard C. Hottelet and Adrian Berwick. For biographical information, see History of the OSS, Box 122A; and Exhibits Illustrating the History of OSS, 3: FIS, Box 99B, both in Donovan Papers; Washington Monthly Reports–COI 1941, COI Members, Oct. 1941 to Apr. 1942, Box 81; COI-Read Hist., pt. 2: COI, and W. Deuel, "The COI as Originally Constituted," both in Box 70; COI Members—July 1941, Box 71, all in Entry 99, RG 226; COI memo, 27 July 1942—London Office Personnel, Box 4, Entry 6G, RG 208; and Troy, *Donovan and CIA*, 78. See also Cave-Brown, *Last Hero*, 170–73, 183–84, 186–87, 275. For specific bio-

graphical sketches, for Murphy, see James G. Rogers, *Wartime Washington: The Secret OSS Journal of James Grafton Rogers, 1942–1943,* ed. Thomas Troy (Frederick, Md.: University Publications of America, 1987), 9, n.6, and Winks, *Cloak and Gown,* 260. For Whitney, see "William Whitney, Lawyer, 74, Dies," *New York Times,* 30 December 1973, 31. For Buxton, see Buxton, G. Edward, *National Cyclopedia of American Biography,* 426–27; Prominent OSS Members, Box 97, Entry 99, RG 226; and Col. G. E. Buxton, OSS Ex-Aide, Dead," *New York Times,* 27 March 1949, 1. For Heppner, see "Richard Heppner, Defense Aide, 49," *New York Times,* 15 May 1958, 29, and OSS Prominent People, Box 97, Entry 99, RG 226. For Baxter, see John E. Sawyer, "Obituary: James Phinney Baxter, 3d," *Proceedings of the American Antiquarian Society* 85 (1975): 357–60. For Doering, see OSS Prominent People, Box 97, Entry 99, RG 226; "Otto Doering, Former OSS Leader," *New York Times,* 14 July 1979, 24; and *Who's Who in America, 1976–1977,* 39:821. For Poole, see OSS Prominent People, Box 97, Entry 99, RG 226, and "Dewitt Poole Dies; Retired Diplomat," *New York Times,* 4 September 1952, 27. For Langer, see OSS Prominent People, Box 97, Entry 99, RG 226, and William L. Langer, *In and Out of the Ivory Tower: The Autobiography of William L. Langer* (New York: N. Watson Academic Publishers, 1977), 181, 184, 188. For McKay, see *New York Times,* 3 April 1959, 27. For Hartshorne, see OSS Prominent People, Box 97, Entry 99, RG 226. For Roper, see "Elmo Roper, Pollster, Is Dead, Predicted '36 Roosevelt Victory," *New York Times,* 1 May 1971, 36. For Wiley, see "John Cooper Wiley Dead at 73; Diplomat Served U.S. 38 Years," *New York Times,* 4 February 1967, 27. For Wilson, see "Hugh R. Wilson Dies; Envoy to Nazis, 61," *New York Times,* 30 December 1946, 19; OSS Prominent People, Box 97, Entry 99, RG 226; and Hugh R. Wilson, *A Career Diplomat* (Westport, Conn.: Greenwood Press, 1973). For Livermore, see OSS Prominent People, Box 97, Entry 99, RG 226, and "R. B. Livermore, Lawyer, 64, Dies," *New York Times,* 23 May 1958, 23. For Ford, see OSS Prominent People, Box 97, Entry 99, RG 226, and "John Ford, the Movie Director Who Won 5 Oscars, Dies at 78," *New York Times,* 1 September 1973, 2. For Lewis, see "Wilmarth S. Lewis, 83, Collector of Material on Horace Walpole," *New York Times Biographical Service,* 8 October 1979, 1376; "Wilmarth S. Lewis, 83, Horace Walpole Expert," *New York Times,* 8 October 1979, 13; and Winks, *Cloak and Gown,* 96–99. For Richards, see Rogers, 9 n.8, and OSS Prominent People, Box 97, Entry 99, RG 226. For Goodfellow, see OSS Prominent People, Box 97, Entry 99, RG 226, and "Col. M. Goodfellow, 81, Dies, Publisher of the Brooklyn Eagle," *New York Times Biographical Edition,* 6 September 1973, 1476.

36. Quote from Troy, *Donovan and CIA,* 87; see also Holly Shulman, "The Voice of Victory: The Development of American Propaganda and the Voice of America, 1920–1942" (Ph.D. diss., University of Maryland, 1984), 259, 268. For Sherwood's recruitment ideas, see memo, Sherwood to Donovan, 16 June 1941; memo, Sherwood to Donovan, 25 July 1941; memo, Sherwood to Donovan, 31 July 1941; memo, Sherwood to Donovan, 18 Aug. 1941; and memo, Sherwood to Donovan, 21 Aug. 1941, all in Box 99b, Donovan Papers. By mid-1942 Sherwood had hired journalist Edmond Taylor, public relations man Louis Cowan, *Newsweek* and former CBS executive Edward W. Barrett, Far Eastern experts Carl Crowe and Owen Lattimore, State Department employee Douglas Miller, James Warburg, journalist Wallace Deuel, the foreign editor of the *New York Herald Tribune* and former Berlin correspondent Joseph Barnes, CBS vice-president Murray Brophy, journalist Morris Gilbert, Nelson Poynter of the *St. Petersburg Times,* lawyer and busi-

nessman Edward Stanley, Scripps-Howard reporter and freelance journalist Edd Johnson then of CBS, Irving Pflaum of the *Chicago Times*, Hobart C. Montee of INS, publisher and Viking Press owner Harold K. Guinzburg, stage producer Werner Michel, Percy Winner of NBC, writer and director John Houseman, writer George Fielding Eliot, businessman Philip Hamblett, correspondent F. M. Fisher, Francis Miller, journalists Pierre J. Huss, Jay Allen, Yvonne Michele, editor and freelance writer Roger Burlingame, James Linen of *Time-Life*, journalists William Harlan Hale, Bjorne Braatoy, Frederick Oechsner, and Joseph C. Harsh, writer Ludwig Bemelmans, journalists Demaree Bess, Edgar A. Mowrer who worked for OFF, and *Foreign Affairs* editor Hamilton Fish Armstrong. For biographical sketches, see, for Cowan, *Who's Who in America, 1974–1975*, 666, and "Louis Cowan Killed with Wife in a Fire; Created Quiz Shows," *New York Times*, 19 November 1976, 1. For Barrett, see *Current Biography, 1947*, 35–36; *International Who's Who*, 108; and "Edward W. Barrett Dies; Started Columbia Journalism Review," *Washington Post*, 23 October 1989. For Lattimore, see Robert Newman, *Owen Lattimore and the Loss of China* (Berkeley: University of California Press, 1992), 92, 97–106. For Warburg, see Ron Chernow, *The Warburgs: The Twentieth Century Odyssey of a Remarkable Jewish Family* (New York: Random House, 1993), 521. For Deuel, see FFFC, 1941–42, *Eyewitnesses*, 12, POF: 4461, Box 1, FDR Papers; *Current Biography, 1942*, 192–94; and *New York Times Biographical Edition*, 12 May 1974, 667; see also Wallace Deuel, *People Under Hitler* (New York: Harcourt, Brace and Company, 1942), v. Deuel declined an offer to join the War Department PWB (see biographical sketch and letter, Deuel to Paul Scott Mowrer, 6 Aug. 1941; letter, Deuel to Black, MID/WDGS, 12 July 1941; and letter, Deuel to parents, 4 Apr. 1943, Wallace Deuel Papers, LC). For Barnes, see Biographical Sketch, Joseph Barnes Papers, LC; *Who Was Who, 1969–73*, 5:37; and "Joseph Barnes, a Senior Editor of Simon and Schuster, Dies at 62," *New York Times*, 2 March 1970, 37. For Gilbert, see *New York Times*, 14 July 1971, 38. For Poynter, see *Newsweek*, 26 June 1978, 47, and *New York Times*, 17 June 1978, 24. For Winner, see "Percy Winner Dies; Correspondent, 74," *New York Times*, 7 January 1974, 34. For Houseman, see *Current Biography, 1959*, 194–96, and *New York Times Biographical Edition*, 14 March 1972, 558–59. For Burlingame, see Roger Burlingame, *I Have Known Many Worlds* (Garden City, N.Y.: Doubleday and Company, 1959), 246–48, and "Roger Burlingame, Writer, Dies; A Biographer and Historian, 67," *New York Times*, 19 March 1967, 31. For Hale, see *New York Times*, 1 July 1974, 32. For Braatoy, see "Bjorne Braatoy, Socialist Leader," *New York Times*, 16 March 1957, 19. For Armstrong, see memo, Sherwood to Donovan, 16 June 1941, Box 71, Entry 99, RG 226.

37. Troy, *Donovan and CIA*, 85–87. During his COI and OWI employment, John Houseman, a Rumanian native, was not an American citizen and was technically an enemy alien (see John Houseman, *Run Through* [New York: Simon and Schuster, 1972], 23). For a biographical sketch, see "Hans Meyer, 77, of E. M. Warburg," *New York Times*, 28 June 1968, 41. For Rauschning and Lazareff, see memo, Sherwood to Donovan, 16 June 1941, Box 71, Entry 99, RG 226, and letter, Blow to Sherwood, 30 Dec. 1941, Box 99b, Donovan Papers.

38. Quote from Houseman, 26–27. See also Supplemental Budget Estimates COI-Fiscal 1942, Box 1, and COI-Read Hist., 2: COI, Box 70, Entry 99, both in RG 226.

39. W. Deuel, "The COI as Originally Constituted," Box 70, Entry 99, RG 226; U.S. Civil Service Commission, *Official Register of the United States, 1942* (Washington,

D.C.: Government Printing Office, 1942), 213–15; Winks, *Cloak and Gown,* 259–60; and Cave-Brown, *Last Hero,* 175–77.

40. In the budget approved on 7 November 1941 Intelligence Activities received $2,546,040, International Broadcasting (Short Wave) received $1.5 million, and International Broadcasting (Medium Wave) received $2 million (see Troy, *Donovan and CIA,* 112).

41. Supplemental Budget Estimates COI-Fiscal 1942, Box 1, Entry 146, RG 226, and 1941 Rept. FIS/COI, Box 5, Entry 6H, RG 208.

42. Sherwood quoted in Roosevelt, *War Report OSS,* 1:41; see also Shulman, "Voice of Victory," 299–300. For efforts to commandeer private transmitters, see memo, Donovan to FDR, 27 Jan. 1942, Box 71, Entry 99, RG 226.

43. COI-FIS Read Hist., Box 72, Entry 99, RG 226; Troy, *Donovan and CIA,* 93; and Roosevelt, *War Report OSS,* 1:14, 31–32, 36–37, 42–44, 46–47.

44. COI-FIS Read Hist., Box 72, Entry 99, RG 226.

45. Roosevelt, *War Report OSS,* 1:14, 31–32, 36–37, 42–44, 46–47; see also Robert L. Bishop, "The Overseas Branch of the Office of War Information" (Ph.D. diss., University of Wisconsin, 1966), 19. OWI outposts in May 1942 included Stockholm, Cape Town, Cairo, Istanbul, Chungking, Manila, New Delhi, Bern, London, Leopoldville, Brazzaville; they were also located in Iceland, Greenland, and Australia.

46. Warburg, *Long Road Home,* 189–91; Roosevelt, *War Report OSS,* 1:34–35; COI-FIS Read Hist., Box 72, Entry 99, RG 226. For FIS Propaganda Directives, Mar. and Apr. 1942, see Box 8, Entry 6E, and FIS and OWI Weekly propaganda directives for Germany, Mar. and Sept. 1942, Box 607, Entry 385, RG 208.

47. Edmond Taylor, *Awakening from History* (Boston: Gambit, 1969), 312, and History of the OSS, Box 122A, Donovan Papers.

Chapter 5. The Self-Destruction of COI

1. Quote from COI-FIS Read Hist., Box 72, Entry 99, RG 226.

2. Donovan quoted in Holly Shulman, "The Voice of Victory: The Development of American Propaganda and the Voice of America, 1920–1942" (Ph.D. diss., University of Maryland, 1984), 336.

3. First quote from Kermit Roosevelt, *War Report of the OSS,* 2 vols. (New York: Walker, 1976), 1:211; second quote from Anthony Cave-Brown, *The Last Hero: Wild Bill Donovan* (New York: Time-Life Books, 1982), 235; see also Ronald T. Farrar, ed., "Elmer Davis: Report to the President," *Journalism Monographs* 7 (August 1968), 11, and History of the OSS, Box 122A, Donovan Papers.

4. Quote from Roosevelt, *War Report OSS,* 1:16.

5. First Taylor quote from Bradley Smith, *The Shadow Warriors: The OSS and the Origins of the CIA* (New York: Basic Books, 1983), 70; other quotes from Edmond Taylor, *Awakening from History* (Boston: Gambit, 1969), 309–10, 314. Sherwood opposed black propaganda for the VOA but recognized it could be effective (see Roosevelt, *War Report OSS,* 1:34).

6. Roosevelt, *War Report OSS,* 1:10, 19, 211.

7. Alfred H. Paddock, Jr., *United States Army Special Warfare, Its Origins: Psychologi-*

cal and Unconventional Warfare, 1941–1962 (Washington, D.C.: National Defense University Press, 1982), 7.

8. Quotes from History of the OSS, Box 122A, Donovan Papers.

9. Ibid.

10. Houseman quoted in John Houseman, *Front and Center* (New York: Simon and Schuster, 1979), 45–46; see also COI-FIS Read Hist., Box 72, and memo, Sherwood to Donovan, 18 Jan. 1942, Box 72, both in Entry 99, RG 226.

11. Letter, Deuel to Bliss, 3 July 1942, Box 1, Wallace Deuel Papers, LC.

12. Quote from Thomas Troy, *Donovan and the CIA* (Frederick, Md.: University Publications of America, 1981), 87; see also Shulman, "Voice of Victory," 259, 268, and William E. Daugherty, "United States Psychological Warfare Organizations in World War II," in *A Psychological Warfare Casebook*, ed. William E. Daugherty and Morris Janowitz (Baltimore: Johns Hopkins University Press, 1958), 127.

13. Taylor quotes from History of OSS, Box 122A, Donovan Papers; Smith, *Shadow Warriors*, 70; and Taylor, *Awakening from History*, 309–10.

14. Quotes from Paddock, *Special Warfare*, 7; see also Cave-Brown, *Last Hero*, 235. For the British view, see Sidney Rogerson, *Propaganda in the Next War* (London: G. Bles, 1938), 47–48, 51–52, 61.

15. Memo, Sherwood to Donovan, 20 Oct. 1941, POF 4485: OSS, FDR Papers.

16. Robert E. Sherwood, Nov. 1942, Box 1, Entry 6E, RG 208.

17. MacLeish quoted in Sydney S. Weinberg, "Wartime Propaganda in a Democracy: America's Twentieth-Century Information Agencies" (Ph.D. diss., Columbia University), 1969, 70.

18. Robert Sherwood, "The Power of Truth," *Vital Speeches* 9 (1 November 1942), 61–62.

19. For Barnes's view, see Robert W. Pirsein, *The VOA: A History of the International Broadcasting Activities of the United States Government, 1940–1962* (New York: Arno Press, 1970), 44, 48. For Childs's view, see Harwood Childs and John Whitton, eds., *Propaganda by Shortwave* (Princeton: Princeton University Press, 1942), 344–45. For Deuel's view, see memo, Deuel to Donovan, 10 Nov. 1941, Box 71, Entry 99, RG 226. For Eliot's view, see report from G. F. Eliot, 11 Jan. 1942, PSF: COI, 1942, FDR Papers.

20. Quote from COI-FIS Read Hist., Box 72, Entry 99, RG 226; for quote on Donovan's management style, see Burton Hersh, *Old Boys: The American Elite and the Origins of the CIA* (New York: Charles Scribner's Sons, 1982), 85; see also Paddock, *Special Warfare*, 7, and Roosevelt, *War Report OSS*, 1:34. Deuel told his parents that "the armed forces haven't thought enough about political and psychological warfare to be very good at running an outfit like ours" (see letter, Deuel to parents, 22 Apr. 1942, Box 1, Deuel Papers).

21. Quotes from COI-FIS Read Hist., Box 72, Entry 99, RG 226; and History of OSS, Box 122A, Donovan Papers; see also Weinberg, "Wartime Propaganda," 218 n.1.

22. Memo, Sherwood to Donovan, 18 Jan. 1942, Box 72, Entry 99, RG 226.

23. Calvin B. Hoover, *Memoirs of Capitalism, Communism and Nazism* (Durham, N.C.: Duke University Press, 1965), 196.

24. History of OSS, Box 122A, Donovan Papers.

25. Letter, Warburg to Donovan, 21 Aug. 1941; letter, Donovan to Warburg, 26 Aug.

1941; letter, Warburg to Donovan, 27 Aug. 1941, Box 99B, Donovan Papers; Houseman, *Front and Center*, 32–33.

26. Quotes from Langer in Walter C. Langer, *The Mind of Adolf Hitler: The Secret Wartime Report* (New York: Basic Books, 1972), v, 3–7, and report, Walter Langer to Donovan, 13 Nov. 1941, Box 71, Entry 99, RG 226. In January 1942 Langer wrote another memo, "Recommendations and suggestions on Shortwave broadcasts to Germany." It outlined what he hoped PFU could do for FIS (see World Situation, 1941–42, Box 5, Entry 6H, RG 208).

27. Memo, Sherwood to Donovan, re: Langer memo of 13 Nov., Box 71, Entry 99, RG 226. For Langer's resignation, see FIS-COI Read Hist., Box 70, and Box 71, both in Entry 99, RG 226; see also Langer, *Mind of Adolf Hitler*, 8.

28. Quote from memo, Sherwood to Donovan, 20 Oct. 1941, POF 4485: OSS, FDR Papers.

29. Memo, Whitney to Donovan, 8 Jan. 1942, Box 99A, Donovan Papers; for Richards's quote, see Hersh, *Old Boys*, 85; for Donovan's reaction, see Troy, *Donovan and CIA*, 117–18.

30. Houseman quote from Houseman, *Front and Center*, 24–25. For the plethora of agencies, see Roger Burlingame, *Don't Let Them Scare You: The Life and Times of Elmer Davis* (Westport, Conn.: Greenwood Press, 1974), 184–85; see also letter, Daniels to FDR, 27 May 1942, POF 5015: OWI, FDR Papers; and Weinberg, "Wartime Propaganda," 208–9.

31. Report and Sherwood quoted in Troy, *Donovan and CIA*, 121–22; see also Weinberg, "Wartime Propaganda," 208–9.

32. Troy, *Donovan and CIA*, 121–22; see also COI-FIS Read Hist., Box 72, Entry 99, RG 226.

33. Memo, Donovan to Branch Heads, 10 February 1942; memo, Roper to Donovan, 11 February 1941, both in Box 99A, Donovan Papers.

34. Memo, Donovan to FDR, 4 Mar. 1942, Box 119A, Donovan Papers, and Roosevelt, *War Report OSS*, 1:21.

35. Memo, Smith to FDR, 7 Mar. 1942, Box 99A, Donovan Papers; and Weinberg, "Wartime Propaganda," 209–10. The agencies Smith used as examples were OFF, the OEM Division of Information, OGR, COI, CIAA, and State, War, and Navy Department programs.

36. Conference with the president, 2:00 P.M., Sat. 7 Mar. 1942, Box 3, Harold D. Smith Papers, FDR Papers.

37. Quotes from Troy, *Donovan and CIA*, 104, 164. For State Department reactions, see James Warburg, *Unwritten Treaty* (New York: Harcourt Brace Jovanovich, 1946), 73, 84–85; Weinberg, "Wartime Propaganda," 215–16; Paul Kramer, "Nelson Rockefeller and British Security Coordination," *Journal of Contemporary History* 16 (January 1981): 73–88; and memo, Smith to FDR, 17 Mar. 1942, re: S. Welles letter, POF 5015: OWI, FDR Papers.

38. For reference to Sherwood's memo to FDR, see Troy, *Donovan and CIA*, 126, 128. For Smith's budget synopsis, see p. 2, item 8, War Information Services, Box 4, Mellett Papers.

39. For Britain's view of psychological warfare, see Robert H. Keyserlingk, "Political Warfare Illusions: Otto Strasser and Britain's World War Two Strategy of National Re-

volts Against Hitler," *Dalhousie Review* 61 (Spring 1981): 72–75, and Troy, *Donovan and CIA*, 129.

40. Joint Chiefs of Staff, *Organization and Development of the Joint Chiefs of Staff, 1942–1987* (Washington, D.C.: Joint Secretariat, JCS, 1987), 2–3, 5, and Vernon E. Davis, *History of the Joint Chiefs of Staff in World War II*, 2 vols. (Washington, D.C.: JCS Historical Section, 1953). For JCS membership, see Troy, *Donovan and CIA*, 129, 131, and James G. Rogers, *Wartime Washington: The Secret OSS Journal of James Grafton Rogers, 1942–1943*, ed. Thomas Troy (Frederick, Md.: University Publications of America, 1987), xxiii–xxiv.

41. Quotes from Troy, *Donovan and CIA*, 131–32, and JCS, 5; see also Paddock, *Special Warfare*, 11. For JSP membership, see JCS, 4. For the definition of psychological warfare, see Roosevelt, *War Report OSS*, 1:33.

42. Smith and Denebrink quoted in Troy, *Donovan and CIA*, 136. For third quote see Hersh, *Old Boys*, 84.

43. Memo, Donovan to FDR, 16 Mar. 1942, Box 119A, Donovan Papers.

44. Troy, *Donovan and CIA*, 132, 137, and Paddock, *Special Warfare*.

45. Troy, *Donovan and CIA*, 138.

46. For Donovan's accident, letter, Donovan to FDR, 14 Apr. 1942, PSF: COI, 1942, FDR Papers; and Cave-Brown, *Last Hero*, 218–22. For activities in Donovan's absence and Smith's quote, see Conference with the President, Sat. 4 Apr. 1942, and White House Conference, Fri. 10 Apr. 1942, 3:30 P.M., both in Box 3, Smith Papers, and memo, Biddle to FDR, 26 Mar. 1942, POF 5015: OWI, all FDR Papers.

47. Quotes from memo, Donovan to FDR, 14 Apr. 1942, PSF: COI, 1942, Box 141, FDR Papers; see also Weinberg, "Wartime Propaganda," 226–27; Cave-Brown, *Last Hero*, 235; and Troy, *Donovan and CIA*, 145.

48. Preliminary Report, Reorganization Committee to Donovan, 2 Mar. 1942. A further list of recommended changes, constituting some fine-tuning, was sent on 24 April, with the final record draft being made on 25 April (see memo, Early to Donovan, 24 Apr. 1942, and memo, Early to Donovan, 25 Apr. 1942, all in Box 99A, Donovan Papers).

49. Memo, Sherwood to Donovan, ca. Apr. 1942; memo, Sherwood and Guinzburg to Donovan, 7 Apr. 1942, Box 99B; and History of OSS, Box 122A, all in Donovan Papers; see also COI-FIS Read Hist., Box 72, and memo, Roper to Donovan, 13 May 1942, Box 71, both in Entry 99, RG 226.

50. Memo, Donovan to FDR, 16 May 1942, PSF: COI, 1942, Box 141, FDR Papers.

51. Donovan quoted in COI-FIS Read Hist., Box 72, Entry 99, RG 226; see also Troy, *Donovan and CIA*, 149–50; letter, MacLeish to FDR, 18 May 1942, POF 4619: OFF, FDR Papers, containing Smith's grievances.

52. Letter, FDR to Sherwood, 13 June 1942, POF 4485: OSS, FDR Papers; see also COI-FIS Read Hist., Box 72, Entry 99, RG 226, and Troy, *Donovan and CIA*, 149–50. For the military order, see Box 80, Entry 99, RG 226.

53. For membership numbers, see COI Statistical Report for Year Ending 30 June 1942, Box 81, Entry 99, RG 226; Cave-Brown, *Last Hero*, 235; and Farrar, ed., "Elmer Davis: Report," 11. For Taylor quote, see Taylor, *Awakening from History*, 319. For Deuel, see letter, Sherwood to Deuel, 2 July 1942; letter, Deuel to Sherwood, 3 July 1942; cable,

Donovan to Deuel, 22 July 1942, Box 61, Deuel Papers; and COI-FIS Read Hist., Box 72, Entry 99, RG 226. Deuel made a career in OSS-CIA, retiring in 1972.

Chapter 6. The Menagerie of the Old Guard of the New Deal

1. For Executive Order 9182 and quotes, see Thomas Troy, *Donovan and the CIA: A History of the Establishment of the CIA* (Frederick, Md.: University Publications of America, 1981), 424–26; see also James Warburg, *Unwritten Treaty* (New York: Harcourt Brace Jovanovich, 1946), 91–95, and Kermit Roosevelt, *War Report of the OSS*, 2 vols. (New York: Walker, 1976), 1:212. For pre-OWI and post-OWI government information services, see Paul M. A. Linebarger, *Psychological Warfare* (Washington, D.C.: Combat Forces Press, 1954), 95.

2. Warburg, *Unwritten Treaty*, 82–83.

3. POF 5015: OWI misc., FDR Papers.

4. Quotes from *New York Times*, 3. Biographical Sketch, Elmer Davis Papers, LC; Mark L. Chadwin, *The Warhawks: American Interventionists Before Pearl Harbor* (New York: W. W. Norton Company, 1968), 55; *National Cyclopedia of American Biography*, 13; and "Elmer Davis, Newsman, Is Dead; Broadcaster, 68, Headed OWI," *New York Times*, 18 May 1958, 3.

5. Quotes from *New York Times*, 3; see also Chadwin, *Warhawks*, 56; "ABC of OWI," *Newsweek*, 20 July 1942, 70; Roger Burlingame, *Don't Let Them Scare You: The Life and Times of Elmer Davis* (Westport, Conn.: Greenwood Press, 1974), 183–86; and Troy, *Donovan and CIA*, 126, 138, 148–49.

6. Quotes from Holly Shulman, "The Voice of Victory: American Propaganda and the Voice of America, 1920–1942" (Ph.D. diss., University of Maryland, 1984), 390–93; see also W. Phillip Davison, "Policy Coordination in OWI," in *A Psychological Warfare Casebook*, ed. William E. Daugherty and Morris Janowitz (Baltimore: Johns Hopkins University Press, 1958), 307.

7. Davison, "Policy Coordination," 307.

8. Letter, Creel to Davis, 4 Aug. 1942, Box 1, Davis Papers. Smith's daily log, for example, shows that he spoke at length with Davis about OWI matters three times in the three days after OWI was formed. No calls were made to Donovan. See Smith daily record, 15, 16, 17 June 1942, daily rec., 1942, Smith Papers.

9. For organization and initial recruiting efforts, see Domestic OWI, Box 27, Pringle Papers. For biographical sketches, see, for Barnes, *Who's Who in America, 1951–1952*, 144. For Eisenhower, see *Current Biography, 1946*, 173–75; *Who's Who in America, 1944–1945*, 611; and Steven Ambrose and Richard H. Immerman, *Milton S. Eisenhower, Educational Statesman* (Baltimore: Johns Hopkins University Press, 1983). For Siepmann, see "Charles Siepmann, Early Critic of Broadcasting," *New York Times Biographical Service*, 22 March 1985, 361–26. For Cowles, see *Current Biography 1943*, 145–48.

10. For members of abolished agencies who joined OWI, see Appendix 7, in Clayton D. Laurie, "Ideology and American Propaganda: The Psychological Warfare Campaign Against Nazi Germany, 1941–1945" (Ph.D. diss., American University, 1990); William E. Daugherty, "United States Psychological Warfare Agencies in World War II," in

Daugherty and Janowitz, eds., *Psychological Warfare Casebook*, 128; OWI Immediate Release, 10 July 1942, Box 38, Arthur Sweetser Papers; Domestic OWI, Box 27, Pringle Papers; and U.S. Civil Service Commission, *Official Register of the United States, 1941, 1942, 1943* (Washington, D.C.: Government Printing Office, 1941–1943), 28–29. For an organization chart of OWI, see Linebarger, *Psychological Warfare*, 180. The most comprehensive account of the OWI Domestic Branch remains Allan M. Winkler, *The Politics of Propaganda: The Office of War Information, 1942–1945* (New Haven: Yale University Press, 1978).

11. For FIS members transferring to the Overseas OWI, see Appendix 7, in Laurie, "Ideology and American Propaganda." For other documents revealing the Overseas OWI membership between 1942 and 1945, see Minutes, 17th meeting Joint Committee of Information Policy, 17 Dec. 1942; 19th meeting, 31 Dec. 1942; 20th meeting, 14 Jan. 1943; 21st meeting, 22 Jan. 1943, Box 11; report, London OWI, 15 Nov. to 15 Dec. 1943, Box 3, both in Entry 6J; Personnel Area 1, OWI, 9 Nov. 1944, Box 1, Entry 6C, all in RG 208; see also memo, Davis to Branch Directors, Bureau Chiefs, Administrative Officers, Heads of Outposts, 20 Sept. 1944, Box 38, Sweetser Papers; and John Pollard, "Words Are Cheaper Than Blood," *Public Opinion Quarterly* 9 (Fall 1945): 296–300. Among OWI personnel recruited after July 1942 were psychology professor Heinz L. Ansbacher and Classics professor Frank E. Brown, both of Brown University; Frick Collection curator H. Harvard Arnason; oilman, investor, and Yale German instructor Jacques Arouet; *New York Post* correspondent Leonard Carlton; *Time Magazine, Fortune,* and *Life Magazine* executive Bernard Barnes; *Detroit News* correspondent Russell Barnes; McClure Syndicate reporter Alan Barth; University of Chicago professor Eric Bellquist; newspaper and magazine editor Harold Berman, *New Yorker* writer Morris Bishop; *Paris Herald* correspondents William Bird, Ralph Jules Frantz, and George Rehm; *Chicago Tribune* and *Paris Times* correspondent Lawrence G. Blochman; *New York Mirror* correspondent and free lance writer Sam Boal; publishers C. D. Jackson, Paul Brooks, Cass Canfield, C. Raymond Everitt, and George Stevens; nightclub entertainer, circus performer, and sometime Shakespearean actor Yul Brynner; *Newsweek* editor and former INS and *New York Herald Tribune* European correspondent Loren Carroll; FBIS propaganda analysts Harwood Childs and Hans Speier; attorney Richard A. Condon; *San Francisco Chronicle* reporter Arthur Eggleston; artist and illustrator Robert Fawcett; *New York World* correspondent William M. Laas, French anthropologist Claude Levi-Strauss; Harvard and Duke University professor and Far Eastern expert Paul M. A. Linebarger; *Buffalo Times* and *PM* writer George H. Lyon; lawyer and *PM* and *New York Herald Tribune* correspondent Leo J. Margolin; CBS executives William S. Paley, Edward Klauber, and Brewster B. Morgan; NBC executive Kenneth D. Fry; NBC foreign language translator Gerald M. Mayer; screen writer and *New York Evening Post* and *New York World* reporter Oliver H. Garrett; Long Island University history professor Leo Gershoy; *Christian Science Monitor* reporter Reuben H. Markham; Cornell Romance Languages professor Charles R. Morey; Interior Department official Saul Padover; managing editor of *Newsweek* Joseph Phillips; U.S. Army Maj. Charles A. H. Thomson; Columbia University psychologist Thomas Reese; *New York Times* London correspondent James Reston; Harvard University fellow Arthur Schlesinger, Jr.; playwright Samuel Spewack; AP correspondent Alfred Stefferud; political science professor, historian, and Far Eastern expert George E. Taylor; educator Hamilton Warren; UP, AP, *Chicago Sun* reporter, and *Newsweek* editor

Llewellyn B. White; *New York Herald Tribune* reporter William Chapman White; and Cornell University sociologist Julian L. Woodward. For biographical information, see, for Arnason, *Who's Who in America, 1974–1975,* 992. For Frantz, see "Ralph Frantz Is Dead at 77," and "*Herald Tribune* Editor," both in *New York Times,* 4 November 1979, 44. For Blochman, see "Lawrence Blochman, 74, Dead; Correspondent, Mystery Writer," *New York Times,* 22 January 1975, 36. For Boal, see "Fire Kills Diner's Club Editor in His Apartment in E. 57th St.," *New York Times,* 29 September 1964, 18. For Jackson, see *Current Biography, 1952,* 298–300. For Carroll, see *Who's Who, 1950–1951,* 437. For Lyon, see "George Lyon Dies; Ex-Editor Was 80," *New York Times,* 17 February 1972, 42. For Paley, see William Paley, *As It Happened: A Memoir* (Garden City, N.Y.: Doubleday and Company, 1979), 155–57, 162–66, and *Who's Who in America, 1984–1994,* 2507. For Klauber, see "Edward Klauber, CBS Official, Dies," *New York Times,* 24 September 1954, 23, and William L. Shirer, *The Nightmare Years, 1930–1940, A Twentieth Century Journey* (Boston: Little, Brown and Company, 1984), 414. For Morgan, see "Brewster Morgan, Radio, TV Producer," *New York Times,* 29 December 1960, 25, and Brewster Morgan, " 'Operation Annie': [The US] Army Radio Station That Fooled the Nazis by Telling Them the Truth," *Saturday Evening Post,* 9 March 1946, 18. For Mayer, see "Gerald Mayer, 74; Honored for His Work in Allied Intelligence," *New York Times,* 7 January 1980, 10. For Garrett, see "O. Garrett, 54, Film Writer Dies," *New York Times,* 24 February 1952, 84. For Markham, see "Reuben Markham, Writer, 62, Dead," *New York Times,* 31 December 1949, 15, and *Eyewitnesses,* POF 4461: FFFC, Box 1, FDR Papers. For White, see "L. B. White Dead; Ex-Aide of U.S., 59," *New York Times,* 16 May 1959, 23.

12. Clayton Koppes and Gregory Black, "What to Show the World," *Journal of American History* 64 (June 1977): 88. For a British perspective of OWI from the leader of PWE, see Robert Bruce Lockhart, *Comes the Reckoning* (London: G. Putnam, 1947), 181–82.

13. James G. Rogers, *Wartime Washington: The Secret OSS Journal of James Grafton Rogers, 1942–1943,* ed. Thomas Troy (Frederick, Md.: University Publications of America, 1987), 17.

14. Quote from Robert L. Bishop, "The Overseas Branch of the Office of War Information" (Ph.D. diss., University of Wisconsin, 1966), 180–81; for the decision to hire Cowles, see Koppes and Black, "What to Show," 88.

15. Joseph Barnes, "Fighting with Information: OWI Overseas," *Public Opinion Quarterly* 7 (Spring 1943): 34–35, 38. For a critique of propaganda policy as it stood, see Stefan T. Possony, "Needed—A New Propaganda Approach to Germany," *Public Opinion Quarterly* 6 (Fall 1942): 335–50.

16. James Warburg, *Foreign Policy Begins at Home* (New York: Harcourt, Brace and World, 1944), v, 4, 6–7, 9, 13–14, 33, 108, 174.

17. "Psychological Warfare," *Life,* 13 December 1945, 81, and Bishop, "Overseas Branch," 95; see also Operations Research Office, *Views of World War II Psychological Warfare Personnel,* Technical Memorandum T-141 (Baltimore: Johns Hopkins University Press, 23 November 1951), 221–30, and James Erdmann, *Leaflet Operations in the Second World War . . .* (Denver: University of Denver, 1969), 214–15. OWI training was conducted at Berkeley, California; the Iranian Institute, Long Island, New York; Camp Ritchie, near Thurmont, Maryland; Quantico, Virginia; Bethesda, Maryland; Camp

Sharpe, near Gettysburg, Pennsylvania; Oshawa, Canada; and Brondesbury and Clevedon, England.

18. "U.S. Arsenal of Words," *Fortune* 27 (March 1943): 83–85.

19. Lester Hawkins, Jr., and George S. Pettee, "OWI Organization and Problems," *Public Opinion Quarterly* 7 (Spring 1943): 15, 28–29, and Establishing Regional Divisions in the Immediate Office of the Director of the Overseas Branch, Memo to All Offices OWI Overseas Branch, 17 Dec. 1942, Box 1, Entry 6B, RG 208; see also Leonard Doob, "The Utilization of Social Scientists in the Overseas Branch of the [U.S.] Office of War Information," *American Political Science Review* 41 (August 1947): 650–51, 654; "U.S. Propaganda," *Time*, 12 October 1942, 44; Bishop, "Overseas Branch," 57–60; Robert W. Pirsein, *The VOA: A History of the International Broadcasting Activities of the United States Government, 1940–1962* (New York: Arno Press, 1979), 51–52; Charles A. H. Thomson, *The Overseas Information Service of the United States Government* (Washington, D.C.: Brookings Institution, 1948), 67–71; and *Civil Service Register, 1943*, 29–30.

20. Winkler, *Politics of Propaganda*, 78.

21. Pirsein, *VOA*, 51–52, 90–91, and Bishop, "Overseas Branch," 75–76. For stations, see "U.S. Takes Over Short Waves to Win Air Propaganda War," *Newsweek*, 19 October 1942, 30–31. For VOA French Desk members, see John Houseman, *Front and Center* (New York: Simon and Schuster, 1979), 53–54; see also Morris Janowitz, "Language and Idiom," in Daugherty and Janowitz, eds., *Psychological Warfare Casebook*, 609–11.

22. Quote from OWI Overseas Operations Branch: Eastern Press and Radio Bureau, Box 1, Entry 6B, RG 208. See also Elmer Davis, "What OWI Is Doing," *Saturday Review of Literature* 25 (5 December 1942): 9; Commentators, Feb. 1943–Dec. 1944, Box 3473, Entry 554, RG 208; "U.S. Takes Over Short Waves," 30; and Lawrence C. Soley, *Radio Warfare: OSS and CIA Subversive Propaganda* (Westport, Conn.: Praeger, 1989). For broadcast transcripts and VOA German texts, see "Hier Spricht der Stimme Amerikas," Box 1, Entry 6C, RG 208.

23. Bishop, "Overseas Branch," 60; Winkler, *Politics of Propaganda*, 78; Linebarger, *Psychological Warfare*, 179, 181, 206–8; and "U.S. Arsenal of Words," 83–85.

24. For this complex, time-consuming, and ultimately failed process, see William E. Daugherty, "Policy Goals and Planning in Psychological Warfare," in Daugherty and Janowitz, eds., *Psychological Warfare Casebook*, 259; and Shulman, "Voice of Victory," 318, 333n, 382–87; see also Establishing Regional Divisions in the Immediate Office of the Director of the Overseas Branch, memo to all Offices OWI Overseas Branch, 17 Dec. 1942, Box 1, Entry 6B, RG 208; Michael Darrocks, "Davis and Goliath," *Harper's* 186 (February 1943): 231; "Elmer Davis Heads OWI," *Publisher's Weekly* 141 (20 June 1942): 2265; and "U.S. Propaganda," *Time*, 12 October 1942, 44.

25. Quote from Overseas Planning and Intelligence Board, Box 1, Entry 6B, RG 208; for an OWI insider's account of the planning board meetings, see Wallace Carroll, *Persuade or Perish* (Boston: Houghton Mifflin Company, 1948), 235–37.

26. Carroll, *Persuade or Perish*, 234–35, and Thomson, *Overseas Information*, 52n, 47–50. Overseas Central and Weekly Directives (Apr. 1943–May 1945) are in Boxes 212, 217, 218, Entry 365; for PWB Directives, see Box 2, Entry 6G, RG 208.

27. Thomson, *Overseas Information*, 52n, 47–50.

28. Quote from Bishop, "Overseas Branch," 401, 404, 408. For OWI administrative output, see suggestions for 9:30 A.M. meeting, Apr. 1943–Sept. 1944, Box 128; 2:30 meeting

notes, Oct. 1942–31 Dec. 1942; 2:30 meeting notes to Lattimore—San Francisco, Jan. to Mar. 1943; Special OWI Guidance, 28 June 1942, Guidance Notes, May 1942–Jan. 1943, all in Box 607, Entry 385; and morning and afternoon reports, Box 129, and cables, Intelligence—London, Box 129, both in Entry 361, RG 208. For more detailed descriptions, see Pirsein, *VOA*, 71, and Thomson, *Overseas Information*, 52n, 47–50.

29. Carroll, *Persuade or Perish*, 234–35; Shulman, "Voice of Victory," 395–97, 401; for examples of Warburg's work, see Overseas Planning and Intelligence Board, Box 1, Entry 6B, RG 208.

30. For complaints and improvements, see memo, Schneider to Barrett, 18 July 1944, and Overseas Planning and Intelligence Board, both in Box 1, Entry 6B, RG 208.

31. Thomson, *Overseas Information*, 69–71; Bishop, "Overseas Branch," 183, 214. For examples of intelligence traffic, see cables, Intelligence—London, Box 129, Entry 361; OWI Official Dispatches, Jan. 1943–4 Dec. 1945, Box 108, Entry 358, RG 208.

32. Carroll, *Persuade or Perish*, 128, 130, 135; Ronald Farrar, ed., "Elmer Davis: Report to the President," *Journalism Monographs* 7 (August 1968): 70–71. For the cost, growth, and eventual size of the London operation, see memo, Kuhn to Barrett and Barnard, re: OWI Budget, 25 Aug. 1944, Box 2, Entry 6G, RG 208; see also Winkler, *Politics of Propaganda*, 125–26; Bishop, "Overseas Branch," 183, 214; Thomson, *Overseas Information*, 69–71; Warburg, *Unwritten Treaty*, 98–100; and Carroll, *Persuade or Perish*, 130–35. Of the 2,537 OWI employees in London on 25 August 1944, only 642 were American citizens; the remainder were British nationals hired for clerical positions.

33. For ABSIE membership and activities, see Budget Justification, Radio Division, OWI London, Box 3, Entry 6J, RG 208; see also Edward Kirby and Jack W. Harris, *Star-Spangled Radio* (Chicago: Ziff Davis, 1948), 58, 121, 271.

34. William Daugherty, "The Role of Intelligence, Research, and Analysis in Psychological Warfare," in Daugherty and Janowitz, eds., in *Psychological Warfare Casebook*, 425–28, and Doob, "Utilization of Social Scientists," 652–53. For examples of combined directives, see Box 830, Entry 363, RG 208. For PWE Directives, see PWE Weekly German Regional Directives for BBC, 13–20 Oct. 1944 / 18–24 February 1945, Box 4, Entry 87, RG 331.

35. Quote from Shulman, "Voice of Victory," 382–88; see also memo, Carroll to Davis, 15 Aug. 1943, re: memo from Bracken to Carroll, 15 Aug. 1943; OWI Official Dispatch to London from Davis, Barrett to Sherwood, Jackson, Hamblet, 23 Mar. 1944; see also OWI Official dispatches from Wash. to N.Y., 12 July to 13 February 1945; memo, Carroll to Thomson, 21 July 1944, re: Relations with British, OWI-PWE Lines; OWI Morning Guidance, cables from Carroll, London, from Thomson, OWI, 31 July 1943 to 20 Apr. 1943; all in Box 830, Entry 363, RG 208. For instructions to OWI personnel regarding British directives, see OWI Official Dispatches, Joint Algiers Directive from London, 16, 23 Aug. 1944, and 22 Feb., 9, 15, 29 Mar., 5, 20 Apr. 1945, and Joint PWE-OWI Dir. to Algiers from London, 25 June 1943–25 May 1945, all in Box 830, Entry 363, RG 208.

Chapter 7. The Bargain Basement of the Military

1. See Military Order, 12 June 1942, Box 75, Entry 99, RG 226; see also James Warburg, *Unwritten Treaty* (New York: Harcourt Brace Jovanovich, 1946), 95–96, and

Thomas Troy, *Donovan and the CIA: A History of the Establishment of the CIA* (Frederick, Md.: University Publications of America, 1981), 427.

2. Quotes from JCS 67 in Troy, *Donovan and CIA*, 428; see also OSS Functions and Organization (June 1945), Box 4, Entry 141, RG 226. One major OSS critic was Budget Director Harold Smith (see memo, Bureau of the Budget, 6 Aug. 1942, Conferences with the President, 1942, Smith Papers).

3. For those transferring to the OSS from the COI, see Appendix 9 in Clayton D. Laurie, "Ideology and American Propaganda: The Psychological Warfare Campaign Against Nazi Germany, 1941–1945" (Ph.D. diss., American University, 1990); first quote from Anthony Cave-Brown, *The Last Hero: Wild Bill Donovan* (New York: Time-Life Books, 1982), 299; second quote from James G. Rogers, *Wartime Washington: The Secret OSS Journal of James Grafton Rogers, 1942–1943*, ed. Thomas Troy (Frederick, Md.: University Publications of America, 1987), xxi.

4. Pearson and Cassini quoted in Cave-Brown, *Last Hero*, 173 and 301; Casey quoted in William Casey, *The Secret War Against Hitler* (Washington, D.C.: Regenery Gateway, 1988), 23; see also Rhodri Jeffreys-Jones, "The Socio-Educational Composition of the CIA Elite: A Statistical Note," *Journal of American Studies* 19 (1985): 421–44.

5. Arthur Krock, "The OSS Gets It Coming and Going," *New York Times*, 31 July 1945, in Box 120B, Donovan Papers.

6. Among those recruited for OSS service after June 1942 were banker and meat-packing firm vice-president Lester Armour; corporate vice-president George C. Atwater; banker and stockbroker Edward L. Bigelow; labor organizer Heber Blankenhorn; Smith-Barney senior partner Charles S. Cheston; Miles Collier, son of a Florida real estate developer; educator and diplomat Frederick Dolbeare; architect and industrialist Alfred Dupont; academic, U.S. Marine, and diplomat William A. Eddy; banker and stockbroker J. Russell Forgan; UCLA psychologist James A. Gengerelli; investment banker Walter Giblin; textile firm vice-president and Office of Price Administration official R. Davis Halliwell; *Fortune*, *Life*, and *New Yorker* writer Geoffrey Hellman; J. Walter Thompson ad agency executive Kenneth W. Hinks; lawyer and corporate director Carl O. Hoffman; Gen. J. J. Pershing's personal aide-de-camp and textile company executive John C. Hughes; lawyer Ellery C. Huntington, Jr.; Harvard psychologist Robert H. Knapp; Seattle lawyer, interventionist, and civic activist Herbert S. Little; former Du-Pont chemist and business executive Stanley P. Lovell; CBS vice-president Lawrence Lowman; U.S. Treasury employee Howard J. Preston; steel company executive K. D. Mann; career diplomat John van Antwerpen MacMurray; university president and former Connecticut lieutenant governor James L. McConaughy; banker and publisher Lanning MacFarland; English-born *New York Herald Tribune* correspondent James Mini-fee; bankers and corporate directors Henry S. and Junius Morgan, the son and grandson of J. P. Morgan, Jr.; Chase Manhattan Bank vice-president Shepard Morgan; Macy's vice-president John E. O'Gara; ad man and novelist Walter O'Meara; Ickes's Interior Department aide Saul Padover; banker, ad man, and stockbroker William L. Rehm; lawyer and former assistant secretary of state James G. Rogers; Pittsburgh investment banker, former New York Stock Exchange president, and OPM official Joseph M. Scribner; railroad president Charles M. Sears, Jr.; public relations executive John M. Shaheen; banker and businessman John E. Toulmin; businessman and stockbroker Archbold van Beuren; salesman and ad agency executive Charles S. Vanderblue; and career Foreign Service officer Edwin

C. Wilson. For biographical sketches, see, for Armour, *National Cyclopedia of American Biography*, 520–21, and "Lester Armour, Chicago Banker," *New York Times*, 27 December 1970, 3. For Bigelow, see OSS Prominent People, Box 97, Entry 99, RG 226; "Edward L. Bigelow," *New York Times*, 21 August 1975, 38; and Rogers, *Wartime Washington*, 135 n.12. For Blankenhorn, see Clayton D. Laurie, "The Chanting of Crusaders: Captain Heber Blankenhorn and AEF Combat Propaganda in World War I," *Journal of Military History*, 59 (July 1995): 457–82, and "H. Blankenhorn, A Labor Advisor," *New York Times*, 2 Jan. 1956, 21. For Cheston, see OSS Prominent People, Box 97, Entry 99, RG 226; "Charles Cheston, Banker, 68, Dies," *New York Times*, 14 February 1960, 84; and Rogers, *Wartime Washington*, 90 n.6. For Preston, see "Howard Preston, 76, Dies; Official with CIA, OSS," *Washington Post*, 22 April 1992. For Mann, see OSS Prominent People, Box 97, Entry 99, RG 226, and *National Cyclopedia of American Biography, 1964*, 73–74. For Minifee, see "James MacDonald Minifee Dies, *Herald Tribune* correspondent," *New York Times Biographical Edition*, 16 June 1974, 864, and Rogers, *Wartime Washington*, 54 n.43. For Henry Morgan, see OSS Prominent People, Box 97, Entry 99, RG 226, and Rogers, *Wartime Washington*, 156 n.12. For Shepard Morgan, see "Shepard Morgan, 84, Former Chase Officer, Aide to World Agencies, Dies," *New York Times*, 18 November 1968, 47. For O'Meara, see *Current Biography, 1958*, 318–19, and Rogers, *Wartime Washington*, 21 n.16. For Padover, see "Saul Padover, Author, Dead at 75," *New York Times Biographical Service*, 24 February 1981, 227, and Daniel Lerner, *Sykewar: Psychological Warfare Against Nazi Germany, D-Day to V-E Day* (New York: Stewart, 1949), 86. For Rogers, see Rogers, *Wartime Washington*, xvii–xxi, 10. For Eddy, see *Who's Who in America*, 4:278; "William Eddy Dies at 66; Educator, Soldier, Diplomat," *New York Times*, 5 May 1962, 27; Robin Winks, *Cloak and Gown: Scholars in the Secret War, 1939–1961* (New York: William Morrow and Company, 1987), 181–82, 188–99; and Rogers, *Wartime Washington*, 23 n.31. For Giblin, see *Who's Who in America, 1961–68*, 4:355, and "Walter Giblin, Broker, 62, Dead," *New York Times*, 2 May 1963, 27. For Hinks, see OSS Prominent People, Box 97, Entry 99, RG 226; *Who's Who in America, 1976–77*, 1:1452; and Rogers, *Wartime Washington*, 116 n.3. For Hughes, see OSS Prominent People, Box 97, Entry 99, RG 226; "John Hughes, NATO Envoy Under Eisenhower, Dead at 79," *New York Times*, 26 May 1971, 46; and Rogers, *Wartime Washington*, 154 n.5. For Little, see *Who Was Who, 1969–73*, 5:435, and Rogers, *Wartime Washington*, 133 n.8. For Lovell, see OSS Prominent People, Box 97, Entry 99, RG 226, and Rogers, *Wartime Washington*, 42 n.61. For Scribner, see *Who Was Who, 1977–1981*, 7:511–12; "Joseph Scribner Is Dead; An Investment Banker," *New York Times*, 25 May 1979, 18; and Rogers, *Wartime Washington*, 145 n.20. For Shaheen, see OSS Prominent People, Box 97, Entry 99, RG 226, and "John Shaheen, 70; Chief of Oil Company," *New York Times Biographical Service*, 4 November 1985, 1330. For Toulmin, see "John E. Toulmin, A Boston Banker," *New York Times*, 12 April 1968, 35. For Wilson, see OSS Prominent People, Box 97, Entry 99, RG 226.

7. Quotes from Troy, *Donovan and CIA*, 431–34.

8. OSS Budget-Planning Group, Box 6, Entry 146, RG 226; Rogers, *Wartime Washington*, xxiii–xxiv; Kermit Roosevelt, *War Report of the OSS*, 2 vols. (New York: Walker, 1976), 1:24, 98, 105–6; Alfred H. Paddock, Jr., *United States Army Special Warfare: Its Origins: Psychological Warfare and Unconventional Warfare, 1941–1952* (Washington, D.C.: National Defense University Press, 1982), 11. For the relationship of the JPWC and OSS to the JCS, see Troy, *Donovan and CIA*, 157, 429–34.

9. For reorganizations, see General Order 9, 3 Jan. 1943, Box 126, Entry 136, and Box 75, Entry 99, both in RG 226; see also Roosevelt, *War Report OSS*, 1:107, 121–23. A directory of OSS R&D people is contained in "Biographical Sketches of R&D Personnel, 1 Sept. 1945, Box 7A, Donovan Papers; see also U.S. Civil Service Commission, *Official Register of the United States, 1943* (Washington, D.C.: Government Printing Office, 1943), 301–2. For historians in OSS R&D, see Winks, *Cloak and Gown*, 495–97 n.19. For a roster as of 20 November 1944, see Troy, *Donovan and CIA*, 223.

10. Roosevelt, *War Report OSS*, 1:130–31; see also Provisional Basic Field Manual—Strategic Services, 1 Dec. 1943, Box 7, Entry 116; and Cairo-MO-Int-1 2, Box 77, Entry 144, both in RG 226. For OSS Planning Group members, 13 Jan. 1943–19 Jan. 1945, see Box 4, Entry 144, RG 226. For Rogers's opinions of these men, see *Wartime Washington*, 21–22, diary entries for 20, 23 November 1943. For MO planning, see meeting PG 118, 3 June 1943, PG mins. 81st to 120th, Box 4, and meetings 570, 592, 1–31 Jan. 1945, PG mins. 570–640, Box 6, all in Entry 144, RG 226. For 155/II/D see Troy, *Donovan and CIA*, 439–42.

11. See Rogers, *Wartime Washington*, 145, 164, 178, 79, diary entries for 15, 17 September, 28 October, 23 November, and April 4, 1943 (quote from 178). Despite Rogers's pessimistic assessment, the planning group completed several score of plans (see Boxes 17, 18, 19, 20, 21, 22, 23, 28, all in Entry 144, RG 226). For minutes, see, for example, meeting 32/2, 22 February 1943, and meeting 64/2, 31 Mar. 1943, Box 8, Entry 144, RG 226. For monthly reports, see Boxes 82–90, Entry 99, RG 226.

12. Wash. MO Drafts, chap. 1: II Read Hist., Box 75, Entry 99; OSS Organization and Functions (June 1945), Box 4, Entry 141; and PG2/ Overall Strategic Plan, 19 February 1943, Box 8, Entry 144, RG 226.

13. MO Field Manual, Strategic Services, 26 Jan. 1943, 1–2, Box 97, and Wash. MO Drafts, chap. 1: Read Hist., Box 75, both in Entry 99, RG 226, and Roosevelt, *War Report OSS*, 1:212–13.

14. OSS Organization and Functions (June 1945), 22, Box 4, Entry 141; and Propaganda Techniques, Box 75, Entry 99, both in RG 226. For MO doctrine, organization, and goals, see MO—Morale Operations OSS, Box 7, Entry 116, RG 226.

15. Quotes from Edmond Taylor, *Awakening from History* (Boston: Gambit, 1969), 302–4; see also Wash. MO Drafts, chaps. 1, 2, Read Hist., Box 75, Entry 99, RG 226.

16. MO Media and Techniques, Box 4, Entry 144, RG 226. For printed propaganda, see Stockholm-MO-OP-5 Production-ETO-Stockholm, Box 136, Entry 148, RG 226; and Howard Becker, "The Nature and Consequences of Black Propaganda," *American Sociological Review* 41 (April 1949): 221–35.

17. MO Media and Techniques, Box 4, Entry 141, and MO—Morale Operations OSS, Box 7, Entry 116, both in RG 226.

18. Wash. MO Drafts, chaps. 1, 2, Read Hist., Box 75, Entry 99, RG 226. People sent to MO from other OSS branches included Frederick Oechsner, David Williamson, Arthur Russell, Joseph Scribner, Robert Knapp, John Toulmin, Herbert Little, Stefan Schnabel, Jack Crutcher, Roland Dulin, Buford Junker, John Whitaker, K. D. Mann, Morton Royse, Edmond Taylor, Vereni Taylor, John Hackett, and Heber Blankenhorn.

19. Houseman quoted in John Houseman, *Front and Center* (New York: Simon and Schuster, 1979), 49–50. For a somewhat mixed assessment of MO alien employees, see memo, Baldwin to Dibert, 17 Aug. 1944, Box 79, Entry 148, RG 226.

20. MO—Morale Operations OSS, Box 7, Entry 116, RG 226.

21. The following people from academe, business, and print and broadcast media joined OSS MO: former foreign correspondent Stuart Raab; former congressional candidate and King Features and free-lance writer James Aswell; UP Balkans correspondent and Ankara UP Bureau chief Ben Ames; CBS and *Time, Fortune, New Yorker, Saturday Evening Post,* and *Reader's Digest* editor and writer John Fistere; CBS publicity director and director of War Programs Charles Vanda; Columbia graduate and AP, *New York Times, Sun, Herald Tribune,* and free-lance correspondent Joseph Peters; newspaper correspondent and ad man Patrick Dolan; *New Yorker* cartoonist Saul Steinberg; author and professor of international law, politics, and political economy Nicholas R. Doman; *New Yorker* ad man Howard Baldwin; University of Wisconsin sociologist Howard Becker; economist and banker Morton Bodfish; millionaire and philanthropist Paul Mellon; U.S. Marine Capt. George H. Owen; Gifford Proctor; Red Cross worker, educator, and Westinghouse employee Harry Dotson; Samuel Scrivner; Hungarian-born free-lance correspondent and Committee for National Morale researcher George O. May; statistician, journalist, and engineer Norman Fournier; Dartmouth sociologist and Committee on National Morale member Michael E. Choukas; U.S. Army soldier Stacey Lloyd; perfume company manager Frederick Shoniniger; Roper Polling employee and businessman Robert Knapp; Robert R. Holt; *Brooklyn Eagle* reporter and CBS ad man and copy writer Edward Cushing; Polish emigré and engineer Severin Kaven; Palestinian-born radio commentator and editor for the Blue and WNEW networks Samuel Cuff; U.S. Army Lt. Col. and Episcopal priest John O. "Buck" Weaver; Capt. Temple H. Fielding; Maj. John Harris; AP editor and public relations officer Lt. Stephen Merrill; and sociologist Edward Shils. For a more complete listing of MO Branch members, see Appendix 10, Laurie, "Ideology and American Propaganda;" see also OSS documents: List of MO Personnel/ Cairo, MO/ME, Box 85, Entry 144; Bari, 3 Apr. 1944, Box 78, Entry 144; memo to Adjutant from Executive Office MO, 23 Oct. 1944, Box 74, Entry 168; MO Personnel, Box 86, Entry 144; memo, Williamson to Chapin, Box 16, Entry 110; memo to Staff, 3 Apr. 1944, Box 78, Entry 148; Weekly Report, HQ 2677 HQ Company, 20 Mar. 1944, Box 29, Entry 165; Special Order 11, 2 July 1944, Box 30, Entry 165; OSS Organization Charts, 20 Nov. 1944, Box 6, Entry 146; METO Personnel, Box 33; OSS ETO 1944, Box 17, Entry 99; Report to Executive Committee on MO Organization, Personnel, 20 Aug. 1943, Box 126, Entry 136; MO Bari, Box 33, Entry 99; memo, Diebert to Casey, 20 Sept. 1944, and Personnel Available for FETO/MO, both in Box 79, Entry 148; memo, Fistere to Johnson, 31 May 1944, Box 85, and Personnel to Dec. 1943, METO, Box 85, both in Entry 144, all in RG 226; see also Deuel, History OSS, Box 61, Deuel Papers.

22. Wash. MO Drafts, chaps. 1, 2 Read Hist., Box 75, Entry 99, RG 226.

23. Wash. MO Drafts, chaps. 1, 2 Read Hist., Box 75, Entry 99, RG 226; see also Roosevelt, *War Report OSS,* 1:216, 236. MO reached a peak membership in Europe in September 1944 of 183 people out of an OSS European establishment of approximately 2,500. In the United States MO was even smaller, consisting of only 72 people of 4,070 total OSS personnel in August 1943. The stateside MO establishment never exceeded 150 people. About eight months later, as of 30 April 1944, the OSS had more than doubled in size to 9,863. Of these, 6,051 were U.S. Army personnel, 747 were U.S. Navy and U.S. Coast Guard personnel, 101 were U.S. Marines, and 2,964 were civilians. Deployments by theater were: ETO (2,329), NATO (1,409), METO (1,085), FETO (829), CO-

NUS (4,070), and "other" (154). Eventually, by V-J Day, over 13,000 people belonged to OSS; see OSS Manpower Report, 30 Apr. 1944, Box 101, Entry 99, RG 226.

24. Wash. MO Ex., MO Reports, 4, 5, 8, Box 75, Entry 99, RG 226.

25. OSS Organization Chart, 6 Dec. 1944, Box 125, Entry 136; MO Branch, Box 17, Entry 99; OSS Organization Chart, 28 Dec. 1944, Box 125, Entry 136; OSS Organization and Functions (June 1945), Box 4, Entry 141; TO&E, no. 1316, Box 125, Entry 136; Wash. MO Exhibits, MO Reports Office, and Propaganda Techniques/Doctrine Behind MO Branch, both in Box 75, Entry 99; and MO—Morale Operations OSS, Box 7, Entry 116, all in RG 226.

26. Washington MO Exhibits, MO Reports Office, 25–29, Box 75, and ETO MO Administration, 1944, Box 17, both in Entry 99; PG meeting 304, 8 Jan. 1944, Box 5, Entry 144, all in RG 226; see also Roosevelt, *War Report OSS*, 2:143–44, and Bradley F. Smith, *The Shadow Warriors: The OSS and the Origins of the CIA* (New York: Basic Books, 1983), 205–6.

27. For planning group activities, see PG meeting 158, 20 July 1943, Box 5, Entry 144, in RG 226, and Roosevelt, *War Report OSS*, 1:106. For MO involvement in planning group sessions, see meeting 122, 8 June 1943; meeting 124/5, 10 June 1943; meeting 137, 25 June 1943, Box 5; minutes, 407th meeting, 17 May 1944; meeting 526, 16 Oct. 1944; meeting 547, 28 Nov. 1944; meeting 548, 29 Nov. 1944, Box 6, both in Entry 144, RG 226. For MO reports from the field, see MO Reports Office Washington, Box 126, Entry 136; Monthly Reports to Director, Boxes 82–90, Entry 99; memo, Department Directors OSS ETO to Donovan, re: Report OSS (Main) for 16–30 Nov. 1944, Box 4, Entry 99, RG 226.

28. For training areas, see Roosevelt, *War Report OSS*, 2:241–43; see also Training Areas, Box 73; Washington S&T Branch History, no. 60, Box 78, all in Entry 99; and MO—Morale Operations OSS, Box 7, Entry 116. For content of MO training, see Boxes 79 and 101, Entry 99, and Boxes 124 and 127, Entry 136, all in RG 226.

29. Rogers, *Wartime Washington*, 164. Negative opinions were evident during and after the war (see Deuel to Donovan, 31 Jan. 1944, Box 120c, and letter, Doering to Shepardson, 21 Oct. 1961, Box 120a, Donovan Papers); see also Report to Executive Committee on MO Organization and Personnel and Operations, 20 Aug. 1943, Box 126, Entry 136, RG 226.

Chapter 8. Controlling a Rear Echelon Insanity

1. For World War I U.S. Army propaganda, see Clayton D. Laurie, "The Chanting of Crusaders: Captain Heber Blankenhorn and AEF Combat Propaganda in World War I," *Journal of Military History* 59 (July 1995): 457–82. Archival documents are in Record Groups 120, 165, 218, NARA. For a published account, see Bruce Bidwell, *History of the Military Intelligence Division, Department of the Army General Staff: 1775–1941* (Frederick, Md.: University Publications of America, 1986), 154, 252–63.

2. Quote from Holly Shulman, "The Voice of Victory: The Development of American Propaganda and the Voice of America, 1920–1942" (Ph.D. diss., University of Maryland, 1984), 162–63; see also Alfred H. Paddock, Jr., *United States Army Special Warfare,*

Its Origins: Psychological and Unconventional Warfare, 1941-1962 (Washington, D.C.: National Defense University Press, 1982), 8-9.

3. For U.S. Army concerns about propaganda after the fall of France, see Andre Morize, "Lessons from the Fall of France," *Sunday Star* (Washington, D.C.), 26 January 1941, editorial section, 1. For concerns about Axis fifth-column activities in Latin America, see Stetson Conn and Byron Fairchild, *The Western Hemisphere: The Framework of Hemispheric Defense* (Washington, D.C.: Office of the Chief of Military History, U.S. Army, 1960), 266, 273-74, 333-36, 415, and Stetson Conn, Rose C. Engelman, and Byron Fairchild, *Western Hemisphere: Guarding the United States and Its Outposts* (Washington, D.C.: Office of the Chief of Military History, U.S. Army, 1964), 382-83.

4. Charles A. H. Thomson, *The Overseas Information Service of the United States Government* (Washington, D.C.: Brookings Institution, 1948), 114n.

5. Bidwell, *History of MID*, 354-55, and Shulman, "Voice of Victory," 160, 167-70.

6. Quotes from memo, Miles to Chief of Staff, 1 February 1941, Box 379, Ickes Papers.

7. Quote from Bidwell, *History of MID*, 354-55.

8. Paul M. A. Linebarger, *Psychological Warfare* (Washington, D.C.: Combat Forces Press, 1954), 175, 183.

9. Shulman, "Voice of Victory," 160-62.

10. Ibid., 170-78, 183, 189-91; William E. Daugherty, "United States Psychological Warfare Agencies in World War II," in *A Psychological Warfare Casebook*, ed. William E. Daugherty and Morris Janowitz (Baltimore: Johns Hopkins University Press, 1958), 130; Thomas Troy, *Donovan and the CIA* (Frederick, Md.: University Publications of America, 1981), 131; H. D. Kehm, "Organization for Military Psychological Warfare in ETO," *Military Review* 26 (February 1947): 10-12; and Paddock, *Special Warfare*, 9-10, 12. For Solbert's efforts and philosophy, see memos, Solbert to Rosenman, 29 May 1942, 11 June 1942, Box 12, Rosenman Papers. For Lee, see Raymond E. Lee, *The London Journal of Gen. Raymond E. Lee, 1940-1941*, ed. James Leutze (Boston: Little, Brown, 1971).

11. James G. Rogers, *Wartime Washington: The Secret OSS Journal of James Grafton Rogers, 1942-1943*, ed. Thomas Troy (Frederick, Md.: University Publications of America, 1987), 9-10, 12, 16-18.

12. James Rogers had written earlier that the concept of theater commander approval "may hamper us. . . . The principle is much overdone" (see Rogers, *Wartime Washington*, 44-45, entries for 24, 31 January, 8 February 1943). Most theater commanders tolerated psychological warfare activities, with the exception of Gen. Douglas MacArthur, who excluded the OSS from areas he controlled; see Linebarger, *Psychological Warfare*, 98. The subsequent PWB G-2 commanders were Col. Charles Blakeney, Lt. Col. Charles Holmes, Col. John Stanley, Lt. Col. Richard Hirsch, Lt. Col. Bruce Buttles, and Col. Dana Johnston. The absence of flag officers in this post indicates the lack of importance attached to PWB; see Linebarger, xiii-xiv.

13. Sherwood quoted in Robert L. Bishop, "The Overseas Branch of the Office of War Information" (Ph.D. diss., University of Wisconsin, 1966), 186, and see also 125-26; "Psychological Warfare in the Mediterranean Theater," part 1: An Overall Review of the Organizational Evolution of the PWB of AFHQ as a Staff Section, 2, Box 12, Entry 6G, RG 208 (hereafter "Hist. of PWB"; James Erdmann, *Leaflet Operations in the Second World War* (Denver: University of Denver, 1969), 82.

14. Quotes from Bishop, "Overseas Branch," 186, 127; see also Wallace Carroll, *Persuade or Perish* (Boston: Houghton Mifflin Company, 1948), 31–32, and Shulman, "Voice of Victory," 195–98.

15. Carroll, *Persuade or Perish*, 27–30; Allan M. Winkler, *The Politics of Propaganda: The Office of War Information, 1942–1945* (New Haven: Yale University Press, 1978), 115–16; Bishop, "Overseas Branch," 137–38. For OWI's TORCH directive, see Overseas Operations Branch, Central Directive A, 7 Nov. 1942, Box 818, Entry 359, RG 208.

16. William E. Daugherty, "The Darlan Story," in Daugherty and Janowitz, eds., *Psychological Warfare Casebook*, 261–62, 291–96.

17. First quote from Winkler, *Politics of Propaganda*, 85–86; Sherwood and Warburg quoted in Sydney S. Weinberg, "Wartime Propaganda in a Democracy: America's Twentieth-Century Information Agencies" (Ph.D. diss., Columbia University, 1969), 371.

18. Quote from Winkler, *Politics of Propaganda*, 87; see also Overseas Operations Branch Central Directive, 20–27 Nov. 1942, Box 818, Entry 359, RG 208, dealing with the Darlan situation.

19. Quote from Daugherty, "Darlan Story," 296–97; see also Weinberg, "Wartime Propaganda," 368–69.

20. Quotes from Winkler, *Politics of Propaganda*, 87–88.

21. For the formation of INC and PWB, and its ramifications, see memo, Williamson to Donovan, 18 Oct. 1943, re: PWB Plans for 1943, Box 32, Entry 99, RG 226; Carroll, *Persuade or Perish*, 31–32; and Thomson, *Overseas Information*, 100–104. McClure's career was utterly lacking in any service relevant to psychological warfare (see Department of Defense Office of Public Information, Press Branch Release; and *New York Times*, 5 January 1957, both in Box 1, Robert A. McClure Papers, MHI).

22. For McClure quote, see Erdmann, *Leaflet Operations*, 194–95; see also Staff memo 56, AFHQ, 1 July 1943, Box 32, Entry 99, RG 226; Bishop, "Overseas Branch," 176–77; "Hist. of PWB," pt. 2, 1–2; Daugherty, "U.S. Psychological Warfare Organizations," 130; and Schematic Organization of PWB, 22 Jan. 1943, Box 32, Entry 99, RG 226.

23. "Hist. of PWB," pt. 2, 2–3; Staff memo 56, AFHQ, 1 July 1943, Box 32, Entry 99, RG 226.

24. "Hist. of PWB," pt. 1, 3–4.

25. Ibid., 4–5.

26. Con O'Neill, "Paper Warfare in Tunisia," *Army Quarterly* (U.K.) 44 (April 1944): 82, 84, 88. For American efforts, see Bishop, "Overseas Branch," 153–54, and Selden C. Menefee, "Propaganda Wins Battles," *Nation* 158 (12 February 1944): 184–85.

27. Kehm, "Organization," 15; Daugherty, "U.S. Psychological Warfare Organizations," 132; Paddock, *Special Warfare*, 10, 14. James Rogers comments on this control controversy in *Wartime Washington*, 33, entry for 4 January 1943.

28. For a detailed look at MRBCs, see U.S. Army, Second Mobile Radio Broadcasting Company, *History of Second Mobile Radio Broadcasting Company, Dec. 1943 to May 1945* (n.p., 1945); and U.S. Army, Fifth Army, Mobile Radio Broadcasting Company, *Psychological Warfare Branch Combat Team* (n.p., n.d.).

29. Anthony Cave-Brown, *The Secret War Report of the OSS* (New York: Berkeley/Medallion Books, 1976), 135–37, and Kermit Roosevelt, *War Report of the OSS*, 2 vols. (New York: Walker, 1976), 2:12, 16. For British operations, see William Stevenson, *A Man*

Called Intrepid (New York: Ballantine Books, 1976), 441. For U.S. diplomatic dealings, see Robert Murphy, *Diplomat Among Warriors* (Garden City, N.Y.: Doubleday, 1964).

30. Hazeltine referred to in PWB-OSS Detachment, re: Relationship of OSS to PWB–U.S. Army; MEDTO-MO-NA, Jan. 43–Apr. 43, both in Box 31; and memo, Williamson to Donovan, 18 Oct. 1943, Box 32, all in Entry 99; British PWE PWB-OSS Detachment Reports, 1 Sept. 1944–14 May 1945, Box 48, Entry 154; all in RG 226; and Roosevelt, *War Report OSS*, 1:213–14; see also David A. Walker, "OSS and Operation TORCH," *Journal of Contemporary History* 22 (1987): 667–79.

31. First quote from Paddock, *Special Warfare*, 31–32; Rogers quoted in Rogers, *Wartime Washington*, 74, entry for 28 March 1943, and 44–45, entry for 31 January 1943.

32. Report, Taylor to Donovan, n.d., re: Psychological Warfare in NATO, Box 32, Entry 99, RG 226.

33. On the VOA, see "U.S. Arsenal of Words," *Fortune* 27 (March 1943): 169, 172; "Beamed to Europe: OWI's Propaganda Paves the Way for Military Advances," *Newsweek*, 27 September 1943, 73; Shulman, "Voice of Victory," 305–6; Roosevelt, *War Report OSS*, 1:37–40; and Leonard Carlton, "Voice of America: The Overseas Radio Bureau," *Public Opinion Quarterly* 7 (Spring 1943): 46–54. For the ideological nature of VOA output, see Central Directive, Overseas Branch, 20–30 July 1943, Box 818, Entry 359, and FIS and OWI directives from 4 Mar. 1942–16 Sept. 1942, Box 607, Entry 385, all in RG 208.

34. Quotes from Shulman, "Voice of Victory," 358–59, 367. For example, see Central Directive, 11–18 Dec. 1942, Box 818; other 1942–43 directives are also in Boxes 818 and 821, all in Entry 359, RG 208.

35. Anne Armstrong, *Unconditional Surrender: The Impact of the Casablanca Policy on World War II* (New Brunswick, N.J.: Rutgers University Press, 1961), 6, 12, and William E. Daugherty, "Unconditional Surrender," in Daugherty and Janowitz, eds., *Psychological Warfare Casebook*, 276.

36. Thomas C. Sorenson, *The Word War: The Story of American Propaganda* (New York: Harper and Row, 1968), 15.

37. Armstrong, *Unconditional Surrender*, 61. For the U.S. Army's opinion of the policy, see Brian L. Villa, "The United States Army, Unconditional Surrender and the Potsdam Proclamation," *Journal of American History* 63 (June 1976): 69–73.

38. Sherwood quoted in Armstrong, *Unconditional Surrender*, 12; see also Daugherty, "Unconditional Surrender," 273–77, and Weinberg, "Wartime Propaganda," 446, 448, 449–50. The Domestic OWI did not share the Overseas OWI view (see Richard W. Steele, "American Popular Opinion and the War Against Germany: The Issue of Negotiated Peace, 1942," *Journal of American History* 65 [December 1978]: 704–23). Warburg was more outspoken against the policy (see Ron Chernow, *The Warburgs: The Twentieth Century Odyssey of a Remarkable Jewish Family* [New York: Random House, 1993], 519).

39. For OWI treatment, see Overseas Operations Branch Weekly Propaganda Directive, Jan. 1943, 29 May 1943, Box 821; Overseas Branch Central Directive 27 Aug., 3–10, 10–17 Sept., Box 818; Overseas Operations Branch Weekly Propaganda Directives, 31 Aug.–7 Sept. 1944, Box 823, all in Entry 359, RG 208; and Daugherty, "Unconditional Surrender," 260. Whether the unconditional surrender policy actually lengthened the war is still debated today; see Raymond G. O'Connor, *Diplomacy for Victory: FDR and Unconditional Surrender* (New York: W. W. Norton, 1971); and J. Glennon, " 'This Time

Germany Is a Defeated Nation': The Doctrine of Unconditional Surrender and Some Unsuccessful Attempts to Alter It, 1943–1944," in *Statesmen and Statecraft of the Modern West*, ed. Gerald N. Grob (Barre, Mass.: Barre Publishers, 1967), 109–51.

40. Winkler, *Politics of Propaganda*, 118–19; Bishop, "Overseas Branch," 141–44; and Robert Pirsein, *The VOA: A History of the International Broadcasting Activities of the United States Government, 1940–1962* (New York: Arno Press, 1979), 80–81.

41. For Garrett quotes, see Field Report of Warner, 8 Sept. 1944, Box 16, and MO Black Radio, Box 69, both in Entry 99, RG 226; see also Cave-Brown, *Secret War Report*, 222. For papers on Balbo, see Box 74B, Donovan Papers.

42. For OSS plans, see Special Military Plan for P.W. in Sicily, PG 14/3rd Draft, 18 Mar. 1943, Box 10, and Plan for P.W. in Italy, Box 9, Entry 144, RG 226.

43. Propaganda Techniques—MO Rumors, Box 75, and memo, Creedy to Wilkins, 5 Oct. 1944, Box 15, both in Entry 99, RG 226; and Roosevelt, *War Report OSS*, 1:214.

44. Project MTO—Italian Newspaper, Box 87, Entry 144, RG 226.

45. Report, Whitaker to Oechsner, Dec. 1943, Box 32, Entry 99, RG 226; Carroll, *Persuade or Perish*, 164; and "Hist. of PWB," pt. 1, 7.

46. Memo, Oechsner to Donovan, 12 Nov. 1943, re: PWB Field Teams—Combat Teams, Box 32, Entry 99, RG 226; see also "Hist. of PWB," pt. 1, 7.

47. "Hist. of PWB," pt. 1, 7–8.

48. Bishop, "Overseas Branch," 177–78.

49. James Warburg, *Unwritten Treaty* (New York: Harcourt Brace Jovanovich, 1946), 105, 107; and Linebarger, *Psychological Warfare*, 177. George Creel commented negatively on U.S. propaganda in *Rebel at Large: Recollections of Fifty Crowded Years* (New York: G. Putnam's Sons, 1947), 319, 321.

Chapter 9. The Final Ideological Clash

1. The 1943–1944 OSS disputes were primarily between Donovan and those members of his organization who felt as William Whitney did in 1942 that the office needed to narrow its mission. To several of these men Donovan was the OSS's greatest liability. James G. Rogers recorded the disputes in *Wartime Washington: The Secret OSS Journal of James Grafton Rogers, 1942–1943*, ed. Thomas F. Troy (Frederick, Md.: University Publications of America, 1987), 86, 140, 143, 145, 153, entries for 24 April 1943, 4, 6, 11, 15 September 1943, 5 October 1943; see also James Rogers questionnaire, Box 120c, Donovan Papers. For Deuel's views, see letter, Deuel to parents, 4 Sept. 1943, Box 1, Deuel Papers. The disputes are also covered in Anthony Cave-Brown, *The Last Hero: Wild Bill Donovan* (New York: Time-Life Books, 1982), 509, 512–17. Among members who resigned from the OSS between 1942 and late 1944 were James Baxter III, Morton Bodfish, Heber Blankenhorn, Wilmarth Lewis, William Maddox, Shepard Morgan, Walter O'Meara, William Phillips, James Rogers, Stefan Schnabel, and John Wiley.

2. For the OWI seal, see Administration Bulletin 17, 9 Nov. 1942, Box 27, and the Strategy of Truth, Box 6, both in Pringle Papers; see also Michael Darrock, "Davis and Goliath," *Harper's*, February 1943, 225, and Ernest S. Pisko, "Words That May Shorten the War," *Christian Century* 59 (24 June 1942): 805–6.

3. OWI Overseas Operations Branch, Box 1, Entry 6B, RG 208; letter, Phillips to FDR, 13 Aug. 1942, PSF: G.B. OSS, FDR Papers; and Allan M. Winkler, *The Politics of Propaganda: The Office of War Information, 1942–1945* (New Haven: Yale University Press, 1978), 27–28.

4. William E. Daugherty, "United States Psychological Warfare Agencies in World War II," in *A Psychological Warfare Casebook*, ed. William E. Daugherty and Morris Janowitz (Baltimore: Johns Hopkins University Press, 1958), 129.

5. Davis quoted in Thomas Troy, *Donovan and the CIA: A History of the Establishment of the CIA* (Frederick, Md.: University Publications of America, 1981), 189; see also PG meeting 28, 17 Feb. 1943, Box 4, Entry 144, RG 226; Rogers, *Wartime Washington*, 29, entries for 20, 31 December 1942, 1 January 1943, and 54, entry for 17 February 1943; and Ronald T. Farrar, "Elmer Davis: Report to the President," *Journalism Monographs* 7 (August 1968): 56–57.

6. Rogers, *Wartime Washington*, 34, 37, 54, entries for 4 January, 15 January, and 17 February 1943.

7. Rogers, *Wartime Washington*, 57, entry for 20 February 1943.

8. Cave-Brown, *The Last Hero*, 342–43.

9. Troy, *Donovan and CIA*, 189.

10. Memo, Donovan to FDR, 23 Feb. 1943, PSF: OSS Donovan, William J., 1941, 1943, FDR Papers.

11. Memo, Davis to Stimson, 9 Mar. 1943, Box 7, Entry 6E, RG 208; see also Robert L. Bishop, "The Overseas Branch of the Office of War Information" (Ph.D. diss., University of Wisconsin, 1966), 49–50; and Kermit Roosevelt, *War Report of the OSS*, 2 vols. (New York: Walker, 1976), 1:107. For the executive order, see Box 126, Entry 136, and Washington MO Exhibits, Box 75, Entry 99, both in RG 226.

12. Rogers, *Wartime Washington*, 67–68, entry for 12 March 1943, and Farrar, "Elmer Davis Report," 56–57.

13. For JCS 155/7/D, see Troy, *Donovan and CIA*, 436–38; see also Bishop, "Overseas Branch," 49–50, and Roosevelt, *War Report OSS*, 1:107.

14. Oechsner quotes Davis in Washington MO Drafts, Read Hist., Box 75, Entry 99, RG 226; see also Troy, *Donovan and CIA*, 207–8.

15. Letter, Deuel to parents, 19 Apr. 1943, Deuel Papers.

16. Strong quoted in Troy, *Donovan and CIA*, 204–5; for the MO manual, see Box 7, Entry 116, RG 226; see also JCS Directive 170 of Dec. 1942, JCS 178/D of 6 May 1943, and JCS 166/3/D of 27 May 1943. For Donovan's definition, see memo, Donovan to JCS, 4 Sept. 1943, sub.: Revised Directive for Functions of OSS and Proposed Directive—Functions of OSS, Box 97, Entry 99, RG 266. For OWI reaction, see Dispatches, Carroll to Sherwood, 29 Sept. and 20 Oct. 1943, Box 829, Entry 359, RG 208.

17. Directive for the OSS approved by JCS at 120th meeting, 26 Oct. 1943, supersedes JCS 155/7/D, Box 127, Entry 136, RG 226; see also Troy, *Donovan and CIA*, 439–42, and Roosevelt, *War Report OSS*, 1:109–10, 216–17. For OWI reactions, see Dispatches, Carroll to Sherwood, Barnes, 22 Nov. 1943; Carroll to Sherwood, Barnes, 23 Nov. 1943; Carroll to Sherwood, Barnes, and Sherwood to Carroll, 23 Nov. 1943; Sherwood to Carroll, McClure, 25 Nov. 1943; Hamblet to Sherwood, 3 Jan. 1944, Box 829, Entry 359, RG 208.

18. Memo, Barrett to Davis, Klauber, Barnard, Thomson, 17 Apr. 1944, Box 829, En-

try 359, RG 208; letter, Davis to Donovan, 6 June 1944; letter, Donovan to Davis, 16 June 1944; letter, Mann to branch chiefs, 14 June 1944, MO, all in Box 79, Entry 144, RG 226; letter, Davis to Rosenman, 17 June 1944, Box 1, Rosenman Papers.

19. Washington MO Exhibits, MO Report Office, Box 75, Entry 99, RG 226.

20. Kenneth Stewart, "OWI and Its Critics," *New Republic* 159 (13 December 1943): 844–46.

21. "Congress Blasts Against OWI: Portends Assault on New Deal," *Newsweek*, 22 February 1943, 25–26.

22. The *Philadelphia Inquirer* remarked, "What are they afraid of—that the Democrats in 1944 will sweep the fifth ward in Casablanca?" (quoted in "Congress Blasts OWI, 26); see also Norman Cousins, "Big Bad OWI," *Saturday Review of Literature* 26 (13 March 1943): 10; "The OWI," *Commonweal* 40 (28 April 1944): 28–29; and Michael Leigh, *Mobilizing Consent: Public Opinion and American Foreign Policy, 1937–1947* (Westport, Conn.: Greenwood Press, 1976), 85–86, 91.

23. "Davis on the Griddle," *Life*, 3 May 1943, 25, and John Houseman, *Front and Center* (New York: Simon and Schuster, 1979), 69–75.

24. James P. Warburg, *Foreign Policy Begins at Home* (New York: Harcourt, Brace and Company, 1944), 158–59; Ralph B. Levering, *American Public Opinion and the Russian Alliance, 1939–1945* (Chapel Hill: University of North Carolina Press, 1976), 95; and Melvin Small, "How We Learned to Love the Russians: American Media and the Soviet Union During World War II," *Historian* 36 (Fall 1974): 455–78.

25. For example, see OWI Weekly Directive 23, 30 Oct. 1943, 6, 13, 10 Nov. 1943, Box 822, Entry 363, and Central Directive 10–17 February 1944, Box 181, Entry 359, RG 208; see also Jeff Peck, "The Heroic Soviet on the American Screen," *Film and History* 9 (1979): 54–63.

26. M. J. Marvick and Elizabeth W. Marvick, "The Katyn Incident," in Daugherty and Janowitz, eds., *Psychological Warfare Casebook*, 352–56, and Levering, *American Opinion*, 111. Pro-Soviet works by OWI members included Wallace Carroll, *We're in This with Russia* (Cambridge, Mass.: Houghton Mifflin Company, 1942), and James Reston, *Prelude to Victory* (New York: Alfred A. Knopf, 1942); see also Jack L. Hammersmith, "The U.S. Office of War Information and the Polish Question, 1943–1945," *Polish Review* 19 (1974): 67–76.

27. Malcolm Cowley, "Sorrows of Elmer Davis," *New Republic* 108 (3 May 1943): 591; see also Robert G. Spivack, "The New Anti-Alien Drive," *New Republic* 159 (29 November 1943): 740–41.

28. Rogers, *Wartime Washington*, 56, 78, entries for 19 February and 1 April 1943.

29. Winkler, *Politics of Propaganda*, 92–94; Sydney S. Weinberg, "Wartime Propaganda in a Democracy: America's Twentieth-Century Information Agencies" (Ph.D. diss., Columbia University, 1969), 397–98, 401–3; Anne Armstrong, *Unconditional Surrender: The Impact of the Casablanca Policy on World War II* (New Brunswick, N.J.: Rutgers University Press, 1961), 83; James Warburg, "The Moronic Little King Incident," in Daugherty and Janowitz, eds., *Psychological Warfare Casebook*, 301–3; and Warburg, *Unwritten Treaty* (New York: Harcourt Brace Jovanovich, 1946), 110, 197–98, 202.

30. Houseman, *Front and Center*, 97–104, and Central Directive Overseas Branch, 30 July to 6 Aug. 1943, Box 818, Entry 359, RG 208.

31. Winner quoted in Winkler, *Politics of Propaganda*, 90; see also Weinberg, "Wartime Propaganda," 398.

32. Warburg quoted in "Moronic Little King Incident," 301–2.

33. Quotes from Winkler, *Politics of Propaganda*, 93–96; see also Warburg, *Unwritten Treaty*, 107–10, and Ted Olson, "The Short Unhappy Life of John Durfee," *Foreign Service Journal* 39 (October 1962): 36–44.

34. For Krock, see Houseman, *Front and Center*, 97–104; for Rogers, see Rogers, *Wartime Washington*, 127, entry for 26 July 1943. The most outspoken OWI critics in the Hearst syndicate were David Lawrence and George Rothwell Brown (see "Opportunity Lost," *Time*, 9 August 1943, 86, for Moley, see Raymond Moley, "Good and Bad Propaganda," *Newsweek*, 9 August 1943, 88. For other press coverage, see "Paging Mr. Durfee: Boner on Italian Situation Lights New Fire Under OWI," *Newsweek*, 9 August 1943, 45–46; "The Strange Case of John Durfee," *Life*, 9 August 1943, 31; "History Unrecognized: Downfall of Mussolini," *Nation* 157 (7 August 1943): 144–45; and Roger Burlingame, *Don't Let Them Scare You: The Life and Times of Elmer Davis* (Westport, Conn.: Greenwood Press, 1974), 229.

35. Rogers, *Wartime Washington*, 128, entry for 28 July 1943; and Weinberg, "Wartime Propaganda," 405.

36. Krock and Brown quoted in Winkler, *Politics of Propaganda*, 96.

37. Memo, Davis to FDR, 10 Aug. 1943; memo, Sherwood to Eisenhower, 7 Aug. 1943, both in PSF: OWI, Box 172; memo, Davis to FDR, 11 Aug. 1943, containing draft of letter from FDR to Davis, POF 5015: OWI, July–Dec. 1943, all in FDR Papers.

38. Warburg quoted in Bishop, "Overseas Branch," 46; see also memo, Barrett to Jackson, 6 May 1944; memo, Barrett to Hamblet, 6 May 1944, Box 3, Entry 6J, RG 208; and Weinberg, "Wartime Propaganda," 412.

39. Quote from Rogers, *Wartime Washington*, 82, entry for 14 April 1943. The emphasis on a strategy of truth permeates all writings on the OWI; see, for example, Manual of Information, ONAF, 1944, Box 5, Entry 6H; Eastern Press and Radio Bureau, Box 1, Entry 6B; and memo, Agar to Sherwood, 30 Nov. 1942, Box 3, Entry 6J, all in RG 208; see also "Truth Joins the AEF," *Nation's Business* 31 (February 1943): 64; and Daniel Lerner, *Sykewar: Psychological Warfare Against Germany, D-Day to V-E Day* (New York: Stewart, 1949), 26, 194.

40. For Warburg's views, see Warburg, *Unwritten Treaty*, 9, 15, 17–19, and William E. Daugherty, "Unconditional Surrender," in Daugherty and Janowitz, eds., *Psychological Warfare Casebook*, 276.

41. First quote from Shulman, "Voice of Victory," 393; second quote from William E. Daugherty, "Short-wave Broadcasts in Psychological Warfare," in Daugherty and Janowitz, eds., *Psychological Warfare Casebook*, 555; see also Charles A. H. Thomson, *The Overseas Information Service of the United States Government* (Washington, D.C.: Brookings Institution, 1948), 40–41.

42. Wallace Carroll, *Persuade or Perish* (Boston: Houghton Mifflin, 1948), 235–37.

43. Quote from Thomson, *Overseas Information*, 36; see also 41–42.

44. Weinberg, "Wartime Propaganda," 202, 206; see also "Victory for Elmer," *Time* 13 September 1943, 50; Elmer Davis and Byron Price, *War Information and Censorship* (Washington, D.C.: American Council on Public Affairs, 1943), 8–9; and Burlingame, *Don't Let Them Scare You*, 188, 195.

45. Deborah E. Lipstadt, *Beyond Belief: The American Press and the Coming of the Holocaust, 1933–1945* (New York: Free Press, 1986), 252, 265–67. For OWI's policy on atrocity stories, see Winkler, *Politics of Propaganda*, 76, and Alfred Kantorowicz, "OWI in Germany," *New Republic* 112 (14 May 1945): 673–74.

46. Winkler, *Politics of Propaganda*, 104–5, and Weinberg, "Wartime Propaganda," 433.

47. "Once More Where's Elmer?" *Newsweek*, 7 February 1944, 53–54, and Farrar, "Elmer Davis Report," 31. For earlier personnel troubles, see Sydney Weinberg, "What to Tell America: The Writer's Quarrel in the Office of War Information," *Journal of American History* 55 (June 1968): 52–59.

48. Sherwood quoted in Winkler, *Politics of Propaganda*, 107–8; see also Farrar, "Elmer Davis Report," 31.

49. Memo, Davis to FDR, 4 Jan. 1944, PSF: OSS OWI, Box 172, FDR Papers; and Bishop, "Overseas Branch," 35.

50. Memo, Davis to FDR, 8 Jan. 1944, PSF: OSS OWI, Box 172, FDR Papers.

51. Memo, Sherwood to FDR, 13 Jan. 1944, PSF: OSS OWI, Box 172, FDR Papers.

52. Agreement between Sherwood and Davis, 5 February 1944, Box 4, Rosenman Papers.

53. Davis quoted in Burlingame, *Don't Let Them Scare You*, 193; see also 240–42. For Warburg's letter of resignation, see letter, Warburg to FDR, 10 February 1944, POF 5015c: OWI Overseas Branch, FDR Papers. Besides Sherwood, Warburg, Barnes, and Johnson, the following people also resigned from OWI in 1943–1944: Alan Barth, Ulric Bell, Roger Burlingame, Loren Carroll, Gardner Cowles, Arthur Eggleston, Milton Eisenhower, Abraham Feller, Bess Furman, Christian Herter, John Houseman, Keith Kane, Owen Lattimore, William B. Lewis, Archibald MacLeish, Edgar A. Mowrer, Henry Pringle, Nicholas Roosevelt, Arthur Schlesinger, Jr., and Percy Winner.

54. Carroll quoted in letter, Carroll to Winant, 25 Mar. 1944, Box 189, Winant Papers; for postpurge changes and reorganizations, see memo, Jackson to McClure, 18 Mar. 1944, Box 21, Entry 87, RG 331; Shulman, "Voice of Victory," 4, 13; and Farrar, "Elmer Davis Report," 64–65.

55. First quote from an article in *Collier's* quoted by Sherwood to Rosenman in letter, Sherwood to Rosenman 3 July 1944; second quote in letter, Sherwood to Rosenman, 5 Mar. 1944, both in Box 4, Rosenman Papers; see also letter of resignation, Sherwood to Davis, 22 Sept. 1944, POF 5015c: OWI Overseas Branch, Box 4, all in FDR Papers. Davis's acceptance is found in the same location, as is the White House notification. The *New York Herald Tribune* article on Sherwood's resignation is contained in Box 1, Entry 6B, RG 208.

56. James Erdmann, *Leaflet Operations in the Second World War* (Denver: University of Denver, 1969), 194–95; Bishop, "Overseas Branch," 177–78, and "Hist. of PWB," pt. 1, 8–10; and pt. 2, Box 12, Entry 6G, RG 208.

57. U.S. Army, Fifth Army, *Functions of the Fifth Army Combat Propaganda Team* (Washington, D.C.: PWB, Headquarters, U.S. Army, 1944), 7, 24–30; and "Hist. of PWB," pt. 1, 10–14, and pt. 2, 3; see also Bishop, "Overseas Branch," 177–78.

58. Allied Forces, Supreme Headquarters, Psychological Warfare Division, *The Psychological Warfare Division of the Supreme Headquarters Allied Expeditionary Force: An Account of Its Operations in the Western European Theater, 1941–1945* (Bad Homburg, Ger-

many: n.p., 1945), 6–7 (hereafter *History of PWD*); see also U.S. Army, Twelfth Army Group, *Report of Operations: Final After Action Report, Twelfth Army Group*, vol. 14: P&PW Section (n.p., 1945), 27–28, and Organization of PWD, Box 20, Entry 87, RG 331.

59. McClure quoted in Erdmann, *Leaflet Operations*, 197–98, 204. For the origins of PWD, see memo, Morgan to Undersecretary of State, 10 May 1944, Box 20, Entry 87, RG 331; Thomson, *Overseas Information*, 102–3; and *History of PWD*, 6–7.

60. For PWD organization, see *History of PWD*, 7–8; Carroll, *Persuade or Perish*, 264–65; and Lerner, *Sykewar*, 59.

61. *History of PWD*, 89–90; see also H. D. Kehm, "Organization for Military Psychological Warfare in ETO," *Military Review* 26 (February 1947): 12–14. Consolidation propaganda was that delivered to liberated peoples or to the populations of occupied enemy nations.

62. PWD/SHAEF Personnel Statistical Return, 18 July 1944, Box 20, Entry 87, RG 331.

63. Organization of PW Division, Box 20, Entry 87, RG 331; *History of PWD*, 7–10; Bishop, "Overseas Branch," 190–92, 196–97, 245; and *Report of Operations, Twelfth AG*, 14:31–32; for an organizational chart of Twelfth AG P&PW, see 37–39; see also P&PW Section, Circular 17, HQ Twelfth AG, APO 655, Extract, 5 Nov. 1944, 14:259–60; for a personnel roster of the Twelfth AG P&PW Division, see 14:12–19.

64. For lower echelon organization, see Kehm, "Organization," 10–15; *Report of Operations, Twelfth AG*, P&PW Section, 14:22–23; U.S. Army, Second Mobile Radio Broadcasting Company, *History of the Second Mobile Radio Broadcasting Company, December 1943 to May 1945* (n.p., 1945), 76; U.S. Army, Third Army, *After Action Report, Third U.S. Army, 1 August 1944 to 9 May 1945*, vol. 2, Staff Section Reports, (n.p., 1945), 13–14; U.S. Army, First Army, *Report of Operations: First U.S. Army, 1 August 1944 to 22 February 1945* (n.p., 1945), 282–83; and First USA, Box 21, Entry 87, RG 331.

65. Bishop, "Overseas Branch," 254–58. For personnel rosters of the Second to Fifth MRBCs, see *Report of Operations, Twelfth AG*, 14:14–19, 33–34, and *History Second MRBC*, 10–14, 17–27.

Chapter 10. The OSS Morale Operations Branch in Action

1. Memo, PWD/SHAEF to Smith, Chief OSS MO ETO, 13 July 1944, Sub. Op. Dir. to MO Branch OSS, Box 79, Entry 148, RG 226.

2. Memo, Donovan to JCS, 13 Sept. 1945, Box 16, Entry 99, RG 226; see also Personnel Strength Rept. OSS, Box 120A, Donovan Papers; and Summary of MO Operations, 23 Apr. 1945, Box 123, Entry 136, RG 226.

3. OSS Planning Group Over-All and Special Programs for the Employment of Rumors Against the Germans, P.G. 79/1, 24 May 1944, Box 23; PG 28 Doctrine re.: Rumors, Box 12, and Rumors, Box 79, all in Entry 144, RG 226. For comebacks see Production METO—Istanbul (Ames), Box 83, Entry 144; and ETO-MO-Comebacks, 1943–45, Box 15, Entry 99, both in RG 226.

4. Rumors disseminated from Cairo, 15 June 1943 to 10 Oct. 1944, METO, Box 79;

rumors for the Balkans, Box 78; rumors for Turkey, Hungary, Rumania, Bulgaria, Box 82; all in Entry 144, RG 226.

5. Creedy to Wintle, 12 March 1945, Box 15, Entry 99, RG 226. The rumor about V-weapons appeared as a comeback in the 12 March 1945 issue of *Stars and Stripes*.

6. Letter, Creedy to Sioux, 27 Apr. 1945, and Creedy to Wintle, 12 Mar. 1945, both in Box 15, Entry 99, RG 226. In his 27 April letter, Wintle wrote that "the planning staff in Washington used to cut out most of the best human sausage meat and human skin decorations stories as implausible. And yet, reading the Belsen concentration camp account, I noted some women had made a lamp shade out of pretty tatoo [*sic*] marks, having preserved the skin of victims. So once again we've turned out to be nearer the truth with our wildest flights of imagination than with some of our more modest creations."

7. ETO MO Operations, 1944–45, Box 16, and Monthly Progress Report, NATO MO, 1 June 1944, Box 86, both in Entry 99; Production-MO-German 1–Cairo MO Operations, Box 31, Entry 154; Production METO-Steinberg Cartoons, Box 83, Entry 144; all in RG 226; see also Kermit Roosevelt, *War Report of the OSS*, 2 vols. (New York: Walker, 1976), 2:93.

8. MO War Diaries, Box 5, Entry 91; and Monthly Report, Feb.–Mar. 1945, Box 94, Entry 99, RG 226.

9. Project MTO, Box 31, Entry 154, and Box 67, Entry 144, RG 226.

10. Roosevelt, *War Report OSS*, 2:97–98, and Anthony Cave-Brown, *The Secret War Report of the OSS* (New York: Berkeley/Medallion Books, 1976), 222.

11. For leaflets to Hungary, Rumania, and Bulgaria, see Box 42; for MO aid to Tito, see Summary of MO Operations, 23 Apr. 1945, Box 123, and Black Propaganda for Tito, Box 126, Entry 136, all in RG 226; see also Roosevelt, *War Report OSS*, 2:131.

12. Apple Mission Rept., Box 42, Entry 136; memo, West to McGlasson, 26 Apr. 1944, Box 79, Entry 144; Summary of MO Operations, 23 Apr. 1945, Box 126, Entry 136, all in RG 226.

13. For Ulysses, see Ulysses Project, Box 42, Entry 136; Project METO–Ulysses parts 1, 2, 3, 4, Box 84, and Project METO–Ulysses, Box 86, both in Entry 144; Summary of MO Operations, 23 Apr. 1945, Box 123, Entry 136; Project METO–Ulysses, Plans Reports, Box 84, Entry 144, RG 226.

14. For leaflets of the Democratic United Austrian Front, see Box 75, Entry 99, and Stockholm-MO-Propaganda, Box 100, Entry 139, RG 226.

15. For the Ludendorff campaign and Driscoll's *New York Herald Tribune* article, see Box 75 and Summary of MO Operations, 23 Apr. 1945, Box 123, both in Entry 136, and Box 16, Entry 99, all in RG 226; Roosevelt, *War Report OSS*, 2:301–2.

16. Roosevelt, *War Report OSS*, 2:301–2; see also U.S. Army, Twelfth Army Group, *Report of Operations: Final After Action Report, Twelfth Army Group*, vol. 14, P&PW Section, (n.p., 1945), 188–89; and MO-PWD-ETO Black Operations—Skorpion, section 1, 3 Leaflets; Annex A for MO Skorpion leaflets, Box 15, Entry 99, RG 226; and Daniel Lerner, *Sykewar: Psychological Warfare Against Germany, D-Day to V-E Day* (New York: Stewart, 1949), 239.

17. Production METO-Kreipe-Krech, Boxes 75, Entry 99, and Boxes 79, 83, Entry 144, RG 226; see also Roosevelt, *War Report OSS*, 2:122.

18. MO Poison Pen Selection, Box 75, Entry 99, RG 226.

19. Folder 470, Box 31, Entry 154, RG 226.

20. OSS Operations, June 1944, MEDTO, Box 93, and OSS Activities, May 1944, Algiers, Box 92, both in Entry 99; Project MTO "Miami," Box 87, Entry 144, RG 226.

21. Propaganda Techniques, Box 75, Entry 99, RG 226.

22. Project ETO DND and Caserta, DND, Box 50, and DND materials, Box 31, all in Entry 154; Production MTO Rome (German), Box 83, Entry 144, all in RG 226; see also Roosevelt, *War Report OSS*, 1:218.

23. Excerpts MO/MEDTO Field Reports—Apr. 1945, Evidence of Effectiveness of DND, 9 July 1945, Box 75, and Boxes 16, 86, 89, all in Entry 99; for newspaper coverage, see Project MTO DND, Box 50, Entry 154, all in RG 226. For OWI interest, see dispatches, Sherwood, Jackson, Carroll to London, 8 July 1944; Thomson to Carroll, 16 July 1944; Carroll to Outposts, 6 July 1944; Box 108, Entry 358, RG 208.

24. MO War Diaries, Box 5, Entry 91; OSS Monthly Activities, MEDTO, Mar. 1945; Background Report, 29 February 1944–METO MO; and ETO MO Operations, 1944–45, Box 16, Entry 99, all in RG 226.

25. Report on Sioux Mission, 15 Mar. to 1 Sept. 1944, Box 79, Entry 148; Box 75, Entry 99; and Leaflets, Box 83, Entry 144, all in RG 226; see also Roosevelt, *War Report OSS*, 1:218, 2:266, and Cave-Brown, *Secret War Report*, 108–9; for Casey's wartime activities, see William Casey, *The Secret War Against Hitler* (Washington, D.C.: Regnery Gateway, 1988), 181.

26. Report on Sioux Mission, 15 Mar.–1 Sept. 1944, Box 75, Entry 99, and Box 79, Entry 148, RG 226.

27. Many examples of stickers survive (see MO Black Stickers, Box 75, Entry 99; MO War Diaries, Box 5, Entry 91; Box 31, Entry 154; and Box 100, Entry 139, all in RG 226).

28. MO poster in MO War Diaries, Publications, Box 5, Entry 91; and Propaganda Techniques, Box 75, Entry 99, RG 226.

29. Information on the missions is extensive (see Clayton D. Laurie, " 'The Sauerkrauts': The OSS and German Prisoners of War as Secret Agents in Europe, 1944–1945," *Prologue* 26 [Spring 1994]: 49–61); see also Boxes 15, 32, 69, 86, 87, 92, 93, 94, 123, all in Entry 99; Project-MTO-Sauerkraut 1–9, and Report on Missions in Box 51, Entry 154; German POWS as Agents, Box 126, Entry 136; memo, Linder to Chief MO, 2 May 1945, sub.: MO Agent Gustav Preuss, Box 67, Entry 144, all in RG 226; and Story of the Sauerkrauts, Box 102A, Donovan Papers.

30. Summary of MO Operations, 23 Apr. 1945, Box 123, Entry 136, and memo, Casey to Donovan, 12 Oct. 1944, Box 15, Entry 99, RG 226. The operation was not well known even after the war. During the writing of the MO War Diaries there was a debate about whether to include Sauerkraut and what to tell the JCS should they learn of the operation (see Report for War Diary, Box 32, Entry 99, RG 226).

31. Project-MTO-Hors d'oeuvre, Box 87, Entry 144; and Washington Branch Progress Reports, 1 Oct.–1 Nov. 1944, MEDTO/ETO, Box 88; OSS Activities, Nov. 1944, Box 93; Washington MO-PWD-ETO Black Operations, section 2—Agents, Box 15; and Report MO-ETO July 1944–Jan. 1945, 3 Feb., Box 16, all in Entry 99, RG 226.

32. Report, Lloyd to Donovan, 23 May 1946, Box 67A, Donovan Papers; see also Agent Infiltration of Front, Box 126; Summary of MO Operations, 23 Apr. 1945, Box 123, all in Entry 136, RG 226; see also *Report of Operations Twelfth AG*, 14:187–88.

33. Reports, Libich to Warner, 21 Aug. 1944, and Libich to Warner, 28 Nov. 1944,

Production-MO "Cornflakes," all in Box 50, Entry 154; MO Progress Report, 16–28 Mar. 1945, Box 67, Entry 144, all in RG 226; see also Walter Skrine and Peter Collins, "Operation Cornflakes," *Philatelist* (May 1971), 250–51; Roosevelt, *War Report OSS*, 2:98–99; and "The Story of Cornflakes, Pig Iron, and Sheet Iron," 3–9, Box 72B, Donovan Papers. For sites of Cornflakes raids, see Skrine and Collins, 254.

34. OSS Activities–ETO, Feb. 1945, Box 94, and MO Forgeries, Box 69, Entry 99, RG 226.

35. "The Story of Cornflakes, Pig Iron, and Sheet Iron," Box 72B, Donovan Papers. For the smaller version of *DND*, see Box 75, Entry 99, RG 226.

36. For stamps, see Skrine and Collins, "Operation Cornflakes," 250–51. Donovan sent FDR several forged stamps for his collection (see letter, FDR to Donovan, 5 Oct. 1944, PPF 6558, Donovan, Gen. W. J., FDR Papers); for forged ration cards, see Black Operations, Box 35, Entry 88, RG 331; for forged documents of all sorts, see Production MTO—German 2 Cairo, Box 31, Entry 154, and Washington MO Exhibits, Box 75, Entry 99, both in RG 226. For plans to counterfeit German currency, see Box 21, and for money leaflets, see Project MTO Banknote, Box 87, both in Entry 144, RG 226.

37. Daniels's idea was quashed because the ammunition might fall into Allied hands and be used with disastrous results by partisan groups or Allied soldiers who, contrary to regulations, often used captured German weapons (see letter, Daniels to Bari MO Chief, and reply, Warner to Daniels, 7 February 1945, Project-MTO-"Brunswick," Box 87, Entry 144, RG 226).

38. Plans Continued, Box 25, Entry 95, RG 331, NARA; see also Daniel Lerner, "Braddock II," in *A Psychological Warfare Casebook*, ed. William E. Daugherty and Morris Janowitz (Baltimore: Johns Hopkins University Press, 1958), 416.

39. Production, METO Broadcasts, Box 84; Production, Broadcasts Morse German I and 2, Box 85; and memo, Vanda to Ames, 6 May 1944, re: Schedule for Morse Broadcasts, Box 79, all in Entry 144. For further Project Morse documents, see Boxes 16, 69, 86, 87, Entry 99, and Clandestine Balkan Morse, Box 126, Entry 136, all in RG 226.

40. Project METO Radio Boston and Production METO Broadcasts German Voice, Box 84; memo, Ames to Warner, 14 Mar. 1944, Box 78; Smyrna, Box 79, all in Entry 144; Clandestine Balkan Radio, Box 126, Entry 136; and Cairo MO INT 3, News Service Greek, Aug. 1944, Box 77, Entry 144; Greek Newscasts, Box 45, Entry 136, and Boxes 16, 45, 69, 86, 87, Entry 99, all in RG 226.

41. Gray propaganda was a term used primarily by the British to denote an operation that was half black and half white. Soldatensender Calais was later called Soldatensender West after Calais was liberated.

42. Summary of MO Operations, 23 Apr. 1945, Box 123, Entry 136; Report MO-ETO, July 44 to Jan. 45, 3 February 1945, Box 16, Entry 99; MO Radio, Soldatensender, Box 5, Entry 91; all in RG 226. Marlene Dietrich received letters from Herbert Little and William Donovan thanking her for her MO work along with the recordings she had made for the OSS (see letters, Little to Dietrich, 31 Aug. 1945, and Donovan to Dietrich, 23 Aug. 1945, Box 123, Entry 136, RG 226).

43. MO War Dairies, Box 5, Entry 91, RG 226. For Nazi warnings and reactions, see Sefton Delmer, *Black Boomerang* (London: Secker and Warburg, 1962), 123–24, 205–6; and Casey, *Secret War Against Hitler*, 28. For overall effectiveness, see U.S. Strategic

Bombing Survey, *The Effects of Strategic Bombing on German Morale* (Washington, D.C.: Government Printing Office, 1948), 1:1–2, 27, 99, 121.

44. For Joker, see Box 16, Entry 99; MO Radio, Box 6, Entry 91; and Summary of MO Operations, 23 Apr. 1945, Box 123, Entry 136, all in RG 226. A letter between MO agents in London and Sweden suggested that news of Beck's existence be planted in Swedish newspapers, which meant that rather than hearing the broadcast itself, the Swedes reported a planted OSS rumor, thereby raising doubts as to actual radio-audience size. In any event, neutral newspapers picked up the gist of the story, and it subsequently appeared in official Allied propaganda (see Cable, 899 to 965, 14 Oct. 1944, Box 136, Entry 148, RG 226).

45. Memo, McClure to Bruce, 11 Nov. 1944, Box 2, Entry 87, RG 331; see also Roosevelt, *War Report OSS*, 2:300.

46. Directive from PWD to Smith, MO, 11 Sept. 1944, Box 79, Entry 148; and Clandestine German Radio, Box 126, Entry 136, RG 226; see also memo, Harris to McClure, 9 Oct. 1944, sub. Black Radio Programs, 10–20 Oct.; memo, Harris to Oechsner, PWD, 30 Sept. 1944; memo, McClure to MO, 26 Oct. 1944; memo, McClure to MO, 11 Sept. 1944, Box 2, Entry 87, all in RG 331. For transcripts, see Broadcasts Voice of SHAEF, Box 4, Entry 87, RG 331, and Box 6, Entry 99, RG 226.

47. MO Radio, Box 5, Entry 91; for Bradley's reaction, see Box 16, Entry 99, RG 226.

48. For Capricorn, see Directive, McClure to MO, 19 February 1945, Box 35, Entry 88, RG 331; Summary of MO Operations, 23 Apr. 1945, Box 123, Entry 136; and Interrogation from Progress Report, 1–30 June, 1945, 30 June 1945, Box 16, Entry 99; see also Boxes 94 and 95, Entry 99, all in RG 226; and *History of PWD*, 54–55.

49. Annex F, Box 15; Annex E, Plan for Covert PW Operation on Radio Luxembourg; Annex G, transcripts; and Section 4, Radio, Box 15, Entry 99, all in RG 226; see also memo, Harris to CO, PWD, n.d., sub.: "Black" Operation on Radio Luxembourg, Box 2, Entry 87, RG 331; and Brewster Morgan, " 'Operation Annie': [The U.S.] Army Radio Station That Fooled the Nazis by Telling Them the Truth," *Saturday Evening Post*, 9 March 1946, 19.

50. For a 1212 Broadcast, see *Report of Operations Twelfth AG*, 14:190–95.

51. Reaction to 1212, 7 Mar. 1945, Annex K, Box 15, Entry 99, RG 226, and memo, Paley to McClure, 6 Apr. 1945, sub.: Final Broadcast of Operation Annie, Reply, 13 Apr. 1945, Box 2, Entry 87, RG 331; see also H. H. Burger, " 'Operation Annie': Now It Can Be Told," *New York Times Magazine*, 17 February 1946, 12–13, and William H. Hale, "Big Noise in Little Luxembourg," *Harper's*, April 1946, 377–84. The perception regarding Strasser could have resulted from the earlier British attempts to use the former Nazi to foment revolution in Germany (see Robert H. Keyserlingk, "Political Warfare Illusion: Otto Strasser and Britain's World War II Strategy of National Revolts Against Hitler," *Dalhousie Review* 61 [Spring 1981]: 71–92).

52. One radio operation code-named Woodland was intended to appeal to Bavarian and Austrian separatist groups (see memo, Baldwin to McClure, n.d., Box 2, Entry 87, RG 331).

53. Goebbels quoted in Joseph Goebbels, *Final Entries, 1945: The Diaries of Joseph Goebbels*, ed. Hugh Trevor-Roper (New York: G. Putnam's Sons, 1978), 223, entry for 28 March 1945; see also memo, McClure to Chief of Staff, SHAEF, 31 Mar. 1945; memo,

Hodgkin to Alms, G-3 (Forward), 26 Mar. 1945, sub.: Aspidistra, Box 35, Entry 88, RG 331. For example, see Transcript, Box 75, Entry 99, RG 226.

54. First quote from memo, Hodgkin to Alms, G-3 (Forward), 16 April 1945; Mc-Clure quote from memo, McClure to Chief of Staff, SHAEF, 31 Mar. 1945; see also memo, Hodgkin to Alms, G-3 (Forward), 26 Mar. 1945, sub.: Aspidistra, all in Box 35, Entry 88, RG 331. For Nazi jamming efforts, see William D. Bayles, "England's Radio Blitz," *Reader's Digest*, April 1944, 61.

55. Memo, McClure to G-2, SHAEF, n.d., sub.: Covert Propaganda Operations, Box 2, Entry 87, RG 331.

56. Roosevelt, *War Report OSS*, 1:222–23.

Chapter 11. White Propaganda Operations

1. Robert Pirsein, *The VOA: A History of the International Broadcasting Activities of the United States Government, 1940–1962* (New York: Arno Press, 1979), 52–55; see also Alfred Kantorowicz, "OWI in Germany," *New Republic* 112 (14 May 1945): 673; Robert L. Bishop, "The Overseas Branch of the Office of War Information" (Ph.D. diss., University of Wisconsin, 1966), 230, 234–38; and Josef Israels, "The Wehrmacht's Yankee Girlfriend," *Collier's*, 3 March 1945, 68. For *Sternenbanner* and *L'Amerique en Guerre*, see Leaflets (Production OWI London), Box 10, Entry 6E, RG 208; Box 1, Entry 112, RG 226; and Public Opinion, Box 7, Entry 87, RG 331.

2. Weekly Propaganda Directives (hereafter WPD), 2, 9, 16, 23, 30 Oct. 1943, Box 822, Entry 363, RG 208.

3. WPD, 24 Dec. 1943, and 1 Jan. 1944, Box 822, Entry 363; and Overseas Operations Branch Central Directive (hereafter OOBCD), 23–30 Dec., Box 818, Entry 359, RG 208.

4. WPD 8, 15, 22, 29 Jan. and 5 Feb. 1944, Box 822, Entry 363, RG 208.

5. OOBCD, 10–17 Feb. 1944, Box 818, Entry 359, RG 208.

6. Ibid., and WPD, 12, 19, 26 Feb. 1944, Box 822, Entry 363, RG 208.

7. WPD, 1 June 1944, Box 823, Entry 359, RG 208.

8. The spring 1944 OWI anti-Luftwaffe operation is a classic example of a successful campaign; see WPD, 4, 9, 16 Mar. 1944, 13, 20, 27 Apr. 1944, 4, 11 May 1944, Boxes 822 and 823 in Entry 363; see also OOBCD, 2–9, 7–13, 18–25 Mar., 2–9 Apr., 16–23 May 1944, Box 818, Entry 359, RG 208; and Wallace Carroll, "Where is the Luftwaffe?" in *A Psychological Warfare Casebook*, ed. William E. Daugherty and Morris Janowitz (Baltimore: Johns Hopkins University Press, 1958), 373–81. For the OSS campaign, see memo, Mann to Smith, London and Warner, Cairo, 10 May 1944, sub.: Plan to Demoralize German Fighter Pilots, Box 16, Entry 110, RG 226.

9. "OWI's ABSIE," *Time*, 16 July 1945, 69; see also Bishop, "Overseas Branch," 217, 219, 222, 224; Pirsein, *VOA*, 81–84; London Newsletter, Radio Division Progress Report, 11 Aug. 1944, Box 3, Entry 6J; and ABSIE: German Operations Plans and Policies, Box 1, Entry 6E, RG 208.

10. OOBCD, 4–11 July 1944, Box 819, Entry 317, RG 208.

11. WPD-Germany, 1, 8, 16, 23, 30 June; 7, 14 July 1944, Box 823, Entry 359, RG 208.

12. WPD, 7 July 1944, Box 823, Entry 359, RG 208.

13. Special Guidance on Long-Range Media for Europe, 14 July 1944, Box 107, Entry 358, RG 208.

14. Ibid.

15. Quotes from OOBCD 11–18 July 1944, Box 819, Entry 317; for themes, see OOBCD, 22–29 Aug., 29 Aug.–5 Sept., 5–14, 12–19, 19–26 Sept., 31 Oct.–7 Nov., 7–14 Nov., 5–12 Dec. 1944, Box 819, Entry 317; and WPD, 24 Aug., 14, 21, 28 Sept., 26 Oct. 1944, Box 823, Entry 359, all in RG 208; see also Wallace Carroll, *Persuade or Perish* (Boston: Houghton Mifflin Company, 1948), 269–70.

16. WPD, 5 Oct. 1944, Box 823, Entry 359; WPD, 7 Dec. 1944, Box 824, Entry 363; WPD, 26 Oct. 1944, Box 823, Entry 35; and WPD, 2, 10, 16, 23, 30 Nov. 1944, Box 824, Entry 363, all in RG 208.

17. OOBCD, 26 Dec. 1944, 3–10 and 17–24 Jan. 1945, Box 819, Entry 317, and WPD, 5, 12, 19, 26 Jan. 1945, Box 824, Entry 363, RG 208.

18. These themes were evident in output for the last year of the war; see OOBCD, 18–25 July, 8–15 Aug., Box 819, Entry 371; WPD, 21, 28 July, 4, 11, 17 Aug., 14 Sept., 5, 12, 19 Oct., Box 823, Entry 359; WPD, 7, 14 Dec. 1944, Box 824, Entry 363; OOBCD, 30 Sept.–7 Oct., 15–22 Oct., 28 Oct.–3 Nov. 1943, Box 818, Entry 359; WPD, 2, 9, 16, 23 Feb., 2, 9 Mar., Box 824, Entry 363; and WPD, 6, 13 Apr. 1945, Box 825, Entry 359, all in RG 208.

19. For quote, see WPD, 31 Aug. 1944, Box 823, Entry 359, see also WPD, 7 Sept. 1944, Box 823, Entry 359; and WPD, 23 Mar. 1945, Box 824, Entry 363, in RG 208. References to general "war news" is found in each OWI directive. For the Teheran Conference, see Overseas Operations Branch Central Directive, 5–12 Sept. 1944, Box 819, Entry 371; for the Dumbarton Oaks Conference, see WPD, 12 Oct. 1944, Box 823, Entry 359; for the Crimea Conference, see OOBCD, 14–21, 21–28 February 1945, Box 819, Entry 371; WPD, 16, 23 February, 2 Mar. 1945, Box 824, Entry 363; for the San Francisco Conference, see OOBCD, 25 Apr.–2 May 1945, Box 819, Entry 371; for general United Nations unity, see OOBCD, 28 Oct.–3 Nov. 1943, Box 818, Entry 359; WPD, 10 Nov., 29 Dec. 1944, Box 824, Entry 363, all in RG 208.

20. Dispatch, Thomson to Carroll, 20 Dec. 1944, re: Whereabouts of Hitler Campaign, Box 830, Entry 363; OWI Overseas Branch Special Guidance on Hitler's Proclamation, 12 Nov. 1944, Box 819, Entry 371; OOBCD, 27 Dec. 1944–3 Jan. 1945, 3–10, 17–24 Jan. 1945, Box 819, Entry 371, RG 208.

21. OOBCD, 14–21, 21–28 Mar., 18–25 Apr., 25 Apr.–2 May 1945, Box 819, Entry 371, and WPD, 4, 11 May 1945, Box 825, Entry 359, RG 208. On 15 July 1945, the OSS, OWI, and PWD/SHAEF, all of which were wartime agencies, turned over the control of propaganda, information services, and communications in Germany to the Allied occupation forces.

22. Pirsein, *VOA*, 77.

23. Holly Shulman, "The Voice of Victory: The Development of American Propaganda and the Voice of America, 1920–1942" (Ph.D. diss., University of Maryland, 1984), 135, and Pirsein, *VOA*, 56.

24. Warburg quoted in Bishop, "Overseas Branch," 381–84; see also 385–87; and Edward W. Barrett, *Truth Is Our Weapon* (New York: Funk and Wagnalls, 1953), 32–33.

25. William E. Daugherty, "Creed of a Modern Propagandist," in Daugherty and

Janowitz, eds., *Psychological Warfare Casebook*, 38–39; see also H. D. Kehm, "Can Psychological Warfare Pay Its Passage?" *Military Review* 26 (March 1947): 41–42; and Kantorowicz, "OWI in Germany," 673.

26. Martin F. Herz, "The Combat Leaflet—Weapon of Persuasion," *Army Information Digest* 5 (June 1950): 37–43; idem, "Mechanics of Surrender, Capture, and Desertion," in Daugherty and Janowitz, eds., *Psychological Warfare Casebook*, 393–96.

27. U.S. Army, Fifth Army, *Functions of the Fifth Army Combat Propaganda Team* (CPT) (Washington, D.C.: PWB Headquarters, U.S. Army, 1944), 8–9; U.S. Army, First Army, *Report of Operations, First U.S. Army, 1 August 1944 to 22 February 1945,* Annex 14 (n.p., 1945), 283–84; and William E. Daugherty, "Military Objectives of Psychological Warfare," in Daugherty and Janowitz, eds., *Psychological Warfare Casebook*, 373.

28. For PWD/SHAEF leaflets, see Leaflets, Box 10, Entry 6E, RG 208, and Box 10, Entry 87, RG 331. See also James Erdmann, *Leaflet Operations in the Second World War* (Denver: University of Denver, 1969), 287–88; Daniel Lerner, *Sykewar: Psychological Warfare Against Germany, D-Day to V-E Day* (New York: Stewart, 1948), 238–40; and *History of PWD*, 90–94, 133–40. For PWD Guidance for Germany and Voice of SHAEF Broadcast texts, see Boxes 2 and 3, Entry 87, RG 331.

29. H. D. Kehm, "The Methods and Functions of Military Psychological Warfare," *Military Review* 26 (January 1947), 11–12; see also memo, Kaufman, 5 Oct. 1944; Report, Garvey to Kaufman, 11 Dec. 1944, Box 30, Entry 87, RG 331; *Report of Operations, First Army*, 285–86; and Caroline Reed, "D-Day Propaganda," *History Today* (U.K.) 34 (June 1984): 27.

30. Memo, Hazeltine to McClure, 15 June 1943, re: Combat Leaflet Distribution to Date, Box 10, Entry 87, RG 331, and Operations of PWB with Seventh Army in Sicily, 18 Aug. 1943, Box 1, Entry 6E, RG 208.

31. Current Combat Leaflets: PWD-SHAEF, 1 Nov. 1944, Box 10, Entry 6E, RG 208; Third USA Leaflets, Box 34, Entry 88; Propaganda, Box 10, Entry 87, RG 331; see also Lerner, *Sykewar*, 238–40. For the safe conduct and "Ei Sorrender" leaflet, see U.S. Army, Twelfth Army Group, *Report of Operations and Final After Action Report, Twelfth Army Group,* Annex 14, P&PW Section (n.p., 1945), 14:126–32.

32. Kehm, "Methods and Functions," 10–12. For leaflet development and air delivery procedures, see *Report of Operations, Twelfth AG*, 14:141–55; for artillery see 14:132–41.

33. Quotes from *Report of Operations, Twelfth AG*, 14:116–22. For *Frontpost*, see Box 108, Entry 358, RG 208, and Box 35, Entry 88, RG 331.

34. *Report of Operations, Twelfth AG*, 122–25; see also William E. Daugherty, "News Sheets as Weapons of War" in Daugherty and Janowitz, eds., *Psychological Warfare Casebook,* 556–62, and Report, Powell to Fitzgerald, 4 Nov. 1944, Box 30, Entry 87, RG 331. For the Seventh Army equivalent of *Frontpost*, *Frontbrief*, see Seventh Army Leaflets, Box 34, Entry 88, RG 331. For *Die Mitteilungen*, see German Miscellaneous, Box 108, Entry 358, RG 208.

35. First Army Leaflets, Box 34, Entry 88, RG 331; and *Report of Operations, First Army*, 14:206, 283–86. For MRBC activities, see U.S. Army, Second MRBC, *History of the Second Mobile Radio Broadcast Company: December 1943 to May 1945* (n.p., 1945), 6, 31–34; see also U.S. Army, Third Army, *After Action Report, Third U.S. Army, August 1944 to May 1945,* vol. 2, Staff Section Reports, pt. 3, G-2, (n.: 1945).

36. Personnel Roster, 20 Oct. 1944, Box 21, Entry 87, RG 331, and William Hale,

"Big Noise in Little Luxembourg," *Harper's*, April 1946, 328–29. For Paley's role, see Sally Bedell Smith, *In All His Glory: The Life of William S. Paley, the Legendary Tycoon and His Brilliant Circle* (New York: Simon and Schuster, 1990), 220.

37. For programming, see Radio Luxembourg schedule for 2 Oct. 1944, Box 29, Entry 87; see also memo, Taylor to Walker, n.d., Box 30, Entry 87; memo, Powell to Fitzgerald, 3 Sept. 1944, re: P.W. Plan 4; PWD/SHAEF Plan by R. H. S. Crossman, both in Box 25, Entry 95; and memo, Operations, Intelligence, and Administration, 15 Sept. 1944, Box 2, Entry 87, all in RG 331; see also *Report of Operations, Twelfth AG*, 14:165–74.

38. *Report of Operations, Twelfth AG*, 14:156–57, 162–65. Historian Omer Bartov discovered, however, that the Wehrmacht provided numerous radios to their front-line troops as early as 1940, more than 134 sets for each division, and that German soldiers were avid radio listeners and newspaper and magazine readers; see Omer Bartov, *The Eastern Front, 1941–1945: German Troops and the Barbarization of Warfare* (New York: St. Martin's, 1986), 69–70, 181 n.98.

39. David Hertz, "The Radio Siege of Lorient," in Daugherty and Janowitz, eds., *Psychological Warfare Casebook*, 384–92; see also Hertz, "The Radio Siege of Lorient," *Hollywood Quarterly*, Jan. 1946, 291–301; *History MRBC*, 52–53; and *Report of Operations, Twelfth AG*, 14:157–60. The German garrison, well supplied by U-boat, did not surrender until after VE Day.

40. Kehm, "Methods and Functions of Military Psychological Warfare," 9; see also Thomas Mahoney, "Words That Win Battles: Psychological Warfare," *Popular Science*, June 1945, 206–7, and *Report of Operations, First Army*, 287–88. Questioned on the shortage by McClure, Paley could provide only a rough estimate of the number of units in existence and had to admit that he was not sure where they were located or what they were doing (see memo, Paley to McClure, 24 Jan. 1945, sub.: PA Systems, Loudspeaker Devices, Box 30, Entry 87, RG 331).

41. For MRBC loudspeaker operations, see *History Second MRBC*, 35, 39, 41, 42, 45, 49–52. For Third Army, see *After Action Report, Third Army*, 2:25, 29, 37, 42.

42. Dolan quoted in Anthony Cave-Brown, *The Last Hero: Wild Bill Donovan* (New York: Time-Life Books, 1982), 551–54; see also Cecil Carnes, "Advertising Paid Off at Cherbourg," *Saturday Evening Post*, 12 August 1944, 84; Text of Surrender Message, Severin Kaven Papers, MHI; and Martin F. Herz, "Ultimatums and Propaganda to Surrounded Units," in Daugherty and Janowitz, eds., *Psychological Warfare Casebook*, 399. The official First Army report claims 2,800 POWs were taken (see *Report of Operations, First Army*, 18:207).

43. One of the best coordinated combat propaganda operations is described in Edward A. Caskey, "Coordinated 'Assault' on the Geilenkirchen Salient," in Daugherty and Janowitz, eds., *Psychological Warfare Casebook*, 627–31; see also Henry F. Pringle, "The Baloney Barrage Pays Off," *Saturday Evening Post*, 31 March 1945, 18–19; *Report of Operations, Twelfth AG*, 14:175–86; and *After Action Report, Third Army*, which contains a loudspeaker broadcast transcript, 87–88.

44. Report, Shotland to HQ, Twelfth AG P&PW, 27 Apr. 1945, sub.: PA Mission Report, Box 30, Entry 87, RG 331.

45. Quote from Operations Research Office, *Views of World War II Psywar Personnel*, Technical Memorandum ORO-T-141 (Baltimore: Johns Hopkins University Press, 1952), 158 and 13–16; report, Powell to Fitzgerald, 4 Nov. 1944, Box 30, Entry 87, RG 331; and

letter, Jackson to Carroll, 25 Sept. 1943, Box 32, Entry 99, RG 226. For a favorable view, see A. T. Hadley, "The Propaganda Tank," *Armor* 60 (January–February 1951): 32–33. For another negative view, see Report of Combat Zone Propaganda Conducted in FUSA sector 3–9 July 1944, Box 10, Entry 87, RG 331.

46. Kehm, "Can Psychological Warfare Pay Its Passage?" 34–35, and Martin F. Herz, "Some Psychological Lessons from Leaflet Propaganda in World War II," *Public Opinion Quarterly* 13 (Fall 1949): 472–73.

47. For Nazi reactions, see Kehm, "Can Psychological Warfare Pay Its Passage?" 38, and Con O'Neill, "Paper Warfare in Tunisia," *Army Quarterly* (UK) 44 (April 1944): 87.

48. Jeffrey Willis, "The Wehrmacht Propaganda Branch: German Military Propaganda and Censorship During World War II" (Ph.D. diss., University of Virginia, 1964), 34–39, 200–201; and *Fifth Army CPT*, 58–61.

49. Goebbels quote from Joseph Goebbels, *Final Entries, 1945: The Diaries of Joseph Goebbels*, ed. Hugh Trevor-Roper (New York: G. P. Putnam's Sons, 1978), 223, entry for 23 March 1945; see also Jay W. Baird, *The Mythical World of Nazi Propaganda, 1939–1945* (Minneapolis: University of Minnesota Press, 1975), 38; Allied Forces, Supreme Headquarters, Psychological Warfare Branch, Monitoring Report: Radio Monitoring Division, *A Record of Axis, Neutral, Clandestine, and Certain Allied Broadcasts* (n.p., n.d.), nos. 106, 118, and 124; and Functions of PWD, Box 32, Entry 99, RG 226.

50. For morale reports, see Box 144, Entry 136, RG 226; see also Murray Gurfein and Morris Janowitz, "Trends in Wehrmacht Morale," *Public Opinion Quarterly* 10 (Spring 1946): 78–84; PWD/SHAEF Report 16, Reaction of POWs to Combat Leaflets, 22 Sept. 1944, Public Opinion, Box 7, and Reports of PWD Interrogation Teams, 1944, Box 26, both in Entry 87, RG 331; and Reactions of POWs to SHAEF leaflets, 17 Aug. 1944, Box 79, Entry 148, RG 226.

51. Eden's impressions are recorded in *History of PWD*, 175, and MO War Diaries, Box 6, Entry 91, RG 226. For reports of effectiveness, see *Report of Operations, First Army*, 18:208–9, 14:286–87, and *Fifth Army CPT*, 37–53, especially 40–49.

52. Quote from "Psychological Warfare Did Not Win the War," *Forum* 104 (October 1945): 168–69, and Kehm, "Can Psychological Warfare Pay Its Passage?" 36–39.

53. McClure quoted in Erdmann, 42; Eisenhower quoted in C. A. H. Thomson, *The Overseas Information Service of the United States Government* (Washington, D.C.: Brookings Institution, 1948), 115–16n; see also *Fifth Army CPT*, 5.

Selected Bibliography

Manuscripts

Archival Collections

National Archives and Records Administration, Washington, D.C.
  Records of American Expeditionary Force, 1917–1919 (RG 120).
  Records of War Department General and Special Staffs (RG 165).
  Records of Office of War Information (RG 208).
  Records of Joint Chiefs of Staff (RG 218).
  Records of Office of Strategic Services (RG 226).
  Records of Foreign Broadcast Information Service (RG 262).
  Records of Allied Operational and Occupational Headquarters, World War II (RG 331).

Private Collections

Joseph Alsop Papers, Library of Congress, Washington, D.C.
Stewart Alsop Papers, Library of Congress, Washington, D.C.
Joseph Barnes Papers, Library of Congress, Washington, D.C.
Wallace Carroll Papers, Library of Congress, Washington, D.C.
Benjamin Cohen Papers, Library of Congress, Washington, D.C.
George Creel Papers, Library of Congress, Washington, D.C.
Elmer Davis Papers, Library of Congress, Washington, D.C.
Wallace Deuel Papers, Library of Congress, Washington, D.C.
William J. Donovan Papers, U.S. Army Military History Institute, Carlisle, Pa.
George F. Eliot Papers, Library of Congress, Washington, D.C.
Corey Ford Papers, Library of Congress, Washington, D.C.
Stanley High Papers, Franklin D. Roosevelt Library, Hyde Park, N.Y.

Harold Ickes Papers, Library of Congress, Washington, D.C.
Severin Kaven Papers, U.S. Army Military History Institute, Carlisle, Pa.
Frank Knox Papers, Library of Congress, Washington, D.C.
Robert A. McClure Papers, U.S. Army Military History Institute, Carlisle, Pa.
Archibald MacLeish Papers, Library of Congress, Washington, D.C.
Lowell Mellett Papers, Franklin D. Roosevelt Library, Hyde Park, N.Y.
Edgar A. Mowrer Papers, Library of Congress, Washington, D.C.
Saul Padover Papers, Franklin D. Roosevelt Library, Hyde Park, N.Y.
Henry Pringle Papers, Library of Congress, Washington, D.C.
Franklin D. Roosevelt Papers, Franklin D. Roosevelt Library, Hyde Park, N.Y.
    President's Official File (POF)
    President's Personal File (PPF)
    President's Secretary File (PSF)
Kermit Roosevelt Papers, Library of Congress, Washington, D.C.
Samuel I. Rosenman Papers, Franklin D. Roosevelt Library, Hyde Park, N.Y.
Whitney H. Shepardson Papers, Franklin D. Roosevelt Library, Hyde Park, N.Y.
Harold D. Smith Papers, Franklin D. Roosevelt Library, Hyde Park, N.Y.
William Standley Papers, Library of Congress, Washington, D.C.
Henry Stimson Papers, Library of Congress, Washington, D.C.
Arthur Sweetser Papers, Library of Congress, Washington, D.C.
John G. Winant Papers, Franklin D. Roosevelt Library, Hyde Park, N.Y.

*Published Primary Sources: Documents, Manuals, and
Reports*

Allied Forces, Supreme Headquarters, Psychological Warfare Branch, Monitoring Report: Radio Monitoring Division. *A Record of Axis, Neutral, Clandestine, and Certain Allied Broadcasts*. N.p., n.d.
Allied Forces, Supreme Headquarters, Psychological Warfare Division. *The Psychological Warfare Division, Supreme Headquarters Allied Expeditionary Force: An Account of Its Operations in the Western European Campaign, 1941–1945*. Bad Homburg, Germany: n.p., 1945.
Committee for National Morale. *A Plan for a National Morale Service, Submitted by the Committee for National Morale*. New York: Committee for National Morale, 1941.
Council on Foreign Relations. *By-Laws and List of Officers and Members*. New York: Council on Foreign Relations, 1938.
———. *Annual Report of the Executive Director*. New York: Council on Foreign Relations, 1943.
———. *War and Peace Studies of the Council on Foreign Relations, 1939–1945*. New York: Council on Foreign Relations, 1946.
———. *The Council on Foreign Relations: A Record of Twenty-Five Years, 1921–1946*. New York: Council on Foreign Relations, 1947.
Institute for Propaganda Analysis. *Propaganda Analysis*. 4 vols. New York: Institute for Propaganda Analysis, 1942.

Joint Chiefs of Staff. *Organization and Development of the Joint Chiefs of Staff, 1942–1987.* Washington, D.C.: Joint Secretariat, JCS, 1987.

Office of War Information. *Office of War Information in the European Theater of Operations: A Report on the Activities of OWI, Jan. 1944 to Jan. 1945.* London: n.p., 1945.

Operations Research Office. *Commentary on Hitler's Theories on Propaganda.* Technical Memorandum ORO-T-135. Baltimore: Johns Hopkins University Press, 21 November 1951.

———. *The Nature of Psychological Warfare.* Technical Memorandum T-214. Baltimore: Johns Hopkins University Press, 5 January 1953.

———. *Target Analysis and Media in Propaganda to Audiences Abroad.* Technical Memorandum T-222. Baltimore: Johns Hopkins University Press, August 1953.

———. *Views of World War II Psywar Personnel.* Technical Memorandum T-141. Baltimore: Johns Hopkins University Press, 23 November 1952.

Rosenman, Samuel I., comp. *The Public Papers and Addresses of F.D.R.* 13 vols. New York: Random House, Macmillan Company, Harper and Brothers, 1938–1950.

U.S. Army. Fifth Army. *Functions of the Fifth Army Combat Propaganda Team.* Washington, D.C.: Psychological Warfare Branch, Headquarters, United States Army, 1944.

———. Fifth Army. Mobile Radio Broadcasting Company. *Psychological Warfare Branch Combat Team.* N.p., n.d.

———. First Army. *Report of Operations, October 1943 to August 1944, August 1944 to February 1945, and 23 February to 8 May 1945.* Annex no. 14. N.p., 1945.

———. Second Mobile Radio Broadcasting Company. *History, Second Mobile Radio Broadcasting Company, December 1943 to May 1945.* N.p., 1945.

———. Third Army. *After Action Report, 1 August 1944 to 9 May 1945.* Staff Section Reports. N.p., 1945.

———. Twelfth Army Group. *Report of Operations: Final After Action Report, Twelfth Army Group.* European Theater of Operations. Vol. 14. N.p., 1945.

U.S. Civil Service Commission. *Official Register of the United States.* Washington, D.C.: Government Printing Office, 1939–1945.

U.S. Congress. House. *Investigation of Un-American Activities and Propaganda.* 76th Congress, 1st sess., 3 January 1939, House Report no. 2.

U.S. Coordinator of Information. Research and Analysis Branch, Psychological Division. *Strategic Aims of Axis versus American Broadcasts.* Washington, D.C.: n.p., 1942.

U.S. Coordinator of Inter-American Affairs. *History of the Office of the Coordinator of Inter-American Affairs.* Washington, D.C.: Government Printing Office, 1947.

U.S. Department of State. *Psychological Warfare in Support of Military Operations.* Washington, D.C.: Government Printing Office, 1951.

U.S. Federal Bureau of Investigation. *Work of the FBI Against Spies and Saboteurs.* Washington, D.C.: Government Printing Office, 1942.

U.S. Strategic Bombing Survey. *The Effects of Strategic Bombing on German Morale.* Vol. 1. Washington, D.C.: Government Printing Office, 1948.

U.S. War Department. Psychological Warfare Branch. *Psychological Warfare in the Mediterranean Theater.* Washington, D.C.: Government Printing Office, 1945.

———. Propaganda Branch. Intelligence Division. *A Syllabus of Psychological Warfare.* Edited by Paul M. A. Linebarger. Washington, D.C.: Government Printing Office, 1946.

Autobiographies, Diaries, Memoirs

Barrett, Edward W. *Truth Is Our Weapon.* New York: Funk and Wagnalls, 1953.

Blankenhorn, Heber. *Adventures in Propaganda: Letters from an Intelligence Officer in France.* Boston: Houghton Mifflin Company, 1919.

Bruce, David K. E. *OSS Against the Reich: The World War II Diaries of Colonel David K. E. Bruce.* Edited by Nelson D. Lankford. Kent, Ohio: Kent State University Press, 1990.

Bullitt, William C. *For the President; Personal and Secret: Correspondence Between Franklin D. Roosevelt and William C. Bullitt.* Boston: Houghton Mifflin Company, 1972.

Burlingame, Roger. *I Have Known Many Worlds.* Garden City, N.Y.: Doubleday and Company, 1959.

Carroll, Wallace. *Persuade or Perish.* Boston: Houghton Mifflin Company, 1948.

Casey, William J. *The Secret War Against Hitler.* Washington, D.C.: Regnery Gateway, 1988.

Colby, William, and Peter Forbath. *Honorable Men: My Life in the CIA.* New York: Simon and Schuster, 1978.

Conant, James B. *My Several Lives: Memoirs of a Social Inventor.* New York: Harper and Row, 1970.

Coon, Carlton Stevens. *A North Africa Story: The Anthropologist as OSS Agent, 1941–1943.* Ipswich, Mass.: Gambit, 1980.

Corvo, Max. *The OSS in Italy, 1942–1945: A Personal Memoir.* Westport, Conn.: Greenwood Press, 1989.

Creel, George. *How We Advertised America: The First Telling of the Amazing Story of the Committee on Public Information That Carried the Gospel of Americanism to Every Corner of the Globe.* New York: Harper Brothers, 1920.

_____. *Rebel at Large: Recollections of Fifty Crowded Years.* New York: G. P. Putnam's Sons, 1947.

de Chambrun, Rene. *I Saw France Fall: Will She Rise Again?* New York: William Morrow and Company, 1940.

Delmer, Sefton. *Black Boomerang.* London: Secker and Warburg, 1962.

Dodd, William E. *Ambassador Dodd's Diary, 1933–1938.* New York: Harcourt, Brace and Company, 1941.

Goebbels, Paul Joseph. *Final Entries, 1945: The Diaries of Joseph Goebbels.* Edited by Hugh Trevor-Roper. New York: Putnam, 1978.

_____. *The Goebbels Diaries, 1942–1943.* Edited and translated by Louis Lochner. New York: Doubleday and Company, 1948.

Hitler, Adolf. *Mein Kampf.* Boston: Houghton Mifflin Company, 1971.

Hoover, Calvin B. *Memoirs of Capitalism, Communism, and Nazism.* Durham, N.C.: Duke University Press, 1965.

Houseman, John. *Front and Center.* New York: Simon and Schuster, 1979.

_____. *Run Through.* New York: Simon and Schuster, 1972.

Howe, Ellic. *The Black Game: British Subversive Operations Against the Germans During the Second World War.* London: Michael Joseph, 1982.

Ickes, Harold. *The Secret Diary of Harold Ickes.* 2 vols. New York: Simon and Schuster, 1954.

Krock, Arthur. *Memoirs: Sixty Years on the Firing Line*. New York: Funk and Wagnalls, 1959.

Langer, William L. *In and Out of the Ivory Tower: The Autobiography of William L. Langer*. New York: N. Watson Academic Publishers, 1977.

Lee, Raymond E. *The London Journal of Gen. Raymond E. Lee, 1940–1941*. Edited by James Leutze. Boston: Little, Brown, 1971.

Lockhart, Robert B. *The Diaries of Sir Robert Bruce Lockhart, 1939–1945*. Edited by Kenneth D. Young. 2 vols. London: St. Martin's Press, 1980.

Lovell, Stanley. *Of Spies and Stratagems*. Englewood Cliffs, N.J.: Prentice-Hall, 1963.

Morgan, William J. *OSS and I*. New York: Norton, 1957.

Mowrer, Edgar A. *A Good Time to Be Alive*. New York: Duell, Sloan and Pearce, 1959.

———. *Triumph and Turmoil*. New York: Weybright and Talley, 1968.

Murphy, Robert. *Diplomat Among Warriors*. Garden City, N.Y.: Doubleday and Company, 1964.

Paley, William S. *As It Happened: A Memoir*. Garden City, N.Y.: Doubleday and Company, 1979.

Phillips, William. *Ventures in Diplomacy*. Boston: Beacon, 1952.

Rogers, James G. *Wartime Washington: The Secret O.S.S. Journal of James Grafton Rogers, 1942–1943*. Edited by Thomas Troy. Frederick, Md.: University Publications of America, 1987.

Sherwood, Robert E. *Roosevelt and Hopkins: An Intimate Biography*. New York: Harper and Brothers, 1950.

———. *There Shall Be No Night*. New York: Charles Scribner's Sons, 1940.

Shirer, William L. *Berlin Diary: The Journal of a Foreign Correspondent, 1934–1941*. New York: Alfred A. Knopf, 1941.

———. *The Nightmare Years, 1930–1940, a Twentieth Century Journey*. Boston: Little, Brown and Company, 1984.

Stimson, Henry L., and McGeorge Bundy. *On Active Service in Peace and War*. New York: G. P. Putnam's Sons, 1948.

Taylor, Edmond. *Awakening from History*. Boston: Gambit, 1969.

Warburg, James P. *The Long Road Home: The Autobiography of a Maverick*. New York: Doubleday and Company, 1964.

Wilson, Hugh R. *A Career Diplomat*. Westport, Conn.: Greenwood Press, 1973.

———. *Diplomat Between Wars*. New York: Longmans, Green and Company, 1941.

———. *The Education of a Diplomat*. New York: Longmans, Green and Company, 1938.

Books and Articles

Abbas, K. A. "India Listens; Fascist Propaganda." *Living Age 357* (September 1939): 55–58.

"ABC of OWI." *Newsweek*, 20 July 1942, 70.

"Addressed to the Germans: Suggestions for Leaflets on Berlin." *Free World* 2 (March 1942): 144–47.

Agar, Herbert. *A Time for Greatness*. London: Eyre and Spottiswoode, 1940.

_____. *World-Wide Civil War*. New York: Freedom House, 1942.

Agar, Herbert, Frank Kingdon, and Lewis Mumford. *Beyond German Victory*. New York: Reynal and Hitchcock, 1940.

Albert, Ernest. "German Propaganda." *Contemporary Review* 157 (January 1940): 84–88.

_____. "The Press in Nazi Germany." *Contemporary Review* 154 (December 1938): 693–99.

Alcorn, Robert H. *No Bugles for Spies: Tales of the OSS*. New York: David McKay, 1962.

Allport, Floyd H., and Mary Mathes Simpson. "Broadcasting to an Enemy Country: What Appeals Are Effective, and Why." *Journal of Social Psychology* 23 (May 1946): 217–24.

Alsop, Stewart, and Thomas Braden. *Sub Rosa: The OSS and American Espionage*. New York: Reynal and Hitchcock, 1946.

Ambrose, Stephen E., and Richard H. Immerman. *Milton S. Eisenhower, Educational Statesman*. Baltimore: Johns Hopkins University Press, 1983.

"American Fascists." *New Republic* 98 (8 March 1939): 117–18.

"Analysis of Propaganda: Institute Teaches How to Bare Influences on Public Opinion." *Newsweek*, 3 April 1939, 32.

Angell, E. "Civilian Morale Agency." *Annals of the American Academy of Political and Social Science* 220 (March 1942): 160–67.

Angell, James R. *War Propaganda and the Radio*. Philadelphia: University of Pennsylvania Press, 1940.

Angoff, Charles. "Nazi Jew-Baiting in America." *Nation* 140 (1 May 1935): 501–3.

Ansbacher, Heinz L. "Attitudes of German Prisoners of War: A Study of National-Socialistic Fellowship." *Psychological Monographs* 288 (1948): 62.

Armstrong, Anne. *Unconditional Surrender: The Impact of the Casablanca Policy on World War II*. New Brunswick, N.J.: Rutgers University Press, 1961.

Armstrong, Hamilton Fish. *Europe Between Wars?* New York: Macmillan Company, 1934.

_____. *Hitler's Reich: The First Phase*. New York: Macmillan Company, 1933.

_____. *The New Balkans*. New York: Harper and Brothers, 1929.

_____. *We or They: Two Worlds in Conflict*. New York: Macmillan Company, 1937.

_____. *When There Is No Peace*. New York: Macmillan Company, 1939.

_____. *Where the West Begins*. New York: Harper and Brothers, 1929.

Armstrong, Hamilton Fish, and Allen Dulles. *Can America Stay Neutral?* New York: Harper and Brothers, 1939.

_____. *Can We Be Neutral?* New York: Harper and Brothers, 1936.

Baird, Jay W. *The Mythical World of Nazi Propaganda, 1939–1945*. Minneapolis: University of Minnesota Press, 1975.

Balfour, Michael. *Propaganda in War, 1939–1945*. London: Routledge and Kegan Paul, 1979.

Barnes, Joseph. "Fighting with Information: OWI Overseas." *Public Opinion Quarterly* 7 (1943): 34–35.

Barron, Gloria J. *Leadership in Crisis: FDR and the Path to Intervention*. Port Washington, N.Y.: Kennikat Press, 1973.

Barth, Alan. "The Bureau of Intelligence." *Public Opinion Quarterly* 7 (Spring 1943): 66–76.

Bartlett, Vernon. "News Abroad; a Ministry of Information." *Forum* 102 (August 1939): 70–71.

Bartov, Omer. *The Eastern Front, 1941–1945: German Troops and the Barbarization of Warfare.* New York: St. Martin's, 1986.

Bayles, William D. "England's Radio Blitz." *Reader's Digest,* April 1944, 61–63.

"Beamed to Europe: OWI Propaganda Paves the Way for Military Advances." *Newsweek,* 27 September 1943, 73.

Beard, Charles A. "Germany Up to Her Old Tricks." *New Republic* 80 (24 October 1934): 299–300.

Becker, Howard. "Intellectuals, Concentration Camps and Black Propaganda." *American Journal of Economics and Sociology* 10 (January 1951): 139–42.

———. "The Nature and Consequences of Black Propaganda." *American Sociological Review* 41 (April 1949): 221–35.

Bell, Leland V. "The Failure of Nazism in America: The German-American Bund, 1936–1941." *Political Science Quarterly* 85 (April 1970): 589–99.

———. *In Hitler's Shadow: The Anatomy of American Nazism.* Port Washington, N.Y.: Kennikat Press, 1973.

Bellquist, Eric C. *On the Position of Democracy in the Present Crisis.* Los Angeles: College Press, 1941.

Berg, Louis. "Hog Callers in Action." *This Week Magazine, New York Herald Tribune,* 27 May 1945, 4–5.

Bernays, Edward L. "Does Propaganda Menace Democracy?" *Forum* 99 (June 1938): 341–45.

———. *Propaganda.* New York: 1928.

———. "War Against Words." *Coast Artillery Journal* 83 (September–October 1940): 460.

Bidwell, Bruce. *History of the Military Intelligence Division, Department of the Army General Staff: 1775–1941.* Frederick, Md.: University Publications of America, 1986.

Bird, Kai. *The Chairman: John J. McCloy and the Making of the American Establishment.* New York: Simon and Schuster, 1992.

Bliven, Bruce, Max Lerner, and George Soule. "America and the Postwar World." *New Republic* 107 (29 November 1943): 763–90.

Bornstein, Joseph, and Paul R. Milton. *Action Against the Enemy's Mind.* Indianapolis: Bobbs-Merrill, 1942.

Braddick, H. B. "A New Look at American Foreign Policy During the Italo-Ethiopian Crisis." *Journal of Modern History* 34 (January 1962): 64–73.

Braden, Tom. "The Birth of the CIA." *American Heritage* 28 (February 1977): 4–13.

Bradford, Saxton. "Deutsche Auslandspropaganda." *Department of State Bulletin* 14 (24 February 1946): 278–84.

Bramsted, Ernest K. *Goebbels and National Socialist Propaganda, 1925–1945.* East Lansing: Michigan State University Press, 1965.

———. "Goebbels and Nazi Propaganda, 1926–1939." *Australian Outlook* 8 (June 1954): 65–93.

Brandt, Albert. "Nazi International." *Catholic World* 138 (January 1934): 394–404.

Breitman, Richard, and Alan Kraut. *American Refugee Policy and European Jewry, 1933–1945.* Bloomington: Indiana University Press, 1987.

Brinkley, Alan. *Voices of Protest: Huey Long, Father Coughlin, and the Great Depression.* New York: Knopf, 1982.

Broughton, Philip S. "Government Agencies and Civilian Morale." *Annals of the American Academy of Political and Social Science* 220 (March 1942): 168–77.

Brown, John M. *The Ordeal of a Playwright: Robert E. Sherwood and the Challenge of War.* New York: Harper and Row, 1970.

———. *The Worlds of Robert Sherwood: Mirror to His Times, 1896–1939.* New York: Harper and Row, 1965.

Bruner, Jerome S. "The Dimensions of Propaganda: German Short-Wave Broadcasts to America." *Journal of Abnormal Psychology* 36 (July 1941): 311–37.

———. "OWI and the American Public." *Public Opinion Quarterly* 7 (Spring 1943): 125–33.

Bruner, Jerome S., and G. Fowler. "Strategy of Terror: Audience Response to Blitzkrieg im Westen." *Journal of Abnormal and Social Psychology* 36 (October 1941): 561–74.

Bruntz, George G. "Allied Propaganda and the Collapse of German Morale in 1918." *Public Opinion Quarterly* 2 (1938): 61–76.

———. *Allied Propaganda and the Collapse of the German Empire in 1918.* Stanford, Calif.: Stanford University Press, 1938.

Bullitt, William C. "America Is in Danger." *Vital Speeches* 6 (1 September 1940): 683–86.

Burdick, Charles B. *An American Island in Hitler's Reich: The Bad Nauheim Internment.* Menlo Park, Calif.: Markgraff, 1987.

Burger, H. H. "Episode on the Western Front: . . . Story of a Psychological Unit." *New York Times Magazine*, 26 November 1944, 5.

———. " 'Operation Annie': Now It Can Be Told." *New York Times Magazine*, 17 February 1946, 12–13.

Burlingame, Roger. *Don't Let Them Scare You: The Life and Times of Elmer Davis.* Westport, Conn.: Greenwood Press, 1974.

Burns, James MacGregor. *Roosevelt: The Lion and the Fox.* New York: Harcourt Brace Jovanovich, 1956.

———. *Roosevelt: The Soldier of Freedom.* New York: Harcourt Brace Jovanovich, 1970.

Butler, J. R. M. *Lord Lothian, Philip Kerr, 1882–1940.* New York: St. Martin's Press, 1960.

Campbell, Kenneth. "William J. Donovan: Leader and Strategist." *American Intelligence Journal* 11 (1989–1990): 31–36.

Campbell, Roy. "Gerald B. Winrod versus the 'Educated Devils,' " *Midwest Quarterly* 16 (Winter 1975): 187–98.

Cantril, Hadley. "Propaganda for Victory." *New Republic* 106 (23 February 1942): 261–63.

———. "Public Opinion in Flux." *Annals of the American Academy of Political and Social Science* 27 (1942): 136–52.

Cantril, Hadley, and Mildred Strunk, eds. *Public Opinion, 1935–1946.* Princeton: Princeton University Press, 1951.

Carlson, John Roy [Arthur Derounian]. *Under Cover: My Four Years in the Nazi Underground of America.* New York: E. P. Dutton, 1943.

Carlton, Leonard. "Voice of America: The Overseas Radio Bureau." *Public Opinion Quarterly* 7 (Spring 1943): 46–54.

Carnes, Cecil. "Advertising Paid Off at Cherbourg." *Saturday Evening Post*, 12 August 1944, 84.

Carroll, Wallace. *We're in This with Russia.* (Cambridge, Mass.: Houghton Mifflin Company, 1942.

Cassidy, William L., ed. *History of the Schools and Training Branch Office of Strategic Services.* San Francisco: Kingfisher, 1983.

Cave-Brown, Anthony. *"C": The Secret Life of Sir Stewart Menzies, Spymaster to Winston Churchill.* New York: Macmillan, 1987.

_____. *The Last Hero: Wild Bill Donovan.* New York: Time-Life Books, 1982.

_____. *The Secret War Report of the OSS.* New York: Berkeley/Medallion Books, 1976.

Chadwin, Mark L. *The Warhawks: American Interventionists Before Pearl Harbor.* New York: W. W. Norton Company, 1968.

Chakhotin, Sergei. *The Rape of the Masses: The Psychology of Totalitarian Propaganda.* London: Routledge, 1940.

Chernow, Ron. *The House of Morgan: An American Banking Dynasty and the Rise of Modern Finance.* New York: Atlantic Monthly Press, 1990.

_____. *The Warburgs: The Twentieth Century Odyssey of a Remarkable Jewish Family.* New York: Random House, 1993.

Childs, Harwood L. *The Nazi Primer.* New York: Harper and Brothers, 1938.

_____. *Pressure Groups and Propaganda.* Philadelphia: American Academy of Political and Social Sciences, 1935.

_____. *Propaganda and Dictatorship.* Princeton: Princeton University Press, 1936.

Childs, Harwood L., and John B. Whitton, eds. *Propaganda by Shortwave.* Princeton: Princeton University Press, 1942.

Chodoff, E. P. "Ideology and Primary Groups." *Armed Forces and Society* 9 (1983): 569-93.

"Clear and Present Danger." *Nation* 150 (29 June 1940): 772.

Clifford, J. Garry. "Both Ends of the Telescope: New Perspectives on FDR and American Entry into World War II." *Diplomatic History* 13 (Spring 1989): 213-30.

Cline, Ray. "U.S. Foreign Intelligence, 1939-1945." *Foreign Service Journal* 53 (1976): 17-20.

Colby, Benjamin. *T'was a Famous Victory.* New Rochelle, N.Y.: Arlington House, 1974.

Cole, Wayne S. *Roosevelt and the Isolationists, 1932-1945.* Lincoln: University of Nebraska Press, 1983.

Collwell, Robert T. "Radio Luxembourg Uses Jokes as Propaganda Against Nazis." *Life,* 5 March 1945, 17-18.

Conant, James B. "Defenses Against Propaganda; History is a Mirror." *Vital Speeches* 4 (15 June 1938): 542-44.

_____. *Speaking as a Private Citizen: Addresses on the Present Threat to Our Nation's Future.* Cambridge: Harvard University Press, 1941.

"Congress Blasts Against OWI: Portends Assault on New Deal." *Newsweek,* 22 February 1943, 25-26.

Conn, Stetson, Rose C. Engelman, and Byron Fairchild. *Western Hemisphere: Guarding the United States and Its Outposts.* Washington, D.C.: Office of the Chief of Military History, U.S. Army, 1964.

Conn, Stetson, and Byron Fairchild. *The Western Hemisphere: The Framework of Hemispheric Defense.* Washington, D.C.: Office of the Chief of Military History, U.S. Army, 1960.

Cooke, A. "British Propaganda in the United States." *Fortnightly* 153 (n.s. 147) (June 1940): 605-13.

Corson, William R. *The Armies of Ignorance: The Rise of the American Intelligence Empire.* New York: Dial Press, 1977.

Cousins, Norman. "Big Bad OWI." *Saturday Review of Literature* 26 (13 March 1943): 10.

———. "Books and Propaganda; Flanders Hall Publishing Outlet for German Propaganda in This Country." *Saturday Review of Literature* 25 (21 February 1942): 10.

———. "Fear and Propaganda." *Saturday Review of Literature* 22 (4 May 1940): 8.

———. "Radio and Morale: We Are Still Behind the Enemy in Recognizing Radio Power." *Saturday Review of Literature* 26 (4 July 1942): 6–7.

Cowley, Malcolm. "Sorrows of Elmer Davis." *New Republic* 108 (3 May 1943): 591–93.

Cranston, Allan. *Adolf Hitler's Own Book Mein Kampf.* Greenwich, Conn.: Noram Publishing Company, 1939.

Creel, George. "Beware the Superpatriots." *American Mercury* 51 (September 1940): 33–41.

———. "Propaganda and Morale." *American Journal of Sociology* 47 (November 1941): 340–51.

Crossman, Richard H. S. "Psychological Warfare." *Journal of the Royal United Service Institution* 98 (August 1953): 351–61.

Cruickshank, Charles G. *The Fourth Arm: Psychological Warfare, 1939–1945.* London: Davis-Poynter, 1977.

Dallek, Robert F. *Franklin D. Roosevelt and American Foreign Policy, 1932–1945.* New York: Oxford University Press, 1979.

"Dangerous for Democracies to Imitate Dictator Propaganda." *Science News Letter* 39 (18 January 1941): 39.

"Dangerous Nazi Campaign in America." *Business Week,* 28 September 1935, 40.

Darilek, Robert E. *A Loyal Opposition in Time of War: The Republican Party and the Politics of Foreign Policy from Pearl Harbor to Yalta.* Westport, Conn.: Greenwood Press, 1976.

Darrock, Michael. "Davis and Goliath; OWI and Its Gigantic Task." *Harper's,* February 1943, 225–37.

Daugherty, William, and Morris Janowitz, eds. *A Psychological Warfare Casebook.* Baltimore: Johns Hopkins University Press, 1958.

Davidson, G. "Whig Propagandists of the American Revolution." *American Historical Review* 39 (April 1934): 442–53.

Davis, Elmer. "Debating This 'Pot and Kettle' War." *Reader's Digest,* April 1940, 17–21.

———. "Is England Worth the Fight?" *New Republic* 103 (15 February 1939): 35–37.

———. "OWI Has a Job." *Public Opinion Quarterly* 7 (Spring 1943): 5–14.

———. "The War and America." *Harper's,* April 1940, 449–62.

———. "What OWI Is Doing." *Saturday Review of Literature* 25 (5 December 1942): 7–9.

Davis, Elmer, et al. "The Office of War Information." *Public Opinion Quarterly* 7 (1943): 3–138.

Davis, Elmer, and Byron Price. *War Information and Censorship.* Washington, D.C.: American Council on Public Affairs, 1943.

"Davis on the Griddle; Press Conference for Senate Judiciary Committee." *Life,* 3 May 1943, 24–25.

Davis, Vernon E. *History of the Joint Chiefs of Staff in World War II.* 2 vols. Washington, D.C.: JCS Historical Section, 1953.

De Jong, Louis. *The German Fifth Column in the Second World War*. Chicago: University of Chicago Press, 1956.

Dennis, Lawrence. "Propaganda for War: Model 1938." *American Mercury* 44 (May 1938): 1–10.

de Rochemont, Richard. "France and Propaganda." *Life*, 25 March 1940, 9–11.

de Saint-Jean, Robert. "Battle of Words: Failure of French Propaganda." *Atlantic* 166 (November 1940): 612–16.

de Santillana, George. "Italy Listening." *Atlantic Monthly* 171 (March 1943): 66–72.

Deuel, Wallace R. *People Under Hitler*. New York: Harcourt, Brace and Company, 1942.

Diamond, Sander A. *The Nazi Movement in the United States, 1924–1941*. Ithaca, N.Y.: Cornell University Press, 1974.

Dies, Martin. *The Trojan Horse in America*. New York: Dodd, Mead, 1940.

Divine, Robert. *Second Chance: The Triumph of Internationalism During World War II*. New York: Athenaeum, 1967.

"Donovan Strategy; Counterpropaganda." *Newsweek*, 17 November 1941, 21.

Donovan, William J. "Foreign Policy Must Be Based on Facts." *Vital Speeches* (1 May 1946): 446–48.

Donovan, William J., and Edgar A. Mowrer. *Fifth Column Lessons for America*. Washington, D.C.: American Council on Public Affairs, 1941.

Doob, Leonard W. "Goebbels' Principles of Propaganda." *Public Opinion Quarterly* 14 (Fall 1950): 419–42.

_____. *Propaganda: Its Psychology and Technique*. New York: H. Holt and Company, 1935.

_____. *Public Opinion and Propaganda*. London: Cresset Press, 1949; reprint, Hamden, Conn.: Archon Books, 1966.

_____. "Strategies of Psychological Warfare." *Public Opinion Quarterly* 13 (Winter 1949): 635–44.

_____. "The Utilization of Social Scientists in the Overseas Branch of the [U.S.] Office of War Information." *American Political Science Review* 41 (August 1947): 649–67.

Dulles, Allen. *Neutrality and International Sanctions*. Chicago: American Bar Association, 1936.

Draper, T. "Psychology of Surrender." *Infantry Journal* 57 (October 1945): 35–38.

Drummond, Donald F. *The Passing of American Neutrality, 1937–1941*. Ann Arbor: University of Michigan Press, 1955.

Dunlop, Richard. *Donovan: America's Master Spy*. Chicago: Rand McNally, 1982.

Dyer, Murray. *The Weapon on the Wall: Rethinking Psychological Warfare*. Baltimore: Johns Hopkins University Press, 1959.

Edwards, John Carver. *Berlin Calling: American Broadcasters in Service to the Third Reich*. New York: Praeger, 1991.

Ekstein, Rudolph. "Ideologies in Psychological Warfare." *Journal of Abnormal Psychology* 37 (July 1942): 369–87.

Eliot, George F. *Defending America*. New York: Foreign Policy Association, 1939.

_____. *If War Comes*. New York: Macmillan Company, 1937.

_____. *The Ramparts We Watch: A Study of the Problems of American National Defense*. New York: Reynal and Hitchcock, 1939.

Ellis, Elmer, ed. *Education Against Propaganda; Seventh Yearbook of the National Council for Social Studies*. Cambridge, Mass.: National Council for Social Studies, 1937.

Ellul, Jacques. *Propaganda: The Formation of Men's Attitudes*. New York: Alfred A. Knopf, 1965.

"Elmer Davis Heads OWI." *Publisher's Weekly* 141 (20 June 1942): 2265.

Erdmann, James. *Leaflet Operations in the Second World War: The Story of the How and the Why of the 6,500,000 Propaganda Leaflets Dropped on the Axis Forces and Homelands in the Mediterranean and European Theaters of Operations*. Denver: University of Denver, 1969.

Esslin, Martin. "The Art of British Black Propaganda." *Encounter* 52 (January 1979): 42–49.

Ettlinger, Harold. *The Axis on the Air*. New York: Bobbs-Merrill, 1943.

Etzold, Thomas H. "The Futility Factor: German Information Gathering in the United States, 1933–1945." *Military Affairs* 39 (April 1975): 77–82.

Farago, Ladislas, ed. *Axis Grand Strategy: Blueprints for Total War*. New York: Farrar, 1942.

———. *German Psychological Warfare: Survey and Bibliography*. New York: U.S. Committee for National Morale, 1942; reprint, New York: Arno Press, 1972.

Farrar, Ronald T. "Elmer Davis: Report to the President." *Journalism Monographs* 7 (August 1968): 1–85.

Feller, Abraham H. "OWI on the Home Front." *Public Opinion Quarterly* 7 (Spring 1943): 55–65.

Field, John C. W. *Aerial Propaganda Leaflets*. Sutton Coldfield, England: F. J. Fields, 1954.

"First Time Up for Elmer Davis." *New Republic* 107 (20 July 1942): 83.

"Flanders Hall Investigated by Grand Jury." *Publisher's Weekly* 140 (4 October. 1941): 1385.

Flannery, Harry. *Assignment to Berlin*. New York: Alfred A. Knopf, 1942.

Flynn, John T. "Mr. Flynn on War Hysteria." *New Republic* 103 (11 November 1940): 660.

Foertsch, Hermann. *The Art of Modern Warfare*. New York: Stechert, 1940.

"Footprints of the Trojan Horse." *Scholastic* 37 (4 November 1940): 12–13.

Ford, Corey. *Donovan of OSS*. Boston: Little, Brown and Company, 1970.

———. "Our German Wehrmacht Is Being Stopped by a Shadow." *American Heritage*, 21 February 1970, 56–57.

Franke, Hermann. "Psychological Warfare and How to Wage it." *Current History* 51 (January 1940): 52–53.

Fraser, Lindley M. *Germany Between Two Wars: A Study of Propaganda and War Guilt*. New York: Oxford University Press, 1945.

———. *Propaganda*. London: Oxford University Press, 1957.

Friedman, R. A. "Alsatian Unrest." *Contemporary Review* 155 (February 1939): 213–21.

Friedrich, Carl J. "Detect Propaganda and Use It." *Independent Woman* 19 (September 1940): 285–86.

———. "Issues of Informational Strategy." *Public Opinion Quarterly* 7 (Spring 1943): 78–89.

Frye, Alton. *Nazi Germany and the American Hemisphere, 1933–1945*. New Haven: Yale University Press, 1967.

Fuchs, M. "Strategy of Persuasion." *Catholic World* 155 (August 1942): 532–38.

Gallup, George H. *The Gallup Poll: Public Opinion, 1935–1971*. Vol. 1: *1935–1948*. New York: Random House, 1972.

Gardner, John W., et al. *Assessment of Men: Selection of Personnel for the OSS.* New York: Rinehart and Company, 1948.

Gedye, George E. R. *Betrayal in Central Europe: Austria and Czechoslovakia.* New York: Harper and Brothers, 1939.

_____. *Fallen Bastions: The Central European Tragedy.* London: Victor Gollancz, 1939.

George, Alexander L. *Propaganda Analysis: A Study of Inferences Made from Nazi Propaganda in World War II.* Evanston, Ill.: Row, Peterson, 1959.

"Germany's Defiance of Britain and France: Nazi Propaganda in Austria." *Literary Digest* 116 (19 Aug. 1933): 13.

"Germany's Psychological Warfare Plan Revealed." *Science News Letter* 39 (7 June 1941): 355.

Gillis, James M. "Propaganda Problem." *Catholic World* 159 (June 1944): 193-201.

Glasgow, George. "Nazi Methods in Memel." *Contemporary Review* 146 (November 1934): 623-24.

Glennon, John P. " 'This Time Germany Is a Defeated Nation': The Doctrine of Unconditional Surrender and Some Unsuccessful Attempts to Alter It, 1943-1944." In *Statesmen and Statecraft of the Modern West,* ed. Gerald Grob, 109-51. Barre, Mass.: Barre Publishers, 1967.

Goldston, Robert. *Sinister Touches: The Secret War Against Hitler.* New York: Dial, 1982.

Gollomb, Joseph. *Armies of Spies.* New York: Macmillan Company, 1939.

Gombrich, Ernest H. *Myth and Reality in German Wartime Broadcasts.* London: Oxford University Press, 1970.

"A Good Man Is Hard to Find." *Fortune* (March 1946): 92-95.

Gordon, Matthew. "What the Axis Thinks of the OWI." *Public Opinion Quarterly* 7 (Spring 1943): 134-38.

Graves, Harold N., Jr. "European Radio and the War." *Annals of the American Academy of Political and Social Sciences* 213 (January 1941): 75-82.

_____. *War on the Short Wave.* New York: Foreign Policy Association, 1941.

Gullahorn, John T. "German Propaganda Techniques." *Sociology and Social Research* 30 (March-April 1946): 290-95.

Gunther, John. *The High Cost of Hitler.* London: Hamilton, 1939.

_____. *Inside Europe.* New York: Harper and Brothers, 1936.

Gurfein, Murray I., and Morris Janowitz. "Trends in Wehrmacht Morale." *Public Opinion Quarterly* 10 (Spring 1946): 78-84.

Hadamovsky, Eugen. *Propaganda und National Macht: Die Organisation der offentlichen meinung für die National Politik.* Oldenburg, Germany: Stalling, 1933.

Hadley, A. "The Propaganda Tank." *Armor* 60 (January-February 1951): 32-33.

Haffner, Sebastian. *Germany: Jekyll and Hyde.* New York: E. P. Dutton, 1941.

_____. *Offensive Against Germany.* London: Secker and Warburg, 1941.

Hale, Julian A. S. *Radio Power: Propaganda and Internal Broadcasting.* Philadelphia: Temple University Press, 1975.

Hale, William H. "Big Noise in Little Luxembourg." *Harper's,* April 1946, 377-84.

Hall, Donald F. "Psychological Warfare Training." *Army Information Digest* 6 (January 1951): 40-46.

Hamilton, T. "What the Germans Told the French." *Harper's,* November 1944, 542-44.

Hammersmith, Jack L. "The U.S. Office of War Information (OWI) and the Polish Question, 1943–1945." *Polish Review* 19 (1974): 67–76.

Hardy, Alexander G. *Hitler's Secret Weapon: The Managed Press and Propaganda Machine of Nazi Germany.* New York: Vantage Press, 1962.

Harris, Elliott. *The "Un-American" Weapon: Psychological Warfare.* New York: M. M. Lads Publishing Company, 1967.

Harsch, Joseph C. *Germany at War: Twenty Key Questions and Answers.* New York: Foreign Policy Association, 1942.

———. *Pattern of Conquest.* London: Heinemann, 1942.

Hartshorne, Edward Y. *The German Universities and Government.* Philadelphia: n.p., 1938.

———. *German Youth and the Nazi Dream of Victory.* New York: Toronto, Farrar, and Rinehart, 1941.

———. "Reactions to the Nazi Threat: A Study of Propaganda and Culture Conflict." *Public Opinion Quarterly* 5 (Winter 1941): 625–39.

Hawkins, Lester G., Jr., and George S. Pettee. "OWI Organization and Problems." *Public Opinion Quarterly* 7 (Spring 1943): 15–32.

Heiber, Helmut. *Goebbels.* New York: Hawthorn, 1972; reprint, New York: DaCapo Press, 1983.

Heinrichs, Waldo. *Threshold of War: Franklin D. Roosevelt and American Entry into World War II.* New York: Oxford University Press, 1988.

Henslow, Miles. *The Miracle of Radio: The Story of Radio's Decisive Contribution to Victory.* London: Evens, 1946.

Herring, E. Pendleton. "Official Propaganda Under the New Deal." *Annals of the American Academy of Political and Social Science* 179 (May 1935): 167–75.

Hersh, Burton. *The Old Boys: The American Elite and the Origins of the CIA.* New York: Charles Scribner's Sons, 1982.

Hertz, David. "The Radio Siege of Lorient." *Hollywood Quarterly* (January 1946): 291–301.

Herz, Martin F. "The Combat Leaflet—Weapon of Persuasion." *Army Information Digest* 5 (June 1950): 37–43.

———. "Psychological Warfare Against Surrounded Troop Units." *Military Review* 30 (Jan. 1950): 3–9.

———. "Some Psychological Lessons from Leaflet Propaganda in World War II." *Public Opinion Quarterly* 13 (Fall 1949): 471–86.

Herzstein, Robert E. *The War That Hitler Won: The Most Infamous Propaganda Campaign in History.* New York: G. P. Putnam, 1978.

High, Stanley. "It Is Not a New Deal War." *Reader's Digest,* November 1942, 25–29.

Hill, C. J. "OWI Cleans House." *Scholastic* 44 (6 March 1944): 9.

Hilton, Stanley E. *Hitler's Secret War in South America.* Baton Rouge: Louisiana State University Press, 1981.

"History Unrecognized; Downfall of Mussolini." *Nation* 157 (7 August 1943): 144–45.

Hollis, Ernest V. "An Antidote for Propaganda." *School and Society* (7 October 1939): 449–52.

Holoway, C. "Fight Fire with Fire: Show the Uninformed People of the Old World the Real America." *Nation* 152 (11 January 1941): 55.

Holt, Robert T., and Robert W. Van der Velds. *Strategic Psychological Operations and American Foreign Policy.* Chicago: University of Chicago Press, 1960.

Hoover, Calvin B. *Germany Enters the Third Reich.* New York: Macmillan Company, 1933.

Hoover, J. Edgar. "Big Scare," *American Magazine,* August 1941, 24.

———. "Enemies Within America," *American Magazine,* August 1940, 18–19.

Horne, Alistair. *To Lose a Battle: France 1940.* Boston: Little, Brown, 1969.

"House Will Make Nazi Inquiry." *Newsweek,* 31 March 1934, 12.

"How Shall We Meet Nazi Propaganda?" *Nation* 137 (8 November 1933): 526.

Hoyt, Palmer. "OWI in 1943 Coordinator and Service Agency." *Journalism Quarterly* 20 (December 1943): 320–25.

Hudson, John, and George Wolfskill. *All but the People: FDR and His Critics.* New York: Macmillan Company, 1969.

Hughes, Barry F. *The Domestic Content of American Foreign Policy.* San Francisco: W. H. Freeman, 1978.

Hulten, Charles M. "How the OWI Operates Its Overseas Propaganda Machine." *Journalism Quarterly* 19 (December 1942): 349–55.

Hummel, William C., and Keith Huntress. *The Analysis of Propaganda.* New York: Sloane, 1949.

Hunt, Michael H. *Ideology and United States Foreign Policy.* New Haven: Yale University Press, 1987.

Huss, Pierre. *The Foe We Face.* Garden City, N.Y.: Doubleday, Doran, and Company, 1942.

Hymoff, Edward. *The OSS in World War II.* New York: Ballantine, 1972.

Hynd, Alan. *Passport to Treason: The Inside Story of Spies in America.* New York: R. M. McBride and Company, 1943.

"Independent Status of OWI Abolished." *Publisher's Weekly* 148 (8 September 1945): 973.

"In Occupied Germany: A Report on Some of the Propaganda Activities of the OWI and PWB." *Tide* (May 1945): 23–25.

Israels, Josef. "The Wehrmacht's Yankee Girlfriend; Music with Margaret, an OWI Activity." *Collier's,* 3 March 1945, 68.

"Italy and Germany in America." *New Republic* 92 (22 September 1937): 173.

Jablin, J. N. "Axis Radio Propaganda in Tunisia." *Infantry Journal* 55 (December 1943): 21–22.

Jacob, Philip E. "Influences of World Events on U.S. 'Neutrality' Opinion." *Public Opinion Quarterly* 4 (March 1940): 48–65.

Jeffreys-Jones, Rhodri. "The Historiography of the CIA." *Historical Journal* 23 (December 1980): 489–96.

———. "The Socio-Educational Composition of the CIA Elite: A Statistical Note." *Journal of American Studies* 19 (December 1985): 421–24.

Johnson, Ronald. "The German-American Bund and Nazi Germany, 1936–1941." *Studies in History and Society* 6 (February 1975): 31–45.

Johnson, T. Walter. *The Battle Against Isolation.* Chicago: University of Chicago Press, 1944.

Jones, Alfred H. "The Making of an Interventionist on the Air: Elmer Davis and CBS News, 1939–1941." *Pacific Historical Review* 42 (February 1973): 74–93.

Jones, F. Elwyn. "The Modern Technique of Aggression." *Fortnightly* 151 (n.s. 145) (April 1939): 378–86.

Jurist, Stewart S. "Leaflets over Europe: Allied Propaganda Used Some Advertising Principles." *Printer's Ink* 213 (26 October 1945): 23–24.

Kamp, Joseph. *Fifth Column in South.* New Haven: Yale University Press, 1940.

———. *Fifth Column in Washington.* New Haven: Yale University Press, 1940.

———. *The Fifth Column vs. the Dies Committee.* New Haven: Yale University Press, 1941.

Kane, R. Keith. "The OFF." *Public Opinion Quarterly* 6 (Summer 1942): 204–20.

Kantorowicz, Alfred. "OWI in Germany." *New Republic* 112 (14 May 1945): 673–74.

———. "The Strategy of Anti-Nazi Propaganda." *Free World* 2 (March 1942): 144–47.

Kecskemeti, Paul. *Strategic Surrender: The Politics of Victory and Defeat.* Stanford, Calif.: Stanford University Press, 1964.

Kehm, Harold D. "Can Psychological Warfare Pay Its Passage?" *Military Review* 26 (March 1947): 35–45.

———. "The Methods and Functions of Military Psychological Warfare." *Military Review* 26 (January 1947): 3–15.

———. "Organization for Military Psychological Warfare in ETO." *Military Review* 26 (February 1947): 10–15.

Ketchum, Richard M. *The Borrowed Years, 1938–1941: America on the Way to War.* New York: Random House, 1989.

Keyserlingk, Robert H. *Austria in World War II: An Anglo-American Dilemma.* Montreal: McGill-Queen's University Press, 1988.

———. "Political Warfare Illusions: Otto Strasser and Britain's World War II Strategy of National Revolts Against Hitler." *Dalhousie Review* 61 (Spring 1981): 71–92.

Kimball, Warren. *The Juggler: Franklin Roosevelt as Wartime Statesman.* Princeton: Princeton University Press, 1991.

Kirby, Edward, and Jack W. Harris. *Star-Spangled Radio.* Chicago: Ziff Davis Publishing Company, 1948.

Knox, Frank. *The Meaning of Munich.* N.p., 1938.

———. *We Planned It That Way.* Toronto: Longmans, Green and Company, 1938.

Koppes, Clayton R., and Gregory D. Black. "What to Show the World: The Office of War Information and Hollywood, 1942–1945." *Journal of American History* 64 (June 1977): 87–105.

Kramer, Paul. "Nelson Rockefeller and British Security Coordination." *Journal of Contemporary History* 16 (January 1981): 73–88.

Kriegsbaum, Hillier. "The OWI and Government News Policy." *Journalism Quarterly* 19 (September 1942): 240–50.

Kries, Wilhelm von. *Strategy and Tactics of the British War Propaganda.* Berlin: E. Zander Druck, 1941.

Kris, Ernst. "German Propaganda Instructions of 1933." *Social Research* 9 (February 1942): 46–81.

———. *German Radio Propaganda.* London: Oxford University Press, 1944.

———. "Morale in Germany." *American Journal of Sociology* 47 (November 1941): 452–61.

Krugman, Morris, and S. Silverman. "Psychological Weapons of War." *Mental Hygiene* 26 (July 1942): 452–61.

Lambert, Richard S. *Propaganda.* New York: Thomas Nelson, 1939.

Landau, Henry. *The Enemy Within: The Inside Story of German Sabotage in America.* New York: G. P. Putnam's Sons, 1937.

Landry, Robert J. "The Impact of OWI on Broadcasting." *Public Opinion Quarterly* 7 (Spring 1943): 111–15.

Lang, Daniel. "Berlin Sends Radio Greetings." *New Republic* 97 (11 January 1939): 279–81.

Langer, Walter C. *The Mind of Adolf Hitler: The Secret Wartime Report.* New York: Basic Books, 1972.

Langer, William L., and S. Everett Gleason. *The Challenge to Isolation: The World Crisis of 1937–1940 and American Foreign Policy.* Gloucester, Mass.: Peter Smith, 1970.

Lasswell, Harold D. "The Relation of Ideological Intelligence to Public Policy." *Ethics* 53 (October 1942): 25–34.

Lasswell, Harold D., and James Wechsler. *Propaganda Technique in the World War.* London: Kegan Paul, Trench, Trubner and Company, 1927.

Lattimore, Owen. *America and Asia: Problems of Today's War and the Peace of Tomorrow.* Claremont, Calif.: Claremont College, 1943.

Laurie, Clayton D. "Black Games, Subversion, and Dirty Tricks: The OSS Morale Operations Branch in Europe, 1943–1945." *Prologue* 25 (Fall 1993): 259–71.

––––––. " 'The Chanting of Crusaders': Captain Heber Blankenhorn and AEF Combat Propaganda in World War I." *Journal of Military History* 59 July 1995): 457–82.

––––––. "Goebbels's Iowan: Frederick W. Kaltenbach and Nazi Short-Wave Radio Broadcasts to America, 1939–45." *Annals of Iowa* 53 (Summer 1994): 219–45.

––––––. " 'The Sauerkrauts': The OSS and German Prisoners of War as Secret Agents in Europe, 1944–1945." *Prologue* 26 (Spring 1994): 49–61.

Lavine, Harold. *Fifth Column in America.* New York: Doubleday, Doran, and Company, 1940.

––––––. "Propagandists Open Fire." *New Republic* 100 (1 November 1939): 360–62.

Lavine, Harold, and James Wechsler. *War Propaganda and the United States.* New Haven: Yale University Press, 1940.

Lawton, G. "Psychological Warfare: Defensive." *Scholastic* (26 October 1942): 27.

"Leaflet Bombs." *New York Times Magazine,* 7 September 1941, 4.

Lean, Edward Tangye. *Voices in the Darkness: The Story of the European Radio War.* London: Secker and Warburg, 1943.

Lee, Alfred M. *The Fine Art of Propaganda.* New York: Institute for Propaganda Analysis, 1939; reprint, New York: Octagon Books, 1972.

Lefever, Ernest W., and Roy Godson. *The CIA and the American Ethic: An Unfinished Debate.* Washington, D.C.: Ethics and Public Policy Center of Georgetown University, 1979.

Leigh, Michael. *Mobilizing Consent: Public Opinion and American Foreign Policy, 1937–1947.* Westport, Conn.: Greenwood Press, 1976.

Leonard, Thomas M. "The United States and World War II: Conflicting Views of American Diplomacy." *Towson State Journal of International Affairs* 7 (Fall 1972): 25–30.

Lerner, Daniel. *Sykewar: Psychological Warfare Against Nazi Germany, D-Day to V-E Day.* New York: Stewart, 1949.

_____, ed. *Propaganda in War and Crisis.* New York: Stewart, 1951.

Lerner, Max. "Propaganda in Our Time." *New Republic* 103 (26 August 1940): 281-82.

_____. "Propaganda's Golden Age." *Nation* 149 (4 November 1939): 495-97.

Leuchtenburg, William. *Franklin Delano Roosevelt and the New Deal, 1932-1940.* New York: Harper and Row, 1963.

Levering, Ralph B. *American Public Opinion and the Russian Alliance, 1939-1945.* Chapel Hill: University of North Carolina Press, 1976.

Lindley, Ernest K. *How War Came to America: From the Fall of France to Pearl Harbor.* London: Allen and Unwin, 1943.

_____. *How War Came to America: White Paper.* New York: Simon and Schuster, 1942.

_____. "Money for OWI Overseas Service." *Newsweek*, 28 September 1942, 30.

Linebarger, Paul M. A. *Psychological Warfare.* Washington, D.C.: Combat Forces Press, 1954.

_____. "Psychological Warfare in World War II." *Infantry Journal* 60 (May-June 1947): 36-39.

Lipset, Seymour Martin, and Earl Raab. *The Politics of Unreason: Right-Wing Extremism in America, 1790-1970.* New York: Harper and Row, 1970.

Lipstadt, Deborah E. *Beyond Belief: The American Press and the Coming of the Holocaust, 1933-1945.* New York: Free Press, 1986.

Little, Douglas. "Antibolshevism and American Foreign Policy, 1919-1939: The Diplomacy of Self-Delusion." *American Quarterly* 35 (Fall 1983): 376-90.

Lockhart, Robert Bruce. *Comes the Reckoning.* London: G. B. Putnam, 1947.

_____. "Political Warfare." *Journal of the Royal United Service Institution* 93 (May 1950): 193-206.

Lore, Ludwig. "Nazi Politics in America." *Nation* 137 (29 November 1933): 615-17.

Lutz, Ralph Haswell. "Studies of World Propaganda." *Journal of Modern History* 5 (1933): 496-516.

McClure, Robert A. "Psychological Warfare." *Army Navy Air Force Journal* 88 (31 January 1951): 517.

Mace, C. A. "Propaganda and Democracy." *Sociology Review* 33 (July-October 1941): 169-71.

McGranahan, Donald V. "U.S. Psychological Warfare Policy." *Public Opinion Quarterly* 4 (1946): 446-50.

McKale, Donald M. *The Swastika Outside Germany.* Kent, Ohio: Kent State University Press, 1977.

McKenzie, Vernon. "United Nations Propaganda in the United States." *Public Opinion Quarterly* 6 (Fall 1942): 351-66.

MacLeish, Archibald. "Address Before a Luncheon of the American Society of Newspaper Editors in New York City, 17 April 1942." Washington, D.C.: n.p., 1942.

_____. *American Opinion and the War: The Rede Lectures Before the University of Cambridge on 30 July 1942.* New York: Macmillan Company, 1942.

_____. *The Irresponsibles.* New York: Duell, Sloan, and Pearce, 1940.

_____. "Munich and the Americans." *Nation* 147 (15 October 1938): 370-71.

———. "Text of Address . . . at Associated Press Annual Luncheon, 20 April 1942." Washington, D.C.: n.p., 1942.

———. *A Time to Act: Selected Addresses*. Boston: Houghton Mifflin Company, 1943.

———. *A Time to Speak: The Selected Prose of Archibald MacLeish*. Boston: Houghton Mifflin Company, 1941.

Maddux, Thomas R. "Red Fascism and Brown Bolshevism: The American Image of Totalitarianism in the 1930s." *Historian* 40 (November 1977): 85–103.

Mahoney, Thomas. "Words That Win Battles: Psychological Warfare." *Popular Science*, June 1945, 121–23, 206–7.

Margolin, Leo J. *Paper Bullets: A Brief History of Psychological Warfare in World War II*. New York: Froeben, 1946.

Martin, Kingsley. *Propaganda's Harvest*. London: Kegan Paul, Trench, Trubner, 1941.

Maurois, Andre. "What Happened to France." *Collier's*, 21 September 1940, 17.

May, Ernest R., ed. *Knowing One's Enemies: Intelligence Assessment Before the Two World Wars*. Princeton: Princeton University Press, 1986.

Mellett, Lowell. "Government Propaganda." *Atlantic* 168 (September 1941): 311–13.

Menefee, Selden C. *Assignment U.S.A.* New York: Reynal and Hitchcock, 1943.

———. "Propaganda Wins Battles: Our Psychological Campaign in the Mediterranean." *Nation* 159 (12 February 1944): 184–86.

Meserve, Walter J. *Robert E. Sherwood: Reluctant Moralist*. New York: Pegasus, 1970.

Meyerhoff, Arthur E. *The Strategy of Persuasion*. New York: Coward, McCann, 1965.

Miller, Clyde R. "Radio and Propaganda." *Annals of the American Academy of Political and Social Sciences* 223 (January 1941): 69–71.

———. *The Process of Persuasion*. New York: Crown, 1946.

———. "Today's Propaganda and Tomorrow's Reality." In *Tomorrow in the Making*, edited by John N. Andrews and Carl A. Marsden. New York: Whittlesey House, 1939.

Miller, Clyde R., and Louis Minsky. "Propaganda—Good and Bad—for Democracy." *Survey Graphic* 28 (November 1939): 706–20.

Miller, Douglas. *Some Regional Views on Our Foreign Policy*. New York: Council on Foreign Relations, 1939.

———. *You Can't Do Business with Hitler*. Boston: Little, Brown and Company, 1941.

Miller, James E. "A Question of Loyalty: American Liberals, Propaganda, and the Italian-American Community, 1939-1943." *Maryland Historian* 9 (1978): 49–71.

Milward, Alan. *The German Economy at War*. London: Athlone Press, 1965.

Mock, James R., and Cedric Larson. *Words That Won the War: The Story of the Committee on Public Information, 1917-1919*. Princeton: Princeton University Press, 1939; reprint, New York: Russell and Russell, 1968.

Moley, Raymond. "Good and Bad Propaganda." *Newsweek*, 9 August 1943, 88.

———. "Propaganda War." *Newsweek*, 26 June 1944, 104.

Morgan, Brewster. " 'Operation Annie': [The U.S.] Army Radio Station That Fooled the Nazis by Telling Them the Truth." *Saturday Evening Post*, 9 March 1946, 18–19.

Morris, B. S. "War and Psychological Services." *Fortnightly* 168 (August 1947): 112–18.

Mowrer, Edgar A. *Germany Puts the Clock Back*. New York: William Morrow and Company, 1933.

———. *Global War*. London: Faber and Faber, 1943.

———. *The Nightmare of American Foreign Policy*. London: Victor Gollancz, 1949.

Mowrer, Lilian. *Rip Tide of Aggression*. New York: William Morrow and Company, 1942.

Mowrer, Paul S. "Bungling the News." *Public Opinion Quarterly* 7 (Spring 1943): 116–22.

Mullen, J. "Goebbels' Guiding Hand." *Nation* 145 (14 August 1937): 179.

Muller, Edwin. "Waging War with Words." *Current History* 50 (August 1939): 24–27.

Munson, Gorham. *Twelve Decisive Battles of the Mind: The Story of Propaganda During the Christian Era*. New York: Greystone Press, 1942.

"Nazi Challenge to American Labor." *Nation* 145 (25 September 1937): 310.

"Nazi Propaganda in the Balkans." *Great Britain and the East* 53 (14 December 1939): 463.

"Nazi Propaganda in the Balkans." *Great Britain and the East* 54 (15 February 1940): 99.

Nelson, R. B. "Hitler's Propaganda Machine." *Current History* 38 (June 1933): 287–94.

Nevins, Allen. "The Centurions Survey a Century." *New York Times Magazine*, 27 April 1947, 16.

"New Bill: U.S. and British Broadcasts in Italian." *Time*, 12 July 1943, 60.

Newman, Robert P. *Owen Lattimore and the Loss of China*. Berkeley: University of California Press, 1992.

Nock, Albert J. "New Dose of British Propaganda." *American Mercury* 42 (December 1937): 482–86.

"Noise over the Nazis." *Current History* 46 (May 1937): 25–30.

Nye, G. "War Propaganda." *Vital Speeches* (15 September 1941): 720–23.

O'Connor, Raymond G. *Diplomacy for Victory: FDR and Unconditional Surrender*. New York: W. W. Norton Company, 1971.

Oechsner, Fredrick et al. *This Is the Enemy*. Boston: Little, Brown and Company, 1942.

Ogden, August R. *The Dies Committee*. Washington, D.C.: Catholic University Press, 1945.

Olberg, Paul. "Scandinavia and the Nazis." *Contemporary Review* 156 (July 1939): 27–34.

Olson, Ted. "The Short Unhappy Life of John Durfee." *Foreign Service Journal* 39 (October 1962): 36–44.

"Once More Where's Elmer?" *Newsweek*, 7 February 1944, 53–54.

O'Neill, Con. "Paper Warfare in Tunisia." *Army Quarterly* (U.K.) 44 (April 1944): 81–91.

"Opportunity Lost." *Time*, 9 August 1943, 86.

"The OWI." *Commonweal* 40 (28 April 1944): 28–29.

"OWI's ABSIE; American Broadcasting Station in Europe." *Time*, 16 July 1945, 69.

Paddock, Alfred H., Jr. *United States Army Special Warfare: Its Origins: Psychological and Unconventional Warfare, 1941–1952*. Washington, D.C.: National Defense University Press, 1982.

Padover, Saul K. *Psychological Warfare*. New York: Foreign Policy Association, 1951.

———. "Psychological Warfare and Foreign Policy." *American Scholar* 19 (Spring 1951): 151–61.

"Paging Mr. Durfee: Boner on Italian Situation Lights New Fire Under OWI." *Newsweek*, 9 August 1943, 42.

Painton, Frederick C. "Fighting with Confetti." *Reader's Digest*, December 1943, 99–101.

Panton, S. "Tuning in the Nazis; Loudest Voice on Earth." *Living Age* 352 (June 1937): 316–18.

"Paris Press: Daladier Goes After Editors in War on Foreign Propaganda." *Newsweek*, 24 July 1939, 20.

Park, Robert E. "Morale and the News." *American Journal of Sociology* 47 (Novemer 1941): 360–77.

Peck, Jeff. "The Heroic Soviet on the American Screen." *Film and History* 9 (1979): 54–63.

Persico, Joseph E. *Casey: From the OSS to the CIA.* New York: Viking, 1990.

Phillips, C. "Shadow Army That Fought in Silence." *New York Times Magazine,* 7 October 1945, 12–13.

———. "War of the Air Waves." *New York Times Magazine,* 28 December 1941, 12.

Pirsein, Robert W. *The VOA: A History of the International Broadcasting Activities of the United States Government, 1940–1962.* New York: Arno Press, 1979.

Pisko, E. S. "Tuning in on the Traitors." *Christian Science Monitor Magazine,* 18 July 1942, 6.

———. "Words That May Shorten the War." *Christian Century* 59 (24 June 1942): 804–6.

Pollard, J. A. "Words Are Cheaper Than Blood: Overseas OWI and the Need for a Permanent Propaganda Agency." *Public Opinion Quarterly* 9 (Fall 1945): 283–304.

Poole, Dewitt C. *Public Opinion.* Princeton: Princeton University Press, 1936.

Possony, Stefan T. "Needed—A New Propaganda Approach to Germany." *Public Opinion Quarterly* 6 (Fall 1942): 335–40.

Powers, Thomas. *The Man Who Kept the Secrets: Richard Helms and the CIA.* New York: Alfred A. Knopf, 1979.

Pringle, Henry F. "The Baloney Barrage Pays Off: The Psychological Warfare Section's Paper Offensive." *Saturday Evening Post,* 31 March 1945, 18–19.

———. *Democracy and National Unity.* Chicago: University of Chicago Press, 1941.

———. *Why . . . ?* New York: Farrar and Rinehart, 1941.

"Problem of Propaganda." *Collier's,* 23 December 1939, 62.

"Propaganda Analysis May Protect You Against It." *Science News Letter* 32 (30 October 1937): 278.

"Propaganda by German Nazis in the United States." *New Republic* 76 (18 October 1933): 264.

"Psychological Warfare: The OWI Runs a School for Propagandists." *Life,* 13 December 1943, 81–84.

"Psychological Warfare Did Not Win the War." *Forum* 104 (October 1945): 168–69.

"Public Opinion: Divide and Rule Is a Potent Device Both for Military Conquest and Internal Dissension." *Scholastic* 38 (5 May 1941): 16.

Qualter, Terence H. *Propaganda and Psychological Warfare.* New York: Random House, 1962.

Rauschning, Hermann. *The Beast from the Abyss.* London: Heineman, 1941.

———. *Hitler and the War.* New York: American Council on Public Affairs, 1940.

———. *Men of Chaos.* New York: G. P. Putnam, 1942.

———. *The Voices of Destruction.* New York: G. P. Putnam, 1940.

Read, J. M. *Atrocity Propaganda.* New Haven: Yale University Press, 1941.

Reed, Caroline. "D-Day Propaganda." *History Today* (U.K.) 34 (June 1984): 27–30.

Reston, James. *Prelude to Victory.* New York: Alfred A. Knopf, 1942.

Reuther, A. "Radio Squadron: To be Attached to Spearheads of the Invading United Nations Armies." *Nation* 150 (31 October 1942): 444–46.

Reynolds, David. *Lord Lothian and Anglo-American Relations, 1939–1940.* Philadelphia: American Philosophical Society, 1983.

Rhodes, Anthony, and Victor Margolin. *Propaganda: The Art of Persuasion in World War II.* New York: Chelsea House, 1976.

Riegel, O. W. *Mobilizing for Chaos: The Story of the New Propaganda.* New Haven: Yale University Press, 1934.

Rigby, Charles A. *War on the Short Waves.* London: Cole, 1944.

Riley, John W., Jr., and Leonard S. Cottrell, Jr. "Research for Psychological Warfare." *Public Opinion Quarterly* 21 (Spring 1957): 147–57.

Roetter, Charles. *Psychological Warfare, 1914–1945.* New York: Stein and Day, 1974.

Rogerson, Sydney. *Propaganda in the Next War.* London: G. Bles, 1938.

Rolo, Charles J. "Germany Calling." *Current History* 52 (22 October 1940): 27–31.

_____. "How to Talk to the Enemy." *Saturday Review of Literature* (11 July 1942): 3–4.

_____. *Radio Goes to War: The Fourth Front.* New York: G. P. Putnam, 1942.

_____. "The Strategy of War by Radio." *Harper's* 181 (November 1940): 640–49.

Rolo, Charles J., and Strauz-Hupe, Robert. "U.S. International Broadcasting." *Harper's* (August 1941): 301–12.

Roosevelt, Kermit. *War Report of the OSS.* 2 vols. New York: Walker, 1976.

Ross, Colin. *Amerikas Schicksalstunde.* Leipzig: F. A. Brockhaus, 1942.

_____. *Unser Amerika.* Leipzig: F. A. Brockhaus, 1941.

Rosten, Leo. *The Washington Correspondents.* New York: Harcourt, Brace and Company, 1937.

Roucek, J. R. "Axis Psychological Strategy Against the United States." *Northern Europe* 2 (October 1942): 331–36.

Royse, Morton W. *Aerial Bombardment and the International Regulation on Warfare.* New York: H. Vinal, 1928.

Rundt, S. J. "Short-Wave Artillery: Still Weaker Than the Enemy's." *Nation* 155 (12 September 1942): 210–13.

Sandeen, Eric J. "Anti-Nazi Sentiment in Film: Confessions of a Nazi Spy and the German-American Bund." *American Studies* 20 (1979): 69–81.

Saunders, Dero. "The Future of Propaganda." *Harper's* 183 (November 1941): 648–55.

Sawyer, John E. "Obituary: James Phinney Baxter 3d." *Proceedings of the American Antiquarian Society* 85 (1975): 357–60.

Sayers, Michael, and Albert E. Kahn. *Sabotage: The Secret War Against America.* New York: Harper and Brothers, 1942.

Schmulowitz, Nat, and Lloyd D. Luckmann. "Foreign Policy by Propaganda Leaflets." *Public Opinion Quarterly* 9 (Fall 1945): 428–29.

Schonback, Morris. *Native American Fascism During the 1930s and 1940s.* New York: Garland, 1985.

Schulzinger, Robert D. "What Ever Happened to the Council on Foreign Relations?" *Diplomatic History* 5 (Fall 1981): 277–90.

_____. *The Wise Men of Foreign Policy: The History of the Council on Foreign Relations.* New York: Columbia University Press, 1984.

Seligmann, Herbert J. "The New Barbarian Invasion: Fascist Propaganda." *New Republic* 95 (22 June 1938): 175–77.

Shepardson, Whitney. *The Early History of the Council on Foreign Relations.* Stanford, Calif.: Stanford University Press, 1960.

_____. *The United States in World Affairs: An Account of American Foreign Relations.* 9 vols. New York: Harper and Brothers, 1939.

Shepardson, Whitney H., ed. *The Interests of the United States as a World Power.* Claremont, Calif.: Claremont University Press, 1942.

Sherwood, Robert E. "The Front Line Is in Our Hearts." *Ladies Home Journal,* August 1941, 21.

_____. "The Power of Truth: Radio a Vital Factor in War." *Vital Speeches* 9 (1 November 1942): 61–62.

_____. "Rush All Possible Aid to Britain!" *Reader's Digest,* September 1940, 12–17.

Shirer, William L. "American Radio Traitors." *Harper's,* October 1943, 397–404.

Short, K. R. M., ed. *Film and Radio Propaganda in World War II.* Knoxville: University of Tennessee Press, 1983.

"Should Congress Pass the Dickstein Bill to Terminate the Stay of Alien Propagandists?" *Congressional Digest* 14 (November 1935): 284–85.

Shoup, Lawrence, and William Minter. *Imperial Brain Trust: The Council on Foreign Relations and United States Foreign Policy.* New York: Monthly Review Press, 1977.

Shulman, Holly. *The Voice of Victory: The Development of American Propaganda and the Voice of America, 1920–1942.* New York: Free Press, 1992.

Siepmann, Charles. *Radio in Wartime.* London: Oxford University Press, 1942.

Sinclair, Andrew. "John Ford's War." *Sight and Sound* 48 (Spring 1979): 99–104.

Singleton, Derrick, and Arthur Weidenfeld. *The Goebbels Experiment: A Study of the Nazi Propaganda Machine.* New Haven: Yale University Press, 1943.

Skrine, Walter, and Peter Collins. "Operation Cornflakes." *Philatelist,* May 1971, 250–55.

Small, Melvin. "How We Learned to Love the Russians: American Media and the Soviet Union During World War II." *Historian* 36 (Fall 1974): 455–78.

Smertenko, Johan T. "Hitlerism Comes to America." *Harper's,* November 1933, 660–70.

Smith, Bradley F. "Admiral Godfrey's Mission to America, June/July 1941." *Intelligence and National Security* 1 (1986): 441–50.

_____. *The Shadow Warriors: The OSS and the Origins of the CIA.* New York: Basic Books, 1983.

Smith, Geoffrey. *To Save a Nation: American Countersubversives, the New Deal, and the Coming of World War II.* New York: Basic Books, 1974.

Smith, R. Harris. *OSS: The Secret History of America's First Central Intelligence Agency.* Los Angeles: University of California Press, 1972.

Smith, Sally B. *In All His Glory: The Life of William S. Paley, the Legendary Tycoon and His Brilliant Circle.* New York: Simon and Schuster, 1990.

Sniegoski, Stephen J. "Unified Democracy: An Aspect of American World War II Interventionist Thought, 1939–1941." *Maryland Historian* 9 (Spring 1978): 33–48.

Sobel, Robert. *The Origins of Interventionism: The United States and the Russo-Finnish War.* New York: Bookman Associates, 1960.

Soley, Lawrence C. *Radio Warfare: OSS and CIA Subversive Propaganda.* Westport, Conn.: Praeger, 1989.

Sondern, F., Jr. "General McClure's Newsboys." *American Mercury* (February 1945): 232–36.

Sorenson, Thomas C. *The Word War: The Story of American Propaganda*. New York: Harper and Row, 1968.

Speier, Hans. "The Future of Psychological Warfare." *Public Opinion Quarterly* (Spring 1948): 5–18.

————. *Treachery in War*. New York: New School for Social Research, 1940.

————. "War Aims in Political Warfare." *Social Research* (May 1945): 157.

————. *War in Our Time*. New York: W. W. Norton Company, 1939.

Speier, Hans, Daniel Lerner, and Harold D. Lasswell, eds. *Propaganda and Communication in World History*. Honolulu: University Press of Hawaii, 1979.

Spivack, Robert G. "New Anti-Alien Drive; Campaign Against Aliens Working for the OWI." *New Republic* 159 (29 November 1943): 740–41.

Spivak, John L. *Secret Armies: The New Technique of Nazi Warfare*. New York: Modern Age Books, 1939.

Squires, James D. "The Problem of Propaganda Today." *Vital Speeches* 5 (15 July 1939): 588–93.

"Station Atlantik: The Phoney Station Set Up by the British." *New Yorker*, 13 October 1945, 20–22.

Steele, Richard W. "American Popular Opinion and the War Against Germany: The Issue of Negotiated Peace, 1942. *Journal of American History* 65 (December 1978): 704–23.

————. "The Great Debate: Roosevelt, the Media, and the Coming of the War, 1940–1941." *Journal of American History* 71 (June 1984): 69–92.

————. "Preparing the Public for War: Efforts to Establish a National Propaganda Agency, 1940–1941." *American Historical Review* 75 (October 1970): 1640–53.

————. *Propaganda in an Open Society: The Roosevelt Administration and the Media, 1933–1941*. Westport, Conn.: Greenwood Press, 1985.

————. "The Pulse of the People: Franklin D. Roosevelt and the Gauging of Public Opinion." *Journal of Contemporary History* 9 (October 1974): 195–216.

Stevenson, William. *A Man Called Intrepid*. New York: Ballantine Books, 1976.

Stewart, Kenneth. "OWI and Its Critics." *New Republic* 159 (13 December 1943): 844–46.

"The Strange Case of John Durfee." *Life*, 9 August 1943, 31.

Strausz-Hupe, Robert. *Axis America: Hitler Plans Our Future*. New York: G. P. Putnam's Sons, 1941.

Strong, Kenneth. *Men of Intelligence: A Study of the Roles and Decisions of Chiefs of Intelligence from World War I to the Present Day*. New York: St. Martin's Press, 1972.

Summers, Robert E. *America's Weapon of Psychological Warfare*. New York: Wilson, 1951.

Sweetser, Arthur. *The Atlantic Declaration, August 14, 1941*. New York: Carnegie Endowment for International Peace, 1941.

————. *The United States and the League*. Geneva, Switzerland: Geneva Research Centre, 1940.

Taylor, Edmond. "How America Can Take the Offensive." *Fortune* 23 (May 1941): 64–65.

————. *Smash Hitler's International*. New York: Greystone Press, 1941.

————. "Strategy of Terror." *Reader's Digest*, September 1940, 89–92.

————. *The Strategy of Terror*. New York: Houghton Mifflin Company, 1942.

Taylor, Philip M. " 'If War Should Come:' Preparing the Fifth Arm for Total War." *Journal of Contemporary History* 16 (January 1981): 7–26.

Teale, Edwin. "America Listens In: Tricks of Germany's War Propagandists." *Popular Science Monthly* (June 1941): 74–77.

"Ten Commandments Offered for Propaganda Protection." *Science News Letter* 36 (14 October 1939): 250.

Thompson, Dean K. "World War II, Intervention, and Henry Pitney van Dusen." *Journal of Presbyterian History* 55 (Winter 1977): 327–45.

Thompson, Dorothy. "Nazi Foreign Missions: German Propaganda in the United States and World." *Vital Speeches* 3 (15 September 1937): 712–14.

———. "Propaganda Bogey." *Ladies Home Journal*, December 1939, 4.

———. "Propaganda in the Modern World." Vital Speeches 2 (4 November 1935): 66–68.

Thomson, Charles A. H. *The Overseas Information Service of the United States Government.* Washington, D.C.: Brookings Institution, 1948.

Thomson, Oliver. *Mass Persuasion in History: An Historical Analysis of the Development of Propaganda Techniques.* Edinburgh, Scotland: Paul Harris, 1977.

Thum, Gladys, and Marcella Thum. *The Persuaders: Propaganda in War and Peace.* New York: Athenaeum, 1972.

Tolischus, Otto D. "Challenge of a Master Propagandist." *New York Times Magazine,* 28 July 1940, 3.

———. *They Wanted War.* New York: Reynal and Hitchcock, 1940.

Tomkins, R. S. "The Propaganda Scare." *Johns Hopkins Alumni Magazine* 28 (November 1939): 1–5.

Trefousse, Hans S. *Germany and American Neutrality, 1939–1941.* New York: Bookman Associates, 1951.

Troy, Thomas F. *Donovan and the CIA: A History of the Establishment of the CIA.* Frederick, Md.: University Publications of America, 1981.

"Truth Joins the AEF; Nation's Psychological Warriors." *Nation's Business* 31 (February 1943): 64.

Tull, Charles J. *Father Charles Coughlin and the New Deal.* Syracuse, N.Y.: Syracuse University Press, 1965.

"Turning the War of Nerves on the Axis: How the Allies Are Using Hitler's Tactics of Propaganda Against His Own People." *U.S. News and World Report,* 19 February 1943, 17.

Turrow, Leon G. *Nazi Spies in America.* New York: Random House, 1939.

Tuttle, William M., Jr. "Aid to the Allies Short-of-War versus American Intervention: A Reappraisal of William Allen White's Leadership." *Journal of American History* 56 (December 1970): 840–58.

"U.S. Arsenal of Words; Overseas Branch Labors Under Handicaps, Many of its Own Making." *Fortune* 27 (March 1943): 83–85, 169–76.

"U.S. Takes Over Short Waves to Win Air Propaganda War." *Newsweek,* 19 October 1942, 30–31.

van Deman, Ralph H. *The Final Memoranda: Major General Ralph H. van Deman, USA, Ret., 1865–1952, Father of Military Intelligence.* Wilmington, Del.: Scholarly Resources, 1988.

Van de Water, Marjorie. "Propaganda: An Insidious Assault upon the Intelligence." *Science News Letter* 34 (8 October 1938): 234–35.

_____. "Selecting Secret Agents for OSS Service." *Science News Letter* 49 (12 January 1946): 26–27.

"The Vanishing Un-American." *New Republic* 103 (26 August 1940): 264.

"Victory for Elmer." *Time*, 13 September 1943, 50.

Vieth, Jane K. "The Donkey and the Lion: The Ambassadorship of Joseph P. Kennedy at the Court of St. James's, 1938–1940." *Michigan Academy of Science, Arts, and Letters* 10 (1978): 273–82.

Villa, Brian L. "The United States Army, Unconditional Surrender and the Potsdam Proclamation." *Journal of American History* 63 (June 1976): 66–92.

"Voice of the Chief; Secret European Radio Station." *Newsweek*, 29 June 1942, 63.

"Voices of Defeat: Some Americans Sow Lies and Hate Inside Our Lines, Abuse Free Speech, and Spread Hitler's Propaganda." *Life*, 13 April 1942, 86.

Walker, David A. "OSS and Operation TORCH," *Journal of Contemporary History* 22 (1987): 667–79.

Wanger, Walter. "OWI and Motion Pictures." *Public Opinion Quarterly* 7 (Spring 1943): 100–110.

Warburg, James P. *Foreign Policy Begins at Home.* New York: Harcourt, Brace and World, 1944.

_____. *The Isolationist Illusion and World Peace.* New York: Toronto, Farrar and Rinehart, 1941.

_____. *Man's Enemy and Man.* New York: Toronto, Farrar and Rinehart, 1942.

_____. *Our War and Our Peace.* New York: Farrar and Rinehart, 1941.

_____. *Peace in Our Time?* New York: Harper and Brothers, 1940.

_____. *Unwritten Treaty.* New York: Harcourt Brace Jovanovich, 1946.

Warner, Geoffrey. "From Teheran to Yalta: Reflections on Franklin D. Roosevelt's Foreign Policy." *International Affairs* 43 (July 1967): 530–36.

Weinberg, Gerhard. "Hitler's Image of the United States." *American Historical Review* 69 (July 1964): 1006–21.

Weinberg, Sydney S. "What to Tell America: The Writer's Quarrel in the Office of War Information." *Journal of American History* 55 (June 1968): 73–89.

Wells, Robert D. "Persuading the U-Boats." *United States Naval Institute Proceedings* 90 (1964): 52–59.

"What's Wrong with American Propaganda." *Free World* 2 (March 1942): 132–43.

Whitaker, John T. *And Fear Came.* New York: Macmillan Company, 1939.

_____. *We Cannot Escape History.* New York: Macmillan Company, 1943.

"Whitewashing Hitlerism." *World Tomorrow* 17 (15 February 1934): 78.

Williams, Margaret H. "The President's Office of Government Reports." *Public Opinion Quarterly* 5 (Winter 1941): 548–62.

Winfield, Betty H. *FDR and the News Media.* New York: Columbia University Press, 1994.

Winkler, Allan M. *The Politics of Propaganda: The Office of War Information, 1942–1945.* New Haven: Yale University Press, 1978.

Winks, Robin W. *Cloak and Gown: Scholars in the Secret War, 1939–1961.* New York: William Morrow and Company, 1987.

Witcover, Jules. *Sabotage at Black Tom: Imperial Germany's Secret War in America, 1914–1917.* Chapel Hill, N.C.: Algonquin Books, 1989.

Wolfe, S. "Berlin, Rome, Tokyo Radio Propaganda." *Contemporary Review* 162 (October 1942): 218–22.

_____. "Goebbels over the Ether." *Contemporary Review* 160 (December 1941): 373–77.

Wood, Edward F. L., Lord Halifax. "Propaganda as a Weapon." *Vital Speeches* 9 (15 January 1943): 129–32.

Zeman, Z. A. B. *Nazi Propaganda.* London: Oxford University Press, 1973.

Dissertations

Bishop, Robert L. "The Overseas Branch of the Office of War Information." Ph.D. diss., University of Wisconsin, 1966.

Kellis, James. "The Development of United States National Intelligence." Ph.D. diss., Georgetown University, 1963.

Laurie, Clayton D. "Ideology and American Propaganda: The Psychological Warfare Campaign Against Nazi Germany, 1941–1945." Ph.D. diss., American University, 1990.

Schwar, Jane H. "Interventionist Propaganda and Pressure Groups in the United States, 1937–1941." Ph.D. diss., Ohio State University, 1973.

Shulman, Holly C. "The Voice of Victory: The Development of American Propaganda and the Voice of America, 1920–1942." Ph.D. diss., University of Maryland, 1984.

Weinberg, Sydney S. "Wartime Propaganda in a Democracy: America's Twentieth Century Information Agencies." Ph.D. diss., Columbia University, 1969.

Willis, Jeffrey R. "The Wehrmacht Propaganda Branch: German Military Propaganda and Censorship During World War II." Ph.D. diss., University of Virginia, 1964.

Index

	DATE DUE